FOOTBALL
LEAGUE YEAR
1·9·8·9

With its colourful trip through the 1987/1988 season of the English Football League's ups-and-downs, this first edition of the *Football League Year: 1989* manages to achieve a statistical balance. It details not only every current Football League player's career record, but also chronicles the 92 League clubs' match-by-match performances.

Football highlights from August 1987 to May 1988 are covered in a lively and entertaining survey, illustrated with action packed photographs. The club section includes all League matches for last season with half-time scores, progressive League positions, attendances, the full teams (including substitutes) and goalscorers. All Cup results are shown separately.

There is also an A-Z of all players who made League appearances during the season. Recorded against each player is his date and place of birth, clubs played for, transfer dates, seasons played, the number of appearances (including substitutions) and the number of goals scored for each club, international appearances, etc.

The fixture list for the 1988/89 season concludes this attractive new presentation which will be an essential item on all soccer fans' shopping lists.

Kenny Dalglish proudly holds the League Championship trophy on behalf of Liverpool, who have won it a record 17 times.   Sporting Pictures (UK) Ltd

FOOTBALL
LEAGUE YEAR
1·9·8·9

EDITED BY BARRY J. HUGMAN

T.A.P./Dalton Watson plc
Russell Chambers
The Piazza
Covent Garden
London WC2E 8AA

First published 1988

British Library Cataloguing in Publication Data

Football League Year 1989.
  1. England. Football League football
  I. Hugman, Barry J. (Barry John)
  796.334'63'0942

  ISBN 1-85443-015-7

Typeset by Area Graphics Ltd, Factory 2, Pixmore
Avenue, Letchworth, Hertfordshire

Made and printed by Netherwood Dalton & Co Ltd.,
Huddersfield, Yorkshire.

Contents

Acknowledgements

The editor would like to thank the many various experts without whose help this book would not have been possible to produce within the time allowed.

Michael Featherstone is a keen sporting statistician and researcher who works in the accounts department of a large public company. He started many years ago by collecting both cricket and soccer information, which he obtained from the Colindale National Newspaper Library. Several years later he joined Ray Spiller's Association of Football Statisticians after being introduced by his very good friend, the late Morley Farror. After meeting Barry Hugman in 1975 he began intensive research into post-war league footballers. This led to Football League Players' Records first published in 1981 with the second edition released in 1984. He has also contributed to the British Boxing Yearbook, The Olympic Games, Complete Track and Field Results, 1896-1988, Cricket Who's Who and many footballing publications.

Alan Platt is a freelance transport planner whose most recent assignments have been overseas. Unlike many schoolboys he did not take an interest in soccer until the age of 14, but once involved he was hooked. From 1960 onwards he has kept detailed records on all Football League clubs and their players and is happy to watch football at any level "provided that there is something at stake and the players are trying". Mostly, he watches his beloved Liverpool whom he has followed since 1961, and his local club Chesterfield, since 1983. From 1985 to 1986 he contributed to the Chesterfield match programme. He first met Barry Hugman in 1981 following the publication of Football League Players' Records and after being impressed by the depth of research and immaculate attention to detail, he volunteered his assistance to all future editions. He is a most worthy addition to the team where his vast expertise can be found among these pages.

Peter Arnold has been a sports enthusiast ever since he can remember. As a boy he would often be drawn to big sporting occasions and even played truant from school to watch the mighty Moscow Dynamos at Stamford Bridge in 1945. He has worked in publishing, editing many books on sports, games, leisure and pastimes, for over 30 years.

Among the books he has written are A History of Boxing, All-Time Greats of Boxing, A History of the Olympic Games, 100 Years of Test Cricket, World Soccer and an Encyclopedia of Gambling. Apart from producing various darts and snooker publications, he was my co-editor on The Olympic Games, Complete Track & Field Results, 1896-1988.

Regarding the photographs used in this book, it gives me great pleasure to personally thank Melvyn Bagnall, the editor of Match Magazine, and his most helpful staff, who kindly put the company's vast library at my disposal. It is easy to see how the magazine has such a vast circulation and not just among the youngsters. The weekly club line-ups are a godsend to any footballing statistician and were of great value in the make-up of this book. They can be reached at Stirling House, Bretton, Peterborough PE3 8DJ.

Once again my good friend Steve Smith of Sporting Pictures (UK) Ltd, 7a Lambs Conduit Passage, London WC1R 4RG, came to our aid with some brilliant colour action shots portraying a selection of matches from last season.

David Jacobs of Action Images Sports Photography, 12 Cambridge Terrace, Bury Street West, London N9 9JJ, who has helped me in the past with boxing photos, also supplied much black/white action for the book.

Other special mentions should go to Chris Ashton and Donald Nannestad, who dug up Vauxhall Conference information on Lincoln City for last season, Deborah and Jennifer Hugman for their great efforts and Dave Clayton for details on internationals.

My thanks must also go to Graham Kelly of The Football League, who yet again made the records available, and Mike Foster and Sheila Murphy who both lent their time and expertise to ensure that the information required was correct. I would also like to show appreciation for the support given by Gordon Taylor of the PFA and Trevor Phillips, the Commercial Director of the Football League.

Finally, as in all my other books, I must congratulate Edwin Cook and Ray Hedley for their expert handling in the area of design.

Preface

This edition of *The Football League Year*, the first of many it is my intention to produce, sets out to provide a good read as well as presenting match-by-match statistics for 1987-88, covering each of the 92 Football League clubs.

An added attraction is that of the A-Z of current English Football League players, which records faithfully, the career record for every player who made an appearance during the 1987-88 season. And introduced by 60 great colour pictures, one attempts to please both young and old alike.

The Football League Year follows the third edition of my *Football League Players' Records, 1946-1988* and it is opportune that one of the Football League's most celebrated records changed hands just before the book went to press. In the penultimate week of the 1987-88 season the record number of Football League appearances passed from Terry Paine (824) to Derby County and England goalkeeper Peter Shilton (826), who now seems set to extend the record to an unsurpassable total before he retires.

Another achievement worthy of mention during 1987-88 was that of Billy Bonds, who at the age of 41, made 22 appearances in West Ham United's beleaguered defence, three years after requesting the management to drop him from the first team pool! Whilst this may not stand comparison with Sir Stanley Matthews turning out for Stoke City at the age of 50, it is nonetheless a remarkable feat for an outfield player. His contribution to the sport was most deservedly recognised with an M.B.E. in the New Years Honours List, a unique award for a player whose international recognition consisted of no more than two England Under-23 caps.

The career of a professional footballer is usually a short and high risk one. For every success story there are hundreds of disappointments and heartaches. Talent or ability is not enough unless allied to a determination to succeed against all the setbacks that the game inevitably throws up. How many players have seen a promising career brought to a halt by a serious injury, an unwise transfer move or, sometimes unforgivably, by a change of manager? Professional football, perhaps more than any other profession, is an "obstacle race" in which many fall by the wayside and those who triumph are not necessarily more talented than those who fail.

Most international players are "spotted" at an early age and graduate from schoolboy to youth international honours and then from Under-21 to full caps. They will inevitably find their way to one of the top clubs. The smooth progression from junior football to international status of players such as Bryan Robson or Ian Rush are too well chronicled to bear any repetition here.

Few, if any, players have had a more tortuous road to the top of their profession than Birmingham City's Peter Withe. No early recognition for him. Quite the contrary

as he progressed from a works team on Merseyside to reserve football with first Southport and then Barrow in 1970/71, both clubs soon to be ejected from the Football League. When discarded, he might have settled for a part-time football career in the North West, but instead he emigrated to try his luck in South Africa where he impressed Derek Dougan sufficiently to recommend him to his former club, Wolves, then in the First Division. However, he did not make the "breakthrough" at Molineux and after two years moved on to Birmingham City and then to Nottingham Forest. Under the management of Brian Clough he formed an effective partnership with Tony Woodcock, which helped to propel Forest first to promotion and, more remarkably, in his second season to the Football League Championship in 1977-78. But if Withe thought he had finally arrived to stay in the "big time" he had a rude shock the following season. First he was dropped and then transferred to Newcastle United, at that time a mediocre Second Division team. After two seasons fate took a hand again and his career was transformed when Ron Saunders signed him for Aston Villa. As with Forest he proved to be a catalyst and his 20 goals assisted the unfancied Villa team to a most unexpected League Championship, followed by an even more surprising European Cup victory, scoring the only goal in the Final. To set the seal on his career he was called up to the England national squad in May 1981, making his international debut at the age of 29.

If Peter Withe's story is unusual, it is not unique. In 1980 Gary Crosby was an associate schoolboy with Lincoln City, but he was not offered an apprentice or professional contract, although he turned out occasionally for the reserves as a non-contract player. In September 1986 whilst performing for Lincoln United, of the Central Midland League, he was offered a second chance by Lincoln City on a one month trial. It did not lead to a professional contract however and Crosby returned to non-league football. The beginning of 1987-88 found him playing with Southern League Grantham, managed by Martin O'Neill, the former Nottingham Forest and Northern Ireland player. O'Neill was so impressed that he recommended Crosby to Forest manager Brian Clough who signed him in December for £15,000. This seemed remarkable enough, but within two months he was playing in the First Division for a championship challenging team! Even Clough, whose record of throwing novices in at the "deep end" and coming up with "pearls" is second to none, must have been amazed by Crosby's progress. In only his ninth League game he caused more problems to Liverpool's near-impregnable defence than any other player in the "Reds" unstoppable march to the championship.

Two years ago Peter Guthrie was a 25-year-old goalkeeper playing for a team called Forest Hall in McEwans Northern Alliance, so obscure that few had heard of them in their native Newcastle. With no prospects of a football career, Guthrie must have felt he had reached the "pinnacle" when he was signed by Blyth Spartans, the "crack" non-league team of the North East. In fact it was only the beginning. His form for Blyth was so impressive that in the summer of 1987 he was persuaded to move to the south coast to play for Weymouth of the Vauxhall Conference. After only 20 games in which he conceded a miserly nine goals, he attracted the interest of two First Division clubs. He opted for Tottenham Hotspur, signing for a fee of £100,000, and seemed set fair to become Ray Clemence's long term successor. But even "fairy tales" don't always go according to plan. Manager Terry Venables decided that Gurthrie wasn't yet ready for the First Division and signed Bobby Mimms from Everton, whilst Guthrie made his League debut on loan to Swansea of the Fourth Division, still a considerable leap from Forest Hall, but it remains to be seen if he makes the grade at First Division level.

Such "romantic" tales are of course the exception. A more typical story would be of the honest journeyman professional who fails to make the grade at the top level, but is a tower of strength in the lower divisions, either clocking up 400 plus appearances with the same club or moving around giving stalwart service wherever he plays. Torquay United's goalie Kenny Allen is such an example.

Allen made his League debut as an amateur for Hartlepool in 1968 but "disappeared" for ten years until he turned up with Bournemouth in 1978. In the interim period he had trials with Aldershot, Burnley and Swindon before emigrating to South Africa to ply his trade. He returned to this country in 1972 and had further unsuccessful trials at West Bromwich and Workington prior to opting for part-time football with Bath City. It seemed that a professional career had passed him by, but after five years at Bath he was signed up by Bournemouth and re-entered League football at the age of 26. He spent five years at Dean Court until he was "freed" to make way for a younger player.

At 31 his League career seemed over especially when trials at Bury and Peterborough led to nothing, but in reality it was the dawn of a new beginning. He was signed up by perennial re-election candidates Torquay United and remained with them 18 months as first choice, until released in September 1985. For most players a "free" transfer from Torquay is the end of the League road, but once again Allen landed on his feet. Swindon Town manager Lou Macari signed him as a "stopgap" while he searched for a young keeper after a disappointing start to the season. The search was deferred as Allen proved to be the answer to a leaky defence, conceding only 32 goals in 40 games (the best keeper's record in the League that season) and earned his first Football League medal as Swindon swept to the Fourth Division title with a record points haul. The following season Macari found his young keeper and Allen was released by mutual consent. He was signed again by Torquay, who no doubt regretted their earlier decision, but at the end of the season his League career seemed over once more as Torquay faced relegation from the Football League. As is now part of football folklore, Torquay saved their Football League status with a last minute equaliser in the final game. Remarkable in the season just ended, Torquay were challengers for promotion, reaching the "play offs" and once again Allen was statistically the safest keeper in the Fourth Division conceding only 41 goals in 46 games.

On the club front, mighty Liverpool won the Championship for the 17th time in their history after going unbeaten for their first 29 matches to equal Leeds United's 1973-74 record. But in the FA Cup final they were thwarted in their bid for the "double" by unfashionable Wimbledon, who once again proved that there are no certainties in soccer.

Professional football once thrived when it was family entertainment and the aims of everyone in the game now must surely be for a return to those memorable days before it is too late. Best of luck for 1988-89.

Barry J. Hugman

A Review of the 1987-88 English Football Season

INTRODUCTION:
The Previous Season and the Summer

The football season of 1986–87 was one in which the changes in the Football League could easily be seen. It was the season before the League's Centenary, and did not promise to be a good one.

Football, of course, had changed a lot in 100 years, as was to be expected, and nothing showed this more than a glance at the record of Preston North End. In the first season of the League they had achieved the "double" without losing a match, and earned for ever the name of "Invincibles". They began 1986–87 in 91st position of the 92 League clubs.

But it was more recent changes that were noticeable and worrying. For the second year English clubs were battling for honours knowing that there was no prospect of European football for the winners. That had ended with the ban on English clubs taking part after the European Cup final tragedy at the Heysel Stadium in Brussels in May 1985. Liverpool fans had sparked off the riot in which many died and Liverpool began season 1986–87 as very much the sufferers from the ban, because they were Champions and Cup-holders.

The European exclusion had had its effect on the Football League as a whole because some prominent players decided to seek European glory with Scottish clubs. Terry Butcher and Chris Woods were two English internationals who did not play in the Football League in 1986–87. They had been transferred to Rangers in Scotland, giving a new meaning to the term "Anglo-Scots", which for years had meant players picked for Scotland from English clubs. These two reversed the usual traffic and went north.

The Football League was also without two of its most exciting strikers. Gary Lineker, after one season with Everton, during which he was Player of the Year and top League scorer in 1985–86, had been transferred to Barcelona, as had Mark Hughes, Manchester United's Welsh international. Ian Rush, his great Welsh partner, appeared for Liverpool, but it was to be his last season, as he was due to join Juventus at the end of it.

Lineker had been the leading scorer in the 1986

World Cup finals, where England had performed on the whole disappointingly, so the Football League prospects for 1986–87 were not good. It was not, by the way, correct to call it the Football League any more. The League had been sponsored for three seasons by Canon, and in 1986–87 a newspaper took over the sponsorship, and it became the *Today* League.

Amid complaints for years of too much football at the top level, the League decided to change the number of clubs in the First Division from 22 to 20, the number to be reduced by one in each of two seasons. It was announced therefore that in 1986–87 there would be play-offs at the end of the season to decide some of the promotion-relegation issues. It was also decided that the bottom club in the Fourth Division could no longer apply for re-election but would automatically be replaced by the winners of the General Motors Vauxhall Conference.

Chris Woods, the English international goalkeeper, now playing for Glasgow Rangers.
Match Magazine

9

Play-offs were not new to the League. They had been used when the Second Division had been formed in 1892–93, and it was not until six years later that promotion and relegation was based solely on League position.

A dream came true for one club on 23 August 1986 as Wimbledon made their first appearance in the First Division at Maine Road. Wimbledon had been admitted to the Fourth Division in 1976–77 and had worked their way to the top flight after only ten years. They lost that opening game 3-1, but a fortnight into the new season they had registered four consecutive wins and were proudly at the top of the First Division.

As the season progressed, the main feature was a great revival in the fortunes of Arsenal, who under a new manager, George Graham, went for 17 League games without defeat from early October into the new year, and set a hot pace at the top of the table. They faltered, however, in a spell of ten games without a win, during which they scored only two goals, and slid to fourth by the season's end.

The team which took over the lead from Arsenal was Everton, but they lost the lead to Liverpool for the whole of March. Liverpool, it seemed, had timed their challenge nicely as usual, but unbelievably they lost three matches running, including a 2-1 home defeat by Wimbledon, and Everton kept going to the end. They won ten of their last 12 games, and secured the title with two matches to spare following a 1-0 victory at Norwich.

The Second Division was won by Derby County, who from the end of January had shared the lead with Portsmouth, who finished second. So two clubs with illustrious histories returned to the top rank, led by managers Arthur Cox and Alan Ball.

The side which finished comfortably in third place, Oldham Athletic, which normally would have claimed the third promotion spot, had to take part in the play-offs. Leicester City, Manchester City and Aston Villa were relegated from the First Division, and Charlton Athletic, fourth from bottom, had to play off with Oldham, Leeds and Ipswich, third, fourth and fifth in the Second Division, for the final spot in the First.

Leeds beat Oldham on away goals in their home-and-away play-offs, the aggregate being 2-2, while Charlton beat Ipswich 2-1. In the final, Charlton and Leeds beat each other 1-0 in the home legs, and Charlton won a replay 2-1 at St Andrews, after extra time, to retain their First Division status. Charlton thus ended their first season at Selhurst Park successfully. They had been forced out of their own ground at The Valley, becoming the first League club in recent times having to share a ground with another. It was a trend which was expected to be followed by others as financial problems began to hit many clubs.

The club with the most severe financial problems as 1986–87 started was Middlesbrough. On 30 July 1986 a judge had ordered their winding-up following a claim of £115,156 in tax arrears from the Inland Revenue. Manager Bruce Rioch was among the staff sacked by the Official Receiver. On 15 August, eight days before they were due to play their first League match, the club was saved by a new consortium who paid off their debts.

The season was a triumph for the newly formed club. They led the Third Division for much of the season, stumbled a little in February and March, but finished strongly to take second place behind Bournemouth and an automatic promotion spot. Grimsby and Brighton were the sides relegated from the Second Division, while Sunderland, third bottom, had to play off with Swindon, Wigan and Gillingham for the last Second Division place. This time justice was done, for Swindon, who would have taken the spot under the old system, won the play-offs. They beat Gillingham in the final after a third match, played at Selhurst Park. Gillingham's semi-final play-off with Sunderland had been won on away goals. They had lost the second leg at Sunderland 4-3 after extra time, having won at home 3-2.

In the Fourth Division, Northampton, Preston (on their way back to the top?) and Southend went up and their places were taken by Carlisle, Darlington and Newport. Bolton Wanderers, from the Third Division, and Wolves, Colchester and Aldershot from the Fourth, played-off for the last Third Division place, won by Aldershot, who in this season of change gained promotion after finishing sixth (they had been 23rd early in the season!)

But the drama in the Fourth Division was at the foot, where half-a-dozen teams were in a prolonged struggle not to finish bottom and lose their League status. Burnley, one of the 12 original members of the Football League, were bottom with one match to go, but they won 2-1 at home to Orient to save themselves. Lincoln were the unlucky side, losing their last match to slide four places to the foot, losing 96 years of League status on goal difference. The team which took their place was Scarborough.

In the FA Cup final, a club with a superb Cup-fighting tradition, unbeaten in seven previous appearances in the final, took on a club without a major trophy in their history. Spurs were overwhelming favourites to beat Coventry, and were ahead after two minutes. But Coventry twice came back from behind, and won the Cup when Gary Mabbutt scored an unlucky own goal in extra time.

In the Littlewoods Challenge Cup (formerly the Milk Cup, originally the Football League Cup) Arsenal found some of their early season form with a late flourish. In a remarkable semi-final, they lost 1-0 at home to Spurs, won the away leg 2-1 after being behind, and won the replay at Tottenham 2-1, again after being behind. In three matches Clive Allen, the season's leading goalscorer with 49 in all matches, three times gave Spurs the lead, but Arsenal went through. In the Wembley final Liverpool took the lead, but again Arsenal came back (with two goals by Charlie Nicholas) to win the Cup.

Liverpool, "double" winners the previous season, ended without a trophy.

Steve Hodge, seen in action for Spurs against Coventry City, was signed from Aston Villa in December 1987 for £650,000.   Match Magazine

Charlie Nicholas scores the first goal for Arsenal in the League Cup final victory over Liverpool.   Sporting Pictures (UK) Ltd

Brilliant action from the FA Cup final at Wembley shows Coventry City's Keith Houchen equalising against the "Spurs". The goal took the game into extra time and the "Sky Blues" eventually won 3-2.
Match Magazine

FINAL FOOTBALL LEAGUE TABLES 1986-87

SECOND DIVISION

		P	Home W	D	L	Goals F	A	Away W	D	L	Goals F	A	Pts
1	Derby Co†	42	14	6	1	42	18	11	3	7	22	20	84
2	Portsmouth†	42	17	2	2	37	11	6	7	8	16	17	78
3	Oldham Ath	42	13	6	2	36	16	9	3	9	29	28	75
4	Leeds U	42	15	4	2	43	16	4	7	10	15	28	68
5	Ipswich T	42	12	6	3	29	10	5	7	9	30	33	64
6	Crystal Palace	42	12	4	5	35	20	7	1	13	16	33	62
7	Plymouth Arg	42	12	6	3	40	23	4	7	10	22	34	61
8	Stoke C	42	11	5	5	40	21	5	5	11	23	32	58
9	Sheffield U	42	10	8	3	31	19	5	5	11	19	30	58
10	Bradford C	42	10	5	6	36	27	5	5	11	26	35	55
11	Barnsley	42	8	7	6	26	23	6	6	9	23	29	55
12	Blackburn Rov	42	11	4	6	30	22	4	6	11	15	33	55
13	Reading	42	11	4	6	33	23	3	7	11	19	36	53
14	Hull C	42	10	6	5	25	22	3	8	10	16	33	53
15	West Bromwich A	42	8	6	7	29	22	5	6	10	22	27	51
16	Millwall	42	10	5	6	27	16	4	4	13	12	29	51
17	Huddersfield T	42	9	6	6	38	30	4	6	11	16	31	51
18	Shrewsbury T	42	11	3	7	24	14	4	3	14	17	39	51
19	Birmingham C	42	8	9	4	27	21	3	8	10	20	38	50
20	Sunderland*	42	8	6	7	25	23	4	6	11	24	36	48
21	Grimsby T*	42	5	8	8	18	21	5	6	10	21	38	44
22	Brighton & HA*	42	7	6	8	22	20	2	6	13	15	34	39

*relegated †promoted

THIRD DIVISION

		P	Home W	D	L	Goals F	A	Away W	D	L	Goals F	A	Pts
1	Bournemouth†	46	19	3	1	44	14	10	7	6	32	26	97
2	Middlesbrough†	46	16	5	2	38	11	12	5	6	29	19	94
3	Swindon T†	46	14	5	4	37	19	11	7	5	40	28	87
4	Wigan Ath	46	15	5	3	47	26	10	5	8	36	34	85
5	Gillingham	46	16	5	2	42	14	7	4	12	23	34	78
6	Bristol C	46	14	6	3	42	15	7	8	8	21	21	77
7	Notts Co	46	14	6	3	52	24	7	7	9	25	32	76
8	Walsall	46	16	4	3	50	27	6	5	12	30	40	75
9	Blackpool	46	11	7	5	35	20	5	9	9	39	39	64
10	Mansfield T	46	9	9	5	30	23	6	7	10	22	32	61
11	Brentford	46	9	7	7	39	32	6	8	9	25	34	60
12	Port Vale	46	8	6	9	43	36	7	6	10	33	34	57
13	Doncaster Rov	46	11	8	4	32	19	3	7	13	24	43	57
14	Rotherham U	46	10	6	7	29	23	5	6	12	19	34	57
15	Chester C	46	7	9	7	32	28	6	8	9	29	31	56
16	Bury	46	9	7	7	30	26	5	6	12	24	34	55
17	Chesterfield	46	11	5	7	36	33	2	10	11	20	36	54
18	Fulham	46	8	8	7	35	41	4	9	10	24	36	53
19	Bristol Rov	46	7	8	8	26	29	6	4	13	23	46	51
20	York C	46	11	8	4	34	29	1	5	17	21	50	49
21	Bolton W*	46	8	5	10	29	26	2	10	11	17	32	45
22	Carlisle U*	46	7	5	11	26	35	3	3	17	13	43	38
23	Darlington*	46	6	10	7	25	28	1	6	16	20	49	37
24	Newport Co*	46	4	9	10	26	34	4	4	15	23	52	37

*relegated †promoted

FIRST DIVISION

		P	Home W	D	L	Goals F	A	Away W	D	L	Goals F	A	Pts
1	Everton	42	16	4	1	49	11	10	4	7	27	20	86
2	Liverpool	42	15	3	3	43	16	8	5	8	29	26	77
3	Tottenham H	42	14	3	4	40	14	7	5	9	28	29	71
4	Arsenal	42	12	5	4	31	12	8	5	8	27	23	70
5	Norwich C	42	9	10	2	27	20	8	7	6	26	31	68
6	Wimbledon	42	11	5	5	32	22	8	4	9	25	28	66
7	Luton T	42	14	5	2	29	13	4	7	10	18	32	66
8	Nottingham F	42	12	8	1	36	14	6	3	12	28	37	65
9	Watford	42	12	5	4	38	20	6	4	11	29	34	63
10	Coventry C	42	14	4	3	35	17	3	8	10	15	28	63
11	Manchester U	42	13	3	5	38	18	1	11	9	14	27	56
12	Southampton	42	11	5	5	44	24	3	5	13	25	44	52
13	Sheffield Wed	42	9	7	5	39	24	4	6	11	19	35	52
14	Chelsea	42	8	6	7	30	30	5	7	9	23	24	52
15	West Ham U	42	10	4	7	33	28	4	6	11	19	39	52
16	Q.P.R.	42	9	7	5	31	27	4	4	13	17	37	50
17	Newcastle U	42	10	4	7	33	29	2	7	12	14	36	47
18	Oxford U	42	8	8	5	30	25	3	5	13	14	44	46
19	Charlton Ath	42	7	7	7	26	22	4	4	13	19	33	44
20	Leicester C*	42	9	7	5	39	24	2	2	17	15	52	42
21	Manchester C*	42	8	6	7	28	24	0	9	12	8	33	39
22	Aston Villa*	42	7	7	7	25	25	1	5	15	20	54	36

*relegated

FOURTH DIVISION

		P	Home W	D	L	Goals F	A	Away W	D	L	Goals F	A	Pts
1	Northampton T†	46	20	2	1	56	20	10	7	6	47	33	99
2	Preston NE†	46	16	4	3	36	18	10	8	5	36	29	90
3	Southend U†	46	14	4	5	43	27	11	1	11	25	28	80
4	Wolverhampton W	46	12	3	8	36	24	12	4	7	33	26	79
5	Colchester U	46	15	3	5	41	20	6	4	13	23	36	70
6	Aldershot†	46	13	5	5	40	22	7	5	11	24	35	70
7	Leyton Orient	46	15	2	6	40	25	5	7	11	24	36	69
8	Scunthorpe U	46	15	3	5	52	27	3	9	11	21	30	66
9	Wrexham	46	8	13	2	38	24	7	7	9	32	27	65
10	Peterborough U	46	10	7	6	29	21	7	7	9	28	29	65
11	Cambridge U	46	12	6	5	37	23	5	5	13	23	39	62
12	Swansea C	46	13	3	7	31	21	4	8	11	25	40	62
13	Cardiff C	46	6	12	5	24	18	9	4	10	24	32	61
14	Exeter C	46	11	10	2	37	17	0	13	10	16	32	56
15	Halifax T	46	10	5	8	32	32	5	5	13	27	42	55
16	Hereford U	46	10	6	7	33	23	4	5	14	27	38	53
17	Crewe Alex	46	8	9	6	38	35	5	5	13	32	37	53
18	Hartlepool U	46	6	11	6	24	30	5	7	11	20	35	51
19	Stockport Co	46	9	6	8	25	27	4	6	13	15	42	51
20	Tranmere Rov	46	6	10	7	32	37	5	7	11	22	35	50
21	Rochdale	46	8	8	7	31	30	3	9	11	23	43	50
22	Burnley	46	9	7	7	31	35	3	6	14	22	39	49
23	Torquay U	46	8	8	7	28	29	2	10	11	28	43	48
24	Lincoln C*	46	8	7	8	30	27	4	5	14	15	38	48

†promoted *replaced by Scarborough

12

It was also an excellent season for attendances, no doubt helped by the play-offs. A total of 17,379,218 watched League football, a rise on the previous season for the first time in eight years.

On the international front, England began their campaign in the 1988 European Championship, with four matches in Group 4. They beat Northern Ireland 3-0 at Wembley, Yugoslavia 2-0 at Wembley, Northern Ireland 2-0 at Belfast, and drew 0-0 with Turkey at Izmir. It looked as if the visit to Yugoslavia in 1987–88 would prove to be the vital match.

In friendlies England lost 1-0 in Sweden, won 4-2 in Spain, with four goals from Gary Lineker, and in the Rous Cup drew 1-1 with Brazil at Wembley and 0-0 with Scotland in Glasgow.

During the summer, the main activity in the transfer market saw Viv Anderson move from Arsenal to Manchester United (his replacement was Nigel Winterburn from Wimbledon), John Barnes from Watford to Liverpool, Chris Fairclough from Nottingham Forest to Spurs, Glenn Hoddle from Spurs to Monaco, Peter Shilton from Southampton to Derby County, Brian McClair from Celtic to Manchester United, Peter Beardsley from Newcastle to Liverpool (for a British record fee of £1.9 million) and David Speedie from Chelsea to Cup-winners Coventry.

Among the managers, Graham Taylor, whose long association with Watford and chairman Elton John had been extremely successful, moved to Aston Villa, while Dave Bassett, who had been the guiding force in Wimbledon's rapid rise, took his place. Howard Kendall, after reviving Everton, left the Champions to become manager of the Spanish club Athletic Bilbao, and was succeeded at Goodison by his assistant, Colin Harvey. Bobby Gould accepted the managership of Wimbledon.

Wimbledon, incidentally, were the second worst-behaved team in the League in 1986–87, and were fined £4,500 by the FA for their disciplinary record. Southend had the worst record. Portsmouth were fined £2,250, including £1,500 suspended from the previous season.

A sadder story concerned Gary Bailey, Manchester United's international goalkeeper, who was forced to give up the game through injury. United received £300,000 compensation.

A story which did not make much impact at the end of May 1987 but which was to return and make the headlines later concerned a chairman, Robert Maxwell, who resigned at Oxford to take over Derby County, previously run by his son Ian, while another son, Kevin, took over at Oxford.

Pat van den Hauwe scores the only goal of the game at Norwich, which gives Everton the League Championship for the ninth time.
Sporting Pictures (UK) Ltd

AUGUST:
The Centenary Season Starts

The 1987–88 season started earlier than ever before: on 1 August to be precise. Part of the reason was fitting in the special Centenary match which was due to be played before the League season started, so the Charity Shield match was moved forward a week.

David Speedie turned out for his new club, Coventry, against the League Champions, Everton. In a close match Everton won the season's traditional curtain-raiser with a 1-0 victory, Wayne Clarke getting the only goal right on half-time.

The evening of the match produced a major shock for the League when Rupert Murdoch, the new owner of the fading *Today* newspaper, announced that he was withdrawing from the sponsorship deal, made only the previous October. The agreement, made for two years with the offer of a third, was potentially worth nearly £5 million to the Football League, whose management committee was naturally shocked. Much of the money was for distribution among the clubs, of which several of those from the Third and Fourth Division were in financial difficulties. A search for a new sponsor was begun, amid murmurings of possible legal action against the newspaper.

The following week was also taken up with the great Maradona question. Would the world's leading footballer dare to play in the forthcoming League Centenary game in view of the fact that he had eliminated England from the World Cup with a goal clearly scored with his hand? The beginning of the week was full of stories of his being overweight and unfit, to prepare for the fact that he would not play, but the British Consulate in Naples was able to give better news — they had issued visas for him and his family and entourage. Meanwhile second thoughts on the sponsorship problems were gloomier than ever: who would want to sponsor the League when its Centenary celebrations were already sold to the Mercantile Credit finance company?

Centre-forwards made the news on the eve of the big Centenary match. Alan Smith, Arsenal's new purchase from Leicester, came into the Football League side, while Newcastle signed Francisco Mirandinha, the Brazilian international for £1 million from Palmeiras. Meanwhile a former million-pound Englishman, Trevor Francis, joined the Glasgow Rangers bandwagon, and Luton sold their Welsh international Peter Nicholas to Aberdeen. Maradona landed at Stansted in his private jet.

The big match did not carry all the football headlines on Saturday, 8 August. The other side of the game was reflected in the announcement that the Football League disciplinary committee had imposed a record £5,000 fine on Portsmouth's Mick Kennedy, who had boasted in the *Sun* newspaper of enjoyment in hurting opponents with his tackling.

The Football League XI beat the Rest of the World 3-0 in the "Centenary Classic". A crowd of 61,000 watched, and 61 countries took the match on television, with an estimated worldwide audience of around one billion. The match was something of an exhibition, with so many substitutes that no fewer than 35 players took part. For the record, they were: Football League XI: Shilton, Gough, Sansom, McClelland, McGrath, Brady, Robson, Webb, C. Allen, Beardsley, Waddle. Subs: Ardiles, A. Smith, Whiteside, Ogrizovic, S. Clarke, Nevin.
Rest of the World: Dasayev, Josimar, Celso, Julio Alberto, Hysen, Bagui, Berthold, Lineker, Platini, Maradona, Futre. Substitutes: Zubizarreta, Elkjaer, Detari, Larsson, Belanov, Stojkovic, Zavarov.

Robson (2) and Whiteside scored the goals, and Maradona played well, despite plenty of token boos at his every touch. Platini was acknowledged as the star of the match, but Maradona was as much in the news afterwards as before, with everybody wondering whether an exhibition match was worth his £90,000 fee and private plane fare.

The fees of the players in the big match, and the cost of the tickets (£6 standing, £17.50 to £30 sitting) was put into perspective before the big League kick-off with the publication of a survey of soccer finances. It revealed that 80 of the 92 League clubs were technically insolvent, including such big names

Francisco Mirandinha, the Brazilian international star, transferred to Newcastle United from Palmeiras for £1 million in time for the new season. Match Magazine

as Arsenal, Manchester United, Chelsea, Aston Villa and Manchester City.

The next day, however, came the best possible financial news. The League sponsorship was taken over by Barclays Bank. That Barclays had outbid three other big companies for the privilege emphasised the continuing status of the national game. In the end it was obvious that *Today* had done the League a favour. Instead of being named after a newspaper, the League was now named after one of the world's great financial institutions.

Not that this was at the forefront of the fans' minds on 15 August. This was the first day of League football, and talk was of prospects. There were 17 clubs beginning the season with new managers, including the Champions and Cup-winners (John Sillett had stepped up from chief coach), and dozens of players had been transferred.

Pride of place, of course, went to Scarborough, the new boys. They began with a match with Wolves, the great team of the 1950s, the side that could claim to have played their part in initiating European club competition. Unfortunately, it was not a happy introduction. Despite spending £120,000 on ground improvements, a section of roofing gave way, a youth was injured, and there was crowd trouble on the terraces with fans fighting. In the end the score of

Everton win the Charity Shield. Wayne Clarke (second left) celebrates after scoring the only goal of the game against Coventry City.
Sporting Pictures (UK) Ltd

Maradona, the world's greatest footballer, comes to Wembley for the League Centenary match.

2-2 was a minor detail of what should have been a happier occasion.

Of the other main results on the first day, Liverpool won 2-1 at Highbury and Coventry beat Spurs by the same score. Derby won and Portsmouth lost on their return to the First Division. Derby were helped when Mick Harford of Luton became the first man to be sent off — after five minutes. Tony Rees of Birmingham scored the first goal, taking only 45 seconds to net against Stoke. The biggest crowd of the day was at Highbury, where Barnes and Beardsley played well to give notice to Liverpool fans that there would be life after Rush.

The new status of the Barclays League was captured by an *Observer* cartoon, showing a pin-striped, bowler-hatted bank manager standing on the terraces shouting: "Deposit it in the net, you fool!"

After the first Saturday, the old story of hooliganism was to the fore again. The serious incident at Scarborough resulted in swift FA/League action, with Wolves' away matches restricted to all-ticket until further notice.

At Robert Maxwell's Derby, where a stabbing was reported, the bigger story was the impending arrival of the England defender Mark Wright from Southampton. Newcastle United, while awaiting their new centre forward from Brazil, knocked down the old West Stand in a £4 million rebuilding project.

Alan Smith, Arsenal's new centre-forward signing from Leicester City.

John Barnes of Liverpool is on the ball in the match against the Arsenal.
Match Magazine

Kerry Dixon of Chelsea (9) seen in the thick of the action against Manchester United.
Sporting Pictures (UK) Ltd

From the same match, which United won 3-1, Remi Moses covers Chelsea's Clive Wilson.

Sporting Pictures (UK) Ltd

Watford start the season by beating Wimbledon at home 1-0. Here the action is in the "Hornets" penalty area with John Fashanu (left) and Carlton Fairweather (11) combining for the "Dons".

Sporting Pictures (UK) Ltd

The League and Littlewoods Cup progressed in mid-week, and on the second Saturday it was announced that Wolves had been fined £5,000 and their supporters banned from six away matches for the Scarborough disturbance.

On the field, after only one week, Liverpool remained the only club in the First Division with a 100 per cent record — but they had played only once, their first few home games being postponed because of extensive repairs to a sewer at the Kop end. Queen's Park Rangers and Nottingham Forest were early League leaders.

Before the last Saturday of August the League were forced to amend one of their Centenary celebrations, a proposed meeting between League Champions Everton and Scottish Champions, Rangers. The Scottish League, frightened of hooliganism and its possible effect on Scottish clubs in Europe, advised that the match, scheduled for 25 November, should be scrapped. The League looked round for Continental opposition.

The goalscorers got off the ground as the first month of the season ended. In the First Division Arsenal hit Portsmouth, 6-0, Everton beat Wednesday 4-0 and Liverpool won 4-1 at Coventry. Pride of place though, went to Gillingham in the Third Division, who scored their first goals of the season — eight of them — in an 8-1 drubbing of Southend, whose only goal was an own goal. Darlington got 5 at Hartlepool, and Scarborough scored their first

League victory with a 4-0 defeat of Bolton Wanderers.

SEPTEMBER:
Queen's Park Rangers Make the Running

On the last day of August, a Monday, Portsmouth earned their first victory in the First Division since 1961, having been down to the Fourth and back again in the meantime. They beat West Ham 2-1 at Fratton Park with two goals by Kevin Dillon. A victory by Manchester United over Chelsea took them to the top of the table for a couple of days.

Mirandinha made his first appearance for Newcastle on the following day and had a quiet debut, although his team earned a welcome draw at Norwich.

Queen's Park Rangers and Nottingham Forest, the two pace-setters in the Championship, played in midweek. While Forest were held at home 3-3 by Southampton, a goal by Martin Allen on Rangers' plastic pitch was enough to defeat Everton 1-0, and Q.P.R. became the first side to pull away at the top of the First Division. Football, however, remains a question of instant success and failure so far as managers are concerned. Ron Saunders, the West Brom manager for 18 months, found his team at the bottom of the Second Division after four games and was sacked. He was replaced by a former West Brom manager in Ron Atkinson, the board no doubt hoping that two Rons would make a right.

Form had begun to settle down a bit by the first Saturday in September. Q.P.R. won 1-0 at Charlton and opened a four-point lead at the top of the First Division. Manchester United and Chelsea came next, Chelsea coming back from 3-1 down at the interval to beat Nottingham Forest 4-3. Liverpool dropped their first point following a 1-1 draw at West Ham, and Luton scored their first victory in emphatic style at Oxford, winning 5-2.

Barnsley, when beating Plymouth 2-1, opened a three-point gap over five teams in the Second Division, where the best result was achieved by Crystal Palace with a 6-0 victory at Birmingham, five goals coming in the second half. West Brom pleased their new manager by beating Shrewsbury 2-1 to climb off the bottom.

Something good seemed to be in the air in Kent, where Gillingham followed their eight against Southend by beating Chesterfield 10-0. They became the League's leading scorers on 19, with 18 of them coming in two games. It was a record victory for Gillingham, and a record defeat for Chesterfield. Southend, incidentally, were at the receiving end of a 6-2 defeat by Notts County, and had conceded 20 in five games, the League's worst record so far.

Talking of the League's worst — the fine imposed on Wimbledon for their behaviour the previous season seemed to be having no effect as six names went into the book at Newcastle, where they won 2-1 to spoil Mirandinha's home debut. Coventry's Nick Pickering was sent off against Manchester United in another rough game and United's manager, Alex Ferguson, was reported to the FA for remarks he made to the referee — the season before he had been fined £500 for a similar offence.

Pat Nevin, Chelsea's brilliant Scottish international wizard of the dribble.
Match Magazine

Already anxieties were appearing around the divisions. Charlton in the First and York in the Third had so far failed to score a point. Scarborough had found their touch, though — a 2-0 defeat of Tranmere allowed them to join Bolton and Exeter at the top of the Fourth Division.

The second week of September brought the England national side back into action for a friendly in Dusseldorf against West Germany. Hoddle of Monaco and Lineker of Barcelona appeared for England, who were thoroughly beaten 3-1 in a dispiriting display and appeared to be well inferior to the World Cup finalists.

On Saturday, 13 September, Liverpool returned to Anfield, the sewer having been mended, and beat Oxford 2-0. Barnes gave glimpses of his potential, received a standing ovation from the fans and became a favourite of the Kop. From then on his form blossomed as it never had at Watford. Pride of place among the day's performances, however, was that of Mirandinha, who dazzled before 45,000 fans at Old Trafford and scored twice as Newcastle drew 2-2 with Manchester United. A Gary Bannister hat-trick against Chelsea kept Q.P.R. at the top and stretched their lead to five points. Spurs were second, with a victory over Southampton by 2-1 giving them their 13th consecutive home win, a club record.

A 2-1 win over Leicester took Crystal Palace, managed by Steve Coppell, to the top of the Second Division. There were also new leaders in the Third Division, with Walsall taking over after a 1-0 victory at Rotherham, Craig Shakespeare's goal being classed as poetry by this team-mates.

Charlton, at Portsmouth, and York, at home to Preston, each drew 1-1 and so earned their first points of the season.

A big programme of football on Tuesday, 15 September, when the European competitions got under way, saw Liverpool have a surprising amount of difficulty in beating Charlton 2-1 at Anfield. But they remained unbeaten and moved up to third, with two games in hand of most of their rivals.

Over 10,000 turned up at Priestfield, to see if Gillingham could maintain their recent average of nine goals per home game, but were disappointed with a 0-0 draw with Sunderland. In the Fourth Division Burnley beat Wrexham 1-0 and moved to the top. Strange to think that four months earlier they were within one goal of dropping out altogether.

The following night an impressive 2-0 win by Aston Villa at West Bromwich, only their second of the season, gave the first indications that under their new manager, Graham Taylor, Villa might turn out to be a force in the Second Division. They won again the following Saturday, 1-0 at Huddersfield.

On that Saturday, Queen's Park Rangers, on the other hand, lost for the first time, 2-0 at Oxford, but stayed top. Wins by Tottenham and Chelsea meant that the top three clubs came from London. To maintain the good London news, Charlton got their first win at the expense of Luton, and relegated

John Barnes of Liverpool (right) and Paul Ince of West Ham (centre) tangle at Upton Park in the 1-1 draw.

Jesper Olsen of Manchester United makes a run at the Newcastle goal with defenders in pursuit. The Danish international scored in the 2-2 draw.

Sheffield Wednesday, still without a win themselves, to bottom.

In the Second Division, Bradford were having a good run and a 2-1 victory over Blackburn kept them one point ahead of Palace.

Wigan won 2-1 at Walsall to take over at the top of the Third Division, Gillingham moving into second, not unnaturally on their goal difference, easily the best in the country. Scarborough, by beating Swansea, moved to the top of the Fourth Division.

This week-end was the first for live Sunday afternoon football television, and the match chosen by the BBC was the Newcastle v Liverpool match at St James' Park: Mirandinha v Barnes, the two players who had made most impact on the season so far. On the day, though, it was the old Liverpool hand Steve Nicol who stole the limelight, netting three times in an easy 4-1 win. Liverpool thus edged comfortably into third place, still with two games in hand.

Midweek soccer concerned the second round, first leg ties of the Littlewoods Cup. On Tuesday night the leading performances were a 1-0 defeat of Derby by Southend, and a 3-1 defeat of Portsmouth by Swindon. Bournemouth beat Southampton 1-0 in a south coast encounter, and Rochdale drew 1-1 with Wimbledon. The best away performances were by Wolves, who won 2-1 at Maine Road, and Rotherham, who held Everton to 3-2 at Goodison.

On Wednesday night Reading beat Chelsea 3-1, Torquay, managed by old Spurs favourite Cyril Knowles, beat Spurs 1-0 (nice one, Cyril) and Blackpool beat Newcastle 1-0. Blackburn drew with Liverpool and Mansfield drew at Oxford.

News from Spain which was expected to have its effect on English football sooner rather than later was the sacking of Terry Venables by Barcelona.

The last Saturday in September saw Q.P.R. get back to winning ways by beating Luton 2-0, and Chelsea shake-off the Littlewoods Cup defeat with a 3-0 win at Watford.

The top six in the four divisions after six weeks of the new season were as follows:

	P	W	D	L	F	A	Pts
First Division							
Q.P.R.	9	7	1	1	14	4	22
Chelsea	9	6	0	3	18	11	18
Nottingham F	9	5	2	2	15	9	17
Tottenham H	9	5	2	2	12	6	16
Liverpool	6	5	1	0	16	6	16
Manchester U	9	4	4	1	14	8	16
Second Division							
Bradford C	9	6	2	1	16	8	20
Crystal Palace	10	5	3	2	25	14	18
Hull C	9	4	5	0	13	8	17
Middlesbrough	9	5	1	3	13	8	16
Swindon T	9	5	1	3	14	10	16
Millwall	9	5	1	3	14	13	16
Third Division							
Northampton T	9	5	2	2	13	4	17
Fulham	9	5	2	2	13	7	17
Walsall	9	5	2	2	13	8	17
Wigan Ath	8	5	2	1	14	11	17
Gillingham	9	4	4	1	27	8	16
Bristol C	9	4	4	1	15	11	16
Fourth Division							
Exeter U	9	5	3	1	17	7	18
Torquay U	9	5	2	2	19	8	17
Cardiff C	9	5	2	2	13	10	17
Leyton Orient	9	4	4	1	20	13	16
Scarborough	9	5	1	3	18	13	16
Scunthorpe U	9	4	3	2	19	15	15

Lee Chapman of Sheffield Wednesday, a centre-forward of the old school.
Match Magazine

At the wrong end of the tables, Charlton, Huddersfield, York and Newport seemed to have the look which promised a season's struggle.

In the last couple of days of September, Liverpool beat Derby 4-0 (Aldridge 3) to move into second place, and Bradford won at Huddersfield to pull further away in the Second Division. In the Third, the top five clubs failed to win Tuesday night matches, and Bristol City, by beating Chesterfield 2-1, leap-frogged over them to the top. Exeter also found themselves beaten, and Leyton Orient and Scarborough, who won at Torquay, took the lead in the Fourth Division.

OCTOBER:
Bradford Try for First Division Status

Transfer news made big headlines in October. Two Scots departed from London to return to their homeland. Richard Gough left Spurs for £1.5 million to join the European glory-seekers of Glasgow Rangers, and West Ham's goalscorer Frank McAvennie also arrived in Glasgow when Celtic paid £750,000 for his services.

On the first Saturday of the month, Liverpool slaughtered Portsmouth 4-0, but Q.P.R. won 2-1 at Wimbledon to stay at the top, although had they been the losers they would by now be feeling Liverpool's breath on their neck. The best individual First Division performance, however, came from Graeme Sharp, who scored all four for Everton at Southampton, suggesting that the Champions were not yet finished with.

In the Second Division Bradford City had their highest crowd of the season to see them beat challengers Middlesbrough 2-0. As their other main rivals lost, they took a six-point lead at the top of the table.

Bristol City's Third Division lead did not last long. They had two men sent off at Northampton, whose 3-0 victory took them to the top of the table. Scarborough, after beating Burnley 1-0, went into the lead on their own in the Fourth Division, as Leyton Orient could only draw at Wrexham.

By an ironic twist, West Ham's programme featured an interview with Frank McAvennie, printed before his transfer, which assured fans that if he were to ask for a move they would be the first to hear about it. Frank Spencer couldn't have timed it better.

The Littlewoods Cup provided the mid-week entertainment again, and the poor West Ham fans must have thought even Frank Spencer couldn't have done worse than their team against Barnsley. Two up in the match at half-time, the Hammers allowed Barnsley to level at 2-2 and then score three in extra time to go through 5-2 on aggregate.

Bournemouth drew 2-2 against their First Division neighbours Southampton to put them out 3-2. The other potential shocks did not materialise in the Tuesday night games. Oxford, Manchester City and Everton all did well enough away from home to squeeze past Mansfield, Wolves and Rotherham respectively. Sheffield Wednesday and Wimbledon each won 2-1 at home to put out Shrewsbury and Rochdale respectively by 3-2 aggregate. Blackburn were the unluckiest side, perhaps. They lost 2-1 to Liverpool on aggregate, Liverpool's winner coming with a minute left. Watford might have done their morale some good with an 8-0 drubbing of Darlington.

The Wednesday matches provided further shocks with three more First Division clubs bowing the knee to lower-class opposition. Chelsea made a complete mess of their home leg with Reading. Durie scored a hat-trick to put Chelsea ahead on aggregate before half-time, and just when everybody expected a big

John Aldridge, who replaced Ian Rush, scored in the first nine matches of the season for Liverpool and promised plenty more. Match Magazine

Graeme Sharp scored all four goals for Everton in the victory over Southampton at the Dell. Match Magazine

score they allowed Reading to net twice and win 5-4 on aggregate. Derby drew 0-0 at home to Southend to go down to a home goal from the first leg, and Portsmouth, having lost 3-1 at Swindon, lost again 3-1 at Fratton Park. Spurs avoided their potential trip-wire by beating Torquay 3-0 and going through.

The draw for the next round of the Littlewoods Cup brought together Liverpool and Everton, a prospect for later in the month.

Amid the disciplinary decisions handed down in early October was a three-match international ban on Tony Cottee for being sent off in an under-21 friendly with West Germany. Alex Ferguson was fined £750 for his abusive language to the referee mentioned earlier. Steve Walsh, of Leicester, was banned for a further six matches (he had been banned for two for being sent off) after fracturing a player's jaw with his elbow. He was also fined £500. Tranmere were fined £2,000 and lost two points for failing to fulful a fixture with Bolton. Everything was happening this season.

Heavy rain caused waterlogged pitches and the postponement of a few games on October's second Saturday. Liverpool and Q.P.R. did not play. Everton and Manchester United popped in four each against Chelsea and Sheffield Wednesday and moved up the table, as did Arsenal, whose 2-0 defeat of Oxford United took them into third place.

Another famous old club, Sunderland, beat Wigan 4-1 in the Third Division to go to the top,

while a new one, Scarborough, maintained their Fourth Division lead with a 3-1 victory over Exeter.

Malcolm Macdonald returned to football from being a publican this month when he was appointed manager of Huddersfield Town, currently propping up the Second Division.

As the England squad prepared for the resumption of the European Championship, and their Wembley meeting with Turkey, football talk speculated on Charlie Nicholas moving to France, and among the lower reaches of the League, analysed the Freight Rover Trophy results. It was strange to see Bolton and Preston meet in the preliminary round — two sides who had graced the great occasions.

England improved their goal difference tremendously with a rout of Turkey by 8-0, Lineker scoring three and Barnes two. The vital match was still going to be the trip to Yugoslavia, but with a goal tally of 15 to nil England at least knew that a draw would be enough.

Saturday 18 October was crunch day for the First Division leaders Queen's Park Rangers. It was the week they were scheduled to go to Anfield, and it proved a humbling experience. Liverpool ran the game and won 4-0 with two from John Barnes, the last a splendid individual effort that put the icing on the cake. The "Reds" took over the top of the table, and as on average they had played two games fewer than everybody else, it was clear that they would take a good deal of dislodging.

In the Second Division Bradford walloped Bir-

Gary Lineker (left) with three goals and John Barnes with two goals, celebrate England's 8-0 rout of Turkey.   Match Magazine

mingham 4-0 and retained their six-point lead. Hull were second, but the other sides were beginning to lose touch. The Third Division was much closer, with two points covering Northampton, Sunderland, Bristol City, Notts County, Fulham and Walsall. Apart from Walsall, who drew at Brentford, the seventh club, all had good wins. Scarborough lost, but retained the Fourth Division lead.

Huddersfield, in the Second Division, and York, in the Third, were beginning to be detached, seven and six points respectively adrift of the rest.

In the televised Sunday match, Arsenal had a good 2-1 win at White Hart Lane and eased themselves into third place.

On 20 October it was revealed that the new League leaders, Liverpool, had signed Ray Houghton from Oxford for £825,000. Houghton's name had been linked with many clubs, including one or two from the Continent. Kenny Dalglish, the Liverpool manager, had now spent more than the £3.2 million he had received for Ian Rush in the summer, principally on Barnes, Beardsley and Houghton. It seemed nothing was to be left to chance in keeping Liverpool at the top.

There was still a full midweek football programme, and the main Tuesday business in England, while Scottish clubs took part in European games, featured mainly the Second, Third and Fourth Divisions. Middlesbrough's 3-1 defeat of Ipswich was the Second Division's best performance, the club which had been bankrupt moving into third place. Sunderland's 1-0 win at Bristol City in the Third took them two points clear, Northampton losing at Mansfield, but Notts County, Walsall and Fulham also had excellent wins to keep right behind them. In the Fourth Division Leyton Orient made the most significant move with an 8-0 thrashing of Rochdale. It was Orient's biggest win (unless one regards 9-2 as bigger) and equalled Rochdale's worst defeat. It moved Leyton Orient into second place.

There was a Second Division turn-up the following night, when Bradford lost 4-2 at home to Manchester City. Their lead was cut to three points. It was City's first away win in 21 months. Villa beat Crystal Palace 4-1 to join Swindon in third place. In the Fourth Division Scarborough drew at Hereford and kept their noses in front by two points.

Off the field Tottenham revealed nearly £1 million in trading profit, after a £662,000 loss the year before. And a nice reminder of perhaps the biggest giant of the past was very appropriate to Centenary year: Sir Stanley Matthews, now coaching in Canada, returned to Hanley, Stoke-on-Trent, to unveil a statue of himself.

The fans at the Saturday games on 24 October had plenty to discuss. Revelations in the *Sun* newspaper about David Pleat's private life had led the Spurs manager to resign. Inevitably there was speculation as to whether Terry Venables would take over. The majority opinion was that it was more a question of when than if.

The managerless Spurs lost 3-0 at Nottingham Forest. Liverpool had a tricky match at Luton, where Dalglish had made rude remarks about the plastic pitch. Liverpool scraped home 1-0, thanks to two amazing misses by Luton in the last few seconds. But the goal was enough to give Liverpool a record of nine wins and a draw in ten matches, and they still led Q.P.R. on goal difference, with two games in hand.

There was little change in the Second Division, where the top four teams drew. In the Third, Sunderland, Walsall and Northampton won, while Notts County, Fulham and Bristol City lost. The six teams ended the day in that order. The Fourth Division was becoming the closest of all. Three points covered the top ten clubs, and the 15th club was only two wins behind the leaders.

On 27 October, the day for Littlewoods and Freight Rover Cup-ties, Terry Venables agreed to join Tottenham, but he would not take over until 1 December, having prior commitments. It was not unexpected news.

In the Littlewoods Cup third round, played on a one-leg basis, there were some shocks. Bury, from the Third Division, beat the long-time Championship leaders, Queen's Park Rangers, 1-0. Bradford won at Charlton 1-0, Manchester City beat Nottingham Forest 3-0 and Stoke beat Norwich 2-1.

The next day came what might be called a shock or not, according to whether one favours red or blue. Everton inflicted upon Liverpool their first defeat of the season, and at Anfield at that. A deflected Gary Stevens shot was enough to take Everton to the next round by 1-0. Aston Villa's 2-1 defeat of Spurs and Swindon's 1-1 draw with Watford were other meritorious performances.

The Saturday League games which ended October saw Spurs' slide continue with a 3-0 home defeat by Wimbledon. Arsenal snatched a 1-0 win at Newcastle, but with Manchester United and Forest drawing, and Q.P.R. being held at Norwich, it was not a day for change. With Liverpool waiting for Sunday, when their home match with Everton was being televised, Arsenal took over the top of the table, at least for 24 hours, having a better goal difference than Q.P.R.

Bradford's 2-0 defeat of Crystal Palace in the Second Division restored their six-point lead, as Hull slipped up at Plymouth. Middlesbrough passed them into second spot on goal difference. Huddersfield won at last, as did York in the Third Division, but both clubs were a long way behind.

Aldershot and Northampton were engaged in a thrilling 4-4 draw in the Third Division, enough to keep Northampton in touch as Sunderland lost at Notts County. In the Fourth Division Scarborough lost at lowly Wrexham and slipped to fourth. Wolves were now the new leaders on 28 points, but there were no fewer than seven teams on 27. Although Liverpool and Bradford had useful leads, all the divisions were being closely fought in the Centenary year.

Steve McMahon of Liverpool gets to the ball ahead of Luton's Brian Stein in the match at Kenilworth Road. Gary Gillespie scored the only goal of the game to send the "Reds" home happy.

The Arsenal goalie, Lukic, is under pressure as Derby attack in quest of the equaliser. The "Gunners" won this Highbury encounter 2-1.

NOVEMBER:
City Score Ten and Elton John "Sells" Watford

November opened with a blistering Sunday televised game at Anfield. If Liverpool were to be halted in the League it seemed necessary for Everton to win this match, but the "Reds" put up a superb dislay. A goal in each half from McMahon and Beardsley put them back on top of the table by two points, with two games in hand, most goals scored and fewest conceded. It was already beginning to look like a question of "who will be second?"

The following Tuesday Arsenal regained the lead temporarily by beating Chelsea 3-1 at Highbury. Heavy scorers in the Second Division were Crystal Palace, reviving their promotion prospects with a 5-1 defeat of Plymouth, and in the Third Division Fulham and Sunderland improved their chances with 5-0 and 7-0 wins over Grimsby and Southend. Watford beat Swindon 4-2 in their Littlewoods Cup replay.

Liverpool appeared at Wimbledon and drew 1-1, thus going back to the top of the table. It was their 12th League game since the start of the season, and they were unbeaten, a record opening run for the club. At the other end of the League, Scarborough could only draw at home to Cardiff and dropped slightly back.

Neither Arsenal nor Liverpool played on the second Saturday in November, and Queen's Park Rangers missed the chance to join them on points at the top of the table by being held 0-0 at home by Watford.

The big story was in the Second Division, where Manchester City slaughtered Malcolm Macdonald's Huddersfield by a 10-1 scoreline. Adcock, Stewart and White all scored three: a hat-trick of hat-tricks, and only the third time it had happened in the League. It was one of City's biggest wins: 11-3 is in the record books, and the reader can choose which he thinks is best. It was certainly the biggest defeat for Huddersfield, who 60 years earlier were the most powerful club in the land, with three consecutive Championships to their name.

Nearer the top of the table Bradford lost 3-0 at Barnsley, and Middlesbrough and Hull halved the gap between them to three points.

The Third Division showed the uncertainty of soccer. Grimsby, who were defeated 5-0 at Fulham in midweek, drew at leaders Sunderland, who had won 7-0 in midweek. Fulham were also held to a 0-0 draw at home by Northampton. Sunderland and Walsall continued to lead.

Scarborough had a good win at Scunthorpe in the Fourth Division to stay in the race, but a two-point gap had opened, with Wolves and Colchester at the top.

With the European Championship and England's vital match with Yugoslavia claiming the attention of the fans, another long-serving manager lost his job in mid-November. Ken Brown, 14 years at Norwich, was dispensed with. The previous season he had

Terry Venables, the former Barcelona manager, joined Tottenham in the same capacity during November. Match Magazine

taken Norwich to fifth in the Championship, their best ever position, but with three wins in 15 matches Norwich found only Watford and Charlton below them this season, and that was that.

Domestic football was confined to the Simod Cup and Freight Rover Trophy as England stepped out before 70,000 onlookers in Belgrade needing to draw to qualify for the European Championship finals. The match began with dithering in the Yugoslav defence after three minutes and Beardsley nipped in to secure the lead. A foolish error by the Yugoslav keeper came in the 16th minute, when he picked the ball up twice in his penalty area. Barnes scored following the free-kick. Four minutes later Robson added another, and soon after Adams headed a fourth. A 4-0 half-time scoreline later became 4-1, but it was a very comfortable victory.

On the same day Wales lost their last chance by losing in Czechoslovakia — the Welsh were a little unlucky as usual. Northern Ireland and Scotland had been eliminated earlier, but Scotland won with a goal five minutes from time in Bulgaria to put the Republic of Ireland through, the first time the country has reached the finals of a big event.

On Saturday Arsenal set up a club record with

In a battle between the "big boys", Viv Anderson of Manchester United gets in an off target header against Liverpool, following a corner.

their tenth consecutive League win (13th in all matches) when they won 4-2 at Norwich. Strange to think that this side had achieved a record that the great teams of Herbert Chapman and Alex James of the 1930s, which dominated football, could not match. Arsenal's victory took them to the top of the table again, because Liverpool had once again been selected for the Sunday televised match. Queen's Park Rangers lost ground with a draw at Tottenham, partly due to their full-back, Mark Dennis, being sent off for the 11th time in his career.

In the Second Division Middlesbrough beat Hull 1-0 and kept three points behind Bradford, with Hull three points further back.

The clubs from the lower divisions were playing in the FA Cup first round. The most nostalgic tie saw Bolton win 1-0 at Burnley — two post-war Cup giants playing alongside the non-Leaguers. There were a few League clubs put out by their humbler opponents. Chester lost 1-0 at home to Runcorn, Crewe lost at Lincoln, the newest non-Leaguers, Carlisle lost 4-2 at Macclesfield (after being two up) and Aldershot crashed 3-0 at Sutton United. York could only manage a draw at home to Burton, and Stockport did likewise away at Telford.

On Sunday, before the cameras, Liverpool were held 1-1 at Old Trafford, so Arsenal, at last, stayed top. They were two points ahead of Liverpool, but the Merseysiders had two games in hand.

FA Cup replays, Littlewoods Cup fourth round ties and a Simod Cup match were the main mid-week fare as November went into its third week. Stockport beat Telford to eliminate a doughty non-League Cup-Fighter in the FA Cup, and there were no surprises in the Tuesday night Littlewoods Cup, although Everton struggled to beat Oldham 2-1 at Goodison. It was much the same on Wednesday, with York winning 2-1 at Burton in the FA Cup replay. In the Littlewoods Cup, Bury led Manchester United for 12 minutes at Old Trafford, but eventually lost 2-1. The Littlewoods Cup now took a rest until January, when the quarter-finals would be played.

The big news before the Saturday games was the resignation of Elton John as Watford chairman. It was reported that he had sold 95 per cent of his shares to publishing magnate Robert Maxwell, who already had substantial connections with Derby and Oxford. However things were not going to be so simple, and this story was going to run and run.

By a coincidence Watford were playing at Oxford, and John and Maxwell watched a draw together. But interest so far as honours were concerned was elsewhere, and surprisingly the big two slipped up together. Arsenal's fine run ended with a 1-0 home defeat by Southampton, while Liverpool, also at home, could only draw with lowly Norwich. Most of the clubs immediately below them did no better, however, so it was only a matter of marking time at the top.

Bradford, Middlesbrough and Hull all won in the Second Division to keep the status quo, there, too.

Sunderland could only draw at Chesterfield in the Third Division, and as most of the chasers won, the table telescoped again. Wolves stayed ahead in the Fourth, but Scarborough had more trouble with hooligans and 25 arrests were made following the visit of Halifax. It seemed that the seaside town had been recognised as a day out for the thugs, and Scarborough must have begun to doubt their wisdom in joining the League. They were held 1-1 on the pitch, and slipped to sixth.

Monday was the day that Terry Venables returned to English football as Spurs manager. He joined a week earlier than intended because of Spurs' poor results. Greeted with a battery of cameras and pressmen he gave away very little but everybody seemed happy.

There were two big games on Merseyside in midweek. Liverpool won the first, beating Watford 4-0 and going back to the top of the table. Meanwhile a host of Freight Rover Trophy preliminary round matches saw Sunderland get six in the first half against Rotherham before easing down to win 7-1.

The next big game in Liverpool was the meeting of Champions Everton and their West German counterparts Bayern Munich. This was billed as the Classic Football Challenge and was part of the League Centenary celebrations. Originally Glasgow Rangers, the Scottish Champions were to be Everton's opponents, but the authorities were afraid of hooliganism if Scots descended in force on Liverpool. It was a good match so far as friendlies go and Everton won 3-1, but a comparison of the 13,000 gate with the 32,000 the night before to see Watford tells its own story.

Meanwhile the League faced a more serious problem than the lack of impact of the Centenary

Bryan Robson of Manchester United, England's captain and general driving force. Match Magazine

Peter Beardsley, shown in his Liverpool colours, scored England's first goal against Yugoslavia. Match Magazine

celebrations. The Management Committee met over the Watford question and came out in opposition to the deal, upholding the regulation that no individual, directly or indirectly, should be in a position to control or influence more than one club. Maxwell, with his powerful media connections, fumed and declared war on the "mismanagement committee", asserting that the purchase of Watford would go ahead as planned on 8 December.

As if they were enjoying the row, Watford beat Arsenal 2-0 on the last Saturday of the month, and the heady days of the Highbury run seemed to have come to an end. Liverpool won at Tottenham by the same score, as if to disappoint those who thought Venables would be able to wave a magic wand. Queen's Park Rangers also lost, and suddenly the gaps between Liverpool and the following clubs were five, eight and ten points, and they still had a game in hand. It seemed all over already.

Bradford lost, too, in the Second Division, 4-2 at home to Aston Villa, whose away record (eight wins in 11 matches) was the best in the country. Villa moved to third, and Middlesbrough took over at the top from Bradford on goal difference.

Sunderland moved two points clear in the Third Division again, beating Port Vale 2-1, and Wolves, despite losing 2-0 at home to Wrexham, remained one point ahead of Leyton Orient in the Fourth.

A sad note was struck by the ten players sent off in one day — the third highest in history. Two of them were Wimbledon representatives. Wimbledon and Portsmouth, two of the most offending teams of 1986–87, had each had two players sent off on successive Saturdays. It seemed that fines and suspensions were not working.

DECEMBER:
Liverpool Stretch Away

Ken Brown, the sacked Norwich manager, took over at Shrewsbury in an acting capacity, during the first week of December. Meanwhile Norwich prepared for the sale of their midfield star Steve Bruce.

The Watford saga took a new turn with the League applying for two temporary injunctions which in effect barred Robert Maxwell from taking over for the time being. However a secret meeting between Maxwell, League president Philip Carter and Arsenal's David Dein, also of the management committee, saw peace. It seemed that the League would raise no objections to Maxwell's acquisition of Watford provided he dispose of his family interest at Oxford, and his 30 per cent share of Reading. The news seemed to please everybody except Oxford, who appeared to have lost an owner at a stroke. By coincidence Watford were visiting Maxwell's "other" club, Derby, and drew 1-1.

Nearer the top of the table, Arsenal returned to winning ways, beating Sheffield Wednesday, and getting to within two points of Liverpool, whose game was again the Sunday television spot. As Queen's Park Rangers lost at home to Manchester

Des Walker, one of Brian Clough's young men at Nottingham Forest, was an ever-present at this stage of the season.   Match Magazine

United, there was now a six-point gap beneath the top two.

There was a shock in the Second Division, where Bradford lost 4-0 at Ipswich. Hull's home draw with Reading dropped them to seventh. The best performance was Crystal Palace's 3-1 win at Maine Road before 23,000 fans, which took them above Manchester City, who had been making a promising run. The Londoners equalised from a penalty after the City keeper, Eric Nixon, had thrown the ball in the face of Palace striker Mark Bright. Nixon was sent off and Palace added two more. The referee was struck by a coin, and there was similar trouble at West Ham, where the referee was given an escort at the end after he had sent off the Hammers' Mark Ward.

There was little activity in the lower divisions, as this was the second round of the FA Cup. There were one or two surprises. Cambridge United lost 1-0 at home to Yeovil, Peterborough lost 3-1 at home to Sutton United and Bristol Rovers could only draw away to Rugby.

On Sunday Liverpool scored two late goals to beat Chelsea 2-1 at Anfield, and Macclesfield beat Rotherham 4-0 in the FA Cup.

Early in the week reservations were voiced by other members of the League management committee over the deal that had been struck the previous Sunday regarding Watford. Ron Noades of Palace and Bill Fox of Blackburn, two management committee representatives of Second Division clubs, were not convinced that Reading's case had been considered sufficiently. According to Noades, a majority of the committee were not in favour of the injunction against Maxwell being dropped. Philip Carter, the League president, had in the meantime gone to Dubai with Everton. On his return the League reserved their position until the committee could meet and Maxwell and John agreed to delay their sale until afterwards.

Ken Brown resigned after eight days at Shrewsbury and Mark Dennis of Q.P.R. was banned by the FA for 53 days, the heaviest punishment given to a League player for 13 years. He was found guilty of bringing the game into disrepute after his 11th sending-off. It was pointed out that he had committed 77 offences in just over ten seasons. The club's chairman, David Bulstrode, described the decision as appalling, and one that did nothing to encourage an honest player — and he didn't mean that the sentence was lenient. The ban was timed to start on Christmas Eve. A happier player was Norwich's England defender Steve Bruce, who was finally permitted to leave for Manchester United for £800,000 plus another £100,000 should he win a full cap.

After all this off-field activity, it was good to get back to the play on Saturday, 12 December, at least initially. It turned out to be the worst day for sendings off since the same Saturday two years earlier. Twelve players took an early bath in a display which had nothing to do with Christmas spirit. Eight of them got marching orders for fighting.

Liverpool came closest to defeat yet, with a 2-2 draw at Southampton, who had a header kicked off the line in the dying seconds. Arsenal were lucky to draw in Sunday's televised match at Coventry, so there was no change. Other interesting Sunday results were Forest's 4-0 defeat of Queen's Park Rangers, which took them to third and Rangers down to sixth, and bottom club Charlton's 1-0 win at White Hart Lane, extending Spurs' run to ten games without a win and proving Terry Venables was no Paul Daniels. Nigel Clough had some magic in his boots, though, for he scored a hat-trick in four minutes against Q.P.R., the fastest in a First Division match.

The League management committee met on 15 December and issued the following four-point statement on the Watford affair:
1. While accepting that the president and Mr Dein acted in good faith, the management committee do not ratify the purported agreement with Mr Maxwell.
2. Mr Maxwell be given management committee blessing for BPCC acquiring Elton John's holding in Watford subject to Mr Maxwell, his family and other interests first disposing of all interests in Oxford, Reading and Derby.
3. A revised and effective regulation to be put to the

Mick Harford of Luton, seen here in action against Aston Villa last season, came back after injury to score the equaliser at Southampton.
Match Magazine

clubs at their extraordinary general meeting on 19 January.
4. The management committee discontinue their court action against Mr Maxwell, BPCC and Watford.

And there, for the time being at least, the matter rested, with Mr Maxwell threatening to turn his back on football altogether if the League refused to honour the agreement he had come to with Mr Carter.

On the Friday, Saturday and Sunday before Christmas, Liverpool extended their unbeaten run to 19 to equal the club record by beating Sheffield Wednesday 1-0, Arsenal drew at home to Everton to drop seven points below them, Tottenham at last won at Derby, 2-1, and Charlton drew 2-2 with Chelsea to climb above Norwich at the bottom.

In the Second Division Bradford lost 2-1 at Plymouth and Middlesbrough, who drew at Bournemouth, took a two-point lead. In the Third, Sunderland beat Rotherham 3-0 and kept two points clear, while in the Fourth Wolves beat Leyton Orient 2-0 and passed over them into top place.

As the 92 clubs prepared for Christmas and the New Year, and the notoriously make-or-break holiday games, the tops and bottoms of the four divisions looked like this:

	P	W	D	L	F	A	Pts
First Division							
Liverpool	19	14	5	0	44	11	47
Arsenal	20	12	4	4	34	15	40
Nottingham F	18	11	4	3	38	15	37
Manchester U	19	9	8	2	33	20	35
Everton	20	9	7	4	29	13	34
Q.P.R.	20	9	5	6	23	24	32
Bottom							
Portsmouth	20	4	7	9	17	36	19
Watford	19	4	5	10	12	24	17
Charlton Ath	20	3	6	11	19	32	15
Norwich C	20	4	3	13	14	28	15
Second Division							
Middlesbrough	24	14	6	4	35	14	48
Bradford C	24	14	4	6	40	27	46
Aston Villa	24	12	8	4	35	21	44
Crystal Palace	23	13	3	7	48	32	42
Ipswich T	23	12	6	5	33	18	42
Hull C	24	11	9	4	35	25	42
Bottom							
Bournemouth	24	5	7	12	28	39	22
Huddersfield T	24	4	7	13	27	57	19
Shrewsbury T	24	3	8	13	19	37	17
Reading	23	3	6	14	22	44	15
Third Division							
Sunderland	22	13	6	3	45	19	45
Notts Co	22	12	7	3	44	26	43
Walsall	22	11	8	3	31	18	41
Brighton & HA	22	10	9	3	31	21	39
Bristol C	22	10	6	6	40	35	36
Northampton T	22	9	8	5	35	23	35
Bottom							
Preston NE	22	4	7	11	17	33	19
Southend U	22	4	6	12	30	52	18
Doncaster Rov	22	5	3	14	18	41	18
York C	22	1	7	14	23	47	10
Fourth Division							
Wolverhampton W	22	12	5	5	37	20	41
Colchester U	22	12	4	6	32	20	40
Leyton Orient	22	11	6	5	50	30	39
Cardiff C	22	11	6	5	30	24	39
Torquay U	22	11	4	7	35	24	37
Scarborough	22	9	8	5	31	23	35
Bottom							
Stockport Co	22	6	4	12	19	29	32
Tranmere Rov	22	7	2	13	24	29	21
Rochdale	22	5	6	11	25	48	21
Newport Co	21	3	2	16	16	45	11

It was clear that Newport's League status was in serious jeopardy — the previous season they had been in the Third Division.

Elton John's Christmas present to football was to ask Robert Maxwell not to buy Watford after all.

Just before festivities began the Mercantile Credit company confirmed that their £750,000 sponsorship of the League Centenary celebrations was going ahead after talks with the League. Manchester United and Liverpool had expressed doubts about the end-of-season knock-out Mercantile Credit Centenary Trophy, originally planned for August, because it would clash with pre-season tours. Bearing this in mind it was put back to October of the following season.

The Boxing Day fixtures went well for Liverpool, who won 3-0 at Oxford. Forest won at Arsenal to go second, but the Merseysider's lead was increased to ten points. At the other end of the table Charlton beat Portsmouth and climbed another place.

In the Second Division Crystal Palace won 3-2 at Ipswich, and with the teams above them all drawing, moved into third position, four points behind Middlesbrough.

The top three teams in the Third Division all won, drawing away from the next three, who all drew, while in the fourth Wolves did not play, and found themselves overtaken by Leyton Orient and Cardiff.

On Monday, 28 December, Liverpool and Forest each netted four against Newcastle and Coventry respectively, while Arsenal lost again, at Wimbledon. Norwich beat Chelsea 3-0 and moved up to fourth from the foot of the table. In the Second Division, Palace, after their excellent win at Ipswich, lost 3-2 at home to bottom club Reading. Luckily for them Middlesbrough also lost, and Bradford and Villa both drew, so it wasn't too expensive a slip. The top three teams in the Third Division all failed to win, thus undoing the good work of Boxing Day, and returning the position to something like what it was before Christmas. Colchester and Wolves won to keep clear in the Fourth Division.

Villa's tricky forward Mark Walters joined Glasgow Rangers at the end of the year, the first black player for many years to play in Scotland's top flight. In England the clubs prepared for two matches in two days over the New Year holiday.

Another ever-present, Tony Adams of Arsenal, impressed many shrewd judges with his fine performances at the centre of the defence.
Match Magazine

JANUARY:
Everton's Cup Draws; Sunderland and Wolves Prosper

The New Year began with most teams playing two games in as many days as the New Year's Day programme was followed by the Saturday fixtures. Liverpool started with a 4-0 defeat of Coventry but torrential rain washed out their Saturday match, along with six others. Their closest rivals did not achieve much, Forest losing twice and Arsenal drawing twice. The only team to pick up six points was Wimbledon, who moved up to sixth. Billy Bonds, who captained West Ham despite being 41 years old, was celebrating being a new MBE in the honours list.

The holiday games were disappointing for Second Division leaders Middlesbrough and Bradford City, who failed to get a point, Middlesbrough losing to Oldham and Bradford to Leeds and at home to Stoke (4-1). Aston Villa collected six points to sweep into the lead, beating Hull 5-0 and winning at Barnsley 3-1, while Crystal Palace and Millwall, with four points each, moved into the top four. Blackburn won twice to climb into fifth place, so the holiday programme had certainly changed the look of the Second Division. Suddenly Villa were three points clear, and long-time leaders Bradford had slipped to seventh. The best match in this division was the 4-4 draw at Leicester, where the home side recovered from 2-4 at half-time. These were Leicester's first League goals in eight matches. They were now under the managership of the ex-Spurs chief, David Pleat.

Most of the leading Third Division clubs did well, Sunderland winning twice to move four points clear of Notts County, who obtained four points, as did Walsall in third place. Wigan and Brentford with six points, and Brighton with four, completed the top six, Bristol City, Northampton and Fulham slipping back.

Leaders Colchester had a disastrous time in the Fourth Division, losing to Scunthorpe and Peterborough. Wolves won twice to go four points above them. Orient joined Colchester on points. Two wins for Scunthorpe moved them up to fifth. Two defeats for Scarborough dropped them down to ninth, and it seemed that dreams of a fairy-tale first League season were disappearing for them.

As the FA Cup third round matches approached, Arsenal finally transferred Charlie Nicholas, four and a half years after the controversial Scot had arrived amid much publicity ballyhoo from Celtic. The fans liked him, but he never properly established himself, and returned to Scotland and Aberdeen.

After the third round Cup-ties, only Sutton United, who drew with Middlesbrough, remained of the non-Leaguers. There were few shocks. Stoke held Liverpool 0-0, and only a goal nine minutes from time saved Watford from losing at home to Hull. A late equaliser from Peter Reid meant a replay between Everton and Sheffield Wednesday, finalists in an epic tie in 1966.

A sad postscript to the FA Cup games concerned trouble reportedly caused by Millwall fans at Highbury, where their team lost to Arsenal. It was particularly significant because it came only a week

Nottingham Forest full-back, Steve Chettle (left), thwarts Orient's Ian Juryeff in the FA Cup fourth round match at Brisbane Road, won by the visitors 2-1.

Sporting Pictures (UK) Ltd

Liam Brady (right) of West Ham, is pictured with his team-mate, 41-year-old Billy Bonds, who was awarded an MBE in the New Year Honours List.
Match Magazine

before the UEFA executive were to discuss the question of the readmittance of English clubs to European competition. The clubs were annoyed by the Minister of Sport for condemning the incidents and giving them much publicity.

Before Watford's Cup replay at Hull, the club and their manager, Dave Bassett, parted by mutual agreement. Bassett's tenure had lasted just eight months. The club appointed Steve Harrison, the assistant that Graham Taylor had taken to Aston Villa with him, as replacement. Harrison reported back in time to see his side recover from a two-goal deficit in the replay to force a further match, and win the toss for choice of venue. Liverpool beat Stoke 1-0 in their replay at Anfield. Sutton finally went out 1-0 at Middlesbrough following extra time, after heading against the bar with three minutes of normal time left.

There was a big upset in the replay at Norwich, where Swindon, having held their First Division opponents at home, won 2-0 with two goals from Dave Bamber. Everton needed another late equaliser to draw again 1-1 with Wednesday.

Back to League business on Saturday, and Arsenal failed to halt Liverpool, who beat them 2-0 at Anfield, Beardsley scoring an excellent individual goal. With Forest drawing at home with lowly Charlton, Liverpool went 15 points clear at the top. Watford won at Wimbledon for their new manager and handed Charlton the bottom spot.

In the Second Division, Villa, Palace, Millwall and Blackburn all won to occupy the top four places, Millwall's defeat of Middlesbrough dropping them down to fifth. Bradford were lucky, their game being abandoned by fog when they were 3-0 adrift at Swindon. Sunderland and Wolves, former giants of the League, maintained their four-point leads in the lower divisions.

During the week Watford finally proceeded to the next round of the FA Cup, beating Hull 1-0 in the

second replay. Luton beat Bradford in the Littlewoods Cup fifth round, and the Simod Cup and Freight Rover Trophy competitions progressed, but the big football news was made by off-the-field proceedings.

The Football League meeting provoked by the Watford sale tightened the regulation concerning a person owning only one club, but did not make the new rule retrospective. It meant that Robert Maxwell could not buy Watford, but could keep his own and family interests in Derby and Oxford. He proposed to sell his holding in Reading. So the storm ended with the status quo maintained, and everybody more or less happy — except, perhaps, Elton John, who still wished to sell his Watford holdings.

The UEFA meeting in Monte Carlo deferred a definite decision on the English clubs' readmittance to Europe, although in principle the members seemed agreeable. They were worried by the situation which might arise if they invited English clubs only to find a European country refusing them entrance. One or two countries had apparently expressed this likelihood. A final decision was put off until a meeting at St Andrews, Birmingham, on 3 May.

In the Littlewoods Cup, Everton, Oxford and Arsenal progressed at the expense of Manchester City, Manchester United and Sheffield Wednesday respectively.

Paul Goddard scored both goals in Newcastle United's 2-2 draw at home to Sheffield Wednesday.
Match Magazine

As Elton John announced that he had decided to take Watford off the market, so the club's old manager, Dave Bassett, took over at Sheffield United, who were having a bad run.

Saturday, 24 January 1988 was a day on which rain and mud postponed 28 League games, forcing the Pools Panel to sit. Liverpool played, and won at Charlton, which meant that they had gone 24 League games without defeat and were 17 points ahead of the field. It was time to talk of imminent records. Villa also played and won — they had a six-point lead for their drive back to the First Division. Middlesbrough scored their first win in six weeks to stay in the hunt.

On Monday Everton and Sheffield Wednesday met for a third time at Goodison to try to resolve their FA Cup third round tie. Once again it ended 1-1 after extra time.

At the end of the month an FA disciplinary committee cleared both Arsenal and Millwall for the trouble at their Cup-tie. It seemed the surges in the crowd were caused by people forcing their way in and not by fighting. The press, so often critical of football crowds, appeared to have over-reacted.

On Wednesday, the long-drawn out Cup-tie between Wednesday and Everton was decided in startling manner, considering the attrition that had gone before. Everton scored five in the first half at Hillsborough, and won 5-0.

Malcolm Allen, seen picking himself up off the ground after scoring for Watford in the 2-1 win at Wimbledon.   Sporting Pictures (UK) Ltd

Everton's Peter Reid scored a late equaliser to force a draw in the third round FA Cup tie against Sheffield Wednesday.   Match Magazine

Gordon Strachan (left) of Manchester United and Arsenal's Graham Rix, in the battle for midfield supremacy at Highbury.   Match Magazine

It was as well the match was settled, for the following Saturday was fourth round day. Everton, believe it or not, drew 1-1 with Middlesbrough. On another Pools Panel day, Bradford knocked out Oxford 4-2 and Port Vale beat Spurs 2-1. Liverpool beat Villa 2-0 in a televised Sunday match.

Blackburn, without Cup duties, won at Ipswich to take second place in the Second Division. Sunderland and Notts County also won to keep alive their hopes of promotion from the Third Division, while Wolves went six points clear in the Fourth.

FEBRUARY:
Arsenal and Luton Book Wembley Spot

The FA Cup fifth-round draw paired Everton (if they could beat Middlesbrough) with Liverpool and Arsenal with Manchester United as big matches for later in February.

Everton took part in a very exciting replay with Middlesbrough at Ayresome Park. Middlesbrough skipper Mowbray equalised in the last minute, the home team then took the lead in extra time and finally Trevor Steven tied it again at 2-2 with only seconds left. A crowd of over 25,000 watched the once-bankrupt club, and brought excitement back to Teeside. Otherwise, in a quiet week, the news that Tommy Docherty had been sacked by Altrincham was a reminder of other days. Another outspoken manager, Brian Clough of Forest, was wanted by the Welsh FA as a part-time manager after their sacking of Mike England, but the Forest Board would not approve such a division of his time.

Liverpool had an off-day on February's first Saturday programme, drawing 0-0 at home to West Ham United. In contrast, Luton and Oxford shared 11 on Kenilworth Road's plastic: Luton 7 Oxford 4. In the Second Division, which was becoming the most interesting contest of all, Villa, Blackburn and Palace all won to occupy the top three places, while

Vinny Jones of Wimbledon gained much publicity from his ill tempered clash with Paul Gascoigne in February. Match Magazine

Middlesbrough, who came next, drew at Swindon, and Bradford kept in the fight with an only goal against rivals Millwall at the Den — an important header by Ormondroyd that squeezed in during injury time. Sunderland and Wolves surrendered a little of their leads in the lower divisions, Sunderland with a home draw with Walsall and Wolves by losing 4-1 at home to Cardiff, who moved into second.

On Sunday, before the TV cameras, Everton played another Cup-tie, this time the Littlewoods Cup semi-final first leg with Arsenal at Goodison. Groves scored for Arsenal but Steven missed a penalty chance to level for the weary home team.

On Tuesday, Everton at last squeezed past Middlesbrough in the FA Cup, winning 2-1 at Goodison, Boro's gallant effort ending with an own goal from Mowbray. It was Everton's seventh match in the competition — enough to win the Cup! Meanwhile the Simod Cup progressed, as did the Sherpa Van Trophy, a new name in mid-season for the Freight Rover Trophy.

Oxford and Luton drew their first leg Littlewoods Cup semi-final on Wednesday night, Dean Saunders netting a penalty for Oxford to earn the home side a 1-1 draw — but Les Sealey saved a second one.

On Saturday Liverpool marched on with a 4-1 win at Watford, while in the Second Division Blackburn won at Barnsley and Bradford beat Oldham 5-3 to

Paul Gascoigne, Newcastle United's star striker, was unable to get on the score sheet at Wimbledon where the match ended 0-0. Match Magazine

Ray Houghton, the Liverpool midfield dynamo, is challenged by Portsmouth's Kevin Ball (6) during the match at Fratton Park. Liverpool won 2-0.
Sporting Pictures (UK) Ltd

in time for a friendly with Monaco, when Glenn Hoddle returned to his old stamping ground and helped his new team beat his old 4-0.

Wolves lost at Halifax in midweek, a slight stutter in their progress. England played a friendly in Tel Aviv and drew 0-0 with Israel, a disappointing result. Portsmouth had a better result in the High Court, where creditors who were owed £1.2 million had petitioned for the wind-up of the club. They were given a fortnight to prove they could keep themselves afloat. Meanwhile Newport County, also in debt, feared that if they dropped out of the League at the end of the season, as seemed probable, they would go out of business, and their ground would be developed for building.

On 20 February Portsmouth were at home in the FA Cup fifth round to Bradford, and duly won 3-0 before 19,000 spectators. In the big match on Saturday, Arsenal beat Manchester United 2-1, after being two up at half-time. Three minutes from the end United's Brian McClair shot over from the penalty spot, so failing to earn a replay. Portsmouth and Arsenal were joined in the quarter-finals by Forest, Manchester City and Wimbledon. Port Vale held Watford 0-0 at home, and Q.P.R. and Luton also drew.

The Merseyside battle was reserved for Sunday and the cameras, and ended in a 1-0 win for Liverpool, when Ray Houghton, the only player afield new to Merseyside derbies, scored the winner during a tight game in which the artistry of Barnes and Beardsley finally prised open the Everton defence. A happy note was the return of Paul Bracewell for Everton after 18 months away with an ankle injury.

Charlton's 3-1 defeat of Sheffield Wednesday to push Watford to the bottom of the First Division, gave them some hope of staying up.

In the big match in the Second Division, Blackburn Rovers beat Aston Villa 3-2 to go to the top of the table. Steve Archibald, on loan to the Lancashire club, scored twice. It was Blackburn's 22nd match without defeat. Sunderland, by beating Brentford 2-0, moved six points clear in the Third Division. And Leyton Orient, following their 4-1 victory over Cardiff, while Bolton lost and Wolves rested, improved their Fourth Division hopes.

Watford ended Port Vale's FA Cup run 2-0 in a

keep on the promotion trail. The television cameras were at Middlesbrough for the important clash with leaders Aston Villa on Sunday. In a stirring match two goals in the last ten minutes gave "The Boro" a 2-1 win to take them to third — but Villa and Blackburn were still clear. In the Third and Fourth Divisions the top clubs kept well ahead: Sunderland, Notts County, Walsall and Wigan were now thirteen, ten, seven and six points clear of Brighton, while Wolves, Cardiff and Bolton led Orient by nine, six and four points respectively. A photograph this weekend of Wimbledon's hard man, Vinny Jones, grabbing Paul Gascoigne of Newcastle, his marker at a free-kick, in a private place provided plenty of jokes for comedians but raised a question for the League's disciplinary committee.

Terry Venables made some purchases to strengthen Spurs' defence and attack this month: Terry Fenwick was bought from Queen's Park Rangers and Paul Walsh from Liverpool, the latter

Goalmouth action in the game between Watford and Liverpool at Vicarage Road.
Sporting Pictures (UK) Ltd

replay in midweek, and Luton beat Q.P.R. 1-0 to go through to the sixth round. Arsenal beat Everton 3-1 in the second leg of the Littlewoods Cup semi-final and booked a place for Wembley. Everton, who had lost to Luton in the Simod Cup, lost their interest in three Cup competitions in the space of days, and their season appeared to be doomed to mediocrity. Meanwhile, also in midweek, Sunderland were thrashed 4-0 at Bristol Rovers, where sadly Rovers' 37-year-old assistant manager, Kenny Hibbitt, broke a leg in the twilight of a distinguished career. Leyton Orient also lost at Scarborough, so there was still plenty to play for in the lower reaches.

Near the end of February, and presumably with the March transfer "deadline" in mind, manager Dave Mackay put the whole Doncaster Rovers senior squad up for transfer.

On the last Saturday of February Liverpool won 2-0 at Portsmouth, who were previously unbeaten for ten games. A crowd of 28,000 fans turned up to see them and help ease the financial problems. Pompey's centre forward Mike Quinn missed three clear openings in the first ten minutes, and that was that. Liverpool had now gone 27 League games unbeaten from the start of the season, and were chasing Leeds' record of 29 made at the start of 1973–74.

Arsenal, with a 4-0 defeat of Charlton, went through February unbeaten, and were back to their most impressive form. Another London club, Chelsea, lost 3-1 at Newcastle after missing two penalties, and had now gone 15 games without a win, sliding from Championship challengers early in the season to near the relegation zone.

Villa beat Plymouth 5-2 to get back to winning ways in the Second Division. Blackburn came back from two down to draw 2-2 at Leeds and stretch their unbeaten run to a club record 23 games. Bradford won a vital match 2-1 at Middlesbrough, and Millwall won, but Palace lost 2-1 at home to their bogey team Shrewsbury. The rest were beginning to lose touch.

Sunderland lost again, 3-2 at Aldershot, and were overtaken in the Third Division by Notts County, but as Walsall, Wigan and Brighton also lost these two stayed six points ahead of the rest. Wolves, who beat Bolton 4-0, took a seven-point lead in the Fourth Division. Their leading scorer, Steve Bull, got two and led the League with 37 overall.

On Sunday, 28 February, Luton comfortably beat Oxford 2-0 in the second leg Littlewoods Cup semi-final to go to Wembley for the first time in 29 years. They were still in the FA Cup and Simod Cup, so were hoping to make Wembley their second home. It was ironic because the previous season Luton had been ejected from the Littlewoods Cup because they would not lift their ban on away supporters, and were threatened with being barred from the FA Cup this season because of their plastic pitch.

MARCH:
Everton End Liverpool's Record Equalling Run

March got under way with Luton taking another step towards Wembley by dismissing Stoke 4-1 at Luton in their Simod Cup quarter-final. This was during a Tuesday evening programme in which Bradford's form continued to fluctuate — after the win at Middlesbrough, they lost 1-0 at home to bottom club Huddersfield, who had won only once away all season. Wolves and Cardiff, on the other hand, registered 1-0 away wins to consolidate themselves at the top of the Fourth Division.

The following day, in a night of European soccer, Reading made history on a much lower level by reaching Wembley for the first time in their 117-year history. They drew 1-1 with Coventry at Elm Park in their Simod Cup semi-final and won the penalty shoot-out.

Off the field, the first week of March saw Portsmouth saved from a winding-up order when their chairman, John Deacon, told the High Court that he would meet the club's debts of £774,000 in tax and VAT.

On 5 March, one of the League's two long runs ended: Blackburn lost 2-1 at Stoke after 23 unbeaten games. It was a blow, as Villa's 2-1 win at Bournemouth took them three points clear in the Second Division.

There were no such problems in the First Division, where Liverpool took their League run to 28 unbeaten games, just one short of Leeds' record. They won 1-0 at Queen's Park Rangers to go 17 points ahead of Manchester United (and also had two games in hand). At the other end Chelsea again snatched a draw from the jaws of victory when they

Kerry Dixon, the Chelsea striker, scored a couple of goals in the 4-4 thriller at Oxford.
Match Magazine

Nigel Clough of Nottingham Forest, wrong foots Manchester United's Steve Bruce during the goaless draw at the City Ground.
Sporting Pictures (UK) Ltd

2-1, but only after extra time, in the Simod Cup semi-final. They would meet Reading. Four Sherpa Van Trophy semi-finals were decided: Burnley beat Halifax (on penalties) and Preston beat Hartlepool in the northern section, and Wolves beat Torquay and Notts County beat Brighton in the southern section.

On 13 March, the sixth round of the FA Cup saw Nottingham Forest put up an excellent performance in winning 2-1 at Arsenal. Luton beat Portsmouth 3-1 to reach yet another semi-final. Wimbledon achieved a remarkable escape against Watford. At half-time they were a goal down and reduced to ten men, but two second-half goals saw the ten men through. The fourth Cup game was at Maine Road on Sunday before the cameras, where Liverpool won easily 4-0.

In the League, Manchester United's 4-1 win over Sheffield Wednesday took them five points ahead of Everton in the race for second spot in the First Division (and a chance of European football if UEFA lifted the ban on all but Liverpool), while Wolves opened a nine-point lead in the Fourth Division.

An unusual soccer story concerned Millwall's threat to sue *The Sun* newspaper over a lead story which they claimed linked a robbery outside The Den with the club by using the club's crest as a graphic. Meanwhile Ken Bates, the Chelsea chairman, returned from a trip to Rio to veto the impending transfers of Dixon and Hazard and indulge in an attack on the tabloid press. His club extended their run to 17 games without a win.

were two up at Coventry but ended at 3-3. It was four months and 16 games since their last League win. Arsenal, who beat Spurs 2-1 at Highbury on Sunday, took their winning sequence to seven.

In midweek, Luton booked their third Wembley appearance (they were already in the Centenary Cup and the League Cup Final) by beating Swindon

Action from Highbury where Arsenal beat their local rivals "Spurs" 2-1. Tony Adams rises above Tottenham's defence with the goalie, Bobby Mimms, unable to take the ball.
Sporting Pictures (UK) Ltd

Liverpool, a club with a chairman of considerably lower profile, equalled Leeds' run of 29 League games without defeat in midweek, but only with a draw at Derby. The home side never ceased trying, and delighted over 26,000 supporters with an equaliser four minutes from time — the second goal conceded by Liverpool in 16 games.

Chelsea and Liverpool were also at the centre of stories the following weekend. Chelsea took a 3-0 half-time lead at Oxford, but two minutes from time Oxford levelled the game at 4-4 to continue the Blues' sequence. The Reds were playing on Sunday with the television audience waiting to see the record broken, but they were disappointed. The Merseyside Blues, Everton, gave their supporters much satisfaction by beating the local enemy 1-0 — the current Champions maintaining some respect against the champions-elect. A nice touch was that the goal was scored by Wayne Clarke, a brother of Allan Clarke, a striker of the Leeds team of 1973-74, whose record Liverpool equalled.

Elsewhere around the divisions, Villa and Blackburn remained favourites for promotion to the First, Notts County and Sunderland to the Second, and Wolves and Cardiff to the Third. They all had at least three points to spare over their nearest challengers, with only seven weeks to go to the play-offs.

John Hollins departed as Chelsea manager during the week. He was replaced as caretaker manager by Bobby Campbell, who had replaced Ernie Walley as coach seven weeks earlier, a decision by Bates which had been against Hollins' wishes.

There were friendly international matches on Wednesday. England drew 2-2 at Wembley with Holland but most of the imaginative football came from Holland, who made England look pedestrian. The Republic of Ireland beat Rumania, Northern Ireland drew with Poland and Yugoslavia beat Wales.

Reading's third goal in their shock Simod Cup final victory over Luton Town at Wembley. Neil Smillie puts the ball in the net after Tim Breaker (2) had failed to clear. Sporting Pictures (UK) Ltd

The transfer deadline arrived with Arsenal making the most expensive buy, paying £600,000 to Sheffield Wednesday for Brian Marwood. Trevor Francis left Glasgow Rangers to join Jim Smith at Queen's Park Rangers for nothing, Smith being a man who once sold him for £1 million when at Birmingham. Ossie Ardiles, the World Cup winning star, joined Blackburn on loan from Tottenham. A sad retirement was Mark Lawrenson, a giant in the Liverpool defence since 1981, who had to give up with Achilles tendon injury. He took on the job of managing Oxford United, who were looking like good prospects for relegation.

Lawrenson saw his team draw 0-0 at Charlton on the last Saturday in March, a draw which left both sides with problems. The sides hoping to take their places showed some nervousness, too, both Villa and Blackburn losing, and none of the top seven

Brian Rice of Forest is seen on the ball with Manchester United's Mike Duxbury in attendance. Sporting Pictures (UK) Ltd

Vince Samways (left), the "Spurs" right-back, is challenged by Nottingham Forest's Neil Webb in the 1-1 draw at White Hart Lane.
Sporting Pictures (UK) Ltd

winning. None of the top seven in the Third Division won either, with the runaway leaders Notts County and Sunderland losing, the former at home and the latter at bottom club York. There was a distinct air of promotion nerves around. Cardiff shared them in the Fourth Division, losing at home to Scunthorpe, who moved above them into second place. Only Wolves, who stretched their lead to eight points, showed the ruthlessness of champions.

Sunday was the day for Reading and their fans, who bought over 30,000 tickets for the Simod Cup final. They were delighted when the relegation-haunted Second Division side played above themselves and surprised Luton 4-1 to take their first trophy. Reading's Cup run earned them nearly £250,000.

The next day showed how football has its tragic side to balance the romance. A benefit match was played at White Hart Lane for full back Danny Thomas, whose career had ended with torn knee ligaments at 26 years of age. Thomas was seeking damages in the High Court over the tackle which put him out of football. Meanwhile, over 20,000 turned out to watch Manchester United play a Spurs XI, enhanced with star guests to help him on his way.

APRIL:
Liverpool Clinch Title, and Luton Win at Last

The Easter programme is always a vital one for clubs involved in promotion and relegation issues, but the match which probably provoked most speculation was the first of three meetings between Nottingham Forest and Liverpool. The teams had not met so far, but two League games and a Cup semi-final were imminent. Forest won the first encounter 2-1 at the City Ground with young winger Gary Crosby having an eye-catching game. Forest kept themselves in the hunt for the First Division's second spot.

After the first Easter games the Second Division race closed right up. Millwall beat Aston Villa 2-1, and although Villa still led, Millwall were now only three points behind in fourth place, and very live promotion candidates themselves. Middlesbrough beat Sheffield United 6-0 to move into second spot above Blackburn, who did not play. In the Third Division, Notts County lost again and their promotion was beginning to look less certain. Wolves kept going in the Fourth Division and Cardiff won at Exeter to keep ahead of the rest.

On Easter Monday, Manchester United drew 3-3 at Anfield to maintain a surprising sequence — they had not lost a League game there since 1979. They came back from 3-1 down and with a man sent off. Alex Ferguson, the United manager, made the headlines next day and risked more FA disciplinary problems by saying on radio that referees were under great pressure at Anfield, made incorrect decisions and that it constituted a miracle if the away side won there.

The surprising result in the Second Division was another defeat for Villa — at home to Oldham. But Blackburn and Middlesbrough only drew, so Villa remained top. These teams, plus Millwall, Bradford and Crystal Palace, made a group of six at the top separated by only five points, so the struggle for promotion and play-off places was promising to last right to the end of the season.

With Notts County losing at home again, 2-1 to

Norman Whiteside made the news in April when his club, Manchester United, agreed to his transfer request. Match Magazine

Brighton, they moved back to the pack. Sunderland only just beat relegation prospects Chesterfield 3-2 at Roker Park, but it was good enough to put them six points clear and they looked good for promotion. Wolves and Cardiff kept going in the Fourth Division, Cardiff beating neighbours Newport 4-0. Newport were certainly dropping out of League football, but there was a good competition going on to replace them. Barnet had led the GM Vauxhall Conference for most of the season, but Lincoln City, attempting to return to the League at the first attempt, were well placed at four points behind with two games in hand.

The subject of English clubs being allowed to play in Europe made news again after Easter, with the Minister of Sport, Colin Moynihan, persuading UEFA to postpone their decision, which was due to be made at a meeting at St Andrews on 3 May, to 25 June, the day of the European Championship final in Munich. It seemed that the British government was reluctant to see English football part of Europe again.

Other Continental news was the agreement of Manchester United to put Norman Whiteside on sale for "around £1½ to £2 million", thereby making a move to Europe likely, while the Italian club Pisa made an offer to Forest for Nigel Clough, the manager's striker son. By the weekend, the Whiteside situation appeared to have unsettled Paul McGrath, United's brilliant central defender, who also asked for, and was granted, a transfer request. Italian clubs were known to be interested.

While European competitions were at the semi-final stage, there was an important Wembley evening result from the only game in England. Millwall won 2-1 at Leeds to join Aston Villa at the top of the Second Division. Although they had an inferior goal difference, they also had a game in hand. More important, Millwall seemed the team least affected by nerves, and were the side in form among the promotion contenders.

Saturday was FA Cup semi-final day. Liverpool won their second encounter with Forest by 2-1 at Hillsborough to put themselves firmly in line to become the first club to perform the "double" twice. There was a similar score in the other semi-final at White Hart Lane, where less than 26,000 saw Wimbledon beat Luton. So Luton did not book a fourth Wembley appearance; the two more muscular sides of the four semi-finalists would dispute the honours on the game's final showpiece occasion.

In the League, the Second Division was providing most interest. Millwall beat Plymouth 3-2 at home and went to the top of the table for the first time. Villa could only draw at Palace, a result which probably disappointed both sides, particularly as Bradford, Blackburn and Middlesbrough all won. The result was that the long-time pacemakers, Villa, dropped to fourth, and had played a game more than the others. They needed a revival.

Chelsea at last staged one, albeit a minor one. They beat Derby 1-0 at Stamford Bridge, their first

Joe McLoughlin, the Chelsea pivot, is seen battling for possession with Arsenal's Perry Groves at Stamford Bridge.

Sporting Pictures (UK) Ltd

win in 22 League games. Because of their excellent start to the season, they now looked likely to avoid relegation.

In the lower divisions, Brighton's 1-0 defeat of Wigan meant that they and Walsall were sorting themselves out as the main challengers to Sunderland and Notts County in the Third Division, while Scunthorpe, Bolton and Torquay joined Cardiff in the fight for the Fourth Division promotion places below Wolves. At the bottom of the Third Division, with Doncaster and York adrift, there was a struggle going on to avoid the other two unwanted spots between Rotherham, Southend, Grimsby, Aldershot and Chesterfield.

The Sherpa Van Trophy reached its divisional finals on 12 April. Burnley drew 0-0 at home to Preston in the Northern final first leg, while Notts County drew 1-1 with Wolves in the Southern final. All to play for at Deepdale and Molineux.

The next night Liverpool played Forest at Anfield in the "rubber" match for the season, and put on an outstanding performance, winning 5-0 with three of the goals being selected for the BBC's "Goal of the Season" competition, which, in fact, uniquely featured only Liverpool goals in a tribute to the magnificent Merseysiders.

The weekend of 16 and 17 April was given over to an event in the Football League's Centenary celebrations, a Mercantile Credit Trophy. Sixteen teams, from all divisions, played a knockout competition at Wembley, the semi-finals and final being played on Sunday. It was a badly conceived interruption to the real League business, ill-attended, and the rain that fell seemed appropriate. The first-round games were 20 minutes each way, decided, if necessary, on penalties. Luckily for the event Tranmere Rovers decided to play some football way above their League position and perform some giant-killing to provide a little interest. Forest won the final on penalties after a 0-0 draw with Sheffield Wednesday. Brian Clough wasn't there, which seemed a reasonable comment on the whole thing.

The Sherpa Van Trophy revealed its finalists on 19 April. Burnley won 3-1 at Preston after extra time before 17,500 spectators to win the Northern final, while Wolves drew about 1,000 more to Molineux and made no mistake with a 3-0 defeat of Notts County in the Southern final.

On the same night, Millwall won 2-1 at Bournemouth and were suddenly four points clear in the Second Division. There was a nasty incident at Huddersfield, however, when a linesman was attacked by spectators after an Oldham equaliser. Huddersfield players apprehended the attackers. The incident prompted the FA and Football League to announce a joint initiative to improve discipline on the field. The League soon came up with a proposition that clubs could lose up to three points a season for bad disciplinary records. The following night, with the issues now on the brink of decision, Liverpool went to Norwich when a win would clinch the Championship on the ground where Everton had

Peter Beardsley of Liverpool is seen centre stage, as the "Reds" put Nottingham Forest out of the FA Cup 2-1 in the semi-final and book their place for Wembley.

Sporting Pictures (UK) Ltd

41

done just that the previous season. However, they could only draw 0-0, and the celebrations were put back for Saturday at Anfield.

A 3-0 defeat of Reading eased Bradford into the second promotion spot in the Second Division, where Crystal Palace had dropped five points below the last play-off position.

On Saturday, 24 April, Liverpool beat Spurs 1-0 and celebrated the Championship. They had lost only two games in 36 and were at the time 15 points clear. At the other end of the table Charlton and Derby won and four clubs were fighting to avoid the play-off spot: those two with Chelsea and West Ham. Watford were sure of relegation, and Portsmouth and Oxford were likely to accompany them.

In the Second Division, Villa just beat Shrewsbury 1-0 to regain second position, while Middlesbrough crashed 4-0 at Ipswich, a bad blow to their hopes. Sunderland lost at home in the Third Division, so still had to compete for one of the two certain promotion places with Notts County, Brighton and Walsall. Wolves and Cardiff now looked good for promotion. In the GM Vauxhall Conference, slight slips by Barnet and Lincoln had allowed Kettering to become a third possibility for League status.

The last Sunday in April was devoted to the Littlewoods Cup Final. Luton led Arsenal for a long time but Arsenal powered ahead 2-1 in the second half, then missed a penalty and peppered the woodwork. They were made to pay when Luton scored two late goals, the winner coming seconds from the finish. It was justice for Luton, the better team, after their Cup runs of this season and particularly after being ejected from the competition the season before because of their ban on visiting supporters.

The England team resumed their friendly build-up to the European Championship with a boring 0-0

When helping Derby County draw at Watford, Peter Shilton broke the Football League appearance record by playing his 825th game.

Match Magazine

draw with Hungary in Budapest in mid-week. Northern Ireland v France and Spain v Scotland produced the same result. The Republic of Ireland beat Yugoslavia 2-0, while Wales, now under the caretaker managership of Terry Yorath, lost 4-1 in Sweden.

On the last day of April, Peter Shilton played his 825th League game, beating Terry Paine's previous record. He helped Derby draw at Watford.

Millwall's 2-0 defeat of Stoke almost certainly saw them promoted. Bradford and Middlesbrough also won, while Palace's 2-0 defeat of Blackburn, restored their chance of easing into a play-off spot.

Sunderland made sure of promotion from the Third Division with a 1-0 win at Port Vale. With Notts County losing at Walsall, Walsall and Brighton looked the most likely candidates for the second certain place.

Wolves, sure of Fourth Division promotion, failed to clinch the Championship when losing at Wrexham. Barnet and Kettering lost in the Vauxhall Conference, leaving Lincoln needing to win their last home match of the season to go back up.

With one week to go in the "regular" League season, there was still a lot to play for.

Wayne Fereday of QPR rises to clear his lines in the 2-0 home victory over the "Spurs".

Sporting Pictures (UK) Ltd

Action from the Littlewoods Cup final where Luton Town had better luck, beating Arsenal 3-2 at Wembley in a thriller. Sporting Pictures (UK) Ltd

Trevor Putney (left) and Jeremy Goss (10) of Norwich clash with Arsenal's David Rocastle at Highbury. The "Gunners" won the match 2-0.
Sporting Pictures (UK) Ltd

Terry Hurlock of Millwall and Tony Henry of Stoke City are shown in aerial confrontation. By winning 2-0, the Londoners virtually assured themselves of First Division football next season. Sporting Pictures (UK) Ltd

Luton Town, in the other FA Cup semi-final, were put out 2-1 by Wimbledon. Dibble, the Luton goalie, is pictured taking a cross.
Sporting Pictures (UK) Ltd

MAY:
Liverpool Fail to Register a Second "Double"

May was the month which would decide it all, and 2 May was a Bank Holiday, with a full League fixture list.

In the First Division, Manchester United's win at Oxford and Everton's dropped point at Derby meant that United would be second and possible European contenders next season. Derby were safe because West Ham beat Chelsea 4-1. It meant that Chelsea's last game with Charlton would decide who needed to play-off for First Division survival.

In the Second Division, Millwall won 1-0 at Hull and were the Champions. Aston Villa beat Bradford 1-0, leaving these clubs on 77 points, one behind Middlesbrough. Blackburn, who drew at home to Reading, and Palace who lost at Leeds, remained in contention for the last play-off place, Blackburn having 74 points to Palace's 72. Reading's brave draw at Blackburn left them still with a faint chance of avoiding relegation.

In the Third Division Brighton drew at Chester, while Walsall lost at Bristol Rovers, so Brighton held the second automatic promotion spot on goal difference. Notts County, three points behind, had a theoretical chance of automatic promotion.

Cardiff made sure of joining Wolves in the move up to the Third Division by beating Crewe 2-0. Bolton's 4-0 defeat of Colchester and Torquay's 3-2 victory at Halifax kept those clubs in the hunt for automatic promotion. In the GM Vauxhall Conference, Lincoln City duly beat Wycombe 2-0 and returned to League football at the first time of asking, replacing Newport, who seemed certain to die altogether as a football club.

The UEFA meeting at St Andrews spent only two minutes on the question of English clubs playing in European competitions, but it was pointed out that only Champions could play in the European Cup, thus dashing any hopes Manchester United might have had for 1988–89. The biggest decision made was one likely to have an even bigger effect on British clubs, but it was not one which the media or clubs treated with much dismay at the time, with the domestic season at its climax. UEFA decided that clubs in European competition would be allowed only four foreign players, and that so far as "foreign" was concerned Scottish, Welsh and Irish players were all foreigners with English clubs. Liverpool's great success in recent years has been built on very cosmopolitan teams, sometimes without an Englishman playing, so if Liverpool were currently in European soccer the decision would completely change their side.

In the middle of soccer's last week, Torquay lost 1-0 at Burnley, when a win would have guaranteed promotion, and a draw given them an odds-on chance. They had one more opportunity to come on the following Saturday, however. Burney retained an outside chance of a play-off place.

Malcolm Macdonald, manager of relegated

Huddersfield for only seven months, resigned despite having a three-year contract.

The last full Saturday of League soccer began with several clubs having their own fates in their hands. Some took their chances, some didn't.

At the bottom of the First Division the issue was simple: Chelsea had to beat Charlton at home to avoid the play-offs, Charlton needed a draw. Chelsea took the lead, Charlton scored a twice-deflected equaliser for the draw. Thus Chelsea had to play-off.

At the top of the Second Division, Middlesbrough needed to beat Leicester at home to join Millwall on the way up. They lost 2-1. This meant that Aston Villa could go up by winning at Swindon. They drew 0-0, enough to pip Middlesbrough, but Bradford could claim the second place by beating Ipswich at home. They lost 3-2. So Villa were promoted with an identical goal difference to Middlesbrough, +27. Villa went up through scoring more goals. Middlesbrough and Bradford were forced to play-off, and would be joined by Blackburn if they won at Millwall. They won 4-1. Crystal Palace were the unlucky side deprived of a place.

At the bottom of the Second Division, Sheffield United needed to win to book themselves a play-off spot. They won at Huddersfield 2-0, and Reading, who only drew with Hull, were relegated.

At the top of the Third Division Brighton needed to win to go up automatically, and they squeezed past Bristol Rovers 2-1 at home to win promotion. Walsall could only draw anyway and joined Notts County in the play-offs. Bristol City needed to win to deprive Northampton of the last play-off place, and beat bottom club Doncaster 1-0.

With four clubs on 52 points (Chesterfield, Southend, Rotherham and Aldershot) and one on 53 (Mansfield), there was great competition to avoid the need to play-off with the Fourth Division clubs at the bottom of the table. All these clubs

One of the key men in getting Wimbledon to Wembley, John Fashanu, received rave reviews throughout the season.
Match Magazine

Dave Beasant makes a magnificent save from Aldridge's spot kick in the FA Cup final.

Sporting Pictures (UK) Ltd

gained at least one point except Rotherham, who lost at home 4-1 to the champions, Sunderland, so Rotherham were left in the hot seat.

Torquay had their second chance to clinch promotion from the Fourth Division. They were at home to Scunthorpe – and lost 2-1. Bolton won 1-0 at Wrexham and squeezed into the promotion place. Leyton Orient lost their play-off place by losing 2-0 at home to champions Wolves. Swansea grabbed it with a 3-0 victory over Darlington to join Torquay and Scunthorpe.

The play-off semi-finals resolved themselves as follows:
For the First Division place: Blackburn v Chelsea, Bradford v Middlesbrough.
For the Second Division place: Bristol City v Sheffield United, Notts. County v Walsall.
For the Third Division place: Swansea v Rotherham, Torquay v Scunthorpe.

Before the FA Cup final, the big news in the transfer market, was that Manchester United agreed to pay Aberdeen £750,000 for the Scottish international goalkeeper Jim Leighton.

Craig Johnston, sensing his opportunities at Liverpool likely to be limited from now on, threatened to return to Australia, but was persuaded to join the Cup final squad with Gillespie and Spackman nursing head injuries. In the event they both played, and Johnston came on as substitute for Aldridge. It was a very disappointing day for Liverpool, who never played up to their real form. Aldridge missed a penalty (the first-ever not converted in a Wembley final) and Beardsley had a goal disallowed for a free-kick to Liverpool. Wimbledon, a muscular team with far less skill than Liverpool, sneaked a goal and won 1-0. Laurie Sanchez scored the winner, but the hero was skipper and goalkeeper David Beasant, whose penalty save was only one of several good stops.

Meanwhile the important play-offs began and resulted as follows:

Blackburn 0   Chelsea 2
Bradford 2   Middlesbrough 1
Bristol City 1   Sheffield United 0
Notts County 1   Walsall 3
Swansea 1   Rotherham 0
Torquay 2   Scunthorpe 1

The following Wednesday the returns took place with the following results:

Chelsea 4   Blackburn 1 (agg 6-1)
Middlesbrough 2   Bradford 0 (agg 3-2)
Sheffield United 1   Bristol City 1 (agg 1-2)
Walsall 1   Notts. County 1 (agg 4-2)
Rotherham 1   Swansea 1 (agg 1-2)
Scunthorpe 1   Torquay 1 (agg 2-3)

Provisional League attendance figures were issued, and indicated a total attendance for the four divisions of 17,960,322, a rise of 577,290 on the previous season – the second season running in which attendances improved, a heartening indication for the future.

The Cup winners, Wimbledon, no strangers to disciplinary inquiries, were charged by the FA with bringing the game into disrepute. At a testimonial match for Alan Cork two days after the final, most of the Wimbledon players lowered their shorts and bowed to the crowd, ie they "mooned".

England played Scotland in the Rous Cup and won 1-0 with a goal from Beardsley. Scotland had already drawn 0-0 with Colombia, and a few days later England drew 1-1 with Colombia to take the Cup. There was terrace trouble at Wembley, however, and the Minister of Sport, Colin Moynihan, was not slow to use it as another example of the unsuitability of lifting the ban on English clubs in European competition.

The next round of the promotion and relegation play-offs resulted in the following first-leg results:

Middlesbrough 2   Chelsea 0
Bristol City 1   Walsall 3
Swansea 2   Torquay 1

A club facing a bigger crisis was Peterborough United, whose directors rejected a £750,000 rescue package as not being enough to settle the club's financial problems – closing down appeared to be a real possibility.

The last Saturday of May saw the play-off returns, resulting as follows:

Chelsea 1   Middlesbrough 0 (agg 1-2)
Walsall 0   Bristol City 2 (agg 3-3)
Torquay 3   Swansea 3 (agg 4-5)

So Chelsea, whose fans demonstrated in ugly fashion after their failure against Middlesbrough, were relegated to the Second Division, and Middlesbrough, a club which was a bankrupt Third Division side only two years earlier, returned to the First Division after six years.

Torquay did not quite complete their fairy story – they avoided relegation from the League altogether in 1986–87 only on goal difference, and just failed this year to get promotion, which went to Swansea. Walsall and Bristol City had to replay at Walsall, who won the toss for venue.

Meanwhile England had a European Championship warm-up in Lausanne against Switzerland and won 1-0, quite impressively apart from the score. Gary Lineker scored the goal.

On Sunday, 80,841 watched the Sherpa Van Trophy final at Wembley, and Wolves completed a fine season, which included promotion from the Fourth Division, by winning 2-0 with goals from Mutch and Dennison.

The last act of the season was the replay between Walsall and Bristol City, played on the Spring Bank Holiday Monday. Walsall got away to an excellent start with three quick goals in the first half and went on to clinch promotion 4-0, three goals coming from David Kelly and the other from Phil Hawker.

Mark Stein (right) appears set to follow his brother Brian, who has been given a free transfer by Luton Town.

The Arsenal goalkeeper John Lukic was an ever-present in League football during the season and conceeded only 39 goals.

Dave Beasant, the Wimbledon goalkeeper, became the hero of the FA Cup final when he defied Liverpool with a string of fine saves, including one from the penalty spot.

Match Magazine

SECOND DIVISION

	P	Home			Goals		Away			Goals		Pts
		W	D	L	F	A	W	D	L	F	A	
1 Millwall†	44	15	3	4	45	23	10	4	8	27	29	82
2 Aston Villa†	44	9	7	6	31	21	13	5	4	37	20	78
3 Middlesbrough†	44	15	4	3	44	16	7	8	7	19	20	78
4 Bradford C	44	14	3	5	49	26	8	8	6	25	28	77
5 Blackburn Rov	44	12	8	2	38	22	9	6	7	30	30	77
6 Crystal Palace	44	16	3	3	50	21	6	6	10	36	38	75
7 Leeds U	44	14	4	4	37	18	5	8	9	24	33	69
8 Ipswich T	44	14	3	5	38	17	5	6	11	23	35	66
9 Manchester C	44	11	4	7	50	28	8	4	10	30	32	65
10 Oldham Ath	44	13	4	5	43	27	5	7	10	29	37	65
11 Stoke C	44	12	6	4	34	22	5	5	12	16	35	62
12 Swindon T	44	10	7	5	43	25	6	4	12	30	35	59
13 Leicester C	44	12	5	5	35	20	4	6	12	27	41	59
14 Barnsley	44	11	4	7	42	32	4	8	10	19	30	57
15 Hull C	44	10	8	4	32	22	4	7	11	22	38	57
16 Plymouth Arg	44	12	4	6	44	26	4	4	14	21	41	56
17 Bournemouth	44	7	7	8	36	30	6	3	13	20	38	49
18 Shrewsbury T	44	7	8	7	23	22	4	8	10	19	32	49
19 Birmingham C	44	7	9	6	20	24	4	6	12	21	42	48
20 West Bromwich A	44	8	7	7	29	26	4	4	14	21	43	47
21 Sheffield U *	44	8	6	8	27	28	5	1	16	18	46	46
22 Reading*	44	5	7	10	20	25	5	5	12	24	45	42
23 Huddersfield T*	44	4	6	12	20	38	2	4	16	21	62	28

* relegated † promoted

THIRD DIVISION

	P	Home			Goals		Away			Goals		Pts
		W	D	L	F	A	W	D	L	F	A	
1 Sunderland†	46	14	7	2	51	22	13	5	5	41	26	93
2 Brighton & H A †	46	15	7	1	37	16	8	8	7	32	31	84
3 Walsall†	46	15	6	2	39	22	8	7	8	29	28	82
4 Notts. Co	46	14	4	5	53	24	9	8	6	29	25	81
5 Bristol C	46	14	6	3	51	30	7	6	10	26	32	75
6 Northampton T	46	12	8	3	36	18	6	11	6	34	33	73
7 Wigan Ath	46	11	8	4	36	23	9	4	10	34	38	72
8 Bristol Rov	46	14	5	4	43	19	4	7	12	25	37	66
9 Fulham	46	10	5	8	36	24	9	4	10	33	36	66
10 Blackpool	46	13	4	6	45	27	4	10	9	26	35	65
11 Port Vale	46	12	8	3	36	19	6	3	14	22	37	65
12 Brentford	46	9	8	6	27	23	7	6	10	26	36	62
13 Gillingham	46	8	9	6	45	21	6	8	9	32	40	59
14 Bury	46	9	7	7	33	26	6	7	10	25	31	59
15 Chester C	46	9	8	6	29	30	5	8	10	22	32	58
16 Preston N E	46	10	6	7	30	23	5	7	11	18	36	58
17 Southend U	46	10	6	7	42	33	4	7	12	23	50	55
18 Chesterfield	46	10	5	8	25	28	5	5	13	16	42	55
19 Mansfield T	46	10	6	7	25	21	4	6	13	23	38	54
20 Aldershot	46	12	3	8	45	32	3	5	15	19	42	53
21 Rotherham U *	46	8	8	7	28	25	4	8	11	22	41	52
22 Grimsby T *	46	6	7	10	25	29	6	7	10	23	29	50
23 York C *	46	4	7	12	27	45	4	2	17	21	46	33
24 Doncaster Rov *	46	6	5	12	25	36	2	4	17	15	48	33

* relegated † promoted

FOURTH DIVISION

	P	Home			Goals		Away			Goals		Pts
		W	D	L	F	A	W	D	L	F	A	
1 Wolverhampton W †	46	15	3	5	47	19	12	6	5	35	24	90
2 Cardiff C †	46	15	6	2	39	14	9	7	7	27	27	85
3 Bolton W †	46	15	6	2	42	12	7	6	10	24	30	78
4 Scunthorpe U	46	14	5	4	42	20	6	12	5	34	31	77
5 Torquay U	46	10	7	6	34	16	11	7	5	32	25	77
6 Swansea T †	46	9	7	7	35	28	11	3	9	27	28	70
7 Peterborough U	46	10	5	8	28	26	10	5	8	24	27	70
8 Leyton Orient	46	13	4	6	55	27	6	8	9	30	36	69
9 Colchester U	46	10	5	8	23	22	9	5	9	24	29	67
10 Burnley	46	12	5	6	31	22	8	2	13	26	40	67
11 Wrexham	46	13	3	7	46	26	7	3	13	23	32	66
12 Scarborough	46	12	8	3	38	19	5	6	12	18	29	65
13 Darlington	46	13	6	4	39	25	5	5	13	32	44	65
14 Tranmere Rov	46	14	2	7	43	20	5	7	11	18	33	64
15 Cambridge U	46	10	6	7	32	24	6	7	10	18	28	61
16 Hartlepool U	46	9	7	7	25	25	6	7	10	25	32	59
17 Crewe Alex	46	7	11	5	25	19	6	8	9	32	34	58
18 Halifax T	46	11	7	5	37	25	3	7	13	17	34	55
19 Hereford U	46	8	7	8	25	24	5	5	12	16	32	54
20 Stockport Co	46	7	7	9	26	26	5	8	10	18	32	51
21 Rochdale	46	5	9	9	28	34	6	6	11	19	42	48
22 Exeter C	46	8	6	9	33	29	3	7	13	20	39	46
23 Carlisle U	48	9	5	9	38	33	3	3	17	19	53	44
24 Newport Co *	46	4	5	14	19	36	2	2	19	16	69	25

* replaced by Lincoln C † promoted

FINAL FOOTBALL LEAGUE TABLES 1987-88

FIRST DIVISION

	P	Home			Goals		Away			Goals		Pts
		W	D	L	F	A	W	D	L	F	A	
1 Liverpool	40	15	5	0	49	9	11	7	2	38	15	90
2 Manchester U	40	14	5	1	41	17	9	7	4	30	21	81
3 Nottingham F	40	11	7	2	40	17	9	6	5	27	22	73
4 Everton	40	14	4	2	34	11	5	9	6	19	16	70
5 Q.P.R.	40	12	4	4	30	14	7	6	7	18	24	67
6 Arsenal	40	11	4	5	35	16	7	8	5	23	23	66
7 Wimbledon	40	8	9	3	32	20	6	6	8	26	27	57
8 Newcastle U	40	9	6	5	32	23	5	8	7	23	30	56
9 Luton T	40	11	6	3	40	21	3	5	12	17	37	53
10 Coventry C	40	6	8	6	23	25	7	6	7	23	28	53
11 Sheffield Wed	40	10	2	8	27	30	5	6	9	25	36	53
12 Southampton	40	6	8	6	27	26	6	6	8	22	27	50
13 Tottenham H	40	9	5	6	26	23	3	6	11	12	25	47
14 Norwich C	40	7	5	8	26	26	5	4	11	14	26	45
15 Derby Co	40	6	7	7	18	17	4	6	10	17	28	43
16 West Ham U	40	6	9	5	23	21	3	6	11	17	31	42
17 Charlton Ath	40	7	7	6	23	21	2	8	10	15	31	42
18 Chelsea*	40	7	11	2	24	17	2	4	14	26	51	42
19 Portsmouth*	40	4	8	8	21	27	3	6	11	15	39	35
20 Watford*	40	4	5	11	15	24	3	6	11	12	27	32
21 Oxford U *	40	5	7	8	24	34	1	6	13	20	46	31

* relegated

The English Football League Clubs

The Complete Barclays League Record for Every Club During 1987–88.

Each club is portrayed match by match and includes the date, venue, opponents, result, half-time (H/T) score, League position (Lge Posn), attendance, full line-ups, substitutes and goalscorers. Lincoln City are also included as they return to the Football League for 1988–89, following a season in the Vauxhall Conference and their 1987–88 record in that League is recorded within these pages.

Please note that the league positions have been determined following each match and that the attendances shown are those which have been reported in the press.

In the Players: League Record table, the substitutes are denoted by an ★ and the players that they replaced are shown in **bold**.

Finally, it is worth noting that the "Play-Offs" are not recorded in this section, but are reported in the review of the 1987–88 season.

ALDERSHOT (Division 3)

Team Manager Len Walker.
Club Address Recreation Ground, High Street, Aldershot GU11 1TW. Tel: (0252) 20211.
Current Ground Capacity 16,000.
Record Attendance 19,138 v Carlisle U., FA Cup 4th Round replay, 28 January 1970.
Year Formed 1926. Turned professional 1927.
Previous Names None.
Club Nickname "The Shots".
Club Colours Red and blue striped shirts, blue edge on collar and cuffs, blue shorts, red stockings and two blue hoops.
Club Honours None.
League History 1932-58 Div. 3(S); 1958-73 Div. 4; 1973-76 Div. 3; 1976-87 Div. 4; 1987- Div. 3.
Most League Points in a Season (2 for a win) 57 in Div. 4, 1978-79. (3 for a win) 75 in Div. 4, 1983-84.
Most League Goals in a Season 83 in Div. 4, 1963-64.
Record Victory 8-1 v Gateshead in Div. 4, 13 September 1958.

Record Defeat 0-9 v Bristol C. in Div. 3(S), 28 December 1946.
Consecutive League Wins 6 in 1961.
Consecutive League Defeats 9 in 1965-66.
Record League Appearances Murray Brodie, 461 between 1970-83.
Record League Goalscorer—Career Jack Howarth, 171 between 1965-77.
Record League Goalscorer—Season John Dungworth, 26 in Div. 4, 1978-79.

Aldershot: League Record, 1987-88 (Division 3)

Match Number	Date	Venue	Opponents	Result		H/T	Lge Posn	Attend
1	15.8.87	A	Port Vale	L	2-4	1-1		3160
2	29.8.87	A	Bristol Rov.	L	1-3	0-3		3390
3	31.8.87	H	Doncaster Rov.	W	2-1	0-1	17	2598
4	5.9.87	A	Chester C.	L	1-4	0-1	21	1700
5	12.9.87	H	Brighton & H.A.	L	1-4	1-2	21	3970
6	15.9.87	H	Notts Co.	L	1-2	1-1	22	4835
7	19.9.87	A	Bury	L	0-1	0-1	22	1744
8	26.9.87	H	Brentford	W	4-1	3-1	21	3651
9	29.9.87	H	Wigan Ath.	W	3-2	2-1	21	2259
10	3.10.87	A	Sunderland	L	1-3	1-1	21	12542
11	17.10.87	A	York C.	D	2-2	0-1	21	1984
12	20.10.87	H	Chesterfield	W	2-0	1-0	20	2054
13	24.10.87	A	Fulham	W	2-1	0-1	19	6530
14	31.10.87	H	Northampton T.	D	4-4	1-3	19	3358
15	3.11.87	A	Walsall	L	0-2	0-1	19	4816
16	7.11.87	H	Bristol C.	W	2-1	1-0	18	4324
17	21.11.87	A	Southend U.	W	1-0	1-0	17	2362
18	28.11.87	H	Rotherham U.	L	1-3	0-2	18	2549
19	12.12.87	A	Preston N.E.	W	2-0	2-0	16	4519
20	19.12.87	H	Grimsby T.	W	3-2	3-1	14	2405
21	26.12.87	A	Brentford	L	0-3	0-2	15	5578
22	28.12.87	H	Gillingham	W	6-0	5-0	12	4734
23	1.1.88	H	Bristol Rov.	W	3-0	3-0	11	4593
24	2.1.88	A	Brighton & H.A.	D	1-1	1-0	11	9420
25	9.1.88	H	Walsall	L	0-1	0-1	11	3270
26	16.1.88	H	Bury	L	0-2	0-0	13	2718
27	31.1.88	A	Doncaster R.	D	0-0	0-0	12	1908
28	6.2.88	H	Chester C.	W	4-1	1-1	11	2578
29	13.2.88	A	Gillingham	L	1-2	0-0	11	4001
30	23.2.88	H	Notts Co.	L	0-2	0-0	13	2880
31	27.2.88	H	Sunderland	W	3-2	2-2	12	5010
32	1.3.88	A	Wigan Ath.	L	0-4	0-0	13	3017
33	5.3.88	H	York C.	L	1-2	0-1	16	2672
34	12.3.88	A	Blackpool	L	2-3	1-1	16	2661
35	19.3.88	A	Northampton T.	D	1-1	1-0	18	4322
36	22.3.88	A	Mansfield T.	L	0-1	0-0	18	2344
37	26.3.88	H	Fulham	L	0-3	0-1	19	4448
38	29.3.88	H	Blackpool	D	0-0	0-0	19	2091
39	2.4.88	A	Bristol C.	L	0-2	0-1	19	8712
40	4.4.88	H	Southend U.	L	0-1	0-0	19	3436
41	9.4.88	A	Chesterfield	L	0-1	0-0	21	1900
42	15.4.88	H	Port Vale	W	3-0	2-0	18	2257
43	19.4.88	H	Mansfield T.	W	3-0	2-0	17	2339
44	30.4.88	A	Rotherham U.	L	0-1	0-0	18	2818
45	2.5.88	H	Preston N.E.	D	0-0	0-0	18	3465
46	7.5.88	A	Grimsby T.	D	1-1	1-1	20	5697

Players: League Record, 1987-88 (Division 3)

Match Number	1	2	3	4	5	6	7	8	9	10	11	12	13	14	15	16	17	18	19	20	21	22	23	24	25	26	27	28	29	30	31	32	33	34	35	36	37	38	39	40	41	42	43	44	45	46	Apps	Subs	Goals
Anderson	4	4	★	★		★			★	★	★			★			5		5¹	5	5	5	5	**5**		6		6				6	6	6	6				★	★	6						16	9	1
Barnes, D.O.	7¹	7	7	7	7	7¹	7	7¹	7³	7¹																																					10	0	7
Barnes, D.			3	3	3	3	3	3	**3**							7	7		★		3	3	7	7	7	7	7				3	3	3	3	3	3	3	3	3				3	3			29	1	0
Bedford																											11	11		7	7	7	7	7	7	7	7	7	7	7	7	7	7	7	7	7	16	0	0
Berry										2	2¹	2	2¹	2	2¹	2	2	2	2	2	2¹	2	2	2	2	2	2	2¹	2	2	2¹	2	2	2	2	2	2	2	2	2	2	2	2	2	2	2	36	0	6
Burvill		★	4	4	4	11	**11**	11	11	11	11	11	11¹	11	11	11	11	11²	11²	11	11¹	11¹	11	11	11	11	11	11¹	11		★	11¹	11	11	**11**	**11**	11	★	11	4	4	4	4				40	3	9
Coles					1	1	1	1	1	1	1	1	1	1	1																																11	0	0
Davis										2																																					1	0	0
Holsgrove																													★		★																0	2	0
Howlett	8																																														1	0	0
Johnson			9	9	9¹	9	9	9	9	9	9	**9**	9	9	9¹	9	9	9	**9**											★	8	8	8														20	1	2
Joseph																																			8	★		4	8	8	11¹	11¹	11	11	11		9	1	2
Lange	1	1	1	1	1							1	1	1	1	1	1	1	1	1	1	1	1	1	1	1	1	1	1	1	1	1	1	1	1	1	1	1	1	1	1	1	1	1	1	1	35	0	0
Langley	9¹	8	8	8	8	8	8	8³	8	8	8¹	8	8	8¹	8	8¹	8	8	8	8	8	8¹	8²		8	**8**	8	8	8	**8**	4¹			8	8	8		8	8		4	8¹	**8¹**	8	8	8¹	41	0	14
McDonald	10	10	10	10	10	10	10	10	10	10	10	10¹	10¹	10	10	10	10	10	10	10¹	10	10	10	10	10	10³	10	10	10	10	10¹	10¹	10	10	10		10	10	10	10				**10**			43	0	8
Ogley											★	★	7	7	7	7	7		6																												6	2	0
Phillips	3	2	2	2	2	2	2	2	2	3	3	3	3	3	3	3	3	3	3	3	3	**3**		3	3	3	3	3	3	**3**									3	3							32	0	0
Riley														★	★	7¹	7	7¹	7		★	9	9²	9	9	9	9	**9**		9¹	9	9	9	9	9	9	9	9	9	9	9¹	9	9	**9**	9	26	3	5
Ring	11	11¹	11²	11	11		★		★	★	7¹	7	7¹	7	7	★	9	9			8	★	★	★¹	9	9	7	7	11		★	★	10	11			★		★			21	11	6
Roberts	2		★	★	4	4	4	4	4	4	4	4	4	4	4	4	4	4	4	4	4	4	4	**4**	4	4	4	4	4	4	4	4	4	**4**						10	10	★			36	3	0
Smith	5	5	5	5	5	5	5	5	5	5	5	5	5	5		5	6		★	★	5	5	5	5	5	5	5	5	5	5	5	5	5	5	5	5	5	5	5	5¹	5	5	5	40	2	1
Wignall	6	6	6	**6**	6	6	6	6	6	**6**	6	6	6	6	6	6		6	6¹	6	6	6		6		6	**6**					6	6	6	6	6		6	6	6	6	6	6	37	0	1
Own Goals							1															1																											2

FA Cup: 1987-88: 1st Round: Sutton U. (A) 0-3.
Littlewoods Cup: 1987-88: 1st Round: Cambridge U. (A) 1-1 (H) 1-4.

ARSENAL (Division 1)

Team Manager   George Graham.
Club Address   Arsenal Stadium, Highbury, London N5. Tel: 01-226 0304.
Current Ground Capacity   57,000.
Record Attendance   73,295 v Sunderland, Div. 1, 9 March 1935.
Year Formed   1886. Turned professional 1891.
Previous Names   Dial Square, Royal Arsenal, Woolwich Arsenal.
Club Nickname   "The Gunners".
Club Colours   Red shirts with white sleeves, white shorts and red and white stockings.
Club Honours   Football League: Div. 1 Champions 1930-31, 1932-33, 1933-34, 1934-35, 1937-38, 1947-48, 1952-53, 1970-71. FA Cup: Winners 1930, 1936, 1950, 1971 and 1979. League Cup: Winners 1987. European Competitions: Fairs Cup: Winners 1969-70, 1970-71.
League History   1893-1904 Div. 2; 1904-13 Div. 1; 1913-19 Div. 2; 1919- Div. 1.
Most League Points in a Season   (2 for a win) 66 in Div. 1, 1930-31. (3 for a win) 71 in Div. 1, 1981-82.

Most League Goals in a Season   127 in Div. 1, 1930-31.
Record Victory   12-0 v Loughborough T., Div. 2, 12 March 1900.
Record Defeat   0-8 v Loughborough T., Div. 2, 12 December 1896.
Consecutive League Wins   9 in 1971.
Consecutive League Defeats   7 in 1977.
Record League Appearances   George Armstrong, 500 between 1961-77.
Record League Goalscorer—Career   Cliff Bastin, 150 between 1930-47.
Record League Goalscorer—Season   Ted Drake, 42 between 1934-35.

Arsenal League Record, 1987-88 (Division 1)

Match Number	Date	Venue	Opponents	Result		H/T	Lge Posn	Attend
1	15.8.87	H	Liverpool	L	1-2	1-1		54703
2	19.8.87	A	Manchester U.	D	0-0	0-0	19	42898
3	22.8.87	A	Q.P.R.	L	0-2	0-1	19	18981
4	29.8.87	H	Portsmouth	W	6-0	4-0	12	30865
5	31.8.87	H	Luton T.	D	1-1	1-1	12	8745
6	12.9.87	A	Nottingham F.	W	1-0	1-0	10	18490
7	19.9.87	H	Wimbledon	W	3-0	3-0	9	27752
8	26.9.87	A	West Ham U.	W	1-0	0-0	7	40127
9	3.10.87	A	Charlton Ath.	W	3-0	1-0	5	15326
10	10.10.87	H	Oxford U.	W	2-0	1-0	3	25244
11	18.10.87	A	Tottenham H.	W	2-1	1-0	3	36680
12	24.10.87	H	Derby Co.	W	2-1	2-1	3	32374
13	31.10.87	H	Newcastle U.	W	1-0	0-0	1	23662
14	3.11.87	H	Chelsea	W	3-1	2-1	1	40230
15	14.11.87	A	Norwich C.	W	4-2	0-1	1	20558
16	21.11.87	H	Southampton	L	0-1	0-0	1	32477
17	28.11.87	A	Watford	L	0-2	0-1	2	19598
18	5.12.87	H	Sheffield Wed.	W	3-1	0-1	2	23670
19	13.12.87	A	Coventry C.	D	0-0	0-0	2	17557
20	19.12.87	H	Everton	D	1-1	0-1	2	34587
21	26.12.87	H	Nottingham F.	L	0-2	0-1	3	31211
22	28.12.87	A	Wimbledon	L	1-3	1-0	3	12473
23	1.1.88	A	Portsmouth	D	1-1	0-1	3	17366
24	2.1.88	H	Q.P.R.	D	0-0	0-0	3	28271
25	16.1.88	A	Liverpool	L	0-2	0-1	3	44294
26	24.1.88	H	Manchester U.	L	1-2	1-1	5	29392
27	13.2.88	H	Luton T.	W	2-1	2-0	5	22615
28	27.2.88	H	Charlton Ath.	W	4-0	1-0	5	25394
29	6.3.88	H	Tottenham H.	W	2-1	1-0	5	37143
30	19.3.88	H	Newcastle U.	D	1-1	1-0	5	25889
31	26.3.88	A	Derby Co.	D	0-0	0-0	6	18382
32	30.3.88	A	Oxford U.	D	0-0	0-0	6	9088
33	2.4.88	A	Chelsea	D	1-1	0-0	6	26084
34	4.4.88	H	Norwich C.	W	2-0	1-0	6	19341
35	9.4.88	A	Southampton	L	2-4	1-3	6	14521
36	12.4.88	A	West Ham U.	W	1-0	0-0	6	26746
37	15.4.88	H	Watford	L	0-1	0-0	6	19541
38	30.4.88	A	Sheffield Wed.	D	3-3	1-3	6	16681
39	2.5.88	H	Coventry C.	D	1-1	1-1	6	16963
40	7.5.88	A	Everton	W	2-1	2-1	6	22445

Players: League Record, 1987-88 (Division 1)

Match Number	1	2	3	4	5	6	7	8	9	10	11	12	13	14	15	16	17	18	19	20	21	22	23	24	25	26	27	28	29	30	31	32	33	34	35	36	37	38	39	40	Apps	Subs	Goals
Adams	6	6	6	6¹	6	6	6	6	6¹	6	6	6	**6**	6	**6**	6	6	6	6	6	6	6	6	6	6	**6**	6	6	6	6	6¹	6		6	6	6	6	6			39	0	3
Caesar							★		★		★						★	5	5	5	**5**		★	5	5	5	5	5	5	5	5	5	5	5	**5**						17	5	0
Campbell																																			★						0	1	0
Davis	8¹	8	8	8¹	8¹	8	8	8	8	8¹	8	8	8	8	8	8	8	**8**		8						★		8	8	8	8	8	8¹	8	8	8			2	2	28	1	5
Dixon																							2				2	2		2									2	2	6	0	0
Groves	★	★		10	10	10	**10**	10	10	10¹	10	**10**	10	10	10	10¹	**10**	10	10¹	10	10	10	**10**	★	★	★	10			10¹	10¹	10	10	10	10¹	**10**			★		28	6	6
Hayes	11	11	11			★		★	★	★	★		★			8			8	8	8	8		8	8	8	11	11			11	11	11		★	★	★	10¹			17	10	1
Lukic	1	1	1	1	1	1	1	1	1	1	1	1	1	1	1	1	1	1	1	1	1	1	1	1	1	1	1	1	1	1	1	1	1	1	1	1	1	1	1	1	40	0	0
Marwood																															11					11	11	11¹			4	0	1
Merson			★			★				★						★¹	★	★	8		★	10					10²					★	10	10	10²	10					7	8	5
Nicholas	10	**10**	10																																						3	0	0
O'Leary	5	5	5	5	5	5	5	5	5	5	5	5	5	5	5	5	5	5	5	**5**			5	5																	23	0	0
Quinn																★				9	9¹	9		10	10¹	★		★	★	★	9										6	5	2
Richardson			★		★		11	11	11¹	11	11²	11	11	11	11¹	**11**	11	11	11	11	11	11	11	11	11	11	**11**	11		★	★				11	**11**	★		8	8	24	3	0
Rix			★	**11**	11	11	11	11	11														8										★							★	7	3	0
Rocastle	7	7	**7**	7¹	7	7	7	**7**	7	7	7¹	7	7	7	7²	7	7	7	7¹	7	7	7	7	**7**	7	7¹	7	7	7	**7**	7	**7**	7	7	7	7	7	7	7	7	40	0	6
Sansom	3	3	3	3	3	3	3	3¹	3	3	3	3	3	3	3	3	3	3	3	3		3	3			3	3		3		3	3	3	3	3	3					34	0	1
Smith	9	9	9	9³	9	9¹	9¹	9	9	**9**	9	9¹	9	9	9	9	9	9	9	9	★	★¹	9	9	9	9¹	9¹	**9**	**9**	9		9¹	9	9	9¹	9	9				36	3	12
Thomas	2	2	2	2	2	2	2¹	2	2¹	2	2	2	2	2¹	2	2	2	2	2	2	2	2	2	2		★	2	4¹	4¹	4	4	4		6	4¹	4	4	4¹			29	1	1
Williams	4	4	4	4	4	4	4	**4**	4	4	4¹	4	4	4	**4**	4	4	4	4	4	4	4	4	4	4					4	4	4									29	0	1
Winterburn																★					3	2	2	3	3	2	2	3	3	2	3	2	2	2	2	2	**2**				16	1	0
Own Goals			1							1																						1												3

FA Cup: 1987-88: 3rd Round: Millwall (H) 2-0; 4th Round: Brighton & H.A. (A) 2-1; 5th Round: Manchester U. (H) 2-1; 6th Round: Nottingham F. (H) 1-2.
Littlewoods Cup: 1987-88: 2nd Round: Doncaster Rov. (A) 3-0 (H) 1-0; 3rd Round: Bournemouth (H) 3-0; 4th Round: Stoke C. (H) 3-0; Quarter Final: Sheffield Wed. (A) 1-0; Semi Final: Everton (A) 1-0; (H) 3-1; Final: Luton T. 2-3.

51

ASTON VILLA (Division 1)

Team Manager   Graham Taylor.
Club Address   Villa Park, Trinity Road, Birmingham B6 6HE. Tel: 021-327 6604.
Current Ground Capacity   48,000.
Record Attendance   76,588 v Derby Co., FA Cup 6th Round, 2 March 1946.
Year Formed   1874. Turned professional 1885.
Previous Names   None.
Club Nickname   "The Villans".
Club Colours   Claret and blue shirts, white shorts and stockings with claret and blue trim.
Club Honours   Football League: Div. 1 Champions 1893-94, 1895-96, 1896-97, 1898-99, 1899-1900, 1909-10, 1980-81; Div. 2 Champions 1937-38, 1959-60; Div. 3 Champions 1971-72. FA Cup: Winners 1887, 1895, 1897, 1905, 1913, 1920, 1957. Football League Cup: Winners 1961, 1975, 1977. European Cup: Winners 1982-83. European Super Cup: Winners 1982-83.
League History   1888-1936 Div. 1; Div. 2; 1938-59 Div. 1; 1959-60 Div. 2; 1960-67 Div. 1; 1967-70 Div. 2; 1970-72 Div. 3; 1972-75 Div. 2; 1975-87 Div. 1; 1987-88 Div. 2; 1988- Div. 1.
Most League Points in a Season   (2 for a win) 70 in Div. 3, 1971-72. (3 for a win) 68 in Div. 1, 1982-83.
Most League Goals in a Season   128 in Div. 1, 1930-31.
Record Victory   13-0 v Wednesbury Old Athletic, FA Cup, 1st Round 1886.
Record Defeat   1-8 v Blackburn Rov. in FA Cup 3rd Round, 16 February 1889.
Consecutive League Wins   9 in 1897.
Consecutive League Defeats   11 in 1910 and 1963.
Record League Appearances   Charlie Aitken, 561 between 1961-76.
Record League Goalscorer—Career   Harry Hampton, 213 between 1904-20 and Billy Walker, 213 between 1919-34.
Record League Goalscorer—Season   "Pongo" Waring, 49 in Div. 1, 1930-31.

Aston Villa: League Record, 1987-88 (Division 2)

Match Number	Date	Venue	Opponents	Result		H/T	Lge Posn	Attend
1	15.8.87	A	Ipswich T.	D	1-1	1-1		14508
2	22.8.87	H	Birmingham C.	L	0-2	0-0		30870
3	29.8.87	A	Hull C.	L	1-2	1-1	22	8315
4	31.8.87	H	Manchester C.	D	1-1	1-0	20	16282
5	5.9.87	A	Leicester C.	W	2-0	1-0	16	10286
6	8.9.87	H	Middlesbrough	L	0-1	0-0	17	12665
7	12.9.87	H	Barnsley	D	0-0	0-0	19	12621
8	16.9.87	A	West Bromwich A.	W	2-0	1-0	16	22072
9	19.9.87	A	Huddersfield T.	W	1-0	1-0	11	6884
10	26.9.87	H	Sheffield U.	D	1-1	1-0	10	14761
11	30.9.87	H	Blackburn Rov.	D	1-1	1-1	7	11772
12	3.10.87	A	Plymouth Arg.	W	3-1	3-1	9	10515
13	10.10.87	A	Leeds U.	W	3-1	1-1	6	20741
14	17.10.87	H	Bournemouth	D	1-1	1-0	7	15145
15	21.10.87	H	Crystal Palace	W	4-1	2-1	5	12755
16	24.10.87	A	Stoke C.	D	0-0	0-0	4	13494
17	31.10.87	H	Reading	W	2-1	0-0	4	13413
18	3.11.87	A	Shrewsbury T.	W	2-1	1-1	3	7089
19	7.11.87	H	Millwall	L	1-2	1-2	5	13255
20	14.11.87	A	Oldham Ath.	W	1-0	1-0	4	8469
21	28.11.87	A	Bradford C.	W	4-2	2-1	3	15006
22	5.12.87	H	Swindon T.	W	2-1	0-0	3	16127
23	12.12.87	A	Birmingham C.	W	2-1	1-1	3	27789
24	18.12.87	H	West Bromwich A.	D	0-0	0-0	3	24437
25	26.12.87	A	Sheffield U.	D	1-1	0-0	4	15809
26	28.12.87	H	Huddersfield T.	D	1-1	1-1	3	20948
27	1.1.88	A	Hull C.	W	5-0	1-0	1	19236
28	2.1.88	A	Barnsley	W	3-1	1-0	1	11562
29	16.1.88	H	Ipswich T.	W	1-0	1-0	1	20201
30	23.1.88	A	Manchester C.	W	2-0	1-0	1	24668
31	6.2.88	H	Leicester C.	W	2-1	2-0	1	18867
32	14.2.88	A	Middlesbrough	L	1-2	1-0	1	16957
33	20.2.88	A	Blackburn Rov.	L	2-3	0-1	2	17356
34	27.2.88	H	Plymouth Arg.	W	5-2	3-1	1	16142
35	5.3.88	A	Bournemouth	W	2-1	1-0	1	10157
36	12.3.88	H	Leeds U.	L	1-2	0-2	1	19677
37	19.3.88	A	Reading	W	2-0	0-0	1	10033
38	26.3.88	H	Stoke C.	L	0-1	0-0	1	20392
39	2.4.88	A	Millwall	L	1-2	1-1	1	13697
40	4.4.88	H	Oldham Ath.	L	1-2	1-0	1	19138
41	9.4.88	A	Crystal Palace	D	1-1	1-0	4	16476
42	23.4.88	H	Shrewsbury T.	W	1-0	1-0	2	18396
43	2.5.88	H	Bradford C.	W	1-0	1-0	3	36423
44	7.5.88	A	Swindon T.	D	0-0	0-0	2	10959

Players: League Record, 1987-88 (Division 2)

Match Number	1	2	3	4	5	6	7	8	9	10	11	12	13	14	15	16	17	18	19	20	21	22	23	24	25	26	27	28	29	30	31	32	33	34	35	36	37	38	39	40	41	42	43	44	Apps	Subs	Goals
Allen					8	8	8			10																																			4	0	0
Aspinall	8	8	8¹	8	★	★	8²	8	8	8¹	8	8²	8	8	8	8¹	8	8	8	8	8	8	8	8	★²	10¹												8	★		11¹	8	8		28	4	11
Birch	7	7					7	7	7	7	7	7	7	7	7	7	7	11¹	7	7	7	7	7¹	7	7¹	7	7	7	7	7	7	7²	7	7	7¹	7	7	7					7		38	0	6
Blair																	★¹	10	10	10																									3	1	1
Burke				★	7	7	7			★							11																												4	2	0
Cooper	4	4	4			★	4	4	4																																				6	1	0
Daley		★	7																								10¹	10	10¹	★	8	8¹	8	8	★	★	8		7						10	4	3
Evans											★	★											5	5	5	5	5¹	5	5	5	5	5	5	5	5	5	5	5	5	5	5	5	5	5	18	2	1
Gage	2	2	2	2¹	2	2	2	2	2	2¹	2	2	2	2	2	2	2	2	2	2	2	2	2	2	2	2	2	2	2	2	2	2	2	2	2	2	2	2	2	2	2	2	2	2	44	0	2
Gallacher	3	3	3	3	3	3	3	3	3	3	3	3	3	3	3	3	3	3	3	3	3	3	3	3	3	3	3	3	3	3	3	3	3	3	3	3			3	3	3	3			43	0	0
Gray, A.																						4	4				4	4¹	4	4	4	4	4	4	4	4				4	4	4			19	0	1
Gray, S.																10²	10	10	10	10	10	10¹								★	10	10¹	10	10	10	10	10¹	10	10	10					19	1	5
Hunt, D.	10	10	10	4	4	4		★	4	10						9		10																											11	1	0
Hunt, S.	★			10	10	10	10	10¹			10	10	10	10¹	10																														10	1	2
Keown	6	6	6	6	6	6	6	6	6	6	6	6	6	6		6¹	6¹	6	6	6	6	6	6	6	6	6	6¹	6	6	6	6	6	6	6	6	6	6	6	6	6	6				42	0	3
Lillis					9¹	9	9	9	9	9	4	4¹	4	4	4	4¹	4	4			4	4		8	8	8	8	8¹	8	8						★	4			8					28	1	4
McInally								9	9	9	9			9	9	9	9	9¹	7		★		★	11¹	11¹	11	11	11	11			★¹	★	8	★	★	★		7						18	7	4
Norton																										★																			1	1	0
Platt																											11¹	11¹	11¹	11	11	11	11	11	11	8¹		11¹	11						11	0	5
Shaw												★		★			★												10																1	3	0
Sims	5	5	5	5	5	5	5	5	5	5	5	5	5	5	5	5	5	5	5	5	5	5	5	5	5												3				6	6			29	0	0
Spink	1	1	1	1	1	1	1	1	1	1	1	1	1	1	1	1	1	1	1	1	1	1	1	1	1	1	1	1	1	1	1	1	1	1	1	1	1	1	1	1	1	1	1	1	44	0	0
Stainrod	9	9	9	9																																									4	0	0
Thompson																		9¹	9²	9²	9	9¹	9	9	9	9	9	9¹	9	9	9	9¹	9¹	9	9	9	9¹	9	9¹	9	9	9	9	9	24	0	11
Walters	11	11	11	11	11¹	11	11	11	11	11	11²	11	11¹	11³		11	11	11		11	11	11	11		11	11	11	11																	24	0	7
Williams																																					11								1	0	0
Own Goals		1													1																																2

FA Cup: 1987-88: 3rd Round: Leeds U. (A) 2-1; 4th Round: Liverpool (H) 0-2.
Littlewoods Cup: 1987-88: 2nd Round: Middlesbrough (A) 1-0 (H) 1-0; 3rd Round: Tottenham H (H) 2-1; 4th Round: Sheffield Wed (H) 1-2.

BARNSLEY (Division 2)

Team Manager Allan Clarke.
Club Address Oakwell Ground, Grove Street, Barnsley. Tel: (0226) 295353.
Current Ground Capacity 36,864.
Record Attendance 40,255 v Stoke C, FA Cup 5th Round, 15 February 1936.
Year Formed 1887. Turned professional 1888.
Previous Names Barnsley St Peter's.
Club Nickname "The Tykes" or "Colliers".
Club Colours Red shirts, white shorts and white stockings.
Club Honours Football League: Div. 3(N) Champions 1933-34, 1938-39, 1954-55. FA Cup: Winners 1912.
League History 1898-1932 Div. 2; 1932-34 Div. 3(N); 1934-38 Div. 2; 1938-39 Div 3(N); 1946-53 Div. 2; 1953-55 Div. 3(N); 1955-59 Div. 2; 1959-65 Div. 3; 1965-68 Div. 4; 1968-72 Div. 3; 1972-79 Div. 4; 1979-81 Div. 3; 1981- Div. 2.
Most League Points in a Season (2 for a win) 67 in Div. 3(N) 1938-39. (3 for a win) 67 in Div. 2, 1981-82.

Most League Goals in a Season 118 in Div. 3(N), 1933-34.
Record Victory 9-0 v Loughborough Town in Div. 2, 28 January 1899 and v Accrington Stanley in Div. 3(N), 3 February 1934.
Record Defeat 0-9 v Notts. County in Div. 2, 19 November 1927.
Consecutive League Wins 10 in 1955.
Consecutive League Defeats 9 in 1953.
Record League Appearances Barry Murphy, 513 between 1962-78.
Record League Goalscorer—Career Ernest Hine, 123 between 1921-38.
Record League Goalscorer—Season Cecil McCormack, 33 in Div. 2, 1950-51.

Barnsley: League Record, 1987-88 (Division 2)

Match Number	Date	Venue	Opponents	Result		H/T	Lge Posn	Attend
1	16.8.87	H	Leeds U.	D	1-1	0-0		9778
2	18.8.87	A	Blackburn Rov.	W	1-0	1-0		6708
3	22.8.87	A	Millwall	L	1-3	0-0	10	6017
4	29.8.87	H	Crystal Palace	W	2-1	0-1	5	4853
5	31.8.87	A	Bournemouth	W	2-1	1-1	2	7480
6	5.9.87	H	Plymouth Arg.	W	2-1	0-0	1	6976
7	12.9.87	A	Aston Villa	D	0-0	0-0	2	12621
8	15.9.87	H	Swindon T.	L	0-1	0-0	4	7773
9	26.9.87	A	Oldham Ath.	L	0-1	0-0	9	5853
10	29.9.87	H	Sheffield U.	L	1-2	1-0	9	10203
11	3.10.87	A	Ipswich T.	L	0-1	0-1	13	10992
12	10.10.87	A	Leicester C.	D	0-0	0-0	13	8665
13	17.10.87	H	Hull C.	L	1-3	0-1	15	7310
14	20.10.87	H	Reading	W	5-2	1-2	12	4396
15	24.10.87	A	Manchester C.	D	1-1	1-1	12	17063
16	31.10.87	H	Stoke C.	W	5-2	2-0	11	5908
17	3.11.87	A	Birmingham C.	L	0-2	0-1	11	6622
18	7.11.87	H	Bradford C.	W	3-0	2-0	10	11569
19	14.11.87	A	Huddersfield T.	D	2-2	2-1	11	8629
20	21.11.87	H	Shrewsbury T.	W	2-1	2-0	11	5364
21	28.11.87	A	Middlesbrough	L	0-2	0-0	11	12732
22	5.12.87	H	West Bromwich A.	W	3-1	1-0	11	5395
23	19.12.87	H	Millwall	W	4-1	2-1	10	5011
24	26.12.87	H	Oldham Ath.	D	1-1	1-1	11	8676
25	1.1.88	A	Crystal Palace	L	2-3	0-1	12	8563
26	2.1.88	H	Aston Villa	L	1-3	0-1	12	11562
27	16.1.88	A	Leeds U.	W	2-0	1-0	12	19028
28	13.2.88	H	Blackburn Rov.	L	0-1	0-0	15	8972
29	20.2.88	A	Sheffield U.	L	0-1	0-0	15	11861
30	27.2.88	H	Ipswich T.	L	2-3	1-2	15	6482
31	5.3.88	A	Hull C.	W	2-1	2-1	13	7622
32	8.3.88	H	Bournemouth	W	2-1	1-1	13	6140
33	12.3.88	H	Leicester C.	D	1-1	1-1	12	7447
34	15.3.88	A	Swindon T.	L	0-3	0-1	13	7558
35	19.3.88	A	Stoke C.	L	1-3	0-0	15	8029
36	26.3.88	H	Manchester C.	W	3-1	2-1	14	9061
37	2.4.88	A	Bradford C.	D	1-1	0-1	14	15098
38	4.4.88	H	Huddersfield T.	W	1-0	1-0	13	7950
39	9.4.88	A	Reading	L	1-2	0-1	13	4849
40	15.4.88	A	Plymouth Arg.	D	0-0	0-0	13	8059
41	23.4.88	H	Birmingham C.	D	2-2	1-0	13	4949
42	30.4.88	A	Shrewsbury T.	D	1-1	0-0	13	4712
43	2.5.88	H	Middlesbrough	L	0-3	0-2	15	13240
44	7.5.88	A	West Bromwich A.	D	2-2	0-1	14	8483

Players: League Record, 1987-88 (Division 2)

Match Number	1	2	3	4	5	6	7	8	9	10	11	12	13	14	15	16	17	18	19	20	21	22	23	24	25	26	27	28	29	30	31	32	33	34	35	36	37	38	39	40	41	42	43	44	Apps	Subs	Goals
Agnew	8	8	8	8	8	8	8	8	8	8^1	8	8	8	8						8	8	8^2	8^2	8	8^1	8	8	8	8																25	0	6
Baker	1	1	1	1	1	1	1	1	1	1	1	1	1	1	1	1	1	1	1	1	1	1	1	1	1	1	1	1	1	1	1	1	1	1	1	1	1	1	1	1	1	1	1	1	44	0	0
Beresford	3			3	3		★		★	★	★	7	7	11	11				11	11	11		10	10	10	★	11	11	11	4^1	4^1	4		10	10^1	10	10	10	10	10	3	3	10		29	5	3
Blair																													8	8	8	8	8	8											6	0	0
Broddle							★	★	11	11	11					★					★	11^1	11	11	11	11	★	10	★			★	★	★					★						9	10	1
Clarke	11	11	11	11	11	11	11	11	11	11											★	★																	10	11					12	2	0
Coatsworth																						2											★	★		★		8	8						3	3	0
Cross		★		★		3	3	3	3	3	3	3	3	3	3	3	3	3	3	3	3	3	3	3	3	3	3	3	3	3	3	3	3	3	3	3	3	3	3						36	2	0
Currie																														7^2	7	7	7	7	7	7	7	7^1	7	7	7^2	7	7	7^2	15	0	7
Dobbin	9									★					8^1	8	8	8		7					10		8	8^1	8	8	8					8									14	2	2
Foreman															★	★			7^1	7	7	7	7^1	7^2		7																			7	2	4
Futcher	6	6	6	6	6	6	6	6	6	6	6	6	6	6		6	6	6	6	6	6	6	6	6	6	6	6	6	6	6	6	6	6	6	6	6	6	6			6	6			41	0	0
Gray	5	5	5	5	5	5	5	5	5	5	5	5	5	5	5	11	11	11^1	11^1	5																									20	0	2
Hedworth																			2	2	2									2						★									4	1	0
Jeffels			3	3																					★	2									6	6			6						6	1	0
Joyce	2	2	2	2	2	2	2	2	2	2	2	2	2	2^1	2	2	2	2	2	2			2	2	2	2		2	2	2	2^1	2	2	2	2	2	2	2	2	2	2	2			38	0	2
Lowndes	★	9	9^1	9	9^1	9	9	9	9	9	9	9	9	9^1	9	9	9	9	9^1	9	9	9		9	9	9^1	9	9	9^1	9	9	9	9	9	9	9	9	9	9	9^1	9	9			43	1	9
MacDonald	10	10^1	10	10^1	10^1	10	10	10	10	10	10	10	10	10^2	10	10	10^1	10	10	10^1	10	10	10				10	★	10	10	10	10	10							★	11	10			31	2	7
McGugan											★			5	5	5		5	5	5^1	5	5	5	5	5	5	5	5			5	5	5	5	5	5	5	5	5	5	5	5			28	1	1
Rees																							11	11	11^1	11	11^1	11	11	11	11	11	11	★	★	11								12	2	2
Robinson			★	★																									8																1	2	0
Rolph																																		★		3									1	1	0
Thomas	4	4	4	4	4	4	4	4	4	4	4	4	4	4^1	4	4	4	4	4	4^1	4	4	4	4^1	4	4	4	★	4		★	4	4	4	4^1	4	4	4	4	4	4	4			40	2	4
Tiler																																										★			0	1	0
Wylde	7^1	7	7	7^1	7	7^2	7	7	7	7	7				7^1	7	7^2	7	7^1	7	7					★			7																19	1	8
Own Goals												1																					1		1												3

FA Cup: 1987-88: 3rd Round: Bolton W. (H) 3-0; 4th Round: Birmingham C. (H) 0-2.
Littlewoods Cup: 1987-88: 2nd Round: West Ham U. (H) 0-0 (A) 5-2; 3rd Round: Sheffield Wed. (H) 1-2.

BIRMINGHAM CITY (Division 2)

Team Manager Gary Pendrey.
Club Address St Andrews, Birmingham B9 4NH. Tel: 021-772 0101/2689.
Current Ground Capacity 43,204.
Record Attendance 66,844 v Everton, FA Cup 5th Round, 11 February 1939.
Year Formed 1875. Turned professional 1885.
Previous Names Small Heath Alliance, Birmingham.
Club Nickname "The Blues".
Club Colours Royal blue shirts, white shorts and blue stockings with white hoops on turnover.
Club Honours Football League: Div. 2 Champions 1892-93, 1920-21, 1947-48, 1954-55. Football League Cup: Winners 1963.
League History 1892-94 Div. 2; 1894-96 Div. 1; 1896-1901 Div. 2; 1901-02 Div. 1; 1902-03 Div. 2; 1903-08 Div. 1; 1908-21 Div. 2; 1921-39 Div. 1; 1939-48 Div. 2; 1948-50 Div. 1; 1950-55 Div. 2; 1955-65 Div. 1; 1965-72 Div. 2; 1972-79 Div. 1; 1979-80 Div. 2; 1980-84 Div. 1; 1984-85 Div. 2; 1985-86 Div. 1; 1986- Div. 2.

Most League Points in a Season (2 for a win) 59 in Div. 2, 1947-48. (3 for a win) 82 in Div. 2, 1984-85.
Most League Goals in a Season 103 in Div. 2, 1893-94.
Record Victory 12-0 v Walsall Town Swifts in Div. 2, 17 December 1892 and v Doncaster Rov. in Div. 2, 11 April 1903.
Record Defeat 1-9 v Sheffield Wed. in Div. 1, 13 December 1930 and v Blackburn Rov. in Div. 1, 5 January 1895.
Consecutive League Wins 13 in 1892-93.
Consecutive League Defeats 8 in 1978-79.
Record League Appearances Gil Merrick, 486 between 1946-60.
Record League Goalscorer—Career Joe Bradford, 249 between 1920-35.
Record League Goalscorer—Season Joe Bradford, 29 in Div. 1, 1927-28.

Birmingham City: League Record, 1987-88 (Division 2)

Match Number	Date	Venue	Opponents	Result	H/T	Lge Posn	Attend
1	15.8.87	H	Stoke C.	W 2-0	1-0		13137
2	22.8.87	A	Aston Villa	W 2-0	0-0		30870
3	29.8.87	H	Bournemouth	D 1-1	0-0	2	8284
4	1.9.87	A	Millwall	L 1-3	1-1	5	6758
5	5.9.87	A	Crystal Palace	L 0-6	0-1	14	7011
6	12.9.87	H	Swindon T.	W 2-0	1-0	10	9128
7	15.9.87	H	Blackburn Rov.	W 1-0	0-0	6	6032
8	19.9.87	H	Shrewsbury T.	D 0-0	0-0	5	7183
9	26.9.87	A	Plymouth Arg.	D 1-1	1-1	8	8912
10	30.9.87	A	West Bromwich A.	L 1-3	0-1	9	15399
11	3.10.87	H	Huddersfield T.	W 2-0	0-0	7	6282
12	10.10.87	H	Reading	D 2-2	0-0	8	6142
13	17.10.87	A	Bradford C.	L 0-4	0-0	9	12256
14	20.10.87	A	Sheffield U.	W 2-0	1-0	9	9287
15	24.10.87	H	Middlesbrough	D 0-0	0-0	9	7404
16	31.10.87	A	Oldham Ath.	W 2-1	1-0	9	5486
17	3.11.87	H	Barnsley	W 2-0	1-0	6	6622
18	7.11.87	A	Hull C.	L 0-2	0-1	7	7901
19	14.11.87	H	Leicester C.	D 2-2	1-1	8	8666
20	21.11.87	A	Manchester C.	L 0-3	0-3	10	22690
21	28.11.87	H	Ipswich T.	W 1-0	0-0	9	6718
22	5.12.87	A	Leeds U.	L 1-4	0-2	10	15977
23	12.12.87	H	Aston Villa	L 1-2	1-1	10	27789
24	19.12.87	A	Blackburn Rov.	L 0-2	0-0	12	8542
25	26.12.87	H	Plymouth Arg.	L 0-1	0-0	15	9166
26	28.12.87	A	Shrewsbury T.	D 0-0	0-0	14	6397
27	1.1.88	H	Bournemouth	L 2-4	0-1	14	7963
28	2.1.88	H	Swindon T.	D 1-1	0-0	15	7829
29	16.1.88	A	Stoke C.	L 1-3	1-1	15	10076
30	6.2.88	A	Crystal Palace	L 0-3	0-1	16	8809
31	9.2.88	H	Millwall	W 1-0	0-0	16	5819
32	27.2.88	A	Huddersfield T.	D 2-2	2-1	16	5441
33	5.3.88	H	Bradford C.	D 1-1	1-1	17	8101
34	8.3.88	H	West Bromwich A.	L 0-1	0-0	17	12331
35	12.3.88	A	Reading	D 1-1	1-1	17	6285
36	19.3.88	H	Oldham Ath.	L 1-3	0-0	17	6012
37	26.3.88	A	Middlesbrough	D 1-1	0-0	17	15465
38	2.4.88	H	Hull C.	D 1-1	0-1	17	7059
39	5.4.88	A	Leicester C.	L 0-2	0-2	18	13541
40	9.4.88	H	Sheffield U.	W 1-0	1-0	17	7046
41	23.4.88	A	Barnsley	D 2-2	0-1	17	4949
42	30.4.88	H	Manchester C.	L 0-3	0-1	17	8014
43	2.5.88	A	Ipswich T.	L 0-1	0-0	18	11067
44	6.5.88	H	Leeds U.	D 0-0	0-0	19	6024

Players: League Record, 1987-88 (Division 2)

Match Number	Apps	Subs	Goals
Ashley	0	1	0
Atkins	8	0	1
Bird	6	3	0
Bremner	37	0	0
Childs	23	9	1
Dicks	32	0	1
Frain	12	2	2
Godden	22	0	0
Handysides	28	2	4
Hansbury	22	0	0
Kennedy	15	13	7
Langley	7	0	0
Morris	0	1	0
Overson	37	0	0
Ranson	38	0	0
Rees	17	6	4
Roberts	26	1	0
Robinson	3	1	1
Russell	6	3	0
Sproston	0	1	0
Starbuck	3	0	0
Tait	0	1	0
Trewick	25	1	0
Whitton	32	1	14
Wigley	43	0	0
Williams	33	0	1
Withe	8	0	2
Yates	1	2	0
Own Goals			2

FA Cup: 1987-88: 3rd Round: Gillingham (A) 3-0; 4th Round: Barnsley (A) 2-0; 5th Round: Nottingham F. (H) 0-1.
Littlewoods Cup: 1987-88: 1st Round: Mansfield T. (A) 2-2 (H) 0-1.

BLACKBURN ROVERS (Division 2)

Team Manager Donald Mackay.
Club Address Ewood Park, Blackburn BB2 4JF. Tel: (0254) 55342.
Current Ground Capacity 21,000.
Record Attendance 61,783 v Bolton W., FA Cup 6th Round, 2 March 1929.
Year Formed 1875. Turned professional 1880.
Previous Names Blackburn Grammar School OB.
Club Nickname "The Blue and Whites".
Club Colours Blue and white halved shirts, white shorts and blue stockings with red and white tops.
Club Honours Football League: Div. 1 Champions 1911-12, 1913-14; Div. 2 Champions 1938-39; Div. 3 Champions 1974-75. FA Cup: Winners 1884, 1885, 1886, 1890, 1891, 1928.
League History 1888-1936 Div. 1; 1936-39 Div. 2; 1946-47 Div. 1; 1947-57 Div. 2; 1957-66 Div. 1; 1966-71 Div. 2; 1971-75 Div. 3; 1975-79 Div. 2; 1979-80 Div. 3; 1980- Div. 2.
Most League Points in a Season (2 for a win) 60 in Div. 3, 1974-75. (3 for a win) 73 in Div. 2, 1984-85.

Most League Goals in a Season 114 in Div. 2, 1954-55.
Record Victory 11-0 v Rossendale U. in FA Cup 1st Round, 1884-85.
Record Defeat 0-8 v Arsenal in Div. 1, 25 February 1933.
Consecutive League Wins 8 in 1980.
Consecutive League Defeats 7 in 1966.
Record League Appearances Derek Fazackerley, 596 between 1970-86.
Record League Goalscorer—Career Tommy Briggs, 140 between 1952-58.
Record League Goalscorer—Season Ted Harper, 43 in Div. 1, 1925-26.

Blackburn Rovers: League Record, 1987-88 (Division 2)

Match Number	Date	Venue	Opponents	Result		H/T	Lge Posn	Attend
1	15.8.87	A	Hull C.	D	2-2	0-0		6462
2	18.8.87	H	Barnsley	L	0-1	0-1		6708
3	22.8.87	H	West Bromwich A.	W	3-1	2-1	7	5619
4	29.8.87	A	Sheffield U.	L	1-3	0-2	14	8540
5	1.9.87	H	Ipswich T.	W	1-0	0-0	10	6074
6	5.9.87	A	Manchester C.	W	2-1	1-1	6	20372
7	12.9.87	H	Huddersfield T.	D	2-2	2-2	6	7109
8	15.9.87	A	Birmingham C.	L	0-1	0-0	9	6032
9	19.9.87	A	Bradford C.	L	1-2	1-1	13	12068
10	26.9.87	H	Middlesbrough	L	0-2	0-0	16	6879
11	30.9.87	A	Aston Villa	D	1-1	1-1	15	11772
12	3.10.87	H	Leeds U.	D	1-1	0-0	18	7675
13	10.10.87	A	Bournemouth	D	1-1	0-0	16	6789
14	17.10.87	H	Stoke C.	W	2-0	1-0	12	7280
15	24.10.87	H	Plymouth Arg.	D	1-1	0-0	15	6014
16	31.10.87	A	Leicester C.	W	2-1	0-0	12	8650
17	7.11.87	H	Oldham Ath.	W	1-0	1-0	12	7519
18	14.11.87	H	Shrewsbury T.	W	2-1	0-0	10	3164
19	21.11.87	H	Crystal Palace	W	2-0	0-0	9	6372
20	28.11.87	A	Reading	D	0-0	0-0	10	4535
21	5.12.87	H	Millwall	W	2-1	1-0	9	6140
22	12.12.87	A	West Bromwich A.	W	1-0	1-0	9	7303
23	19.12.87	H	Birmingham C.	W	2-0	0-0	7	8542
24	26.12.87	A	Middlesbrough	D	1-1	1-1	8	23536
25	28.12.87	H	Bradford C.	D	1-1	1-0	9	14123
26	1.1.88	H	Sheffield U.	W	4-1	3-0	7	10493
27	2.1.88	A	Huddersfield T.	W	2-1	2-0	5	10735
28	16.1.88	H	Hull C.	W	2-1	2-0	4	9692
29	30.1.88	A	Ipswich T.	W	2-0	2-0	2	12604
30	6.2.88	H	Manchester C.	W	2-1	1-0	2	13508
31	13.2.88	A	Barnsley	W	1-0	0-0	2	8972
32	20.2.88	H	Aston Villa	W	3-2	1-0	1	17356
33	27.2.88	A	Leeds U.	D	2-2	0-2	2	23843
34	5.3.88	A	Stoke C.	L	1-2	0-1	2	14100
35	12.3.88	H	Bournemouth	W	3-1	1-1	2	10807
36	19.3.88	H	Leicester C.	D	3-3	0-0	2	12506
37	26.3.88	A	Plymouth Arg.	L	0-3	0-1	2	12359
38	1.4.88	A	Oldham Ath.	L	2-4	2-2	3	14853
39	4.4.88	H	Shrewsbury T.	D	2-2	2-0	3	13741
40	9.4.88	A	Swindon T.	W	2-1	0-1	3	9373
41	25.4.88	H	Swindon T.	D	0-0	0-0	4	13536
42	30.4.88	A	Crystal Palace	L	0-2	0-1	5	13059
43	2.5.88	H	Reading	D	1-1	0-0	5	11373
44	7.5.88	A	Millwall	W	4-1	2-0	5	15467

Players: League Record, 1987-88 (Division 2)

Match Number	1	2	3	4	5	6	7	8	9	10	11	12	13	14	15	16	17	18	19	20	21	22	23	24	25	26	27	28	29	30	31	32	33	34	35	36	37	38	39	40	41	42	43	44	Apps	Subs	Goals
Ainscow	★	★	★	★	★	★						★	★	★	4	4	4					11				★	★	7	4¹	4	4	4			★		9	9	4	★		7	3	8	16	12	1
Archibald																					9	9	9	9	9	10¹	9	9	9	9²	9	9	9¹	9	9	8	8	8²	8	8					20	0	6
Ardiles																																	7				9	9	9	9					5	0	0
Barker	4	4	4	4	4	4	4¹	4		4¹	4	4	4			4	4¹	4	4	4	4	4	4	4¹	4¹	4			★	4	4¹	4	4	4¹	4¹	★					4¹				31	2	9
Curry			9¹	9	9	9¹	9		9¹		9	9	9		★	★	★	9¹	9	9	9	9¹				9																			15	5	5
Dawson	6	6	6	6	6	6	6			6	6	6	6		★			7	7	7	7	7			7	7				★	7	7													20	2	0
Diamond	9	9					★																										★	★				★	★						2	5	0
Garner	10¹	10	10¹	10¹	10			10	10	10¹	10	10¹	10	10¹	10		10	10	10	10	10	10	10¹	10	10¹	10¹	10¹		10	10¹	10	10¹	10¹	10	10	10	10	10	10	10	10	10²			40	0	14
Gayle	7	7	7	7	7			11¹	7	7															★	★					★											8	9	10	3	1
Gennoe						1	1	1	1	1	1	1	1	1	1	1	1	1	1	1	1	1	1	1	1	1	1	1	1	1	1	1	1	1	1	1	1	1	1	1	1	1	1	1	39	0	0
Hendry	5	5	5¹	5	5¹	5	5	5	9	5	5	5	5	5	5	5¹	5	5	5	5	5¹	5	5¹	5	5¹	5	5	5	5	5	5	5¹	5	5	5¹	5	5¹	5	5	5	5	5¹	5		44	0	12
Hill									5																																				1	0	0
Johnrose																			★																										0	1	0
Mail				★	6	6	4			7	6	6	6	6	6	6	6	6	6	6	6	6	6	6	6	6	6	6	6	6	6	6	6	6	★	6	6	6	6	6	6				34	2	0
Millar							7	7	11		★		7													★	3	3							3	3		3	3	3	3		3		13	2	0
Miller									★	7	7				7	7	7	7						7	7	7				★	7	7	7	7		7	★	7		7	7	★	7		19	4	0
O'Keefe	1	1	1	1	1																																								5	0	0
Patterson	11¹	11	11	11	11	11¹						9	9	9	9	10	★									★																			11	2	2
Price	2	2	2	2	2		2	2	2	2	2	2¹	2	2	2	2¹	2¹	2	2	2	2	2	2¹	2	2¹	2	2¹	2	2	2	2¹	2¹	2	2	2		2	2	2	2¹					43	0	9
Reid	8	8	8	8	8		8	8	8	8	8	8	8	8	8	8¹	8	8	8	8	8	8	8	8	8	8	8	8	8	8	8	8	8	8	8	6	7	2	4	4	4	7			44	0	1
Sellars	★	★		★	★	10	10	9	11	11	11	11	11	11¹	11¹	11	11	11	11	11	11¹		11¹	11	11	11	11	11¹	11	11¹	11¹	11	11	11	11¹	11	11	11	11¹	11	11	11	11	11	38	4	7
Sulley	3	3	3	3	3	3	3	3	3	3	3	3	3	3	3	3	3	3	3	3	3	3	3			3	3	3	3	3	3				3	3									34	0	0
Own Goals																																			1												1

FA Cup: 1987-88: 3rd Round: Portsmouth (H) 1-2.
Littlewoods Cup: 1987-88: 2nd Round: Liverpool (H) 1-1 (A) 0-1.

BLACKPOOL (Division 3)

Team Manager Sam Ellis.
Club Address Bloomfield Road Ground, Blackpool FY1 6JJ. Tel: (0253) 404331.
Current Ground Capacity 12,696.
Record Attendance 38,098 v Wolverhampton W., Div. 1, 17 September 1955.
Year Formed 1887. Turned professional 1887.
Previous Names South Shore.
Club Nickname "The Seasiders".
Club Colours Tangerine shirts with white stripe on sleeves, white collar and cuffs, white shorts and tangerine stockings with white tops.
Club Honours Football League: Div. 2 Champions 1929-30. FA Cup: Winners 1953.
League History 1896-99 Div. 2; 1899 Failed re-election; 1900-30 Div. 2; 1930-33 Div. 1; 1933-37 Div. 2; 1937-67 Div. 1; 1967-70 Div. 2; 1970-71 Div. 1; 1971-78 Div. 2; 1978-81 Div. 3; 1981-85 Div. 4; 1985- Div. 3.
Most League Points in a Season (2 for a win) 58 in Div. 2, 1929-30. (3 for a win) 86 in Div. 4, 1984-85.
Most League Goals in a Season 98 in Div. 2, 1929-30.

Record Victory 10-0 v Lanerossi Vicenza in Anglo-Italian Tournament, 10 June 1972.
Record Defeat 1-10 v Small Heath in Div. 2, 2 March 1901 and v Huddersfield T. in Div. 1, 13 December 1930.
Consecutive League Wins 9 in 1936-37.
Consecutive League Defeats 8 in 1898-99.
Record League Appearances Jimmy Armfield, 568 between 1954-71.
Record League Goalscorer—Career Jimmy Hampson, 247 between 1927-38.
Record League Goalscorer—Season Jimmy Hampson, 45 in Div. 2, 1929-30.

Blackpool: League Record, 1987-88 (Division 3)

Match Number	Date	Venue	Opponents	Result		H/T	Lge Posn	Attend
1	15.8.87	A	Gillingham	D	0-0	0-0		4430
2	22.8.87	H	Walsall	L	1-2	0-1		4614
3	29.8.87	A	Bury	L	1-3	1-0	19	3053
4	31.8.87	H	Bristol Rov.	W	2-1	0-0	15	3319
5	5.9.87	A	Brighton & H.A.	W	3-1	1-0	15	7166
6	12.9.87	H	Chester C.	L	0-1	0-0	16	4035
7	15.9.87	A	Doncaster Rov.	L	1-2	0-0	17	1558
8	19.9.87	A	Brentford	L	1-2	0-1	20	3886
9	26.9.87	H	Preston N.E.	W	3-0	2-0	16	8406
10	29.9.87	A	York C.	W	3-1	2-1	14	2559
11	3.10.87	H	Fulham	W	2-1	1-0	13	4973
12	17.10.87	H	Sunderland	L	0-2	0-0	14	8476
13	20.10.87	A	Grimsby T.	D	1-1	1-1	12	2260
14	24.10.87	H	Wigan Ath.	D	0-0	0-0	18	4821
15	31.10.87	H	Mansfield T.	D	0-0	0-0	16	3221
16	3.11.87	H	Bristol C.	W	4-2	1-1	13	3140
17	7.11.87	H	Rotherham U.	W	3-0	1-0	12	3447
18	21.11.87	A	Port Vale	D	0-0	0-0	12	3594
19	28.11.87	H	Northampton T.	W	3-1	2-1	10	3593
20	12.12.87	A	Chesterfield	D	1-1	1-0	11	2279
21	19.12.87	H	Southend U.	D	1-1	1-0	11	3277
22	26.12.87	A	Preston N.E.	L	1-2	1-0	12	11155
23	28.12.87	H	Notts Co.	D	1-1	0-0	11	4627
24	1.1.88	H	Bury	W	5-1	2-1	9	4240
25	2.1.88	A	Chester C.	D	1-1	1-0	10	3093
26	16.1.88	H	Brentford	L	0-1	0-1	12	3911
27	6.2.88	H	Brighton & H.A.	L	1-3	0-0	14	4081
28	13.2.88	A	Notts Co.	W	3-2	0-1	12	5794
29	20.2.88	H	Gillingham	D	3-3	0-0	12	3045
30	23.2.88	A	Walsall	L	2-3	0-0	12	4252
31	27.2.88	A	Fulham	L	1-3	0-1	15	4072
32	1.3.88	H	York C.	W	2-1	1-1	12	2249
33	5.3.88	H	Sunderland	D	2-2	1-2	14	15513
34	12.3.88	H	Aldershot	W	3-2	1-1	12	2661
35	19.3.88	H	Mansfield T.	W	2-0	1-0	12	2847
36	25.3.88	A	Wigan Ath.	D	0-0	0-0	11	4505
37	29.3.88	A	Aldershot	D	0-0	0-0	11	2091
38	2.4.88	A	Rotherham U.	W	1-0	0-0	9	3001
39	4.4.88	H	Port Vale	L	1-2	0-2	11	5516
40	9.4.88	A	Bristol C.	L	1-2	0-1	12	6460
41	15.4.88	H	Doncaster Rov.	W	4-2	1-0	10	2291
42	23.4.88	H	Grimsby T.	W	3-0	1-0	9	2555
43	27.4.88	A	Bristol Rov.	L	0-2	0-2	9	3546
44	30.4.88	A	Northampton T.	D	3-3	0-0	10	5730
45	2.5.88	H	Chesterfield	W	1-0	1-0	10	2950
46	7.5.88	A	Southend U.	L	0-4	0-1	10	5541

Players: League Record, 1987-88 (Division 3)

Match Number	1	2	3	4	5	6	7	8	9	10	11	12	13	14	15	16	17	18	19	20	21	22	23	24	25	26	27	28	29	30	31	32	33	34	35	36	37	38	39	40	41	42	43	44	45	46	Apps	Subs	Goals
Bradshaw				2										4	4	4	4	4	4	4	4	4														★	★		11		6	6	11				14	2	0
Butler		★	7	8		★								★			★	★			★	★	2	2¹	2		★		★		4	4				6	7										9	9	1
Coughlin																				7	8	8	8¹	8	8	8	8	8¹	8	8	8				7	7	8	8	4		4	4	4	4	10		24	0	0
Cunningham	7	7¹		7²	7²	7¹	7	7	7¹	7		7	7	7	7		6	8¹	8	7	7	7	7¹	7	7	9	9			10	10	10	10	10¹	10	10		10	10	10	10	10	10	10	6		40	0	10
Davies	2	2	2	2	2		2		2	2	2	2				2	2	2		2	2		★	2	2	2	2	2	2	2	2	2	2	2			2	2	2	2	2		36	2	0
Deary	10	10	10	10	10	10			7	8	8	8	6	6¹	7	7			★	★¹	10	10	10			7	7	4	4	4	10	10¹	7	7	7	7	7	7	7	7		34	3	3
Hutchinson								2	9	9	★	★																														3	3	0
Jones	6	6	★			★		10	10	10				6			★	★	5	6	6	6	6	6	6	6	6	5	★	6	5			8	8	8	8	6	6				★				23	6	0
Lancashire									★	★			2		★	7	★				★																									2	5	0
Lester							★	★	5	5	10	10	10	10	10	10	10	10	10		4	4	4	4¹	4	4	4				7	7				4											11	0	1
McAteer																									11		★																				18	3	0
Madden	8	8	8			8	8	8	8	8¹	8¹	8²	8	★		2	8²	8¹	8	2		★	2¹	9	9¹	9¹	9	★	★	10	★	★					★	6¹	6	6	★		★				25	9	11
Matthews	4	4	4	4	4	4	4	4	4	4	4	4	4																			6	6	6	4	4	2	8	8	8	8	8	4		27	0	0
Methven	5	5	5	5	5	5	5	★	★	5	5	5	5	5	5	5	5	★		5	5	5	5	5		★	5		5¹	5	5	5	5	5	5	5	5	5	5	★	★¹	★		35	5	2
Morgan	3	3	3	3	3	3	3	3	3	3¹	3	3	3	3	3¹	3	3	3¹	3	3	3	3	3¹	3	3	3	3¹	3	3	3	3	3	3	3	3	3	3	3	3	3	3	3¹	3	3			46	0	6
Muggleton																															1	1															2	0	0
Powell																																								1	1	1	1	1	1		6	0	0
Rooney			★																							★			★			8		★		11	11	8								4	4	0
Shaw																					7	7	7	7		★	★																				4	2	0
Siddall	1	1	1	1	1	1	1	1	1	1	1	1	1	1	1	1	1	1	1	1	1	1	1	1	1				1	1	1	1	1	1	1	1	1	1	1	1		38	0	0
Taylor	11	11	11	11	11¹	11	11	11	11	11	11	11¹	11	11	11¹	11¹	11	11	11¹	11	11	11		11	11²	11¹	11²	11	11¹	11¹	11²	11	11	11¹	11²	11²		41	0	21
Walsh		★	6	6	6	6	6	6	6	6	6	6	6				6	6						5	5	6	6	5	6	6	6				★	★	6			★	5	5	5				26	4	0
Walwyn	9	9	9¹	9	9	9	9	9¹	9¹		★	9	9	9	9	9	9	9¹	9	9				9¹	9	9¹	9¹	9¹	9	9	9	9	9¹	9	9¹	9¹	9¹	9¹	9		38	1	13
Wright																																									★		0	1	0
Own Goals															1																																		1

FA Cup: 1987-88: 1st Round: Bishop Auckland (A) 4-1; 2nd Round: Northwich (A) 2-0; 3rd Round: Scunthorpe U. (A) 0-0 Replay (H) 1-0; 4th Round: Manchester C. (H) 1-1 Replay (A) 1-2.
Littlewoods Cup: 1987-88: 1st Round: Chester C. (H) 2-0 (A) 0-1; 2nd Round: Newcastle U. (H) 1-0 (A) 1-4.

BOLTON WANDERERS (Division 3)

Team Manager Phil Neal.
Club Address Burnden Park, Bolton BL3 2QR. Tel: (0204) 389200.
Current Ground Capacity 43,000.
Record Attendance 69,912 v Manchester C., FA Cup 5th Round, 18 February 1933.
Year Formed 1874. Turned professional 1880.
Previous Names Christ Church FC.
Club Nickname "The Trotters".
Club Colours White shirts, navy blue shorts and white stockings.
Club Honours Football League: Div. 2 Champions 1908-09, 1977-78. Div. 3 Champions 1972-73. FA Cup: Winners 1923, 1926, 1929, 1958.
League History 1888-99 Div. 1; 1899-1900 Div. 2; 1900-03 Div.1; 1903-05 Div. 2; 1905-08 Div. 1; 1908-09 Div. 2; 1909-10 Div. 1; 1910-11 Div. 2; 1911-33 Div. 1; 1933-35 Div. 2; 1935-64 Div 1; 1964-71 Div. 2; 1971-73 Div. 3; 1973-78 Div. 2; 1978-80 Div. 1; 1980-83 Div. 2; 1983-87 Div. 3; 1987-88 Div. 4; 1988- Div.3.

Most League Points in a Season (2 for a win) 61 in Div. 3, 1972-73. (3 for a win) 78 in Div. 4, 1987-88.
Most League Goals in a Season 96 in Div. 2, 1934-35.
Record Victory 13-0 v Sheffield U. in FA Cup 2nd Round, 1 February 1890.
Record Defeat 0-7 v Manchester C. in Div. 1, 21 March 1936.
Consecutive League Wins 11 in 1904.
Consecutive League Defeats 10 in 1902-03.
Record League Appearances Eddie Hopkinson, 519 between 1956-70.
Record League Goalscorer—Career Nat Lofthouse, 255 between 1946-61.
Record League Goalscorer—Season Joe Smith, 38 in Div. 1, 1920-21.

Bolton Wanderers: League Record, 1987-88 (Division 4)

Match Number	Date	Venue	Opponents	Result		H/T	Lge Posn	Attend
1	15.8.87	H	Crewe Alex.	D	1-1	1-0		4792
2	22.8.87	H	Cardiff C.	W	1-0	1-0		4530
3	29.8.87	A	Scarborough	L	0-4	0-2	16	4462
4	31.8.87	H	Peterborough U.	W	2-0	1-0	6	3746
5	5.9.87	A	Hereford U.	W	3-0	2-0	3	2541
6	12.9.87	H	Halifax T.	W	2-0	1-0	2	4445
7	15.9.87	A	Scunthorpe U.	D	1-1	1-0	2	2501
8	19.9.87	A	Torquay U.	L	1-2	0-2	6	2211
9	26.9.87	H	Hartlepool U.	L	1-2	0-0	10	4398
10	3.10.87	H	Wolverhampton W.	W	1-0	0-0	9	3833
11	10.10.87	A	Darlington	L	0-1	0-0	13	1763
12	17.10.87	H	Carlisle U.	W	5-0	2-0	11	4184
13	20.10.87	H	Exeter C.	W	1-0	0-0	7	4165
14	24.10.87	A	Rochdale	D	2-2	0-1	8	4294
15	31.10.87	H	Swansea C.	D	1-1	0-1	10	4607
16	3.11.87	A	Newport Co.	W	1-0	1-0	8	1566
17	7.11.87	H	Leyton Orient	W	1-0	0-0	3	5189
18	21.11.87	A	Burnley	L	1-2	0-0	7	7489
19	28.11.87	H	Cambridge U.	D	2-2	1-1	7	4294
20	11.12.87	A	Colchester U.	L	0-3	0-1	8	1725
21	15.12.87	A	Tranmere Rov.	L	0-2	0-0	8	3064
22	19.12.87	H	Wrexham	W	2-0	1-0	7	3701
23	26.12.87	A	Hartlepool U.	D	0-0	0-0	7	4102
24	28.12.87	H	Stockport Co.	W	2-1	1-0	5	6607
25	1.1.88	H	Scarborough	W	3-1	1-0	6	6295
26	12.1.88	A	Halifax T.	D	0-0	0-0	4	2689
27	16.1.88	H	Torquay U.	L	1-2	1-1	8	5996
28	30.1.88	A	Peterborough U.	W	4-0	2-0	5	3485
29	6.2.88	H	Hereford U.	W	1-0	0-0	3	4559
30	12.2.88	H	Stockport Co.	W	2-1	1-0	3	4814
31	20.2.88	A	Crewe Alex.	L	1-2	1-1	3	4305
32	27.2.88	A	Wolverhampton W.	L	0-4	0-4	5	12430
33	1.3.88	H	Tranmere Rov.	W	2-0	0-0	4	3979
34	5.3.88	H	Carlisle U.	W	2-0	1-0	3	2796
35	11.3.88	H	Darlington	D	1-1	1-0	3	4948
36	18.3.88	A	Swansea C.	L	0-1	0-0	5	3980
37	26.3.88	H	Rochdale	D	0-0	0-0	4	4875
38	2.4.88	H	Leyton Orient	W	2-1	0-1	4	4537
39	4.4.88	H	Burnley	W	2-1	1-1	4	9921
40	9.4.88	A	Exeter C.	D	1-1	0-1	4	1962
41	15.4.88	A	Cardiff C.	L	0-1	0-0	4	6703
42	19.4.88	H	Scunthorpe U.	D	0-0	0-0	5	6669
43	23.4.88	H	Newport Co.	W	6-0	4-0	4	4357
44	29.4.88	A	Cambridge U.	D	2-2	1-1	5	2063
45	2.5.88	H	Colchester U.	W	4-0	2-0	4	5540
46	7.5.88	A	Wrexham	W	1-0	0-0	3	5977

Players: League Record, 1987-88 (Division 3)

Match Number	1	2	3	4	5	6	7	8	9	10	11	12	13	14	15	16	17	18	19	20	21	22	23	24	25	26	27	28	29	30	31	32	33	34	35	36	37	38	39	40	41	42	43	44	45	46	Apps	Subs	Goals
Barnes												11	11																																			2	0	0
Brookman	★		11	11	11			★		4		7²	7	7	7	7	7	7	7	7		4					★	11¹	11	11¹	11	11		5¹	5¹	4	4										23	3	6
Callaghan																		8																													1	0	0
Came	5	5	5	5	5	5	5	5¹	5	5	5	5¹	5	5	5	5	5	5	5	5	5	5	5	5¹	5	5¹	5	5		5	5	5		5	5	5	5	5	5	5	5	5	5¹	5			43	0	5
Chandler	11	11¹																																									★¹				2	1	2
Crombie	3	3	3	3	3	3	3	3	3	3	3	3	3	3	3	3	6	3															3	3	3	3		3									24	0	0
Darby	2	2					2	2			★¹	11	11	11	11	11	11	11	11	11	11	11	11	11	11	11			5			11	11	11	11	11	11	11¹	11	11	11	11	11	11	11	11	34	1	2
Elliott			★					★	★		10	10¹	10	10	10	10¹	10	10	10	10	10	10															10	10	10		10						17	3	2
Felgate	1	1	1	1	1	1	1	1	1	1	1	1	1	1	1	1	1	1	1	1	1	1	1	1	1	1	1	1	1	1	1	1	1	1	1	1	1	1	1	1	1	1	1	1	1	1	46	0	0
Henshaw	7¹	7	7	7	7	7	7¹	7	7	7	7	7				3		★	7	7	4	4	4	4	4	★			★	★	7	7	7		★			★	4	★							23	8	2
Hughes																		2			2	2	2	2	2	2	2	2				2															11	0	0
Joyce	8	8	8	8	8	8	8	8	8	8	8	8																																			11	0	0
May																														★		7¹	7¹	7	7	7	7	7	7	7	7						9	1	2
Morgan	9	9	9	9	9¹	9	9¹	9	9	9	9				★	★		★	★	★	★¹	10	10¹	10	10	10	10	10	10	10¹	10¹	10	10	10	10	10			10		10¹	10	10	10			31	7	7
Neal																	6	3							3															3	3	3	3				7	1	0
Savage						11	11	11¹	11	11		4	4	4	4	4	4	4	4	4	3	3	3		6	4	4¹	4	4	4	4	4	3	3	4	4	4		4	4¹	4¹	4¹					39	0	5
Scott			2	2	2	2			2	2	2	2	2	2	2	2	2	2	2	2	2²	2	2			2	2	3	3	3	3	3	3	3	3	2	2	2		2	2	2	2	2	2		40	0	0
Stevens												★	★	★																					★	★	★			★							2	7	0
Storer																		7	7¹	7	7	7	7	7	7	7	7	7			★		7	7				★	★								12	3	1
Sutton	6	6	6	6	6	6	6	6	6	6	6	6	6	6			6	6	6	6	6	6			6	6	6	6	6	6	6	6	6	6	6	6	6	6	6								36	0	0
Thomas	10	10	10	10¹	10²	10¹	10	10	10	10¹	★	9	9	9²	9	9¹	9¹	9²	9	9	9	9	9	9¹		9³	9	9	9	9	9¹	9¹	9	9	9	9	9¹	9	9	9³	9¹	9¹	9				43	1	23
Thompson	4	4	4	4¹	4	4	4	4		4	★	8	8	8	8¹	8	8	8		8	8¹	8	8	8¹	8	8	8	8¹	8	8	8	8¹	8	8	8	8	8	8	8	6	8¹	8	8	8			43	1	6
Winstanley													6	6				3																						6	6¹	6	6	6			8	0	1
Own Goals											1																							1															2

FA Cup: 1987-88: 1st Round: Burnley (A) 1-0; 2nd Round: Wrexham (A) 2-1; 3rd Round: Barnsley (A) 1-3.
Littlewoods Cup: 1987-88: 1st Round: Wigan Ath. (A) 3-2 (H) 1-3.

AFC BOURNEMOUTH (Division 2)

Team Manager Harry Redknapp.
Club Address Dean Ground Ground, Bournemouth. Tel: (0202) 35381.
Current Ground Capacity 12,038.
Record Attendance 28,799 v Manchester U., FA Cup 6th Round, 2 March 1957.
Year Formed 1899. Turned professional 1912.
Previous Names Boscome St Johns , Boscombe FC, Bournemouth and Boscombe FC.
Club Nickname ''The Cherries''.
Club Colours Red shirts with white pinstripe, red shorts and red stockings.
Club Honours Football League: Div. 3 Champions 1986-87.
League History 1923-58 Div. 3(S); 1958-70 Div. 3; 1970-71 Div. 4; 1971-75 Div. 3; 1975-82 Div. 4; 1982-87 Div. 3; 1987- Div. 2.
Most League Points in a Season (2 for a win) 62 in Div. 3, 1971-72. (3 for a win) 97 in Div. 3, 1986-87.
Most League Goals in a Season 88 in Div. 3(S), 1956-57.

Record Victory 11-0 v Margate in FA Cup 1st Round, 20 November 1971.
Record Defeat 0-9 v Lincoln C. in Div. 3, 18 December 1982.
Consecutive League Wins 7 in 1970.
Consecutive League Defeats 7 in 1955.
Record League Appearances Ray Bumstead, 414 between 1958-70.
Record League Goalscorer—Career Ron Eyre, 202 between 1924-33.
Record League Goalscorer—Season Ted MacDougall, 42 in 1970-71.

Bournemouth: League Record, 1987-88 (Division 2)

Match Number	Date	Venue	Opponents	Result		H/T	Lge Posn	Attend
1	15.8.87	A	Sheffield U.	W	1-0	0-0		9757
2	22.8.87	H	Bradford C.	W	2-0	0-0		7407
3	29.8.87	A	Birmingham C.	D	1-1	0-0	3	8284
4	31.8.87	H	Barnsley	L	1-2	1-1	4	7480
5	5.9.87	A	Hull C.	L	1-2	0-1	13	5807
6	12.9.87	H	Reading	W	3-0	1-0	7	7597
7	15.9.87	A	Middlesbrough	L	0-3	0-0	10	9660
8	19.9.87	A	West Bromwich A.	L	0-3	0-1	15	7749
9	26.9.87	H	Leicester C.	L	2-3	1-1	18	7969
10	29.9.87	H	Plymouth Arg.	D	2-2	1-1	12	6491
11	3.10.87	A	Stoke C.	L	0-1	0-0	21	8104
12	10.10.87	H	Blackburn Rov.	D	1-1	0-0	20	6789
13	17.10.87	A	Aston Villa	D	1-1	0-1	20	15145
14	20.10.87	H	Shrewsbury T.	W	2-0	2-0	15	5587
15	24.10.87	A	Leeds U.	L	2-3	0-3	19	15253
16	31.10.87	H	Ipswich T.	D	1-1	0-1	18	8105
17	3.11.87	A	Millwall	W	2-1	0-0	13	5734
18	7.11.87	H	Crystal Palace	L	2-3	2-3	18	9083
19	21.11.87	H	Huddersfield T.	L	0-2	0-1	19	6419
20	28.11.87	A	Swindon T.	L	2-4	1-2	19	7934
21	1.12.87	A	Manchester C.	L	0-2	0-1	19	9499
22	5.12.87	H	Oldham Ath.	D	2-2	1-1	19	5377
23	12.12.87	A	Bradford C.	L	0-2	0-0	19	10763
24	19.12.87	H	Middlesbrough	D	0-0	0-0	20	6392
25	26.12.87	A	Leicester C.	W	1-0	1-0	17	11452
26	28.12.87	H	West Bromwich A.	W	3-2	1-0	16	8969
27	1.1.88	H	Birmingham C.	W	4-2	1-0	17	7963
28	16.1.88	H	Sheffield U.	L	1-2	0-1	17	6466
29	6.2.88	H	Hull C.	W	6-2	3-1	17	5901
30	13.2.88	A	Manchester C.	L	0-2	0-1	17	16161
31	27.2.88	H	Stoke C.	D	0-0	0-0	19	6871
32	5.3.88	H	Aston Villa	L	1-2	0-0	20	10157
33	8.3.88	A	Barnsley	L	1-2	1-1	20	6140
34	12.3.88	A	Blackburn Rov.	L	1-3	1-1	21	10807
35	19.3.88	A	Ipswich T.	W	2-1	2-0	18	10208
36	26.3.88	H	Leeds U.	D	0-0	0-0	18	9147
37	2.4.88	A	Crystal Palace	L	0-3	0-2	20	9557
38	8.4.88	A	Shrewsbury T.	L	1-2	0-1	20	7106
39	13.4.88	A	Reading	D	0-0	0-0	20	10037
40	19.4.88	H	Millwall	L	1-2	1-2	21	9204
41	26.4.88	A	Plymouth Arg.	W	2-1	1-0	20	6310
42	30.4.88	A	Huddersfield T.	W	2-1	2-0	18	2794
43	2.5.88	H	Swindon T.	W	2-0	2-0	17	5212
44	7.5.88	A	Oldham Ath.	L	0-2	0-0	17	6009

Players: League Record, 1987-88 (Division 2)

Match Number	1	2	3	4	5	6	7	8	9	10	11	12	13	14	15	16	17	18	19	20	21	22	23	24	25	26	27	28	29	30	31	32	33	34	35	36	37	38	39	40	41	42	43	44	Apps	Subs	Goals
Armstrong	10	10¹	10¹	10	10																									★	★	★	10													6	3	2
Aylott	9	9	9	9	9	9¹	9		9¹	9¹	9	9	9¹	9¹	9	9	9	9	9	9	9	9	9	9	9¹	9	9	9	9	9	9	9	9¹	9	9	9	9	9	9	9	9¹	9	9		43	0	9
Brooks	4¹	4	4	4	4¹	4	4	4	4¹	4	★		★	4¹	4	4	★			4	4		4	4	4¹	4	4	4	4	4	4	4	★		4¹	4	4	4							33	4	6
Clark					5	5																																							2	0	0
Close																			8	11²	11	11	11		11¹	11¹	11	11	11	11	11	11	11	11¹	11¹	★									15	1	6
Coleman									4	4	3																	3									★								4	1	0
Cooke		11	11	11	★		★	9	10	10	11		10	10	10			★	10	10	★		★	10	10	10¹	10	10²	10	10¹	10	10			10	10	10	10¹	10	10	10				29	5	5
Goulet															★		10		★									★	★									11							2	4	0
Heffernan								★	8		6	★	2	2¹	2	2	2		2						5																				9	2	1
Keane							8	★																																					1	1	0
Langan																2	2	2	2	2	2	2	2	2	2	2	2	2	2	2	2	2	2	★											19	1	0
Morrell	3	3	3	3	3	3	3	3	3	3	3	3	3	3	3	3	3	3	3	3		3	3	3	3	3	3	3	3	3	3	3		3	3	3	3	3	3	3					42	0	0
Newson	2	2	2	2	2	2¹	2	2	2¹	2	2	2											8	8	8	8	8	8	8	8	8	8	8	8	8	8	8	8	8	8	8¹	8			29	0	3
O'Connor	11			11	11¹	11	11	11	★	11	11	11	11	11	11	11	11	11	11¹	11	11	11	11	11	11	11	11	★	7	★	7	7	7	7	7				10	10	10				34	3	2
O'Driscoll	7	7	7	7	7	7	7	7	7	7	7	7¹	7	7	7¹	7	7	7¹	7	7	7	7	7	7	7	7	7	7	7	7	7		★	4	4	4	7	7	7	7					39	0	4
Peyton	1		1	1	1	1	1	1	1	1	1	1	1	1	1	1	1	1	1	1	1	1	1	1	1	1	1	1	1	1	1	1	1	1	1	1	1	1	1	1	1	1			42	0	0
Puckett					★							★	8	8¹	8	8²	8	8	8	8	★	4¹	★																						8	4	4
Pulis	★		★		10	10	10		10	10	4	4	4	8	8	8	2	4		4			4¹	★	★							7	6	6	6	6	6	2¹	2¹	2	2				25	4	3
Randall																																										2			1	0	0
Richards	8	8¹	8	8¹	8	8	8	★	8		8			★	★	10										11¹	10		★	★	★	★	★												12	8	4
Shearer												8	8	8	8	★	10¹	10		10		★	★¹	8¹																					8	3	3
Smeulders		1																																										1	2	0	0
Whitlock	6	6	6	6	6	6	6	6	6	6		6	6	6	6		6	6	6	6	6		6	6	6	6	6	6		6	6	6	6		5		5	5	6	6	6	6			41	0	0
Williams	5	5	5	5	5		5	5	5	5	5	5	5	5	5	5	5	5¹	5	5	5	5	5	5		5	5¹	5	5	5	5	5	5		5			5	5	5	5	5			38	0	2
Own Goals																							1			1																					2

FA Cup: 1987-88: 3rd Round: Brighton & H.A. (A) 0-2.
Littlewoods Cup: 1987-88: 1st Round: Exeter C. (H) 1-1 (A) 3-1; 2nd Round: Southampton (H) 1-0 (A) 2-2; 3rd Round: Arsenal (A) 0-3.

BRADFORD CITY (Division 2)

Team Manager Terry Dolan.
Club Address Valley Parade Ground, Bradford BD8 7DY. Tel: (0274) 306062.
Current Ground Capacity 15,500.
Record Attendance 39,146 v Burnley, FA Cup 4th Round, 11 March 1911.
Year Formed 1903. Turned professional 1903.
Previous Names None.
Club Nickname "The Bantams".
Club Colours Claret and amber shirts, black shorts and amber stockings.
Club Honours Football League: Div. 2 Champions 1904-08; Div. 3 Champions 1984-85; Div. 3(N) Champions 1928-29. FA Cup: Winners 1911.
League History 1903-08 Div. 2; 1908-22 Div. 1; 1922-27 Div. 2; 1927-29 Div. 3(N); 1929-37 Div. 2; 1937-61 Div. 3; 1961-69 Div. 4; 1969-72 Div. 3; 1972-77 Div. 4; 1977-78 Div. 3; 1978-82 Div. 4; 1982-85 Div. 3; 1985- Div. 2.
Most League Points in a Season (2 for a win) 63 in Div. 3(N) 1928-29. (3 for win) 94 in Div. 3, 1984-85.

Most League Goals in a Season 128 in Div. 3(N), 1928-29.
Record Victory 11-1 v Rotherham U. in Div. 3(N), 25 August 1928.
Record Defeat 1-9 v Colchester U. in Div. 4, 30 December 1961.
Consecutive League Wins 10 in 1983-84.
Consecutive League Defeats 8 in 1933.
Record League Appearances Cec Podd, 502 between 1970-84.
Record League Goalscorer—Career Bobby Campbell, 121 between 1981-86.
Record League Goalscorer—Season David Layne, 34 in Div. 4, 1961-62.

Bradford City: League Record, 1987-88 (Division 2)

Match Number	Date	Venue	Opponents	Result		H/T	Lge Posn	Attend
1	15.8.87	H	Swindon T.	W	2-0	0-0		10553
2	18.8.87	A	Oldham Ath.	W	2-0	1-0		8087
3	22.8.87	A	Bournemouth	L	0-2	0-0	3	7407
4	29.8.87	H	Leeds U.	D	0-0	0-0	4	11428
5	5.9.87	H	Millwall	W	3-1	1-0	3	8658
6	12.9.87	A	Stoke C.	W	2-1	1-0	3	9571
7	16.9.87	H	Plymouth Arg.	W	3-1	1-0	1	11009
8	19.9.87	H	Blackburn Rov.	W	2-1	1-1	1	12068
9	26.9.87	A	Shrewsbury T.	D	2-2	0-0	1	4247
10	29.9.87	A	Huddersfield T.	W	2-1	1-0	1	11671
11	3.10.87	H	Middlesbrough	W	2-0	0-0	1	14222
12	10.10.87	A	West Bromwich A.	W	1-0	1-0	1	12241
13	17.10.87	H	Birmingham C.	W	4-0	0-0	1	12256
14	21.10.87	H	Manchester C.	L	2-4	0-1	1	14818
15	24.10.87	A	Reading	D	1-1	1-0	1	5920
16	31.10.87	H	Crystal Palace	W	2-0	0-0	1	13012
17	3.11.87	A	Hull City	D	0-0	0-0	1	15443
18	7.11.87	A	Barnsley	L	0-3	0-2	1	11569
19	14.11.87	H	Sheffield U..	W	2-0	1-0	1	13694
20	21.11.87	A	Leicester C.	W	2-0	1-0	1	11543
21	28.11.87	H	Aston Villa	L	2-4	1-2	2	15006
22	5.12.87	A	Ipswich T.	L	0-4	0-1	2	13307
23	12.12.87	H	Bournemouth	W	2-0	0-0	2	10763
24	20.12.87	A	Plymouth Arg.	L	1-2	0-2	2	11350
25	26.12.87	H	Shrewsbury T.	D	1-1	0-0	2	12474
26	28.12.87	H	Blackburn Rov.	D	1-1	0-1	2	14123
27	1.1.88	A	Leeds U.	L	0-2	0-1	5	36004
28	2.1.88	H	Stoke C.	L	1-4	0-3	7	12223
29	6.2.88	A	Millwall	W	1-0	0-0	6	8201
30	13.2.88	H	Oldham Ath.	W	5-3	3-1	5	13862
31	27.2.88	A	Middlesbrough	W	2-1	1-0	5	21079
32	1.3.88	H	Huddersfield T.	L	0-1	0-0	5	12782
33	5.3.88	H	Birmingham C.	D	1-1	1-1	6	8101
34	12.3.88	H	West Bromwich A.	W	4-1	1-0	4	12502
35	19.3.88	A	Crystal Palace	D	1-1	0-0	6	9801
36	30.3.88	A	Swindon T.	D	2-2	0-0	5	8203
37	2.4.88	A	Barnsley	D	1-1	1-0	6	15098
38	4.4.88	A	Sheffield U.	W	2-1	1-0	6	13888
39	9.4.88	H	Hull C.	W	2-0	1-0	5	13659
40	20.4.88	H	Reading	W	3-0	3-0	2	13608
41	23.4.88	H	Manchester C.	D	2-2	2-2	3	20335
42	30.4.88	H	Leicester C.	W	4-1	4-1	2	14393
43	2.5.88	A	Aston Villa	L	0-1	0-1	4	36423
44	7.5.88	H	Ipswich T.	L	2-3	2-2	4	16017

Players: League Record, 1987-88 (Division 2)

Match Number	1	2	3	4	5	6	7	8	9	10	11	12	13	14	15	16	17	18	19	20	21	22	23	24	25	26	27	28	29	30	31	32	33	34	35	36	37	38	39	40	41	42	43	44	Apps	Subs	Goals
Abbott	10	10¹	10		★	10³	10	10	10			2	3	3	3	3		10	★	★	★	10	10	10		8	8	8	8	2	2	11	11			★				★¹					25	7	5
Ellis	11	11	11	11	11	11¹	11				★	★	★		★	11	11		★		11¹	11	11	11	11	11	★	11																	16	6	2
Evans			6	6	6	6	6	6	6	6	6	6	6	6	6¹	6	6	6	6	6	6	6	6	6	6	6	6	6	6	6	6	6	6	6	6	6	6	6	6	6	6	6	6	6	43	0	1
Futcher	9¹	9	9	9	9²	9¹	9	9	9¹	9		6	★			★		9¹	9¹	9²	9	9	9	9	9			★	★		★¹	★	★	11¹	11¹	11¹	11¹	11¹	11	11					25	7	14
Goddard	3			3	3	3	3	3	3	3	3	3													3	3		3	3	3	3	3	3	3	3	3	3	3	3	3	3	3			29	0	0
Hendrie	7	7¹	7	7	7	7	7	7	7¹	7	7	7	7	7	7¹	7	7	7	7	7¹	7	7	7	7	7	7	7	7	7³	7	7	7¹	7¹	7	7	7¹	7	7	7¹	7	7¹	7	7¹	7	43	0	13
Kennedy																									10	10¹	10		10	10	10	10	10	10	10	10	10	10	10	10	10	10	10	10	15	0	1
Leonard	★	★	★						★	★	9¹	9	9²	9	9	9¹	9	9		★	11	11²	11	★		★	9				11²		★¹	11	11		★¹	★	★	7					16	12	10
Litchfield																					1											1													2	0	0
McCall	4¹	4	4	4	4	4	4	4	4¹	4	4¹	4	4¹	4	4	4¹	4	4	4	4	4	4	4¹	4	4	4	4¹	4	4	4	4	4	4	4	4	4¹	4	4	4	4¹	4	4	4	4¹	44	0	9
Mitchell	2	2	2	2	2	2	2	2¹	2	2¹	2	2		2¹	2	2	2	2	2¹	2	2	2	2	2	2	2	2¹	2	2	2	2	2		5	2	2	2	2	2	2	2¹	2	2		42	0	6
Oliver	5	5	5	5	5	5	5	5	5	5	5	5	5	5	5	5	5	5	5	5	5	5	5	5	5	5	5	5		5	5	5	5	5	5	5	5	5	5	5	5	5	5	5	43	0	0
Ormondroyd		★	★			★	★	11¹	11	11	11	11	11	11	11	11	11			11			★	★	★	★	8¹	9¹	9	9²	9	9	9	9¹	9	9	9	9¹	9¹	9	9¹	9	9	★	28	9	9
O'Shaughnessy														★																															0	1	0
Palin			10	10¹	10								10¹	10	10¹	10	10	10	10	10			10	10	10¹	10				10		★		10		★									18	2	3
Savage	6	3	3																																										3	0	0
Sinnott	8	8	8	8	8	8	8	8	8	8	8	8	8	8	8	8	8	8	8	8	8	8	8	8	8	8	8	3			11	11	8	8¹	8	8	8	8	8	8	8	8	8	8	42	0	1
Staunton																			3	3	3	3	3	3	3		★																		7	1	0
Thorpe							★	11																																					1	1	0
Tomlinson	1	1	1	1	1	1	1	1	1	1		1	1	1	1	1	1	1	1	1	1	1	1	1		1	1	1	1	1	1	1	1	1	1	1	1	1	1	1	1	1	1	1	42	0	0
Withe								★	★																																				0	2	0

FA Cup: 1987-88: 3rd Round: Wolverhampton W. (H) 2-1; 4th Round: Oxford U. (H) 4-2; 5th Round: Portsmouth (A) 0-3.
Littlewoods Cup: 1897-88: 2nd Round: Fulham (A) 5-1 (H) 2-1; 3rd Round: Charlton Ath. (A) 1-0; 4th Round: Reading (A) 0-0 Replay (H) 1-0; Quarter Final: Luton T. (A) 0-2.

BRENTFORD (Division 3)

Brentford FC

Team Manager Steve Perryman.
Club Address Griffin Park, Braemer Road, Brentford, Middlesex TW8 0NT. Tel: 01-847 2511.
Current Ground Capacity 10,500.
Record Attendance 39,626 v Preston N.E., FA Cup 6th Round, 5 March 1938.
Year Formed 1889. Turned professional 1899.
Previous Names None.
Club Nickname "The Bees".
Club Colours Red and white striped shirts, black shorts and red stockings with white tops.
Club Honours Football League: Div. 2 Champions 1934-35; Div. 3(S) Champions 1932-33; Div. 4 Champions 1962-63.
League History 1920-33 Div. 3(S); 1933-35 Div. 2; 1935-47 Div. 1; 1947-54 Div. 2; 1954-62 Div. 3(S); 1962-63 Div. 4; 1963-66 Div. 3; 1966-72 Div. 4; 1972-73 Div. 3; 1973-78 Div. 4; 1978- Div. 3.
Most League Points in a Season (2 for a win) 62 in Div. 3(S), 1932-33 and 62 in Div. 4, 1962-63. (3 for a win) 68 in Div. 3, 1981-82.

Most League Goals in a Season 98 in Div. 4, 1962-63.
Record Victory 9-0 v Wrexham in Div. 3, 15 October 1963.
Record Defeat 0-7 v Swansea T. in Div. 3(S), 8 November 1924 and v Walsall, Div. 3(S), 19 January 1957.
Consecutive League Wins 9 in 1932.
Consecutive League Defeats 9 in 1925 and 1928.
Record League Appearances Ken Coote, 513 between 1949-64.
Record League Goalscorer—Career Jim Towers, 153 between 1954-61.
Record League Goalscorer—Season Jack Holliday, 38 in Div. 3(S), 1932-33.

Brentford: League Record, 1987-88 (Division 3)

Match Number	Date	Venue	Opponents	Result		H/T	Lge Posn	Attend
1	15.8.87	H	Sunderland	L	0-1	0-0		7509
2	29.8.87	H	Bristol C.	L	0-2	0-0		4328
3	31.8.87	A	Grimsby T.	W	1-0	1-0	20	3361
4	5.9.87	A	Rotherham U.	D	1-1	0-0	18	3604
5	9.9.87	A	Northampton T.	L	1-2	0-0	18	5748
6	12.9.87	A	Southend U.	W	3-2	3-1	17	2335
7	15.9.87	H	Chesterfield	W	2-0	2-0	12	3183
8	19.9.87	H	Blackpool	W	2-1	1-0	11	3886
9	26.9.87	A	Aldershot	L	1-4	1-3	13	3651
10	29.9.87	A	Preston N.E.	W	2-1	0-1	12	4241
11	3.10.87	H	Port Vale	W	1-0	0-0	6	4013
12	10.10.87	A	Bury	D	2-2	1-1	6	2300
13	17.10.87	H	Walsall	D	0-0	0-0	7	5056
14	20.10.87	H	Chester C.	D	1-1	0-0	8	4027
15	24.10.87	A	Brighton & H.A.	L	1-2	1-0	10	7600
16	31.10.87	H	Bristol Rov.	D	1-1	1-0	12	4487
17	3.11.87	A	Gillingham	W	1-0	1-0	9	4529
18	7.11.87	A	Notts Co.	L	0-3	0-0	11	5364
19	21.11.87	H	Wigan Ath.	W	2-1	1-0	9	3625
20	28.11.87	A	Doncaster Rov.	W	1-0	0-0	7	1360
21	12.12.87	H	Mansfield T.	D	2-2	1-2	8	3729
22	18.12.87	A	York C.	D	1-1	0-1	9	1801
23	26.12.87	H	Aldershot	W	3-0	2-0	7	5578
24	28.12.87	A	Fulham	D	2-2	0-0	7	9340
25	1.1.88	A	Bristol C.	W	3-2	3-0	6	12877
26	2.1.88	A	Southend U.	W	1-0	0-0	6	5752
27	9.1.88	H	Northampton T.	L	0-1	0-0	6	6025
28	16.1.88	A	Blackpool	W	1-0	1-0	5	3911
29	14.2.88	H	Fulham	W	3-1	1-0	6	8712
30	17.2.88	A	Rotherham U.	L	0-2	0-1	6	2572
31	20.2.88	A	Sunderland	L	0-2	0-2	7	15458
32	23.2.88	H	Grimsby T.	L	0-2	0-1	7	3534
33	27.2.88	A	Port Vale	L	0-1	0-0	7	3876
34	1.3.88	H	Preston N.E.	W	2-0	1-0	7	3505
35	5.3.88	A	Walsall	L	2-4	1-2	7	4494
36	12.3.88	H	Bury	L	0-3	0-1	7	3920
37	19.3.88	A	Bristol Rov.	D	0-0	0-0	7	3380
38	26.3.88	A	Brighton & H.A.	D	1-1	0-1	8	5331
39	2.4.88	H	Notts Co	W	1-0	1-0	8	4388
40	4.4.88	A	Wigan Ath.	D	1-1	1-1	9	3597
41	9.4.88	H	Gillingham	D	2-2	0-0	9	3875
42	19.4.88	A	Chesterfield	L	1-2	0-2	9	2010
43	23.4.88	A	Chester C.	D	1-1	0-0	10	1777
44	30.4.88	H	Doncaster Rov.	D	1-1	1-0	11	3122
45	2.5.88	A	Mansfield T.	L	1-2	1-0	12	2663
46	7.5.88	H	York C.	L	1-2	0-2	12	4180

Players: League Record, 1987-88 (Division 3)

Match Number	1	2	3	4	5	6	7	8	9	10	11	12	13	14	15	16	17	18	19	20	21	22	23	24	25	26	27	28	29	30	31	32	33	34	35	36	37	38	39	40	41	42	43	44	45	46	Apps	Subs	Goals
Bates		2	2	10		5	10		5	5	5	5	5¹	5	5	5	5			4	4	4	4		★			★			★														4	4	20	3	1
Birch																					★	9¹	9¹	9	9		10	9	9	9	9	9	9	9			★						★				13	3	2
Blissett	10	10	10¹	10	★	10¹			10	10	10	10	10	10	10	10	10		10	10¹	10	10	10	10²	10	10		10¹	10	10		10	10¹	10¹	10	10	10	10	10	10	10	10	10	10	10	10	40	1	9
Booker					★	★	10						★	★									★						★			★				★	★	★		★		★					1	11	0
Buckle																																															0	1	0
Carroll	★	11							★	7¹		7							9¹	9				★	★															9			9¹	9¹			8	4	4
Cockram																																					7	7	9	9¹	9¹		11			7	0	2
Cooke	9	9	9	9	9¹	9	9¹	9¹	9	9	9	9	9	9¹	9	★																															15	1	4
Evans																5	5	5			5	5	5	5¹	5		5	5	5	5	5	5	5	5	5	5¹	5¹	5	5	5	5	5	5	5	5	5	29	0	4
Feeley	7	6	6	6	3	3	3	3		★			★	★		★	7	6	6	6	6	6	6		6	6		★	10	11	11	11	11	11				3	★	★	7						27	7	0
Ferdinand																																						9	9	9							3	0	0
Gravette			★				★	★																					★	9																	1	4	0
Holloway	11																																														1	0	0
Howard																																													★		0	1	0
Jones			5¹	11		6		6	6	6	6	6	6	6	6	6	6	6	6			★	★	6			6	6	6	6	6	6	6	6	6	6	6	6	6	6	6	6	6	6	6	6	34	2	1
Joseph	2	2		2	2	2	2	2	2	2	2	2	2	2	2	2	2	2	2	2	2	2	2	2	2	2	2	2	2	2	2	2	2	2			2	★¹	11	11	11	11	11	11	2	2	43	0	0
Lee	5	5	5		5		5			★	7								9	★	5	11				9	9												2								19	3	1
Millen	4	4	4		4		4	4	4	4	4	4	4	4	4	4		4¹	4	4	4	4	4¹	4¹	4	4	4	4	4		4	4	4	4	4	4	4	4	4	4	4	4	4	4	4	4	40	0	3
Murray	3	3	3	3																																											4	0	0
Oliver																												1	1	1	1	1	1	1	1	1	1	1									11	0	0
Perryman		★	11	11		6					★	11	11	11	11	11	11	11	11	11	11	11	11		★		★	6	★																		16	5	0
Phillips	1	1	1	1	1		1	1	1	1	1	1	1	1	1	1	1	1	1	1	1	1	1	1	1	1	1	1	1	1	1	1	1	1									1	1	1		35	0	0
Priddle	6						11	11	11	11	★																																				5	1	0
Rix																						11	11	11	11	11	11																				6	0	0
Sinton	8	8	8	8	8	8¹	8	8¹	8¹	8¹	8¹	8¹	8	8	8	8	8	8	8	8¹	8	8	8¹	8	8	8¹	8	8	8	8	8	8	8	8	8	8	8	8	8	8²	8	8	8	8	8	8	46	0	11
Smith		7	7	7	7	7	7	7¹	7		7		★		★	7								★		★	★	★			★			★													10	7	1
Stanislaus					3	3	3	3	3	3	3	3¹	3	3	3	3	3	3	3	3	3	3	3¹	3	3	3	3	3	3	3	3	3	3	3	3	3	3	3	3	★	3	3	3				36	1	2
Stewart																									11	11	11	11	★		★	★															4	3	0
Thorne											7¹																																				1	0	1
Turner												7	7	7	7¹	7	7	7	7	7	7	7	7	7	7	7	7	7	7	7	7	7	7	7							7¹	7	7	7			24	0	0
Williams							7	7	9¹	9	9	10¹	9¹																																		7	0	3
Own Goals								1																					1																		2

FA Cup: 1987-88: 1st Round: Brighton & H.A. (H) 0-2.
Littlewoods Cup: 1987-88: 1st Round: Southend U. (H) 2-1 (A) 2-4.

BRIGHTON & HOVE ALBION (Division 2)

Team Manager Barry Lloyd.
Club Address Goldstone Ground, Old Shoreham Road, Hove, Sussex BN3 7DE. Tel: (0273) 739535.
Current Ground Capacity 29,026.
Record Attendance 36,747 v Fulham, Div. 2, 27 December 1958.
Year Formed 1900. Turned professional 1900.
Previous Names Brighton and Hove Rangers.
Club Nickname "The Seagulls".
Club Colours Blue and white striped shirts, white shorts and blue stockings.
Club Honours Football League: Div. 3(S) Champions 1957-58; Div. 4 Champions 1964-65.
League History 1920-58 Div. 3(S); 1958-62 Div. 2; 1962-63 Div. 3; 1963-65 Div. 4; 1965-72 Div. 3; 1972-73 Div. 2; 1973-77 Div. 3; 1977-79 Div. 2; 1979-83 Div. 1; 1983-87 Div. 2; 1987-88 Div. 3; 1988- Div. 2.
Most League Points in a Season (2 for a win) 65 in Div. 3(S), 1955-56 and Div. 3, 1971-72. (3 for a win) 84 in Div. 3, 1987-88.

Most League Goals in a Season 112 in Div. 3(S), 1955-56.
Record Victory 10-1 v Wisbech in FA Cup 1st Round, 13 November 1965.
Record Defeat 0-9 v Middlesbrough in Div. 2, 23 August 1958.
Consecutive League Wins 9 in 1926.
Consecutive League Defeats 12 in 1972-73.
Record League Appearances "Tug" Wilson, 509 between 1922-36.
Record League Goalscorer—Career Tommy Cook, 113 between 1922-29.
Record League Goalscorer—Season Peter Ward, 32 in Div. 3, 1976-77.

Brighton and Hove Albion: League Record, 1987-88 (Division 3)

Match Number	Date	Venue	Opponents	Result		H/T	Lge Posn	Attend
1	15.8.87	H	York C.	W	1-0	0-0		6068
2	22.8.87	A	Chesterfield	D	0-0	0-0		2286
3	29.8.87	H	Fulham	W	2-0	1-0	4	8773
4	31.8.87	A	Northampton T.	D	1-1	0-0	5	7934
5	5.9.87	H	Blackpool	L	1-3	0-1	10	7166
6	12.9.87	A	Aldershot	W	4-1	2-1	5	3970
7	16.9.87	H	Rotherham U.	D	1-1	0-1	8	6945
8	19.9.87	H	Sunderland	W	3-1	2-0	4	8949
9	26.9.87	A	Southend U.	L	1-2	0-0	9	3789
10	28.9.87	A	Port Vale	L	0-2	0-0	10	3789
11	3.10.87	H	Bury	W	2-1	1-1	8	6509
12	10.10.87	A	Walsall	D	1-1	0-1	9	5020
13	17.10.87	H	Preston N.E.	D	0-0	0-0	10	6043
14	20.10.87	A	Wigan Ath.	D	3-3	0-1	10	2392
15	24.10.87	H	Brentford	W	2-1	0-1	8	7600
16	31.10.87	A	Grimsby T.	W	1-0	1-0	5	2711
17	4.11.87	H	Doncaster Rov.	W	2-0	1-0	5	7142
18	7.11.87	A	Gillingham	D	1-1	0-0	5	6437
19	21.11.87	A	Mansfield T.	D	1-1	0-1	6	3284
20	28.11.87	H	Notts Co.	D	1-1	0-0	6	8725
21	12.12.87	H	Chester C.	W	1-0	0-0	4	6738
22	19.12.87	A	Bristol Rov.	W	2-1	1-1	4	3589
23	26.12.87	H	Southend U.	D	0-0	0-0	4	11147
24	28.12.87	A	Bristol C.	L	2-5	0-3	5	16058
25	1.1.88	A	Fulham	W	2-1	0-1	5	6530
26	2.1.88	H	Aldershot	D	1-1	0-1	5	9420
27	16.1.88	A	Sunderland	L	0-1	0-1	7	17404
28	6.2.88	A	Blackpool	W	3-1	0-0	6	4081
29	13.2.88	H	Bristol C.	W	3-2	1-1	5	8781
30	17.2.88	H	Chesterfield	D	2-2	1-1	5	8182
31	20.2.88	A	York C.	W	2-0	1-0	5	2576
32	27.2.88	A	Bury	L	1-2	0-0	5	2557
33	2.3.88	H	Port Vale	W	2-0	0-0	5	7296
34	5.3.88	A	Preston N.E.	L	0-3	0-3	6	5834
35	12.3.88	H	Walsall	W	2-1	1-0	6	8345
36	16.3.88	A	Rotherham U.	L	0-1	0-0	6	2562
37	19.3.88	H	Grimsby T.	D	0-0	0-0	6	7269
38	26.3.88	H	Brentford	D	1-1	1-0	6	5331
39	2.4.88	A	Gillingham	W	2-0	2-0	6	9256
40	4.4.88	A	Notts Co.	W	2-1	1-1	6	7522
41	9.4.88	H	Wigan Ath.	W	1-0	0-0	4	9423
42	15.4.88	H	Northampton T.	W	3-0	1-0	4	14421
43	23.4.88	A	Doncaster Rov.	W	2-0	0-0	4	1683
44	30.4.88	H	Mansfield T.	W	3-1	2-1	3	11493
45	2.5.88	A	Chester C.	D	2-2	2-1	2	3345
46	7.5.88	H	Bristol Rov.	W	2-1	1-0	2	19800

Players: League Record, 1987-88 (Division 3)

Match Number	1	2	3	4	5	6	7	8	9	10	11	12	13	14	15	16	17	18	19	20	21	22	23	24	25	26	27	28	29	30	31	32	33	34	35	36	37	38	39	40	41	42	43	44	45	46	Apps	Subs	Goals
Armstrong	★		★¹	★		★		★		★	★	★			★			★				★																									0	11	1
Bremner	9		9²	9	9	9	9¹	9	9	9	9	9	9	9	9²	9¹	9	9	9	9	9	9	9	9	9	9	9	9	9	9	9	9	9	9		★	★	9	9	9	9	9	9	9	9	9¹	42	2	8
Brown	2	2	2	2	2	2	2	2	2	2	2	2	2	2	2	2	2	2	2	2	2	2	2	2	2	2	2	2	2	2	2	2	2	2													35	0	0
Chivers																																			2	2	2	2	2	2	2	2	2	2			10	0	0
Cooper																																															0	2	0
Crumplin			7	7	7	7		★			★	11	11	11	11	11	11	11						★	11	11	11¹	11	11	11	11	★¹	★	★				★									19	7	2
Curbishley		★	4	4	4	4¹	4	4	4	4	4¹	4	4	4	4¹	4	4	4							4	4	4	4	4	4	4	4	4¹	4	4	4	4	4	4	4¹	4	4¹	4			4	34	0	6
Dublin	3	3	3	3	3	3	3	3	3	3	3	3	3	3	3	3	3	3¹	3	3¹	3	3	3	3	3¹	3	3	3	3	3	3	3	3¹	3	3	3	3	3	3	3	3	3¹	3	3			46	0	5
Gatting	6	6	6	6	6	6	6¹	6	6	6	6	6	6	6	6	6	6	6	6	6	6	6	6	6	6	6	6	6	6	6	6	6	6	6	6	6	6	6	6	6	6	6¹	6	6¹	6	6	46	0	3
Gipp					10																																				★						1	1	0
Horscroft														5	5																																2	0	0
Hutchings	8	8	8	8	8	8	8	8¹	8	8	8	8	8	8	8	8	8	8	8	8																											20	0	1
Isaac																									2	5	5			5	5	5	5	5	5	5											10	0	0
Jasper														★					4	4	4	4¹	4	4	4¹	4		★¹	8¹	8	8	8															12	2	4
Keeley	1	1	1	1	1	1	1	1	1	1	1	1	1	1	1	1	1	1	1	1	1	1	1	1	1	1	1	1	1	1	1	1	1	1	1	1	1	1	1	1	1	1	1	1	1	1	46	0	0
Nelson	10¹					7²	7	7¹	7	7	7	7¹	7	7	7	7	7²	7	7¹	7	7	7	7	7	7	7	7	7²	7²	7¹	7¹	7	7	7	7	7	7	7¹	7	7¹	7	7	7	7	7	7¹	42	0	21
Owers																																		8	8	8¹	8	8	8¹	8	8	8	8			9	0	2
Penney	7																								11	11	11	11¹	11	11¹	11¹	11	11	11	11	11	11¹	11	11								13	0	3
Rougvie	5	5	5	5	5	5	5	5¹	5	5	5	5	5	5	5	5	5	5	5			5	5	5	5	5	5¹	5	5	5	5	5	5			5											35	0	2
Rowell	4							★																																							1	1	0
Tiltman		9																																													1	0	0
Trusson																	8¹	8	8	8	8¹	8	8	8	8					8	8	8											★	★			13	2	2
Wilkins	11	11	11	11	11	11	11	11	11	11		★			10¹	10	10	10	10	10	10	10	10	10	10	10	10	10	10	10	10	10	10	10	10	10	10	10	10	10	10	10	10	10²	10		43	1	3
Wood			10	10	10	10	10	10	10¹	10	10	10						11	11	11	11	11	11¹	11		★			★	★	11	11	9¹	9	9			★	4¹	4	4	★					26	5	4
Own Goals							1																	1																									2

FA Cup: 1987-88: 1st Round: Brentford (A) 2-0; 2nd Round: Northampton T. (A) 2-1; 3rd Round: Bournemouth (H) 2-0; 4th Round: Arsenal (H) 1-2.
Littlewoods Cup: 1987-88: 1st Round: Gillingham (A) 0-1 (H) 1-0.

BRISTOL CITY (Division 3)

Team Manager Joe Jordan.
Club Address Ashton Gate, Bristol BS3 2EJ. Tel: (0272) 632812.
Current Ground Capacity 30,868.
Record Attendance 43,335 v Preston N.E., FA Cup 5th Round, 16 February 1935.
Year Formed 1894. Turned professional 1897.
Previous Names Bristol South End.
Club Nickname "The Robins".
Club Colours Red shirts, white shorts and red stockings.
Club Honours Football League: Div. 2 Champions 1905-06; Div. 3(S) Champions 1922-23, 1926-27, 1954-55.
League History 1901-06 Div. 2; 1906-11 Div. 1; 1911-22 Div. 2; 1922-23 Div. 3(S); 1923-24 Div. 2; 1924-27 Div. 3(S); 1927-32 Div. 2; 1932-55 Div. 3(S); 1955-60 Div. 2; 1960-65 Div. 3; 1965-76 Div. 2; 1976-80 Div. 1; 1980-81 Div. 2; 1981-82 Div. 3; 1982-84 Div. 4; 1984- Div. 3.
Most League Points in a Season (2 for a win) 70 in Div. 3(S), 1954-55. (3 for a win) 82 in Div. 4, 1983-84.
Most League Goals in a Season 104 in Div. 3(S), 1926-27.

Record Victory 11-0 v Chichester in FA Cup 1st Round, 5 November 1960.
Record Defeat 0-9 v Coventry C in Div. 3(S), 28 April 1934.
Consecutive League Wins 14 in 1905.
Consecutive League Defeats 7 in 1931 and 1970.
Record League Appearances John Atyeo, 596 between 1951-66.
Record League Goalscorer—Career John Atyeo, 314 between 1951-66.
Record League Goalscorer—Season Don Clark, 36 in Div. 3(S), 1946-47.

Bristol City: League Record, 1987-88 (Division 3)

Match Number	Date	Venue	Opponents	Result		H/T	Lge Posn	Attend
1	15.8.87	A	Mansfield T.	L	0-2	0-2		5441
2	22.8.87	H	Preston N.E.	W	3-1	1-0		7655
3	29.8.87	A	Brentford	W	2-0	0-0	7	4328
4	31.8.87	H	Port Vale	W	1-0	0-0	3	8716
5	5.9.87	A	Bury	D	1-1	1-1	4	2376
6	12.9.87	H	Bristol Rov.	D	3-3	1-1	7	14746
7	15.9.87	A	Walsall	D	1-1	0-0	7	6425
8	19.9.87	A	Notts Co.	W	1-0	0-0	5	5705
9	26.9.87	H	Gillingham	D	3-3	1-2	6	10070
10	29.9.87	H	Chesterfield	W	2-1	1-0	6	9088
11	3.10.87	A	Northampton T.	L	0-3	0-1	5	6234
12	10.10.87	H	Southend U.	W	3-2	1-1	3	8606
13	17.10.87	A	Grimsby T.	W	4-1	4-1	3	3100
14	20.10.87	H	Sunderland	L	0-1	0-1	4	15109
15	24.10.87	A	Rotherham U.	L	1-4	1-3	8	3397
16	3.11.87	A	Blackpool	L	2-4	1-1	11	3140
17	7.11.87	A	Aldershot	L	1-2	0-1	14	4324
18	21.11.87	H	Chester C.	D	2-2	1-2	12	8103
19	28.11.87	A	Wigan Ath.	D	1-1	1-0	13	2879
20	12.12.87	H	York C.	W	3-2	2-1	12	6238
21	15.12.87	H	Fulham	W	4-0	3-0	7	6150
22	19.12.87	A	Doncaster Rov.	W	2-1	1-1	5	1819
23	26.12.87	A	Gillingham	D	1-1	1-0	5	6457
24	28.12.87	H	Brighton & H.A.	W	5-2	3-0	4	16058
25	1.1.88	H	Brentford	L	2-3	0-3	7	12877
26	9.1.88	A	Preston N.E.	L	0-2	0-1	8	5729
27	16.1.88	H	Notts Co.	W	2-1	0-1	8	9558
28	6.2.88	H	Bury	W	3-2	0-1	8	9158
29	9.2.88	H	Walsall	D	0-0	0-0	7	8454
30	13.2.88	A	Brighton & H.A.	L	2-3	0-1	7	8781
31	20.2.88	H	Mansfield T.	L	1-2	1-2	8	8528
32	27.2.88	H	Northampton T.	D	2-2	1-2	9	8578
33	1.3.88	A	Chesterfield	W	4-1	2-1	8	1657
34	5.3.88	A	Grimsby T.	D	1-1	0-0	8	8343
35	11.3.88	A	Southend U.	L	0-2	0-1	8	3664
36	19.3.88	A	Fulham	D	0-0	0-0	8	4896
37	26.3.88	H	Rotherham U.	W	2-0	0-0	7	7517
38	2.4.88	H	Aldershot	W	2-0	1-0	7	8712
39	4.4.88	A	Chester C.	L	0-1	0-1	7	2849
40	9.4.88	H	Blackpool	W	2-1	1-0	7	6460
41	12.4.88	A	Bristol Rov.	L	0-1	0-0	8	5947
42	18.4.88	A	Port Vale	D	1-1	0-0	8	2671
43	23.4.88	A	Sunderland	W	1-0	1-0	8	18225
44	30.4.88	H	Wigan Ath.	W	4-1	2-1	7	7340
45	2.5.88	A	York C.	W	1-0	0-0	6	2616
46	7.5.88	H	Doncaster Rov.	W	1-0	0-0	5	18373

Players: League Record, 1987-88 (Division 3)

Player	Apps	Subs	Goals
Bromage	28	2	0
Caldwell	8	8	3
Curle	3	0	0
Fitzpatrick	22	2	5
Galliers	35	0	6
Gordon	6	0	4
Harvey	0	1	0
Hawkins	1	0	0
Honor	14	3	0
Humphries	24	0	0
Jordan	17	11	4
Llewllyn	36	6	1
McClaren	16	0	1
Mardon	8	0	0
Marshall	13	6	1
Milne	19	0	4
Moyes	15	0	1
Neville	37	3	5
Newman	44	0	11
Owen	17	1	6
Pender	28	0	2
Prudhoe	3	0	0
Shutt	18	4	9
Tanner	10	2	0
Vaughan	3	0	0
Walsh	39	3	12
Waugh	40	0	0
Own Goals			2

FA Cup: 1987-88: 1st Round: Aylesbury (H) 1-0; 2nd Round: Torquay U. (H) 0-1.
Littlewoods Cup: 1987-88: 1st Round: Swindon T. (A) 0-3 (H) 3-2.

BRISTOL ROVERS (Division 3)

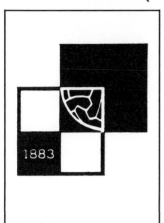

1883

Team Manager   Gerry Francis.
Club Address   Twerton Park, Twerton, Bath (shared with Bath City). Tel: (0225) 23087.
Current Ground Capacity   6,600.
Record Attendance   38,472 v Preston N.E., FA Cup 4th Round, 30 January 1960.
Year Formed   1883. Turned professional 1897.
Previous Names   Black Arabs, Eastville Rovers, Bristol Eastville Rovers, Bristol Rovers.
Club Nickname   "The Pirates".
Club Colours   Blue and white quartered shirts, white shorts and blue stockings with two white rings on top.
Club Honours   Football League: Div. 3(S) Champions 1952-53.
League History   1920-53 Div. 3; 1921-53 Div 3(S); 1953-62 Div. 2; 1962-74 Div. 3; 1974-81 Div. 2; 1981- Div. 3.
Most League Points in a Season   (2 for a win) 64 in Div. 3(S), 1952-53. (3 for a win) 79 in Div. 3, 1983-84.
Most League Goals in a Season   92 in Div. 3(S), 1952-53.
Record Victory   7-0 v Swansea T. in Div. 2, 2 October

1954, and v Brighton and H.A. in Div. 3(S), 29 November 1952 and v Shrewsbury T. in Div. 3, 21 March 1964.
Record Defeat   0-12 v Luton T. in Div. 3(S), 13 April 1936.
Consecutive League Wins   12 in 1952-53.
Consecutive League Defeats   8 in 1961.
Record League Appearances   Stuart Taylor, 546 between 1965-80.
Record League Goalscorer—Career   Geoff Bradford, 242 between 1949-64.
Record League Goalscorer—Season   Geoff Bradford, 33 in Div. 3(S), 1952-53.

Bristol Rovers: League Record, 1987-88 (Division 3)

Match Number	Date	Venue	Opponents	Result		H/T	Lge Posn	Attend
1	15.8.87	H	Rotherham U.	W	3-1	2-0		3399
2	22.8.87	A	Sunderland	D	1-1	0-0		13059
3	29.8.87	H	Aldershot	W	3-1	3-0	1	3390
4	31.8.87	H	Blackpool	L	1-2	0-1	6	3319
5	5.9.87	H	Wigan Ath.	L	2-3	2-2	12	3168
6	12.9.87	A	Bristol C.	D	3-3	1-1	14	14746
7	16.9.87	H	York C.	W	2-1	1-0	11	3177
8	19.9.87	A	Northampton T.	L	0-2	0-1	14	3655
9	26.9.87	A	Fulham	L	1-3	0-1	15	4614
10	29.9.87	A	Notts Co.	D	1-1	0-0	16	4334
11	3.10.87	H	Mansfield T.	W	2-1	1-0	16	2980
12	10.10.87	A	Gillingham	L	0-3	0-0	16	4399
13	17.10.87	A	Chester C.	D	2-2	2-1	15	3083
14	19.10.87	A	Port Vale	L	1-2	1-1	15	3598
15	24.10.87	H	Doncaster Rov.	W	4-0	3-0	16	2817
16	31.10.87	A	Brentford	D	1-1	0-1	15	4487
17	4.11.87	H	Preston N.E.	L	1-2	0-1	17	2804
18	7.11.87	H	Chesterfield	W	2-0	2-0	15	2633
19	21.11.87	A	Bury	L	1-4	0-1	15	2356
20	28.11.87	H	Grimsby T.	W	4-2	2-1	15	2787
21	12.12.87	A	Walsall	D	0-0	0-0	14	4234
22	19.12.87	H	Brighton & H.A.	L	1-2	1-1	15	3589
23	26.12.87	H	Fulham	W	3-1	1-1	13	4718
24	28.12.87	A	Southend U.	L	2-4	1-2	14	4094
25	1.1.88	A	Aldershot	L	0-3	0-3	18	4593
26	16.1.88	A	Northampton T.	L	1-2	1-1	19	4473
27	6.2.88	A	Wigan Ath.	L	0-1	0-0	20	3827
28	13.2.88	H	Southend U.	D	0-0	0-0	20	3092
29	20.2.88	A	Rotherham U.	D	1-1	0-0	20	2966
30	24.2.88	H	Sunderland	W	4-0	1-0	20	4501
31	27.2.88	A	Mansfield T.	L	0-1	0-0	20	3191
32	2.3.88	H	Notts Co.	D	1-1	0-0	20	4075
33	5.3.88	A	Chester C.	W	3-0	2-0	19	2067
34	12.3.88	H	Gillingham	W	2-0	0-0	17	3846
35	19.3.88	H	Brentford	D	0-0	0-0	19	3380
36	25.3.88	A	Doncaster Rov.	W	1-0	1-0	18	1311
37	2.4.88	A	Chesterfield	W	1-0	1-0	15	2208
38	4.4.88	H	Bury	D	0-0	0-0	16	4264
39	8.4.88	A	Preston N.E.	L	1-3	1-2	16	5386
40	12.4.88	H	Bristol C.	W	1-0	0-0	14	5947
41	15.4.88	A	York C.	W	4-0	2-0	12	1834
42	23.4.88	H	Port Vale	W	1-0	0-0	11	3780
43	27.4.88	H	Blackpool	W	2-0	2-0	9	3546
44	30.4.88	A	Grimsby T.	D	0-0	0-0	9	2025
45	2.5.88	H	Walsall	W	3-0	3-0	8	6328
46	7.5.88	A	Brighton & H.A.	L	1-2	0-1	8	19800

Players: League Record, 1987-88 (Division 3)

Match Number	1	2	3	4	5	6	7	8	9	10	11	12	13	14	15	16	17	18	19	20	21	22	23	24	25	26	27	28	29	30	31	32	33	34	35	36	37	38	39	40	41	42	43	44	45	46	Apps	Subs	Goals
Alexander	2	2	2	2	2	2	2	2	2	2	2	2			2	2	2	2	2	2	2	2	2	2	2	2	2¹	2	2	2	2	2	2	2	2	2	2	2	2	2	2	2	2	2	2	2	45	0	1
Carr	5	5	5	5	5						4	4	4																																		8	0	0
Carter							1	1	1	1	1	1	1																																		7	0	0
Clark													4	4	4	4	4	5	5	5	5	5				4	4	4	4	4	4	4	4	4	4	4	4	4	4	4	4	4	4	4	4	4¹	31	0	1
Dryden	3	3	3	3	3								3																																		6	0	0
Eaton	★																★		★																												0	3	0
Francis																		8																													1	0	0
Hibbitt	4	4	4	4	4	4	4	4					5	5	5¹	4	4¹	4	4	4	4	4	4		8	5	5	5																			24	0	2
Holloway		7			7	7¹	7	7	7	7	7	7	7	7	7	7	7	7	7	7	7¹	7¹	7	7	7	7	7	7	7¹	7	7	7	7	7	7	7	7	7	7	7	7¹	7					43	0	5
Jones	6	6	6	6	6	6¹	6¹	6	6	6	6	6	6	6¹	6	6	3	3	6	6	6	6	6	6	6	6	6	6	6	6	6	6	6	6	6	6	6	6	6	6	6	6	6	6	6	6	46	0	3
Joseph																									9	9	8																				2	0	0
McClean																																	9	9	★		★			★		★					2	4	0
Martyn	1	1	1	1	1								1	1	1	1	1	1	1	1	1	1	1	1	1	1	1	1	1	1	1	1	1	1	1	1	1	1	1	1	1	1	1	1	1	1	39	0	0
Meacham		★	7¹	7							★¹	9		★	★		★	8¹	8	8¹	★	8				★																					7	7	4
Mehew																									★	8¹	5	5	5¹	5	5	5	5	5¹	5	5³	5	5¹	5	5	5¹	5					17	1	8
Penrice	10²	10¹	10¹	10	10	10	10	10¹	10	10	10¹	10¹	10	10¹	10¹	10	10	10	10	10¹	10	10	10¹	10	10	10	10	10	10	10¹	10	10	10¹	10	10¹	10¹	10	10¹	10	10¹	10	10	10	10		10	46	0	17
Purnell	11	11	11	11	11¹	11	11	11	11	11	11	11	11	11²	11	11	11¹	11	11¹	11	11	11	11	11	11	11	11	11	11	11	11	11¹	11¹	11	11	11	11	11	★				11	11		11	40	1	8
Reece	8	8	8			8¹	8	8	8	8	8	8	8	8	8	★		8	★	8	8	★		★	8		★	8	8	8	8	8	8	8	8	8	8	8	8	8	8				8	8	35	5	1
Tanner				3	3	3	3	3	3	3	3	3	3	2	3	3	3				3	3	3	3	3	3	3									★					11	11	11	11	11	11	25	1	4
Turner	9¹	9		★	★		★	★	★		★	5																																			3	6	1
Twentyman			★		5	5	5	5	5	5	5						3	6	6		★	5	5	5	5	5	5	3	3	3	3¹	3	3	3	3	3	3	3	3	3	3	3	3	3	3	3	35	3	0
Weston				8																	8							8			★						★					★					2	3	0
White			9¹	9¹	9¹	9	9	9	9¹	9	9		9¹	9	9¹	9	9	9	9	9¹	9	9	9¹	9¹	9	9			9¹	9¹	9	9	9	9¹	9	9			9	9	9¹	9	9¹	9	9¹	9	39	0	15
Wiffill	7			8																																											2	0	0
Own Goals													1																																				1

FA Cup: 1987-88: 1st Round: Merthyr Tydfil (H) 6-0; 2nd Round: VS Rugby (A) 1-1 Replay (H) 4-0; 3rd Round: Shrewsbury T. (A) 1-2.
Littlewoods Cup: 1987-88: 1st Round: Hereford U. (H) 1-0 (A) 0-2.

BURNLEY (Division 4)

Team Manager Brian Miller.
Club Address Turf Moor, Burnley BB10 4BX. Tel: (0282) 27777/38021.
Current Ground Capacity 25,000.
Record Attendance 54,775 v Huddersfield T., FA Cup 3rd Round, 23 February 1924.
Year Formed 1882. Turned professional 1883.
Previous Names Burnley Rovers.
Club Nickname "The Clarets".
Club Colours Claret shirt with light blue sleeves, white shorts and stockings.
Club Honours Football League: Div. 1 Champions 1920-21, 1959-60; Div. 2 Champions 1897-98, 1972-73; Div. 3 Champions 1981-82. FA Cup: Winners 1914.
League History 1888-97 Div. 1; 1897-98 Div. 2; 1898-1900 Div. 1; 1900-13 Div. 2; 1913-30 Div. 1; 1930-47 Div. 2; 1947-71 Div. 1; 1971-73 Div. 2; 1973-76 Div. 1; 1976-80 Div. 2; 1980-82 Div. 3; 1982-83 Div. 2; 1983-85 Div. 3; 1985- Div. 4.
Most League Points in a Season (2 for a win) 62 in Div. 2, 1972-73. (3 for a win) 80 in Div. 3, 1981-82.

Most League Goals in a Season 102 in Div. 1, 1960-61.
Record Victory 9-0 v Darwen in Div. 1, 9 January 1892 , v Crystal Palace in FA Cup replay 1908-09, v New Brighton in FA Cup 4th Round, 26 January 1957 and v Penrith in FA Cup 1st Round, 17 November 1984.
Record Defeat 0-10 v Aston Villa, Div. 1, 29 August 1925, and v Sheffield U., Div. 1, 19 January 1929.
Consecutive League Wins 10 in 1912-13.
Consecutive League Defeats 8 in 1889-90, 1895.
Record League Appearances Jerry Dawson, 530 between 1906-29.
Record League Goalscorer—Career George Beel, 178 between 1923-32.
Record League Goalscorer—Season George Beel, 35 in Div. 1, 1927-28.

Burnley: League Record, 1987-88 (Division 4)

Match Number	Date	Venue	Opponents	Result		H/T	Lge Posn	Attend
1	15.8.87	H	Colchester U.	L	0-3	0-2		5369
2	22.8.87	A	Newport Co.	W	1-0	0-0		2006
3	29.8.87	H	Carlisle U.	W	4-3	3-1	4	5781
4	1.9.87	A	Leyton Orient	L	1-4	0-1	12	3560
5	5.9.87	H	Swansea C.	W	1-0	0-0	6	4778
6	11.9.87	A	Tranmere Rov.	W	1-0	0-0	4	4209
7	15.9.87	H	Wrexham	W	1-0	0-0	1	5642
8	19.9.87	H	Cambridge U.	L	0-2	0-2	3	5789
9	26.9.87	A	Rochdale	L	1-2	0-1	7	4426
10	29.9.87	H	Crewe Alex.	D	0-0	0-0	7	5404
11	3.10.87	A	Scarborough	L	0-1	0-1	10	4782
12	10.10.87	H	Hartlepool U.	W	1-0	0-0	6	5215
13	17.10.87	A	Exeter C.	W	2-1	1-1	4	2780
14	20.10.87	H	Scunthorpe U.	D	1-1	0-0	8	6323
15	24.10.87	A	Torquay U.	W	3-1	1-0	3	2740
16	31.10.87	H	Stockport Co.	D	1-1	1-1	8	6645
17	3.11.87	A	Halifax T.	L	1-2	1-1	9	3419
18	7.11.87	A	Wolverhampton W.	L	0-3	0-0	11	10002
19	21.11.87	H	Bolton W.	W	2-1	0-0	9	7489
20	28.11.87	A	Peterborough U.	L	0-5	0-3	10	3550
21	12.12.87	H	Hereford U.	D	0-0	0-0	12	4216
22	19.12.87	A	Cardiff C.	L	1-2	0-0	15	3401
23	26.12.87	H	Rochdale	W	4-0	3-0	9	7013
24	28.12.87	A	Darlington	L	2-4	1-1	14	3325
25	1.1.88	A	Carlisle U.	W	4-3	2-2	9	4262
26	2.1.88	H	Tranmere Rov.	D	1-1	0-1	10	7317
27	9.1.88	H	Newport Co.	W	2-0	0-0	9	5305
28	16.1.88	A	Cambridge U.	L	0-2	0-0	9	2148
29	2.2.88	A	Wrexham	W	3-1	0-0	8	1821
30	6.2.88	A	Swansea C.	D	0-0	0-0	8	3498
31	13.2.88	H	Darlington	W	2-1	1-0	5	6432
32	19.2.88	A	Colchester U.	W	1-0	0-0	5	2520
33	27.2.88	H	Scarborough	L	0-1	0-0	7	7845
34	1.3.88	A	Crewe Alex.	W	1-0	0-0	5	3720
35	5.3.88	H	Exeter C.	W	3-0	1-0	4	6052
36	12.3.88	A	Hartlepool U.	L	1-2	0-2	6	2891
37	18.3.88	A	Stockport Co.	L	0-2	0-1	8	4423
38	22.3.88	H	Leyton Orient	W	2-0	1-0	5	5878
39	2.4.88	H	Wolverhampton W.	L	0-3	0-1	7	10341
40	4.4.88	A	Bolton W.	L	1-2	1-1	6	9921
41	8.4.88	H	Halifax T.	W	3-1	1-1	6	5766
42	23.4.88	A	Scunthorpe U.	D	1-1	0-0	8	5347
43	30.4.88	H	Peterborough U.	L	1-2	1-0	11	6305
44	2.5.88	A	Hereford U.	L	1-2	1-1	11	2304
45	4.5.88	H	Torquay U.	W	1-0	0-0	10	5075
46	7.5.88	H	Cardiff C.	L	1-2	0-0	10	8525

Players: League Record, 1987-88 (Division 4)

Match Number	1	2	3	4	5	6	7	8	9	10	11	12	13	14	15	16	17	18	19	20	21	22	23	24	25	26	27	28	29	30	31	32	33	34	35	36	37	38	39	40	41	42	43	44	45	46	Apps	Subs	Goals
Britton	11														9¹	★		★	7¹	7	★		4	4¹	4	4	4	4		4	4	4	4	4	4	4	4	4	4	4	4¹	4	4	4			29	3	4
Comstive	10	10	10	**10**	10	10¹	10	10	10	10	10¹	10	10	10¹	10	10	10	10	10	10	10	10	10¹	10	10	10¹	10¹	10		10	10	10	10	10		10	10	10	10	10¹	10	10¹	10	10			44	0	8
Daniel	4	4	4	4	4	4	4	★			2	2	2	2	2		2							2	2	2	**2**	2	2	2						2					2	2	2				26	1	0
Davis									5	5	5	5	5	5	5¹	5	5	4	4	5	5¹	5	5	5¹	5	5	5	5	5				5¹	5	5	5	5	5¹	5	5	5						33	0	5
Deakin	6	6	3¹	3	3	3	3	3	3									3	3	3	3	3	3	3¹	3	3	3	3			3	10	3	3	3	3	6	3	3¹	3	5		5				37	0	3
Devaney																											★					★		★			★										0	4	0
Farrell	8	8	8	8¹	7	7	7¹	7	7	7	7	7	7	7	**7**	7	7	2	2	7	7¹	7	7	7	7	2	7	7	7	**7**	7	7	6	7	7	7	7	7	7	7		7	7	7	7		45	0	3
Gardner	★	3	6	6	6	6	6	6	6	6	6	6	6	6	6	6	6	6	6	6	6	6					6	6	6	6					6	6	6			6	6	6	6				41	1	0
Grewcock	7	7	7	7	8	8	8	8	8	8	8	8	8	8	8	8	8	8	8		8	8	8	8	8	8	8			★	★	★	★	11													28	4	0
Hoskin	★			★				★	★	★							11	★			★	★	7	11¹	11	**11**	11	11	11			11	11	11	11			11	11	11							15	9	1
James					5	5	5	5	3	4	4	4	4	4	4					4										5	5		6			11								3			19	0	0
Leebrook	2	2	2	2	2	2	2	2	**2**	**2**	2	2									2	2	2	2	2	**2**									2		2	2	2								22	0	0
McGrory	3											3	3	3	3									10					3	3			3	2				2	3	2	11	11¹	11				16	0	1
Malley									4	4	4			★	3	3																7	★							8	8						6	2	0
Oghani	9	9¹	9¹	9¹	9	9	9	9	9¹	9	9	9	9²	9		9	9	9		9	9	9¹	9		9¹	9		★				8¹	8	8²	8	8¹	8	8	8	8	8	8¹					36	1	14
Pearce	1	1	1	1	1	1	1	1	1	1	1	1	1	1	1	1	1	1	1	1	1	1	1	1	1	1	1	1	1	1	1	1	1	1	1	1	1	1	1	1	1	1	1	1	1	1	46	0	0
Reeves																			9¹	9	11	8	11	11²	11	11	11¹	11		8	8²	8¹	8	8	8¹												16	0	8
Taylor			11	11¹	11	11	11	11	11	11	11	11	11	11¹	11¹	11	11¹	11	11	★		★	★		★		9	9	8		9	9	**9**	9	9	9¹	9	9	9	9	9¹	9	9	9	9	9	38	4	6
Zelem	5	5	5¹	5	5									★					5	5				6	6																						9	1	1
Own Goals																			1			1				1																							3

FA Cup: 1987-88: 1st Round: Bolton W. (H) 0-1.
Littlewoods Cup: 1987-88: 1st Round: Wrexham (A) 0-1 (H) 3-0; 2nd Round: Norwich C. (H) 1-1 (A) 0-1.

BURY (Division 3)

Team Manager Martin Dobson.
Club Address Gigg Lane, Bury BL9 9HR, Tel: 061-764 4881/2.
Current Ground Capacity 8,000.
Record Attendance 35,000 v Bolton W., FA Cup 3rd Round, 9 January 1960.
Year Formed 1885. Turned professional 1885.
Previous Names None.
Club Nickname "The Shakers".
Club Colours White shirts, royal blue shorts and white stockings.
Club Honours Football League: Div. 2 Champions 1894-95. Div. 3 Champions 1960-61. FA Cup: Winners 1900, 1903.
League History 1894-95 Div. 2; 1895-1912 Div. 1; 1912-24 Div. 2; 1924-29 Div. 1; 1929-57 Div 2; 1957-61 Div. 3; 1961-67 Div. 2; 1967-68 Div. 3; 1968-69 Div. 2; 1969-71 Div. 3; 1971-74 Div. 4; 1974-80 Div. 3; 1980-85 Div. 4; 1985- Div. 3.
Most League Points in a Season (2 for a win) 68 in Div. 3, 1960-61. (3 for a win) 84 in Div. 4, 1984-85.

Most League Goals in a Season 108 in Div. 3, 1960-61.
Record Victory 12-1 v Stockton in FA Cup 1st Round replay 1896-97.
Record Defeat 0-10 v Blackburn Rov. in FA Cup preliminary Round, 1st October 1887 and v West Ham U. in Milk Cup, 2nd Round, 2nd leg, 25 October 1983.
Consecutive League Wins 9 in 1960.
Consecutive League Defeats 6 in 1953 and 1967.
Record League Appearances Norman Bullock, 506 between 1920-35.
Record League Goalscorer—Career Craig Madden, 129 between 1977-86.
Record League Goalscorer—Season Craig Madden, 35 in Div. 4, 1981-82.

Bury: League Record, 1987-88 (Division 3)

Match Number	Date	Venue	Opponents	Result		H/T	Lge Posn	Attend
1	15.8.87	H	Southend U.	D	2-2	1-0		1937
2	22.8.87	A	Rotherham U.	W	1-0	0-0		3017
3	29.8.87	H	Blackpool	W	3-1	0-1	2	3053
4	31.8.87	A	Chesterfield	L	0-1	0-0	7	2411
5	5.9.87	H	Bristol C.	D	1-1	1-1	9	2376
6	12.9.87	A	Sunderland	D	1-1	1-1	13	13227
7	15.9.87	H	Grimsby T.	L	0-2	0-2	15	1899
8	19.9.87	H	Aldershot	W	1-0	1-0	13	1744
9	26.9.87	A	Wigan Ath.	W	2-0	1-0	10	3664
10	29.9.87	A	Walsall	D	2-2	1-2	11	2449
11	3.10.87	A	Brighton & H.A.	L	1-2	1-1	14	6509
12	10.10.87	H	Brentford	D	2-2	1-1	13	2300
13	17.10.87	A	Port Vale	L	0-1	0-1	13	3235
14	20.10.87	A	Notts Co.	L	0-3	0-1	15	4044
15	24.10.87	H	Preston N.E.	W	4-0	1-0	12	4316
16	31.10.87	A	Doncaster Rov.	W	2-1	1-0	10	1403
17	3.11.87	H	Mansfield T.	W	1-0	1-0	7	2248
18	7.11.87	A	York C.	D	1-1	1-0	8	2641
19	21.11.87	H	Bristol Rov.	W	4-1	1-0	7	2356
20	28.11.87	A	Gillingham	D	3-3	1-1	8	3981
21	12.12.87	H	Fulham	D	1-1	1-1	9	2643
22	18.12.87	A	Chester C.	D	4-4	0-1	10	1772
23	26.12.87	H	Wigan Ath.	L	0-2	0-1	10	4555
24	28.12.87	A	Northampton T.	D	0-0	0-0	10	6067
25	1.1.88	A	Blackpool	L	1-5	1-2	13	4240
26	2.1.88	H	Sunderland	L	2-3	1-1	13	4883
27	9.1.88	H	Rotherham U.	D	2-2	0-0	13	2230
28	16.1.88	A	Aldershot	W	2-0	0-0	10	2718
29	26.1.88	A	Grimsby T.	L	0-2	0-1	10	2525
30	30.1.88	H	Chesterfield	W	2-0	2-0	9	2071
31	6.2.88	A	Bristol C.	L	2-3	1-0	10	9158
32	13.2.88	H	Northampton T.	D	0-0	0-0	10	2172
33	20.2.88	A	Southend U.	L	0-1	0-1	10	3003
34	27.2.88	H	Brighton & H.A.	W	2-1	0-0	10	2557
35	1.3.88	A	Walsall	L	1-2	1-1	9	3920
36	5.3.88	H	Port Vale	L	0-1	0-0	12	2635
37	12.3.88	A	Brentford	W	3-0	1-0	11	3920
38	19.3.88	H	Doncaster Rov.	W	2-1	1-1	10	2431
39	26.3.88	A	Preston N.E.	L	0-1	0-1	12	6456
40	2.4.88	H	York C.	L	0-1	0-0	13	2277
41	4.4.88	A	Bristol Rov.	D	0-0	0-0	14	4264
42	9.4.88	H	Notts Co.	L	0-1	0-0	14	2527
43	23.4.88	A	Mansfield T.	D	0-0	0-0	15	2381
44	30.4.88	H	Gillingham	W	2-1	1-1	15	1433
45	2.5.88	A	Fulham	W	1-0	1-0	13	5283
46	7.5.88	H	Chester C.	L	0-1	0-0	14	1952

Players: League Record, 1987-88 (Division 3)

Match Number	1	2	3	4	5	6	7	8	9	10	11	12	13	14	15	16	17	18	19	20	21	22	23	24	25	26	27	28	29	30	31	32	33	34	35	36	37	38	39	40	41	42	43	44	45	46	Apps	Subs	Goals
Bishop							★		4	4	4																																				13	4	0
Brotherston	11	11	11¹	11	11	11	11	11		11¹	11	11¹	11	11	11	11¹	11	11	11	11	11	11	11	11	11	11		★		★	11	11	11	11	5	11	11				2	2				★	30	6	4
Clements																																															9	0	1
Collins																									★											5	5	5	5	5	5	5¹	5	5			
Colville	9				★	★																																									0	1	0
Fairbrother			★					★	★						★								★²	9	10	10	10	10	10		11	★		★	★	★											1	2	0
Farnworth	1						1	1	1	1		1	1	1	1	1	1	1	1	1	1	1	1	1	1	1	1	1	1		1	1	1	1	1	1	1	1	1	1	1	1	1	1	1	1	8	9	2
Greenwood	8	8	8	8							★		9¹	9	9	9	9	9	9	9¹	9	★			9	9			★	★	★	11	★		★	10¹	10¹	10	10	10			★	9			39	0	0
Hart		6	6²	6	6	6	6	4		★	4	4	★	★	★	4	★	★	★	★	7	7	★	5			★	5	4	4	4	11	11	11			★	★	11	2	22	8	4
Higgins	6			★	7		6	6	6	6	6	6	6	6	6	6	6	6	6	6	6	6	6	6	6	6	6	6	6	6	6	6	6	6	6	6	6	6	6		★	★	11	2	23	11	2
Hill	2	2	2	2	2	2	2	2	2	2	2	2¹	2	2	2	2	2	2	2	2	2	2	2	2	2	2	2	2	2	2	2	2	2	2	2			2	2¹	2			6	6	6	6	40	1	0
Hoyland	4¹	4	4	4	4	4	9	9	9	9	9	9	4	4	4¹	4	4¹	4	4¹	4	4	4	4¹	4	4	4	4	4	4¹	4			10	10	4	4	4	4	4	4	4¹	4					43	0	2
Hughes		1	1	1	1	1								1																																	44	1	8
Lee	7	7	7	7	7		7	7	7	7	7	7	7	7	7¹	7	7	7	7	7	7	7	★	7	7	7	7	7	7¹	7	7	7	7	7¹	7		★	11			11	11	7	7			7	0	0
McIlroy	10¹	10	10	10	10	10	10	10	10	10	10¹	10	10	10	10	10	10	10	10¹	10¹	10	10	10	10	10	10	10	10																			38	2	3
Parkinson																																			7¹	7	7	7	7	7					9	11	28	0	4
Pashley	3	3	3	3		3	3	3	3	3	3	3	3	3	3	3	3	3	3	3	3	3	3	3	3	3	3¹	3	3	3	3	3	3	3	3	3	3	3	3	3	3	3	3	3	3	3	8	0	1
Robinson	★		★		8¹	8	8¹	8²	8	8¹	8	8	8	8²	8¹	8	8¹	8	8²	8	8¹	8	8	8	8	8²	8	8¹	8	8¹	8	8	8	8²	8	8	8	8	8	8	8	8	8	8	8	8	46	0	1
Taylor		9¹	9	9	9	9	9	★	11		★				★		★	★	★		★²	9	9	9		★	9	9	9	9	9	9	9	9	9¹	9	9	9	9	9	9	9	★				41	2	19
Valentine	5	5	5	5	5	5	5	5	5	5	5	5	5	5	5	5	5	5	5	5	5¹	5	5	5	5		5	5	5	5¹	★	5	5	5	★		6	10	7	7	10	10					26	7	4
Walsh																																														★	40	2	2
																																																0	1	0
Own Goals																																			1														1

FA Cup: 1987-88: 1st Round: Scunthorpe U. (A) 1-3.

Littlewoods Cup: 1987-88: 1st Round: Preston N.E. (H) 2-2 (A) 3-2; 2nd Round: Sheffield U. (H) 2-1 (A) 1-1; 3rd Round: Q.P.R. (H) 1-0; 4th Round: Manchester U. (H) 1-2.

CAMBRIDGE UNITED (Division 4)

Team Manager   Chris Turner.
Club Address   Abbey Stadium, Newmarket Road, Cambridge. Tel: (0223) 241237.
Current Ground Capacity   10,150.
Record Attendance   14,000 v Chelsea, Friendly, 1 May 1970.
Year Formed   1919. Turned professional 1946.
Previous Names   Abbey United.
Club Nickname   "United".
Club Colours   Black and amber striped shirts, black shorts and stockings.
Club Honours   Football League: Div. 4 Champions 1976-77.
League History   1970-73 Div. 4; 1973-74 Div. 3; 1974-77 Div. 4; 1977-78 Div. 3; 1978-84 Div. 2; 1984-85 Div. 3; 1985- Div. 4.
Most League Points in a Season   (2 for a win) 65 in Div. 4, 1976-77. (3 for a win) 62 in Div. 4, 1986-87.
Most League Goals in a Season   87 in Div. 4, 1976-77.
Record Victory   6-0 v Darlington in Div. 4, 18 September 1971.

Record Defeat   0-6 v Aldershot in Div. 3, 13 April 1974 and v Darlington in Div. 4, 28 September 1974 and v Chelsea in Div. 2, 15 January 1983.
Consecutive League Wins   7 in 1977 and 1984.
Consecutive League Defeats   7 in 1983, 1984-85, 1985.
Record League Appearances   Steve Fallon, 410 between 1974-86.
Record League Goalscorer—Career   Alan Biley, 74 between 1975-86.
Record League Goalscorer—Season   David Crown, 24 in Div. 4, 1985-86.

Cambridge United: League Record, 1987-88 (Division 4)

Match Number	Date	Venue	Opponents	Result	H/T	Lge Posn	Attend
1	15.8.87	A	Exeter C.	L 0-3	0-2		2650
2	22.8.87	H	Crewe Alex.	W 4-1	2-1		1523
3	29.8.87	A	Peterborough U.	L 0-1	0-0	18	4623
4	1.9.87	H	Cardiff C.	D 0-0	0-0	18	2079
5	5.9.87	A	Torquay U.	W 1-0	0-0	13	2676
6	12.9.87	H	Scunthorpe U.	D 3-3	1-2	13	1830
7	16.9.87	A	Hartlepool U.	L 1-2	0-2	14	1376
8	19.9.87	A	Burnley	W 2-0	2-0	13	5789
9	26.9.87	H	Halifax T.	W 2-1	1-1	9	1805
10	29.9.87	H	Wrexham	L 0-1	0-0	13	2257
11	3.10.87	A	Swansea C.	D 1-1	1-0	12	3378
12	10.10.87	H	Newport Co.	W 4-0	1-0	9	1874
13	17.10.87	A	Leyton Orient	W 2-0	0-0	7	4059
14	20.10.87	A	Wolverhampton W.	L 0-3	0-3	11	6492
15	24.10.87	H	Colchester U.	L 0-1	0-0	14	2450
16	30.10.87	A	Tranmere Rov.	W 1-0	0-0	12	2240
17	3.11.87	H	Hereford U.	L 0-1	0-1	15	2257
18	8.11.87	A	Darlington	W 1-0	0-0	13	2463
19	20.11.87	H	Rochdale	L 1-2	1-2	11	2104
20	28.11.87	A	Bolton W.	D 2-2	1-1	13	4294
21	11.12.87	H	Stockport Co.	W 2-0	2-0	10	1475
22	18.12.87	A	Carlisle U.	L 1-2	0-2	12	1843
23	26.12.87	A	Halifax T.	D 1-1	1-1	13	1667
24	28.12.87	H	Scarborough	W 1-0	0-0	11	3243
25	1.1.88	H	Peterborough U.	L 1-3	0-2	13	3975
26	2.1.88	A	Scunthorpe U.	L 2-3	2-3	15	3253
27	16.1.88	H	Burnley	W 2-0	0-0	11	2148
28	30.1.88	A	Cardiff C.	L 0-4	0-3	13	4012
29	6.2.88	H	Torquay U.	W 1-0	0-0	13	1948
30	13.2.88	A	Scarborough	D 0-0	0-0	14	1879
31	19.2.88	H	Exeter C.	W 2-1	0-0	13	1878
32	27.2.88	H	Swansea C.	L 0-3	0-2	14	2080
33	1.3.88	A	Wrexham	L 0-3	0-2	14	1025
34	5.3.88	H	Leyton Orient	W 2-0	0-0	13	2500
35	12.3.88	A	Newport Co.	D 0-0	0-0	13	1208
36	19.3.88	H	Tranmere Rov.	D 1-1	1-0	13	1514
37	25.3.88	A	Colchester U.	D 0-0	0-0	15	2146
38	1.4.88	H	Darlington	W 1-0	1-0	14	2242
39	4.4.88	A	Rochdale	L 1-2	0-0	15	1596
40	10.4.88	H	Wolverhampton W.	D 1-1	0-0	15	5107
41	15.4.88	A	Crewe Alex.	D 0-0	0-0	15	1546
42	19.4.88	H	Hartlepool U.	D 1-1	0-1	15	1492
43	23.4.88	A	Hereford U.	L 0-1	0-1	15	1666
44	29.4.88	H	Bolton W.	D 2-2	1-1	17	2063
45	2.5.88	A	Stockport Co.	W 2-0	0-0	15	1842
46	7.5.88	H	Carlisle U.	L 1-2	1-0	15	1738

Players: League Record, 1987-88 (Division 4)

Match Number	1	2	3	4	5	6	7	8	9	10	11	12	13	14	15	16	17	18	19	20	21	22	23	24	25	26	27	28	29	30	31	32	33	34	35	36	37	38	39	40	41	42	43	44	45	46	Apps	Subs	Goals
Bastock																																				1	1	1	1	1	1	1	1	1	1	1	10	0	0
Beattie			4	4	4	4	4	4	4	4	4	4	4	4	4	4	4							6¹		★			5	5																	20	1	1
Beck	6	6	6	6	6	6¹		6	6	6	6¹	6		6	6	6	6	6	6	6		6	6		6	6	★	6	6	6	6	6	6	6	6	6	6	6	6								34	1	2
Benjamin									9	9	9	9	9¹	9	9¹	9	10	10	10	10	10	10	10	7	7	7	★			★			★	9	9	★	9										20	5	2
Branagan	1	1	1	1	1	1	1	1	1	1	1	1	1	1	1	1	1	1	1	1	1	1	1	1	1	1	1	1	1	1	1	1	1	1		1	1	1									35	0	0
Brattan	★				7	7	6				7	11	11	6																																	7	1	0
Bull																																						7	7	7	7	7	7	7¹	7¹	7¹	9	0	3
Butler	7	7	7	7	7			7	7	7	7¹		7¹	7	7	7	7	7	7	7	7¹	7	7¹	7	7	7	7	7	7	7¹	7	7															26	0	5
Casey																									1																						1	0	0
Chapple																																	★	★			5	5	5¹	5							4	2	1
Clayton	8	8¹	8	8	8	8	8	8	8	8	8	8	8	8	8¹	8	8	8		8	8	8	8	8	8¹	8	8	8	8	8¹	8	8	8	8	8	8	8	8¹	8	8	8	8	8	8	8	8	45	;0	5
Crowe	4	4									5	5	5	5	4	4	4	4	4	4	4	4	4	4	4	4	4	4	4	4	4	4															27	0	0
Crown	10	10³	10	10	10¹	10	10	10¹	10	10²	10	10	10¹	10	10	10	10																														17	0	8
Ebanks	2	2	2		★																																										3	1	0
Fuccillo																									★	6	10	10	10	10	10	10	10	10	10	10¹	10	10	10¹	10	10	10					18	1	2
Goble																													6	★																	1	1	0
Hamilton																																		11¹	11	11	11	11	11	11	11	11					9	0	1
Hildersley																									11	11¹	11	11	11¹	11	11	11¹	11	11													9	0	3
Hollis																																		11				2	2								3	0	0
Horwood	9	★			★		★									★¹		★	★			9¹	★	★		★	9																				4	10	2
Kimble, A.	3	3	3	3	3	3	3	★				★¹	6		★	11	★	11	11		3	3	3	3	3	3	3	3	3	3	3	3	3	3	3	3	3	3	3	3	3	3	3¹	3	3		37	4	2
Kimble, G.	11	11	11	11	11	11	11	11	11	11	11																																				12	0	0
Lawrence																										★	9	9	9	9	9	9	9	9	9	9	9		★								11	2	0
Murray							3	3	3	3	3	3	3	3	3	3	3	3																													13	0	0
Neal																							9	9	9	9																					4	0	0
Poole					2	2	2	2	2	2	2	2	2	2	2		2	2	2	2	2	2	2	2	2	2	2	2	2	2	2	2	2	2	2	2	2	2	2		★	2	2	2	2		41	1	0
Pugh																							11	11	11¹	11	11	11																			6	0	1
Purdie													11	11	11		11	11	10¹	10¹	10																										7	0	2
Rigby		9	9	9	9	9²	9	9²	9	9	9	9	9	9	9	9	★	10																7	7¹	7	7										19	1	5
Ryan																																													9	9	2	0	0
Sayer																									9	★		★	7		★																2	3	0
Smith	5	5	5	5	5	5		5	5	5	5¹	5	5	5	5	5	5	5	4	4	4¹	4	5	5	5¹	5¹	5	5	5		5	5	5¹	5	5	5	5	5				4	4				42	0	5
Turner							6					★		6	★	★	8	★	★		6	★																★		6	6	6					7	6	0
Williams																																						★		9							1	0	0

FA Cup: 1987-88: 1st Round: Farnborough (H) 2-1; 2nd Round: Yeovil T. (H) 0-1.
Littlewoods Cup: 1987-88: 1st Round: Aldershot (H) 1-1 (A) 4-1; 2nd Round: Coventry C. (H) 0-1 (A) 1-2.

CARDIFF CITY (Division 3)

Team Manager Frank Burrows.
Club Address Ninian Park, Cardiff CF1 8SX. Tel: (0222) 398636/7/8.
Current Ground Capacity 42,000.
Record Attendance 61,566 Wales v England, 14 October 1961.
Year Formed 1899. Turned professional 1910.
Previous Names Riverside, Riverside Albion, Cardiff.
Club Nickname "The Bluebirds".
Club Colours Royal blue shirts and stockings and white shorts.
Club Honours Football League: Div. 3(S) Champions 1946-47. FA Cup: Winners 1927.
League History 1920-21 Div. 2; 1921-29 Div. 1; 1929-31 Div. 2; 1931-47 Div. 3(S); 1947-52 Div. 2; 1952-57 Div. 1; 1957-60 Div. 2; 1960-62 Div. 1; 1962-75 Div. 2; 1975-76 Div. 3; 1976-82 Div. 2; 1982-83 Div. 3, 1983-85 Div. 2; 1985-86 Div. 3; 1986-88 Div. 4; 1988- Div. 3.
Most League Points in a Season (2 for a win) 66 in Div. 3(S), 1946-47. (3 for a win) 86 in Div. 3, 1982-83.
Most League Goals in a Season 93 in Div. 3(S), 1946-47.

Record Victory 9-2 v Thames in Div. 3(S), 6 February 1932.
Record Defeat 2-11 v Sheffield U. in Div. 1, 1 January 1926.
Consecutive League Wins 9 in 1946.
Consecutive League Defeats 7 in 1933.
Record League Appearances Phil Dwyer, 471 between 1972-85.
Record League Goalscorer—Career Len Davies, 128 between 1920-31.
Record League Goalscorer—Season Stan Richards, 31 in Div. 3(S), 1946-47.

Cardiff City: League Record, 1987-88 (Division 4)

Match Number	Date	Venue	Opponents	Result		H/T	Lge Posn	Attend
1	15.8.87	H	Leyton Orient	D	1-1	1-1		3357
2	22.8.87	A	Bolton W.	L	0-1	0-1		4530
3	29.8.87	H	Swansea C.	W	1-0	0-0	13	6010
4	1.9.87	A	Cambridge U.	D	0-0	0-0	13	2079
5	5.9.87	H	Wolverhampton W.	W	3-2	1-1	10	2258
6	12.9.87	A	Wrexham	L	0-3	0-0	15	2212
7	15.9.87	H	Darlington	W	3-1	1-0	18	2201
8	19.9.87	H	Carlisle U.	W	4-2	1-2	7	2659
9	25.9.87	A	Tranmere Rov.	W	1-0	0-0	3	2543
10	29.9.87	H	Halifax T.	D	0-0	0-0	4	3666
11	2.10.87	H	Stockport Co.	W	1-0	1-0	2	2332
12	10.10.87	H	Hereford U.	L	0-1	0-0	4	4420
13	17.10.87	A	Peterborough U.	L	3-4	2-1	9	3473
14	20.10.87	H	Torquay U.	W	2-1	0-1	6	3503
15	24.10.87	A	Scunthorpe U.	L	1-2	0-2	9	2872
16	31.10.87	H	Rochdale	W	1-0	0-0	7	3046
17	4.11.87	A	Scarborough	D	1-1	1-1	8	2599
18	7.11.87	H	Exeter C.	W	3-2	1-1	5	3474
19	21.11.87	H	Newport Co.	W	2-1	0-0	2	4022
20	28.11.87	H	Hartlepool U.	D	1-1	0-1	3	3232
21	12.12.87	A	Crewe Alex.	D	0-0	0-0	4	2010
22	19.12.87	H	Burnley	W	2-1	0-0	4	3401
23	26.12.87	H	Tranmere Rov.	W	3-0	1-0	3	5233
24	28.12.87	A	Colchester U.	L	1-2	1-1	4	2599
25	1.1.88	A	Swansea C.	D	2-2	0-0	4	10300
26	16.1.88	A	Carlisle U.	D	0-0	0-0	6	2344
27	30.1.88	H	Cambridge U.	W	4-0	3-0	3	4012
28	2.2.88	A	Darlington	D	0-0	0-0	3	2332
29	6.2.88	A	Wolverhampton W.	W	4-1	0-0	2	9077
30	13.2.88	H	Colchester U.	W	1-0	0-0	2	5458
31	20.2.88	A	Leyton Orient	L	1-4	1-1	2	3523
32	27.2.88	H	Stockport Co.	D	0-0	0-0	2	4008
33	1.3.88	A	Halifax T.	W	1-0	0-0	2	1128
34	4.3.88	H	Peterborough U.	D	0-0	0-0	2	4172
35	13.3.88	A	Hereford U.	W	2-1	1-1	2	3210
36	16.3.88	H	Wrexham	D	1-1	0-1	2	4083
37	26.3.88	H	Scunthorpe U.	L	0-1	0-0	3	4527
38	29.3.88	A	Rochdale	D	2-2	0-1	2	1435
39	2.4.88	A	Exeter C.	W	2-0	2-0	2	2649
40	4.4.88	H	Newport Co.	W	4-0	1-0	2	6536
41	9.4.88	A	Torquay U.	L	0-2	0-2	2	3082
42	15.4.88	H	Bolton W.	W	1-0	0-0	2	6703
43	23.4.88	H	Scarborough	W	2-0	1-0	2	5751
44	30.4.88	A	Hartlepool U.	W	1-0	1-0	2	1097
45	2.5.88	H	Crewe Alex.	W	2-0	0-0	2	10125
46	7.5.88	A	Burnley	W	2-1	0-0	2	8525

Players: League Record, 1987-88 (Division 4)

Match Number	1	2	3	4	5	6	7	8	9	10	11	12	13	14	15	16	17	18	19	20	21	22	23	24	25	26	27	28	29	30	31	32	33	34	35	36	37	38	39	40	41	42	43	44	45	46	Apps	Subs	Goals
Abrahams						5	5¹																																								2	0	1
Bartlett		★			8¹	8	8²	8	8	8	8¹	8	★			★		★	11	8		★		★	11	11¹	11	11	11	11¹		11¹	11	11¹	11	11	11¹	11²	11	11	11	11	11	11¹	11		30	7	12
Bater					3	3	2	2		2	2	2	2	2	2	2	2	2	2	2	2	2	2	2	2	2	2	2	2	2	2	2	2	2	2	2	2	2	2	2	2	2	2	2	2	2	40	0	0
Boyle	6	6	6	6	6¹	6	6	6¹	6	6	6	6	6	6	6	6	6¹	6	6	6	6	6	6	6	6	6¹	6	6	6	6	6	6	6	6	6	6	6	6	6	6	6	6	6	6	6	6	46	0	4
Curtis	7	7	7	7	7	7	7	7	7	7	7	7	7			7	7	7	7			7	7	7	7	7	7	7	7			7	7	7	7	7	7	7	7¹	7	7	7	7¹	7	7	7¹	40	0	2
Endersby																				1	1	1	1	1																							4	0	0
Ford	3	3	3	3	2	2	2	3¹	3	2	3	11	11²	11¹	11	5	4	8	8	8	5	8	8	8	8¹	8	8	8	8	8¹	8	8	8	8	8	8	8	8	8	8¹	8	8		4	4	8	45	0	7
Gilligan	9¹	9	9¹	9	9	9	9	9¹	9	9	9	9	9	9¹	9	9¹	9	9²	9	9	9	9²	9²	9	9	9	9²	9	9	9	9²	9	9	9	9¹	9¹	9	9	9	9	9	9¹	9	9¹	9	9¹	46	0	19
Gummer	4																																														1	0	0
Judge													★			1	1	1	1	1		1	1	1																							1	1	0
Kelly	11	11	11	11	11	11	11	11	11	11		★	5	5	11	11	★	5	5	11		★	★	11¹	★				3	3	3	3	3	★		★		★	10	10	10	10	4				28	8	1
McDermott	10	10	10	10	10¹	10	10	10	10	10	10	10	10¹	10	10	10	10	10	10¹	10	10	10	10	10	10	10	10	10¹	10	10	10	10	10	10	10	10	10	10	10	10	10¹	10		8¹	8	8¹	10	45	0	7
Mardenborough	★		2	2	4						8	8	8	8		★	★	★	7	7					★	★		★	★		★					★			★	★		9	12	0
Moseley	1	1	1	1	1	1	1	1	1	1	1	1																																			13	0	0
Perry	2	2			5																																										3	0	0
Platnaeur		4	4	4	3			5	5	3	11	3	3	3	3	3	3	3	3	3¹	3	3	3	3	3	3	3	3	3							3	3	3	3	3	3	3	3	3	3	38	0	1
Roberts																														1	1	1	1	1	1	1											8	0	0
Sanderson	8	8	8	8	★	★		★		★	★	★	★	★¹		11	11		★			★	★		★			★	7	7																	8	0	1
Stevenson	5	5	5	5				5	5		5	5		★	5	5			5	5	5	5	5	5	5	5	5	5	5	5	5	5	5	5	5	5	5	5¹	5	5	5	5	5	5	5	5	35	1	1
Walsh																													★	11						★	★	★	★								1	5	0
Wheeler		★							★					★	7	7				11	11	11	★	11		★															★			★	★		6	10	0
Wimbleton					4	4	4¹	4¹	4	4	4	4	4		4¹	4	4	4	4¹	4	4	4	4¹	4	4	4¹	4	4²	4	4	4	4	4	4	4	4	4¹	4	4	4							37	0	9
Wood																									1	1	1	1	1														1	1	1	1	1	1	1	1	13	0	0
Own Goals																														1																			1

FA Cup: 1987-88: 1st Round: Peterborough U. (A) 1-2.
Littlewoods Cup: 1987-88: 1st Round: Newport Co. (A) 1-2 (H) 2-2.

CARLISLE UNITED (Division 4)

Team Manager   Clive Middlemass.
Club Address   Brunton Park, Carlisle CA1 1LL. Tel: (0228) 26237.
Current Ground Capacity   18,035.
Record Attendance   27,500 v Birmingham C., FA Cup 3rd Round, 5 January 1957 and v Middlesbrough, FA Cup 5th Round, 7 February 1970.
Year Formed   1904. Turned professional 1921.
Previous Names   None.
Club Nickname   "The Cumbrians" or "Blues".
Club Colours   Blue shirts with white pinstripe and red and white trim, white shorts and blue stockings.
Club Honours   Football League: Div. 3 Champions 1964-65.
League History   1928-58 Div. 3(N); 1958-62 Div. 4; 1962-63 Div. 3; 1963-64 Div. 4; 1964-65 Div. 3; 1965-74 Div. 2; 1974-75 Div. 1; 1975-77 Div. 2; 1977-82 Div. 3; 1982-86 Div. 2; 1986-87 Div. 3; 1987- Div. 4.
Most League Points in a Season   (2 for a win) 62 in Div. 3(N), 1950-51. (3 for a win) 80 in Div. 3, 1981-82.

Most League Goals in a Season   113 in Div. 4, 1963-64.
Record Victory   8-0 v Hartlepool U. in Div. 3(N), 1 September 1928 and v Scunthorpe U. in Div. 3(N), 25 December 1952.
Record Defeat   1-11 v Hull C. in Div. 3(N), 14 January 1939.
Consecutive League Wins   6 in 1937 and 1981-82.
Consecutive League Defeats   8 in 1935.
Record League Appearances   Alan Ross, 466 between 1963-79.
Record League Goalscorer—Career   Jimmy McConnell, 126 between 1928-32.
Record League Goalscorer—Season   Jimmy McConnell, 42 in Div. 3(N), 1928-29.

Carlisle United: League Record, 1987-88 (Division 4)

Match Number	Date	Venue	Opponents	Result		H/T	Lge Posn	Attend
1	15.8.87	A	Peterborough U.	L	0-1	0-1		4000
2	22.8.87	H	Scunthorpe U.	W	3-1	0-0		2074
3	29.8.87	A	Burnley	L	3-4	1-3	17	5781
4	31.8.87	H	Hereford U.	W	3-1	1-1	7	2708
5	4.9.87	A	Stockport Co.	L	0-3	0-1	16	2257
6	12.9.87	H	Hartlepool U.	L	1-3	0-2	20	2463
7	16.9.87	A	Exeter C.	D	1-1	1-1	20	3347
8	19.9.87	A	Cardiff C.	L	2-4	2-1	21	2659
9	26.9.87	H	Scarborough	W	4-0	1-0	18	2693
10	29.9.87	H	Darlington	D	3-3	2-2	19	2996
11	3.10.87	A	Rochdale	W	2-1	0-0	16	1940
12	10.10.87	H	Wolverhampton W.	L	0-1	0-1	18	2620
13	17.10.87	A	Bolton W.	L	0-5	0-2	18	4184
14	20.10.87	A	Colchester U.	L	0-1	0-0	19	1328
15	24.10.87	H	Tranmere Rov.	W	3-2	1-2	20	2160
16	31.10.87	A	Crewe Alex.	L	1-4	0-3	20	2124
17	3.11.87	H	Leyton Orient	L	1-2	1-1	20	2139
18	7.11.87	H	Newport Co.	W	3-1	2-0	20	1766
19	21.11.87	A	Wrexham	L	0-4	0-1	21	1485
20	28.11.87	H	Torquay U.	D	3-3	3-2	20	2017
21	12.12.87	A	Swansea C.	L	1-3	0-1	21	3876
22	18.12.87	H	Cambridge U.	W	2-1	2-0	20	1843
23	26.12.87	A	Scarborough.	L	1-3	0-1	20	3261
24	1.1.88	H	Burnley	L	3-4	2-2	21	4262
25	2.1.88	A	Hartlepool U.	D	0-0	0-0	21	3135
26	9.1.88	A	Darlington	L	1-2	0-1	21	2517
27	16.1.88	H	Cardiff C.	D	0-0	0-0	21	2344
28	23.1.88	H	Exeter C.	D	0-0	0-0	21	1699
29	30.1.88	A	Hereford U.	L	0-2	0-1	23	1904
30	6.2.88	A	Stockport Co.	W	2-0	1-0	22	1852
31	20.2.88	H	Peterborough U.	L	0-2	0-2	23	2026
32	27.2.88	H	Rochdale	W	2-0	2-0	22	1983
33	5.3.88	H	Bolton W.	L	0-1	0-1	23	2796
34	12.3.88	A	Wolverhampton W.	L	1-3	0-1	23	9262
35	19.3.88	H	Crewe Alex.	L	0-1	0-1	23	1834
36	25.3.88	A	Tranmere Rov.	L	0-3	0-2	23	3093
37	2.4.88	A	Newport Co.	W	2-1	2-1	23	1376
38	4.4.88	H	Wrexham	L	0-4	0-2	23	2284
39	9.4.88	A	Leyton Orient	L	1-4	0-2	23	2861
40	12.4.88	A	Scunthorpe U.	L	0-1	0-0	23	3514
41	19.4.88	H	Halifax T.	D	1-1	0-0	23	1517
42	23.4.88	H	Colchester U.	W	4-0	2-0	23	1496
43	26.4.88	A	Halifax T.	D	1-1	0-0	23	1002
44	30.4.88	A	Torquay U.	L	0-1	0-1	23	3537
45	2.5.88	H	Swansea C.	L	0-1	0-1	23	1854
46	7.5.88	A	Cambridge U.	W	2-1	0-1	23	1738

Players: League Record, 1987-88 (Division 4)

Match Number	1	2	3	4	5	6	7	8	9	10	11	12	13	14	15	16	17	18	19	20	21	22	23	24	25	26	27	28	29	30	31	32	33	34	35	36	37	38	39	40	41	42	43	44	45	46	Apps	Subs	Goals
Bishop	10	10	10	10	10	10	10¹	10¹	10	10	10¹	10	10			10	10	10																				7	7	7	7	7	7	7	7	7	24	0	3
Carter																																		1	1	1	1									4	0	0
Clark	★	3	3	7	7	7	7	7	7	7¹	7	7		7	7	7	7	7		7	7	7	7	7		9	9	2	3	3	3	2	3	2	3	2	2	2	2	10	2	10	3				40	1	1
Cooke	8	8	8¹	8¹	8	8	8	8	8	8	8	8	8	8	8¹	8	8	8¹	8	8	8	8	8	8	8	8	8		8	7	7	7	7	7					★	11¹	11						36	1	5
Crompton	1	1	1	1	1	1	1	1	1			1	1																																		10	0	0
Fulbrook											3				3	3	10	3	3																												6	0	0
Fyfe																																	★	★	★	★		★¹	8²	8	8	8	8¹				5	5	4
Gorman	4	4	4	4	4	4	4	4					7	3	4		★	★	4	4			6	6	2	2	2	2	2	9	2	2	9			3	3	3	3	3	3	3	10				35	2	0
Halpin																					10	10¹	10	10¹	10	10	10	10	10	10	10	10	10	10	10	10	10	10	10	10¹		10					23	0	3
Hampton																					3	3	3	3	3	3	3	3	3				3		3												12	0	0
Harbach			★	★		★		★							★	★				★																											0	7	0
Harrison														6	★																																1	1	0
Hetherington	11	11¹	11	11¹	11	11	11	11	11¹	11¹	11	11		11	11	11¹	11¹	11¹	11¹	11¹	11	11	11	11	★		★	11	★	8	11	11			11	11	11	★	★	★			11¹				31	6	10
Holdsworth																									9	9¹	9	9								★											4	0	1
Houston												★	6	6¹	4	4	4	10	10		★						★		★						★			★				★	11	★			8	8	1
Hutchinson																									7	7	7	7	4	★	8¹	8	8	8	8	8¹	8	8									12	1	2
McCaffery			3	3	3	3	3	3	3		3	3		3			2	2	2	2	2	2	2						★													4					14	0	0
McNeil	3			3	3	3	3	3	3	3			3				2	2	2	2	2	2	2		★																						18	1	0
Mills																													★																		0	1	0
Ogley																																			2							4	4			3	0	0
Patterson	2	2	2	2	2	2	2	2	2	2	2	2	2	2	2	2																															16	0	0
Poskett	9	9	9²	9¹	9	9	9	9	9	9¹	9¹	9²	9	9	9	9	9	9	9¹	9	9	★¹	11¹	11	11				11	11	11			9²	9	9	9	9	9	9	9	9	9				38	1	12
Prudhoe														1	1	1	1	1	1	1	1	1	1	1	1	1	1	1	1	1							1	1	1	1	1	1	1				22	0	0
Robertson																	★																	2						2			2	2		4	1	0
Robinson	7	7¹	7			★	4	4	4	4	4	4	★		2	3	7	7¹	4¹	4	4	4	4	4	4	4	4		8	8	★						6	6	6	6	6	6	6	6			32	3	3
Rowell																																			7	7	11	11	11	11	11						7	0	0
Saddington																														4	4	4	4	4	4	4	4	4	4	4	4	4¹	4				13	0	1
Saunders	6	6	6	6	6	6	6	6¹	6¹	6	6			6	6	6¹	6	6	6	6¹		6	6	6	6	6	6¹																				25	0	5
Stephens																					9	9¹	9	9¹	9																			★			5	1	2
Taylor										1	1	1	1	1				1	1	1	1	1																									10	0	0
Tynan												★	10	10					★		★																										2	3	0
Wright	5	5	5	5	5	5	5	5	5¹	5	5	5	5	5	5	5	5	5	5	5	5	5	5	5	5	5¹	5	5	5¹	5	5¹	5	5	5	5	5	5	5	5	5	5	5	5	5	5	5	46	0	3
Own Goals			1																																														1

FA Cup: 1987-88: 1st Round: Macclesfield (A) 2-4.

Littlewoods Cup: 1987-88: 1st Round: Stockport Co (A) 1-0 (H) 3-0; 2nd Round: Oldham Ath (H) 4-3 (A) 1-4.

CHARLTON ATHLETIC (Division 1)

Team Manager Lennie Lawrence.
Club Address Selhurst Park, London SE25 6PH. Tel: 01-771 6321.
Current Ground Capacity 36,000.
Record Attendance 75,031 v Aston Villa, FA Cup 5th Round, 12 February 1938 (at the Valley).
Year Formed 1905. Turned professional 1920.
Previous Names None.
Club Nickname "The Haddicks", "Robins", or "Valiants".
Club Colours Red shirts, white shorts and black stockings.
Club Honours Football League: Div. 3(S) Champions 1928-29, 1934-35. FA Cup: Winners 1947.
League History 1921-29 Div. 3(S); 1929-33 Div.2; 1933-35 Div. 3(S); 1935-36 Div. 2; 1936-57 Div. 1; 1957-72 Div. 2; 1972-75 Div. 3; 1975-80 Div. 2; 1980-81 Div. 3; 1981-86 Div. 2; 1986- Div. 1.
Most League Points in a Season (2 for a win) 61 in Div. 3(S), 1934-35. (3 for a win) 77 in Div. 2, 1985-86.

Most League Goals in a Season 107 in Div. 2, 1957-58.
Record Victory 8-1 v Middlesbrough in Div. 1, 12 September 1953.
Record Defeat 1-11 v Aston Villa in Div. 2, 14 November 1959.
Consecutive League Wins 7 in 1980.
Consecutive League Defeats 9 in 1957.
Record League Appearances Sam Bartram, 583 between 1934-56.
Record League Goalscorer—Career Stuart Leary, 153 between 1951-62.
Record League Goalscorer—Season Ralph Allen, 32 in Div. 3(S), 1934-35.

Charlton Athletic: League Record, 1987-88 (Division 1)

Match Number	Date	Venue	Opponents	Result		H/T	Lge Posn	Attend
1	15.8.87	H	Nottingham F.	L	1-2	1-0		6021
2	29.8.87	H	Manchester U.	L	1-3	0-3		14046
3	1.9.87	A	Wimbledon	L	1-4	1-1	21	5184
4	5.9.87	H	Q.P.R.	L	0-1	0-1	21	7726
5	12.9.87	A	Portsmouth	D	1-1	0-1	21	13136
6	15.9.87	A	Liverpool	L	2-3	1-1	21	36637
7	19.9.87	H	Luton T.	W	1-0	1-0	20	5003
8	26.9.87	A	Sheffield Wed.	L	0-2	0-2	21	16850
9	3.10.87	H	Arsenal	L	0-3	0-1	21	15326
10	10.10.87	A	West Ham U.	D	1-1	1-1	21	15757
11	17.10.87	H	Derby Co.	L	0-1	0-1	21	5432
12	24.10.87	A	Oxford U.	L	1-2	0-0	21	7325
13	31.10.87	H	Southampton	D	1-1	0-1	21	5158
14	7.11.87	A	Norwich C.	W	2-0	2-0	21	5044
15	14.11.87	A	Watford	L	1-2	0-1	21	12093
16	21.11.87	H	Coventry C.	D	2-2	1-0	21	4936
17	28.11.87	A	Newcastle U.	L	1-2	1-1	21	19453
18	5.12.87	H	Everton	D	0-0	0-0	21	7208
19	13.12.87	A	Tottenham H.	W	1-0	0-0	21	20392
20	20.12.87	H	Chelsea	D	2-2	0-1	21	10893
21	26.12.87	H	Portsmouth	W	2-1	1-1	19	6686
22	28.12.87	A	Luton T.	L	0-1	0-1	20	7243
23	1.1.88	A	Manchester U.	D	0-0	0-0	20	37257
24	16.1.88	A	Nottingham F	D	2-2	0-0	21	15363
25	23.1.88	H	Liverpool	L	0-2	0-1	21	28095
26	6.2.88	H	Q.P.R.	L	0-2	0-1	21	11512
27	13.2.88	H	Wimbledon	D	1-1	1-0	21	5520
28	20.2.88	H	Sheffield Wed.	W	3-1	3-0	20	4517
29	27.2.88	A	Arsenal	L	0-4	0-1	20	25394
30	5.3.88	A	Derby Co.	D	1-1	0-1	20	16139
31	12.3.88	H	West Ham U.	W	3-0	2-0	19	8118
32	19.3.88	A	Southampton	W	1-0	0-0	18	12103
33	26.3.88	H	Oxford U.	D	0-0	0-0	18	6245
34	2.4.88	A	Norwich C.	L	0-2	0-0	19	15015
35	4.4.88	H	Watford	W	1-0	1-0	18	6196
36	9.4.88	A	Coventry C.	D	0-0	0-0	18	14313
37	23.4.88	H	Newcastle U.	W	2-0	2-0	18	7402
38	30.4.88	A	Everton	D	1-1	0-0	17	20372
39	2.5.88	H	Tottenham H.	D	1-1	0-0	17	13977
40	7.5.88	A.	Chelsea	D	1-1	0-1	17	33701

Players: League Record, 1987-88 (Division 1)

Match Number	1	2	3	4	5	6	7	8	9	10	11	12	13	14	15	16	17	18	19	20	21	22	23	24	25	26	27	28	29	30	31	32	33	34	35	36	37	38	39	40	Apps	Subs	Goals
Bennett			★					★						7[1]	7	7	7				★	★	7	7	7	7									★	★	★	9			9	7	1
Bolder	1	1	1						1	1	1	1	1	1	1	1	1	1	1	1	1	1	1	1	1	1	1	1	1	1	1	1	1	1	1	1	1	1	1	1	35	0	0
Campbell										10	10	10	8	8	8	8	8	8	8[1]	8	8	8	8	8	8	8	8	8		10											21	0	1
Crooks	11	11	11	11	11	11[1]	11[1]		11	11[1]	11	11			★					★	★	★	11[2]	11	11	11[2]	11[1]	11	11	11	11	11	11[2]	11	11	11					24	4	10
Gritt	★	★			★	4	3	3					3	4	4	4	4	4	4	4		★	★				9	9	9	9	9	9	9	9	9	9					22	5	0
Humphrey	2	2	2	2	2	2	2	2	2	2	2	2	2	2	2	2	2	2	2	2	2	2	2	2	2	2	2	2	2	2	2	2	2	2	2	2	2	2	2	2	40	0	0
Johns				1	1	1	1	1																																	5	0	0
Jones									9	9	9	9	★[1]	9	9[1]	9	9[1]	9[1]	10	10	10	9[1]	9	9	9[1]	9	9	9	9												21	4	6
Leaburn																							★	★	8	8	8	8	8	8	8	8	8	8	8						10	2	0
Lee		★	7					7	7	8	7						★	10	10[1]	10	10	10	10	10	10	10	10	10		10[1]	10	10	10	10	10						22	1	2
Mackenzie	4	4	10	10	10	10	10	10			★			11	11		11		7	4	4	4	4	4	4	4	4[1]	4	4	4	4	4	4	4	4	4[1]	4	4			31	1	2
Melrose	9	9	9																																						3	0	0
Miller			6	4	6	6	6	6	6	★	6	6						★	8	6	6	6	6	6	6	6	6	6	6	6[1]											21	2	1
Milne	★		7	7	7	7	8	8		7	7				11																					★					9	1	0
Mortimer									3	3			11	11	11		11	11	11	11	11	11													★					11	1	0
Peake	7	10	7	4		4	4	4	4	4	4	4		★	7	7	7																								15	1	0
Pender	6		6																																						2	0	0
Reid	3[1]	3	3	3	3			3	3	3	3		11	3	3	3	3	3	3	3	3	3	3	3[1]	3	3	3[1]	3	3	3	3	3	3	3[1]	3						36	0	4
Shirtliff				5	5	5	5	5	5	5	5	5	5	5	5	5	5	5[1]	5[1]	5	5	5	5	5	5	5	5	5		5	5	5	5	5	5						36	0	2
Stuart	8	8[1]	8[1]	8	8[1]	8	8		10	7	8	8		★	★[1]	★		★[1]	11	7			7	7	7	7[1]	7	7	7	7	7	7	7	7	7						27	4	6
Thompson	5	5	5						6	6			6	6	6	6	6	6	6	6	6	6	6	6	6	6	6	6	6		5										23	0	0
Walsh	10			9	9[1]	9	11		9	10[1]	10	10[1]	10	10													★				★	★	★								11	0	3
Williams		★	9		★							9	9	9	10	10									★					★	★	★									6	6	0

FA Cup: 1987-88: 3rd Round: West Ham U (A) 0-2.
Littlewoods Cup: 1987-88: 2nd Round: Walsall (H) 3-0 (A)0-2; 2nd Round: Bradford C (H) 0-1.

CHELSEA (Division 2)

Team Manager   Bobby Campbell.
Club Address   Stamford Bridge, London SW6. Tel: 01-385 5545/6.
Current Ground Capacity   43,900.
Record Attendance   82,905 v Arsenal, Div. 1, 12 October 1935.
Year Formed   1905. Turned professional 1905.
Previous Names   None.
Club Nickname   "The Blues".
Club Colours   All royal blue.
Club Honours   Football League: Div. 1 Champions 1954-55. Div. 2 Champions 1983-84. FA Cup: Winners 1970. Football League Cup: Winners 1965. European Cup-winners Cup: Winners 1970-71.
League History   1905-07 Div. 2; 1907-10 Div. 1; 1910-12 Div. 2; 1912-24 Div. 1; 1924-30 Div. 2; 1930-62 Div. 1; 1962-63 Div. 2; 1963-75 Div. 1; 1975-77 Div. 2; 1977-79 Div. 1; 1979-84 Div. 2; 1984-88 Div. 1; 1988- Div. 2.
Most League Points in a Season   (2 for a win) 57 in Div 2, 1906-07. (3 for a win) 88 in Div. 2, 1983-84.

Most League Goals in a Season   98 in Div. 1, 1960-61.
Record Victory   13-0 v Jeunesse Hautcharage, European Cup-winners Cup 1st Round, 29 September 1971.
Record Defeat   1-8 v Wolverhampton W. in Div. 1, 26 September 1953.
Consecutive League Wins   8 in 1927.
Consecutive League Defeats   7 in 1952.
Record League Appearances   Ron Harris, 655 between 1962-80.
Record League Goalscorer—Career   Bobby Tambling, 164 between 1958-70.
Record League Goalscorer—Season   Jimmy Greaves, 41 in 1960-61.

Chelsea: League Record, 1987-88 (Division 1)

Match Number	Date	Venue	Opponents	Result		H/T	Lge Posn	Attend
1	5.8.87	H	Sheffield Wed.	W	2-1	1-0		21929
2	8.8.87	A	Portsmouth	W	3-0	1-0		16917
3	2.8.87	A	Tottenham H.	L	0-1	0-0	3	37079
4	9.8.87	H	Luton T.	W	3-0	1-0	3	16075
5	1.8.87	A	Manchester U.	L	1-3	1-1	4	46478
6	5.9.87	H	Nottingham F.	W	4-3	1-3	3	18414
7	12.9.87	A	Q.P.R.	L	1-3	0-0	5	22583
8	19.9.87	H	Norwich C.	W	1-0	1-0	3	15242
9	26.9.87	A	Watford	W	3-0	1-0	2	16213
10	3.10.87	H	Newcastle U.	D	2-2	2-1	4	22071
11	10.10.87	A	Everton	L	1-4	0-2	7	32004
12	17.10.87	H	Coventry C.	W	1-0	0-0	5	16699
13	24.10.87	A	Southampton	L	0-3	0-0	7	11890
14	31.10.87	H	Oxford U.	W	2-1	0-1	6	15027
15	3.11.87	A	Arsenal	L	1-3	1-2	6	40230
16	22.11.87	A	Derby Co.	L	0-2	0-0	7	18644
17	28.11.87	H	Wimbledon	D	1-1	0-0	7	15608
18	6.12.87	A	Liverpool	L	1-2	1-0	7	31211
19	12.12.87	H	West Ham U.	D	1-1	0-1	7	22850
20	20.12.87	A	Charlton Ath.	D	2-2	1-0	8	10893

Match Number	Date	Venue	Opponents	Result		H/T	Lge Posn	Attend
21	26.12.87	H	Q.P.R.	D	1-1	0-0	8	18020
22	28.12.87	A	Norwich C.	L	0-3	0-0	8	19668
23	1.1.88	A	Luton T.	L	0-3	0-1	11	8018
24	2.1.88	H	Tottenham H.	D	0-0	0-0	11	29317
25	16.1.88	A	Sheffield Wed.	L	1-3	0-1	13	19859
26	23.1.88	H	Portsmouth	D	0-0	0-0	13	15856
27	6.2.88	A	Nottingham F.	L	2-3	0-1	14	18203
28	13.2.88	H	Manchester U.	L	1-2	0-0	14	25014
29	27.2.88	A	Newcastle U.	L	1-3	0-2	15	17858
30	5.3.88	H	Coventry C.	D	3-3	3-2	16	16816
31	12.3.88	H	Everton	D	0-0	0-0	16	17390
32	19.3.88	A	Oxford U.	D	4-4	3-0	17	8468
33	26.3.88	H	Southampton	L	0-1	0-0	17	15380
34	29.3.88	H	Watford	D	1-1	0-1	17	11240
35	2.4.88	H	Arsenal	D	1-1	0-0	16	26084
36	9.4.88	H	Derby Co.	W	1-0	1-0	15	16996
37	23.4.88	A	Wimbledon	D	2-2	0-1	16	15128
38	30.4.88	H	Liverpool	D	1-1	0-0	16	35625
39	2.5.88	A	West Ham U.	L	1-4	0-2	18	28521
40	7.5.88	H	Charlton	D	1-1	1-0	18	33701

Players: League Record, 1987-88 (Division 1)

Match Number	1	2	3	4	5	6	7	8	9	10	11	12	13	14	15	16	17	18	19	20	21	22	23	24	25	26	27	28	29	30	31	32	33	34	35	36	37	38	39	40	Apps	Subs	Goals
Bodley						4	4	4	4											4¹										6											6	0	1
Bumstead																					6	6	6	6	6	6			11	11	11¹	11	11	11	11	11	11	11	8		17	0	1
Clarke	2	2	2	2		2¹	2	2	2	2	2	2	2	2	2	2	2	2	2	2		4	4	4	4	2	2	2	5	2	2	2	2	2	6	6	6	6	2		38	0	1
Coady					11¹	11				★	★		★			9	9			★		★																			4	6	1
Digweed																									1	1	1														3	0	0
Dixon	9¹	9¹	9	9¹	9	9			9¹	9¹	9¹	9¹	9¹				9	9	9	9		9	9	9	9	9¹	9	9	9	9²	9	9	9		9	9	9	9			33	0	11
Dorigo	3	3	3	3	3	3	3	3	3	3	3	3	3	3	3	3	3	3	3	3	3	3	3	3	3	3	3	3	3	3	3	3	3	3	3	3	3	3	3	3	40	0	0
Durie	10¹	10	10	10	10	10²	10¹			10²	10	10		9	10	10	10	10	10¹	10¹		10	10	10	10					10	9	10²	10¹	10	10¹						26	0	12
Freestone													1	1	1	1	1	1	1	1	1	1	1	1		1	1	1	1												15	0	0
Hall												4	★			2	2	2			★	2		★	★		★		2	2	2										8	5	0
Hazard	8	8	8			8	8	8	8	8	8	8	8		8			8			8	8	8	8		8	8	8	8	8	8	8¹	8¹	8	8	8					28	0	2
Hitchcock																														1	1	1	1	1	1	1	1 ·	1			8	0	0
McAllister																★		7	7	7	7																				4	1	0
McLaughlin	5	5	5	5	5	5	5	5	5	5	5	5	5	5	5	5	5	5	5	5	5¹	5	5	5	5	5	5	5			5	5	5	5	5	5	5				36	0	1
McNaught						6																																			1	0	0
Murphy															8	8																									2	0	0
Nevin	7	7¹	7	7¹	7	7	7	7	7	7	7	7	7	7¹	7¹	7	7	7	7¹	7	7		★	7	7	7	7¹	7	7¹	7	7	7	7	7	7	7	7	7			36	1	6
Niedzwieckl	1	1	1	1	1	1	1	1	1	1	1	1	1	1	1																										14	0	0
Pates													4	4	4	4			4	4	4				★	4	4	4	4	4	4	4							6		16	1	0
Wegerle												8¹	8	★			★	8		8		★	10		11	11	11														8	3	1
West									★				★							★¹	10					10¹	★	10			★¹	★									3	6	3
Wicks	4	4	4	4	4	4																					5	5	5	4	4	4	4	4	4	4					17	0	0
Wilson C.	11	11¹	11	8	8	11¹	11	11	11	11	11	11	11	11	11	11	11	11	11	11	11	11	11	11	11¹	★	★			6		★	★					11			27	4	2
Wilson K.	★		★		★	★	9	10		★	10	10	9	★	★		10¹	10	8	9		10	8¹	8	★¹	10²	10	10	10	10			★								16	9	5
Wood	6	6	6	6	2	6	6	6	6	6	6	6	6	6	6	6	6	6¹	6	6	2	2	2	2	11	10	10			6	6	6	6	6	6						34	0	1
Own Goals				1					1																																		2

FA Cup: 1987-88: 3rd Round: Derby Co (A) 3-1; 4th Round: Manchester U (A) 0-2.
Littlewoods Cup: 1987-88: 2nd Round: Reading (A) 1-3 (H) 3-2.

CHESTER CITY (Division 3)

Team Manager   Harry McNally.
Club Address   The Stadium, Sealand Road, Chester CH1 4LW. Tel: (0244) 371376.
Current Ground Capacity   22,000.
Record Attendance   20,500 v Chelsea, FA Cup 3rd Round replay, 16 January 1952.
Year Formed   1884. Turned professional 1902.
Previous Names   Chester.
Club Nickname   "The Blues".
Club Colours   Royal blue shirts with white pinstripe, white shorts and stockings.
Club Honours   None.
League History   1931-58 Div. 3(N); 1958-75 Div. 4; 1975-82 Div. 3; 1983-86 Div. 4; 1986- Div. 3.
Most League Points in a Season   (2 for a win) 56 in Div. 3(N), 1946-47 and Div. 4, 1964-65. (3 for a win) 84 in Div. 4, 1985-86.
Most League Goals in a Season   119 in Div. 4, 1964-65.
Record Victory   12-0 v York C. in Div. 3(N), 1 February 1936.

Record Defeat   2-11 v Oldham Ath. in Div. 3(N), 19 January 1952.
Consecutive League Wins   8 in 1934, 1936 and 1978.
Consecutive League Defeats   7 in 1955, 1956 and 1982.
Record League Appearances   Ray Gill, 406 between 1951-62.
Record League Goalscorer—Career   Gary Talbot, 83 between 1963-69.
Record League Goalscorer—Season   Dick Yates, 36 in Div. 3(N), 1946-47.

Chester City: League Record, 1987-88 (Division 3)

Match Number	Date	Venue	Opponents	Result	H/T	Lge Posn	Attend
1	15.8.87	H	Northampton T.	L 0-5	0-1		3458
2	22.8.87	A	Southend U.	D 2-2	1-1		2369
3	29.8.87	H	York C.	W 1-0	0-0	14	2010
4	31.8.87	A	Rotherham U.	L 2-5	0-1	17	2551
5	5.9.87	H	Aldershot	W 4-1	1-0	16	1700
6	12.9.87	A	Blackpool	W 1-0	0-0	11	4035
7	16.9.87	H	Fulham	L 1-2	1-1	14	2469
8	19.9.87	H	Grimsby T.	W 1-0	0-0	12	1897
9	26.9.87	A	Sunderland	W 2-0	0-0	7	12760
10	29.9.87	A	Gillingham	W 1-0	0-0	2	5193
11	3.10.87	H	Notts Co.	L 1-2	1-0	7	3365
12	17.10.87	A	Bristol Rov.	D 2-2	1-2	11	3083
13	20.10.87	A	Brentford	D 1-1	0-0	11	4027
14	24.10.87	H	Mansfield T.	L 0-2	0-0	11	2453
15	31.10.87	A	Preston N.E.	D 1-1	0-1	13	5657
16	4.11.87	H	Port Vale	W 1-0	0-0	12	2789
17	7.11.87	H	Walsall	D 1-1	0-0	10	3269
18	21.11.87	A	Bristol C. ·	D 2-2	2-1	10	8103
19	28.11.87	H	Chesterfield	D 1-1	1-0	10	1843
20	5.12.87	H	Doncaster Rov.	D 1-1	1-0	11	1853
21	12.12.87	A	Brighton & H.A.	L 0-1	0-0	13	6738
22	18.12.87	H	Bury	D 4-4	1-0	13	1772
23	26.12.87	H	Sunderland	L 1-2	0-2	14	6663
24	28.12.87	A	Wigan Ath.	L 0-1	0-0	15	4394
25	1.1.88	A	York C.	L 0-2	0-1	17	2686
26	2.1.88	H	Blackpool	D 1-1	0-1	17	3093
27	9.1.88	H	Southend U.	D 1-1	0-1	16	2065
28	16.1.88	A	Grimsby T.	L 1-2	0-0	16	2594
29	30.1.88	H	Rotherham U.	W 1-0	0-0	14	2059
30	6.2.88	A	Aldershot	L 1-4	1-1	15	2578
31	13.2.88	H	Wigan Ath.	W 1-0	0-0	14	3088
32	20.2.88	A	Northampton T.	L 0-2	0-0	17	4285
33	27.2.88	A	Notts Co.	L 0-1	0-0	18	5868
34	2.3.88	H	Gillingham	W 3-1	0-0	16	1638
35	5.3.88	H	Bristol Rov.	L 0-3	0-2	18	2067
36	11.3.88	A	Doncaster Rov.	D 2-2	1-1	19	1482
37	19.3.88	H	Preston N.E.	W 1-0	1-0	17	3724
38	26.3.88	A	Mansfield T.	W 2-1	1-1	16	2918
39	2.4.88	A	Walsall	L 0-1	0-1	17	4978
40	4.4.88	H	Bristol C.	W 1-0	1-0	15	2849
41	9.4.88	A	Port Vale	D 1-1	1-1	15	4278
42	15.4.88	A	Fulham	L 0-1	0-0	16	4131
43	23.4.88	H	Brentford	D 1-1	0-0	16	1777
44	30.4.88	A	Chesterfield	D 0-0	0-0	16	2225
45	2.5.88	H	Brighton & H.A.	D 2-2	1-2	16	3345
46	7.5.88	A	Bury	W 1-0	0-0	15	1952

Players: League Record, 1987-88 (Division 3)

Match Number	1	2	3	4	5	6	7	8	9	10	11	12	13	14	15	16	17	18	19	20	21	22	23	24	25	26	27	28	29	30	31	32	33	34	35	36	37	38	39	40	41	42	43	44	45	46	Apps	Subs	Goals
Abel	5	2	2	5	2	2	5	5	5	5	5	5	5	5	5			5	5	5	5	5	5^1	5	5	5	5	5	5	5	5	5	5	5	5	5	5	5	5	5	5	10	5	5^1	5		45	0	2
Astbury																		1	1	1	1	1																									5	0	0
Banks																★	2																														1	1	0
Barrow		8	8	8	8	8	8	8	8	8	8	8	8	8	8	8	8	8		8	8	8	8	8	8	8	8^1	8^1	8	8	8					8	8	8	8	8^1	8	8^1	8				38	0	4
Bennett	10	10	10	10^1	10	10	10	10	10	10	10^1	10	10	10		★	10	10	10	10	10^1	10	10	9^1	★		7	7	7	7	7	7	9^2	9^1	9^1	9	9^1	9	9	9	9	9	9^1				41	2	10
Butler	7							6	7	7		2	7												6				6	6	6	7		★	2	2	5										15	1	0
Caldwell																										10	10	10	10																		4	0	0
Croft	★		5	4	7^1	7	7	7	7^1	7	7	★	★	★	7	7	11	11	11	★			★	11	11	11	★					8	★	7	10	10	10	10	10★	★		11					26	11	2
Fazackerley	4	4			5	5	4	4	4	4		4	4	4	4	4	4	4	4	4	4	4	4	4	4	4	4	4	4	4	4	4	4	4	4	4	4	4	4	4	4	4	4	4			43	0	0
Glenn																					★	★	2	2	2	2	2	2	2	2	2	2	2	2	2	2					2	2	2				19	2	0
Graham	11	11^1	11	11	11	11	11^1	11															★	11	11	11	11	11	11	11	8		8	11	11	11	11	11	11	11		11					24	1	2
Greenhough	2		4	2	4	4	2	6	6	6	2	2	2	2	10	10	2	2	2	2	2	2	2	11	10					★	★	★								6	6	6					28	3	0
Hawtin											★	2	2	2																																	3	1	0
Hetzke	6	6	6	6	6	6					4	6	6	6	6	6													6	6																	14	0	0
Houghton	10																8	8	8	11	11	11								★	11					★		10									9	2	0
Howlett												11	6^1	6	7	7	7																														6	1	1
Langley																								6	6	10	10	10	10	10	10	10															9	0	0
Lightfoot								6									5^1		6					6	6	6	6					6	6	6	6	6	6	6					★				15	1	1
Lowey																																8	7	7	7	7	7	7	7								9	0	0
Lundon	8	5					6					6	6	3	3	3	3	3	3								11	7^1	3	3	3^1	3	3	3	3												22	0	2
Maddy					6		11	11	11	11	11	11	11	11	11		7	7	7	7	7	7			7^1	7	★																				17	1	1
Moore	★																																														0	0	0
Newhouse																																												★			0	1	0
Painter																	★		★																												0	2	0
Parry			7^1	7	7				★				7																																		4	1	1
Rimmer	9	9	9^1	9^2	9^2	9^1	9	9^1	9^1	9^1	9^1	9	9	9^1	9	9^1	9^1	9	9^2	9^1	9^1	9	9^2	9	9	9		9	9^1	9	9	9^1	9	9	9^3	9											34	0	25
Stewart	1	1	1	1		1													1	1	1	1	1	1	1	1	1	1	1	1	1	1	1	1	1	1	1	1	1	1	1	1	1				27	0	0
Stowell						1		1	1	1	1	1	1	1	1	1	1	1																													14	0	0
Woodthorpe	3	3	3	3	3	3	3	3	3	3	3	3	3	3	3	3	3	3	3	3		★	3	3	3	3	3	3	3	3	3	3	3									11	10	10			34	1	0

FA Cup: 1987-88: 1st Round: Runcorn (H) 0-1.
Littlewoods Cup: 1987-88: 1st Round: Blackpool (A) 0-2 (H) 1-0.

CHESTERFIELD (Division 3)

Team Manager   Kevin Randall.
Club Address   Recreation Ground, Chesterfield S40 4SX.
Tel: (0246) 31535.
Current Ground Capacity   11,200.
Record Attendance   30,561 v Tottenham H., FA Cup 5th
Round, 12 February 1938.
Year Formed   1866. Turned professional 1891.
Previous Names   None.
Club Nickname   "The Blues" or "Spireites".
Club Colours   Royal blue shirts with white pinstripe,
white shorts with blue side stripes and white stockings.
Club Honours   Football League: Div. 3(N) Champions
1930-31, 1935-36; Div. 4 Champions 1969-70, 1984-85.
League History   1908-09 Div. 2; 1909 Failed re-election;
1921-31 Div. 3(N); 1931-33 Div. 2; 1933-36 Div. 3(N);
1936-51 Div. 2; 1951-58 Div. 3(N); 1958-61 Div. 3; 1961-70
Div. 4; 1970-83 Div. 3; 1983-85 Div. 4; 1985- Div. 3.
Most League Points in a Season   (2 for a win) 64 in Div. 4,
1969-70. (3 for a win) 91 in Div. 4, 1984-85.
Most League Goals in a Season   102 in Div. 3(N), 1930-31.

Record Victory   10-0 v Glossop N.E. in Div. 2, 17 January
1903.
Record Defeat   0-10 v Gillingham in Div. 3, 5 September
1987.
Consecutive League Wins   10 in 1933.
Consecutive League Defeats   9 in 1960.
Record League Appearances   Dave Blakey, 617 between
1948-67.
Record League Goalscorer—Career   Ernie Moss, 161
between 1969-86.
Record League Goalscorer—Season   Jimmy Cookson, 44
in Div. 3(N), 1925-26.

Chesterfield: League Record, 1987-88 (Division 3)

Match Number	Date	Venue	Opponents	Result		H/T	Lge Posn	Attend
1	15.8.87	A	Preston N.E	W	1-0	0-0		6509
2	22.8.87	H	Brighton & H.A.	D	0-0	0-0		2286
3	29.8.87	A	Mansfield T.	W	1-0	0-0	5	5224
4	31.8.87	H	Bury	W	1-0	0-0	2	2411
5	5.9.87	A	Gillingham	L	0-10	0-5	5	4099
6	12.9.87	H	Port Vale	L	1-3	1-1	12	2406
7	15.9.87	A	Brentford	L	0-2	0-2	14	3183
8	18.9.87	A	Doncaster Rov.	L	0-1	0-1	16	1952
9	26.9.87	H	Notts Co.	W	2-0	1-0	14	3466
10	29.9.87	A	Bristol C.	L	1-2	0-1	15	9088
11	3.10.87	H	Rotherham U.	W	3-2	1-2	15	2993
12	10.10.87	H	Grimsby T.	L	0-3	0-1	15	2072
13	17.10.87	A	Northampton T.	L	0-4	0-2	16	5073
14	20.10.87	A	Aldershot	L	0-2	0-1	18	2054
15	24.10.87	H	Southend U.	W	3-1	2-0	17	1726
16	31.10.87	A	York C.	L	0-1	0-1	18	2316
17	3.11.87	H	Wigan Ath.	L	0-1	0-1	18	1725
18	7.11.87	A	Bristol Rov.	L	0-2	0-2	19	2633
19	21.11.87	H	Sunderland	D	1-1	0-0	19	5700
20	28.11.87	A	Chester C.	D	1-1	0-1	19	1843
21	12.12.87	H	Blackpool	D	1-1	0-1	19	2279
22	19.12.87	A	Fulham	W	3-1	1-1	17	4006
23	26.12.87	A	Notts Co.	L	0-2	0-2	19	8675
24	28.12.87	H	Walsall	W	2-1	1-0	18	3916
25	1.1.88	H	Mansfield T.	W	3-1	1-0	15	5070
26	2.1.88	A	Port Vale	W	1-0	0-0	14	3495
27	16.1.88	H	Doncaster Rov.	L	0-1	0-0	15	2715
28	30.1.88	A	Bury	L	0-2	0-2	17	2071
29	6.2.88	H	Gillingham	L	1-4	0-1	17	2141
30	13.2.88	A	Walsall	D	0-0	0-0	19	4162
31	17.2.88	A	Brighton & H.A.	D	2-2	1-1	19	8182
32	20.2.88	H	Preston N.E.	D	0-0	0-0	19	2864
33	27.2.88	A	Rotherham U.	D	1-1	0-0	19	3440
34	1.3.88	A	Bristol C.	L	1-4	1-2	19	1657
35	5.3.88	H	Northampton T.	L	0-2	0-2	20	2400
36	12.3.88	A	Grimsby T.	D	1-1	0-0	21	3464
37	19.3.88	H	York C.	W	2-1	1-0	20	1966
38	25.3.88	A	Southend U.	L	0-3	0-1	21	3315
39	2.4.88	H	Bristol Rov.	L	0-1	0-1	22	2208
40	4.4.88	A	Sunderland	L	2-3	2-2	22	21886
41	9.4.88	H	Aldershot	W	1-0	0-0	22	1900
42	19.4.88	H	Brentford	W	2-1	2-0	19	2010
43	23.4.88	A	Wigan Ath.	W	2-1	1-1	18	3303
44	30.4.88	H	Chester C.	D	0-0	0-0	17	2225
45	2.5.88	A	Blackpool	L	0-1	0-1	21	2950
46	7.5.88	H	Fulham	W	1-0	1-0	18	3084

Players: League Record, 1987-88 (Division 3)

Match Number	1	2	3	4	5	6	7	8	9	10	11	12	13	14	15	16	17	18	19	20	21	22	23	24	25	26	27	28	29	30	31	32	33	34	35	36	37	38	39	40	41	42	43	44	45	46	Apps	Subs	Goals
Alleyne																																					8¹	8	8	8	8	8	8¹	8	8	8		10	0	2
Arnott																			10	10	10	10	10	10	10	10	10¹	10	10	10	10	10	10	10	10	10											19	0	1
Benjamin	5	5	5	5	5	5	5	5	5	5	5	5	5	5	5	5	5								★	★	5	5	5	5	5	5	5	5					10	10	10	10	10				32	2	0
Bloomer	3	11	11	11	11	11	11	11	11	11	11	11	11	11	★	★		6	8	8	6		★	★	★	11¹	11		8	3	3	3	3	3	★	3			5	5	5	5	5	5			32	6	1
Bradshaw	6	4	4	4	4	4	4	4	4	4	4	4	4	4	4	4	4																														18	0	0
Brown	1	1	1	1	1														1	1	1	1	1	1	1	1	1	1	1	1	1	1	1	1	1	1	1	1	1	1	1	1	1	1	1	1	29	0	0
Caldwell			10	10				10	10	10	10	10			10	10	10																														10	0	0
Coyle	7	6				10			7¹	7	7	7		7	7	7	7	7	7	7	7	7	7	7	7	7	7	7	7¹	7	7	7	★		★	★	7	7	7	7	7	7	7	7			35	3	2
Curran																																★															0	1	0
Eley	10	7	7	7	7		★	7			★	★	★	★	11¹	11	11	11	11	11	11¹	11	11	11	11		11	11	11	11	11	11	11	11	11	11	11	11		★							30	6	2
Grayson																			8	★	8	8	8	8	8	8																					7	1	0
Henderson	4	3	3¹	3	3	3	3	3	3	3		7																												4	4	4¹	4	4	4	4	19	0	2
Hewitt	2			★	6						★	10	10	3	3	3	3	3¹	3									★	★	★	★		7	3	3	3	3	3	3	3¹	3	3	3			22	6	2
Hunter																		8	6	6	6	6¹	6	6	6	6	6	6	6	6	6	6¹	6	6		6	6	6¹	6	6	6						25	0	3
McGeeney	8	8	8	8	8	8	8	8		★	3	3	3			10	4	4	4	4	4	4	4	4	4	8	8¹	8	8	3		★	10	10	10	10		★	5	5	5						35	3	1
Morris																															★	★				★	11	11	11	11	11	11	11				7	0	0
Muggleton					1	1	1	1	1	1	1	1	1	1	1	1	1	1	1	1	1																										17	0	0
Perry			★		★														5	3	3	3	3	3	3	3									6												10	2	0
Phillips																										9	9	9	9	9	9¹	8¹	8	8													9	0	2
Reid									8	8	8	8	8	8	8	8	8																														9	0	0
Rogers		2	2	2	2	2	2	2	2	2	2	2	2	2	2	2	2	2	2	2	2	2	2	2	2	2	2	2	2	2	2	2	2	2	2	2	2	2	2	2	2	2	2	2	2	2	43	0	0
Taylor	11¹	10	★	★	10	★	10							★							★																										4	5	1
Thompson																																				7	7	7	7								4	0	0
Travis			6	6	6		★	★					★			★		5		6				9	★																						6	5	0
Walker							7	★											★																												1	3	0
Waller	9	9	9	9¹	9	9	9	9	9¹	9¹	9³	9	9	9	9²	9	9	9	9	9¹	9	9²	9	9¹	9								★	9	9	9	9¹	9	9	9²	9¹	9	9	9	9	9¹	39	1	19
Wood				7		6	6	6	6	6	6	6	6	6		6	6			6	6		5	5	5	5	5	5	8¹	4	4	4	4	4	4	4	4	4	4		4			★	2	2	34	1	1
Own Goals																					1				1																								2

FA Cup: 1987-88: 1st Round: Notts Co (A) 3-3 Replay (H) 0-1.
Littlewoods Cup: 1987-88: 1st Round: Peterborough U. (H) 2-1 (A) 0-2.

COLCHESTER UNITED (Division 4)

Team Manager Roger Brown.
Club Address Layer Road Ground, Colchester. Tel: (0206) 574042.
Current Ground Capacity 4,900.
Record Attendance 19,072 v Reading, FA Cup 1st Round, 27 November 1948.
Year Formed 1937. Turned professional 1937.
Previous Names None.
Club Nickname "The U's".
Club Colours Blue and white striped shirts, blue shorts and white stockings.
Club Honours None.
League History 1950-58 Div. 3(S); 1958-61 Div. 3; 1961-62 Div. 4; 1962-65 Div. 3; 1965-66 Div. 4; 1966-68 Div. 3; 1968-74 Div. 4; 1974-76 Div. 3; 1976-77 Div. 4; 1977-81 Div. 3; 1981- Div. 4.
Most League Points in a Season (2 for a win) 60 in Div. 4, 1973-74. (3 for a win) 81 in Div. 4, 1982-83.
Most League Goals in a Season 104 in Div. 4, 1961-62.
Record Victory 9-1 v Bradford C., Div. 4, 30 December 1961.

Record Defeat 0-7 v Leyton Orient, Div. 3(S), 5 January 1952 and v Reading, Div. 3(S), 18 September 1957.
Consecutive League Wins 7 in 1968-69.
Consecutive League Defeats 8 in 1954.
Record League Appearances Mickey Cook, 613 between 1969-84.
Record League Goalscorer—Career Martyn King, 131 between 1956-65.
Record League Goalscorer—Season Bobby Hunt, 37 in Div. 4, 1961-62.

Colchester United: League Record, 1987-88 (Division 4)

Match Number	Date	Venue	Opponents	Result		H/T	Lge Posn	Attend
1	15.8.87	A	Burnley	W	3-0	2-0		5369
2	21.8.87	H	Torquay U.	L	0-1	0-0		1372
3	29.8.87	A	Scunthorpe U.	D	2-2	0-1	9	2003
4	31.8.87	H	Scarborough	L	1-3	1-0	16	1525
5	4.9.87	A	Crewe Alex.	D	0-0	0-0	20	1843
6	12.9.87	H	Peterborough U.	W	4-1	1-0	9	1164
7	16.9.87	A	Hereford U.	L	0-1	0-1	14	1951
8	19.9.87	A	Hartlepool U.	L	1-3	0-1	19	1698
9	25.9.87	H	Exeter C.	L	0-2	0-1	22	1443
10	29.9.87	H	Swansea C.	W	2-1	1-0	21	1140
11	3.10.87	A	Newport Co.	W	2-1	1-0	17	1200
12	9.10.87	H	Leyton Orient	D	0-0	0-0	15	1665
13	17.10.87	A	Wrexham	W	1-0	1-0	17	1493
14	20.10.87	H	Carlisle U.	W	1-0	0-0	16	1328
15	24.10.87	A	Cambridge U.	W	1-0	0-0	10	2450
16	30.10.87	H	Darlington	W	2-1	0-0	6	1659
17	3.11.87	A	Rochdale	W	4-1	2-1	5	1399
18	6.11.87	H	Halifax T.	W	2-1	1-1	2	1432
19	21.11.87	A	Wolverhampton W.	L	0-1	0-0	5	2413
20	27.11.87	A	Stockport Co.	D	1-1	0-1	5	1703
21	11.12.87	H	Bolton W.	W	3-0	1-0	3	1725
22	18.12.87	A	Tranmere Rov.	W	2-0	1-0	2	2642
23	26.12.87	A	Exeter C.	W	2-0	0-0	1	2675
24	28.12.87	H	Cardiff C.	W	2-1	1-1	1	2599
25	1.1.88	H	Scunthorpe U.	L	0-3	0-0	2	2287
26	2.1.88	A	Peterborough U.	L	0-2	0-0	3	3665
27	15.1.88	A	Hartlepool U.	D	0-0	0-0	3	1768
28	30.1.88	A	Scarborough	L	1-3	0-0	4	2155
29	5.2.88	H	Crewe Alex.	L	1-4	0-2	5	1822
30	13.2.88	A	Cardiff C.	L	0-1	0-0	6	5458
31	19.2.88	H	Burnley	L	0-1	0-1	10	2520
32	27.2.88	H	Newport Co.	D	0-0	0-0	12	1780
33	1.3.88	A	Swansea C.	W	2-1	0-0	8	4011
34	4.3.88	H	Wrexham	L	1-2	1-2	12	1797
35	12.3.88	A	Leyton Orient	D	0-0	0-0	12	3125
36	19.3.88	A	Darlington	L	0-2	0-2	12	2034
37	25.3.88	H	Cambridge U.	D	0-0	0-0	12	2146
38	1.4.88	H	Halifax T.	W	2-1	0-1	12	1992
39	4.4.88	A	Wolverhampton W.	L	0-2	0-1	13	13443
40	8.4.88	H	Rochdale	W	1-0	0-0	12	1864
41	15.4.88	A	Torquay U.	D	0-0	0-0	12	3508
42	19.4.88	H	Hereford U.	W	1-0	0-0	8	1367
43	23.4.88	A	Carlisle U.	L	0-4	0-2	10	1496
44	29.4.88	H	Stockport Co.	W	2-0	0-0	7	1607
45	2.5.88	A	Bolton W.	L	0-4	0-2	10	5540
46	6.5.88	H	Tranmere Rov.	D	0-0	0-0	14	1660

Players: League Record, 1987-88 (Division 4)

Match Number	1-46 appearances	Apps	Subs	Goals
Angell	(5 at match 25)	1	0	0
Baker	5 5 5 5 ... 5 5 5 5 5 5 5 5 5 ... 5	15	0	0
Benstead	1 1 1 1 1 1 1 1 1 1 1 1 1 1 1 1 1 1	18	0	0
Chatterton	4 4 4 4 4 4¹ 4 4 4 4 4¹ 4 4 4 4¹ 4¹ 4¹ 4¹ 4 4¹ 4 4 4 4 4	26	0	7
Coleman	3 3 3 3¹ 3 3	6	0	1
Daniels	★	0	1	0
English	8¹ 8 8 8 5 5 5 5 5 10 10 10 10 10 10 10 10 10 10 10 10¹ 10 6 6 10 10 10 10 10 10 10 10 10 10 10 6 6 6 6	43	0	2
Farrell	★ ★¹ 7 7 7 ★ ★ 10	4	5	1
Forrest	1 1 1 1 ★ 1 1 1 1 1 1	11	0	0
Grenfell	★ 3 3 3 3 3 3 3 3 3 3 3 3 3 3 3 3 11 ★ 11 11 11 10 11 3 11 11 11 11 11 11 11 11 11 3 3 11	39	2	0
Hedman	6 6 6 6 6 6 6 6 6 6 6 6 6 6 6 6 6 2 2 3 3 3 3 3 2 3 ★ 2 2 2 2 2 2 2 4 4 2	41	1	0
Hetzke	5 5 5 5 2	5	0	0
Hicks	5 5 5 5 5 5 5	7	0	0
Hill	★ ★ ★ 5 6 5 5 5 6 5 6 6 6 6 6 6 6 6 6 6 6	22	3	0
Hinshelwood	2 2 2 2 2 2 2 2¹ 2 2¹ 2 2 2 2 2 2 2¹ 2 6 6 2 2 2 2 2 11¹ 2 2 4 4 4 4 4 4¹ 4 11	40	0	5
Hunter	4	1	0	0
Keane	★ ★ 10 10 ★ 8 ★ ★ 7 7 7 ★ ★ 10 10 10	9	7	0
Keeley	5 5 5 5	4	0	0
Lowe	9¹ 10 10 10 10 10 ★ 10 ★ ★	7	3	1
Norman	3 3 3 ★ ★ 10 10 10	6	2	0
Radford	11 11 4 4 3 3 3 3 3 3 3 ★ ★ 3	12	2	0
Ray	★	0	1	0
Reeves	★ 11 11 11 11 11 11 11¹ 11 11 11¹ 11 11 11 11	18	2	1
Smith	6 ★ 11 11 11 11	18	2	1
Tempest	9 9¹ 9 9¹ 9 9 9 9¹ 9 9 9 9¹ 9 9 2 2 2 2 4 4 4 2 2	11	0	0
Walsh	10¹ 9 ★ ★¹ 10 10 ★ ★ 9 9 9 9 9 9 9¹ 9¹ 9 9 9 9 9 9 9 9 9 9¹ 9 9¹ 9 9¹ 9 9	44	0	11
Walton	1 1 1 1 1 1 1 1 1 1 ★	4	7	2
White	7 7 7¹ 7 7 7 7¹ 7 7 7 7 7 7 7 7 7 7 7 7² 2¹ 7 7 7 7 7 7 7 7 7 7¹ 7 7 7 ★ 7 7 7 7 1 1	17	0	0
Wilkins	11 11 11¹ 11 8 8 8 8 8 8 8 8¹ 8 8 8 8 8¹ 8² 8¹ 8 8 8 8 8 8 4 8 8 8 8 8 8 8 8¹ 8 8	40	1	7
Williams	6 11 6 6 6 11 4 5 5 ★	46	0	9

FA Cup: 1987-88: 1st Round: Tamworth (H) 3-0; 2nd Round: Hereford U. (H) 3-2; 3rd Round: Plymouth Arg. (A) 0-2.
Littlewoods Cup: 1987-88: 1st Round: Fulham (A) 1-3 (H) 0-2.

COVENTRY CITY (Division 1)

Team Manager John Sillett.
Club Address Highfield Road Stadium, King Richard Street, Coventry CV2 4FW. Tel: (0203) 57171.
Current Ground Capacity 28,273.
Record Attendance 51,455 v Wolverhampton W., Div. 2, 29 April 1967.
Year Formed 1883. Turned professional 1893.
Previous Names Singers FC.
Club Nickname "The Sky Blues".
Club Colours Sky blue and white striped shirts, sky blue shorts and stockings.
Club Honours Football League: Div. 2 Champions 1966-67; Div. 3 Champions 1963-64; Div. 3(S) Champions 1935-36. FA Cup: Winners 1987.
League History 1919-25 Div. 2; 1925-26 Div. 3(N); 1926-36 Div. 3(S); 1936-52 Div. 2; 1952-58 Div. 3(S); 1958-59 Div. 4; 1959-64 Div. 3; 1964-67 Div. 2; 1967- Div. 1.
Most League Points in a Season (2 for a win) 60 in Div. 4, 1958-59 and in Div. 3, 1963-64. (3 for a win) in Div. 1, 1986-87.

Most League Goals in a Season 108 in Div. 3(S), 1931-32.
Record Victory 9-0 v Bristol C. in Div. 3(S), 28 April 1934.
Record Defeat 2-10 v Norwich C. in Div. 3(S), 15 March 1930.
Consecutive League Wins 6 in 1964.
Consecutive League Defeats 9 in 1919.
Record League Appearances George Curtis, 486 between 1956-70.
Record League Goalscorer—Career Clarrie Bourton, 171 between 1931-37.
Record League Goalscorer—Season Clarrie Bourton, 49 in Div. 3(S), 1931-32.

Coventry City: League Record, 1987-88 (Division 1)

Match Number	Date	Venue	Opponents	Result		H/T	Lge Posn	Attend
1	15.8.87	H	Tottenham H.	W	2-1	2-0		23947
2	18.8.87	A	Luton T.	W	1-0	0-0		7506
3	22.8.87	A	Norwich C.	L	1-3	0-1	5	13726
4	29.8.87	H	Liverpool	L	1-4	0-1	8	27637
5	31.8.87	A	Sheffield Wed.	W	3-0	2-0	5	17171
6	5.9.87	H	Manchester U.	D	0-0	0-0	8	27125
7	19.9.87	H	Nottingham F.	L	0-3	0-1	10	17519
8	26.9.87	A	Everton	W	2-1	2-1	8	28153
9	3.10.87	H	Watford	W	1-0	0-0	8	16111
10	17.10.87	A	Chelsea	L	0-1	0-0	9	16699
11	20.10.87	H	Southampton	L	2-3	2-1	9	14552
12	24.10.87	H	Newcastle U.	L	1-3	1-2	11	18585
13	31.10.87	A	Derby Co.	L	0-2	0-0	12	15738
14	7.11.87	A	Oxford U.	L	0-1	0-0	13	7856
15	14.11.87	H	Wimbledon	D	3-3	1-0	14	14966
16	21.11.87	A	Charlton Ath.	D	2-2	0-1	14	4936
17	28.11.87	H	West Ham U.	D	0-0	0-0	15	16740
18	5.12.87	A	Portsmouth	D	0-0	0-0	17	13002
19	13.12.87	H	Arsenal	D	0-0	0-0	16	17557
20	18.12.87	A	Q.P.R.	W	2-1	0-1	15	7299
21	28.12.87	A	Nottingham F.	L	1-4	1-1	16	31061
22	1.1.88	A	Liverpool	L	0-4	0-1	17	38790
23	16.1.88	A	Tottenham H.	D	2-2	0-1	15	25650
24	6.2.88	A	Manchester U.	L	0-1	0-1	17	37144
25	13.2.88	H	Sheffield Wed.	W	3-0	0-0	17	14382
26	20.2.88	H	Norwich C.	D	0-0	0-0	17	15557
27	27.2.88	A	Watford	W	1-0	1-0	14	12052
28	5.3.88	H	Chelsea	D	3-3	2-3	15	16816
29	12.3.88	A	Southampton	W	2-1	0-0	14	12914
30	15.3.88	H	Luton T.	W	4-0	2-0	9	13723
31	19.3.88	H	Derby Co.	L	0-3	0-2	11	19871
32	26.3.88	A	Newcastle U.	D	2-2	0-0	11	19050
33	2.4.88	H	Oxford U.	W	1-0	0-0	9	15748
34	5.4.88	A	Wimbledon	W	2-1	2-1	9	5920
35	9.4.88	H	Charlton Ath.	D	0-0	0-0	8	14313
36	19.4.88	H	Everton	L	1-2	1-0	10	15641
37	23.4.88	A	West Ham U.	D	1-1	0-0	9	17733
38	30.4.88	H	Portsmouth	W	1-0	0-0	9	14296
39	2.5.88	A	Arsenal	D	1-1	1-1	9	16963
40	7.5.88	H	Q.P.R.	D	0-0	0-0	10	16089

Players: League Record, 1987-88 (Division 1)

Match Number	1	2	3	4	5	6	7	8	9	10	11	12	13	14	15	16	17	18	19	20	21	22	23	24	25	26	27	28	29	30	31	32	33	34	35	36	37	38	39	40	Apps	Subs	Goals
Bannister																												8	8[1]	8	8		★				★	8	8	8		7	1	1
Bennett	7	7	7	7	7			7	7	7	7[1]	7	7	7	7	7	7	7	7	**7**	**7**	7	7[1]		7[2]	7	7	7	7	★											27	1	4
Borrows	2	2	2	2			★	2	2	2	2	2	2	2	2	2	2	2	2	2	2	2	2	2					2	2	2	2	2	2	2	2					32	1	0
Dobson											11																														1	0	0
Downs	3[1]	3	3	3	3	3	3					3	3	3	3	3[1]	3	3	3	3	3	3	3	3	3	3	3	3	3	3	3	3									27	0	2
Emerson													4	4	4	4	4	4	4	**4**					9		★	7	7	7	7	7		7	7	7	7	7			19	1	0
Gynn	8	8	8	8		★	11	11	11	11[1]	6	6	★	11[1]	6[1]	6	★	11	11	11	11[1]	11	11	9					★	★											19	6	3
Houchen	★	9	★	★	9	9	8	★	10[1]	10	10		11	11		9	9		★[1]		★	★					9[1]	7					★								13	8	3
Kilcline	5	5[1]	5[1]	5							5	5[1]			5	5	5	5	5	5	5	5	5	5	5[1]	5[1]	5[1]		5	5	5[1]	5	5	5	5	5[1]	5	5			28	0	8
Lane														★			★																								0	2	0
Livingstone													9				10	10		★																					3	1	0
McGrath	4	4	4	4	4	4	4	4	4	4	4			8						4	4	4																			17	0	0
Ogrizovic	1	1	1	1	1	1	1	1	1	1	1	1	1	1	1	1	1	1	1	1	1	1	1	1	1	1	1	1	1	1	1	1	1	1	1	1	1	1	1	1	40	0	0
Peake	6	6	6	6	6	6	6	6	6							6	6	6	6		6	6	6	6	**6**	6	6	6	6	6	6	6	6	6	6	6	6	6	6	6	31	0	0
Phillips			★	★	2	2	2	8[1]	8	8	8	8	8	**8**	★	8	8	8	8	8	8	8	8	**8**	8[1]	8	2	2	2	8	8	8	8								32	3	2
Pickering	11	11	11	11	11	11		3	3	3	3	11		11	11	11	11						11	11		★	3	3	3	3	3	3	3	3							26	1	0
Regis	9		9	9[1]	★	9	9[1]	9	9		9[1]	9	9	9			9	9[1]	9[1]	9	9[1]	9		9	9	9	9[1]	9	9	9[1]		9	9[1]	9[1]	9	9					30	1	10
Rodger			5[1]	5	5			5	5	5	5							★			★				2		★	5													9	3	1
Sedgley			8[1]	8	7	5	5	6	6	★				★				10	7	4	4	4	4	4[1]	4	4	4	4	4	4	4	4	4	4	4	4	4	4			25	2	2
Smith, D.																				★	11	11		★[1]	11[1]	11	11	11[1]	**11**	11	11	11	11	11	11	11[1]	11	11			14	2	4
Smith, K.							6	6	5	5	5							6					★																		5	1	0
Speedie	10[1]	10	10	10	10[1]	**10**	10	10		★	9	10	**10**	10	10	10[1]	10	10	**10**		10	10		10	10	10[1]	10[1]	10	10	10	10[1]	10	10	10	10	10	10	10	10	10	35	1	6

FA Cup: 1987-88: 3rd Round: Torquay U. (H) 2-0; 4th Round: Watford (H) 0-1.

Littlewoods Cup: 1987-88: 2nd Round: Cambridge U. (A) 1-0 (H) 2-1; 3rd Round Luton T. (A) 1-3.

CREWE ALEXANDRA (Division 4)

Team Manager Dario Gradi.
Club Address Football Ground, Gresty Road, Crewe.
Tel: (0270) 213014.
Current Ground Capacity 5,000.
Record Attendance 20,000 v Tottenham H., FA Cup 4th
Round, 30 January 1960.
Year Formed 1877. Turned professional 1893.
Previous Names None.
Club Nickname "The Railwaymen".
Club Colours Red shirts, white shorts and red stockings.
Club Honours None.
League History 1892-96 Div. 2; 1896 Failed re-election;
1921 Re-entered Div. 3(N); 1958-63 Div. 4; 1963-64 Div. 3;
1964-68 Div. 4; 1968-69 Div. 3; 1969- Div. 4.
Most League Points in a Season (2 for a win) 59 in Div. 4,
1962-63. (3 for a win) 66 in Div. 4 1984-85.
Most League Goals in a Season 95 in Div. 3(N), 1931-32.
Record Victory 8-0 v Rotherham U. in Div. 3(N), 1
October 1932.
Record Defeat 2-13 v Tottenham H. in FA Cup 4th
Round Replay, 3rd February 1960.

Consecutive League Wins 7 in 1928-29 and 1986-87.
Consecutive League Defeats 10 in 1923, 1957-58 and 1979.
Record League Appearances Tommy Lowry, 436 between
1966-78.
Record League Goalscorer—Career Bert Swindells, 126
between 1928-37.
Record League Goalscorer—Season Terry Harkin, 34 in
Div. 4, 1964-65.

Crewe Alexandra: League Record, 1987-88 (Division 4)

Match Number	Date	Venue	Opponents	Result		H/T	Lge Posn	Attend
1	15.8.87	A	Bolton W.	D	1-1	0-1		4792
2	22.8.87	A	Cambridge U.	L	1-4	1-2		1523
3	29.8.87	H	Wrexham	W	2-0	1-0	15	2210
4	31.8.87	A	Rochdale	D	2-2	2-1	15	2346
5	4.9.87	H	Colchester U.	D	0-0	0-0	17	1843
6	12.9.87	A	Wolverhampton W.	D	2-2	1-1	17	6285
7	15.9.87	H	Tranmere Rov.	D	0-0	0-0	16	1839
8	18.9.87	A	Leyton Orient	D	3-3	1-0	17	2150
9	26.9.87	A	Swansea C.	W	4-2	2-0	13	3832
10	29.9.87	A	Burnley	D	0-0	0-0	13	5404
11	3.10.87	H	Hartlepool U.	D	1-1	0-0	15	2128
12	10.10.87	A	Torquay U.	L	0-1	0-1	17	2499
13	17.10.87	H	Scarborough	W	1-0	1-0	16	2723
14	20.10.87	H	Stockport Co.	W	3-1	2-0	13	2251
15	24.10.87	A	Exeter C.	L	1-3	0-1	16	2149
16	31.10.87	H	Carlisle U.	W	4-1	3-0	13	2124
17	3.11.87	A	Darlington	L	0-1	0-0	15	1720
18	7.11.87	A	Hereford U.	D	1-1	0-0	14	2272
19	21.11.87	H	Scunthorpe U.	D	2-2	0-1	15	2045
20	27.11.87	A	Halifax T.	W	2-1	0-0	12	1412
21	12.12.87	H	Cardiff C.	D	0-0	0-0	13	2010
22	18.12.87	A	Peterborough U.	W	4-0	3-0	8	2540
23	26.12.87	H	Swansea C.	D	2-2	1-0	10	2976
24	28.12.87	A	Newport Co.	W	2-1	1-0	8	1918
25	1.1.88	A	Wrexham	L	1-2	0-0	10	2939
26	2.1.88	H	Wolverhampton W.	L	0-2	0-1	12	4629
27	16.1.88	A	Leyton Orient	D	1-1	0-0	14	4082
28	29.1.88	H	Rochdale	L	0-1	0-1	14	2107
29	5.2.88	A	Colchester U.	W	4-1	2-0	14	1822
30	13.2.88	H	Newport Co.	W	2-1	0-1	12	2080
31	20.2.88	H	Bolton W.	W	2-1	1-1	11	4305
32	27.2.88	A	Hartlepool U.	L	1-2	1-2	13	2165
33	1.3.88	H	Burnley	L	0-1	0-0	13	3720
34	5.3.88	A	Scarborough	L	0-2	0-1	14	2260
35	11.3.88	H	Torquay U.	L	0-1	0-1	15	1858
36	19.3.88	A	Carlisle U.	W	1-0	1-0	14	1834
37	26.3.88	H	Exeter C.	D	0-0	0-0	16	1665
38	1.4.88	H	Hereford U.	D	0-0	0-0	16	1313
39	4.4.88	A	Scunthorpe U.	L	1-2	0-0	17	4091
40	9.4.88	A	Darlington	W	3-1	1-1	16	1482
41	15.4.88	H	Cambridge U.	D	0-0	0-0	16	1546
42	22.4.88	A	Stockport Co.	D	1-1	0-0	16	1520
43	25.4.88	A	Tranmere Rov.	D	2-2	1-2	15	2962
44	29.4.88	H	Halifax T.	D	0-0	0-0	16	1403
45	2.5.88	A	Cardiff C.	L	0-2	0-2	17	10125
46	7.5.88	H	Peterborough U.	L	0-1	0-1	17	1533

Players: League Record, 1987-88 (Division 4)

Match Number	1	2	3	4	5	6	7	8	9	10	11	12	13	14	15	16	17	18	19	20	21	22	23	24	25	26	27	28	29	30	31	32	33	34	35	36	37	38	39	40	41	42	43	44	45	46	Apps	Subs	Goals
Allatt																						8^1	8	8^1	8	★																					4	1	2
Billing	5	5				5	5	5	5	5	5	**5**	5	5	5	5	5	5	5	5	5	5	5		5		5	5	5	5	5	5	5	5	5		5				5						32	0	0
Bodak	8	8	8	8	**8**	8	8	8	8	**8**	8	8	8	**8**	8	8				8				★	★		8	8	8	8	8	8	★														24	3	0
Cutler	9	9	9	9	9	9		★	★	★	10	10	10	10^1	10	10^1	10	**10**						4	4	11	11^1	11^1	11^1	11		8	9	7	9	9	9	9	★	9^1	9	9	9				32	4	6
Davis		★	★		★																																						10	10	10	★	3	1	0
Doyle																															★	7	11	**11**	11^1	★	★	11			3	3	3	3	11	10	3	1
Edwards, P																																															4	2	1
Edwards, R.																						9	11^1	11	★	4				★																	4	2	1
Eli						★	9	9^1	9	9	9	9	9	9	9	9	9		9		★	9	9	4		9^1	★				★	★	4		9	2	2	★		**10**			★				20	7	1
Fishenden																					7^1	7	7	7		7	7						7	7	7	7	7^1	7^1	7	7							15	0	3
Gage	6		6	6	6	6	6	6^1	6	6	6	6	6	6	6	6	6	6	**6**		★				6	6	6	6	6	6	6	6	6	6	6	6	6	6	6	6	6						39	1	1
Goodison	2	2		★	10			2	2	2	2	2	2	2	2	2	2	2	2	2	2	2	2	2	2	2	2		2	2									★	★	2	2	2				31	3	0
Goulet																								9^1	★		9^2																				2	1	3
Greygoose		1	1	1	1	1	1	1	1	1	1		1	1	1	1	1	1	1	1	1	1	1	1	1	1	1	1	1	1	1	1	1	1	1	1	1	1	1	1	1	1	1	1	1	1	43	0	0
Gymer	★		★	★	★	10	10	10^2	10^1	10		7	11		★	11^2	11	11																													10	5	5
Harris																																							8			8	8				3	0	0
Healey													11	11	4	11										★		★		★		8^1	11^1	11										★			7	3	2
Jones																																	2	2	2	2					★						4	1	0
Macowat			3	3	3	3	3	3									★		11	11	3	3	**3**		3	11	3		★	3	3	3	3	3	3	3	3	3		★		5	3				26	3	0
Milligan	4	4^1	4	4	4	★	9		★	★	★		★	8	8	10	10	10	10	10	10	10	10	10	10	10	10	10^1	**10**	10	10	10	10	10	10	10	10	10									31	6	2
Morton																		★	★	4	4		9		7	★	9	9^1	9	9	9	9	9	8	8	★	8	★	8	8	★	★	8				17	7	1
Murphy	★	10	・			★	★				★	★	11	11			9^1			4^1	11				9	4	4	4	4	4	4		4	4	4												15	5	2
Nuttell																		★		9^1		8																									2	1	1
Parker																		8	9				★														2		★	★	11	11	11	11		7	4	0
Parkin	1	1												1																																	3	0	1
Pemberton	3		2	2	2	2	2	3	3	3	3	3	3	3	3	3			3	3	3			5	3	6^1	3	6	3	3	3	3						2	2								31	0	1
Platt	7^1	7	7^1	7^2	7	7^2	7	7	7^1	7	7^1		7^1	7^2	7^1	7	7^1	7^2	7^1	7	7^1	7^2	7	7	7																						26	0	19
Ritchie		★	10	10													★				★	4		4	★			★											4	4	4	4	4	4	4	**4**	13	4	0
Wakenshaw	11	11	**11**	11	11	11	11	11^1	**11**	11	11														11			★		8	★	7	11	11													17	3	1
Walters																																												10			1	0	0
Wright	10	6	5	5	5	4	4	4	4	4	4	4	4	4	4	4	4	★		8	6	6	6	5	6	★		★		2		★		5		5	5	5^2	5	9	5	5		5			34	3	2
Own Goals			1																		1							1																			3

FA Cup: 1987-88: 1st Round: Lincoln C. (A) 1-2.
Littlewoods Cup: 1987-88: 1st Round: Shrewsbury T. (H) 3-3 (A) 1-4.

CRYSTAL PALACE (Division 2)

Team Manager Steve Coppell.
Club Address Selhurst Park, London SE25 6PU. Tel: 01-653 4462.
Current Ground Capacity 36,000.
Record Attendance 51,482 v Burnley, Div. 2, 11 May 1979.
Year Formed 1905. Turned professional 1905.
Previous Names None.
Club Nickname "The Eagles".
Club Colours All white with 4″ diagonal red and blue band across shirt from left shoulder.
Club Honours Football League: Div. 2 Champions 1978-79, Div. 3(S) Champions 1920-21.
League History 1920-21 Div. 3(S); 1921-25 Div. 2; 1925-58 Div. 3(S); 1958-61 Div. 4; 1961-64 Div. 3; 1964-69 Div. 2; 1969-73 Div. 1; 1973-74 Div. 2; 1974-77 Div. 3; 1977-79 Div. 2; 1979-81 Div. 1; 1981- Div. 2.
Most League Points in a Season (2 for a win) 64 in Div. 4, 1960-61. (3 for a win) 75 in Div. 2, 1987-88.
Most League Goals in a Season 110 in Div. 4; 1960-61.

Record Victory 9-0 v Barrow in Div. 4, 10 October 1959.
Record Defeat 4-11 v Manchester C. in FA Cup 5th Round, 20 February 1926.
Consecutive League Wins 8 in 1921.
Consecutive League Defeats 8 in 1925.
Record League Appearances Jim Cannon, 571 between 1973-88.
Record League Goalscorer—Career Peter Simpson, 154 between 1930-36.
Record League Goalscorer—Season Peter Simpson, 46 in Div. 3(S), 1930-31.

Crystal Palace: League Record, 1987-88 (Division 2)

Match Number	Date	Venue	Opponents	Result		H/T	Lge Posn	Attend
1	15.8.87	A	Huddersfield T.	D	2-2	1-0		6132
2	22.8.87	H	Hull C.	D	2-2	0-2		6688
3	29.8.87	A	Barnsley	L	1-2	1-0	18	4853
4	1.9.87	H	Middlesbrough	W	3-1	1-0	14	6866
5	5.9.87	A	Birmingham C.	W	6-0	1-0	9	7011
6	8.9.87	H	West Bromwich A.	W	4-1	1-0	2	8554
7	12.9.87	H	Leicester C.	W	2-1	1-1	1	8925
8	15.9.87	A	Sheffield U.	D	1-1	0-0	1	7767
9	19.9.87	A	Reading	W	3-2	0-1	2	6819
10	26.9.87	H	Ipswich T.	L	1-2	0-0	2	10828
11	3.10.87	A	Shrewsbury T.	L	0-2	0-1	4	3999
12	10.10.87	H	Millwall	W	1-0	0-0	3	10678
13	21.10.87	A	Aston Villa	L	1-4	1-2	8	12755
14	24.10.87	H	Swindon T.	W	2-1	1-1	6	9077
15	31.10.87	A	Bradford C.	L	0-2	0-0	8	13012
16	3.11.87	H	Plymouth Arg.	W	5-1	1-0	7	7424
17	7.11.87	A	Bournemouth	W	3-2	3-2	6	9083
18	14.11.87	H	Stoke C.	W	2-0	0-0	5	8309
19	21.11.87	A	Blackburn Rov.	L	0-2	0-0	6	6372
20	28.11.87	H	Leeds U.	W	3-0	1-0	5	8749
21	5.12.87	A	Manchester C.	W	3-1	0-0	4	23161
22	13.12.87	H	Sheffield U.	W	2-1	0-1	4	8174
23	19.12.87	A	Hull C.	L	1-2	1-2	4	6780
24	26.12.87	A	Ipswich T.	W	3-2	1-1	3	17200
25	28.12.87	H	Reading	L	2-3	1-1	4	12449
26	1.1.88	H	Barnsley	W	3-2	1-0	3	8563
27	2.1.88	A	Leicester C.	D	4-4	4-2	2	10104
28	16.1.88	H	Huddersfield T.	W	2-1	2-1	2	9013
29	23.1.88	H	Middlesbrough	L	1-2	0-1	2	12597
30	29.1.88	A	Oldham Ath.	L	0-1	0-0	4	6169
31	6.2.88	H	Birmingham C.	W	3-0	1-0	3	8809
32	13.2.88	A	West Bromwich A.	L	0-1	0-0	3	8944
33	27.2.88	A	Shrewsbury T.	L	1-2	1-1	6	8210
34	5.3.88	H	Oldham Ath.	W	3-1	2-0	4	7032
35	12.3.88	A	Millwall	D	1-1	0-0	6	12815
36	19.3.88	H	Bradford C.	D	1-1	0-0	5	9801
37	27.3.88	H	Swindon T.	D	2-2	0-0	6	12915
38	2.4.88	H	Bournemouth	W	3-0	2-0	5	9557
39	4.4.88	A	Stoke C.	D	1-1	0-1	6	9613
40	9.4.88	H	Aston Villa	D	1-1	0-1	6	16476
41	23.4.88	A	Plymouth Arg.	W	3-1	1-0	6	8370
42	30.4.88	H	Blackburn Rov.	W	2-0	1-0	6	13059
43	2.5.88	A	Leeds U	L	0-1	0-1	6	13217
44	7.5.88	H	Manchester C.	W	2-0	0-0	6	17555

Players: League Record, 1987-88 (Division 2)

Match Number	1	2	3	4	5	6	7	8	9	10	11	12	13	14	15	16	17	18	19	20	21	22	23	24	25	26	27	28	29	30	31	32	33	34	35	36	37	38	39	40	41	42	43	44	Apps	Subs	Goals
Bailey																				★		★	★¹	★			★																		0	5	1
Barber	★			★		★		★		★	★		★	★		11	11	11	11	11	9¹	9¹	9	9	9	9¹	11¹	11	11	10¹	10	11	11	11	11¹	11	11	11	11	11	10¹	11	11	11	28	9	7
Bright	9²	9	9¹	9²	9¹	9²	9	9	9¹	9	9	9¹	9	9¹	9	9	9²	9¹	9	9¹	9²					9	9	9	9¹	9	9	9	9	9	9¹	9¹	9¹	9	9²	9	9				38	0	24
Brush	3	3	3	3	3	3	3	3																																					9	0	0
Burke													3			3	3	3	3	3	3	3	3	3	3	3	3	3	3	3	3	3	3	3	3	3	3	3	3	3	3	3	3	3	31	0	0
Cannon	6	6	6	6	6¹	6	6	6	6		6	6	6	6	6		6	6	6	6	6	6¹	6	6	6¹	6	6	6	6	6	6¹	6	6	6	6	6	6	6	6	6	6	6	6	6	40	0	4
Finnigan		★																				★					★	5	5	5	2	2	2	2	2	2	2	2	2	2					14	3	0
Gray	4	4²	4	4²	4	4	4	4	4	4	4	4	4	4¹	4	4¹	4																												17	0	6
Hone												5	3	3																															3	0	0
Nebbeling	5	5	5	5	5	5	5	5	5	5¹	5¹	5		5	5	5	5¹	5	5	5	5	5	5	5	5	5					★	5²	5	5	5	5	5	5	5	5	5	5	5	5¹	38	1	6
O'Doherty						★	2	2	6	2	2	2	2	2	2	6	6									5	5	2	2	2															16	1	0
O'Reilly				★	★	2	2																																						2	2	0
Pardew																	4	4	4	4	4	4	★			7	4	4	4	7	★	4	4	4	4	4		★	★						16	4	0
Pemberton																																					★	★							0	2	0
Pennyfather																	★		11	11	4	4	4	4¹	8	8	8	4	4						7	4	4	4	4	4	4	4		18	1	1
Redfearn	7	7	7	7	7¹	7¹	7	7	7	7	7	7	7	7	7	7	7	7	7	7¹	7¹	7	7¹	7	7	11	7	7	7	11	11	7¹	7	7	7	7²	7		7	7	7	7			42	0	6
Salako	11	11	11	11	11	11	11	11	11	11	11	11	11	11	11		★		11		11	11	11		★¹	7	★		★	★			★	7	11	★	★								23	8	1
Shaw								★		3	2																																		2	1	0
Stebbing	2	2	2	2	2	2										★	★	2	2	2	2	2	2	2	2	2	2	2	2	2															19	2	0
Suckling																									1	1	1	1	1	1	1	1	1	1	1	1	1	1	1	1	1	1	1	1	17	0	0
Taylor												6	8																																2	0	0
Thomas	8	8	8	8¹	8¹	8	8	8¹	8	8	3	8	8	8	8	8¹	8	8	8	8	8	8	8				8	8	8	8	8	8	8	8		8	8	8	8	8	8¹	8	8¹	41	0	6
Wood	1	1	1	1	1	1	1	1	1	1	1	1	1	1	1	1	1	1	1	1	1	1	1	1																					27	0	0
Wright	10	10	10	10	10	10¹	10¹	10¹	10¹	10¹	10	10	10¹	10	10	10³	10¹	10	10	10¹	10	10	10²	10¹	10¹	10²	10	10¹	10		10	10¹	10	10	10¹	10	10¹	10¹		10	10	10			41	0	20
Own Goals																				1							1																					2

FA Cup: 1987-88: 3rd Round: Newcastle U. (A) 0-1.
Littlewoods Cup: 1987-88: 2nd Round: Newport Co. (H) 4-0 (A) 2-0; 3rd Round: Manchester U. (A) 1-2.

DARLINGTON (Division 4)

Formed 1883

Team Manager David Booth.
Club Address Feethams Ground, Darlington. Tel: (0325) 465097.
Current Ground Capacity 13,511.
Record Attendance 21,023 v Bolton W., League Cup 3rd Round, 14 November 1960.
Year Formed 1883. Turned professional 1908.
Previous Names None.
Club Nickname "The Quakers".
Club Colours All white with black and red trim.
Club Honours Football League: Div. 3(N) Champions 1924-25.
League History 1921-25 Div. 3(N); 1925-27 Div. 2; 1927-58 Div. 3(N); 1958-66 Div. 4; 1966-67 Div. 3; 1967-85 Div. 4; 1985-87 Div. 3; 1987- Div. 4.
Most League Goals in a Season 108 in Div. 3(N), 1929-30.
Most League Points in a Season (2 for a win) 59 in Div. 4, 1965-66. (3 for a win) 85 in Div. 4, 1984-85.
Record Victory 9-2 v Lincoln C. in Div. 3(N), 7 January 1928.

Record Defeat 0-10 v Doncaster Rov. in Div. 4, 25 January 1964.
Consecutive League Wins 5 in 1922, 1924, 1928, 1975 and 1985.
Consecutive League Defeats 8 in 1985.
Record League Appearances Ron Greener, 442, between 1955-67.
Record League Goalscorer—Career Alan Walsh, 87 between 1978-84.
Record League Goalscorer—Season David Brown, 39 in Div. 3(N), 1924-25.

Darlington: League Record, 1987-88 (Division 4)

Match Number	Date	Venue	Opponents	Result		H/T	Lge Posn	Attend
1	15.8.87	A	Halifax T.	D	2-2	1-0		1342
2	22.8.87	H	Stockport Co.	L	1-2	1-0		1744
3	29.8.87	A	Hartlepool U.	W	5-2	1-0	7	2106
4	31.8.87	H	Torquay U.	D	1-1	0-0	10	2251
5	5.9.87	A	Peterborough U.	W	2-1	2-1	8	3200
6	12.9.87	H	Scarborough	W	2-1	1-0	5	3187
7	15.9.87	A	Cardiff C.	L	1-3	0-1	7	2201
8	19.9.87	A	Hereford U.	L	0-1	0-1	12	2102
9	26.9.87	H	Scunthorpe U.	L	1-4	1-1	15	1638
10	29.9.87	H	Carlisle U.	D	3-3	2-2	16	2996
11	3.10.87	H	Tranmere Rov.	D	0-0	0-0	18	1612
12	10.10.87	H	Bolton W.	W	1-0	0-0	14	1763
13	17.10.87	A	Rochdale	W	3-1	1-1	13	1417
14	20.10.87	A	Wrexham	W	1-0	0-0	9	1278
15	24.10.87	H	Wolverhampton W.	D	2-2	2-2	11	2282
16	30.10.87	A	Colchester U.	L	1-2	0-0	14	1659
17	3.11.87	H	Crewe Alex.	W	1-0	0-0	11	1720
18	8.11.87	H	Cambridge U.	L	0-1	0-0	12	2463
19	20.11.87	A	Leyton Orient	L	3-4	2-1	15	3644
20	8.12.87	H	Exeter C.	W	4-1	3-0	11	1107
21	19.12.87	H	Swansea C.	W	2-0	1-0	9	1726
22	26.12.87	A	Scunthorpe U.	L	0-1	0-1	12	3140
23	28.12.87	H	Burnley	W	4-2	1-1	10	3325
24	1.1.88	H	Hartlepool U.	D	1-1	0-0	11	4735
25	2.1.88	A	Scarborough	W	1-0	1-0	8	3377
26	9.1.88	H	Carlisle U.	W	2-1	1-0	7	2517
27	12.1.88	A	Newport Co.	L	1-2	1-1	7	1402
28	17.1.88	A	Hereford U.	W	3-1	0-0	4	2621
29	2.2.88	H	Cardiff C.	D	0-0	0-0	6	2332
30	13.2.88	A	Burnley	L	1-2	0-1	8	6432
31	20.2.88	H	Halifax T.	W	4-1	2-1	6	1824
32	27.2.88	A	Tranmere Rov.	L	1-2	0-1	9	2756
33	5.3.88	H	Rochdale	W	2-1	1-1	8	1773
34	12.3.88	A	Bolton W.	D	1-1	0-1	10	4948
35	15.3.88	H	Peterborough U.	W	2-1	2-1	8	1618
36	19.3.88	H	Colchester U.	W	2-0	0-0	6	2034
37	26.3.88	A	Wolverhampton W.	L	3-5	0-2	7	9349
38	1.4.88	A	Cambridge U.	L	0-1	0-1	9	2242
39	4.4.88	H	Leyton Orient	D	2-2	1-1	8	2730
40	9.4.88	A	Crewe Alex.	L	1-3	1-1	10	1482
41	19.4.88	A	Stockport Co.	D	1-1	0-1	10	1625
42	23.4.88	H	Wrexham	W	2-1	1-0	7	1711
43	27.4.88	A	Torquay U.	D	0-0	0-0	7	3939
44	30.4.88	A	Exeter C.	L	1-4	0-0	9	1515
45	2.5.88	H	Newport Co.	L	0-2	0-2	11	1675
46	7.5.88	A	Swansea C.	L	0-3	0-1	13	4071

Players: League Record, 1987-88 (Division 4)

Match Number	1	2	3	4	5	6	7	8	9	10	11	12	13	14	15	16	17	18	19	20	21	22	23	24	25	26	27	28	29	30	31	32	33	34	35	36	37	38	39	40	41	42	43	44	45	46	Apps	Subs	Goals
Anderson																																						★				★	★	★			0	4	0
Bell	11	★	11	11	11	11	11¹	11	11		★	★¹	7	7	7	7	7	7	7		★				★	★		★			★		4	★	★	★				10	11					18	11	2
Bonnyman		2	4	4	4	4	4	4	6	6	6	6	6	6¹	6	6		6	6	6	6	6	6	6	6	6	6	6	6	6	6	6¹	6	6	6	6¹		10²	10	10	10¹	10	10		10	10	10	★	10	38	0	3
Clayton																																											11	1	3
Crichton					1	1	1																																								3	0	0
Currie	10¹	10	10²	10	10²	10	10	10	10¹	10	10	10¹	10¹	10¹	10	10	10	10	10²	10²	10	10²	10	10¹	10	10¹	10	10²	10	10¹	10																31	0	21
Granger																								1	1	1	1	1	1	1	1	1	1	1	1	1	1	1	1	1	1	1	1	1	1	1	23	0	0
Hinchley	2						★		2	2																																3					4	1	0
Hine	4	4	2	2	2	2	2	2	2	4	4	4	4	4	4	4	4	4¹	4¹	4	4	4	4¹	4	4	4	4	4	4	4	4	4	4	4¹		4	4	4	4	4	4	4	4	4	4	4	45	0	4
Hyde																																							★							★	0	2	0
McAughtrie	6	6	6	6	6	6	6	6	6							★	6			★																	9	6	6	6	6	6					17	0	7
MacDonald	9¹	9¹	9¹	9¹	9	9	9	9¹	9	9	9	9	9	9	9		9	9	9	9	9		9	9	9	9	9	9	9	9¹	9	9	9	9	9¹	9¹	9	9		9	9	9	9	9	9	9	42	0	7
Morgan	3	3	3	3	3	3	3	3	3	3	3	3	3	3	3	3	3	3	3	3	3	3	3	3	3	3	3	3	3	3	3	3	3	3	3	3	3	3	3	3		3	3	3	3	3	45	0	0
O'Dell									★																				★		8																1	2	0
Outterside	7	★						7	2	2	2	2	2	2	2	2	2	2	2	2	2	2	2	2	2	2	2	2	2		2	2	2	2	2	2	2	2	2	2	2	2	2	2	2	2	37	1	0
Roberts A.		7	7²	7	7	7	7	7	7		7				★			7¹	7	7	7	7	7	7	7	7	7	7¹	7	7	7	7	7	7¹	7	7	7	7	7¹	7	7	7²	7	7	7	7	37	1	7
Roberts J.	1	1	1	1	1	1	1	1	1	1		1	1	1	1	1	1	1	1	1	1	1	1																								20	0	0
Robinson	5	5	5	5	5	5	5	5	5	5	5	5	5	5	5	5	5	5	5	5	5	5	5	5	5	5	5	5	5	5	5	5	5	5	5	5		10	★		★						38	2	0
Stonehouse	★	11	★		★¹	★		★	11²	11	11	11²	11	11	11	11	11	11²	11	11	11	11¹	11	11	11¹	11	11	11	11¹	11	11¹	11	11	11¹	11	11¹	11	11	11	11	11	11	11	10	11		38	5	13
Ward	8	8	8¹	8	8	8	8	8	8	8	8	8	8	8	8	8	8	8	8	8	8	8	8	8	8	8	8	8²	8¹	8	8	8	8	8	8	8¹	8¹	8	8	8							45	0	6
Willis																																						5	5	5	5	5	5	5	5		9	0	0
Worthington	★											★¹	9¹	9			★¹	9		★		★				10																					4	5	3
Own Goals																						1																		1									2

FA Cup: 1987-88: 1st Round: Sunderland (A) 0-2.
Littlewoods Cup: 1987-88: 1st Round: Grimsby T. (A) 2-3 (H) 2-1; 2nd Round: Watford (H) 0-3 (A) 0-8.

DERBY COUNTY (Division 1)

Team Manager   Arthur Cox.
Club Address   Baseball Ground, Shaftesbury Crescent, Derby DE3 8NB. Tel: (0332) 40105.
Current Ground Capacity   26,500.
Record Attendance   41,826 v Tottenham H., Div. 1, 20 September 1969.
Year Formed   1884. Turned professional 1884.
Previous Names   None.
Club Nickname   "The Rams".
Club Colours   White shirts, blue shorts and blue stockings.
Club Honours   Football League: Div 1. Champions 1971-72, 1974-75. Div. 2 Champions 1911-12, 1914-15, 1968-69, 1986-87; Div. 3(N) Champions 1956-57. FA Cup: Winners 1946.
League History   1888-1904 Div. 1; 1904-12 Div. 2; 1912-14 Div. 1; 1914-15 Div. 2; 1915-21 Div. 1; 1921-26 Div. 2; 1926-53 Div. 1; 1953-55 Div. 2; 1955-57 Div. 3(N); 1957-69 Div. 2; 1969-80 Div. 1; 1980-84 Div. 2; 1984-86 Div. 3; 1986-87 Div. 2; 1987- Div. 1.

Most League Points in a Season   (2 for a win) 63 in Div. 2, 1968-69, Div. 3(N) 1955-56 and 1956-57. (3 for a win) 84 in Div. 3, 1985-86 and Div. 3, 1986-87.
Most League Goals in a Season   111 in Div. 3(N), 1956-57.
Record Victory   12-0 v Finn Harps in UEFA Cup 3rd Round 1st Leg, 15 September 1976.
Record Defeat   2-11 v Everton, FA Cup 1st Round, 1889-90.
Consecutive League Wins   9 in 1969.
Consecutive League Defeats   8 in 1965 and 1988.
Record League Appearances   Kevin Hector, 486 between 1966-82.
Record League Goalscorer—Career   Steve Bloomer, 291 between 1892-1914.
Record League Goalscorer—Season   Jack Bowers, 37 in Div. 1, 1930-31 and Ray Straw, 37 in Div. 3(N), 1956-57.

Derby County: League Record, 1987-88 (Division 1)

Match Number	Date	Venue	Opponents	Result		H/T	Lge Posn	Attend
1	15.8.87	H	Luton T.	W	1-0	1-0		17204
2	19.8.87	A	Q.P.R.	D	1-1	1-1		11651
3	29.8.87	H	Wimbledon	L	0-1	0-0	13	15165
4	5.9.87	H	Portsmouth	D	0-0	0-0	13	15071
5	12.9.87	A	Norwich C.	W	2-1	0-0	11	14402
6	19.9.87	A	Sheffield Wed.	D	2-2	2-0	11	15869
7	26.9.87	H	Oxford U.	L	0-1	0-1	13	15711
8	29.9.87	A	Liverpool	L	0-4	0-1	13	43405
9	3.10.87	A	West Ham U.	D	1-1	0-1	12	17226
10	10.10.87	H	Nottingham F.	L	0-1	0-1	13	22394
11	17.10.87	A	Charlton Ath.	W	1-0	1-0	11	5432
12	24.10.87	A	Arsenal	L	1-2	1-2	13	32374
13	31.10.87	H	Coventry C.	W	2-0	0-0	12	15738
14	14.11.87	A	Newcastle U.	D	0-0	0-0	13	21698
15	22.11.87	H	Chelsea	W	2-0	0-0	13	18644
16	28.11.87	A	Southampton	W	2-1	0-0	10	15201
17	5.12.87	H	Watford	D	1-1	1-0	9	14516
18	12.12.87	A	Everton	L	0-3	0-1	11	26224
19	20.12.87	H	Tottenham H.	L	1-2	0-1	13	17593
20	26.12.87	H	Norwich C.	L	1-2	0-1	14	15452
21	28.12.87	A	Sheffield Wed.	L	1-2	0-2	15	26191
22	1.1.88	A	Wimbledon	L	1-2	1-1	16	5479
23	16.1.88	A	Luton T.	L	0-1	0-0	17	7175
24	6.2.88	A	Portsmouth	L	1-2	0-1	18	14790
25	10.2.88	H	Manchester U.	L	1-2	0-0	18	20016
26	20.2.88	A	Oxford U.	D	0-0	0-0	18	8924
27	27.2.88	H	West Ham U.	W	1-0	0-0	18	16301
28	1.3.88	A	Tottenham H.	D	0-0	0-0	18	15986
29	5.3.88	H	Charlton Ath.	D	1-1	1-0	17	16139
30	16.3.88	H	Liverpool	D	1-1	0-0	17	26356
31	19.3.88	A	Coventry C.	W	3-0	2-0	16	19871
32	26.3.88	H	Arsenal	D	0-0	0-0	16	18382
33	30.3.88	A	Nottingham F.	L	1-2	0-1	16	25017
34	2.4.88	A	Manchester U.	L	1-4	0-2	17	40146
35	4.4.88	H	Newcastle U.	W	2-1	0-1	15	18591
36	9.4.88	A	Chelsea	L	0-1	0-1	16	16996
37	13.4.88	H	Q.P.R.	L	0-2	0-1	16	14214
38	23.4.88	H	Southampton	W	2-0	2-0	15	14291
39	30.4.88	A	Watford	D	1-1	1-1	15	14181
40	2.5.88	H	Everton	D	0-0	0-0	15	17974

Players: League Record, 1987-88 (Division 1)

Match Number	1	2	3	4	5	6	7	8	9	10	11	12	13	14	15	16	17	18	19	20	21	22	23	24	25	26	27	28	29	30	31	32	33	34	35	36	37	38	39	40	Apps	Subs	Goals
Blades		★		2	2	2		6	6	6	6	6	6	6	6	6	6	6	6	6		2	2	2	2	2	2	2	2	2	2	2									30	1	0
Callaghan	11	11	11	11	11	11	11	11	7	7	7	7	7	7	7	7	7	7	7	7	7¹	7	11	11	11	11¹	11	11¹	11	11	11	11	11	11	11	11	11	11¹	11		40	0	4
Cross						★		11	11	11¹	11	11	11	11¹	11	11	11	11													★¹		★	★							11	4	3
Davison	9	9	9	9	9¹	9	9	9	9		9	9	9	9																											13	0	1
Forsyth	3	3	3	3	3	3	3	3	3	3	3	3	3	3	3	3	3	3	3	3	3	3	3	3	3	3	3	3¹	3¹	3	3	3	3	3			3	3			39	0	3
Garner			★	★	★	★	★		9	8	8¹	8²	8	8	8¹	8	8	8	8	8		8	8	★		★	★	★	★												14	10	4
Gee	8	8¹	8	8	8	8	8	8	8¹	8		★		★	9	9¹	9	9	9	9¹	9	9	9	9	9	9	9	9	9	9	9	9¹	9	9	9¹	9	9	9	9		36	2	6
Gregory	10¹	10	10	10¹	10¹	10	10	10	10	10	10	10	10	10¹	10	10		10¹	10	10	10	10	10	10	10	10	10	10	10	10	10	10	10	10¹	10	10					39	0	6
Hindmarch	5	5	5																					6	6	6	6	6	6	6	6	6	6	6	6	6	6	6	6	6	19	0	0
Lewis											★				★	★	10	★		★		★	8	8	8	8	8	8	8	8											10	6	0
Lillis			★																																						0	1	0
McCord																		11																							1	0	0
McClaren																	★		11																						1	1	0
MacLaren	6	6		6	6	6	6	6	★	2	2	2	2	2	2	2	2	2	2	2	2	2	2		★	★		★		★		★	★	★	2	★	2				25	9	0
McMinn																					7	7¹	7	7	7	7	7														7	0	1
Micklewhite	7	7	7	7	7																					★	★	★	★	7	7¹	7	7	7	7	7					12	4	1
Penney													★	★	★	★	11	11	8		★	★																			3	6	0
Sage	2	2	2	2	2	7	7	7	2	2								★																			3	2		12	1	0
Shilton	1	1	1	1	1	1	1	1	1	1	1	1	1	1	1	1	1	1	1	1	1	1	1	1	1	1	1	1	1	1	1	1	1	1	1	1	1	1	1	1	40	0	0
Stapleton																												7	7	7	8	8	8	8	8¹	8	8				10	0	1
Williams	4	4	4	4	4	4	4	4	4	4	4	4	4	4	4	4	4	4	4	4	4	4	4	4	4	4	4	4	4	4¹	4	4	4	4	4	4	4	4	4	4	40	0	1
Wright			6	5	5	5	5	5	5	5	5	5	5	5	5	5	5	5	5¹	5	5	5	5¹	5	5	5	5¹	5	5	5	5	5	5	5	5	5	5	5	5	5	38	0	3
Own Goals																								1																			1

FA Cup: 1987-88: 3rd Round: Chelsea (H) 1-3.

Littlewoods Cup: 1987-88: 2nd Round: Southend U. (A) 0-1 (H) 0-0.

DONCASTER ROVERS (Division 4)

Team Manager Dave Mackay.
Club Address Belle Vue Ground, Doncaster. Tel: (0302) 539441.
Current Ground Capacity 4,859.
Record Attendance 37,149 v Hull C., Div. 3(N), 2 October 1948.
Year Formed 1879. Turned professional 1885.
Previous Names None.
Club Nickname "Rovers".
Club Colours Red shirts, white shorts and red stockings.
Club Honours Football League: Div. 3(N) Champions 1934-35, 1946-47, 1949-50, Div. 4 Champions 1965-66, 1968-69.
League History 1901-03 Div. 2; 1903 Failed re-election; 1904-05 Div. 2; 1905 Failed re-election; 1923-35 Div. 3(N); 1935-37 Div. 2; 1937-47 Div. 3(N); 1947-48 Div. 2; 1948-50 Div. 3(N); 1950-58 Div. 2; 1958-59 Div. 3; 1959-66 Div. 4; 1966-67 Div. 3; 1967-69 Div. 4; 1969-71 Div. 3; 1971-81 Div. 4; 1981-83 Div. 3; 1983-4 Div. 4; 1984-88 Div. 3; 1988- Div. 4.

Most League Points in a Season (2 for a win) 72 in Div. 3(N), 1946-47. (3 for a win) 85 in Div. 4, 1983-84.
Most League Goals in a Season 123 in Div. 3(N), 1946-47.
Record Victory 10-0 v Darlington in Div. 4, 25 January 1964.
Record Defeat 0-12 v Small Heath in Div. 2, 11 April 1903.
Consecutive League Wins 10 in 1947.
Consecutive League Defeats 9 in 1905.
Record League Appearances Fred Emery, 406 between 1925-36.
Record League Goalscorer—Career Tom Keetley, 180 between 1923-29.
Record League Goalscorer—Season Clarrie Jordan, 42 in Div. 3(N), 1946-47.

Doncaster Rovers: League Record, 1987-88 (Division 3)

Match Number	Date	Venue	Opponents	Result		H/T	Lge Posn	Attend
1	15.8.87	H	Grimsby T.	W	1-0	1-0		2482
2	22.8.87	A	Fulham	L	0-4	0-3		4157
3	29.8.87	H	Sunderland	L	0-2	0-1	17	2740
4	31.8.87	A	Aldershot	L	1-2	1-0	21	2598
5	5.9.87	H	Northampton T.	L	0-2	0-0	22	1873
6	12.9.87	A	Wigan Ath.	L	1-2	1-1	22	2764
7	15.9.87	H	Blackpool	W	2-1	0-0	19	1558
8	18.9.87	H	Chesterfield	W	1-0	1-0	18	1952
9	26.9.87	A	York C.	D	1-1	0-0	19	2702
10	29.9.87	A	Mansfield T.	L	0-2	0-2	19	3159
11	3.10.87	H	Gillingham	W	4-2	2-0	17	1647
12	17.10.87	H	Notts Co.	L	0-1	0-1	20	2649
13	20.10.87	A	Walsall	L	0-4	0-1	21	1387
14	24.10.87	A	Bristol Rov.	L	0-4	0-3	22	2817
15	31.10.87	H	Bury	L	1-2	0-1	22	1403
16	4.11.87	A	Brighton & H.A.	L	0-2	0-1	22	7142
17	7.11.87	H	Port Vale	D	1-1	1-0	22	1365
18	21.11.87	A	Preston N.E.	W	2-1	2-0	22	5178
19	28.11.87	H	Brentford	L	0-1	0-0	22	1360
20	5.12.87	A	Chester C.	D	1-1	0-1	22	1853
21	11.12.87	A	Southend U.	L	1-4	1-1	22	2268
22	19.12.87	H	Bristol C.	L	1-2	1-1	23	1819
23	26.12.87	H	York C.	W	2-0	0-0	21	2409
24	28.12.87	A	Rotherham U.	L	0-1	0-0	23	5840
25	1.1.88	A	Sunderland	L	1-3	1-3	23	19419
26	2.1.88	H	Wigan Ath.	L	3-4	2-1	23	2464
27	9.1.88	H	Fulham	D	2-2	0-1	23	1827
28	16.1.88	A	Chesterfield	W	1-0	0-0	23	2715
29	31.1.88	H	Aldershot	D	0-0	0-0	23	1908
30	6.2.88	A	Northampton T.	L	0-1	0-1	23	4359
31	13.2.88	H	Rotherham U.	D	2-2	1-1	23	2769
32	20.2.88	A	Grimsby T.	D	0-0	0-0	23	3890
33	27.2.88	A	Gillingham	L	1-3	1-1	23	4041
34	1.3.88	H	Mansfield T.	L	0-2	0-0	23	1987
35	5.3.88	A	Notts Co.	L	0-2	0-1	23	5816
36	11.3.88	H	Chester C.	D	2-2	1-1	23	1482
37	19.3.88	A	Bury	L	1-2	1-1	23	2431
38	25.3.88	H	Bristol Rov.	L	0-1	0-1	23	1311
39	2.4.88	A	Port Vale	L	0-5	0-2	23	3680
40	4.4.88	H	Preston N.E.	W	3-2	0-1	23	2167
41	9.4.88	A	Walsall	L	1-2	0-0	23	6631
42	15.4.88	A	Blackpool	L	2-4	0-0	23	2291
43	23.4.88	H	Brighton & H.A.	L	0-2	0-0	23	1683
44	30.4.88	A	Brentford	D	1-1	0-1	23	3122
45	2.5.88	H	Southend U.	L	0-1	0-0	23	1306
46	7.5.88	A	Bristol C.	L	0-1	0-0	24	18373

Players: League Record, 1987-88 (Division 3)

Match Number	Apps	Subs	Goals
Beattie	2	0	0
Brannigan	15	0	1
Brevett	16	1	0
Buckley	6	0	0
Burke	14	6	3
Chamberlain	22	7	4
Cusack	17	0	1
Deane	42	1	10
Flynn	18	6	1
Gaughan	0	4	0
Gaynor	7	3	3
Gorman	1	6	1
Hall	0	1	0
Harbottle	4	0	0
Holmes	22	4	0
Humphries	8	0	0
James	7	1	0
Joyce	10	2	1
Kimble	34	0	1
Kinsella	21	0	3
Mendonca	2	0	0
Miller	41	0	1
Nesbitt	2	1	0
Peckett	2	0	0
Raffell	11	3	0
Rankine	14	4	2
Raven	17	0	3
Rhodes	35	0	0
Robinson, L.	7	0	1
Robinson, R.	37	0	1
Russell	6	0	0
Samways	11	0	0
Stead	23	0	0
Stubbs	8	1	1
Turnbull	24	6	1
Own Goals			1

FA Cup: 1987-88: 1st Round: Rotherham U. (H) 1-1 Replay (A) 0-2.
Littlewoods Cup: 1987-88: 1st Round: Scarborough (A) 0-1 (H) 3-1; 2nd Round: Arsenal (H) 0-3 (A) 0-1.

EVERTON (Division 1)

Team Manager Colin Harvey.
Club Address Goodison Park, Liverpool L4 4EL. Tel: 051-521 2020.
Current Ground Capacity 52,691.
Record Attendance 78,299 v Liverpool, Div. 1, 18 September 1948.
Year Formed 1878. Turned professional 1885.
Previous Names St Domingo FC.
Club Nickname "The Toffeemen".
Club Colours Royal blue shirts, white shorts and blue stockings with white turnovers.
Club Honours Football League: Div. 1 Champions 1890-91, 1914-15, 1927-28, 1931-32, 1938-39, 1962-63, 1969-70, 1984-85, 1986-87; Div. 2 Champions 1930-31. FA Cup: Winners 1906, 1933, 1966, 1984. European Cup-winners Cup: 1984-85.
League History 1888-1930 Div. 1; 1930-31 Div. 2; 1931-51 Div. 1; 1951-54 Div. 2; 1954- Div. 1.
Most League Points in a Season (2 for a win) 66 in Div. 1, 1969-70. (3 for a win) 90 in Div. 1, 1984-85.
Most League Goals in a Season 121 in Div. 2, 1930-31.

Record Victory 11-2 v Derby Co. in FA Cup 1st Round, 1889-90.
Record Defeat 4-10 v Tottenham H. in Div. 1, 11 October 1958.
Consecutive League Wins 12 in 1894.
Consecutive League Defeats 6 in 1929-30, 1958 and 1972.
Record League Appearances Ted Sagar, 465 between 1929-53.
Record League Goalscorer—Career "Dixie" Dean, 349 between 1925-37.
Record League Goalscorer—Season "Dixie" Dean, 60 in Div. 1, 1927-28 (League record).

Everton: League Record, 1987-88 (Division 1)

Match Number	Date	Venue	Opponents	Result	H/T	Lge Posn	Attend
1	15.8.87	H	Norwich C.	W 1-0	1-0		31728
2	18.8.87	A	Wimbledon	D 1-1	0-1		7763
3	22.8.87	A	Nottingham F.	D 0-0	0-0	9	20445
4	29.8.87	H	Sheffield Wed.	W 4-0	1-0	4	29649
5	2.9.87	A	Q.P.R.	L 0-1	0-1	8	15380
6	5.9.87	H	Tottenham H.	D 0-0	0-0	8	32389
7	12.9.87	A	Luton T.	L 1-2	1-1	9	8124
8	19.9.87	H	Manchester U.	W 2-1	1-0	7	38439
9	26.9.87	H	Coventry C.	L 1-2	1-2	9	28153
10	3.10.87	A	Southampton	W 4-0	3-0	9	15719
11	10.10.87	H	Chelsea	W 4-1	2-0	8	32004
12	17.10.87	A	Newcastle U.	D 1-1	1-1	8	20266
13	24.10.87	H	Watford	W 2-0	1-0	7	28501
14	1.11.87	A	Liverpool	L 0-2	0-1	7	44760
15	14.11.87	H	West Ham U.	W 3-1	3-0	5	29405
16	21.11.87	A	Portsmouth	W 1-0	0-0	5	17724
17	28.11.87	H	Oxford U.	D 0-0	0-0	5	25443
18	5.12.87	A	Charlton Ath.	D 0-0	0-0	5	7208
19	12.12.87	H	Derby Co.	W 3-0	1-0	3	26224
20	19.12.87	A	Arsenal	D 1-1	1-0	5	34587
21	26.12.87	H	Luton T.	W 2-0	1-0	4	32242
22	28.12.87	A	Manchester U.	L 1-2	0-0	5	47024
23	1.1.88	A	Sheffield Wed.	L 0-1	0-1	7	26433
24	3.1.88	H	Nottingham F.	W 1-0	1-0	5	21680
25	16.1.88	A	Norwich C.	W 3-0	1-0	3	15750
26	13.2.88	H	Q.P.R.	W 2-0	1-0	4	24724
27	27.2.88	H	Southampton	W 1-0	1-0	4	20754
28	5.3.88	H	Newcastle U.	W 1-0	1-0	4	25674
29	9.3.88	A	Tottenham H.	L 1-2	0-1	4	18262
30	12.3.88	A	Chelsea	D 0-0	0-0	3	17390
31	20.3.88	H	Liverpool	W 1-0	1-0	3	44162
32	26.3.88	A	Watford	W 2-1	1-0	3	13503
33	29.3.88	H	Wimbledon	D 2-2	2-2	4	20351
34	4.4.88	A	West Ham U.	D 0-0	0-0	4	21195
35	9.4.88	H	Portsmouth	W 2-1	1-1	3	21292
36	19.4.88	A	Coventry C.	W 2-1	0-1	3	15641
37	23.4.88	A	Oxford U.	D 1-1	1-1	3	7619
38	30.4.88	A	Charlton Ath.	D 1-1	0-0	3	20372
39	2.5.88	H	Derby Co.	D 0-0	0-0	3	17974
40	7.5.88	H	Arsenal	L 1-2	1-2	4	22445

Players: League Record, 1987-88 (Division 1)

Match Number	1	2	3	4	5	6	7	8	9	10	11	12	13	14	15	16	17	18	19	20	21	22	23	24	25	26	27	28	29	30	31	32	33	34	35	36	37	38	39	40	Apps	Subs	Goals
Adams	10	7				9														★					7	10	10						11								7	1	0
Clarke	8	8	8	8¹	8	8		9¹	8¹	8			8		★			★	★	9¹		8	8¹	8	8	8¹	8¹	8	8		8	8¹	9	9	8						24	3	9
Harper	6	6	7	2	2	2	2	2	6	★		★		★		7					★	★		4	6	6	6	10	6	4	10	10		★	10	8	★				21	7	0
Heath				★	8	8	★	★	8²	8	8¹		8	8	8	8	8¹	8	8²	8	8	8	8¹	8	6		★		★		9	9	9¹	★¹	10	8					23	6	9
Jones																						8						★													0	1	0
Marshall		10	★			★																	8																		1	3	0
Mimms	1	1	1	1	1	1			1	1																															8	0	0
Mountfield		★			★		★						★												5	5	5					4									4	5	0
Pointon	3	3	3	3	11	11¹	11	3				3			★		3	3	3	3	3		3	3¹	3	3	3	3	3	3	3¹	3	3	3	3	3	3	3			32	1	3
Power	11¹	11	11	11	11		4	4	4	4	4	4	4	4	4	4	4		11	11¹		★	10	★	10	10						11	11								12	2	2
Ratcliffe	4	4	4	4		4												4	4	4	4	4	4	4	4	4															24	0	0
Reid			6	6	6	6	6		6	6	6	6	6¹	6	6	6	6	6	6	6	6	6	6	6				6			6	6	6	6	6	6					32	0	1
Sharp	9	9¹	9	9	9	9			9	9⁴	9²	9	9¹	9	9¹	9¹	9	9	9	9	9	9	9		9²	9	9	9	9	9	9		9¹	9		9					32	0	13
Sheedy			★	★								11	11	11	11	11	11					11	11	11	11	11¹	11	11	11						★					14	3	1
Snodin		10	10	10	10	10	10	10	10	10	10¹	10	10	10¹	10	10	10	10¹	10	10	10	10		★	8	10	★		10						1						29	2	2
Southall			1	1	1		1	1	1	1	1	1	1	1	1	1	1	1	1	1	1	1		1	1	1	1	1	1	1	1	1		1	1	1	1	1			32	0	0
Steven	7			7²	7	7	7	7	7	7	7	7	7	7		7	7	7¹	7	7	7	7	7	7		7	7	7	7	7	7¹	7	7¹	7	7¹	7	7				36	0	6
Stevens								2	2	2	2	2	2	2	2	2	2	2	2	2	2	2	2	2	2	2	2	2	2	2	2	2	2	2	★	2	2				31	0	0
Van den Hauwe	2	2	2		3	3	3	2	3	3	3		3	3	3	3					3	4		4	4	4	4		4	4	4	4	4	4	4	4					28	0	0
Watson	5	5	5	5	5	5	5	5	5	5	5	5	5	5	5	5¹	5	5	5	5	5¹	5	5	5¹	5	5	5	5	5	5	5		5	5	5	5	5¹				37	0	4
Wilson						11	11	11	11	11	11	★		★		★	11	11	11	11	11										11	11									13	3	0
Own Goals				1															1			1																					3

FA Cup: 1987-88: 3rd Round: Sheffield Wed. (A) 1-1 Replay (H) 1-1 2nd Replay (H) 1-1 3rd Replay (A) 5-0; 4th Round: Middlesbrough (H) 1-1 Replay (A) 2-2 2nd Replay (H) 2-1; Fifth Round: Liverpool (H) 0-1.
Littlewoods Cup: 1987-88: 2nd Round: Rotherham U. (H) 3-2 (A) 0-0; 3rd Round: Liverpool (A) 1-0; 4th Round: Oldham Ath. (H) 2-1; Quarter Final: Manchester C. (H) 2-0; Semi Final: Arsenal (H) 0-1 (A) 1-3.

EXETER CITY (Division 4)

Team Manager Terry Cooper.
Club Address St James Park, Exeter EX4 6PX. Tel: (0392) 54073.
Current Ground Capacity 17,086.
Record Attendance 20,984 v Sunderland, FA Cup 6th Round Replay, 4 March 1931.
Year Formed 1904. Turned professional 1908.
Previous Names None.
Club Nickname "The Grecians".
Club Colours Red and white striped shirts, black shorts and black stockings with red turnovers.
Club Honours None.
League History 1920-58 Div. 3(S); 1958-64 Div. 4; 1964-66 Div. 3; 1966-77 Div. 4; 1977-84 Div. 3; 1984- Div. 4.
Most League Points in a Season (2 for a win) 62 in Div. 4, 1976-77. (3 for a win) 57 in Div. 3, 1981-82.
Most League Goals in a Season 88 in Div. 3(S), 1932-33.
Record Victory 8-1 v Coventry C. in Div. 3(S), 4 December 1926 and v Aldershot in Div. 3(S), 4 May 1935.
Record Defeat 0-9 v Notts Co. in Div. 3(S), 16 October 1948 and v Northampton T. in Div. 3(S), 12 April 1958.

Consecutive League Wins 7 in 1977.
Consecutive League Defeats 7 in 1936 and 1984.
Record League Appearances Arnold Mitchell, 493 between 1952-66.
Record League Goalscorer—Career Tony Kellow, 128 between 1976-88.
Record League Goalscorer—Season Fred Whitlow, 34 in Div. 3(S), 1932-33.

Exeter City: League Record, 1987-88 (Division 4)

Match Number	Date	Venue	Opponents	Result		H/T	Lge Posn	Attend
1	15.8.87	H	Cambridge U.	W	3-0	2-0		2650
2	22.8.87	A	Swansea C.	W	2-0	1-0		5557
3	29.8.87	H	Newport Co.	W	3-0	0-0	1	2628
4	31.8.87	A	Tranmere Rov.	L	1-2	0-1	1	3107
5	5.9.87	H	Wrexham	D	1-1	0-0	1	2719
6	12.9.87	A	Leyton Orient	W	3-2	1-0	1	3613
7	16.9.87	H	Carlisle U.	D	1-1	1-1	2	3347
8	19.9.87	H	Rochdale	D	1-1	0-1	2	2628
9	25.9.87	A	Colchester U.	W	2-0	1-0	1	1443
10	30.9.87	A	Hartlepool U.	L	1-3	1-1	3	2973
11	3.10.87	H	Torquay U.	L	0-1	0-1	5	6281
12	10.10.87	A	Scarborough	L	1-3	1-1	7	2472
13	17.10.87	H	Burnley	L	1-2	1-1	14	2780
14	20.10.87	A	Bolton W.	L	0-1	0-0	14	4165
15	24.10.87	H	Crewe Alex.	W	3-1	1-0	13	2149
16	31.10.87	A	Hereford U.	D	1-1	0-0	15	2200
17	7.11.87	A	Cardiff C.	L	2-3	1-1	18	3474
18	21.11.87	H	Stockport Co.	W	2-1	1-0	16	2217
19	8.12.87	A	Darlington	L	1-4	0-3	16	1107
20	12.12.87	H	Scunthorpe U.	D	1-1	0-0	17	1831
21	18.12.87	A	Halifax T.	L	0-2	0-1	18	1302
22	26.12.87	H	Colchester U.	L	0-2	0-0	18	2675
23	28.12.87	A	Wolverhampton W.	L	0-3	0-1	18	15588
24	1.1.88	A	Newport Co.	D	1-1	1-1	20	1691
25	2.1.88	H	Leyton Orient	L	2-3	1-1	20	2568
26	9.1.88	H	Swansea C.	W	3-1	1-0	18	2225
27	16.1.88	A	Rochdale	D	0-0	0-0	18	1431
28	23.1.88	A	Carlisle U.	D	0-0	0-0	19	1699
29	30.1.88	H	Tranmere Rov.	L	0-1	0-1	19	2261
30	13.2.88	H	Wolverhampton W.	L	2-4	0-2	21	3483
31	19.2.88	A	Cambridge U.	L	1-2	0-0	21	1878
32	27.2.88	A	Torquay U.	D	1-1	0-1	21	3383
33	2.3.88	H	Hartlepool U.	W	1-0	0-0	20	1573
34	5.3.88	A	Burnley	L	0-3	0-1	20	6052
35	9.3.88	H	Peterborough U.	L	0-1	0-0	20	1584
36	12.3.88	H	Scarborough	W	1-0	0-0	20	1738
37	19.3.88	A	Hereford U.	D	2-2	0-2	20	1628
38	22.3.88	A	Wrexham	L	0-3	0-0	20	963
39	26.3.88	A	Crewe Alex.	D	0-0	0-0	21	1665
40	2.4.88	H	Cardiff C.	L	0-2	0-2	22	2649
41	4.4.88	A	Stockport Co.	L	1-2	1-0	22	2161
42	9.4.88	H	Bolton W.	D	1-1	1-0	22	1962
43	23.4.88	A	Peterborough U.	L	1-2	0-1	22	2278
44	30.4.88	H	Darlington	W	4-1	0-0	21	1515
45	2.5.88	A	Scunthorpe U.	D	1-1	0-0	21	6736
46	7.5.88	H	Halifax T.	L	1-2	1-0	22	1602

Players: League Record, 1987-88 (Division 4)

Match Number	1	2	3	4	5	6	7	8	9	10	11	12	13	14	15	16	17	18	19	20	21	22	23	24	25	26	27	28	29	30	31	32	33	34	35	36	37	38	39	40	41	42	43	44	45	46	Apps	Subs	Goals
Batty	7	7	7¹	7	7¹	7	7	7	7¹	7	7	★	7	7	7¹	7	7¹		7	7	7	7	7	7	7¹	7	7	7	7	11														★	★		29	3	6
Carter	6²	6	6	6	6	6	6	6	6	6			4	4	4	4	4	4	4	4	4	4	4	4	4	4	7	7	7	7	7		★	★			★	★	4	4	4	4					37	4	2
Collins													7	6	11	11		★	11	11	11	11																6	6	6	6	6	6	6			8	1	0
Cooper	★	5	5¹	5								★	7	2	2	2	2	★	8	8	8	8	8		8					8	8	8	8		8	8	8	★						8		8¹	30	3	1
Delve													10	10	10									8	8	8		8			★	4	4	4									8		8¹		12	1	1
Edwards	8	8	8	8	8	8	8²	8	8	8¹	8¹	8	8	8¹	8	8	8	8	8	9	9	9	9	9¹	9¹	9	9	9	9	9	9	9	9	★	★	★	9	9	9	9³	9¹	9					40	3	12
Gwinnett													1	1	1									1	1	1	1	1	1	1	1	1	1	1	1	1	1	1	1	1	1	1	1	1	1	1	24	0	0
Harris																	★				★												★	9¹	9	9	9										5	4	1
Harrower	11	11	11¹	11	11	★	★	★	11	11	11	11	11	11	11	11	11	11	11	2	2	2	2	2	2	2	2	2	2	2	2	2	2	2	2	2	2	2	2	2	2¹	2	2	2			43	3	2
Hiley														★	10															★	11			11		7	7¹	7	7	7	7	7	★	7			12	3	1
Kellow		★¹	★	★	★	★	★	★¹		★		10	9	9¹					11	9		★	★		★																						5	11	3
Marker	4	4	4	4	4	4	4	4	4	4	4																																				11	0	0
Massey						5				5			4	★	6	6¹	★		2	6	6				★		★	★	★	4	4	4	4				4	4	4								17	6	1
Milton													10²		10¹																																2	0	3
Nisbet	2	2	2	2	2	2	2	2	2	2	2	2																																			12	0	0
O'Connell	9¹	9¹	9	9¹	9	9¹	9	9						9¹	9	9	9	10¹	10	10	10	10	10	10	10¹	10	10	10	10²	10	10	10¹	10	10	10	10	10	10	10	10	10¹	10	10¹	10	10		39	0	12
Olsson	10	10	10	10	10	10	11			10	10	10	★	6			★			★		6¹	6	6¹	6	6	6	6			★	6			8	8	8	8	8	8	8	7	8	7			30	5	2
Phillips									9	9	9	9	9¹	9	★																																5	1	1
Rowbotham													6	6¹	6		★	11						11	11	11	★	★	11	11			11	11	11	11	11	11¹	11	11	11	11	11	11			20	3	2
Shaw	1	1	1	1	1	1	1	1	1	1	1	1					1	1	1	1	1	1	1	1	1	1																					22	0	0
Taylor	5				5	5	5		5	5	5	5	5	5	5	5	5	5	5	5	5	5	5	5	5	5	5	5	5	5¹	5	5	5	5	5	5	5	5	5	5	5	5	5	5	5	5	41	0	1
Viney	3	3	3	3	3	3	3	3	3	3	3	3	3	3	3	3	3	3	3	3	3	3	3	3	3	3	3	3	3	3	3	3	3	3	3	3	3	3	3	3	3	3	3	3	3	3	46	0	0
Watson									11		11			6							6	6							8	6	6	6			6	6	6		★								12	1	0
Williams				★		10¹	10		★	6	10																																				4	2	1
Own Goals																																				1													1

FA Cup: 1987-88: 1st Round: Leyton Orient (A) 0-2.
Littlewoods Cup: 1987-88: 1st Round: Bournemouth (A) 1-1 (H) 1-3.

FULHAM (Division 3)

FULHAM F.C.

Team Manager Ray Lewington.
Club Address Craven Cottage, Stevenage Road, London SW6. Tel: 01-736 6561.
Current Ground Capacity 25,680.
Record Attendance 49,335 v Millwall, Div. 2, 8 October 1938.
Year Formed 1879. Turned professional 1898.
Previous Names Fulham St Andrew's.
Club Nickname "The Cottagers".
Club Colours White shirts with black collar, black shorts and white stockings with three black hoops on turnover.
Club Honours Football League: Div. 2 Champions 1948-49; Div. 3(S) Champions 1931-32.
League History 1907-28 Div. 2; 1928-32 Div. 3(S); 1943-49 Div. 2; 1949-52 Div. 1; 1952-59 Div. 2; 1959-68 Div. 1; 1968-69 Div. 2; 1969-71 Div. 1; 1971-80 Div. 2; 1980-82 Div. 3; 1982-86 Div. 2; 1986- Div. 3.
Most League Points in a Season (2 for a win) 60 in Div. 2, 1958-59 and Div. 3, 1970-71. (3 for a win) 78 in Div. 3, 1981-82.
Most League Goals in a Season 111 in Div. 3(S), 1931-32.
Record Victory 10-1 v Ipswich T., in Div. 1, 26 December 1963.
Record Defeat 0-10 v Liverpool in League Cup 2nd Round 1st leg, 23 September 1986.
Consecutive League Wins 8 in 1963.
Consecutive League Defeats 11 in 1961-62.
Record League Appearances Johnny Haynes, 594 between 1952-70.
Record League Goalscorer—Career Bedford Jezzard, 154 between 1948-56.
Record League Goalscorer—Season Frank Newton, 43 in Div. 3(S), 1931-32.

Fulham: League Record, 1987-88 (Division 3)

Match Number	Date	Venue	Opponents	Result		H/T	Lge Posn	Attend
1	15.8.87	A	Walsall	W	1-0	0-0		4691
2	22.8.87	H	Doncaster Rov.	W	4-0	3-0		4157
3	29.8.87	A	Brighton & H.A.	L	0-2	0-1	6	8773
4	1.9.87	H	Notts Co.	D	0-0	0-0	7	4767
5	4.9.87	A	Mansfield T.	W	2-0	0-0	2	3536
6	12.9.87	H	Gillingham	L	0-2	0-0	10	7404
7	16.9.87	A	Chester C.	W	2-1	1-1	5	2469
8	19.9.87	A	Port Vale	D	1-1	1-0	8	3894
9	26.9.87	H	Bristol Rov.	W	3-1	1-1	2	4614
10	29.9.87	H	Sunderland	L	0-2	0-1	5	6996
11	3.10.87	A	Blackpool	L	1-2	0-1	11	4973
12	10.10.87	H	York C.	W	3-1	2-1	5	4057
13	17.10.87	A	Wigan Ath.	W	3-1	2-0	5	2806
14	20.10.87	A	Southend U.	W	2-0	1-0	5	3419
15	24.10.87	H	Aldershot	L	1-2	1-0	6	6530
16	3.11.87	H	Grimsby T.	W	5-0	3-0	5	3493
17	17.11.87	H	Northampton T.	D	0-0	0-0	6	6717
18	21.11.87	A	Rotherham U.	W	2-0	1-0	5	3427
19	28.11.87	H	Preston N.E.	L	0-1	0-1	5	5324
20	12.12.87	A	Bury	D	1-1	1-1	5	2643
21	15.12.87	A	Bristol C.	L	0-4	0-3	5	6150
22	19.12.87	H	Chesterfield	L	1-3	1-1	7	4006
23	26.12.87	A	Bristol Rov.	L	1-3	1-1	9	4718
24	28.12.87	H	Brentford	D	2-2	0-0	9	9340
25	1.1.88	H	Brighton & H.A.	L	1-2	1-0	10	6530
26	2.1.88	A	Gillingham	D	2-2	1-2	10	6001
27	9.1.88	A	Doncaster Rov.	D	2-2	1-0	9	1827
28	16.1.88	H	Port Vale	L	1-2	1-0	11	3748
29	30.1.88	A	Notts Co.	L	1-5	1-2	11	6107
30	6.2.88	H	Mansfield T.	D	0-0	0-0	12	3330
31	14.2.88	A	Brentford	L	1-3	0-1	13	8712
32	20.2.88	H	Walsall	W	2-0	1-0	11	3718
33	27.2.88	H	Blackpool	W	3-1	1-0	11	4072
34	1.3.88	A	Sunderland	L	0-2	0-2	11	11379
35	5.3.88	H	Wigan Ath.	W	3-2	3-2	10	3860
36	12.3.88	A	York C.	W	3-1	2-1	9	2560
37	19.3.88	H	Bristol C.	D	0-0	0-0	11	4896
38	26.3.88	A	Aldershot	W	3-0	1-0	10	4448
39	2.4.88	A	Northampton T.	L	2-3	1-1	11	6211
40	4.4.88	H	Rotherham U.	W	3-1	2-0	9	4402
41	9.4.88	A	Grimsby T.	W	2-0	1-0	8	3123
42	15.4.88	H	Chester C.	W	1-0	0-0	7	4131
43	23.4.88	H	Southend U.	W	3-1	1-0	7	5043
44	30.4.88	A	Preston N.E.	L	1-2	0-1	8	4192
45	2.5.88	H	Bury	L	0-1	0-1	9	5283
46	7.5.88	A	Chesterfield	L	0-1	0-1	9	3084

Players: League Record, 1987-88 (Division 3)

Match Number	1	2	3	4	5	6	7	8	9	10	11	12	13	14	15	16	17	18	19	20	21	22	23	24	25	26	27	28	29	30	31	32	33	34	35	36	37	38	39	40	41	42	43	44	45	46	Apps	Subs	Goals
Achampong					★																	★			★	10		★	★			★				10	10[1]	10	10	10[1]	10	10[1]	10				9	6	3
Barnett	11	11	11	11	11	11	11	11	11[1]	11	11	★			11[1]	11	7	7	7		7[1]	7	★	7	7	7	7	7	7	7	7	7	7	7	7	7[1]	7[1]	7[2]	7	7	7[1]	★[1]	7	7			39	3	9
Cole																																		11	11	11	11	11[1]	11	11	11	11				9	0	1
Davies	10	10[2]	10	10	10[1]	10	10	10		10	10	10[1]	10	10[1]	10[1]	10[1]	10	10		10	10	10[1]		10[1]	10	10	★	10[1]	10	10	10	10[1]			★				★	★	10	10				35	4	13
Donnellan	★	★	★	★	★	★	★	★		★				★	★		★			★																											0	11	0
Eckhardt																5	5	5	5	5	5	5	5	5	5	5	2	2	2	2	2	2	2	2	2	2	2	2	2	2[1]	2	2	2				29	0	1
Elkins											2	2	2	2	2	2	2	2				6	6	6	6				3	3	3	3	3	3	3	3	3	3	3	3	3	3	3	3			29	0	0
Gore																						6	6	6	6	6	6	★																			7	1	0
Greaves																																										★					0	1	0
Hicks							6									6	6	6	6	6	6	6		★	6																						9	1	0
Hoddy																							9												★	★		4			★						2	3	0
Hopkins	6	5	5	5	5	5	5	5	5	5	5	5	5	5																		6	6	6	6	6	6	5	6	6	6	6	6	6			26	0	0
Kerrins	★	★	★	★	2	2	2	2	★				3	★								8	2	6																							8	6	0
Langley	2	2	2	2									3	2	2	2	2	2	2	2	2	2	2																								15	0	0
Lewington	4	4	4	4	4	4	4	4	4	4	4	4	4	4	4	4	4	4	4	4	4	4	4	4	4[1]	4	4	4																			31	0	1
Marshall	7	7	7	7	7	7	7	7				8	8	8	8	7	7																		★	9	9[1]	9	9	9[1]	9	9	9	9	9		24	1	2
Oakes	5	6	6	6	6	6	6		6	6	6	6	6	6	6	5	5							5	5	5	5	5	5	5	5	5	5	5	5	5	5	6	5	5	5	5	5	5		35	0	0
Pike																		★							★	★																					0	3	0
Rosenior	9[1]	9[2]	9	9	9[1]	9	9[2]	9	9[1]	9	9	9	9[2]	9[1]	9	9[1]	9	9	9	9	9[1]	9	9	9[2]	9[1]			9	9	9[1]	9[1]	9	9[1]	9[1]													34	0	20
Scott																								★	7[1]	11	11	8		8	8	8	8	8[1]	8	8[1]	8	8	8	8	8	8	8	8	8		22	1	3
Skinner	8	8	8	8	8	8	8[1]	8	8	8		★	8[2]	8	★		7	10					8	9	★	10		★	★	4	4	4	4[1]	4[1]		4	4	4									27	5	5
Stannard	1	1	1	1	1	1	1	1	1	1	1	1	1	1	1	1	1	1	1	1	1	1	1	1	1	1	1	1	1	1	1	1	1	1	1	1	1	1	1	1	1	1	1	1	1	1	46	0	0
Thomas	3	3	3	3	3	3	3	3	3	3	3	3	3	3		3	3	3	3	3	3	3	3	3	3	3	3	3																			27	0	0
Walker											11[2]	11	11[1]	11			11	11[1]	11	11	11	11	11		11	11	11[1]	11	11	11	11[1]	11	11[1]	11	11								★		7	4	4	25	1	8
Wilson									7	7	7[1]	7	7	7	7		8	8	8	8	8	8[1]	8		★	★[1]	4	4	4																		18	2	3

FA Cup: 1987-88: 1st Round: Gillingham (A) 1-2.
Littlewoods Cup: 1987-88: 1st Round: Colchester U. (H) 3-1 (A) 2-0; 2nd Round: Bradford C. (H) 1-5 (A) 1-2.

82

GILLINGHAM (Division 3)

Team Manager Paul Taylor.
Club Address Priestfield Stadium, Gillingham. Tel: (0634) 51854.
Current Ground Capacity 19,581.
Record Attendance 23,002 v Q.P.R., FA Cup 3rd Round, 10 January 1948.
Year Formed 1893. Turned professional 1894.
Previous Names New Brompton.
Club Nickname "The Gills".
Club Colours Royal blue shirts, white shorts and stockings with blue trim.
Club Honours Football League: Div. 4 Champions 1963-64.
League History 1920-38 Div. 3(S); 1938 Failed re-election; 1938-44 Southern League; 1944-46 Kent League; 1946-50 Southern League; 1950-58 Div. 3(S); 1958-64 Div. 4; 1964-71 Div. 3; 1971-74 Div. 4; 1974- Div. 3.
Most League Points in a Season (2 for a win) 62 in Div. 4, 1973-74. (3 for a win) 83 in Div. 3, 1984-85.
Most League Goals in a Season 90 in div. 4, 1973-74.

Record Victory 10-0 v Chesterfield in 3rd Div., 5 September 1987.
Record Defeat 2-9 v Nottingham F. in Division 3(S), 18 November 1950.
Consecutive League Wins 7 in 1954-55.
Consecutive League Defeats 9 in 1951-52.
Record League Appearances John Simpson, 571 between 1957-72.
Record League Appearances Brian Yeo, 135 between 1963-75.
Record League Goalscorer—Season Ernie Morgan, 31 in Div. 3(S), 1954-55 and Brian Yeo, 31 in Div. 4, 1973-74.

Gilingham: League Record, 1987-88 (Division 3)

Match Number	Date	Venue	Opponents	Result		H/T	Lge Posn	Attend
1	15.8.87	H	Blackpool	D	0-0	0-0		4430
2	22.8.87	A	Grimsby T.	L	0-2	0-1		2901
3	29.8.87	H	Southend U.	W	8-1	4-0	10	4154
4	31.8.87	A	Wigan Ath	D	1-1	1-0	9	3412
5	5.9.87	H	Chesterfield	W	10-0	5-0	7	4099
6	12.9.87	A	Fulham	W	2-0	0-0	4	7404
7	15.9.87	H	Sunderland	D	0-0	0-0	6	9184
8	19.9.87	H	York C.	W	3-1	0-1	2	5507
9	26.9.87	A	Bristol C.	D	3-3	2-1	5	10070
10	29.9.87	H	Chester C.	L	0-1	0-0	8	5193
11	3.10.87	A	Doncaster Rov.	L	2-4	0-2	12	1647
12	10.10.87	H	Bristol Rov.	W	3-0	0-0	7	4399
13	17.10.87	A	Mansfield T.	D	2-2	2-1	8	2957
14	20.10.87	A	Preston N.E.	D	1-1	1-1	9	5676
15	24.10.87	H	Notts Co.	W	3-1	0-1	7	5551
16	31.10.87	A	Port Vale	D	0-0	0-0	7	3495
17	3.11.87	H	Brentford	L	0-1	0-1	10	4529
18	7.11.87	H	Brighton & H.A.	D	1-1	0-0	9	6437
19	21.11.87	A	Northampton T.	L	1-2	0-0	11	5151
20	28.11.87	H	Bury	D	3-3	1-1	12	3981
21	12.12.87	A	Rotherham U.	W	2-1	2-0	10	2557
22	18.12.87	H	Walsall	L	0-1	0-0	12	4020
23	26.12.87	H	Bristol C.	D	1-1	0-1	11	6457
24	28.12.87	A	Aldershot.	L	0-6	0-5	13	4734
25	1.1.88	A	Southend U.	W	3-1	2-0	12	5254
26	2.1.88	H	Fulham	D	2-2	2-1	12	6001
27	16.1.88	A	York C.	W	2-0	0-0	9	2129
28	23.1.88	H	Wigan Ath.	L	0-1	0-1	9	4256
29	30.1.88	A	Sunderland	L	1-2	0-2	10	16195
30	2.2.88	H	Grimsby T.	D	1-1	1-0	10	2993
31	6.2.88	A	Chesterfield	W	4-1	0-0	9	2141
32	13.2.88	H	Aldershot	W	2-1	0-0	9	4001
33	20.2.88	A	Blackpool	D	3-3	0-0	9	3045
34	27.2.88	H	Doncaster Rov.	W	3-1	1-1	8	4041
35	2.3.88	A	Chester C.	L	1-3	0-0	9	1638
36	5.3.88	H	Mansfield T.	D	0-0	0-0	9	3720
37	12.3.88	A	Bristol Rov.	L	0-2	0-0	10	3846
38	19.3.88	H	Port Vale	D	0-0	0-0	9	3459
39	26.3.88	A	Notts Co.	W	1-0	0-0	9	6473
40	2.4.88	A	Brighton & H.A.	L	0-2	0-2	10	9256
41	4.4.88	H	Northampton T.	L	1-2	0-0	12	4126
42	9.4.88	A	Brentford	D	2-2	0-0	11	3875
43	23.4.88	H	Preston N.E.	W	4-0	1-0	12	2721
44	30.4.88	A	Bury	L	1-2	1-1	13	1433
45	2.5.88	H	Rotherham U.	L	0-2	0-1	14	3015
46	7.5.88	A	Walsall	D	0-0	0-0	13	8850

Players: League Record, 1987-88 (Division 3)

Player	Apps	Subs	Goals
Berry	15	5	0
Cooper	24	7	8
Docker	0	1	0
Elsey	37	2	6
Eves	9	6	7
Gernon	19	2	1
Greenall	25	0	2
Haines	0	1	0
Haylock	32	0	0
Hillyard	18	0	0
Kite	26	0	0
Lillis	3	4	0
Lovell	46	0	25
Luff	0	1	0
Palmer	2	0	0
Parks	2	0	0
Peacock	26	0	2
Pearce	32	0	0
Pritchard	40	2	8
Quow	33	7	1
Shearer	11	0	5
Shipley	15	0	7
Smith, D.	34	1	7
Smith, M.	1	1	0
Walker	7	0	0
Weatherley	8	9	0
West	42	0	2
Own Goals			1

FA Cup: 1987-88: 1st Round: Fulham (H) 2-1; 2nd Round: Walsall (H) 2-1; 3rd Round: Birmingham C. (H) 0-3.
Littlewoods Cup: 1987-88: 1st Round: Brighton & H.A. (H) 1-0 (A) 0-1; 2nd Round: Stoke C. (A) 0-2 (H) 0-1.

GRIMSBY TOWN (Division 4)

Team Manager Alan Buckley
Club Address Blundell Park, Cleethorpes, South Humberside DN35 7PY. Tel: (0472) 697111.
Current Ground Capacity 20,865.
Record Attendance 31,651 v Wolverhampton W., FA Cup 5th Round, 20 February 1937.
Year Formed 1878. Turned professional 1890.
Previous Names Grimsby Pelham.
Club Nickname ''The Mariners''.
Club Colours Black and white vertical striped shirts, black shorts and stockings.
Club Honours Football League: Div. 2 Champions 1900-01, 1933-34; Div. 3(N) Champions 1925-26, 1955-56; Div. 3 Champions 1979-80; Div. 4 Champions 1971-72.
League History 1892-1901 Div. 2; 1901-03 Div. 1; 1903-10 Div 2; 1910 Failed re-election; 1911-20 Div. 2; 1920-21 Div. 3; 1921-26 Div. 3(N); 1926-29 Div. 2; 1929-32 Div. 1; 1932-34 Div. 2; 1934-48 Div. 1; 1948-51 Div. 2; 1951-56 Div. 3(N); 1956-59 Div. 2; 1959-62 Div. 3; 1962-64 Div. 2; 1964-68 Div. 3; 1968-72 Div. 4; 1972-77 Div. 3; 1977-79

Div. 4; 1979-80 Div. 3; 1980-87 Div. 2; 1987-88 Div. 3; 1988- Div. 4.
Most League Points in a Season (2 for a win) 68 in Div. 3(N), 1955-56. (3 for a win) 70 in Div. 2, 1983-84.
Most League Goals in a Season 103 in Div. 2, 1933-34.
Record Victory 9-2 v Darwen in Div. 2, 15 April 1899.
Record Defeat 1-9 v Arsenal in Div. 1, 28 January 1931.
Consecutive League Wins 11 in 1952.
Consecutive League Defeats 9 in 1907-08.
Record League Appearances Keith Jobling, 448 between 1953-69.
Record League Goalscorer—Career Pat Glover, 182 between 1930-39.
Record League Goalscorer—Season Pat Glover, 42 in Div. 2, 1933-34.

Grimsby Town: League Record, 1987-88 (Division 3)

Match Number	Date	Venue	Opponents	Result		H/T	Lge Posn	Attend
1	15.8.87	A	Doncaster Rov.	L	0-1	0-1		2482
2	22.8.87	H	Gillingham	W	2-0	1-0		2901
3	29.8.87	A	Notts Co.	D	0-0	0-0	13	5322
4	31.8.87	H	Brentford	L	0-1	0-1	14	3361
5	5.9.87	A	Preston N.E.	W	3-1	2-0	14	5522
6	12.9.87	H	Mansfield T.	L	2-3	1-1	15	3410
7	15.9.87	A	Bury	W	2-0	2-0	10	1899
8	19.9.87	A	Chester C.	L	0-1	0-0	15	1897
9	26.9.87	H	Walsall	L	0-2	0-1	18	3311
10	29.9.87	A	Rotherham U.	D	0-0	0-0	17	3375
11	3.10.87	H	Southend U.	L	1-3	0-3	20	2900
12	10.10.87	A	Chesterfield	W	3-0	1-0	17	2072
13	17.10.87	H	Bristol C.	L	1-4	1-4	17	3100
14	20.10.87	H	Blackpool	D	1-1	1-1	19	2260
15	24.10.87	A	Northampton T.	L	1-2	1-1	20	5388
16	31.10.87	H	Brighton & H.A.	L	0-1	0-1	20	2711
17	3.11.87	A	Fulham	L	0-5	0-3	20	3493
18	7.11.87	H	Sunderland	D	1-1	1-0	20	18197
19	21.11.87	H	York C.	W	5-1	2-1	20	2200
20	28.11.87	A	Bristol Rov.	L	2-4	1-2	20	2787
21	12.12.87	H	Wigan Ath.	L	0-2	0-1	20	2127
22	19.12.87	A	Aldershot	L	2-3	1-3	20	2405
23	26.12.87	A	Walsall	L	2-3	1-0	22	6272
24	28.12.87	H	Port Vale	W	3-1	1-1	21	2941
25	1.1.88	H	Notts Co.	D	0-0	0-0	20	5297
26	2.1.88	A	Mansfield T.	L	0-1	0-1	21	3315
27	16.1.88	H	Chester C.	W	2-1	0-0	22	2594
28	26.1.88	H	Bury	W	2-0	1-0	21	2525
29	2.2.88	A	Gillingham	D	1-1	0-1	21	2993
30	6.2.88	H	Preston N.E.	L	0-1	0-1	21	2907
31	13.2.88	A	Port Vale	L	0-2	0-0	21	3417
32	20.2.88	H	Doncaster Rov.	D	0-0	0-0	22	3890
33	23.2.88	A	Brentford	W	2-0	1-0	20	3534
34	26.2.88	A	Southend U.	D	0-0	0-0	21	3409
35	5.3.88	A	Bristol C.	D	1-1	0-1	21	8343
36	8.3.88	H	Rotherham U.	W	2-1	1-0	20	3423
37	12.3.88	H	Chesterfield	D	1-1	0-0	20	3464
38	19.3.88	A	Brighton & H.A.	D	0-0	0-0	21	7269
39	26.3.88	H	Northampton T.	D	2-2	2-0	20	3406
40	2.4.88	H	Sunderland	L	0-1	0-1	21	7001
41	4.4.88	A	York C.	W	2-0	1-0	20	3215
42	9.4.88	H	Fulham	L	0-2	0-1	20	3123
43	23.4.88	A	Blackpool	L	0-3	0-1	22	2555
44	30.4.88	H	Bristol Rov.	D	0-0	0-0	22	2025
45	2.5.88	A	Wigan Ath.	W	1-0	0-0	22	2705
46	7.5.88	H	Aldershot	D	1-1	1-1	22	5697

Players: League Record, 1987-88 (Division 3)

Match Number	1	2	3	4	5	6	7	8	9	10	11	12	13	14	15	16	17	18	19	20	21	22	23	24	25	26	27	28	29	30	31	32	33	34	35	36	37	38	39	40	41	42	43	44	45	46	Apps	Subs	Goals
Agnew	3	3	3	3	3	3	3	3		3			3	3	3					3	3	3	3	3	3	3	3	3		3	3	3	3	3	3	3	3	3	3¹	3	3	3	3	3			38	0	1
Burgess	6	6		6	6	6	6	6	6			6	6	6	6			5		6	5	5	5	5	5	5	5		5	5	5	5	5	5	5	5	5	5	5	5	5	5	5	5	5	5	38	0	0
Cunnington																															4	4	4	4	4¹	4	4	4¹	4	4	4	4	4	4	4	4	15	0	2
Curran																	7	7	7		★	7	★	7	7	9	7	7				7															10	2	0
Dixon					3									★	★	3	3	3	3		9	2	2	2	2	2	2	2	2	2	2	2	2	2	2	2	2	2	2	2	2	2	2	2	2	2	30	2	0
Grocock			★¹		★	★		★		★	★	★	4	★	6	★	5		★			★		★	9		★	11	★					11	11	11	11		11	★	★					10	15	1
Jobling																								6	6¹	6	6	6	6	6	6	6	6¹	6	6	6	6	6	6								15	0	1
Lever																												★																			0	1	0
McDermott	2	2			★			2	2	2	2				2	2	2	2	2	2								7	7	3		★	9	★		★	★	★	★	9	9			9	11		21	7	0
McGarvey	11	11	11	11	11	11	11²	11	11	11	11	11¹	11	11	11	11	11	11	11	11	11	11	11	11¹	11	11	11	11²	11	11	11		11	11	11	11	11			11	★	11					38	1	6
Moore																							★																								0	1	0
North	9	9	9	9		9	8	8	8	8	8	9¹		9	9	9	9	9¹	9²	9	9		9¹	9³	9		9		9	9	9	9	9		9	9¹	9	9	9	9			9	9	★¹	9¹	37	1	11
O'Riordan	10	10	10	10	10¹	10¹	10	10	10	10	10¹	10	10	10	10	10	10¹	10²	10	10	10	10	10	10	10	10	10	10¹	10	10	10	10	10	10	10	10	10¹	10	10	10	10	10	10	10	10	10	46	0	8
Rawcliffe																	★		★																												0	2	0
Robinson	7	4	7	7			9	9				6	8	8	8	8	4		6²	6	6	7	6	6	6	6	6	6	7	11	7	7	7	7	7	7	7¹	7	7	7	7	7	7				40	0	3
Saunders	★		6		7¹			9	9	9			3	8	8	8	8	8	8¹	8	8	8	8	8	8	8	8	8	8	8¹	8	8	8	8	8	8			8	8	8	8					34	1	3
Sherwood	1	1	1	1	1	1	1	1	1	1	1	1	1	1	1	1	1	1	1	1	1	1	1	1	1	1	1	1	1	1	1	1	1	1	1	1	1	1	1	1	1	1	1	1	1	1	46	0	0
Slack	5	5	5	5		5	5	5	5	5	5	5	5	5	5	5	5	5			5	5																									21	0	0
Stubbs																																★		★¹	★		★	8¹	8	★							2	5	2
Toale		★	2	2	2	2	2	7		6	3	2	2	2				7	7	★	★		7				6										★			★							16	4	0
Turner	4	7	4	4	4	4	4	4	4	4	4	4	4¹	4¹		4	4	4	4¹	4	4	4	4	4¹	4¹	4	4																				28	0	5
Walsh	8	8²	8	8	8¹	8	★	★		★	8²	9																																			8	3	5
Watson			9	7	7	7		7	7	7	7	7	7	7	7	6	4			★	★	★	★		★	★																					13	6	0

FA Cup: 1987-88: 1st Round: Scarborough (A) 2-1; 2nd Round: Halifax T. (H) 0-0 Replay (A) 0-2.
Littlewoods Cup: 1987-88: 1st Round: Darlington (H) 3-2 (A) 1-2.

HALIFAX TOWN (Division 4)

Team Manager Billy Ayre.
Club Address Shay Ground, Halifax HX1 2YS. Tel: (0422) 53423.
Current Ground Capacity 16,500.
Record Attendance 36,885 v Tottenham H, FA Cup 5th Round, 14 February 1953.
Year Formed 1911. Turned professional 1911.
Previous Names None.
Club Nickname "The Shaymen".
Club Colours Royal blue shirts with white trim, white shorts with blue trim and blue stockings with white tops.
Club Honours None.
League History 1921-58 Div. 3(N); 1958-63 Div 3; 1963-69 Div. 4; 1969-76 Div. 3; 1976- Div. 4.
Most League Points in a Season (2 for a win) 57 in Div. 4, 1968-69. (3 for a win) 60 in Div. 4, 1982-83.
Most League Goals in a Season 83 in Div. 3(N), 1957-58.
Record Victory 7-0 v Bishop Auckland in FA Cup 2nd Round Replay, 10 January 1967.
Record Defeat 0-13 v Stockport Co. in Div. 3(N), 6 January 1934.

Consecutive League Wins 7 in 1964.
Consecutive League Defeats 8 in 1946-47.
Record League Appearances John Pickering, 367 between 1965-74.
Record League Goalscorer—Career Ernest Dixon, 129 between 1922-30.
Record League Goalscorer—Season Albert Valentine, 34 in Div. 3(N), 1934-35.

Halifax Town: League Record, 1987-88 (Division 4)

Match Number	Date	Venue	Opponents	Result	H/T	Lge Posn	Attend
1	15.8.87	H	Darlington	D 2-2	0-1		1342
2	22.8.87	A	Wolverhampton W.	W 1-0	0-0		7223
3	28.8.87	H	Rochdale	L 1-2	1-0	11	2275
4	31.8.87	A	Wrexham	D 2-2	0-1	14	1661
5	4.9.87	H	Newport Co.	W 3-1	0-0	9	1095
6	12.9.87	A	Bolton W.	L 0-2	0-1	12	4445
7	16.9.87	H	Swansea C.	W 3-1	2-0	9	1236
8	18.9.87	H	Tranmere Rov.	W 2-1	0-0	5	1754
9	26.9.87	A	Cambridge U.	L 1-2	1-1	8	1805
10	29.9.87	A	Cardiff C.	D 0-0	0-0	9	3666
11	3.10.87	H	Hereford U.	W 2-1	1-1	7	1414
12	10.10.87	A	Scunthorpe U.	L 0-1	0-0	11	2105
13	16.10.87	H	Stockport Co.	W 2-0	2-0	12	1696
14	21.10.87	A	Hartlepool U.	L 1-2	0-1	11	2768
15	24.10.87	H	Peterborough U.	D 0-0	0-0	12	1615
16	31.10.87	A	Leyton Orient	L 1-4	1-3	16	3208
17	3.11.87	H	Burnley	W 2-1	1-1	13	3419
18	6.11.87	H	Colchester U.	L 1-2	1-1	15	1432
19	21.11.87	A	Scarborough	D 1-1	0-1	16	2892
20	27.11.87	H	Crewe Alex.	L 1-2	0-0	17	1412
21	12.12.87	A	Torquay U.	W 2-1	1-1	16	2422
22	18.12.87	H	Exeter C.	W 2-0	1-0	13	1302
23	26.12.87	H	Cambridge U.	D 1-1	1-1	14	1667
24	1.1.88	A	Rochdale	D 0-0	0-0	16	2050
25	12.1.88	H	Bolton W.	D 0-0	0-0	16	2689
26	15.1.88	A	Tranmere Rov.	L 0-2	0-1	16	3317
27	23.1.88	A	Swansea C.	D 1-1	1-1	16	5064
28	5.2.88	A	Newport Co.	L 0-1	0-1	16	1509
29	16.2.88	H	Wolverhampton W.	W 2-1	1-1	17	2281
30	20.2.88	A	Darlington	L 1-4	1-2	17	1824
31	23.2.88	H	Wrexham	W 2-0	1-0	16	1284
32	27.2.88	A	Hereford U.	L 1-2	0-2	18	1905
33	1.3.88	H	Cardiff C.	L 0-1	0-0	18	1128
34	4.3.88	A	Stockport Co.	L 0-1	0-0	18	2171
35	12.3.88	H	Scunthorpe U.	D 2-2	2-0	17	1807
36	26.3.88	A	Peterborough U.	L 0-1	0-0	19	2308
37	1.4.88	A	Colchester U.	L 1-2	1-0	19	1992
38	4.4.88	H	Scarborough	D 2-2	1-0	21	1747
39	8.4.88	A	Burnley	L 1-3	1-1	21	5766
40	14.4.88	H	Leyton Orient	W 1-0	1-0	19	1006
41	19.4.88	A	Carlisle U.	D 1-1	0-0	19	1517
42	23.4.88	H	Hartlepool U.	W 3-1	2-1	18	866
43	26.4.88	H	Carlisle U.	D 1-1	1-0	18	1002
44	29.4.88	A	Crewe Alex.	D 0-0	0-0	18	1403
45	2.5.88	H	Torquay U.	L 2-3	1-1	18	1218
46	7.5.88	A	Exeter C.	W 2-1	0-1	18	1602

Players: League Record, 1987-88 (Division 4)

Player	Apps	Subs	Goals
Allison	29	6	4
Barr	25	5	0
Black	19	8	5
Blain	2	1	0
Brown	44	0	5
Duffield	12	0	6
Ferebee	6	6	0
Fleming	7	2	0
Galloway	17	0	2
Harrison	18	0	0
Heathcote	7	0	1
Holden	35	0	10
Kendall	9	1	0
McPhillips	11	14	3
Martin	38	2	3
Matthews, M.	45	0	3
Matthews, N.	29	3	10
Richardson	20	10	1
Robinson	32	0	0
Roche	46	0	0
Shaw	21	3	0
Thornber	34	1	0
Willis	0	1	0
Own Goals			1

FA Cup: 1987-88: 1st Round: Billingham (A) 4-2, 2nd Round: Grimsby T. (A) 0-0 Replay (H) 2-0; 3rd Round: Nottingham F. (H) 0-4.
Littlewoods Cup: 1987-88: 1st Round: York C. (H) 1-1 (A) 0-1.

HARTLEPOOL UNITED (Division 4)

Team Manager John Bird.
Club Address The Victoria Ground, Clarence Road, Hartlepool. Tel: (0429) 272584.
Current Ground Capacity 5,620.
Record Attendance 17,426 v Manchester U., FA Cup 3rd Round, 5 January 1957.
Year Formed 1908. Turned professional 1908.
Previous Names Hartlepools United, Hartlepool.
Club Nickname "The Pool".
Club Colours Blue shirts, white shorts and stockings.
Club Honours None.
League History 1921-58 Div. 3(N); 1958-68 Div. 4; 1968-69 Div. 3; 1969- Div. 4.
Most League Points in a Season (2 for a win) 60 in Div. 4, 1967-68. (3 for a win) 70 in Div. 4, 1985-86.
Most League Goals in a Season 90 in Div. 3(N), 1956-57.
Record Victory 10-1 v Barrow in Div. 4, 4 April 1959.
Record Defeat 1-10 v Wrexham in Div. 4, 3 March 1962.
Consecutive League Wins 7 in 1956 and 1968.
Consecutive League Defeats 8 in 1950.

Record League Appearances Wattie Moore, 448 between 1948-60.
Record League Goalscorer—Career Ken Johnson, 98 between 1949-64.
Record League Goalscorer—Season William Robinson, 28 in Div. 3(N), 1927-28.

Hartlepool United: League Record, 1987-88 (Division 4)

Match Number	Date	Venue	Opponents	Result		H/T	Lge Posn	Attend
1	15.8.87	H	Newport Co.	D	0-0	0-0		1926
2	22.8.87	A	Wrexham	L	1-2	0-0		1816
3	29.8.87	H	Darlington	L	2-5	0-1	23	2106
4	31.8.87	A	Swansea C.	L	1-2	1-0	23	3569
5	5.9.87	H	Leyton Orient	D	2-2	1-1	23	1197
6	12.9.87	A	Carlisle U.	W	3-1	2-0	22	2463
7	16.9.87	H	Cambridge U.	W	2-1	2-0	17	1376
8	19.9.87	H	Colchester U.	W	3-1	1-0	14	1698
9	26.9.87	A	Bolton W.	W	2-1	0-0	11	4398
10	30.9.87	H	Exeter C.	W	3-1	1-1	6	2973
11	3.10.87	A	Crewe Alex.	D	1-1	0-0	6	2128
12	10.10.87	A	Burnley	L	0-1	0-0	10	5215
13	17.10.87	H	Torquay U.	D	0-0	0-0	8	2870
14	21.10.87	H	Halifax T.	W	2-1	1-0	9	2768
15	24.10.87	A	Scarborough	D	1-1	0-0	10	3909
16	31.10.87	H	Scunthorpe U.	W	1-0	1-0	9	2763
17	3.11.87	A	Stockport Co.	L	0-1	0-0	10	1408
18	7.11.87	A	Peterborough U.	W	1-0	0-0	9	3200
19	21.11.87	H	Tranmere Rov.	L	1-2	1-1	10	2507
20	28.11.87	A	Cardiff C.	D	1-1	1-0	9	3232
21	12.12.87	H	Wolverhampton W.	D	0-0	0-0	11	2760
22	19.12.87	A	Hereford U.	L	2-4	1-3	14	1655
23	26.12.87	H	Bolton W.	D	0-0	0-0	15	4102
24	28.12.87	A	Rochdale	W	2-0	1-0	12	1851
25	1.1.88	A	Darlington	D	1-1	0-0	12	4735
26	2.1.88	H	Carlisle U.	D	0-0	0-0	11	3135
27	15.1.88	A	Colchester U.	D	0-0	0-0	13	1768
28	26.1.88	H	Wrexham	W	1-0	0-0	9	1692
29	30.1.88	H	Swansea C.	L	0-2	0-2	11	2092
30	6.2.88	A	Leyton Orient	W	2-0	1-0	10	4102
31	13.2.88	H	Rochdale	D	1-1	0-0	10	2186
32	19.2.88	A	Newport Co.	W	3-2	2-1	9	1880
33	27.2.88	H	Crewe Alex.	W	2-1	2-1	6	2165
34	2.3.88	A	Exeter C.	L	0-1	0-0	8	1573
35	5.3.88	A	Torquay U.	D	1-1	0-1	10	2867
36	12.3.88	H	Burnley	W	2-1	2-0	8	2891
37	19.3.88	A	Scunthorpe U.	L	0-3	0-3	10	3784
38	26.3.88	H	Scarborough	W	1-0	1-0	9	2443
39	2.4.88	H	Peterborough U.	L	0-1	0-1	10	2315
40	4.4.88	A	Tranmere Rov.	L	1-3	0-1	10	3921
41	9.4.88	H	Stockport Co.	L	1-3	1-2	13	1317
42	19.4.88	A	Cambridge U.	D	1-1	1-0	14	1492
43	23.4.88	A	Halifax T.	L	1-3	1-2	14	866
44	30.4.88	H	Cardiff C.	L	0-1	0-1	15	1097
45	2.5.88	A	Wolverhampton W.	L	0-2	0-1	16	17895
46	7.5.88	H	Hereford U.	L	1-2	0-1	16	1002

Players: League Record, 1987-88 (Division 4)

Match Number	1	2	3	4	5	6	7	8	9	10	11	12	13	14	15	16	17	18	19	20	21	22	23	24	25	26	27	28	29	30	31	32	33	34	35	36	37	38	39	40	41	42	43	44	45	46	Apps	Subs	Goals
Baker	9	9	9¹	9	9¹	9²	9²	9³	9¹	9²	9¹	9	9	9	**9**	9	9	9	**9**	9	9			9¹	9¹	9	9	9	**9**	9¹	9		9¹	9	9	9¹				**9**	**9**	**9**	★	9¹	9		38	1	19
Barratt	2	2	11	★	★	★			11	11	11	11	**11**	2	2¹	2		11		★	11¹	11	11	11	11	11	11	2	2	2	2	2	2¹	2	2	2	2	2	2	2	2	2	2	2	2	2	39	4	3
Borthwick		★				10	10	10	10	10	**10**	10		★			★	10	10	10	10			11	11¹	11	11	11¹	11²	11	11	11	11¹	11	11¹	11	11	11	11	11	**11**	★	9	10			30	4	5
Butler	11	11	★	11	★		★						11			11	11	11																													6	3	0
Carr															1	1	1	1	1	1	1	1	1	1	1	1	1	1	1	1	1	1	1	1	1	1	1	1	1	1	1	1	1	1	1	1	31	0	0
Danskin																												7	7	7																	3	0	0
Dixon			★	¹	10	**10**	10						10							9							★				★				★		★	10	10	★							7	6	1
Doig																															10	10	10	10	**10**	10	11	11	11								9	0	0
Gibb	★											★		10	10	10	10	10	★		★	9		★	★		10		9		★		★	9						★							9	9	0
Grayson																																														9	1	0	0
Haigh	4	4	4			4	4	4	4	4	4	4		11	2	2	2	2	2	2	2	2	2	2	2	2	6	6	6	6	6	6	**6**			6	6	6	6	6	6	6	3	3			39	0	0
Hall																						★																									0	1	0
Honour	7	7	7	7	7	7	7	7	7	7	7	7	7	7	7	7	7	7	7	7	7	7	7	7		★	7	7	7	7	7	7	7	7	7	7	★	7	7	7	7	7	7	7			42	2	0
Kennedy											★		3	3		3	3																														4	1	0
McCarthy																																													★		0	1	0
McKinnon			3¹	3		3	3	3	3	3	3¹	3	3	3	11	11	3		★	3	3	3	3	3	3	3	3	3	3	3	3	3	3	3	3	3	3	3	3	3	3	3	3	3			41	1	2
Nobbs	3		2	2	2	2	2	2	2	2	2	2	4	4	4	4	4	4	4			4	4	4	4	4	4	4	4	4	4	4	4	4	4	**4**	4	4	4	4	★	4	4	4	4	4	42	1	0
Owers	1	1																																													2	0	0
Prudhoe				1	1	1	1	1	1	1	1	1	1	1	1																																13	0	0
Shoulder	10	10				11	11	11																																							5	0	0
Smith	5	5	5	5	5	5	5	5	5	5	5	5	5	5	5	5	5	5	5	5	5	5	5	5	5	5	5	5	5	5	5	5	5	5	5	5	5	5	5	5	5	5	5	5	5	5	46	0	0
Stokes	6	6	6	6	6	6	6	6	6	6	6	6	6	6	6	6	6	6	6	6	6	6	6	6																							24	0	0
Stokle																																	6	6	6												3	0	0
Thomson			10	4		★																																									2	1	0
Tinkler														4	4					6	6	★	★	10	10	10	10	6	10	10	**10**		★	7				4			6	6					16	4	0
Toman	8	8	**8**	8¹	8¹	8	8	8	8	8	8	8	8	8¹	8¹	8¹	8	8¹	8¹	8	8	8¹	8²	8	8	8	8	8	8	8¹	8¹	8¹	8¹	8	8	8	8	8	8¹	8	8	8	8	8¹			46	0	17
Whellans																							10¹	10	10	10	10				★	10				9	★	★		9							8	3	1
Own Goals							1																																		1									2

FA Cup: 1987-88: 1st Round: Chorley (A) 2-0; 2nd Round: York C. (A) 1-1 Replay (H) 3-1; 3rd Round: Luton T. (H) 1-2.
Littlewoods Cup: 1987-88: 1st Round: Scunthorpe U. (A) 1-3 (H) 0-1.

HEREFORD UNITED (Division 4)

Team Manager   Ian Bowyer.
Club Address   Edgar Street, Hereford. Tel: (0432) 276666.
Current Ground Capacity   11,914.
Record Attendance   18,114 v Sheffield Wed., FA Cup 3rd Round, 4 January 1958.
Year Formed   1924. Turned professional 1924.
Previous Names   None.
Club Nickname   "United".
Club Colours   White shirts with black pinstripe, black shorts and white stockings.
Club Honours   Football League: Div. 3 Champions 1975-76.
League History   1972-73 Div. 4; 1973-76 Div. 3; 1976-77 Div. 2; 1977-78 Div. 3; 1978- Div. 4.
Most League Points in a Season   (2 for a win) 63 in Div. 3, 1975-76. (3 for a win) 77 in Div. 4, 1984-85.
Most League Goals in a Season   86 in Div. 3, 1975-76.
Record Victory   11-0 v Thynnes in FA Cup Preliminary Round September 1947.

Record Defeat   0-5 v Wrexham in Div. 3, 22 December 1973; 1-6 v Tranmere Rov. in Div. 3, 29 November 1975; 1-6 v Wolverhampton W. in Div. 2, 2 October 1976; 2-7 v Arsenal in FA Cup 3rd Round replay, 22 January 1985.
Consecutive League Wins   5 in 1984.
Consecutive League Defeats   7 in 1976.
Record League Appearances   Chris Price, 330 between 1976-86.
Record League Goalscorer—Career   Dixie McNeil, 88 between 1974-83.
Record League Goalscorer—Season   Dixie McNeil, 35 in 1975-76.

Hereford United: League Record, 1987-88 (Division 4)

Match Number	Date	Venue	Opponents	Result		H/T	Lge Posn	Attend
1	15.8.87	H	Rochdale	D	0-0	0-0		2652
2	21.8.87	A	Tranmere Rov.	W	1-0	0-0		2824
3	29.8.87	H	Wolverhampton W.	L	1-2	0-2	14	2628
4	31.8.87	A	Carlisle U.	L	1-3	1-1	18	2708
5	5.9.87	H	Bolton W.	L	0-3	0-2	22	2541
6	12.9.87	A	Swansea C.	L	0-3	0-0	24	3794
7	16.9.87	H	Colchester U.	W	1-0	0-0	22	1951
8	19.9.87	H	Darlington	W	1-0	1-0	16	2102
9	27.9.87	A	Newport Co.	D	0-0	0-0	18	1480
10	30.9.87	H	Peterborough U.	L	0-1	0-1	19	2010
11	3.10.87	A	Halifax T.	L	1-2	1-1	20	1414
12	10.10.87	A	Cardiff C.	W	1-0	0-0	19	4420
13	17.10.87	H	Scunthorpe U.	L	2-3	0-2	19	2092
14	21.10.87	H	Scarborough	D	1-1	0-0	19	2359
15	23.10.87	A	Stockport Co.	W	2-0	1-0	19	1566
16	31.10.87	H	Exeter C.	D	1-1	0-0	18	2200
17	3.11.87	A	Cambridge U.	W	1-0	1-0	17	2257
18	7.11.87	H	Crewe Alex.	D	1-1	0-0	17	2272
19	21.11.87	A	Torquay U.	L	0-1	0-1	18	2305
20	28.11.88	H	Leyton Orient	L	0-3	0-2	19	1853
21	12.12.87	A	Burnley	D	0-0	0-0	19	4216
22	19.12.87	H	Hartlepool U.	W	4-2	3-1	17	1655
23	26.12.87	H	Newport Co.	W	4-2	1-1	16	3203
24	28.12.87	A	Wrexham	D	0-0	0-0	16	2443
25	1.1.88	A	Wolverhampton W.	L	0-2	0-1	17	14577
26	2.1.88	H	Swansea C.	D	0-0	0-0	17	3504
27	9.1.88	H	Tranmere Rov.	D	1-1	1-0	17	2209
28	17.1.88	A	Darlington	L	1-3	0-0	17	2621
29	30.1.88	A	Carlisle U.	W	2-0	2-0	16	1904
30	6.2.88	A	Bolton W.	L	0-1	0-0	17	4559
31	13.2.88	H	Wrexham	L	0-2	0-2	17	2002
32	20.2.88	A	Rochdale	L	1-3	0-2	18	1568
33	24.2.88	A	Peterborough U.	W	2-1	0-1	18	2065
34	27.2.88	H	Halifax T.	W	2-1	2-0	16	1905
35	5.3.88	A	Scunthorpe U.	L	0-3	0-1	17	3413
36	13.3.88	H	Cardiff C.	L	1-2	1-1	18	3210
37	19.3.88	A	Exeter C.	D	2-2	2-0	18	1628
38	26.3.88	H	Stockport Co.	L	0-1	0-1	18	1695
39	1.4.88	A	Crewe Alex.	D	0-0	0-0	18	1313
40	4.4.88	H	Torquay U.	D	0-0	0-0	17	2425
41	9.4.88	A	Scarborough	L	1-2	0-2	19	2154
42	19.4.88	A	Colchester U.	L	0-1	0-0	20	1367
43	23.4.88	H	Cambridge U.	W	1-0	1-0	20	1666
44	30.4.88	A	Leyton Orient	L	0-4	0-3	20	3444
45	2.5.88	H	Burnley	W	2-1	1-1	19	2304
46	7.5.88	A	Hartlepool U.	W	2-1	1-0	19	1002

Players: League Record, 1987-88 (Division 4)

Match Number	1	2	3	4	5	6	7	8	9	10	11	12	13	14	15	16	17	18	19	20	21	22	23	24	25	26	27	28	29	30	31	32	33	34	35	36	37	38	39	40	41	42	43	44	45	46	Apps	Subs	Goals
Benbow			★	7					★	8	8		8[1]		★	9					8	★		★				★	★	9	9	9[1]	9		★	11	10			★							12	9	2
Bowyer	8	8	8	6	8	8	8	8	8	8			8[1]		8	8	8	8	8	8	8	8	★	8	8	8	8	8	8																		28	1	1
Campbell																									7	11	11	7																			4	0	0
Dalziel	11		★	3	3	3			★	3								7		11[1]	11	11	2			★			8	8	8		★	9	9	9	9	3	3	3							21	4	1
Devine	3	3	3			3	3	3	3	4	3	3	3	3	3	3	3	3	3	3	3	3	3	3	3	3	3	3	3	3	3	3	3	3	3	3	3	3	3	3	4	4	4	4			43	0	0
Jones	2	2	2	2	2	2	2	2	2	2	2	2	2	2	2		2	2	2		2	2	2		2	2		2		★	2																27	1	0
Kearns	10	10	10	10[1]	10	10			10	10		★		★				10																													9	2	1
Leadbitter	★			6	11	★	11	11	11								11	11	11	11	11	11			11	11	11[1]	7	7	11	11	11	11	11	11	11	11	11	11	11	11	11		★			27	3	1
Leonard																																		8	8	8	8	8	8	8	7	11	11[1]	11			11	0	1
McLoughlin	7	11[1]	11	7	11	7			11	11	11	11	11	11	11	11												★	7	7	7	7	7	7	7	7	7	7	11	7	7	7					28	1	2
Maddy																															6	6				★	★	6	6	6	6						6	2	0
Mallender																																	★														0	1	0
Pejic	5	5	5	5	5	5	5	5	5	5	5	5		★	2		★	5	2	5	5	5	5	5		5	5	5	5	5	5	5	5[1]	5	5	5	5	5	5	5	5	5	5	5[1]	5		42	2	1
Phillips	9	9	9	9	9	9	9	9	9[1]	9	9	9	9	9	9	9	9	9[1]	9		9	9			9	9	9	9	9[1]	9	9	9	9														30	0	3
Powell																	5	4	4	4	4	4																									7	0	0
Rodgerson			7	7	8		7	7	7	7	7[1]	7	7[1]	7	7	7	7[1]	7			7	7	7	7				2	2	2	7	2	2	2		2	2	2	2	2	2	2	2	2			37	0	3
Rose	1	1	1	1	1	1	1	1	1	1	1	1	1	1	1	1	1	1	1	1	1	1	1	1	1	1	1	1	1	1	1	1	1	1			1	1	1	1	1	1	1	1			42	0	0
Spooner	6	6			6	6	6	6	6	6	6[1]	6	6	6	6	6[1]	6	6	6	6	6	6	6	6[1]	6	6[1]	6	6	6	6	6[1]	6[1]	6		6	6	6	6[1]	6	8	8	8	8				42	0	8
Stant			★[1]			★	10[1]	10		★		10	10	10	10[1]	10	10	10	10	7	10	10[2]	10	10	10		7	10	10	10	10	10	10[1]	10	10	10[1]	10[1]	10	10	10		9	9	9[1]			36	3	9
Stevens	4	4	4		4	4	4	4	4		4	4	4	4	10	4	4[1]	4	4	4	4	4	4	9[1]	9[2]	9		10	10	4	4	4	4[1]	4	4[1]	4	4	4	4	4	9	10	10	10[1]			45	0	7
Wassall															5	5	5	5																													5	0	0
Own Goals																		1																				1											2

FA Cup: 1987-88: 1st Round: Barnet (A) 1-0; 2nd Round: Colchester U. (A) 2-3.
Littlewoods Cup: 1987-88: 1st Round: Bristol Rov. (A) 0-1 (H) 2-0; 2nd Round: Nottingham F. (A) 0-5 (H) 1-1.

HUDDERSFIELD TOWN (Division 3)

Team Manager Eoin Hand.
Club Address Leeds Road, Huddersfield HD1 6PE. Tel: (0484) 20335/6.
Current Ground Capacity 32,000.
Record Attendance 67,037 v Arsenal, FA Cup 6th Round, 27 February 1932.
Year Formed 1908. Turned professional 1908.
Previous Names None.
Club Nickname "The Terriers".
Club Colours Blue and white striped shirts, white shorts and white stockings.
Club Honours Football League: Div.1 Champions 1923-24, 1924-25, 1925-26; Div. 2 Champions 1969-70; Div. 4 Champions 1979-80. FA Cup: Winners 1922.
League History 1910-20 Div. 2; 1920-52 Div. 1; 1952-53 Div. 2; 1953-56 Div. 1; 1956-70 Div. 1; 1970-72 Div. 1; 1972-73 Div. 2; 1973-75 Div. 3; 1975-80 Div. 4; 1980-83 Div. 3; 1983-88 Div. 2; 1988- Div. 3.
Most League Points in a Season (2 for a win) 66 in Div. 4, 1979-80. (3 for a win) 82 in Div. 3, 1982-83.

Most League Goals in a Season 101 in Div. 4, 1979-80.
Record Victory 10-1 v Blackpool in Div. 1, 13 December 1930.
Record Defeat 0-8 v Middlesbrough in Div. 1, 30 September 1950.
Consecutive League Wins 11 in 1920.
Consecutive League Defeats 7 in 1913-14, 1955.
Record League Appearances Billy Smith, 520 between 1914-34.
Record League Goalscorer—Career George Brown, 142 between 1921-29 and Jimmy Glazzard, 142 between 1946-56.
Record League Goalscorer—Season Sam Taylor, 35 in Div. 2, 1919-20 and George Brown, 35 in Div. 1, 1925-26.

Huddersfield Town: League Record, 1987-88 (Division 2)

Match Number	Date	Venue	Opponents	Result	H/T	Lge Posn	Attend
1	15.8.87	H	Crystal Palace	D 2-2	0-1		6132
2	22.8.87	A	Plymouth Arg.	L 1-6	0-2		8811
3	29.8.87	H	Shrewsbury T.	D 0-0	0-0	20	4478
4	31.8.87	A	Oldham Ath.	L 2-3	1-1	23	7377
5	12.9.87	A	Blackburn Rov.	D 2-2	2-2	23	7109
6	15.9.87	H	Leeds U.	D 0-0	0-0	23	9085
7	19.9.87	H	Aston Villa	L 0-1	0-1	23	6884
8	26.9.87	A	Stoke C.	D 1-1	1-0	23	8665
9	29.9.87	H	Bradford C.	L 1-2	0-1	23	11671
10	3.10.87	A	Birmingham C.	L 0-2	0-0	23	6282
11	10.10.87	H	Middlesbrough	L 1-4	0-2	23	6169
12	17.10.87	A	Reading	L 2-3	0-2	23	4678
13	20.10.87	H	Hull C.	L 0-2	0-0	23	8033
14	24.10.87	A	West Bromwich A.	L 2-3	2-2	23	8450
15	31.10.87	H	Millwall	W 2-1	1-0	23	5504
16	3.11.87	A	Ipswich T.	L 0-3	0-2	23	9984
17	7.11.87	A	Manchester C.	L 1-10	0-4	23	19583
18	14.11.87	H	Barnsley	D 2-2	1-2	23	8629
19	21.11.87	A	Bournemouth	W 2-0	1-0	23	6419
20	28.11.87	H	Leicester C.	W 1-0	1-0	22	6704
21	1.12.87	A	Swindon T.	L 1-4	0-2	22	6963
22	5.12.87	A	Sheffield U.	D 2-2	1-1	22	9269
23	12.12.87	H	Plymouth Arg.	W 2-1	1-0	21	5574
24	19.12.87	A	Leeds U.	L 0-3	0-1	21	20111
25	26.12.87	H	Stoke C.	L 0-3	0-0	21	9500
26	28.12.87	A	Aston Villa	D 1-1	1-1	21	20948
27	1.1.88	A	Shrewsbury T.	L 1-3	0-1	23	5448
28	2.1.88	H	Blackburn Rov.	L 1-2	0-2	23	10735
29	16.1.88	A	Crystal Palace	L 1-2	1-2	23	9013
30	13.2.88	H	Swindon T.	L 0-3	0-1	23	5458
31	27.2.88	H	Birmingham C.	D 2-2	1-2	23	5441
32	1.3.88	A	Bradford C.	W 1-0	0-0	23	12782
33	5.3.88	H	Reading	L 0-2	0-2	23	6094
34	12.3.88	A	Middlesbrough	L 0-2	0-1	23	13866
35	19.3.88	A	Millwall	L 1-4	1-2	23	6181
36	26.3.88	H	West Bromwich A.	L 1-3	1-0	23	4503
37	2.4.88	H	Manchester C.	W 1-0	0-0	23	7835
38	4.4.88	A	Barnsley	L 0-1	0-1	23	7950
39	8.4.88	H	Ipswich T.	L 1-2	1-0	23	4023
40	19.4.88	A	Oldham Ath.	D 2-2	2-0	23	5547
41	23.4.88	A	Hull C.	L 0-4	0-4	23	5221
42	30.4.88	H	Bournemouth	L 1-2	0-2	23	2794
43	2.5.88	A	Leicester C.	L 0-3	0-2	23	9803
44	7.5.88	H	Sheffield U.	L 0-2	0-0	23	8644

Players: League Record, 1987-88 (Division 2)

Match Number	Apps	Subs	Goals
Banks	41	0	9
Barham	24	2	1
Bent	5	2	0
Bray	29	1	0
Brown	23	2	0
Burke	10	0	0
Chapman	4	2	0
Cooper	20	5	5
Cork	36	0	8
Cowling	5	1	0
Cox	20	0	0
France	5	3	0
Hutchings	23	0	0
Kirkham	0	1	0
McDonagh	6	0	0
McStay	4	4	0
Madrick	3	5	1
Martin	18	0	0
May	27	1	2
Mitchell	28	1	1
Shearer	31	2	10
Shotton	14	0	0
Trevitt	31	6	1
Tucker	19	4	0
Walford	12	0	0
Ward	19	7	2
Webster	22	0	0
Winter	5	2	0

FA Cup: 1987-88: 3rd Round: Manchester C. (H) 2-2 Replay (A) 0-0 2nd Replay (H) 0-3.
Littlewoods Cup: 1987-88: 1st Round: Rotherham U. (A) 4-4 (H) 1-3.

HULL CITY (Division 2)

Team Manager Dennis Booth and Tom Wilson (joint).
Club Address Boothferry Park, Hull HU4 6EU. Tel: (0482) 51119/563750.
Current Ground Capacity 28,000.
Record Attendance 55,019 v Manchester U., FA Cup 6th Round, 26 February 1949.
Year Formed 1904. Turned professional 1905.
Previous Names None.
Club Nickname "The Tigers".
Club Colours Amber shirts with red pinstripe, black collar and cuffs, black shorts with amber and red stripe down side and red stockings.
Club Honours Football League: Div. 3(N) Champions 1932-33, 1948-49; Div. 3 Champions 1965-66.
League History 1905-30 Div. 2; 1930-33 Div. 3(N); 1933-36 Div. 2; 1936-49 Div. 3(N); 1949-56 Div. 3(N); 1956-58 Div. 3(N); 1958-59 Div. 3; 1959-60 Div. 2; 1960-66 Div. 3; 1966-78 Div. 2; 1978-81 Div. 3; 1981-83 Div. 4; 1983-85 Div. 3; 1985- Div. 2.
Most League Points in a Season (2 for a win) 69 in Div. 3, 1965-66. (3 for a win) 90 in Div. 4 1982-83.

Most League Goals in a Season 109 in Div. 3, 1965-66.
Record Victory 11-1 v Carlisle U. in Div. 3(N), 14 January 1939.
Record Defeat 0-8 v Wolverhampton W. in Div. 2, 4 November 1911.
Consecutive League Wins 10 in 1948 and 1966.
Consecutive League Defeats 8 in 1934.
Record League Appearances Andy Davidson, 520 between 1952-67.
Record League Goalscorer—Career Chris Chilton, 193 between 1960-71.
Record League Goalscorer—Season Bill McNaughton, 39 in Div. 3(N), 1932-33.

Hull City: League Record, 1987-88 (Division 2)

Match Number	Date	Venue	Opponents	Result		H/T	Lge Posn	Attend
1	15.8.87	H	Blackburn Rov.	D	2-2	0-0		6462
2	18.8.87	A	Stoke C.	D	1-1	1-0		9139
3	22.8.87	A	Crystal Palace	D	2-2	2-0	12	6688
4	29.8.87	H	Aston Villa	W	2-1	1-1	7	8315
5	31.8.87	A	Swindon T.	D	0-0	0-0	10	9600
6	5.9.87	H	Bournemouth	W	2-1	1-0	10	5807
7	12.9.87	A	Leeds U.	W	2-0	0-0	4	18205
8	15.9.87	H	Shrewsbury T.	D	1-1	0-0	2	7939
9	19.9.87	H	Oldham Ath.	W	1-0	1-0	3	7183
10	29.9.87	H	Manchester C.	W	3-1	2-0	2	9650
11	3.10.87	A	Sheffield U.	L	1-2	1-1	2	10446
12	10.10.87	H	Ipswich T.	W	1-0	0-0	2	6962
13	17.10.87	A	Barnsley	W	3-1	1-0	2	7310
14	20.10.87	A	Huddersfield T.	W	2-0	0-0	2	8033
15	24.10.87	H	Leicester C.	D	2-2	1-1	2	8826
16	31.10.87	A	Plymouth Arg.	L	1-3	1-3	3	8550
17	3.11.87	H	Bradford C.	D	0-0	0-0	2	15443
18	7.11.87	H	Birmingham C.	W	2-0	1-0	3	7901
19	14.11.87	A	Middlesbrough	L	0-1	0-1	3	15709
20	21.11.87	H	West Bromwich A.	W	1-0	0-0	3	7654
21	28.11.87	A	Millwall	L	0-2	0-0	3	6743
22	5.12.87	H	Reading	D	2-2	0-1	7	5797
23	12.12.87	A	Shrewsbury T.	D	2-2	2-1	8	2588
24	19.12.87	H	Crystal Palace	W	2-1	2-1	6	6780
25	28.12.87	A	Oldham Ath.	W	2-1	0-1	6	8080
26	1.1.88	A	Aston Villa	L	0-5	0-1	8	19236
27	3.1.88	H	Leeds U.	W	3-1	3-1	6	14694
28	16.1.88	A	Blackburn Rov.	L	1-2	0-2	7	9692
29	6.2.88	A	Bournemouth	L	2-6	1-3	8	5901
30	13.2.88	H	Stoke C.	D	0-0	0-0	8	6424
31	27.2.88	H	Sheffield U.	L	1-2	1-0	9	8832
32	2.3.88	A	Manchester C.	L	0-2	0-0	9	16040
33	5.3.88	H	Barnsley	L	1-2	1-2	11	7622
34	12.3.88	A	Ipswich T.	L	0-2	0-1	11	9726
35	19.3.88	H	Plymouth Arg.	D	1-1	0-1	11	5172
36	26.3.88	A	Leicester C.	L	1-2	0-1	11	10353
37	1.4.88	A	Birmingham C.	D	1-1	1-0	13	7059
38	4.4.88	H	Middlesbrough	D	0-0	0-0	15	10758
39	9.4.88	A	Bradford C.	L	0-2	0-1	15	13659
40	12.4.88	H	Swindon T.	L	1-4	1-2	15	4583
41	23.4.88	H	Huddersfield T.	W	4-0	4-0	14	5221
42	30.4.88	A	West Bromwich A.	D	1-1	0-1	14	8004
43	2.5.88	H	Millwall	L	0-1	0-1	16	10811
44	7.5.88	A	Reading	D	0-0	0-0	15	6710

Players: League Record, 1987-88 (Division 2)

Match Number	1	2	3	4	5	6	7	8	9	10	11	12	13	14	15	16	17	18	19	20	21	22	23	24	25	26	27	28	29	30	31	32	33	34	35	36	37	38	39	40	41	42	43	44	Apps	Subs	Goals
Askew	10	10	10	10	10	10¹	10	10	10	10	10	10¹	10	10	10	10	10	10	10¹	10	10	10		10	10	10	10	10	10																30	0	3
Barnes																											11	11	11	11	11	11	11	7	11	11	11								11	0	0
Brown																							★		2	2	6					5	2	2	2	2	2								9	1	0
Bunn	8¹	8	8¹	8	8	8	8	8	8	8²	8¹			★	★		8	8	8	8																10¹	10¹	10	10						16	2	5
Daniel	11	11	11	11	11	11	11	11¹	11						3	3	3	3	3	3	3		★		★	10		3	★																23	1	0
De Mange																	10	10	10	10	10	10	10	6				★																	8	1	0
Dyer	9			9¹	9	9¹	9	9	9				★	8		9	9	9	9	9	9¹	9	9	9¹	9	9¹	9	9¹	9	9	9	9	9	9	9										27	1	8
Edwards																														9¹	9	9	9	9	9²	9	9	9							9	0	3
Heard	3	3	3	3¹	3	3	3	3	3	3	3	3¹	3	3	3	3					10¹	11	3	3	3	3	3	3	3		6¹	6	6		3	3	3							35	0	4
Hotte																																				★	★	★	6						1	3	0
Jacobs																																3	3	3	3				11						6	0	0
Jenkinson																				11								★	11¹																2	1	1
Jobson	4	4	4	4	4	4	4	4	4	4	4	4	4	4	4	4	4	4	4	4	4	4	4	4	4	4¹	4¹	4	4	4	4	4	4	4	4	4	4	4	4	4	4	4	4	4	44	0	2
McEwan	6																																												1	0	0
Norman	1	1	1	1	1	1	1	1	1	1	1	1	1	1	1	1	1	1	1	1	1	1	1	1	1	1	1	1	1	1	1	1	1	1	1	1	1	1	1	1	1	1	1	1	44	0	0
Owen																	11	11		11																									3	0	0
Palmer	2	2	2	2	2	2	2	2	2	2	2	2	2	2	2	2	2	2	2	2	2	2	2	2	2	2	2	2	2						2	2	2	2							35	0	1
Parker	7	6¹	6¹	6	6	6	6¹	6	6	6¹	6	6	6	6¹	6	6	6	6	6	6	6	6	6¹	6	6	6	★	6	6	6	6			6¹											33	1	8
Payton							★										★		★	★					★	8¹	8	8¹	8	★		★	★	★	6	★		8	8	8	6	6	6	★	11	11	2
Roberts	11	7	7	7	7	7	7	7¹	7	7	7	7	7	7¹	7	7	7	7	7	7	7	7	7¹	7	7	7	7	7	7	7	7	7	7	7	7	7	★	7	7	7	7				43	1	3
Saville		9	9		★		★	★	9	9	9	9¹	9	9	9¹						8	8¹	8		8				★	★	8¹	8	8¹	8	8	8	8		★	★	8¹	8	8	8	24	7	6
Skipper	5¹	5	5	5	5	5	5	5	5¹	5	5	5	5	5	5	5	5	5	5	5	5	5	5	5	5	5	5	5	5	5	5			★						5	5	5	5	5	43	0	2
Thompson								8¹	8	8¹	8																										10	★							5	2	1
Williams				★	★	11	11	11	11¹	11	11	11¹	11	11	11	11¹	11	11	11	11	★	★	8	★	6	11	11	11		11		2	2												21	4	2
Own Goals																		1																														1

FA Cup: 1987-88: 3rd Round: Watford (A) 1-1 Replay (H) 2-2 2nd Replay (A) 0-1.
Littlewoods Cup: 1987-88: 2nd Round: Manchester U. (A) 0-5 (H) 0-1.

89

IPSWICH TOWN (Division 2)

Team Manager John Duncan.
Club Address Portman Road, Ipswich, Suffolk IP1 2DA. Tel: (0473) 219211.
Current Ground Capacity 37,000.
Record Attendance 38,010 v Leeds U., FA Cup 6th Round, 8 March 1975.
Year Formed 1878. Turned professional 1936.
Previous Names None.
Club Nickname "The Blues" or "Town".
Club Colours Blue shirts with red band and white trim, white shorts and blue stockings.
Club Honours Football League: Div. 1 Champions 1961-62; Div. 2 Champions 1960-61, 1967-68; Div. 3(S) Champions 1953-54, 1956-57. FA Cup: Winners 1978. UEFA Cup: Winners 1980-81.
League History 1938-54 Div. 3(S); 1954-55 Div. 2; 1955-57 Div. 3(S); 1957-61 Div. 2; 1961-64 Div. 1; 1964-68 Div. 2; 1968-86 Div. 1; 1986- Div. 2.
Most League Points in a Season (2 for a win) 64 in Div. 3(S), 1953-54 and 1955-56. (3 for a win) 83 in Div. 1, 1981-82.

Most League Goals in a Season 106 in Div. 3(S), 1955-56.
Record Victory 10-0 v Floriana in European Cup 1st Round, 25 September 1962.
Record Defeat 1-10 v Fulham in Div. 1, 26 December 1963.
Consecutive League Wins 8 in 1953.
Consecutive League Defeats 10 in 1954.
Record League Appearances Mick Mills, 591 between 1966-82.
Record League Goalscorer—Career Ray Crawford, 204 between 1958-69.
Record League Goalscorer—Season Ted Phillips, 41 in Div. 3(S), 1956-57.

Ipswich Town: League Record, 1987-88 (Division 2)

Match Number	Date	Venue	Opponents	Result		H/T	Lge Posn	Attend
1	15.8.87	H	Aston Villa	D	1-1	1-1		14508
2	18.8.87	A	Plymouth Arg.	D	0-0	0-0		11901
3	22.8.87	A	Shrewsbury T.	D	0-0	0-0	14	3610
4	29.8.87	H	Stoke C.	W	2-0	1-0	6	11149
5	1.9.87	A	Blackburn Rov.	L	0-1	0-0	13	6074
6	5.9.87	H	Leeds U.	W	1-0	0-0	7	11016
7	12.9.87	A	Millwall	L	1-2	0-1	11	6356
8	19.9.87	H	Swindon T.	W	3-2	3-1	10	10460
9	26.9.87	A	Crystal Palace	W	2-1	0-0	7	10828
10	30.9.87	H	Leicester C.	D	1-1	1-1	8	11533
11	3.10.87	H	Barnsley	W	1-0	1-0	3	10992
12	10.10.87	A	Hull C.	L	0-1	0-0	7	6962
13	17.10.87	H	Manchester C.	W	3-0	2-0	4	12711
14	20.10.87	A	Middlesbrough	L	1-3	1-0	6	10491
15	24.10.87	H	Sheffield U.	W	1-0	0-0	5	11949
16	31.10.87	A	Bournemouth	D	1-1	1-0	5	8105
17	3.11.87	H	Huddersfield T.	W	3-0	2-0	5	9984
18	7.11.87	H	Reading	W	2-1	0-1	4	11508
19	14.11.87	A	West Bromwich A.	D	2-2	1-0	6	8457
20	21.11.87	H	Oldham Ath.	W	2-0	1-0	4	11007
21	28.11.87	A	Birmingham C.	L	0-1	0-0	6	6718
22	5.12.87	H	Bradford C.	W	4-0	1-0	5	13307
23	18.12.87	H	Shrewsbury T.	W	2-0	0-0	5	9930
24	26.12.87	H	Crystal Palace	L	2-3	1-1	5	17200
25	28.12.87	A	Swindon T.	L	2-4	0-2	8	12429
26	1.1.88	A	Stoke C.	W	2-1	1-1	6	9976
27	2.1.88	H	Millwall	D	1-1	0-0	8	13710
28	16.1.88	A	Aston Villa	L	0-1	0-1	8	20201
29	30.1.88	H	Blackburn Rov.	L	0-2	0-2	9	12604
30	6.2.88	A	Leeds U.	L	0-1	0-1	9	19564
31	13.2.88	H	Plymouth Arg.	L	1-2	1-1	9	10476
32	20.2.88	H	Leicester C.	L	0-2	0-1	9	11084
33	27.2.88	A	Barnsley	W	3-2	2-1	8	6482
34	5.3.88	A	Manchester C.	L	0-2	0-1	10	17402
35	12.3.88	H	Hull C.	W	2-0	1-0	9	9726
36	19.3.88	H	Bournemouth	L	1-2	0-2	10	10208
37	26.3.88	A	Sheffield U.	L	1-4	1-2	10	8753
38	2.4.88	A	Reading	D	1-1	0-0	11	9953
39	4.4.88	H	West Bromwich A.	D	1-1	0-1	11	10665
40	8.4.88	A	Huddersfield T.	W	2-1	0-1	11	4023
41	23.4.88	H	Middlesbrough	W	4-0	3-0	9	12773
42	30.4.88	A	Oldham Ath.	L	1-3	1-1	11	5018
43	2.5.88	H	Birmingham C.	W	1-0	0-0	9	11067
44	7.5.88	A	Bradford C.	W	3-2	2-2	8	16017

Players: League Record, 1987-88 (Division 2)

Match Number	1	2	3	4	5	6	7	8	9	10	11	12	13	14	15	16	17	18	19	20	21	22	23	24	25	26	27	28	29	30	31	32	33	34	35	36	37	38	39	40	41	42	43	44	Apps	Subs	Goals
Atkins					★	★	4				★	10									4	4			4	4	4	4	4	4	4	4	4^1	4											13	3	1
Atkinson								10	7														★	★				★		10	10^2	10	10	10		★	9	9^2	10^3	10	10^1	10		13	4	8
Bernal																						★		★										★	6	6	6	6		★	★			4	5	0
Brennan	8	8		8	8	8	8^1	8^1	8	8	8	8	8	8	8	8^1	8^1	8	8	8^1	8	8	8	8	8^1	8	8	8	8	★	8	8	8		★	8									34	2	6
Carson																											1																		1	0	0
Cole																							★		9																				1	1	0
Cranson	6	6	6	6	6	6	6		6^1	6	6	6	6	6	6	6	6	6				4	6	6	6	6	6		6	6	6														29	0	1
D'Avray		★	9	9	9	9	9^1	9			9	9	9	9^1	9		9	★	9			9^1			9^1	9^1	9	9					5	5	★		5	5	9^1	9	9	9^1		26	3	7
Deehan																			★	★	9	9		9				9	9^1	9	9	9	★	10	10	10	10	6	6	6	6			16	4	1
Dozzell	5	5	5	5	5	5	5	5	5	5	5		5	5	5	5	5	5	5	5		10	10	10	10	★		★	6		★	★	8	8	5	8	8	5	5	5	5^1				35	4	1
Fearon																																		1	1	1	1	1	1	1	1	1	1	10	0	0
Gleghorn	11^1	11	11	11	11									★	★		10			5^1	5	5	5			★	★	11			★														11	5	2
Hallworth	1	1	1	1	1	1	1	1	1	1	1	1	1	1	1	1	1	1	1	1	1	1	1	1	1	1	1	1	1	1	1	1	1	1											33	0	0
Harbey	3	3	3	3	3	3	3	3	3	3	3	3	3^1	3	3	3	3	3	3	3	3	3	3	3	3	3	3	3	3	3	3	★		3	3	3									34	1	1
Humes				★	11	11	6		4	4	4		★		★	2	2				6	6	6	6		5	5		5	5	5	5	5		5							3	3		23	4	0
Lowe	7	7	7	7^1	7	7^1			7^1	7	7^1	7	7	7	7^1	7	7^1	7	7^2	7^1	7^1	7		7^2	7^1	7^1	7	7	7	7	7	7	7	7	7^1	7	7	7	7	7^1	7	7			41	0	17
Milton																							4															★	6	4	4	4	4^1		7	1	1
O'Donnell	4													★																															1	1	0
Rimmer							10	10	★	4	4				5	4^2	4	4	4	4	4^1	4	4							5			11	11	11						★			18	1	1
Stockwell	★	2	2	2	2	2	2	11	11	11	11	11	11	11	11	11	11	11	11	11	11	11	11	11^1	11	11	11	11	11	11	11^1	11	8	3		3	11	11	11	11	11	11^1	11	11	42	1	1
Wark																									10	10	10	10		3									★	★					5	2	0
Wilson																						★													3	3	3	3	3						5	1	0
Woods	9	9	9				★			9^1	★	★	★			9^1	9	9			7								★	★			9^1	9^1	9	9		★							12	7	4
Yallop	2	4	4		4	4		2^1	2	2	2	2	2	2	2			2	2	2	2	2	2	2	2	2	2	2	2	2	2	2	2	2	2	2	2^1	2	2	2	2	2	2	2	41	0	2
Zondervan	10	10	10	10			7	10	10	10	10		10	10	10	10	10		10	10	10	10	10^2	10^1									4	4	4^1	4	4	4	4	8	8	8	8	29	0	4
Own Goals			1																																												1

FA Cup: 1987-88: 3rd Round: Manchester U. (H) 1-2.
Littlewoods Cup: 1987-88: 2nd Round: Northampton T. (H) 1-1 (A) 4-2; 3rd Round: Southend U. (H) 1-0; 4th Round: Luton T. (H) 0-1.

LEEDS UNITED (Division 2)

Team Manager Billy Bremner.
Club Address Elland Road, Leeds LS11 0ES. Tel: (0532) 716037.
Current Ground Capacity 39,423.
Record Attendance 57,892 v Sunderland, FA Cup 5th Round replay, 15 March 1967.
Year Formed 1919. Turned professional 1920.
Previous Names None.
Club Nickname "The Whites".
Club Colours All white with blue and yellow stripe.
Club Honours Football League: Div. 1 Champions 1968-69, 1973-74; Div. 2 Champions 1923-24, 1963-64. FA Cup: Winners 1972. Football League Cup: Winners 1968. European Fairs Cup: Winners 1967-68, 1970-71.
League History 1920-24 Div. 2; 1924-27 Div. 1; 1927-28 Div.2; 1928-31 Div.1; 1931-32 Div.2; 1932-47 Div. 1; 1947-56 Div 2; 1956-60 Div. 1; 1960-64 Div. 2; 1964-82 Div 1; 1982- Div. 2.
Most League Points in a Season (2 for a win) 67 in Div. 1, 1968-69. (3 for a win) 69 in Div. 2, 1984-85.

Most League Goals in a Season 98 in Div. 2, 1927-28.
Record Victory 10-0 v Lyn Oslo in European Cup 1st Round 1st Leg, 17 September 1969.
Record Defeat 1-8 v Stoke C. in Div. 1, 27 August 1934.
Consecutive League Wins 9 in 1931.
Consecutive League Defeats 6 in 1947.
Record League Appearances Jack Charlton, 628 between 1953-73.
Record League Goalscorer—Career Peter Lorimer, 168 between 1962-86.
Record League Goalscorer—Season John Charles, 42 in Div. 2, 1953-54.

Leeds United: League Record, 1987-88 (Division 2)

Match Number	Date	Venue	Opponents	Result		H/T	Lge Posn	Attend
1	16.8.87	A	Barnsley	D	1-1	0-0		9778
2	19.8.87	H	Leicester C.	W	1-0	0-0		21034
3	22.8.87	H	Reading	D	0-0	0-0	4	19286
4	29.8.87	A	Bradford C.	D	0-0	0-0	9	11428
5	31.8.87	H	West Bromwich A.	W	1-0	0-0	3	19847
6	5.9.87	A	Ipswich T.	L	0-1	0-0	8	11016
7	12.9.87	H	Hull C.	L	0-2	0-0	12	18205
8	15.9.87	A	Huddersfield T.	D	0-0	0-0	12	9085
9	19.9.87	A	Middlesbrough	L	0-2	0-1	16	12051
10	26.9.87	H	Manchester C.	W	2-0	1-0	11	25358
11	30.9.87	H	Stoke C.	D	0-0	0-0	10	17208
12	3.10.87	A	Blackburn Rov.	D	1-1	0-0	12	7675
13	10.10.87	H	Aston Villa	L	1-3	1-1	14	20741
14	17.10.87	A	Plymouth Arg.	L	3-6	2-2	16	9358
15	20.10.87	A	Oldham Ath.	D	1-1	0-1	16	6312
16	24.10.87	H	Bournemouth	W	3-2	3-0	13	15253
17	31.10.87	A	Sheffield U.	D	2-2	0-1	14	12095
18	7.11.87	H	Shrewsbury T.	W	2-1	1-0	13	13760
19	14.11.87	A	Millwall	L	1-3	0-0	13	8014
20	21.11.87	H	Swindon T.	W	4-2	3-1	12	15457
21	28.11.87	A	Crystal Palace	L	0-3	0-1	13	8749
22	5.12.87	H	Birmingham C.	W	4-1	2-0	13	15977
23	12.12.87	A	Reading	W	1-0	0-0	12	6505
24	19.12.87	H	Huddersfield T.	W	3-0	1-0	11	20111
25	26.12.87	A	Manchester C.	W	2-1	1-1	10	30153
26	28.12.87	H	Middlesbrough	W	2-0	1-0	10	33606
27	1.1.88	H	Bradford C.	W	2-0	1-0	9	36004
28	3.1.88	A	Hull C.	L	1-3	1-3	9	14694
29	16.1.88	H	Barnsley	L	0-2	0-1	9	19028
30	30.1.88	A	West Bromwich A.	W	4-1	2-0	8	9008
31	6.2.88	H	Ipswich T.	W	1-0	1-0	7	19564
32	13.2.88	A	Leicester C.	L	2-3	1-1	7	11937
33	23.2.88	A	Stoke C.	L	1-2	0-1	7	10129
34	27.2.88	H	Blackburn Rov.	D	2-2	2-0	7	23843
35	5.3.88	H	Plymouth Arg.	W	1-0	0-0	7	18115
36	12.3.88	H	Aston Villa	W	2-1	2-0	7	19677
37	19.3.88	H	Sheffield U.	W	5-0	1-0	7	22376
38	26.3.88	A	Bournemouth	D	0-0	0-0	6	9147
39	2.4.88	A	Shrewsbury T.	L	0-1	0-0	7	7369
40	6.4.88	H	Millwall	L	1-2	0-1	7	24241
41	23.4.88	A	Oldham Ath.	D	1-1	0-0	7	13442
42	30.4.88	A	Swindon T.	W	2-1	2-1	7	8299
43	2.5.88	H	Crystal Palace	W	1-0	1-0	7	13217
44	6.5.88	A	Birmingham C.	D	0-0	0-0	7	6024

Players: League Record, 1987-88 (Division 2)

Match Number	1	2	3	4	5	6	7	8	9	10	11	12	13	14	15	16	17	18	19	20	21	22	23	24	25	26	27	28	29	30	31	32	33	34	35	36	37	38	39	40	41	42	43	44	Apps	Subs	Goals
Adams	3	3	3	3	3	3	3	3	3	3	3	3	3	3	3	3			3	3	3	3	3	3	3	3	3	3	3	3	3	3	3				3	3	3	3	3	3			40	0	0
Aizlewood	4	4	4	4	4	4	4																									4	4	4	4	4	4	4	4	4		★			16	1	0
Ashurst	5	5	5	5	5	5	5	5	5	5	5	5	5	5	5	5	5	5	5	5	5	5	5	5	5	5	5	5	5	5	5	5	5	5	5	5	5	5	5	5					41	0	0
Aspin	2	2	2	2	2	2	2	2	2	2	2	2	★	2	2						2	2	2	2	2	2	2	2	2	2															25	1	0
Baird																														9¹	9	9	9	9	9	9	9²	9	9						10	0	3
Batty							7	7	7	7	7	7	7¹	7	7	7		7		11		7	7	7	7	7	★	7	7	7	7	7													22	1	1
Brockie																																										2	2		2	0	1
Buckley		★																																											0	1	0
Davison										10¹	10¹	10¹	10	10¹	10	10¹	10	10¹	10	10	10	10¹	10	10							★		10												15	1	6
Day	1	1	1	1	1	1	1	1	1	1	1	1	1	1	1	1	1	1	1	1	1	1	1	1	1	1	1	1	1	1	1	1	1	1	1	1	1	1	1	1	1	1	1	1	44	0	0
De Mange									7¹	7	7	7	7	7	7	4	4	4	4	4		4				★	7																		14	1	1
Doig				★										7																															1	0	0
Edwards	★	★	10			9	9	11	★	★																																			4	4	0
Grayson								4																																				4	2	0	0
Haddock		★	11	11	11	★	11	4	4	4	2	4	6	2	6	6	6	6¹	6	6	6	6	6	6	6	6	6	6	6	6	6	6		3	3	8	7	2	2	2					38	2	1
McDonald															3																														1	0	0
Maguire																																							10	10					2	0	0
Melrose									9	9	9	★																																	3	1	0
Mumby									10	7	★		10															★																	3	2	0
Noteman																																											★		0	1	0
Pearson	9	9	9	9	★	★	9	9	9	★	9		10	10			7										9¹	9¹	9	9¹	9	10	10	10³	10	★		★	★						21	7	6
Rennie	6	6	6	6	6	6	6	6	6	6	6	6	6		6¹		7	3	8¹	8							11	7	7		★	★	★				10	6	6	6					25	3	2
Sheridan	8	8¹	8	8	8¹	8	8	8	8	8	8	8		8	8				8¹	8¹	8²	8	8	8	8	8	8¹	8	8¹	8	8¹	8		★¹	★	8	8¹	8	8	8¹	8				36	2	12
Snodin	11	11					11	7	11	11¹	11	11	11	11²	11	11	11	11¹	11	11	11	11		11	11	11¹	11		11	11	11	★	★	11	11¹	11	11	11							33	2	7
Stiles								7	★	★					4	4		4			★																		4	4					7	6	1
Swan										★	★¹	10¹	10¹	10	10			★	★¹	11	11	9	9	9¹	9¹	11					6	6¹	6¹	6	6	6	5	5	5						21	4	8
Taylor	10¹	10		10	10	10		10	10	10	★	9¹	9¹	9	9¹	9	9¹	9	9¹	9	9	9			★	9	★		★		10		8¹	8		11	11	★	10						27	5	8
Williams	7	7	7	7	7	7					6	8	4	2	2	2	2	4		4	4	4	4¹	4	4	4¹	4	4¹	2	2	2	2	2	2	2										31	0	3
Own Goals													1								1																										2

FA Cup: 1987-88: 3rd Round: Aston Villa (H) 1-2.
Littlewoods Cup: 1987-88: 2nd Round: York C. (H) 1-1 (A) 4-0; 3rd Round: Oldham Ath. (H) 2-2 Replay (A) 2-4.

LEICESTER CITY (Division 2)

Team Manager David Pleat.
Club Address City Stadium, Filbert Street, Leicester LE2 7FL. Tel: (0533) 555000.
Current Ground Capacity 31,000.
Record Attendance 47,298 v Tottenham H., FA Cup 5th Round, 18 February 1928.
Year Formed 1884. Turned professional 1894.
Previous Names Leicester Fosse.
Club Nickname "The Filberts" or "Foxes".
Club Colours Blue shirts with white pinstripe, white shorts and stockings with blue trim.
Club Honours Football League: Div. 2 Champions 1924-25, 1936-37, 1953-54, 1956-57, 1970-71, 1979-80. Football League Cup: Winners 1964.
League History 1894-1908 Div. 2; 1908-09 Div. 1; 1909-25 Div. 2; 1925-35 Div. 1; 1935-37 Div. 2; 1937-39 Div. 1; 1946-54 Div. 2; 1954-55 Div. 1; 1955-57 Div. 2; 1957-69 Div. 1; 1969-71 Div. 2; 1971-78 Div. 1; 1978-80 Div. 2; 1980-81 Div. 1; 1981-83 Div. 2; 1983-87 Div. 1; 1987- Div. 2.
Most League Points in a Season (2 for a win) 51 in Div. 2, 1956-57. (3 for a win) 70 in Div. 2, 1982-83.

Most League Goals in a Season 109 in Div. 2, 1956-57.
Record Victory 10-0 v Portsmouth in Div. 1, 20 December 1928.
Record Defeat 0-12 v Nottingham F. in Div. 1, 21 April 1909.
Consecutive League Wins 7 in 1908, 1925 and 1962-63.
Consecutive League Defeats 7 in 1931-32.
Record League Appearances Adam Black, 528 between 1920-35.
Record League Goalscorer—Career Arthur Chandler, 259 between 1923-35.
Record League Goalscorer—Season Arthur Rowley, 44 in Div. 2, 1956-57.

Leicester City: League Record, 1978-88 (Division 2)

Match Number	Date	Venue	Opponents	Result		H/T	Lge Posn	Attend
1	15.8.87	H	Shrewsbury T.	L	0-1	0-0		8469
2	19.8.87	A	Leeds U.	L	0-1	0-0		21034
3	29.8.87	H	Millwall	W	1-0	0-0	17	7553
4	31.8.87	A	Stoke C.	L	1-2	1-2	18	9948
5	5.9.87	A	Aston Villa	L	0-2	0-1	22	10286
6	12.9.87	A	Crystal Palace	L	1-2	1-1	22	8925
7	16.9.87	H	Oldham Ath.	W	4-1	4-0	20	7358
8	19.9.87	H	Plymouth Arg.	W	4-0	3-0	17	8872
9	26.9.87	A	Bournemouth	W	3-2	1-1	13	7969
10	30.9.87	H	Ipswich T.	D	1-1	1-1	12	11533
11	3.10.87	A	Manchester C.	L	2-4	1-1	15	16481
12	10.10.87	H	Barnsley	D	0-0	0-0	15	8665
13	17.10.87	A	Sheffield U.	L	1-2	0-2	17	10593
14	21.10.87	H	West Bromwich A.	W	3-0	1-0	14	9262
15	24.10.87	A	Hull C.	D	2-2	1-1	14	8826
16	31.10.87	H	Blackburn Rov.	L	1-2	0-0	17	8650
17	7.11.87	H	Swindon T.	W	3-2	0-1	15	8346
18	14.11.87	A	Birmingham C.	D	2-2	1-1	15	8666
19	21.11.87	H	Bradford C.	L	0-2	0-1	15	11543
20	28.11.87	A	Huddersfield T.	L	0-1	0-1	16	6704
21	5.12.87	H	Middlesbrough	D	0-0	0-0	16	9411
22	12.12.87	A	Oldham Ath.	L	0-2	0-1	17	4785
23	26.12.87	H	Bournemouth	L	0-1	0-1	19	11452
24	28.12.87	A	Plymouth Arg.	L	0-4	0-0	19	15581
25	1.1.88	A	Millwall	L	0-1	0-1	19	7220
26	2.1.88	H	Crystal Palace	D	4-4	2-4	21	10104
27	16.1.88	A	Shrewsbury T.	D	0-0	0-0	21	5025
28	30.1.88	A	Reading	W	2-1	1-1	19	6645
29	6.2.88	A	Aston Villa	L	1-2	0-2	20	18867
30	13.2.88	H	Leeds U.	W	3-2	1-1	19	11937
31	20.2.88	A	Ipswich T.	W	2-0	1-0	17	11084
32	27.2.88	H	Manchester C.	W	1-0	0-0	17	13852
33	5.3.88	H	Sheffield U.	W	1-0	0-0	16	12256
34	12.3.88	A	Barnsley	D	1-1	1-1	16	7447
35	16.3.88	H	Stoke C.	D	1-1	1-0	16	10502
36	19.3.88	A	Blackburn Rov.	D	3-3	0-0	16	12506
37	26.3.88	H	Hull C.	W	2-1	1-0	16	10353
38	2.4.88	A	Swindon T.	L	2-3	1-1	16	9450
39	5.4.88	H	Birmingham C.	W	2-0	2-0	16	13541
40	9.4.88	A	West Bromwich A.	D	1-1	1-1	16	11031
41	23.4.88	H	Reading	W	1-0	1-0	16	9603
42	30.4.88	A	Bradford C.	L	1-4	1-4	16	14393
43	2.5.88	H	Huddersfield T.	W	3-0	2-0	13	9803
44	7.5.88	A	Middlesbrough	W	2-1	1-0	13	27645

Players: League Record, 1987-88 (Division 2)

Match Number	1	2	3	4	5	6	7	8	9	10	11	12	13	14	15	16	17	18	19	20	21	22	23	24	25	26	27	28	29	30	31	32	33	34	35	36	37	38	39	40	41	42	43	44	Apps	Subs	Goals
Andrews	1	1	1	1	1															1	1	1	1	1	1																				12	0	0
Brien							★	5	2	2	★						5	5	5	5	5	5	5	5¹	5		★	★																	11	4	1
Brown																																									4	4		2	0	0
Cooper						1	1	1	1	1	1	1	1	1	1	1	1	1	1	1						1	1	1	1	1	1	1	1	1	1	1	1	1	1	1	1	1			32	0	0
Cross																							8	8	8¹	8	8¹	8¹	8	8	8	8	8	8	8	8¹	8	8	8²	8					17	0	6
Cusack	9	9							★				★				★¹	★	9	9	9	★	★			★				★				★			★								5	11	1
Ford	7	7	7	7	7	★		7¹	7¹						11	11	11	11	10	10	11	7																							15	1	2
Groves																																								★¹					0	1	1
Horner			5	5	★				5	5											4	4																							6	1	0
James	3	2	2	2	9	2	3	3	3	3	3	3	3	3			3	3		★	2	2	2	★	2	2																			21	2	0
Jobling																				★				6	★			6	10	★															3	3	0
Langan															2	2	2	2	2																										5	0	0
McAllister	8	10	10	10¹	10	10¹	★	★	7	7	7	7	7¹	7	7¹	7	7	7	7	7	10	7	7¹	7	7	7	7	7²	7	7	7	7	7	7	7	7	7¹	7			7	7	7¹		40	2	9
MacDonald																					8	6	11																						3	0	0
Mauchlen						7	10	10	10¹	10	10	10	10	10	10	10	10	★	★	2	★	6	6	8	6			2	2	2	2	2	2	2¹	2	2	2	2	2	2	2	2			33	3	2
Moran	★	8	8¹	8	8	8	★	★	★	11¹	★	9	9	9²	9	9¹																													11	5	5
Morgan	2	★	★	★	2	★	2	2	2	2	2	★	★	2	3	★		3	3	3			4	4		★	2	2	3	3	3	3	3	3	3	3	3	3	3	3	3	3	3	3	32	8	0
Newell							8¹	8¹	8¹	8	8¹	8	8	8	8	8	8	8	8	8¹	8	8	8			9	9	9	9	9	9¹	9	9¹	9	9	9	9	9¹	9¹		9	9	9	9	36	0	8
Osman	4	4	4	4	4	4	4	4	4¹	4	4	4	4	4	4	4	4	4	4					4¹	4	4	4	4	4	4	4	4	4	4¹	4²	4					4				37	0	5
Osvold											11	11	★	11																															3	1	0
Prindiville																						★																							0	1	0
Ramsey	6	6	6	6	6	6	6	6	6	6	6	6	6	6	6	★¹	9	10	10		10	2	10	10	6	6	6	6	6	6	6	6	6	6	6	6	6'	6	6	6	6	6			41	1	1
Rantanen			9	9¹	9¹	9	9	9¹							9	10	9	★	★		9			★																					10	3	3
Reid			9	9							★	11	★	11	11	11				★	11¹			10	10	10	10¹	10	10	10	10	10²	10	10	10	10	10	10¹	10						23	3	5
Russell	11			★	★				11																													★							2	3	0
Turner																																			★	★	9		7	7	★	★	10		4	4	0
Venus	★	3	3	3	3	3			★		11		11				6¹	6	6	6	3	3	3	3	3	3	3																		19	2	1
Walsh	5	5			5	5	5	5			5	5	5¹	5¹	5¹	5¹	5¹	5						4	5¹	5	5	5	5	5	5	5¹	5	5	5	5	5¹	5	5	5					32	0	7
Weir																					11	11	11	11	11	11	11	11	11	11	11	11¹	11	11	11	11	11	11	11	11	11¹				18	0	2
Wilkinson		★																		★			8	8¹	8																				3	2	1
Wilson	10	11	11	11	11	11	11¹	11¹																																					8	0	2

FA Cup: 1987-88: 3rd Round: Oxford U. (A) 0-2.
Littlewoods Cup: 1987-88: 2nd Round: Scunthorpe U. (H) 2-1 (A) 2-1; 3rd Round: Oxford U. (A) 0-0 Replay (H) 2-3.

LEYTON ORIENT (Division 4)

Team Manager Frank Clark.
Club Address Leyton Stadium, Brisbane Road, Leyton, London E10 5NE. Tel: 01-539 2223/4.
Current Ground Capacity 26,500.
Record Attendance 34,345 v West Ham U., FA Cup 4th Round, 25 January 1964.
Year Formed 1881. Turned professional 1903.
Previous Names Glyn Cricket and Football Club, Eagle Football Club, Orient Football Club, Clapton Orient, Orient.
Club Nickname "The O's".
Club Colours All red.
Club Honours Football League: Div. 3 Champions 1969-70; Div.3(S) Champions 1955-56.
League History 1905-29 Div. 2; 1929-56 Div. 3(S); 1956-62 Div. 2; 1962-63 Div. 1; 1963-66 Div. 2; 1966-70 Div. 3; 1970-82 Div. 2; 1982-85 Div. 3; 1985- Div. 4.
Most League Points in a Season (2 for a win) 66 in Div. 3(S), 1955-56. (3 for a win) 72 in Div. 4, 1985-86.
Most League Goals in a Season 106 in Div. 3(S), 1955-56.

Record Victory 9-2 v Aldershot in Div. 3(S), 10 February 1934 and v Chester in League Cup 3rd Round, 15 October 1962.
Record Defeat 0-8 v Aston Villa in FA Cup 4th Round, 30 January 1929.
Consecutive League Wins 10 in 1956.
Consecutive League Defeats 8 in 1927-28.
Record League Appearances Peter Allen, 430 between 1965-78.
Record League Goalscorer—Career Tom Johnston, 119 between 1956-61.
Record League Goalscorer—Season Tom Johnston, 35 in Div. 2, 1957-58.

Leyton Orient: League Record, 1987-88 (Division 4)

Match Number	Date	Venue	Opponents	Result		H/T	Lge Posn	Attend
1	15.8.87	A	Cardiff C.	D	1-1	1-1		3357
2	22.8.87	H	Scarborough	W	3-1	0-1		3540
3	29.8.87	A	Torquay U.	D	1-1	0-0	5	2705
4	1.9.87	H	Burnley	W	4-1	1-0	3	3560
5	5.9.87	A	Hartlepool U.	D	2-2	1-1	4	1197
6	12.9.87	H	Exeter C.	L	2-3	0-1	7	3613
7	15.9.87	A	Stockport Co.	W	2-1	2-1	4	2560
8	18.9.87	A	Crewe Alex.	D	3-3	0-1	8	2150
9	26.9.87	H	Peterborough U.	W	2-0	0-0	4	3426
10	29.9.87	H	Newport Co.	W	4-1	3-1	1	3761
11	3.10.87	A	Wrexham	D	2-2	1-1	3	2123
12	9.10.87	A	Colchester U.	D	0-0	0-0	3	1665
13	17.10.87	H	Cambridge U.	L	0-2	0-0	5	4059
14	20.10.87	H	Rochdale	W	8-0	4-0	2	2995
15	24.10.87	A	Swansea C.	L	0-3	0-1	6	3895
16	31.10.87	H	Halifax T.	W	4-1	3-1	2	3208
17	3.11.87	A	Carlisle U.	W	2-1	1-1	2	2139
18	7.11.87	A	Bolton W.	L	0-1	0-0	6	5189
19	20.11.87	H	Darlington	W	4-3	1-2	3	3644
20	28.11.87	A	Hereford U.	W	3-0	2-0	2	1853
21	12.12.87	H	Tranmere Rov.	W	3-1	1-0	1	3684
22	19.12.87	A	Wolverhampton W.	L	0-2	0-0	3	12051
23	26.12.87	A	Peterborough U.	W	2-1	1-0	2	3371
24	28.12.87	H	Scunthorpe U.	D	1-1	1-1	3	5542
25	1.1.88	H	Torquay U.	L	0-2	0-1	3	4589
26	2.1.88	A	Exeter C.	W	3-2	1-1	2	2568
27	16.1.88	H	Crewe Alex.	D	1-1	0-0	2	4082
28	23.1.88	H	Stockport Co.	D	1-1	0-1	2	4205
29	6.2.88	H	Hartlepool U.	L	0-2	0-1	4	4102
30	13.2.88	A	Scunthorpe U.	L	2-3	1-0	4	2951
31	20.2.88	H	Cardiff C.	W	4-1	1-1	4	3523
32	24.2.88	A	Scarborough	L	1-3	0-1	4	2116
33	27.2.88	H	Wrexham	W	2-1	2-0	3	3448
34	1.3.88	A	Newport Co.	D	0-0	0-0	3	1656
35	5.3.88	A	Cambridge U.	L	0-2	0-0	6	2500
36	12.3.88	H	Colchester U.	D	0-0	0-0	7	3125
37	22.3.88	A	Burnley	L	0-2	0-1	9	5878
38	26.3.88	H	Swansea C.	W	3-0	1-0	6	3390
39	2.4.88	H	Bolton W.	L	1-2	1-0	8	4537
40	4.4.88	A	Darlington	D	2-2	1-1	7	2730
41	9.4.88	H	Carlisle U.	W	4-1	2-0	6	2861
42	14.8.88	A	Halifax T.	L	0-1	0-1	6	1006
43	23.4.88	A	Rochdale	W	3-1	1-1	6	1390
44	30.4.88	H	Hereford U.	W	4-0	3-0	6	3444
45	2.5.88	A	Tranmere Rov.	L	1-2	0-1	6	3604
46	7.5.88	H	Wolverhampton W.	L	0-2	0-1	8	7738

Players: League Record, 1987-88 (Division 4)

Match Number	1	2	3	4	5	6	7	8	9	10	11	12	13	14	15	16	17	18	19	20	21	22	23	24	25	26	27	28	29	30	31	32	33	34	35	36	37	38	39	40	41	42	43	44	45	46	Apps	Subs	Goals
Baker																																					6	6	6	6¹	6	6	6¹	6	6	9	0	2
Castle	8	8	8¹	8	8	8	8	8	8	8	8	8	8	8	8	8	8	8	8¹	8²	8	8¹	8	8	8	8	8	8	8¹	8¹	8¹	8	8	8	8	8	8	8	8	8	8¹	8	8¹				42	0	10
Comfort	11	11¹	11	11¹	11	11	11	11	11¹	11	11¹	11	11	11²	11	11	11	11	11¹	11	11	11	11	11	11	11¹	11	11	11	11	11	11	11	11	11¹	11	11	11	11	11¹	11¹	11	11	11	11	11	46	0	11
Conroy																												★																			2	1	0
Day	5	5¹	5	5	5	5¹	5¹	5	5	5	5	5	5	5	5	5	5	5	5	5	5	5	5	5	5	5	5	5	5		5		5		5	5	5	5	5	5	5	5	5	5	5		41	0	3
Dickenson							6	3	3	3¹	3	3	3	3	3	3	3	3	3	3	3	3	3	3	3	3	3	3	3																		22	0	1
Godfrey	10	10	10	10¹	10¹	10¹	10	10²	10	10	10	10	10	★	10	10	10¹	10	10	10		10		9	6		★		★				★	★		9¹	9	9									28	6	7
Hales	6	6	6	6	6	6	6	6	6	6		2	2	7²	7	7¹	7	7	7¹	7	7	7	7	7	6	7	6¹	6	6	6	7	7	7	7		7	7	7	7	7							42	0	6
Harvey				★	★	★	★	★	★¹	★	★	★	★		10	10	★			★	★	★	10	★	6	★	6	9	★			★															6	17	1
Howard	2	2	2	2		2	2	2	2	2¹	2		2	2	2	2	2	2	2	2	2	2	2	2		2	2	2	2	2¹	2	2	2	2	2	2	2	2	2	2	2	2	2	2	2	2	41	0	2
Hughton	3				★	2	2																								★	3	3	3													3	3	0
Hull	★	★		3²	3	3	3¹	3	3	3¹	3		6	6	6	6¹	6	6	6	6	6	6	6	6	6	★		★	★	9	9	9	★	9	9	9						★	★	★			27	9	5
Juryeff	9	9															9¹			9²	9	10¹	10	10¹	10¹	10¹	10	10		10	10	10	10	10¹	10	10²	10	10²	10	10²	10²	10¹	10				23	0	16
Ketteridge	7	7	7	7	7	7	7	7	7¹	7	7	7	7	7					★	★	2	★		7	7	7	7	7	7				7				9			★	★			★			21	5	1
Marks																																9	10														3	0	0
Nugent			3¹	3				9					9¹	6										★	9	10	8¹								9		9										10	1	3
Shinners			9	9	9¹		9	9	9	9¹		9	9	9²	9	9²	9²	9	9¹	9¹	9¹	9	9															9	9	9	9¹						24	0	11
Sitton				★																							4	4	4	4	4¹	4	4	4	4	4		4	4	4	4	4	4	4	4	4	19	1	1
Smalley	4¹	4	4	4	4	4	4	4¹	4	4	4	4¹	4	4	4	4	4	4	4	4	4	4	4	4	5	★	5	5	★	5	5	5															33	2	3
Stimson																															3	3	3	3	3	3	3	3	3	3							10	0	0
Sussex					★										★			★		8¹											6											8	8	8			5	3	1
Wells	1	1	1	1	1	1	1	1	1	1	1	1	1	1	1	1	1	1	1	1	1	1	1	1	1	1	1	1	1	1	1	1	1	1	1	1	1	1	1	1	1	1	1	1	1	1	46	0	0
Own Goals																																				1													1

FA Cup: 1987-88: 1st Round: Exeter C. (H) 2-0; 2nd Round: (H) Blackpool 2-0; 3rd Round: Stockport Co. (A) 2-1; 4th Round: Nottingham F. (H) 1-2.
Littlewoods Cup: 1987-88: 1st Round: Millwall (H) 1-1 (A) 0-1.

LINCOLN CITY (Division 4)

Team Manager Colin Murphy.
Club Address Sincil Bank, Lincoln LN5 8LD. Tel: (0522) 22224.
Current Ground Capacity 9,500.
Record Attendance 23,196 v Derby Co., Football League Cup, 4th Round, 15 November 1967.
Year Formed 1884. Turned professional 1892.
Previous Names None.
Club Nickname "The Imps".
Club Colours Red and white striped shirts, white shirts and stockings.
Club Honours Football League: Div. 3(N) Champions 1931-32, 1947-48, 1951-52; Div. 4 Champions 1975-76. Vauxhall Conference Champions 1987-88.
League History 1892-1921 Div. 2; 1921-32 Div. 3(N); 1932-34 Div. 2; 1934-48 Div. 3(N); 1948-49 Div. 2; 1949-52 Div. 3(N); 1952-61 Div. 2; 1961-62 Div. 3; 1962-76 Div. 4; 1976-79 Div. 3; 1979-81 Div. 4; 1981-86 Div. 3; 1986-87 Div. 4; 1987-88 Vauxhall Conference; 1988- Div. 4.
Most League Points in a Season (2 for a win) 74 in Div. 4, 1975-76. (3 for a win) 77 in Div. 3, 1981-82.

Most League Goals in a Season 121 in Div. 3(N), 1951-52.
Record Victory 11-1 v Crewe Alex., Div. 3(N), 29 September 1951.
Record Defeat 3-11 v Manchester C., Div. 2, 23 March 1895.
Consecutive League Wins 10 in 1930-31 and 1974-75.
Consecutive League Defeats 12 in 1896-97.
Record League Appearances Tony Emery, 402 between 1946-59.
Record League Goalscorer—Career Andy Graver, 144 between 1950-61.
Record League Goalscorer—Season Allan Hall, 42 in Div. 3(N), 1931-32.

Lincoln City: League Record, 1987-88 (Vauxhall Conference)

Match Number	Date	Venue	Opponents	Result	H/T	Lge Posn	Attend
1	22.8.87	A	Barnet	L 2-4	1-3		2589
2	26.8.87	A	Weymouth	L 0-3	0-0		3500
3	29.8.87	H	Dagenham	W 3-0	1-0		1995
4	31.8.87	H	Runcorn	W 1-0	0-0		2330
5	5.9.87	H	Stafford R.	W 4-1	2-0		2111
6	8.9.87	A	Altrincham	D 0-0	0-0	8	2398
7	19.9.87	H	Enfield	W 4-0	1-0	7	2503
8	22.9.87	A	Runcorn	L 1-4	1-1		970
9	26.9.87	A	Telford U.	W 1-0	0-0	6	2025
10	30.9.87	H	Kettering T.	L 0-1	0-0		3145
11	3.10.87	H	Bath C.	W 3-0	1-0	5	2494
12	10.10.87	A	Maidstone U.	W 2-1	1-1	4	1101
13	17.10.87	A	Wealdstone	D 0-0	0-0	6	1107
14	28.10.87	H	Barnet	W 2-1	1-0		4624
15	31.10.87	H	Cheltenham	W 5-1	3-1	3	2241
16	7.11.87	A	Wycombe W.	W 2-1	1-1	3	2105
17	21.11.87	H	Weymouth	D 0-0	0-0	3	3890
18	25.11.87	H	Macclesfield T.	W 3-0	2-0		2544
19	28.11.87	A	Sutton U.	L 1-4	1-2	3	1013
20	12.12.87	H	Northwich Victoria	W 3-2	0-1	3	2301
21	26.12.87	A	Boston U.	W 2-1	0-0	3	5822
22	28.12.87	H	Kidderminster Harriers	W 5-1	3-1	2	4121
23	2.1.88	A	Northwich Victoria	W 3-2	0-1	2	1207
24	9.1.88	H	Fisher Ath.	W 3-0	1-0	2	3751
25	16.1.88	A	Welling U.	W 4-1	3-1	2	1339
26	17.2.88	H	Sutton U.	D 1-1	0-1	2	3201
27	20.2.88	H	Telford U.	D 0-0	0-0	2	3500
28	27.2.88	A	Dagenham	W 3-0	2-0	2	832
29	2.3.88	H	Welling U.	W 2-1	2-0	2	3218
30	12.3.88	A	Kidderminster Harriers	D 3-3	1-2	2	2635
31	19.3.88	A	Enfield	D 0-0	0-0	2	1390
32	26.3.88	H	Altrincham	W 5-0	2-0	2	2720
33	1.4.88	A	Fisher Ath.	D 1-1	1-0	2	765
34	4.4.88	H	Boston U.	W 5-1	3-1	2	7542
35	9.4.88	A	Cheltenham T.	D 3-3	3-3	2	1715
36	12.4.88	A	Macclesfield T.	L 0-2	0-1	2	2050
37	16.4.88	H	Wealdstone	W 3-0	3-0	2	4159
38	19.4.88	A	Bath C.	L 1-2	1-2	2	1336
39	23.4.88	A	Kettering T.	L 0-2	0-1	2	4135
40	27.4.88	H	Maidstone U.	D 1-1	0-0	2	4892
41	30.4.88	H	Stafford R.	W 2-1	1-1	1	4402
42	2.5.88	H	Wycombe W.	W 2-0	1-0	1	9432

Players: League Record, 1987-88 (Vauxhall Conference)

Match Number	1	2	3	4	5	6	7	8	9	10	11	12	13	14	15	16	17	18	19	20	21	22	23	24	25	26	27	28	29	30	31	32	33	34	35	36	37	38	39	40	41	42	Apps	Subs	Goals
Batch	1	1	1	1	1	1	1	1	1	1	1	1	1	1	1	1	1	1	1	1	1	1	1			1				1	1	1	1				1	1	1				32	0	0
Bressington													4		★	4	4	4											★	★	6		★										9	4	0
Brown	7	4	4	4	7	7			★	★	4^1	4	4	4	4	4^1	4	9^1	9	9^2	9	9	9^1	9	9	9^1	9	9	9	9	9	9^2	9	9	9	9	9^1	9^1					38	2	16
Buckley	3	3											6	6	6	6	6	6	6	6	6	6	6	6	6	**6**		6	**6**			6	6	6									22	0	0
Casey																								7	4	7	7	7	7	4	7	7	7	7									10	0	0
Clarke				★¹	3	4	4	4	**4**					★	★	4			★¹	8	4^1	4	8	8^1	8	8	3	3^1	3	3	3	3	3	8	4	4	4						26	4	5
Crombie																					7																						1	0	0
Cummings	9^1			9	8	8	8^1	8	**8**	8	8	8	8	8^1	8^1	8	8	8^1	8	8	8^1		8	**8**					4	8	8	8^1	8	8		**8**	8		8	8	8		33	0	7
Evans				2	2	2	2	2	2	2	2	2^2	2	2	2	2	2	2	2	2^1	2^1	2^1	2	2	2	2	2^1	2^1	2	2	2	2	2	2	2	2	2	2	2	2^1	2		36	0	8
Franklin		2	2	2																						★																	3	1	0
Gamble																								10																			1	0	0
Hunter	6	9	9^1																																								3	0	1
McGinley	11	11	11	11	11	11	11^1	11	11	11	11	11	11	11^1	11^1	11	11	11^2	11	11^1	11		11^1	11	11^2	11	11		11		11^2	11	11^1	11^1	11	11^1	**11**	11	11^1	**11**	**11**		38	0	15
Matthewson	5	5	5	5	5	5	5	5	5	5	5	5	5^1	5	5	5	5	5	5	5	5		5^1	5^1	5	5	5	5			5^1	5^1	5	5	5^1	5	5	5					40	0	6
Moore	2	6	6	6	6	6	6	6	6	6	6	6	6	6	6	6	6	6				★			4	4^1	4		4	4	4		4										27	1	1
Mossman			7^2	7	2	2	7	7	7	7	7	**7**	7	7	7	7	7	7										7			★		7										20	1	2
Nicholson	4	7	3	3	3		3	3	3	3	3	3	3	3	3	3	3	3	3	3^1	3	3	3	3	3	3	3								3	3	3	3					33	0	1
Parkin		★																																									0	1	0
Scott																																★	6										1	1	0
Sertori	8	8	8	8	4	4					★		★¹	9	9			9		11			★	★	11	11^1		11	10	10	10^2	10^1	10	★	★	★	★	★	$★^1$				18	10	6
Simmonite													7	7	7	7	7		**7**	7	7	7	7	5	5	**7**																	13	0	0
Smith			10	10	10^2	10^1	10^1	10	10	10^1	10	10	10	10	10	10	10	10	10^1	10	10^1	10	10	10	10	10	10^1						8	10	10	10	10	10					33	0	8
Waitt	10^1	10	10	10^1	9^3	9	9	9	9	9	9^2	9^1	9	9	**9**																												15	0	8
Wilson																						1	1		1	1	1					1	1	1	1	1							10	0	0
Own Goals																	1										2																		2

FA Cup: 1987-88: 4th Qualifying Round: Brigg T. (A) 4-1; 1st Round: Crewe Alex. (H) 2-1; 2nd Round: Mansfield T. (A) 3-4.

LIVERPOOL (Division 1)

Team Manager Kenny Dalglish.
Club Address Anfield Road, Liverpool 4. Tel: 051-263 2361.
Current Ground Capacity 45,600.
Record Attendance 61,905 v Wolverhampton W., FA Cup 4th Round, 2 February 1952.
Year Formed 1892. Turned professional 1892.
Previous Names None.
Club Nickname "The Reds" or "Pool".
Club Colours All red with white trim.
Club Honours Football League: Div. 1 Champions 1900-01, 1905-06, 1921-22, 1922-23, 1946-47, 1963-64, 1965-66, 1972-73, 1975-76, 1976-77, 1978-79, 1979-80, 1981-82, 1982-83, 1983-84, 1985-86, 1987-88; Div. 2 Champions 1893-94, 1895-96, 1904-05, 1961-62. FA Cup: Winners 1965, 1974, 1986. Football League Cup: Winners 1981, 1982, 1983, 1984. League Super Cup: Winners 1985-86. European Cup: Winners 1976-77, 1977-78, 1980-81, 1983-84. UEFA Cup: Winners 1972-73, 1975-76. Super Cup: Winners 1977.

League History 1893-94 Div. 2; 1894-95 Div. 1; 1895-96; Div. 2; 1896-1904 Div. 1; 1904-05 Div. 2; 1905-54 Div. 1; 1954-62 Div. 2; 1962 Div. 1.
Most League Points in a Season (2 for a win) 68 in Div. 1, 1978-79. (3 for a win) 90 in Div. 1, 1987-88.
Most League Goals in a Season 106 in Div. 2, 1895-96.
Record Victory 11-0 v Stromsgodset in European Cup-winners Cup 1st Round 1st Leg, 17 September 1974.
Record Defeat 1-9 v Birmingham C. in Div. 2, 11 December 1954.
Consecutive League Wins 11 in 1982.
Consecutive League Defeats 9 in 1899.
Record League Appearances Ian Callaghan, 640 between 1960-78.
Record League Goalscorer—Career Roger Hunt, 245 between 1959-69.
Record League Goalscorer—Season Roger Hunt, 41 in Div. 2, 1961-62.

Liverpool: League Record, 1987-88 (Division 1)

Match Number	Date	Venue	Opponents	Result		H/T	Lge Posn	Attend
1	15.8.87	A	Arsenal	W	2-1	1-1		54703
2	22.8.87	A	Coventry C.	W	4-1	1-0		27637
3	5.9.87	A	West Ham U.	D	1-1	0-0	9	29865
4	12.9.87	H	Oxford U.	W	2-0	2-0	7	42266
5	15.9.87	H	Charlton Ath.	W	3-2	1-1	5	36637
6	20.9.87	A	Newcastle U.	W	4-1	2-0	5	24141
7	29.9.87	H	Derby Co.	W	4-0	1-0	2	43405
8	3.10.87	H	Portsmouth	W	4-0	1-0	2	43665
9	17.10.87	H	Q.P.R.	W	4-0	1-0	1	43735
10	24.10.87	A	Luton T.	W	1-0	0-0	3	12452
11	1.11.87	H	Everton	W	2-0	1-0	1	44760
12	4.11.87	A	Wimbledon	D	1-1	0-0	2	13454
13	15.11.87	A	Manchester U.	D	1-1	1-0	2	47106
14	21.11.87	H	Norwich C.	D	0-0	0-0	2	37446
15	24.11.87	H	Watford	W	4-0	0-0	1	32396
16	28.11.87	A	Tottenham H.	W	2-0	0-0	1	47362
17	6.12.87	H	Chelsea	W	2-1	0-1	1	31211
18	12.12.87	A	Southampton	D	2-2	2-1	1	19502
19	19.12.87	H	Sheffield Wed.	W	1-0	0-0	1	35383
20	26.12.87	A	Oxford U.	W	3-0	1-0	1	13680

Match Number	Date	Venue	Opponents	Result		H/T	Lge Posn	Attend
21	28.12.87	H	Newcastle U.	W	4-0	1-0	1	44637
22	1.1.88	H	Coventry C.	W	4-0	1-0	1	38790
23	16.1.88	H	Arsenal	W	2-0	1-0	1	44294
24	23.1.88	A	Charlton Ath.	W	2-0	1-0	1	28095
25	6.2.88	H	West Ham U.	D	0-0	0-0	1	42049
26	13.2.88	A	Watford	W	4-1	1-0	1	23838
27	27.2.88	A	Portsmouth	W	2-0	0-0	1	28197
28	5.3.88	A	Q.P.R.	W	1-0	1-0	1	23171
29	16.3.88	A	Derby Co.	D	1-1	0-0	1	26356
30	20.3.88	A	Everton	L	0-1	0-1	1	44162
31	26.3.88	H	Wimbledon	W	2-1	1-0	1	36464
32	2.4.88	A	Nottingham F.	L	1-2	0-1	1	29188
33	4.4.88	H	Manchester U.	D	3-3	2-1	1	43497
34	13.4.88	H	Nottingham F.	W	5-0	2-0	1	39535
35	20.4.88	A	Norwich C.	D	0-0	0-0	1	22509
36	23.4.88	H	Tottenham H.	W	1-0	1-0	1	44798
37	30.4.88	A	Chelsea	D	1-1	0-0	1	35625
38	2.5.88	H	Southampton	D	1-1	1-0	1	37610
39	7.5.88	A	Sheffield Wed.	W	5-1	2-0	1	35893
40	9.5.88	H	Luton T.	D	1-1	1-1	1	30374

Players: League Record, 1987-88 (Division 1)

Match Number	1	2	3	4	5	6	7	8	9	10	11	12	13	14	15	16	17	18	19	20	21	22	23	24	25	26	27	28	29	30	31	32	33	34	35	36	37	38	39	40	Apps	Subs	Goals
Ablett																	★				★			2	2	2	3	3	3	3	3	3		3	3	3					15	2	0
Aldridge	8[1]	8[1]	8[1]	8[1]	8[1]	8[1]	8[3]	8[1]	8[1]	8	8	8	8[1]	8	8[1]	8	8	8	8[1]	8[2]	8[1]	8[1]	8	8	8[1]	8		8[1]	8[1]	8	8[2]	8	8	8	8[1]						36	0	26
Barnes	10	10	10	10[1]	10	10	10	10	10[2]	10	10	10	10	10	10[1]	10	10	10[2]	10	10[1]	10	10	10	10	10[1]	10	10[1]	10[2]	10[1]	10	10	10[1]	10	10			10[1]	10	10[1]	10	38	0	15
Beardsley	7	7[1]	7	7	7	7[1]	7	7[1]	7	7	7	7[1]	7	7	7		7	7	7	7	7	7[2]	7[1]	7[1]	7	7[2]	7	7	7	7	★	7[1]	7[1]	7	7[1]	★	7	7[2]			36	2	15
Dalglish																										★												★			0	2	0
Gillespie	2	2	2	2	2	2	2	2	2	2[1]	2	2	2	2	2	2	2	2	2[1]	2	2	2	2			2	2	2	2	2[1]	2[1]	2	2			2	2	2			35	0	4
Grobbelaar	1	1	1	1	1	1	1	1	1	1	1	1	1	1	1	1	1	1	1	1		1	1	1	1	1	1	1	1	1	1	1	1	1	1	1	1	1	1	1	38	0	0
Hansen	6	6	6	6	6[1]	6	6	6	6	6	6	6	6	6	6	6	6	6	6	6	6	6	6	6	6	6	6	6	6	6	6	6	6	6	6	6	6	6	6	6	39	0	1
Hooper																							1	1																	2	0	0
Houghton									9		★[1]		9	9[1]	9	9	9	9	9	9	9[1]	9[1]	9	9	9	9	9	9	9	9	★	9	9[1]	9	9	9	9	9	9		26	2	5
Johnston	9	9					9	9	9[1]		9	9	9	★		★[1]	★		★	★	★			★	★	★		8	8[1]	8	9	9	★	★	10	10	7	★	8[2]	7	18	12	5
Lawrenson				★	9	★	★	★		3	3	3	3	3	3	3	3					3																			10	4	0
MacDonald																																★									0	1	0
McMahon	11	11	11	11	11[1]	11	11	11[1]	11	11	11[1]	11	11	11	11[1]	11[1]	11[1]	11	11	11[1]	11[1]	11	11	11	11	11[1]	11	11	11	11[1]	11	11	11	11	11[1]	11	11	11	11[1]	11	40	0	9
Molby																								★			★	★	★	7	★					★					1	6	0
Nicol	4[1]	4[2]	4	4	4	4[3]	4	4	4	4	4	4	4	4	4	4	4	4	4	4	4	4	4	4	4	4	4	4	4	4	4	4	4	4	4	4	4	4	4	4	40	0	6
Spackman			9	9	9	★											★	★			★	★	★	★	★	★	5	5	5	5	5	5	5	5	5	5	5	5	5	5	19	8	0
Venison	3	3	3	3		3	3	3	3	3							3	3	3	3		3	3	3	3																18	0	0
Walsh	★	★		★			★	★	★							★	7																								1	7	0
Wark				★																																					0	1	0
Watson																									3									2							2	0	0
Whelan	5	5	5	5	5	5	5	5[1]	5	5	5	5	5	5	5	5	5	5	5	5	5	5	5	5									3	★	★	6					26	2	1

FA Cup: 1987-88: 3rd Round: Stoke C. (A) 0-0 Replay (H) 1-0; 4th Round: Aston Villa (A) 2-0; 5th Round: Everton (A) 1-0; 6th Round: Manchester U. (A) 4-0; Semi-Final: Nottingham F. 2-1; Final: Wimbledon: 0-1.
Littlewoods Cup: 1987-88: 2nd Round: Blackburn Rov. (A) 1-1 (H) 1-0; 3rd Round: Everton (H) 0-1.

LUTON TOWN (Division 1)

Team Manager   Ray Harford.
Club Address   70-72 Kenilworth Road, Luton. Tel: (0582) 411622.
Current Ground Capacity   14,700.
Record Attendance   30,069 v Blackpool, FA Cup 6th Round Replay, 4 March 1959.
Year Formed   1885. Turned professional 1890.
Previous Names   None.
Club Nickname   "The Hatters".
Club Colours   White shirts with navy and orange trim, navy shorts and white stockings with orange and navy turnovers.
Club Honours   Football League: Div. 2 Champions 1981-82; Div. 3(S) Champions 1936-37; Div. 4 Champions 1967-68. Football League Cup: Winners 1988.
League History   1897-1900 Div. 2; 1900 Failed re-election, 1920-37 Div. 3(S); 1937-55 Div. 2; 1955-60 Div. 1; 1960-63 Div. 2; 1963-65 Div. 3; 1965-68 Div 4; 1968-70 Div. 3; 1970-74 Div. 2; 1974-75 Div. 1; 1975-82 Div. 2; 1982- Div. 1.

Most League Points in a Season   (2 for a win) 66 in Div. 4, 1967-68. (3 for a win) 88 in Div. 2, 1981-82.
Most League Goals in a Season   103 in Div. 3(S), 1936-37.
Record Victory   12-0 v Bristol Rov. in Div. 3(S), 13 April 1936.
Record Defeat   0-9 v Small Heath in Div. 2, 12 November 1898.
Consecutive League Wins   9 in 1977.
Consecutive League Defeats   8 in 1899-1900.
Record League Appearances   Bob Morton, 494 between 1948-64.
Record League Goalscorer—Career   Gordon Turner, 243 between 1950-64.
Record League Goalscorer—Season   Joe Payne, 55 in Div. 3(S), 1936-37.

Luton Town: League Record, 1987-88 (Division 1)

Match Number	Date	Venue	Opponents	Result		H/T	Lge Posn	Attend
1	15.8.87	A	Derby Co.	L	0-1	0-1		17204
2	18.8.87	H	Coventry C.	L	0-1	0-0		7506
3	22.8.87	H	West Ham U.	D	2-2	1-2	16	8073
4	29.8.87	A	Chelsea	L	0-3	0-1	18	16075
5	31.8.87	H	Arsenal	D	1-1	1-1	19	8745
6	5.9.87	A	Oxford U.	W	5-2	2-1	14	6804
7	12.9.87	H	Everton	W	2-1	1-1	12	8124
8	19.9.87	A	Charlton Ath.	L	0-1	0-1	12	5003
9	26.9.87	A	Q.P.R.	L	0-2	0-0	14	11175
10	3.10.87	H	Manchester U.	D	1-1	1-0	14	9137
11	10.10.87	A	Portsmouth	L	1-3	0-0	16	12391
12	17.10.87	H	Wimbledon	W	2-0	1-0	14	7018
13	24.10.87	H	Liverpool	L	0-1	0-0	17	12452
14	7.11.87	H	Newcastle U.	W	4-0	1-0	14	7638
15	14.11.87	A	Sheffield Wed.	W	2-0	1-0	12	16960
16	21.11.87	H	Tottenham H.	W	2-0	1-0	11	10091
17	5.12.87	H	Norwich C.	L	1-2	1-0	14	7002
18	12.12.87	A	Watford	W	1-0	1-0	9	12152
19	18.12.87	H	Southampton	D	1-1	1-1	10	6618
20	26.12.87	A	Everton	L	0-2	0-1	11	32242
21	28.12.87	H	Charlton Ath.	W	1-0	1-0	9	7243
22	1.1.88	H	Chelsea	W	3-0	1-0	8	8018
23	2.1.88	A	West Ham U.	D	1-1	0-0	8	16716
24	16.1.88	A	Derby Co.	W	1-0	0-0	8	7175
25	6.2.88	H	Oxford U.	W	7-4	3-2	8	8063
26	13.2.88	A	Arsenal	L	1-2	0-2	8	22615
27	5.3.88	A	Wimbledon	L	0-2	0-1	9	5058
28	15.3.88	A	Coventry C.	L	0-3	0-2	12	13723
29	29.3.88	H	Portsmouth	W	4-1	1-0	10	6740
30	2.4.88	A	Newcastle U.	L	0-4	0-2	13	20565
31	5.4.88	H	Sheffield Wed.	D	2-2	0-0	13	7337
32	12.4.88	A	Manchester U.	L	0-3	0-1	13	28830
33	19.4.88	H	Q.P.R.	W	2-1	1-0	11	6735
34	30.4.88	A	Norwich C.	D	2-2	0-0	12	12700
35	2.5.88	H	Watford	W	2-1	2-0	11	10409
36	4.5.88	A	Tottenham H.	L	1-2	1-1	11	15437
37	7.5.88	A	Southampton	D	1-1	1-0	11	12722
38	9.5.88	A	Liverpool	D	1-1	1-1	11	30374
39	13.5.88	H	Nottingham F.	D	1-1	1-0	11	9108
40	15.5.88	A	Nottingham F.	D	1-1	1-0	9	13106

Players: League Record, 1987-88 (Division 1)

Match Number	1	2	3	4	5	6	7	8	9	10	11	12	13	14	15	16	17	18	19	20	21	22	23	24	25	26	27	28	29	30	31	32	33	34	35	36	37	38	39	40	Apps	Subs	Goals
Allinson												★	10	11	11¹	11²	11	11	11	11	11	11	11	11	11	11	11	11	11	11	★	★	11		9	8	8	★	8	11	23	4	3
Black										11	10		10										9		★		11		★		11	11		11	11	11	★				10	3	0
Breaker	2	2	2	2	2	2¹	2	2	2	2	2	2	2	2	2	2	2	2	2	2	2	2	2	2	2	2	2	2	2	2	2	2	2	2	2	2	2	2	2	2	40	0	1
Cobb			8	8																					★				★	8	★			4							4	3	0
Dibble																													1	1	1	1	1	1	1	1	1				9	0	0
Donaghy	6			6	6	6	6	6	6	6	6		6	6	6	6	6	6	6	6	6	6	6	6	6	6	6	6	6		6					6¹					32	0	1
Foster	5	5	5	5	5	5	5	5	5	5	5	5	5	5	5	5	5	5¹	5	5	5	5	5	5	5		5	5	5	5¹	5	5	5	5	5	5	5	5			39	0	2
Grimes	3	3	3	3	3	3		3	3	3	3	3	3	3	3	3	3	3			★	3	3	3	3	3	3			10	3	10¹	3	4	3						31	1	1
Harford	9	9	9²		9¹	9	9	9	9	9¹	9	9						★¹	9	9	9¹	9		9²	9	9	9		9	9	9				9						24	1	9
Hill	4	4	4	4	4	4¹	4¹	4	4	4	4					★	9	9	10											4	10										16	1	2
James																																★	★		.						0	3	0
Johnson, M.																					5								6	★	6	6	6	6	★	6					7	2	0
Johnson, R.					★	★	★		10				7					★	3	3	3	3	3		4	8	9	8	11	3	3	3	4	3	4	3	4	3			21	4	0
McDonough	★	6	6				3		★	★	4	4	4	4	4	4	4	4¹	4	4	4	4	4¹	4¹	4		4	4	4	4¹	4	4									24	3	4
Newell	★	8	10	9	9																																				4	1	0
North			★																																						0	1	0
Nwajiobi		★		10	10	10¹	10					★					9¹	9	9	9											7	10									10	2	2
Oldfield																									★			★	9¹	9	9	9¹	9	9¹							6	2	3
Preece	11	11	11	11	11	11	11	11																	11			11		10·	10	10									13	0	0
Sealey	1	1	1	1	1	1	1	1	1	1	1	1	1	1	1	1	1	1	1	1	1	1	1	1	1	1	1	1													31	0	0
Stein, B.	8			8	8¹	8¹	8	8	8	8	8	8¹	8	8	8	8¹	8	8	8	8	8	8¹	8	8	8¹	8		8¹		8¹	8	8									28	0	9
Stein, M.			★	★	★	10		★					10²	10¹	10		10	★	10	10¹	10¹	10	10	10³	10¹	10	10	10¹	10	10	10	10	8¹			8					20	5	11
Weir					★	10	11	11	11	11			10	10																											7	1	0
Wilson, D.	7	7	7		7¹	7	7	7	7	7	7	7¹	7	7	7		7	7	7	7	7¹	7	7	7	7	7	7	7	7	7¹	7	7	7¹	7¹	7¹	4	7¹	7	7	7	38	0	8
Wilson, R.	10	10		7																																					3	0	0
Own Goals																				1																							1

FA Cup: 1987-88: 3rd Round: Hartlepool U. (A) 2-1; 4th Round: Southampton (H) 2-1; 5th Round: QPR (A) 1-1 Replay (H) 1-0; 6th Round: Portsmouth (H) 3-1; Semi-Final: Wimbledon 1-2.
Littlewoods Cup: 1987-88: 2nd Round: Wigan Ath. (A) 1-0; (H) 4-2; 3rd Round: Coventry C. (H) 3-1; Fourth Round: Ipswich T. (A) 1-0; Quarter Final: Bradford C. (H) 2-0; Semi-Final: Oxford U. (A) 1-1 (H) 2-0; Final: Arsenal 3-2.

96

MANCHESTER CITY (Division 2)

Team Manager Mel Machin.
Club Address Maine Road, Moss Side, Manchester M14 7WN. Tel: 061-226 1191/2.
Current Ground Capacity 52,600.
Record Attendance 84,569 v Stoke C, FA Cup 6th Round, 3 March 1934.
Year Formed 1887. Turned professional 1887.
Previous Names Ardwick.
Club Nickname "City" or "The Blues".
Club Colours Sky blue shirts with white collar and cuffs, sky blue shorts with white trim and sky blue stockings with white rings on top.
Club Honours Football League: Div. 1 Champions 1936-37, 1967-68; Div. 2 Champions 1898-99, 1902-03, 1909-10, 1927-28, 1946-47, 1965-66. FA Cup: Winners 1904, 1934, 1956, 1969, Football League Cup: Winners 1970, 1976. European Cup-Winners Cup: Winners 1969-70.
League History 1892-99 Div. 2; 1899-1902 Div. 1; 1902-03 Div. 2; 1903-09 Div. 1; 1909-10 Div. 2; 1910-26 Div. 1; 1926-28 Div. 2; 1928-38 Div. 1; 1938-47 Div. 2; 1947-50 Div. 1; 1950-51 Div. 2; 1951-63 Div. 1; 1963-66 Div. 2; 1966-83 Div. 1; 1983-85 Div. 2, 1985-87 Div. 1; 1987- Div. 2.
Most League Points in a Season (2 for a win) 62 in Div. 2, 1946-47. (3 for a win) 74 in Div. 2, 1984-85.
Most League Goals in a Season 108 in Div. 2, 1926-27.
Record Victory 11-3 v Lincoln City in Div. 2, 23 March 1895.
Record Defeat 1-9 v Everton in Div. 1, 3 September 1906.
Consecutive League Wins 9 in 1912.
Consecutive League Defeats 6 in 1910 and 1960.
Record League Appearances Alan Oakes, 564 between 1959-76.
Record League Goalscorer—Career Tommy Johnson, 158 between 1919-30.
Record League Goalscorer—Season Tommy Johnson, 38 in Div. 1, 1928-29.

Manchester City: League Record, 1987-88 (Division 2)

Match Number	Date	Venue	Opponents	Result		H/T	Lge Posn	Attend
1	15.8.87	H	Plymouth Arg.	W	2-1	0-1		20046
2	22.8.87	A	Oldham Ath.	D	1-1	1-1		15984
3	31.8.87	A	Aston Villa	D	1-1	0-1	7	16282
4	5.9.87	H	Blackburn Rov.	L	1-2	1-1	15	20372
5	12.9.87	A	Shrewsbury T.	D	0-0	0-0	17	6280
6	16.9.87	H	Millwall	W	4-0	2-0	14	15430
7	19.9.87	H	Stoke C.	W	3-0	2-0	9	19322
8	26.9.87	A	Leeds U.	L	0-2	0-1	12	25358
9	29.9.87	A	Hull C.	L	1-3	0-2	14	9650
10	3.10.87	H	Leicester C.	W	4-2	1-1	11	16481
11	10.10.87	H	Sheffield U.	L	2-3	2-1	11	18377
12	17.10.87	H	Ipswich T.	L	0-3	0-2	14	12711
13	21.10.87	A	Bradford C.	W	4-2	1-0	11	14818
14	24.10.87	H	Barnsley	D	1-1	1-1	11	17063
15	31.10.87	A	Swindon T.	W	4-3	2-1	10	11536
16	4.11.87	H	Middlesbrough	D	1-1	0-1	10	18434
17	7.11.87	H	Huddersfield T.	W	10-1	4-0	9	19583
18	14.11.87	A	Reading	W	2-0	0-0	9	10052
19	21.11.87	H	Birmingham C.	W	3-0	3-0	8	22690
20	28.11.87	A	West Bromwich A.	D	1-1	0-1	8	15425
21	1.12.87	A	Bournemouth	W	2-0	1-0	5	9499
22	5.12.87	H	Crystal Palace	L	1-3	0-0	8	23161
23	12.12.87	A	Millwall	W	1-0	1-0	4	10477
24	19.12.87	H	Oldham Ath.	L	1-2	0-1	8	22518
25	26.12.87	H	Leeds U.	L	1-2	1-1	9	30153
26	28.12.87	A	Stoke C.	W	3-1	2-0	7	18020
27	2.1.88	H	Shrewsbury T.	L	1-3	1-0	10	21455
28	16.1.88	A	Plymouth Arg.	L	2-3	2-0	10	13291
29	23.1.88	H	Aston Villa	L	0-2	0-1	10	24668
30	6.2.88	A	Blackburn Rov.	L	1-2	0-1	10	13508
31	13.2.88	H	Bournemouth	W	2-0	1-0	10	16161
32	27.2.88	A	Leicester C.	L	0-1	0-0	11	13852
33	2.3.88	H	Hull C.	W	2-0	0-0	10	16040
34	5.3.88	H	Ipswich T.	W	2-0	1-0	8	17402
35	8.3.88	A	Sheffield U.	W	2-1	0-1	8	13906
36	19.3.88	H	Swindon T.	D	1-1	0-0	8	17022
37	26.3.88	A	Barnsley	L	1-3	1-2	9	9061
38	2.4.88	H	Huddersfield T.	L	0-1	0-0	9	7835
39	4.4.88	H	Reading	W	2-0	0-0	8	15172
40	9.4.88	A	Middlesbrough	L	1-2	0-1	8	19443
41	23.4.88	H	Bradford C.	D	2-2	2-1	10	20335
42	30.4.88	A	Birmingham C.	W	3-0	1-0	8	8014
43	2.5.88	H	West Bromwich A.	W	4-2	2-1	8	16490
44	7.5.88	A	Crystal Palace	L	0-2	0-0	9	17555

Players: League Record, 1987-88 (Division 2)

Match Number	1	2	3	4	5	6	7	8	9	10	11	12	13	14	15	16	17	18	19	20	21	22	23	24	25	26	27	28	29	30	31	32	33	34	35	36	37	38	39	40	41	42	43	44	Apps	Subs	Goals
Adcock	★		9	9				★									★	9³	9	9		9¹	9	9	9	9¹	9			8		9													12	3	5
Beckford																																								9	7	7	7	7	5	0	0
Brightwell	5	5	5	5	5					11	11	11¹	5	5	5	5	5		3		★			2	2¹	2	5	5	2			3	4	4	2	2	5	5	5¹	5²	5	5			32	1	5
Clements	4	4	4	4									★	4	4	4	4	4	4	4	4	4	4		4	4	4	4	4			2	2	2											24	1	0
Gidman	2	2	2	2	2	2¹	2	2	2	2		2	2	2	2	2	2	2	2	2	2	2			2	2		2	2						2	2	2	★				3	3	3	30	1	1
Hinchcliffe	3	3	3	3	3	3	3	3	3	3	3	3	3	3	3	3	3¹	3		3	3	3	3	3	3	3	3	3	3	3	3		3	3	3	3	3	3	3	3	3	3	3	3	42	0	1
Lake					4	4	4	4	★	5	5	9	7		★	★	5	5	5	5	5	5¹	5	5	5	5	5¹	11	10	5	5		5	5	4	4	10			2					30	3	2
Lennon																																					2								1	0	0
McNab	11	11	11	11	11	11	11	11	★	7	7	7	10	10	10	10	10¹	10	10	10	10	10	10				10	10	10¹		4	4	5	4		10	10		10		10	10	10	10	36	1	2
Mimms												1	1	1																															3	0	0
Morley																												9	10		★	★	8¹	8¹	5	5	11	9	10	9¹	9	9¹	9		13	2	4
Moulden																																★		★	★	8	★	11					1	2	4	0
Nixon	1	1	1	1	1	1	1			1	1	1	1	1	1	1	1	1	1	1	1	1			1	1	1	1																	25	0	0
Redmond	6	6	6	6	6	6	6	6	6	6	6	6	6	6	6	6	6	6	6	6	6	6	6	6	6	6	6	6	6	6	6	6	6	6	6	6	6	6	6	6	6	6	6	6	44	0	3
Scott	10	10	10¹	10¹	10	10¹	10	10	10	10	10		7								10	10	★	★		10	10	10	10	10						★	4	4	4	4	4	4	★		19	4	3
Seagraves	★		★	★	5	5	5	5		★	10	11	11	11¹	11	11	11	11	11	11	11	11	11	11	11	★	11	11	11	11	11	11	11	★	11	11	★	11	11					★	31	7	1
Simpson																4					4		★	★					★	4	4	4	4	★	4										13	4	0
Stewart	8¹	8	8	8	8	8¹	8	8	8	8¹	8²	8	8	8³	8	8	8³	8²	8¹	8	8¹	8	8	8	8²		8¹	8	8	8¹	8	8				8¹	8	8	8²		8	8	8²	8	40	0	25
Stowell																															1	1	1	1	1	1	1	1	1	1	1	1	1	1	14	0	0
Suckling																	1	1																											0	1	1
Thompstone																															★¹													0	1	1
Varadi	9¹	9¹			9	9	9³	9	9	9²	★		9	9¹	9¹	9			★	★			★	9	9	9	★	★		9¹	9¹	9	9²	9¹	9	9	9¹	9			11¹	11¹			26	6	17
White	7	7	7	7	7	7¹	7	7	7	★		9¹	2	★¹	★	7²	7	7³	7	7²	7	7¹	7	7	7	7¹	7	7	7	7	7	7	7	7	7¹	7	7	7	7	7	11	★	2	2	40	4	13

FA Cup: 1987-88: 3rd Round: Huddersfield T. (A) 2-2 Replay (H) 0-0 2nd Replay (A) 3-0; 4th Round: Blackpool (A) 1-1 Replay (H) 2-1; 5th Round: Plymouth Arg. (H) 3-1; 6th Round: Liverpool (H) 0-4.

Littlewoods Cup: 1987-88: 2nd Round: Wolverhampton W. (H) 1-2 (A) 2-0; 3rd Round: Nottingham F. (H) 3-0; 4th Round: Watford (H) 3-1; Quarter Final: Everton (A) 0-2.

MANCHESTER UNITED (Division 1)

Team Manager Alex Ferguson.
Club Address Old Trafford, Manchester M16 0RA. Tel: 061-872 1661/2.
Current Ground Capacity 56,385.
Record Attendance 76,962 Wolverhampton W. v Grimsby T., FA Cup Semi-final, 25 March 1939.
Year Formed 1878. Turned professional 1885.
Previous Names Newton Heath.
Club Nickname "The Red Devils".
Club Colours Red shirts with red, white and black trim, white shorts and black stockings with red tops with three white bands on top.
Club Honours Football League: Div. 1 Champions 1907-08, 1910-11, 1951-52, 1955-56, 1956-57, 1964-65, 1966-67; Div. 2 Champions 1935-36, 1974-75. FA Cup: Winners 1909, 1948, 1963, 1977, 1983, 1985. European Cup: Winners 1967-68.
League History 1892-94 Div. 1; 1894-1906 Div. 2; 1906-22 Div. 1; 1922-25 Div. 2; 1925-31 Div. 1; 1931-36 Div. 2; 1936-37 Div. 1; 1937-38 Div. 2; 1938-74 Div. 1; 1974-75 Div. 2; 1975- Div. 1.

Most League Points in a Season (2 for a win) 64 in Div. 1, 1956-57. (3 for a win) 81 in Div. 1, 1987-88.
Most League Goals in a Season 103 in Div. 1, 1956-57 and 1958-59.
Record Victory 10-0 v Anderlecht in European Cup preliminary round, 26 September 1956.
Record Defeat 0-7 v Blackburn Rov. in Div. 1, 10 April 1926 and v Aston Villa in Div. 1, 27 December 1930 and v Wolverhampton W. Div. 2, 26 December 1931.
Consecutive League Wins 14 in 1904-05.
Consecutive League Defeats 14 in 1930.
Record League Appearances Bobby Charlton, 606 between 1956-73.
Record League Goalscorer—Career Bobby Charlton, 199 between 1956-73.
Record League Goalscorer—Season Dennis Viollet, 32 in 1959-60.

Manchester United: League Record 1988-88 (Division 1)

Match Number	Date	Venue	Opponents	Result		H/T	Lge Posn	Attend
1	15.8.87	A	Southampton	D	2-2	2-1		21214
2	19.8.87	H	Arsenal	D	0-0	0-0		42898
3	22.8.87	H	Watford	W	2-0	0-0	7	38582
4	29.8.87	A	Charlton Ath.	W	3-1	3-0	5	14046
5	31.8.87	H	Chelsea	W	3-1	1-1	1	46478
6	5.9.87	A	Coventry C.	D	0-0	0-0	2	27125
7	12.9.87	H	Newcastle U.	D	2-2	2-2	3	45137
8	19.9.87	A	Everton	L	1-2	0-1	6	38439
9	26.9.87	H	Tottenham H.	W	1-0	1-0	6	47601
10	3.10.87	A	Luton T.	D	1-1	0-1	7	9137
11	10.10.87	A	Sheffield Wed.	W	4-2	1-1	4	32779
12	17.10.87	H	Norwich C.	W	2-1	1-0	4	39345
13	25.10.87	A	West Ham U.	D	1-1	1-0	5	19863
14	31.10.87	H	Nottingham F.	D	2-2	0-1	5	44699
15	15.11.87	H	Liverpool	D	1-1	0-1	5	47106
16	21.11.87	A	Wimbledon	L	1-2	0-0	6	11532
17	5.12.87	A	Q.P.R.	W	2-0	1-0	6	20632
18	12.12.87	H	Oxford U.	W	3-1	2-0	4	34709
19	19.12.87	A	Portsmouth	W	2-1	1-0	4	22207
20	26.12.87	A	Newcastle U.	L	0-1	0-1	5	26461
21	28.12.87	H	Everton	W	2-1	0-0	4	47024
22	1.1.88	H	Charlton Ath.	D	0-0	0-0	4	37257
23	2.1.88	A	Watford	W	1-0	1-0	4	18038
24	16.1.88	H	Southampton	L	0-2	0-1	5	35716
25	24.1.88	A	Arsenal	W	2-1	1-1	3	29392
26	6.2.88	H	Coventry C.	W	1-0	1-0	3	37144
27	10.2.88	A	Derby Co.	W	2-1	0-0	2	20016
28	13.2.88	A	Chelsea	W	2-1	0-0	2	25014
29	23.2.88	A	Tottenham H.	D	1-1	0-1	2	25731
30	5.3.88	A	Norwich C.	L	0-1	0-0	2	19129
31	12.3.88	H	Sheffield Wed.	W	4-1	2-0	2	33318
32	19.3.88	A	Nottingham F.	D	0-0	0-0	2	27598
33	26.3.88	H	West Ham U.	W	3-1	0-0	2	37269
34	2.4.88	H	Derby Co.	W	4-1	2-0	2	40146
35	4.4.88	A	Liverpool	D	3-3	1-2	2	43497
36	12.4.88	H	Luton T.	W	3-0	1-0	2	28830
37	30.4.88	H	Q.P.R.	W	2-1	1-0	2	35733
38	2.5.88	A	Oxford U.	W	2-0	2-0	2	8966
39	7.5.88	H	Portsmouth	W	4-1	3-0	2	35105
40	9.5.88	H	Wimbledon	W	2-1	0-1	2	28040

Players: League Record, 1987-88 (Division 1)

Match Number	1	2	3	4	5	6	7	8	9	10	11	12	13	14	15	16	17	18	19	20	21	22	23	24	25	26	27	28	29	30	31	32	33	34	35	36	37	38	39	40	Apps	Subs	Goals
Albiston	★		★		3	3									★	3	★					3			★	★	3														5	6	0
Anderson	2	2	2	2	2	2	2	2	2			2	2	2		★	2	2	2	2	2	2	2	2		2	2¹	2	2	2	2¹	2									30	1	2
Blackmore							★	2	★¹	8	★		5	5¹				★		5			★	8	2	2¹	3	3	3	3	3	3	★	★	3						15	7	3
Bruce												4	4	4	4	4	4	4	4	4	4	4	4¹	4	4	4	4			4	4	4¹	4	4	4						21	0	2
Davenport	★		★	★		★	★	★		★	6¹	10	8	★		10¹	6	★	11	★	10	★	10		★	8	7	10	10¹	10	10	10	10¹	10	10	10¹	10				21	13	5
Duxbury	3	3	3	3	7	7	3	6	6	6	4	4	4	4	3	2	2	2	2	6	5	6	8	3	3	3		3	3	5	5	6	6	6	6	6	6	2			39	0	0
Garton								★	4	4	2	2		5																											5	1	0
Gibson			★	★	★			3	3	3	3	3¹	3	3		3	3	3	3	3	11	3			11	11	11	3	11	11	11¹	11	11		3	3	11				26	3	0
Graham															8																										1	0	0
Hogg							6													6	6	6	6	6		6	6		4					★							9	1	0
McClair	9	9	9¹	9¹	9	9	9¹	9	9¹	9¹	9²	9	9	9	9	9	9	9¹	9	9²	9	9¹	9	9¹	9	9	9	9¹	9	9²	9	9	9³	9	9¹	9	9	9²	9²		40	0	24
McGrath	5	5	5¹	5¹	5	5	5	5	5	5	5	5	5													★	5	5	5	5	5	5	5	★	5						21	1	2
Martin																																			★					0	1	0
Moran	6	6	6	6	6	6		6	★	6	6	6	6	5	5	5	5		5	5						6								6						20	1	0
Moses	4	4	4	4	4	4	4					4	4	4	6	6★	★	6			6														6						16	1	0
O'Brien								★		★				★	6			★	★	★	5¹	5	5¹	5	5	★	★		★												6	11	2
Olsen	11	11	11	11	11	11	11¹	11	11	11	11	11	11	11	11	11¹	11	★	11	11			11	11	11	11		★	11	8	★	★	★	★	11	11	11				30	7	2
Robson	7	7	7	7¹			7	7	7	7	7	7¹	7¹	7	7	7¹	7	7¹	7	7	7	7	7	7	7		7	7		7¹	7	7¹	7¹	7	7	7¹	7				36	0	10
Strachan	8	8	8	8	8¹	8	8	8	8	8	8		8	★	8		8	8²	8	8	8	8	★	8¹	8	8¹		★	8	8		8¹	8	8¹	8	8	8¹	8	8		33	3	8
Turner																1	1	1	1	1	1	1	1	1	1	1	1	1	1	1	1	1	1	1	1	1	1				24	0	0
Walsh	1	1	1	1	1	1	1	1	1	1	1	1	1	1	1																										16	0	0
Whiteside	10²	10	10	10	10¹	10	10	10¹	10	10	10		10¹	10¹	10		10	10	10	10		10		10	10	10¹	10	10			7		★								26	1	7
Own Goals																										1		1															2

FA Cup: 1987-88: 3rd Round: Ipswich T. (A) 2-1; 4th Round: Chelsea (H) 2-0; 5th Round: Arsenal (A) 1-2.

Littlewoods Cup: 1987-88: 2nd Round: Hull C. (H) 5-0 (A) 1-0; 3rd Round: Crystal Palace (H) 2-1; 4th Round: Bury (A) 2-1; Quarter Final: Oxford U. (A) 0-2.

MANSFIELD TOWN (Division 3)

Team Manager Ian Greaves.
Club Address Field Mill Ground, Quarry Lane, Mansfield. Tel: (0623) 23567.
Current Ground Capacity 24,000.
Record Attendance 24,467 v Nottingham F., FA Cup 3rd Round, 10 January 1963.
Year Formed 1905. Turned professional 1905.
Previous Names None.
Club Nickname "The Stags".
Club Colours Amber shirts, blue shorts and stockings.
Club Honours Football League: Div. 3 Champions 1976-77; Div. 4 Champions 1974-75.
League History 1931-32 Div. 3(S); 1932-37 Div. 3(N); 1937-47 Div. 3(S); 1947-58 Div. 3(N); 1958-60 Div. 3; 1960-63 Div. 4; 1963-72 Div. 3; 1972-75 Div. 4; 1975-77 Div. 3; 1977-78 Div. 2; 1978-80 Div. 3; 1980-86 Div. 4; 1986- Div. 3.
Most League Points in a Season (2 for a win) 68 in Div. 4, 1974-75. (3 for a win) 81 in Div. 4, 1985-86.
Most League Goals in a Season 108 in Div. 4, 1962-63.

Record Victory 9-2 v Rotherham U. in Div. 3(N), 27 December 1932 and v Hounslow T. in FA Cup 1st Round Replay, 5 November 1962.
Record Defeat 1-8 v Walsall in Div. 3(N), 19 January 1933.
Consecutive League Wins 7 in 1962.
Consecutive League Defeats 7 in 1947.
Record League Appearances Sandy Pate, 413 between 1967-78.
Record League Goalscorer—Career Harry Johnson, 104 between 1931-36.
Record League Goalscorer—Season Ted Harston, 55 in Div. 3(N), 1936-37.

Mansfield: League Record, 1987-88 (Division 3)

Match Number	Date	Venue	Opponents	Result		H/T	Lge Posn	Attend
1	15.8.87	H	Bristol C.	W	2-0	2-0		5441
2	29.8.87	H	Chesterfield	L	0-1	0-0		5224
3	31.8.87	A	Sunderland	L	1-4	1-0	18	13994
4	4.9.87	H	Fulham	L	0-2	0-0	19	3536
5	12.9.87	A	Grimsby T.	W	3-2	1-1	18	3410
6	15.9.87	H	Wigan Ath.	L	0-1	0-0	18	3261
7	19.9.87	A	Southend U.	W	1-0	1-0	17	2854
8	26.9.87	A	Rotherham U.	L	1-2	1-1	20	3839
9	29.9.87	H	Doncaster Rov.	W	2-0	2-0	16	3159
10	3.10.87	A	Bristol Rov.	L	1-2	0-1	18	2980
11	11.10.87	H	Notts Co.	D	1-1	0-0	18	8564
12	17.10.87	H	Gillingham	D	2-2	1-2	18	2957
13	20.10.87	H	Northampton T.	W	3-1	2-1	15	3645
14	24.10.87	A	Chester C.	W	2-0	0-0	13	2453
15	31.10.87	H	Blackpool	D	0-0	0-0	14	3221
16	3.11.87	A	Bury	L	0-1	0-1	15	2248
17	7.11.87	H	Preston N.E.	D	0-0	0-0	16	3631
18	21.11.87	H	Brighton & H.A.	D	1-1	1-0	15	3284
19	28.11.87	A	Walsall	L	1-2	0-1	16	4227
20	12.12.87	A	Brentford	D	2-2	2-1	18	3729
21	20.12.87	H	Port Vale	W	4-0	2-0	15	3173
22	26.12.87	H	Rotherham U.	L	0-1	0-1	16	4763
23	28.12.87	A	York C.	D	2-2	2-1	17	2781
24	1.1.88	A	Chesterfield	L	1-3	0-1	18	5070
25	2.1.88	H	Grimsby T.	W	1-0	1-0	17	3315
26	15.1.88	A	Southend U.	L	1-2	1-1	17	3091
27	6.2.88	A	Fulham	D	0-0	0-0	18	3330
28	13.2.88	H	York C.	W	2-1	0-1	17	2749
29	20.2.88	H	Bristol C.	W	2-1	2-1	16	8528
30	27.2.88	H	Bristol Rov.	W	1-0	0-0	14	3191
31	1.3.88	A	Doncaster Rov.	W	2-0	0-0	10	1987
32	5.3.88	A	Gillingham	D	0-0	0-0	11	3720
33	12.3.88	H	Notts Co.	D	1-1	1-1	13	7997
34	19.3.88	A	Blackpool	L	0-2	0-1	14	2847
35	22.3.88	H	Aldershot	W	1-0	0-0	13	2344
36	26.3.88	H	Chester C.	L	1-2	1-1	14	2918
37	28.3.88	A	Wigan Ath.	L	1-2	1-1	14	3217
38	2.4.88	A	Preston N.E.	L	0-1	0-0	16	6254
39	5.4.88	H	Walsall	L	1-3	1-2	17	4900
40	10.4.88	A	Northampton T.	L	0-2	0-0	17	6917
41	19.4.88	A	Aldershot	L	0-3	0-2	18	2339
42	23.4.88	H	Bury	D	0-0	0-0	19	2381
43	26.4.88	H	Sunderland	L	0-4	0-2	19	6930
44	30.4.88	A	Brighton & H.A.	L	1-3	1-2	19	11493
45	2.5.88	H	Brentford	W	2-1	0-1	17	2663
46	7.5.88	A	Port Vale	D	1-1	0-0	19	3617

Players: League Record, 1987-88 (Division 3)

Match Number	1	2	3	4	5	6	7	8	9	10	11	12	13	14	15	16	17	18	19	20	21	22	23	24	25	26	27	28	29	30	31	32	33	34	35	36	37	38	39	40	41	42	43	44	45	46	Apps	Subs	Goals
Anderson			★		★												★		★	★	5	★																	★			★	★	7	8		3	9	0
Beasley																					1	1													1	1	1	1	1	1							8	0	0
Cassells	10¹	10	10	10	10¹	10	10	10			10	10	10¹	10	10¹	10	10	10	10	10	10¹	10	10	10	10¹	10	10¹	10	10	10	10¹	10¹	10	10	10	10	10	10	10						10	10	40	0	9
Chambers	★					★	★	★		★				★		8	★																														1	7	0
Charles	11	11	11	11	11¹	11	11	11	11¹	11	11	11¹	11¹	11	11	11	11	11	11	11	11	11	11	11	11	11	11	11¹	11	11	11	11	11	11	11	11¹	11¹	11	11	11	11	11	11	11¹	11	11	46	0	12
Coleman	6	6	6			3	3	3	3	6	6	6	6¹	6	6	6	6	6	6	6	6	6	6	6	6	6	6	6	6	6¹	6	6	6	6	6	6	6	6	6	6	6	6	6	6	6	6	44	0	2
Eves									9	9	9																																				3	0	0
Foster	5	5	5	5		5	5	5	5	5	5	5	5	5	5	5	5	5	5	5			5	5	5	5	5	5	5	5	5	5	5	5	5	5	5	5	5	5	5	5	5	5	5	5	44	0	0
Garner			★	3																★	★	3	3	3	3	3	3	★		3	3	3	★	★	3	3	3		3								14	5	0
Graham	2	2	2	2		2	2	2	2	2	2	2	2	2	2	2	2	2	2	2	2	2	2	2	2	2	2	2¹	2	2	2	2	2	2	2	2	2	2	2	2	2	2	2	2	2	2	46	0	1
Hitchcock	1	1	1	1	1	1	1	1	1	1	1	1	1	1	1	1	1	1	1	1				1	1	1	1	1	1	1	1	1	1	1	1	1	1										33	0	0
Hodges	8	8	8	8	8¹	8	8	8	8	8	8	8	8¹	★					9	9	9		9															7	7	7	7						21	1	2
Kearney	3	3	3	3																																											4	0	0
Kent	7	7	7	7	7	7	7	7¹	10	7	7	7		7	7	7	7	7¹	7	7 ·	7⁴	7	7¹	7	7	7	7	8	7	9¹	9	9	9	9	9	9	9¹	9	4	9	9	10	10	10	9¹	9	45	0	10
Kenworthy		★	6	6	6	6	6	6									8	8	8	8	8	8				8	8	8	8	8	8	8	8	8	8	8	8	8	8	8	8						29	1	0
Lowery	4	4	4	4			4	4	4	4	4	4	4	4	4	4	4	4		4	4	4	4	4	4	4	4	**4**	4	4	4	4		4	4	4	4	4	4	4	4	4	4	4	4		44	0	0
McKernon	★				★	7	★	9	9	7	8	8		8								★		8					4			★															9	5	0
Marks																									8																						0	1	0
Owen																									8	7¹	7	7	7	7	7	7¹	7	7	7	7	7	7	★					★	7¹		15	2	3
Ryan				3	3	3	3	3	3	3	3	3	3	3	3	3	3	5	8	8¹	9	9	9	3	3				3	3	★		★	★	3	3		3	3	3	3	3					30	2	1
Steele																																							1	1	1	1	1				5	0	0
Stringfellow	9¹	9	9¹	9	9	9	9¹	9	9²	9		★¹	9	9			9	9	9¹			9					★			★	★	★		★		9	10	10	9	9	9¹						22	8	8
Whatmore																	★		★		★																★										0	4	0
Williams			★		★								★																													★					0	4	0

FA Cup: 1987-88: 1st Round: Preston N.E. (A) 1-1 Replay (H) 4-2; 2nd Round: Lincoln C. (H) 4-3; 3rd Round: Bath C. (H) 4-0; 4th Round: Wimbledon (H) 1-2.
Littlewoods Cup: 1987-88: 1st Round: Birmingham C. (H) 2-2 (A) 1-0; 2nd Round: Oxford U. (A) 1-1 (H) 0-2.

MIDDLESBROUGH (Division 2)

Team Manager Bruce Rioch.
Club Address Ayresome Park, Middlesbrough, Cleveland TS1 4PB. Tel: (0642) 819659/815996.
Current Ground Capacity 42,000.
Record Attendance 53,596 v Newcastle U., Div. 1, 27 December 1949.
Year Formed 1876. Turned professional 1889.
Previous Names None.
Club Nickname "The Boro".
Club Colours Red shirts with white shoulders and sleeves, white shorts and red stockings with white and blue hooped turnovers.
Club Honours Football League: Div. 2 Champions 1926-27, 1928-29 and 1973-74.
League History 1899-1902 Div. 2; 1902-24 Div. 1; 1924-27 Div. 2; 1927-28 Div. 1; 1928-29 Div. 2; 1929-54 Div. 1; 1954-66 Div. 2; 1966-67 Div. 3; 1967-74 Div. 2; 1974-82 Div. 1; 1982-86 Div. 2; 1986-87 Div. 3; 1987-88 Div. 2; 1988- Div. 1.
Most League Points in a Season (2 for a win) 65 in Div. 2, 1973-74. (3 for a win) 94 in Div. 3, 1986-87.

Most League Goals in a Season 122 in Div. 2, 1926-27.
Record Victory 9-0 v Brighton & H.A. in Div. 2, 23 August 1958.
Record Defeat 0-9 v Blackburn Rov. in Div. 2, 6 November 1954.
Consecutive League Wins 9 in 1974.
Consecutive League Defeats 8 in 1954.
Record League Appearances Tim Williamson, 563 between 1902-23.
Record League Goalscorer—Career George Camsell, 326 between 1925-39.
Record League Goalscorer—Season George Camsell, 59 in Div. 2, 1926-27 (Div. 2 record).

Middlesbrough: League Record, 1987-88 (Division 2)

Match Number	Date	Venue	Opponents	Result		H/T	Lge Posn	Attend
1	15.8.87	H	Millwall	D	1-1	0-1		11535
2	22.8.87	A	Stoke C.	L	0-1	0-0		9345
3	29.8.87	H	Oldham Ath.	W	1-0	0-0	13	10551
4	1.9.87	A	Crystal Palace	L	1-3	0-1	18	6866
5	5.9.87	H	Swindon T.	L	2-3	1-2	20	9324
6	8.9.87	A	Aston Villa	W	1-0	0-0	14	12665
7	15.9.87	H	Bournemouth	W	3-0	0-0	11	9660
8	19.9.87	H	Leeds U.	W	2-0	1-0	6	12051
9	26.9.87	A	Blackburn Rov.	W	2-0	0-0	4	6879
10	29.9.87	H	Reading	D	0-0	0-0	4	10903
11	3.10.87	A	Bradford C.	L	0-2	0-0	8	14222
12	10.10.87	A	Huddersfield T.	W	4-1	2-0	5	6169
13	17.10.87	H	West Bromwich A.	W	2-1	0-0	3	10684
14	20.10.87	A	Ipswich T.	W	3-1	0-1	3	10491
15	27.10.87	A	Birmingham C.	D	0-0	0-0	3	7404
16	31.10.87	H	Shrewsbury T.	W	4-0	1-0	2	10183
17	4.11.87	A	Manchester C.	D	1-1	1-0	2	18434
18	7.11.87	H	Sheffield U.	W	2-0	0-0	2	11278
19	14.11.87	H	Hull C.	W	1-0	1-0	2	15709
20	21.11.87	A	Plymouth Arg.	W	1-0	1-0	2	9428
21	28.11.87	H	Barnsley	W	2-0	0-0	1	12732
22	5.12.87	A	Leicester C.	D	0-0	0-0	1	9411
23	12.12.87	H	Stoke C.	W	2-0	0-0	1	12289
24	19.12.87	A	Bournemouth	D	0-0	0-0	1	6392
25	26.12.87	H	Blackburn Rov.	D	1-1	1-1	1	23536
26	28.12.87	A	Leeds U.	L	0-2	0-1	1	33606
27	1.1.88	A	Oldham Ath.	L	1-3	0-2	3	8181
28	16.1.88	A	Millwall	L	1-2	0-0	5	8517
29	23.1.88	H	Crystal Palace	W	2-1	1-0	3	12597
30	6.2.88	A	Swindon T.	D	1-1	1-1	4	9941
31	14.2.88	H	Aston Villa	W	2-1	0-1	3	16957
32	20.2.88	A	Reading	D	0-0	0-0	3	6446
33	27.2.88	H	Bradford C.	L	1-2	0-1	4	21079
34	5.3.88	A	West Bromwich A.	D	0-0	0-0	5	8316
35	12.3.88	H	Huddersfield T.	W	2-0	1-0	3	13866
36	19.3.88	A	Shrewsbury T.	W	1-0	0-0	3	5603
37	26.3.88	H	Birmingham C.	D	1-1	0-0	3	15465
38	2.4.88	H	Sheffield U.	W	6-0	3-0	2	17340
39	4.4.88	A	Hull C.	D	0-0	0-0	2	10758
40	9.4.88	H	Manchester C.	W	2-1	1-0	2	19443
41	23.4.88	A	Ipswich T.	L	0-4	0-3	4	12773
42	30.4.88	H	Plymouth Arg.	W	3-1	1-0	3	16615
43	2.5.88	A	Barnsley	W	3-0	2-0	2	13240
44	7.5.88	H	Leicester C.	L	1-2	0-1	3	27645

Players: League Record, 1987-88 (Division 2)

Match Number	1	2	3	4	5	6	7	8	9	10	11	12	13	14	15	16	17	18	19	20	21	22	23	24	25	26	27	28	29	30	31	32	33	34	35	36	37	38	39	40	41	42	43	44	Apps	Subs	Goals
Burke																							★	★		2	★				★	★	★	★	9			11	11	11	11	11	★	11	8	8	0
Cooper	3	3	3	3	3	3	3	3	3	3	3	3	3^1	3	3	3	3	3	3	3	3	3	3	3	3	3	3	3	3	3^1	3	3	3	3	3	3	3	3	3	3	3	3	3	3	43	0	2
Gill				2	2																			★																					2	1	0
Glover	2	2	2				2	2	2	2	2	2	2	2	2	2	2^1	2	2	2	2	2	2	2		2	2^1	2	2	2	2	2	2^1	2^1	2	2	2		2	★		★			36	2	4
Hamilton	9	9	9	9	9	9	9	9^2	9	9	9	9	9	9	9	9	9	9	9	9	9^1	9	9	9	9	9	9	9	9	9	10		9	2^1	★		5^1	5	5						40	1	6
Kernaghan		★	★		★		★	★	8^1	8	8	8	8	8^1	8	8^1	8	8	8	8	8^1	8	8	8	8	8	8	★	★^{1}	★	★	11		★		★			9^1	9	9				24	11	6
Kerr	10	10	10	10	10	10	10^1	10	10^1	10^1	10	10	10	10	10	10	10	10	10	10	10	10	10	10	10	10^1	10	10	**10**	**10**	**10**	10	10^1	**10**	★	10	10	10	10	10	10	10	10	10	43	1	5
Laws											11^1	11	11	★	★						★		5	5	5	5	**2**	11	11	11	11	11	★	11	11	11	11	5	5	5	5		11	3	24	4	1
Mowbray	4	4	4	4	4	4	4	4	4	4	4	4	4	4	4	4	4	4	4	4	4	4	4	4	4	4	4	4	4^1	4^1	4^1	4	4	4	4	4	4	4	4	4	4	4	4	4	44	0	3
Pallister	6	6	6	6	6	6	6	6^1	6	6	6	6	6	6^1	6	6	6	6	6	6	6	6	6	6	6	6	6	6	6	6	6	6	6	6	6	6	6^1	6	6	6	6	6	6	6	44	0	3
Parkinson	5	5	5	5	5	5	5	5	5	5	5	5	5	5	5	5	5	5	5	5	5	5	★		★	★	5	5	5	5	5	5	5	5	5	5				2	2	2			35	3	0
Pears	1	1	1	1	1	1	1	1	1	1	1	1	1	1	1	1	1	1	1	1	1	1	1	1	1	1		1	1	1	1	1	1	1	1	1	1	1	1	1	1	1	1	1	43	0	0
Poole																											1																		1	0	0
Proudlock				★																																									0	1	0
Ripley	11	11	**11**	11	**11**	11	11	11	11	11	★	★	★	11	11	11	11^1	11^1	11	11	11	**11**	11		8	8	**8**	8	8	8	8	8	8	8	8^3	8	8^1	8	8^1	8^1	8				40	3	8
Senior																														9	9^2	9	9	9		★									5	1	2
Slaven	7	7	7^1	7^1	7^1	7	7^1	7	7	7	7	7^3	7^1	7^1	7	7^3	7	7^1	7	7	7	7^1	7	7^1	**7**	7	7^1	7	7	**7**	7	7	7	7	7^1	7	7	7	7	7	7^2	7^1			44	0	21
Stephens	8^1	8	8	8	8^1	8	**8**	8		★						★				8		★																							8	3	2

FA Cup: 3rd Round: Sutton U. (A) 1-1 Replay (H) 1-0; 4th Round: Everton (A) 1-1 Replay (H) 2-2 2nd Replay (A) 1-2.
Littlewoods Cup: 1987-88: 1st Round: Sunderland (A) 0-1 (H) 2-0; 2nd Round: Aston Villa (H) 0-1 (A) 0-1.

MILLWALL (Division 1)

Team Manager   John Docherty.
Club Address   The Den, Cold Blow Lane, London SE14 5RH. Tel: 01-639 3143/4.
Current Ground Capacity   18,900.
Record Attendance   48,672 v Derby Co., FA Cup 5th Round, 20 February 1937.
Year Formed   1885. Turned professional 1893.
Previous Names   Millwall Rovers, Millwall Athletic.
Club Nickname   "The Lions".
Club Colours   All royal blue.
Club Honours   Football League: Div. 2 Champions 1987-88; Div. 3(S) Champions 1927-28, 1937-38; Div. 4 Champions 1961-62.
League History   1920-28 Div. 3(S); 1928-34 Div. 2; 1934-38 Div. 3(S); 1938-48 Div. 2; 1948-58 Div. 3(S); 1958-62 Div. 4; 1962-64 Div. 3; 1964-65 Div. 4; 1965-66 Div. 3; 1966-75 Div. 2; 1975-76 Div. 3; 1976-79 Div. 2; 1979-85 Div. 3; 1985-88 Div. 2; 1988- Div. 1.
Most League Points in a Season   (2 for a win) 65 in Div. 3(S), 1927-28, and Div. 3, 1965-66. (3 for a win) 90 in Div. 3, 1984-85.

Most League Goals in a Season   127 in Div. 3(S), 1927-28.
Record Victory   9-1 v Torquay U. in Div. 3(S), 29 August 1927, and Coventry C. in Div. 3(S), 19 November 1927.
Record Defeat   1-9 v Aston Villa in FA Cup 4th Round, 28 January 1946.
Consecutive League Wins   10 in 1928.
Consecutive League Defeats   11 in 1929.
Record League Appearances   Barry Kitchener, 523 between 1967-82.
Record League Goalscorer—Career   Derek Possee, 79 between 1967-73.
Record League Goalscorer—Season   Richard Parker, 37 in Div. 3(S), 1926-27.

Millwall: League Record, 1987-88 (Division 2)

Match Number	Date	Venue	Opponents	Result		H/T	Lge Posn	Attend
1	15.8.87	A	Middlesbrough	D	1-1	1-0		11535
2	22.8.87	H	Barnsley	W	3-1	0-0		6017
3	29.8.87	A	Leicester C.	L	0-1	0-0	11	7553
4	1.9.87	H	Birmingham C.	W	3-1	1-1	4	6758
5	5.9.87	A	Bradford C.	L	1-3	0-1	12	8658
6	12.9.87	H	Ipswich T.	W	2-1	1-0	8	6356
7	16.9.87	A	Manchester C.	L	0-4	0-2	13	15430
8	19.9.87	A	Sheffield U.	W	2-1	1-0	8	8048
9	26.9.87	H	West Bromwich A.	W	2-0	1-0	6	6564
10	29.9.87	A	Oldham Ath.	D	0-0	0-0	6	4840
11	3.10.87	H	Swindon T.	D	2-2	1-0	6	7018
12	10.10.87	A	Crystal Palace	L	0-1	0-0	10	10678
13	17.10.87	H	Shrewsbury T.	W	4-1	2-1	8	5202
14	20.10.87	A	Plymouth Arg.	W	2-1	1-1	8	8958
15	31.10.87	A	Huddersfield T.	L	1-2	0-1	9	5504
16	3.11.87	H	Bournemouth	L	1-2	0-0	9	5734
17	7.11-87	A	Aston Villa	W	2-1	2-1	8	13255
18	14.11.87	H	Leeds U.	W	3-1	0-0	7	8014
19	21.11.87	A	Stoke C.	W	2-1	0-1	7	7998
20	28.11.87	H	Hull C.	W	2-0	0-0	7	6743
21	1.12.87	H	Reading	W	3-0	2-0	3	6762
22	5.12.87	A	Blackburn Rov.	L	1-2	0-1	6	6140
23	12.12.87	H	Manchester C.	L	0-1	0-1	7	10477
24	19.12.87	A	Barnsley	L	1-4	1-2	9	5011
25	26.12.87	A	West Bromwich A.	W	4-1	2-1	7	9291
26	28.12.87	H	Sheffield U.	W	3-1	3-0	5	7255
27	1.1.88	H	Leicester C.	W	1-0	1-0	4	7220
28	2.1.88	A	Ipswich T.	D	1-1	0-0	4	13710
29	16.1.88	H	Middlesbrough	W	2-1	0-0	3	8517
30	6.2.88	H	Bradford C.	L	0-1	0-0	5	8201
31	9.2.88	A	Birmingham C.	L	0-1	0-0	5	5819
32	13.2.88	A	Reading	W	3-2	1-2	4	6050
33	20.2.88	H	Oldham Ath.	D	1-1	0-0	5	6839
34	27.2.88	A	Swindon T.	W	1-0	1-0	3	9570
35	5.3.88	H	Shrewsbury T.	D	0-0	0-0	3	5408
36	12.3.88	H	Crystal Palace	D	1-1	0-0	5	12815
37	19.3.88	H	Huddersfield T.	W	4-1	2-1	4	6181
38	2.4.88	H	Aston Villa	W	2-1	1-1	4	13697
39	6.4.88	A	Leeds U.	W	2-1	1-0	2	24241
40	9.4.88	H	Plymouth Arg.	W	3-2	3-2	1	11052
41	19.4.88	A	Bournemouth	W	2-1	2-1	1	9204
42	30.4.88	H	Stoke C.	W	2-0	0-0	1	12636
43	2.5.88	A	Hull C.	W	1-0	1-0	1	10811
44	7.5.88	H	Blackburn Rov.	L	1-4	0-2	1	15467

Players: League Record, 1987-88 (Division 2)

Match Number	1	2	3	4	5	6	7	8	9	10	11	12	13	14	15	16	17	18	19	20	21	22	23	24	25	26	27	28	29	30	31	32	33	34	35	36	37	38	39	40	41	42	43	44	Apps	Subs	Goals
Anthrobus													11	11	11																														3	0	0
Briley	★	8	8	8	8	8	8	8	8	8	8	8	8	8	8	8	8¹	8	8	8	8	8	8	8¹	8¹	8¹	8	8	8	8	8	8	8	8	8	8	8	8	8	8	8	8	8	8	43	1	4
Byrne	11	11	11				7	★	7¹			★		★	★	7	7	7	7¹	7			10	★	7	7	7	7	7	★															17	6	2
Carter												11	11	11	11	11	11	11	11	11	11	11	11	11	11	11			7	7				7	7	★	7	7	7	7	7	7			25	1	0
Cascarino	10	10¹		10	10	10	10	10	10¹	10	10	10	10¹	10¹	10¹	10³	10²	10	10²	10¹			10	10	10¹	10	10	10	10¹	10	10¹	10	10¹	10	10	10	10	10	10	10	39	0	20
Coleman					3	3	3	3	3	3	3	3	3	3	3	3	3	3	3		3	3	3	3	3	3	3	3	3	3	3	3	3	3	3	3					3	3			36	0	0
Cooke																							7	7	7	10¹																			4	0	1
Horne	1	1	1	1	1	1	1	1	1	1	1	1	1	1	1	1	1	1	1	1	1	1		1	1	1	1	1	1	1	1	1	1	1	1	1	1	1	1	1	1	1	1	1	43	0	1
Horrix																																★¹													0	2	1
Hurlock	4	4	4	4	4¹	4	4	4	4	4	4	4	4			★	10												7¹	4	4			7	4¹	4	4¹	4	4	4					27	1	4
Lawrence	7	7¹	7	7¹	7		9	7	9	7	7	7¹	7	7	7	7			★¹	7								6	6	6	6	6	6	6	6	6	6	6	6	6	6	6	6		16	1	4
McLeary	6						6	6	6	6	6	6	6	6	6	6	6	6	6	6	6	6			6	6	6	6	6	6	6	6	6	6	6	6	6	6	6						31	0	0
Mehmet	8																																												1	0	0
Morgan																								6	6							★				3									3	1	0
O'Callaghan						6¹	11	11¹	11	11	11	11	11¹										10							11	11	11	11	11	11	11¹	11¹	11¹	11¹	11			22	1	7
Salman		10	11	11	11	6	2	2	2	2	2	2	2	2	2	2	2	2	2	2	2	2	2	2	2	2	2	2	2	2	2	2	2	2	2¹										36	0	1
Sansome																						1																						1	0	0
Sheringham	9¹	9¹	9	9	9	9	9		9¹	9	9	9¹	9¹	9	9	9	9	9	9¹	9	9	9	9¹	9³	9¹	9	9	9¹	9	9²	9	9	9¹	9²	9¹	9	9	9	9¹	9	9¹	43	0	22
Sparham	3	3	3	3	3	3																																					7	0	0
Stevens	2	2	2	2¹	2	2	2		★					4	4	4	4	4	4	4	4	4	4	4	4	4	4	4	4				7	4	4	4	2	2	2	2	2	2			34	1	1
Thompson																							5	5	5	5	5																		5	0	0
Walker	5	5	5	5¹	5	5¹	5		6	5	5	5	5	5	5¹	5	5	5	5	5	5	5							5¹	5	5														26	0	4
Wood		6	6	6	6				6	6	6											6	6						5	5	5	5	5	5	5	5	5	5	5	5					22	0	0
Own Goals													1																																		1

FA Cup: 1987-88: 3rd Round: Arsenal (A) 0-2.
Littlewoods Cup: 1987-88: 1st Round: Leyton Orient (A) 1-1 (H) 1-0; 2nd Round: Q.P.R (A) 1-2 (H) 0-0.

NEWCASTLE UNITED (Division 1)

Team Manager Willie McFaul.
Club Address St James' Park, Newcastle-upon-Tyne NE1 4ST. Tel: (091) 232 8361.
Current Ground Capacity 36,585.
Record Attendance 68,386 v Chelsea, Div. 1, 3rd September 1930.
Year Formed 1882. Turned professional 1889.
Previous Names Newcastle East End.
Club Nickname "The Magpies".
Club Colours Black and white striped shirts, black shorts and black stockings with two white hoops on the top.
Club Honours Football League: Div. 1 Champions 1904-05, 1906-07, 1908-09, 1926-27; Div. 2 Champions 1964-65. FA Cup: Winners 1910, 1924, 1932, 1951, 1952, 1955. European Fairs Cup: Winners 1968-69.
League History 1893-98 Div. 2; 1898-1934 Div. 1; 1934-48 Div. 2; 1948-61 Div. 1; 1961-65 Div. 2; 1965-78 Div. 1; 1978-84 Div. 2; 1984- Div. 1.
Most League Points in a Season (2 for a win) 57 in Div. 2, 1964-65. (3 for a win) 80 in Div. 2, 1983-84.

Most League Goals in a Season 98 in Div. 1, 1951-52.
Record Victory 13-0 v Newport Co. in Div. 2, 5 October 1946.
Record Defeat 0-9 v Burton Wanderers in Div. 2, 15 April 1895.
Consecutive League Wins 7 in 1904, 1909 and 1964-65.
Consecutive League Defeats 10 in 1977.
Record League Appearances Jim Lawrence, 432 between 1904-22.
Record League Goalscorer—Career Jackie Milburn, 177 between 1946-57.
Record League Goalscorer—Season Hughie Gallacher, 36 in Div. 1, 1926-27.

Newcastle United: League Record, 1987-88 (Division 1)

Match Number	Date	Venue	Opponents	Result		H/T	Lge Posn	Attend
1	19.8.87	A	Tottenham H.	L	1-3	0-3		26261
2	22.8.87	A	Sheffield Wed.	W	1-0	1-0		22031
3	29.8.87	H	Nottingham F.	L	0-1	0-1	17	20111
4	1.9.87	A	Norwich C.	D	1-1	0-0	15	16636
5	5.9.87	H	Wimbledon	L	1-2	0-2	18	22684
6	12.9.87	A	Manchester U.	D	2-2	2-2	19	45137
7	20.9.87	H	Liverpool	L	1-4	0-2	19	24141
8	26.9.87	H	Southampton	W	2-1	0-0	15	18093
9	3.10.87	A	Chelsea	D	2-2	1-2	15	22071
10	17.10.87	H	Everton	D	1-1	1-1	16	20266
11	24.10.87	H	Coventry C.	W	3-1	2-1	12	18585
12	31.10.87	H	Arsenal	L	0-1	0-0	15	23662
13	7.11.87	A	Luton T.	L	0-4	0-1	18	7638
14	14.11.87	H	Derby Co.	D	0-0	0-0	19	21698
15	21.11.87	A	Q.P.R.	D	1-1	0-1	16	11794
16	28.11.87	H	Charlton Ath.	W	2-1	1-1	16	19453
17	5.12.87	A	Oxford U.	W	3-1	1-0	15	8190
18	12.12.87	H	Portsmouth	D	1-1	0-1	14	20455
19	19.12.87	A	West Ham U.	L	1-2	0-0	15	18679
20	26.12.87	H	Manchester U.	W	1-0	1-0	12	26461

Match Number	Date	Venue	Opponents	Result		H/T	Lge Posn	Attend
21	28.12.87	A	Liverpool	L	0-4	0-1	14	44637
22	1.1.88	A	Nottingham F.	W	2-0	1-0	13	28583
23	2.1.88	H	Sheffield Wed.	D	2-2	0-0	12	25503
24	23.1.88	H	Tottenham H.	W	2-0	1-0	12	24616
25	6.2.88	A	Wimbledon	D	0-0	0-0	10	10505
26	13.2.88	H	Norwich C.	L	1-3	1-1	12	21068
27	27.2.88	H	Chelsea	W	3-1	2-0	11	17858
28	1.3.88	A	Southampton	D	1-1	0-0	11	13380
29	5.3.88	A	Everton	L	0-1	0-1	11	25674
30	19.3.88	A	Arsenal	D	1-1	0-1	13	25889
31	26.3.88	H	Coventry C.	D	2-2	0-0	12	19050
32	2.4.88	H	Luton T.	W	4-0	2-0	11	20565
33	4.4.88	A	Derby Co.	L	1-2	1-0	11	18591
34	9.4.88	A	Q.P.R.	D	1-1	1-1	11	18403
35	12.4.88	H	Watford	W	3-0	1-0	10	16318
36	19.4.88	A	Watford	D	1-1	0-1	9	12075
37	23.4.88	A	Charlton Ath.	L	0-2	0-2	10	7402
38	30.4.88	H	Oxford U.	W	3-1	1-0	10	16617
39	2.5.88	A	Portsmouth	W	2-1	1-0	8	12468
40	7.5.88	H	West Ham U.	W	2-1	0-1	8	23731

Players: League Record, 1987-88 (Division 1)

Match Number	1	2	3	4	5	6	7	8	9	10	11	12	13	14	15	16	17	18	19	20	21	22	23	24	25	26	27	28	29	30	31	32	33	34	35	36	37	38	39	40	Apps	Subs	Goals
Anderson			★	10	7	3	3	2	2		★	2	2	2	2	2	2	2	2	5	5	2	2	2	2	2			2	5	5	5	5	2	5	5¹	5	5	5	5	33	2	1
Bailey	3	3	3																																	★					3	1	0
Bogie													10			8	8		★	★							★									★					3	4	0
Cornwell							11	11	11	11	11		11		11¹	11	11	11	11	11	★		★	7	7		7			★			7	3	3	3					20	4	1
Craig													11				★		★																						1	2	0
Gascoigne	8	8	8	8	8			8	8	8	8¹	8	8	8	8			8	8	8	8¹	8	8²	8	8¹	8¹	8	8	8	8	8	8		★	8	8	8				34	1	6
Goddard	9	9	9		9	9	9	9¹	9¹	9	9¹	9	9			9	9	9	9	9²	9	9	9	9	9	9	9¹	9	9¹	9	9	9	9	9¹		9					35	0	8
Hodges	11	11	11	11	11	11	11																																		7	0	0
Jackson, D.	7	7¹	7	7		★	★	★	★	7	7¹	10	11	10			★		7	7		11	4	4	4	★		★	10	10			11	7	8	8	7	7	7		24	7	2
Jackson, P.	5	5	5	5¹	5	5	5	5	5	5	5	5	5	5	5¹	5	5	5			5	5	5	5	5	5	5			5											28	0	2
Kelly	1	1			1	1	1	1	1	1	1	1	1	1	1	1	1	1	1	1	1	1	1	1	1	1	1	1	1	1	1	1	1	1	1	1	1	1	1	1	37	0	0
Lormor																											★					★	11¹	11¹	11						3	2	2
McCreery	4¹	4	4	4	4	4	4	4	4	4	4			4	4	4	4	4	4	4			4	4	4	4	4	4	4	4	4	4	4	4	4	4	4	4	4	4	35	0	1
McDonald	2	2	2	2	2¹	2	2¹	7	7	2	2	7	7	7	7	7¹	7	7	2	2	7	7	7	7	7	2	2	7	2	2	2	2	7	2	2	2	2	2			40	0	3
Mirandinha				9	10	10²	10	10¹	10	10¹	10		10			10	10¹	10¹	10¹	10	10	10¹	10	10¹	10	10	10	10¹	10	10²	10		★	10							25	1	11
O'Neill											★	★		9	9¹						11	11	11	11	11¹	11	11	11²	10³	10¹	10¹	10¹	11	10	10¹	10	10¹				19	2	12
Roeder	6		6	6	6	6	6	6	6	6	6	6	6	6	6	6	6	6	6	6¹	6	6	6	6	6	6	6	6	6	6	6	6	6	6	6	6	6				37	0	1
Scott		6																															7			6¹	6				4	0	1
Stephenson					7	7																						★	7	7	7	★									5	2	0
Thomas, A.	★		★																													★	9								1	3	0
Thomas, M.			1	1	1																																				3	0	0
Tinnion					★			3	3	3	3	3	3	3			3						3	3	3	3	3	3	3				3¹		3						15	1	1
Wharton	10	10	10	3	3	8	8		★¹	★	★		4	4	3	3	3	3		3	3	3	3	3	3	3	3	3			11	11	3	11¹	3	11					28	3	2
Own Goals																																					1						1

FA Cup: 1987-88: 3rd Round: Crystal Palace (H) 1-0; 4th Round: Swindon T. (H) 5-0; 5th Round: Wimbledon (H) 1-3.
Littlewoods Cup: 1987-88: 2nd Round: Blackpool (A) 0-1 (H) 4-1; 3rd Round: Wimbledon (A) 1-2.

NEWPORT COUNTY (Vauxhall Conference)

Team Manager David Williams
Club Address Somerton Park, Newport, Gwent. Tel: (0633) 277543/277472.
Current Ground Capacity 8,000.
Record Attendance 24,268 v Cardiff C., Div. 3(S), 16 October 1937.
Year Formed 1912. Turned professional 1912.
Previous Names None.
Club Nickname "The Ironsides".
Club Colours Amber shirt, black shorts and amber stockings.
Club Honours Football League: Div. 3(S) Champions 1938-39.
League History 1920-31 Div. 3(S); 1931 Failed to be re-elected; 1932-39 Div. 3(S); 1946-47 Div. 2; 1947-58 Div. 3(S); 1958-62 Div. 3; 1962-80 Div. 4; 1980-87 Div. 3; 1987-88 Div. 4.
Most League Points in a Season (2 for a win) 61 in Div. 4, 1979-80. (3 for a win) 78 in Div 3, 1982-83.
Most League Goals in a Season 85 in Div. 4, 1964-65.

Record Victory 10-0 v Merthyr T. in Div. 3(S), 10 April 1930.
Record Defeat 0-13 v Newcastle U. in Div. 2, 5 October 1946.
Consecutive League Wins 10 in 1980.
Consecutive League Defeats 10 in 1970.
Record League Appearances Len Weare, 526 between 1955-70.
Record League Goalscorer—Career Reg Parker, 99 between 1948-54.
Record League Goalscorer—Season Tudor Martin, 34 in Div. 3(S), 1929-30.

Newport County: League Record, 1987-88 (Division 4)

Match Number	Date	Venue	Opponents	Result		H/T	Lge Posn	Attend
1	15.8.87	A	Hartlepool U.	D	0-0	0-0		1926
2	22.8.87	H	Burnley	L	0-1	0-0		2006
3	29.8.87	A	Exeter C.	L	0-3	0-0	24	2628
4	31.8.87	H	Stockport Co.	L	1-2	1-0	24	1626
5	4.9.87	A	Halifax T.	L	1-3	0-0	24	1095
6	12.9.87	H	Torquay U.	W	3-1	2-1	23	1368
7	16.9.87	A	Scarborough	L	1-3	1-1	24	2345
8	19.9.87	A	Scunthorpe U.	L	1-3	1-2	24	2004
9	27.9.87	H	Hereford U.	D	0-0	0-0	24	1480
10	29.9.87	A	Leyton Orient	L	1-4	1-3	24	3761
11	3.10.87	H	Colchester U.	L	1-2	0-1	24	1200
12	10.10.87	A	Cambridge U.	L	0-4	0-1	24	1874
13	17.10.87	A	Swansea C.	W	2-1	1-0	24	3739
14	21.10.87	H	Peterborough U.	L	0-3	0-2	24	3163
15	24.10.87	H	Wrexham	W	2-0	1-0	22	1470
16	31.10.87	A	Wolverhampton W.	L	1-2	0-0	22	6467
17	3.11.87	H	Bolton W.	L	0-1	0-1	24	1566
18	7.11.87	A	Carlisle U.	L	1-3	0-2	24	1766
19	21.11.87	H	Cardiff C.	L	1-2	0-0	24	4022
20	27.11.87	A	Tranmere Rov.	L	0-4	0-3	24	3252
21	19.12.87	A	Rochdale	L	0-3	0-2	24	1491
22	26.12.87	A	Hereford U.	L	2-4	1-1	24	3203
23	28.12.87	H	Crewe Alex.	L	1-2	0-1	24	1918
24	1.1.88	H	Exeter C.	D	1-1	1-1	24	1691
25	9.1.88	A	Burnley	L	0-2	0-0	24	5305
26	12.1.88	A	Darlington	W	2-1	1-1	24	1402
27	16.1.88	H	Scunthorpe U.	D	1-1	1-0	24	1760
28	29.1.88	A	Stockport Co.	L	1-5	1-1	24	2509
29	5.2.88	H	Halifax T.	W	1-0	0-0	24	1509
30	13.2.88	A	Crewe Alex.	L	1-2	0-0	24	2080
31	19.2.88	A	Hartlepool U.	L	2-3	1-2	24	1880
32	26.2.88	A	Colchester U.	D	0-0	0-0	24	1780
33	1.3.88	H	Leyton Orient	D	0-0	0-0	24	1656
34	5.3.88	H	Swansea C.	L	1-2	1-0	24	2235
35	12.3.88	H	Cambridge U.	D	0-0	0-0	24	1208
36	26.3.88	A	Wrexham	L	1-4	1-1	24	1627
37	2.4.88	H	Carlisle U.	L	1-2	1-2	24	1376
38	4.4.88	A	Cardiff C.	L	0-4	0-1	24	6536
39	9.4.88	H	Peterborough U.	L	0-4	0-1	24	988
40	12.4.88	H	Scarborough	L	0-4	0-1	24	1025
41	19.4.88	A	Torquay U.	L	1-6	1-2	24	3416
42	23.4.88	A	Bolton W.	L	0-6	0-4	24	4357
43	26.4.88	H	Wolverhampton W.	L	1-3	0-2	24	3409
44	30.4.88	H	Tranmere Rov.	L	0-3	0-1	24	1110
45	2.5.88	A	Darlington	W	2-0	2-0	24	1675
46	7.5.88	H	Rochdale	L	0-1	0-0	24	2560

Players: League Record, 1987-88 (Division 4)

Player	Appearances (by match 1–46)	Apps	Subs	Goals
Abruzzese	6(6) 6(7) 6(8) 3(12) 9(13) ★(14) 5(19) 2(20) 2(21) 7(22) 7(23) 2(29–37)	21	1	0
Bodin	11(29) 11(30) 11^1(31) 11(32) 11(33) 11(34)	6	0	1
Bradshaw	1(1–10) 1(12–19) 1(42–46)	23	0	2
Brook	9(22–35), 9^1 in matches 26 & 34	14	0	2
Carr	5(13–15) 5(17) 5(29–30) 4(33–35)	9	0	0
Clement	3(24) 3(25) 3^1(26) 3(27) 3(28)	5	0	1
Coles	1(23–36)	14	0	0
Collins	★(3) 10(4) 10^1(5) 9(6) ★(18) 9(19) 9(36)	5	2	1
Dillon	1(13) 1(24) 1(25) 1(26)	5	0	0
Evans	10(1) 10(2) 10(3) 10^1(7) 10^1(8) 10(9) 10(10) 10(11) ★(14) 10(20)	9	1	2
Gibbins	4(1–4) 6(5) 4(6–8) 5(9) 9(10) 10(11) 6(12) 5(13–15) 3(19–23) 8(24) 8^1(25) 8(26–33) 5(34)	33	0	1
Giles	7(1–3) 7^1(4) 7(5) 7(12–19) ★(20)	15	1	1
Hamer	6(6) ★(29) 4(35–39) 4^1(40) 4(41–45)	12	1	1
Hodson	2(1–9) 2^1(10) 2(11–18) 4(20) 2(21–36)	34	0	1
Jones	7(7) 7(8) 7(9) 4(10) 6(11) ★(19) 9(20) ★(21) ★(22) 7(23–30) 7^1(27) 7(31–33) 5(34–40) 11(45) 11(46)	28	3	1
Lewis	3(1–3) 3(24–33)	8	0	1
Mann	11(19) 11(20) 6(22) 10(23–38), 10^1 in match 32	17	0	1
Miller	9(12) 10(13) 10^1(14) 10(15) 10(16) 10^1(17)	6	0	2
Millett	★(3) ★(7) 8(8) ★(13) 9(15) ★(16) 10(19) 10(20) ★(21) ★(22) ★(23) 9(24) 9(25) ★(31) ★(32) ★(36) 11(37) 7^1(38) 7(39–46)	18	10	1
Osborne	11(20) 11(22–24) 8(25) 6(27–34) 6(36)	15	0	0
Peacock	3(43) 3(44) 5(45)...	5	0	0
Preece	3(13) 9^1(19) 9(20) $★^1$(22) ★(24) ★(37) 11(38) 11(39) 3(40) 3(41)	7	3	2
Sherlock	★(2) 3(3) 3(4) 3^1(5) 3(6–9) 6(14–21) 6(22) 5(24) 3(25) 11(26) 11(27) 11(28) 11^1(29) 3(30–37)	31	2	2
Taylor	9(1–5) ★(7) 9(8) 8(9) 7(10) 9(11) 11(12) 11^2(13) 11(14) 11(15) 11(16) ★(17) ★(18) 9(19) 11(22) ★(23) ★(30) ★(31) 8(38) 10(39) 10^1(40) 10(41–45) 10^1(45) 10(46)	28	6	4
Thackeray	8(1–4) 4(5) ★(7) 8(8) 7(9) 4(10–13) 4^1(14) 4(15–23) 8(24) 4(25–33) 11(34) 4(35) 8(36–46)	42	1	1
Thompson	4^1(13) ★(21) 9(29–31) ★(32) 9(33–38) 9^1(39) 9(40)	10	3	2
Tupling	11(1–5) 8(6) 8(7) 11^1(8) ★(9) 8(11) 8(12–19) ★(20) 6(35–44) 6^1(43) 6(45) 6(46)	30	3	2
Williams	5(1–8) 5(12) 5(13) 5(14) 3(15) 3(16–18) 5^1(24) 5(25–28) 5(34) 5^2(35) 5(36–38)	26	0	3

Also Played: **Bennett** 4 apps (11 in match 43, 3 in matches 44, 45 & 46) 1 sub (match 41)—**Boughen** 1 app (11 in match 46)—**Brignull** 3 apps (6 in matches 1, 2 & 3)—**Carter** 1 app (1 in match 21)—**Davies** 2 subs (matches 40 & 42)—**Downes** 4 apps/2 goals (7 in match 21, 6 in matches 22¹, 23¹ & 24)—**Griffiths** 1 sub (match 36)—**Holtham** 4 apps (9 in matches 9 & 11, 8 in match 10, 11 in match 19)—**Hopkins** 2 apps (11 in matches 39 & 40) 4 subs (matches 38, 41, 42 & 44)—**Morgan** 2 subs (matches 37 & 38)—**O'Hagan** 3 apps (1 in match 39, 40 & 41)—**Parselle** 4 apps (10 in match 14, 11 in matches 38, 41 & 42) 6 subs (matches 4, 12, 13, 37, 39 & 46)—**Withers** 4 apps (10 in match 7, 9 in match 12 & 3 in matches 40 & 41) 3 subs (matches 5, 6¹ & 8).

FA Cup: 1987-88: 1st Round: Northampton T. (A) 1-2.
Littlewoods Cup: 1987-88: 1st Round: Cardiff C. (H) 2-1 (A) 2-2; 2nd Round: Crystal Palace (A) 0-4 (H) 0-2.

NORTHAMPTON TOWN (Division 3)

Team Manager   Graham Carr.
Club Address   County Ground, Abington Avenue, Northampton NN1 4PS. Tel: (0604) 721103/39500.
Current Ground Capacity   11,150.
Record Attendance   24,523 v Fulham, Div. 1, 23 April 1966.
Year Formed   1897. Turned professional 1901.
Previous Names   None.
Club Nickname   "The Cobblers"
Club Colours   All maroon with white pinstripe on shirts and white trim.
Club Honours   Football League: Div. 3 Champions 1962-63; Div. 4 Champions 1986-87.
League History   1920-58 Div. 3(S); 1958-61 Div. 4; 1961-63 Div. 3; 1963-65 Div. 2; 1965-66 Div. 1; 1966-67 Div. 2; 1967-69 Div 3; 1969-76 Div 4; 1976-77 Div. 3; 1977-78 Div. 4; 1987- Div. 3.
Most League Points in a Season   (2 for a win) 68 in Div. 4, 1975-76. (3 for a win) 99 in Div. 4, 1986-87.
Most League Goals in a Season   109 in Div.3, 1962-63, and Div. 3(S), 1952-53.

Record Victory   10-0 v Walsall in Div. 3(S), 5 November 1927.
Record Defeat   0-10 v Bournemouth in Div. 3(S), 2 September 1939.
Consecutive League Wins   8 in 1960.
Consecutive League Defeats   8 in 1935.
Record League Appearances   Tommy Fowler, 521 between 1946-61.
Record League Goalscorer—Career   Jack English, 135 between 1947-60.
Record League Goalscorer—Season   Cliff Holton, 36 in Div. 3, 1961-62.

Northampton Town: League Record, 1987-88 (Division 3)

Match Number	Date	Venue	Opponents	Result	H/T	Lge Posn	Attend
1	15.8.87	A	Chester C.	W 5-0	1-0		3458
2	29.8.87	A	Walsall	L 0-1	0-1		5993
3	31.8.87	H	Brighton & H.A.	D 1-1	0-0	12	7934
4	5.9.87	A	Doncaster Rov.	W 2-0	0-0	11	1873
5	9.9.87	H	Brentford	W 2-1	0-0	2	5748
6	12.9.87	H	Notts Co.	L 0-1	0-1	8	6023
7	15.9.87	A	Preston N.E.	D 0-0	0-0	8	5179
8	19.9.87	A	Bristol Rov.	W 2-0	1-0	6	3655
9	26.9.87	H	Port Vale	W 1-0	0-0	1	5072
10	29.9.87	H	Southend U.	D 1-1	1-1	2	3407
11	3.10.87	H	Bristol C.	W 3-0	1-0	1	6234
12	11.10.87	A	Rotherham U.	D 2-2	2-0	2	5244
13	17.10.87	H	Chesterfield	W 4-0	2-0	1	5073
14	20.10.87	A	Mansfield T.	L 1-3	1-2	5	3645
15	24.10.87	H	Grimsby T.	W 2-1	1-1	3	5388
16	31.10.87	A	Aldershot	D 4-4	3-1	3	3358
17	4.11.87	A	York C.	D 0-0	0-0	3	4950
18	7.11.87	H	Fulham	D 0-0	0-0	4	6717
19	21.11.87	H	Gillingham	W 2-1	0-1	3	5151
20	28.11.87	A	Blackpool	L 1-3	1-2	4	3593
21	12.12.87	H	Sunderland	L 0-2	0-0	6	7279
22	19.12.87	A	Wigan Ath.	D 2-2	1-1	6	2692
23	26.12.87	A	Port Vale	D 1-1	0-1	8	4446
24	28.12.87	H	Bury	D 0-0	0-0	8	6067
25	1.1.88	H	Walsall	D 2-2	0-2	8	5832
26	2.1.88	A	Notts. Co.	L 1-3	0-1	8	8149
27	9.1.88	A	Brentford	W 1-0	0-0	7	6025
28	16.1.88	A	Bristol Rov.	W 2-1	1-1	6	4473
29	27.1.88	H	Preston N.E.	L 0-1	0-1	6	5052
30	30.1.88	H	Wigan Ath.	D 1-1	0-1	6	4825
31	6.2.88	H	Doncaster Rov.	W 1-0	1-0	5	4359
32	13.2.88	A	Bury	D 0-0	0-0	6	2172
33	20.2.88	H	Chester C.	W 2-0	0-0	6	4285
34	27.2.88	A	Bristol C.	D 2-2	2-1	6	8578
35	2.3.88	H	Southend U.	W 4-0	1-0	6	4249
36	5.3.88	A	Chesterfield	W 2-0	2-0	5	2400
37	11.3.88	H	Rotherham U.	D 0-0	0-0	5	5432
38	19.3.88	H	Aldershot	D 1-1	0-1	5	4322
39	26.3.88	A	Grimsby T.	D 2-2	0-2	5	3406
40	2.4.88	H	Fulham	W 3-2	1-1	5	6211
41	4.4.88	H	Gillingham	W 2-1	0-0	5	4126
42	10.4.88	H	Mansfield T.	W 2-0	0-0	4	6917
43	15.4.88	A	Brighton & H.A.	L 0-3	0-1	6	14421
44	23.4.88	A	York C.	D 2-2	0-1	5	2048
45	30.4.88	H	Blackpool	D 3-3	0-0	5	5730
46	2.5.88	A	Sunderland	L 1-3	1-1	6	29454

Players: League Record, 1987-88 (Division 3)

Match Number	1	2	3	4	5	6	7	8	9	10	11	12	13	14	15	16	17	18	19	20	21	22	23	24	25	26	27	28	29	30	31	32	33	34	35	36	37	38	39	40	41	42	43	44	45	46	Apps	Subs	Goals
Adcock																													10	10^1	10^1	**10**	10^1	10^1	10^1	10	10	10^1	10	10	10	10^1	10^1				18	0	10
Benjamin	8	8	8	8	8	**8**	8	8	8	8	★	11^1	11																																		13	1	1
Bunce				★			7	7	7	7^1					★							★	8	★															★							5	5	1
Carter																																															0	1	0
Chard	11^1	**11**		★	4	4	4^1	4^1	4	4^2	**11**		11	3	3	10	3	3	11	2	2	2^1	2	9^1	6	2	2	**11**	**11**	**11**	11^1	2	2	2	4												33	1	8
Culpin												8^1	8^2	8^1	8^1	8^1	8	8		★	8	8	8													★	8^1	8^1	8^1	8	8	8^1	8	8			18	2	10
Donald	4	4	4	4	**4**			★			4	4	4	4	4	4	4	4	4	4^1	4	4	4	4	4	4^1	4	4	4	4	4	4	4	4	4	4	4	4	4	4	4	4	4	4	4	4	39	1	2
Donegal																				★	$★^1$	9		★	11		★			★									★	★	★						2	8	1
Gilbert	9^1	9	9	9	9^1	9	9	9	9	9	9	9	9	9	9^1	9	9	9	9	9	**9**			9		9^1	9	9	9	9	9	9	9^1	9	9	9	9	9	9	9	9	9	9	9^1	9		41	0	6
Gleasure	1	1	1	1	1	1	1	1	1	1	1	1	1	1	1	1	1	1	1	1	1	1	1	1	1	1	1	1	1	1	1	1	1	1	1	1	1	1	1	1	1	1	1	1	1	1	46	0	0
Logan	3	3	3	3	3	3	3	3	3	3	3	3	3	**3**			3	★	★	3	3	3	3	3	3	3		3																			24	2	0
Longhurst	7^1	7	7	7^1	7^1						★	11^1	11	11	11	11	11^1	★	11	11	11	**11**	11	11	11			8	8	8	8^1	8	8	**8**	11	11	11	**11**	**11**	11^1	11						33	2	7
McGoldrick	★	★	**11**	11	11	11	11	11	11	11	11	7	7	7	7	7	7	★	**8**	8	7	9	9	9	**8**	8	8	8	8	**8**	8	★	★	★	11^1	11^1	11	11	2	2	2	2	2	2	2	2	40	6	2
McPherson	6	6	6	6	6	6	6	6	6	6	6	6	6	6	6	6	6	6	6	6	6	6	6	6	6	6	6		6	6	6					6	6										32	0	0
Mann							7																																								1	0	0
Morley	10^1	10	10^1	10^1	10^1	10	10	10	10^1	10	10^1	10	10^1	10^1	10	10	10^1	**10**			10^1	10	10	10	10	10	10	10^1	10	10																	27	0	10
O'Donnell																														10																	1	0	0
Reed	2	**2**	2	2	2	2	2	2	2	2	2	2	2	2	2	2	2	2	2	2	2	**2**			★	2				2	2	2	2			2	★	★		★							27	4	0
Sandeman																												★	★																		0	2	0
Senior	★	★					7			★																																					1	3	0
Singleton													7	7	7	★	7^1	7^1	7	7	7	7	7	7	7	7	7	7	7	7	7	7	7	7	7	7^1	7	7	7	7	7	7					28	1	3
Slack																								6	6^1	6	6	6	6	6						6	6	**6**	6	6							13	0	1
Wilcox	5^1	5	5	5	5	5	5	5	5	5	5	5	5	5	5	5	5	5	5^1	5	5	5	5	5	5	5	5	5	5	5	5	5	5	5^1	5	5	5	5	5	5^1	5	5	5	5			46	0	4
Williams																						3	3	★	3																						3	1	0
Wilson																														3	3	3	3	3	3	3	3	3	3	3	3	3	3^1	3	3		15	0	1
Own Goals																		1																	1		1												3

FA Cup: 1987-88: 1st Round: Newport Co. (H) 2-1; 2nd Round: Brighton & H.A. (H) 1-2.
Littlewoods Cup: 1987-88: 1st Round: Port Vale (A) 1-0 (H) 4-0; 2nd Round: Ipswich T. (A) 1-1 (H) 2-4.

NORWICH CITY (Division 1)

Team Manager Dave Stringer.
Club Address Carrow Road, Norwich NR1 1JE. Tel: (0603) 612131.
Current Ground Capacity 26,812.
Record Attendance 43,984 v Leicester C., FA Cup 6th Round, 30 March 1963.
Year Formed 1905. Turned professional 1905.
Previous Names None.
Club Nickname "The Canaries".
Club Colours Yellow shirts with green pinstripe, green shorts with yellow trim and yellow stockings.
Club Honours Football League: Div. 2 Champions 1971-72, 1985-86; Div. 3(S) Champions 1933-34; Football League Cup: Winners 1962, 1985.
League History 1920-34 Div. 3(S); 1934-39 Div. 2; 1946-60 Div. 3; 1960-72 Div. 2; 1972-74 Div. 1; 1974-75 Div. 2; 1975-81 Div. 1; 1981-82 Div. 2; 1982-85 Div. 1; 1985-86 Div. 2; 1986- Div. 1.
Most League Points in a Season (2 for a win) 64 in Div. 3(S), 1950-51. (3 for a win) 84 in Div. 2, 1985-86.
Most League Goals in a Season 99 in Div. 3(S), 1952-53.
Record Victory 10-2 v Coventry C. in Div. 3(S), 15 March 1930.
Record Defeat 2-10 v Swindon T. in Southern League, 5 September 1908.
Consecutive League Wins 9 in 1985-86.
Consecutive League Defeats 7 in 1935 and 1957.
Record League Appearances Ron Ashman, 592 between 1947-64.
Record League Goalscorer—Career Johnny Gavin, 122 between 1948-58.
Record League Goalscorer—Season Ralph Hunt, 31 in Div. 3(S), 1955-56.

Norwich City: League Record, 1987-88 (Division 1)

Match Number	Date	Venue	Opponents	Result		H/T	Lge Posn	Attend
1	15.8.87	A	Everton	L	0-1	0-1		31728
2	19.8.87	H	Southampton	L	0-1	0-0		14429
3	22.8.87	H	Coventry C.	W	3-1	1-0	12	13726
4	29.8.87	A	West Ham U.	L	0-2	0-0	16	16394
5	1.9.87	H	Newcastle U.	D	1-1	0-0	14	16636
6	5.9.87	A	Watford	W	1-0	0-0	11	11724
7	12.9.87	H	Derby Co.	L	1-2	0-0	14	14402
8	19.9.87	A	Chelsea	L	0-1	0-1	16	15242
9	26.9.87	H	Nottingham F.	L	0-2	0-2	18	13755
10	3.10.87	A	Oxford U.	L	0-3	0-1	19	6847
11	10.10.87	H	Tottenham H.	W	2-1	1-1	14	18669
12	17.10.87	H	Manchester U.	L	1-2	1-0	18	39345
13	24.10.87	A	Sheffield Wed.	L	0-1	0-1	18	15861
14	31.10.87	H	Q.P.R.	D	1-1	0-0	19	14522
15	7.11.87	A	Charlton Ath.	L	0-2	0-2	19	5044
16	14.11.87	H	Arsenal	L	2-4	1-0	20	20558
17	21.11.87	A	Liverpool	D	0-0	0-0	20	37446
18	28.11.87	H	Portsmouth	L	0-1	0-1	20	13099
19	5.12.87	A	Luton T.	W	2-1	0-1	20	7002
20	18.12.87	A	Wimbledon	L	0-1	0-1	20	4026
21	26.12.87	A	Derby Co.	W	2-1	1-0	20	15452
22	28.12.87	H	Chelsea	W	3-0	0-0	18	19668
23	1.1.88	H	West Ham U.	W	4-1	0-1	15	20059
24	16.1.88	H	Everton	L	0-3	0-1	18	15750
25	23.1.88	A	Southampton	D	0-0	0-0	16	12002
26	6.2.88	H	Watford	D	0-0	0-0	16	13316
27	13.2.88	A	Newcastle U.	W	3-1	1-1	16	21068
28	20.2.88	A	Coventry C.	D	0-0	0-0	15	15557
29	5.3.88	H	Manchester U.	W	1-0	0-0	14	19129
30	12.3.88	A	Tottenham H.	W	3-1	1-0	13	19322
31	16.3.88	H	Oxford U.	W	4-2	1-0	9	12260
32	19.3.88	A	Q.P.R.	L	0-3	0-1	10	9033
33	26.3.88	H	Sheffield Wed.	L	0-3	0-1	13	13280
34	2.4.88	H	Charlton Ath.	W	2-0	0-0	12	15015
35	4.4.88	A	Arsenal	L	0-2	0-1	14	19341
36	20.4.88	H	Liverpool	D	0-0	0-0	14	22509
37	23.4.88	A	Portsmouth	D	2-2	1-0	13	12762
38	30.4.88	H	Luton T.	D	2-2	1-0	13	12700
39	4.5.88	A	Nottingham F.	L	0-2	0-2	13	11610
40	7.5.88	H	Wimbledon	L	0-1	0-0	14	11782

Players: League Record, 1987-88 (Division 1)

Match Number	1	2	3	4	5	6	7	8	9	10	11	12	13	14	15	16	17	18	19	20	21	22	23	24	25	26	27	28	29	30	31	32	33	34	35	36	37	38	39	40	Apps	Subs	Goals
Benstead																								1	1																2	0	0
Biggins	9	9	9	9	9¹	9	9	9			9¹	9	9	9¹	9	★													★		★¹	★		8	9						15	5	5
Bowen		11	11	11	11	11	11	11			11	11	11				★			3	3	3¹	3	3	3	3	3	3	3	3	3¹	3									23	1	1
Brown	2									2			2	2	2	2	2																								7	0	0
Bruce	4	4	4¹	4	4	4¹	4	4	4	4	4	4	4	4	4	4	4	4	4																						19	0	2
Butterworth	6	6	6	6	6	6	6	6		★	6	6	6	6	6	6	6	6	6	6	6	6	6	6	6		6	6	6	6	6	6	6	6	6	6	6	6	6	6	34	1	0
Crook	★	10	10	10	10	10	10	10	10		★	★	★	11	11	7	7	7	7¹	7							★	★		★	5										16	7	1
Culverhouse	2	2	2	2	2	2	2	2			2	2	2					2	2	2	2	2	2	2	2	2	2	2	2	2	2	2	2	2	2	2	2	2	2	2	33	0	0
Drinkell	8	8	8²	8	8	8	8	8	8	8	8¹	8	8	8	8	8²	8	8	8	8	8	8	8¹	8¹	8	8	8¹	8	8	8¹	8	8		8¹		8					38	0	12
Elliott				3	3	3	3	3					3	3	3	3	3	4	4		★		★	10	10																14	2	0
Fleck																	9	9¹				9	9	9	9²	9	9¹	9¹	9²	9	9	9	9	9	9	9	9				18	0	7
Fox		7	7	7	7	7	7	7	7		7	7	7	7				★		7	7¹	7	7	7	7	7	7	7	7	7	7¹	7	7	7	7	7	7	7			33	1	2
Gordon	7		★					★	7					11	11	11	11¹	11	11¹	11	11¹	11	11	11	11	11						★			★	★					16	5	3
Goss											10						★	10	10¹	10	10	10	10	★		4	10	10¹	10	10	10	10	10	10	10	10	10	10	10	10	20	2	2
Gunn	1	1	1	1	1	1	1	1	1	1	1	1	1	1	1	1	1	1	1	1	1	1	1			1	1	1	1	1	1	1	1	1	1	1	1	1	1	1	38	0	0
Linighan																								4	4	4¹	4	4	4	4	4	4	4¹	4	4	4					12	0	2
O'Neill																4																									1	0	0
Phelan	5	5	5	5	5	5	5	5	5	5	5	5	5	5	5	5	5	5	5	5	5	5	5	5	5	5	5	5	5	5	5					5	5	5	5	5	37	0	0
Putney	11							11	11			10					10	10	10	10	★		4	4	4	4		6	11	11	11	11	11	11	11	11	11¹	11	11		25	1	1
Ratcliffe				★				★	6	6	6	6	6	10																				8					★		6	3	0
Rosario		★					★¹	★	9	9				★	9	9	9	9	★		9	9¹														8					9	5	2
Spearing	3	3	3	3	3	3	3	3					3	3											★	3	3	3	3	3	3	3									17	1	0
Williams	10								★	10	10	10	10		★											5	5														7	2	0

FA Cup: 1987-88: 3rd Round: Swindon T. (A) 0-0 Replay (H) 0-2.
Littlewoods Cup: 1987-88: 2nd Round: Burnley (A) 1-1 (H) 1-0; 3rd Round: (A) Stoke C. 1-2.

NOTTINGHAM FOREST (Division 1)

Team Manager   Brian Clough.
Club Address   City Ground, Nottingham NG2 5FJ. Tel: (0602) 822202.
Current Ground Capacity   35,507.
Record Attendance   49,945 v Manchester U., Div. 1, 28 October 1967.
Year Formed   1865. Turned professional 1889.
Previous Names   None.
Club Nickname   "The Reds".
Club Colours   Red shirts with white pinstripe, white shorts and red stockings.
Club Honours   Football League: Div. 1 Champions 1977-78; Div. 2 Champions 1906-07, 1921-22; Div. 3(S) Champions 1950-51. FA Cup: Winners 1898, 1959. Football League Cup: Winners 1978, 1979. European Cup: Winners 1978-79, 1979-80. Super Cup: Winners 1979-80.
League History   1892-1906 Div. 1; 1906 Div. 2; 1907 Div. 1; 1911-22 Div. 2; 1922-25 Div. 1; 1925-49 Div. 2; 1949-51 Div. 3(S); 1951-57 Div. 2; 1957-72 Div. 1; 1972-77 Div. 2; 1977- Div. 1.

Most League Points in a Season   (2 for a win) 70 in Div. 3(S), 1950-51. (3 for a win) 74 in Div. 1, 1983-84.
Most League Goals in a Season   110 in Div. 3(S), 1950-51.
Record Victory   14-0 v Clapton in FA Cup 1st Round, 1890-91.
Record Defeat   1-9 v Blackburn Rov. in Div. 2, 10 April 1937.
Consecutive League Wins   7 in 1892, 1906, 1921 and 1979.
Consecutive League Defeats   14 in 1913.
Record League Appearances   Bob McKinlay, 614 between 1951-70.
Record League Goalscorer—Career   Grenville Morris, 199 between 1898-1913.
Record League Goalscorer—Season   Wally Ardron, 36 in Div. 3(S), 1950-51.

Nottingham Forest: League Record, 1987-88 (Division 1)

Match Number	Date	Venue	Opponents	Result		H/T	Lge Posn	Attend
1	15.8.87	A	Charlton Ath.	W	2-1	0-1		6021
2	19.8.87	H	Watford	W	1-0	1-0		14527
3	22.8.87	H	Everton	D	0-0	0-0	2	20445
4	29.8.87	A	Newcastle U.	W	1-0	1-0	2	20111
5	2.9.87	H	Southampton	D	3-3	2-1	3	14173
6	5.9.87	A	Chelsea	L	3-4	3-1	6	18414
7	12.9.87	H	Arsenal	L	0-1	0-1	6	18490
8	19.9.87	A	Coventry C.	W	3-0	1-0	4	17519
9	26.9.87	A	Norwich C.	W	2-0	2-0	3	13755
10	10.10.87	A	Derby Co.	W	1-0	1-0	5	22394
11	17.10.87	H	Sheffield Wed.	W	3-0	1-0	3	17685
12	24.10.87	H	Tottenham H.	W	3-0	1-0	4	23543
13	31.10.87	A	Manchester U.	D	2-2	1-0	4	44699
14	14.11.87	H	Portsmouth	W	5-0	3-0	4	15851
15	21.11.87	H	West Ham U.	L	2-3	1-1	4	17216
16	5.12.87	A	Wimbledon	D	1-1	1-0	6	5170
17	13.12.87	H	Q.P.R.	W	4-0	1-0	3	18130
18	19.12.87	A	Oxford U.	W	2-0	0-0	3	7891
19	26.12.87	A	Arsenal	W	2-0	1-0	2	31211
20	28.12.87	H	Coventry C.	W	4-1	1-1	2	31061

Match Number	Date	Venue	Opponents	Result		H/T	Lge Posn	Attend
21	1.1.88	H	Newcastle U.	L	0-2	0-1	2	28583
22	3.1.88	A	Everton	L	0-1	0-1	2	21680
23	16.1.88	A	Charlton Ath.	D	2-2	0-0	2	15363
24	23.1.88	A	Watford	D	0-0	0-0	2	13158
25	6.2.88	H	Chelsea	W	3-2	1-0	2	18203
26	13.2.88	A	Southampton	D	1-1	1-1	3	13314
27	5.3.88	A	Sheffield Wed.	W	1-0	1-0	3	19509
28	16.3.88	A	Q.P.R.	L	1-2	0-1	4	8316
29	19.3.88	H	Manchester U.	D	0-0	0-0	3	27598
30	26.3.88	H	Tottenham H.	D	1-1	0-1	5	25306
31	30.3.88	H	Derby Co.	W	2-1	1-0	4	25017
32	2.4.88	H	Liverpool	W	2-1	1-0	3	29188
33	4.4.88	A	Portsmouth	W	1-0	0-0	3	17528
34	13.4.88	A	Liverpool	L	0-5	0-2	5	39535
35	20.4.88	H	West Ham U.	D	0-0	0-0	5	15775
36	30.4.88	H	Wimbledon	D	0-0	0-0	5	14341
37	4.5.88	H	Norwich C.	W	2-0	2-0	4	11610
38	7.5.88	H	Oxford U.	W	5-3	4-1	3	12762
39	13.5.88	A	Luton T.	D	1-1	0-1	3	9108
40	15.5.88	H	Luton T.	D	1-1	0-1	3	13106

Players: League Record, 1987-88 (Division 1)

Match Number	1	2	3	4	5	6	7	8	9	10	11	12	13	14	15	16	17	18	19	20	21	22	23	24	25	26	27	28	29	30	31	32	33	34	35	36	37	38	39	40	Apps	Subs	Goals
Campbell	6	6	6	6	6	6	6	★																																	7	1	0
Carr	7	7	7	7	7	7	7	7^1	7	7	7^1	7^1	7	7	7					7									10	7	7	7^1	7	7							22	0	4
Chettle					★			2	2	2	2	2	2	2		2	2	2	2	2	2	★				2	2	3	2	2	2	2	4	4	4	4	5	3			28	2	0
Clough	9^1	9	9	9^1	9^1	9^1	9	9	9	9	9^1	9	9^1	9^1	9^1	9^3	9			9^1	9^1	9	9	9	9^1	9^2	9	9	9		9	9^2	9	9							34	0	19
Crosby																	★	7^1	7	7	7	7	7	7	7	7						11	★								12	2	1
Fleming	2	2	2	2	2	2	2	2					2	2	★	★	★		2	2	2			2						2	2	2	2	2							19	3	0
Foster	5	5	5	5	5	5^1	5	5	5	5	5	5	5	5	5	5	5	5	5	5	5	5	5	5^1		5	5	5	5	5	5	5	5	5	★	5					38	1	2
Gaynor												★	10	10^1	10	10	10^2	10	10	10		10	★						9												10	2	3
Glover	11^1	11	11	11	11	11	11	★				★					9	9		9	9							11	10		★	10^1	10	10^1	10						17	3	3
Osvold									★	★											1																				1	2	0
Parker																														10	★										1	1	0
Pearce	3	3^1	3	3	3^1	3	3	3^1	3	3	3	3^1	3	3	3	3	3^1	3	3	3	3	3		3	3	3	3			3	3	3	3								34	0	5
Plummer															7	7	7^1	7	7	7		7^1	7																		8	0	2
Rice						11	11	11	11	11	11	11	11^1	11	11	11	11^1	11	11	11	11	11	**11**		11	11	11	11	11		11	11	11	11	11		11				30	0	2
Segers				1	1	1	1	1																																	5	0	0
Starbuck					★									★	★		★	★	★	★	9			★																	1	9	0
Sutton	1	1							1	1	1	1	1	1	1	1	1	1	1	1	1	1	1	1	1	1	1	1	1	1	1	1	1	1	1	1	1	1	1	1	35	0	0
Walker	4	4	4	4	4	4	4	4	4	4	4	4	4	4	4	4	4	4	4	4	4	4	4	4	4	4	4	4	4	4					4	4					35	0	0
Wassall																														4	★										2	1	0
Webb	8	8	8	8	8^1	8	8	8	8^2	8	8	8^1	8	8^1	8^1	8	8	8	8	8	8	8^1	8	8	8^1	8	8	8	8	8	8^1	8	8	8	8^1	8^2	8	8^1			40	0	13
Wilkinson	10	10	10	10	10	10^1	**10**	10	10	10	10^1	10^1	10	10^1	10^1	10					★	10		10	10	10	10	10	10	10					★						24	2	0
Williams																																	3	3	3	3					4	0	0
Wilson			★	★	★	6^1	6	6	6	6	6^1	6	6	6	6	6^1	6^1	6	6	6	6	6	6	6	6	6	6	6	6	6^1	6	6	**6**	6	6	6					33	3	5
Own Goals														1									1					1															3

FA Cup: 1987-88: 3rd Round: Halifax T. (A) 4-0; 4th Round: Leyton Orient (A) 2-1; 5th Round: Birmingham C. (A) 1-0; 6th Round: Arsenal (A) 2-1; Semi Final: Liverpool 1-2.
Littlewoods Cup: 1987-88: 2nd Round: Hereford U. (H) 5-0 (A) 1-1; 3rd Round: Manchester C. (A) 0-3.

106

NOTTS. COUNTY (Division 3)

Team Manager John Barnwell.
Club Address County Ground, Meadow Lane, Nottingham NG2 3HJ. Tel: (0602) 861155.
Current Ground Capacity 24,045.
Record Attendance 47,310 v York C., FA Cup 6th Round, 12 March 1955.
Year Formed 1862. Turned professional 1885.
Previous Names None.
Club Nickname "The Magpies".
Club Colours Black and white striped shirts, black shorts with white stripe down the side and white stockings with black hoops at the top.
Club Honours Football League: Div. 2 Champions 1896-97, 1913-14, 1922-23; Div. 3(S) Champions 1930-31, 1949-50; Div. 4 Champions 1970-71. FA Cup: Winners 1894.
League History 1888-93 Div. 1; 1893-97 Div. 2; 1897-1913 Div. 1; 1913-14 Div. 2; 1914-20 Div. 1; 1920-23 Div. 2; 1923-26 Div. 1; 1926-30 Div. 2; 1930-31 Div. 3(S); 1931-35 Div. 2; 1935-50 Div. 3(S); 1950-58 Div. 2; 1958-59 Div. 3; 1959-60 Div. 4; 1960-64 Div. 3; 1964-71 Div. 4; 1971-73 Div. 3; 1973-81 Div. 2; 1981-84 Div. 1; 1984-85 Div. 2; 1985- Div. 3.
Most League Points in a Season (2 for a win) 69 in Div. 4, 1970-71. (3 for a win) 81 in Div. 3, 1987-88.
Most League Goals in a Season 107 in Div. 4, 1959-60.
Record Victory 15-0 v Thornhill U., FA Cup 1st Round, 24 October 1885.
Record Defeat 1-9 v Blackburn Rov., Div. 1, 16 November 1889 and v Aston Villa, Div. 1, 29 September 1888 and v Portsmouth, Div. 2, 9 April 1927.
Consecutive League Wins 8 in 1914.
Consecutive League Defeats 7 in 1888-89, 1912, 1933 and 1983.
Record League Appearances Albert Iremonger, 564 between 1904-26.
Record League Goalscorer—Career Les Bradd, 125 between 1967-78.
Record League Goalscorer—Season Tom Keetley, 39 in Div. 3(S), 1930-31.

Notts County: League Record, 1987-88 (Division 3)

Match Number	Date	Venue	Opponents	Result		H/T	Lge Posn	Attend
1	15.8.87	H	Wigan Ath.	D	4-4	2-3		6344
2	22.8.87	A	York C.	W	5-3	4-2		2878
3	29.8.87	H	Grimsby T.	D	0-0	0-0	9	5322
4	1.9.87	A	Fulham	D	0-0	0-0	9	4767
5	5.9.87	H	Southend U.	W	6-2	3-2	6	4166
6	12.9.87	A	Northampton T.	W	1-0	1-0	2	6023
7	15.9.87	H	Aldershot	W	2-1	1-1	1	4835
8	19.9.87	H	Bristol C.	L	0-1	0-0	3	5705
9	26.9.87	A	Chesterfield	L	0-2	0-1	8	3466
10	29.9.87	H	Bristol Rov.	D	1-1	0-0	9	4334
11	3.10.87	A	Chester C.	W	2-1	0-1	3	3365
12	11.10.87	H	Mansfield T.	D	1-1	0-0	5	8564
13	17.10.87	A	Doncaster Rov.	W	1-0	1-0	4	2649
14	20.10.87	H	Bury	W	3-0	1-0	2	4044
15	24.10.87	A	Gillingham	L	1-3	1-0	4	5551
16	31.10.87	H	Sunderland	W	2-1	1-1	4	8854
17	3.11.87	A	Rotherham U.	D	1-1	1-1	3	4157
18	7.11.87	H	Brentford	W	3-0	0-0	3	5364
19	21.11.87	H	Walsall	W	3-1	2-1	2	7211
20	28.11.87	A	Brighton & H.A.	D	1-1	0-0	2	8725
21	12.12.87	A	Port Vale	W	3-1	0-0	2	3358
22	19.12.87	H	Preston N.E.	W	4-2	2-1	1	5730
23	26.12.87	H	Chesterfield	W	2-0	2-0	2	8675
24	28.12.87	A	Blackpool	D	1-1	0-0	2	4627
25	1.1.88	A	Grimsby T.	D	0-0	0-0	2	5297
26	2.1.88	H	Northampton T.	W	3-1	1-0	2	8149
27	9.1.88	H	York C.	W	3-0	1-0	2	5924
28	16.1.88	A	Bristol C.	L	1-2	1-0	2	9558
29	30.1.88	H	Fulham	W	5-1	2-1	2	6107
30	5.2.88	A	Southend U.	W	2-1	0-1	2	3904
31	13.2.88	H	Blackpool	L	2-3	1-0	2	5794
32	20.2.88	A	Wigan Ath.	L	1-2	1-1	2	5182
33	23.2.88	A	Aldershot	W	2-0	0-0	2	2880
34	27.2.88	H	Chester C.	W	1-0	0-0	1	5868
35	2.3.88	A	Bristol Rov.	D	1-1	0-0	2	4075
36	5.3.88	H	Doncaster Rov.	W	2-0	1-0	1	5816
37	12.3.88	A	Mansfield T.	D	1-1	1-1	1	7997
38	19.3.88	A	Sunderland	D	1-1	0-1	1	24071
39	26.3.88	H	Gillingham	L	0-1	0-0	1	6473
40	2.4.88	A	Brentford	L	0-1	0-1	2	4388
41	4.4.88	H	Brighton & H.A.	L	1-2	1-1	2	7522
42	9.4.88	A	Bury	W	1-0	0-0	3	2527
43	23.4.88	A	Rotherham U.	W	4-0	0-0	2	7021
44	30.4.88	A	Walsall	L	1-2	1-0	4	11913
45	2.5.88	H	Port Vale	L	1-2	0-1	4	7702
46	7.5.88	A	Preston N.E.	W	2-1	0-0	4	5822

Players: League Record, 1987-88 (Division 3)

Match Number	1	2	3	4	5	6	7	8	9	10	11	12	13	14	15	16	17	18	19	20	21	22	23	24	25	26	27	28	29	30	31	32	33	34	35	36	37	38	39	40	41	42	43	44	45	46	Apps	Subs	Goals
Barnes					★															★		★													★	★^{1}	★	★		11^1	11	8	8				4	7	2
Belford		1																																													1	0	0
Birtles	9^2	9	6	9	**9**	9	9	9	9	9^1	**9**	**9**	9	9^1	9	9^2	9	9	6	9	9	6	6		6	6	6	6	6			9	6	6	**6**	6	6	9	9^1	6	6	6	6				43	0	7
Davis	3	3	3	3	3	3	3						4	4	4	4	4	4	★	★		4							3			3				11		3								18	2	0
Fairclough			★	★	★		3	3	3	★	★	11	11	11	11	11	11	**11**		4		★			★	★		★	★		★	★		★		★			★	★			★	★		4	11	18	0
Gray	6	6	★	11																																											3	1	0
Hart				6	6	6	6	6	6	6	6	6	6	6	6	6	6		6	6				6						6	6	6				6		6									23	0	0
Kevan	4	4	4	4	4	4	4	4	4	4	4					4			4	4	4	4	4	**4**	4	4	4	4				4	4	4	4	4		4		4	4	4					32	0	0
Leonard	1		1	1	1	1	1	1	1	1	1	1	1	1	1	1	1	1	1	1	1	1	1	1	1	1	1	1	1	1	1	1	1	1	1	1	1	1	1	1	1	1	1	1	1	1	45	0	0
Lund	8	★	9	★	★^{1}	11^1	11^1	11	★		★	★	8^1	8^2	8				9^1	★		9	9^1	9	9^1	9^1	9^1	9	9	9	9	9	★^{1}	9	9^2	9	9	9	11	9		9^3	9^1	9	9		32	8	20
McParland	7	8^2	8	8	8^2	8	8	8	8	8	8	8		★	8	8	8^2	8	8^2	8	8^2	8	8	8	8	8	8	8	8^3	8^1	8^1	8^1	8^2	8	8	**8**	8	8	8	8	★	8	8^1				41	2	21
McStay																																		4	4	4		11			★	4	★		★	2	6	3	0
Mills	11	7	7	7	7	7	7	7	7	7^1	7^1	7	7	7	7	7	7	7	7	7	7	7	7	7	7^1	7	7	7	7^1	**7**	7	7	7	7	7	7	7	7	7	7	7	7	7	7	7	7	46	0	5
Pike	10^2	10^1	10	10	10	10^3	10	10^1	10	10	10^1	10	10	10	10	10	10	10	10	10	10^1	10^2	10	10	10	10	**10**	10	10	10^1	10	10	10	10	10	10	10	10	10	10^1	10	10	10	10	10	10^1	46	0	14
Smalley	2	2	2	2	2	2	2	2	2	2	2	2	2	2	2	2	2	2	2	2	2	2	2	2	2	2	2	2	2	2	2	2	2	2	2	2	2	2	2	2	2	2	2	2	2	★	45	1	0
Thompson	★	11^1	11		11			★	11	11	11	11																																			7	2	1
Thorpe																			★	11	11	11	**11**	11	11	11	**11**	11^2	11^1	11	**11**	11	11^1	11	11	11						11	11	11^1	11		22	1	5
Withe				3	3	3	3	3^1	3	3	3^1	3	3	3	3	3	3	3	3	3		3	3	4	3	3	3	3	3	11	3	3	3	3													35	0	2
Yates	5	5	5	5	5	5	5	5	5	5	**5**	5	5	5	5	5	5	5	5^1	5	5	5	5	5	5	5	5	5^1	5	5	5	5	5^1	5	5	5	5	5	5	5	5	5	5	5	5	5	46	0	2
Own Goals		1											1																						1														3

FA Cup: 1987-88: 1st Round: Chesterfield (H) 3-3 Replay (A) 1-0; 2nd Round: Port Vale (A) 0-2.
Littlewoods Cup: 1987-88: 1st Round: Wolverhampton W. (A) 0-3 (H) 1-2.

OLDHAM ATHLETIC (Division 2)

Team Manager Joe Royle.
Club Address Boundary Park, Oldham. Tel: 061-624 4972.
Current Ground Capacity 25,793.
Record Attendance 47,671 v Sheffield Wed., FA Cup 4th Round, 25 January 1930.
Year Formed 1894. Turned professional 1899.
Previous Names Pine Villa, Oldham Athletic.
Club Nickname "The Latics".
Club Colours All blue.
Club Honours Football League: Div. 3(N) Champions 1952-53; Div. 3 Champions 1973-74.
League History 1907-10 Div. 2; 1910-23 Div. 1; 1923-35 Div. 2; 1935-53 Div. 3(N); 1953-54 Div. 2; 1954-58 Div. 3; 1958-63 Div. 4; 1963-69 Div. 3; 1969-71 Div. 4; 1971-74 Div. 3; 1974- Div. 2.
Most League Points in a Season (2 for a win) 62 in Div. 3, 1973-74. (3 for a win) 75 in Div. 2, 1986-87.
Most League Goals in a Season 95 in Div. 4, 1962-63.
Record Victory 11-0 v Southport in Div. 4, 26 December 1962.

Record Defeat 4-13 v Tranmere Rov. in Div. 3(N), 26 December 1935.
Consecutive League Wins 10 in 1974.
Consecutive League Defeats 8 in 1932-33, 1934-35.
Record League Appearances Ian Wood, 525 between 1966-80.
Record League Goalscorer—Career Eric Gemmell, 110 between 1947-54.
Record League Goalscorer—Season Tom Davis, 33 in Div. 3(N), 1936-37.

Oldham Athletic: League Record, 1987-88 (Division 2)

Match Number	Date	Venue	Opponents	Result		H/T	Lge Posn	Attend
1	15.8.87	A	West Bromwich A.	D	0-0	0-0		8873
2	18.8.87	H	Bradford C.	L	0-2	0-1		8087
3	22.8.87	H	Manchester C.	D	1-1	1-1	16	15984
4	29.8.87	A	Middlesbrough	L	0-1	0-0	19	10551
5	31.8.87	H	Huddersfield T.	W	3-2	1-1	13	7377
6	5.9.87	A	Reading	L	0-3	0-1	18	4798
7	12.9.87	H	Sheffield U.	W	3-2	2-2	14	5730
8	16.9.87	A	Leicester C.	L	1-4	0-4	17	7358
9	19.9.87	A	Hull C.	L	0-1	0-1	20	7183
10	26.9.87	H	Barnsley	W	1-0	0-0	17	5853
11	29.9.87	H	Millwall	D	0-0	0-0	20	4840
12	10.10.87	A	Swindon T.	L	0-2	0-0	22	8160
13	20.10.87	H	Leeds U.	D	1-1	1-0	21	6312
14	24.10.87	A	Shrewsbury T.	W	3-2	0-2	20	3337
15	31.10.87	H	Birmingham C.	L	1-2	0-1	20	5486
16	7.11.87	A	Blackburn Rov.	L	0-1	0-1	20	7519
17	14.11.87	H	Aston Villa	L	0-1	0-1	20	8469
18	21.11.87	A	Ipswich T.	L	0-2	0-1	21	11007
19	28.11.87	H	Plymouth Arg.	L	0-1	0-0	21	4516
20	5.12.87	A	Bournemouth	D	2-2	1-1	20	5377
21	8.12.87	A	Stoke C.	D	2-2	1-1	20	6740
22	12.12.87	H	Leicester C.	W	2-0	1-0	20	4785
23	19.12.87	A	Manchester C.	W	2-1	1-0	16	22518
24	26.12.87	A	Barnsley	D	1-1	1-1	18	8676
25	28.12.87	H	Hull C.	L	1-2	1-0	18	8080
26	1.1.88	H	Middlesbrough	W	3-1	2-0	17	8181
27	2.1.88	A	Sheffield U.	W	5-0	3-0	16	9574
28	16.1.88	H	West Bromwich A.	W	2-1	0-0	16	5557
29	29.1.88	H	Crystal Palace	W	1-0	0-0	15	6169
30	6.2.88	H	Reading	W	4-2	0-1	13	5388
31	13.2.88	A	Bradford C.	L	3-5	1-3	14	13862
32	20.2.88	A	Millwall	D	1-1	0-0	14	6839
33	5.3.88	A	Crystal Palace	L	1-3	0-2	15	7032
34	12.3.88	H	Swindon T.	W	4-3	0-1	15	5193
35	19.3.88	A	Birmingham C.	W	3-1	0-0	13	6012
36	26.3.88	H	Shrewsbury T.	D	2-2	0-1	15	5379
37	1.4.88	H	Blackburn Rov.	W	4-2	2-2	12	14853
38	4.4.88	A	Aston Villa	W	2-1	0-1	12	19138
39	9.4.88	A	Stoke C.	W	5-1	2-1	10	6505
40	19.4.88	A	Huddersfield T.	D	2-2	0-2	9	5547
41	23.4.88	A	Leeds U.	D	1-1	0-0	11	13442
42	30.4.88	H	Ipswich T.	W	3-1	1-1	9	5018
43	2.5.88	A	Plymouth Arg.	L	0-1	0-0	10	6084
44	7.5.88	H	Bournemouth	W	2-0	0-0	10	6009

Players: League Record, 1987-88 (Division 2)

Match Number	1	2	3	4	5	6	7	8	9	10	11	12	13	14	15	16	17	18	19	20	21	22	23	24	25	26	27	28	29	30	31	32	33	34	35	36	37	38	39	40	41	42	43	Apps	Subs	Goals
Atkinson			★	★	★				11	11	11					★																												3	4	0
Barlow	3	3	3							★							★	★	★	3	3	3	3	3	3	3	3	3	★		6		★	6	★	6	9	9						19	7	0
Barrett												3	3	3	3											★	★	5	3	3	3	3	3	3	3	3	3	3						16	2	0
Blundell																																						★						0	1	0
Bunn																			9	9¹		9	9¹	9	9	9²	9	9	9²	9	9¹	9	9¹	9	9	9	9¹	9	9	9				21	0	9
Callaghan									4¹	4	4	4	4	4		3									6					2		5¹	★											10	1	2
Cecere	9	9	9	9	9	9	9	9	★	★	9	9	9	★		★	★			★	★			6			★	★¹		★					★¹		★	9						14	11	2
Donachie			3	3	3	3	3	3	3	3	3	3	3	3						★	8	8	8	8	8	8¹	8	8	8	8	8¹	8	8	8	8	8	8¹	8	8					30	1	3
Edmonds			★	3	3																												★					★						2	2	0
Ellis							★		9	9																																		2	1	0
Flynn		★		★			4						4	4	4	4	4	4	4	4	4	4	4	4	4	4	4¹	4	4	4	4	4	4	★	4	4	4	4	4	4	4	4	4	29	2	1
Goram	1	1	1	1	1	1	1	1	1																																			9	0	0
Gorton											1	1	1	1	1	1	1	1	1	1	1	1	1	1	1	1	1	1	1	1	1	1	1											24	0	0
Henry, A.	8	8	8	8	8¹	8	8	8	8	8	8	★	8¹	8	8	9	9	9	8	8¹	8¹																							20	1	4
Henry, N.					10					★	10	10		★																														3	2	0
Irwin	2	2	2	2	2	2	2	2	2	2	2	2	2	2	2	2	2	2	2	2	2	2	2	2	2	2	2	2	2	2	2	2	2		2	2	2	2	2	2	2	2	2	43	0	0
Keeley	4	4	4	4	4	4	4	4						★	9	9																												10	1	0
Kelly, J.																			8	8	6	7	7	8	8	8	8	8																10	0	0
Kelly, N.																																				★								0	1	0
Linighan	5	5	5¹	5	5	5	5	5¹	5	5	5	5	5	5	5	5	5	5	5	5	5	5	5	5	5	5	5	5	5	5	5	5												32	0	2
Marshall																																		5	5	5	5	5		5	5	5	5	10	0	0
Milligan	6	6	6	6	6	6	6	6	6	6	6	6	6	6	6	6	6		6	6	6	6	6	6	6		6	6¹	6	6	6	6		6	6		6	6	6					39	0	1
Morgan														★																														0	1	0
Palmer	7	7	7	7	7	7	7¹	7	7	7	7	7	7³	7	7	7	7		7¹	7	7	7¹	7¹	7¹	7	7	7	7	7¹	7¹	7¹	7²	7	7³	7	7	7¹	7	7					42	0	17
Rhodes																														1	1	1	1	1	1	1	1	1	1	1	1			11	0	0
Ritchie	11	11	11	11	11²	11	11	11¹	11		8							9	11	11	11	11	11	11	11	11²	11	11¹	11	11²	11	11	11²	11	11²	11	11¹	11¹	11	11¹	11	11	11¹	36	0	19
Williams											10	11	11	11¹	11	11	11	11		9																								9	0	1
Wright	10	10	10	10	10	10	10	10	★	10	10			10	10	10	10	10	10	10	10¹	10	10¹	10¹	10	10¹	10¹	10	10¹	10¹	10	10¹	10	10	10	10	10¹	10	10¹	10¹	10	10	10	40	1	8
Own Goals					1																1																			1						3

FA Cup: 1987-88: 3rd Round: Tottenham H. (H) 2-4.
Littlewoods Cup: 1987-88: 2nd Round: Carlisle U. (A) 3-4 (H) 4-1; 3rd Round: Leeds U. (A) 2-2 Replay (H) 4-2; 4th Round: Everton (A) 1-2.

OXFORD UNITED (Division 2)

Team Manager Mark Lawrenson.
Club Address Manor Ground, Headington, Oxford. Tel: (0865) 61503.
Current Ground Capacity 14,232.
Record Attendance 22,730 v Preston N.E., FA Cup 6th Round, 29 February 1964.
Year Formed 1896. Turned professional 1949.
Previous Names Headington U.
Club Nickname "The U's".
Club Colours Yellow shirts with blue trim, blue shorts and yellow stockings.
Club Honours Football League: Div. 2 Champions 1984-85; Div. 3 Champions 1967-68, 1983-84. Football League Cup: Winners 1986.
League History 1962-65 Div. 4; 1965-68 Div. 3; 1968-76 Div. 2; 1976-84 Div. 3; 1984-85 Div. 2; 1985-88 Div. 1; 1988- Div. 2.
Most League Points in a Season (2 for a win) 61 in Div. 4, 1964-65. (3 for a win) 95 in Div. 3, 1983-84.
Most League Goals in a Season 91 in Div. 3, 1983-84.

Record Victory 7-0 v Barrow in Div. 4, 19 December 1964.
Record Defeat 0-6 v Liverpool in Div. 1, 22 March 1986.
Consecutive League Wins 6 in 1968, 1982-83 and 1985.
Consecutive League Defeats: 6 in 1968-69 and 1975.
Record League Appearances John Shuker, 480 between 1962-77.
Record League Goalscorer—Career Graham Atkinson, 75 between 1962-73.
Record League Goalscorer—Season John Aldridge, 30 in Div. 2, 1984-85.

Oxford United: League Record, 1987-88 (Division 1)

Match Number	Date	Venue	Opponents	Result		H/T	Lge Posn	Attend
1	15.8.87	H	Portsmouth	W	4-2	1-0		9174
2	18.8.87	A	Sheffield Wed.	D	1-1	1-1		17868
3	22.8.87	A	Wimbledon	D	1-1	1-0	6	4229
4	1.9.87	A	Tottenham H.	L	0-3	0-2	11	21811
5	5.9.87	H	Luton T.	L	2-5	1-2	16	6804
6	12.9.87	A	Liverpool	L	0-2	0-2	19	42266
7	19.9.87	H	Q.P.R.	W	2-0	2-0	14	9800
8	26.9.87	A	Derby Co.	W	1-0	1-0	11	15711
9	3.10.87	H	Norwich C.	W	3-0	1-0	10	6847
10	10.10.87	A	Arsenal	L	0-2	0-1	10	25244
11	17.10.87	H	West Ham U.	L	1-2	1-2	10	9092
12	24.10.87	H	Charlton Ath	W	2-1	0-0	9	7325
13	31.10.87	A	Chelsea	L	1-2	1-0	10	15027
14	7.11.87	H	Coventry C.	W	1-0	0-0	9	7856
15	14.11.87	A	Southampton	L	0-3	0-1	11	12095
16	21.11.87	H	Watford	D	1-1	0-1	12	7811
17	28.11.87	A	Everton	D	0-0	0-0	12	25443
18	5.12.87	H	Newcastle U.	L	1-3	0-1	13	8190
19	12.12.87	A	Manchester U.	L	1-3	0-2	15	34709
20	19.12.87	H	Nottingham F.	L	0-2	0-0	16	7891
21	26.12.87	H	Liverpool	L	0-3	0-1	17	13680
22	28.12.87	A	Q.P.R.	L	2-3	0-2	17	9125
23	2.1.88	H	Wimbledon	L	2-5	0-3	19	6926
24	16.1.88	H	Portsmouth	D	2-2	1-0	19	13417
25	6.2.88	A	Luton T.	L	4-7	2-3	20	8063
26	13.2.88	H	Tottenham H.	D	0-0	0-0	19	9906
27	20.2.88	H	Derby Co.	D	0-0	0-0	19	8924
28	5.3.88	A	West Ham U.	D	1-1	0-0	19	14980
29	16.3.88	A	Norwich C.	L	2-4	0-1	20	12260
30	19.3.88	H	Chelsea	D	4-4	0-3	20	8468
31	26.3.88	A	Charlton Ath.	D	0-0	0-0	20	6245
32	30.3.88	H	Arsenal	D	0-0	0-0	20	9088
33	2.4.88	A	Coventry C.	L	0-1	0-0	20	15748
34	4.4.88	H	Southampton	D	0-0	0-0	20	7657
35	9.4.88	A	Watford	L	0-3	0-2	20	10045
36	13.4.88	H	Sheffield Wed.	L	0-3	0-2	21	5727
37	23.4.88	H	Everton	D	1-1	1-1	21	7619
38	30.4.88	A	Newcastle U.	L	1-3	0-1	21	16617
39	2.5.88	H	Manchester U.	L	0-2	0-2	21	8966
40	7.5.88	A	Nottingham F.	L	3-5	1-4	21	12762

Players: League Record, 1987-88 (Division 1)

Match Number	1	2	3	4	5	6	7	8	9	10	11	12	13	14	15	16	17	18	19	20	21	22	23	24	25	26	27	28	29	30	31	32	33	34	35	36	37	38	39	40	Apps	Subs	Goals
Bardsley							2	2	2	2	2	2	2	2	2	2	2	2	2	2	2	2	2	2	2	2	2^1	2	2	2	2	2	2	2	2						34	0	1
Briggs	5	5	5	5		5																	5^1	5	5	5	5	5	5	5	5	5	5	5			5	5	5	5	18	0	1
Caton	6^1	6	6	6	6	6	6	6	6	6	6	6	6	6	6	6	6	6	6	6	6	6	6	**6**	**6**	6		6	**6**		★	★	★	5	5	5	5				33	3	1
Denton																																				★	★				0	2	0
Dreyer	★	3	3	3	**3**	3	3	3	3	3	3	3	3	3	3	3	3	3	3	3	3	3		3	3	3	3	3	3	**3**				3	3	**3**	3				34	1	0
Foyle	8	8^1	8^1	8	8^1	8	**8**	8	8	8^1	**8**	8	8^1	8	★		★		★		11	8^1	8	8^1	8	8	8	8^1	8	8	**8**			8	8	8	8	8^2			30	3	10
Greenall																							6		4	6	6	6	6	6	6	6	6	6	6	6					12	0	0
Hardwick							1	1															1	1																	4	0	0
Hebberd	10	10	**10**	10	10	10	10	10		11	11	7	7^1	7	7	7	7	7	7	7	7	7	7	7	7	7	7^1	7	7	7	7	7	7	7	7	7	7^1				39	0	3
Hill									11	11^1	11	11^1	★	11		★		5	5	5	5	5		★	3^2	4	4	11	11	★	★	3	★	★	★						15	9	4
Houghton	7	7	7	7	7	7	7^1	7	7	7	**7**																														11	0	1
Hucker	1	1	1	1	1	1				1	1	1	1	1	1	1	1	1	1	1	1	1								1	1	1	1	1	1						27	0	0
Judge																							1	1	1	1	1							1	1	1	1				9	0	0
Langan	2^1				2																																				2	0	1
Mustoe			★									★				★	★	5		★						10	11	10	10	10	10	**10**	10	**10**	10	10					12	5	0
Nogan																												★	8	8											2	1	0
Phillips				★			10	10	10	10	10	10	10	10^1	10	10	10	**10**	10	10	10	10	10^1	10		10					3	3	3	4	4^1	4	4				29	1	4
Reck					4																						★														1	1	0
Rhoades-Brown	11				★				★		★	11	11	**11**	11	11	11	11	11	★	$★^1$	11	11	11	11	★	★	11^1		11	11	11	**11**	11	11	11	11^1	11			25	6	2
Saunders			★	11	**11**	★	9	9	9	9^1	9	9^1	9	9^1	9	9	9	9	9^1	9^1	9	9^1	9^1	9	9	9	9	9^2	9	9	9	9	9	9	9^1	9	9				35	2	11
Shelton	4	4	4	4		4	4	4	4	4	**4**	4	4	4	4	4	4	4	4	4	4	4		4	4				4	4		4	4	4	4	4	**4**				32	0	0
Shotton			★																																						0	1	0
Slatter	3	2	2	2	5^1	2	5	5^1	5^1	5	5	5	5	**5**	5	5																									16	0	3
Trewick		11	11	11																																					3	0	0
Whitehurst	9^2	9	9	9	9	9	9		★	★				8	8	8	8	8	8	8	8	8	5		★																17	3	2

FA Cup: 1987-88: 3rd Round: Leicester C. (H) 2-0; 4th Round: Bradford C. (A) 2-4.

Littlewoods Cup: 1987-88: 2nd Round: Mansfield T. (H) 1-1 (A) 2-0; 3rd Round: Leicester C. (H) 0-0 Replay (A) 3-2; 4th Round: Wimbledon (H) 2-1; Quarter Final: Manchester U. (H) 2-0; Semi Final Luton T. (H) 1-1 (A) 0-2.

PETERBOROUGH UNITED (Division 4)

Team Manager Noel Cantwell.
Club Address London Road Ground, Peterborough PE2 8AL. Tel: (0733) 63947.
Current Ground Capacity 28,000.
Record Attendance 30,096 v Swansea T., FA Cup 5th Round, 20 February 1965.
Year Formed 1934. Turned professional 1934.
Previous Names None.
Club Nickname "The Posh".
Club Colours Blue shirts, white shorts and blue stockings.
Club Honours Football League: Div. 4 Champions 1960-61.
League History 1960-61 Div. 4; 1961-68 Div. 3; 1968-74 Div. 4; 1974-79 Div. 3; 1979- Div. 4.
Most League Points in a Season (2 for a win) 66 in Div. 4, 1960-61. (3 for a win) 82 Div. 4, 1981-82.
Most League Goals in a Season 134 in Div. 4, 1960-61.
Record Victory 8-1 v Oldham Ath. in Div. 4, 26 November 1969.
Record Defeat 1-8 v Northampton T. in FA Cup 2nd Round 2nd Replay, 18 December 1946.

Consecutive League Wins 7 in 1960-61, 1973.
Consecutive League Defeats 4 in 1967-68, 1971, 1972, 1977, 1978, 1982 and 1985.
Record League Appearances Tommy Robson, 482 between 1968-81.
Record League Goalscorer—Career Jim Hall, 122 between 1967-75.
Record League Goalscorer—Season Terry Bly, 52 in Div. 4, 1960-61.

Peterborough United: League Record, 1987-88 (Division 4)

Match Number	Date	Venue	Opponents	Result		H/T	Lge Posn	Attend
1	15.8.87	H	Carlisle U.	W	1-0	1-0		4000
2	22.8.87	A	Rochdale	D	1-1	1-1		1808
3	29.8.87	H	Cambridge U.	W	1-0	0-0	3	4623
4	31.8.87	A	Bolton W.	L	0-2	0-1	6	3746
5	5.9.87	H	Darlington	L	1-2	1-2	14	3200
6	12.9.87	A	Colchester U.	L	1-4	0-1	18	1164
7	16.9.87	H	Wolverhampton W.	D	1-1	0-1	19	3089
8	19.9.87	H	Wrexham	W	1-0	1-0	15	2805
9	26.9.87	A	Leyton Orient	L	0-2	0-0	17	3426
10	30.9.87	H	Hereford U.	W	1-0	1-0	14	2010
11	3.10.87	H	Scunthorpe U.	D	1-1	1-0	14	3594
12	10.10.87	A	Stockport Co.	W	1-0	0-0	12	1594
13	17.10.87	H	Cardiff C.	W	4-3	1-2	10	3473
14	21.10.87	H	Newport Co.	W	3-0	2-0	7	3163
15	24.10.87	A	Halifax T.	D	0-0	0-0	5	1615
16	31.10.87	H	Torquay U.	L	0-2	0-0	11	3500
17	7.11.87	H	Hartlepool U.	L	0-1	0-0	13	3200
18	21.11.87	A	Swansea C.	L	1-2	1-1	17	4033
19	28.11.87	H	Burnley	W	5-0	3-0	14	3550
20	12.12.87	A	Scarborough	D	1-1	0-1	15	2525
21	18.12.87	H	Crewe Alex.	L	0-4	0-3	16	2540
22	26.12.87	H	Leyton Orient	L	1-2	0-1	17	3371
23	28.12.87	A	Tranmere Rov.	L	1-3	0-1	17	3193
24	1.1.88	A	Cambridge U.	W	3-1	2-0	16	3975
25	2.1.88	H	Colchester U.	W	2-0	0-0	15	3665
26	9.1.88	H	Rochdale	D	1-1	1-1	14	3212
27	16.1.88	A	Wrexham	L	1-3	0-1	15	1506
28	30.1.88	H	Bolton W.	L	0-4	0-2	15	3485
29	13.2.88	H	Tranmere Rov.	W	2-1	1-1	15	2230
30	20.2.88	A	Carlisle U.	W	2-0	2-0	15	2026
31	24.2.88	H	Hereford U.	L	1-2	1-0	15	2065
32	27.2.88	A	Scunthorpe U.	L	0-5	0-1	15	3378
33	4.3.88	A	Cardiff C.	D	0-0	0-0	16	4172
34	9.3.88	A	Exeter C.	W	1-0	0-0	14	1584
35	12.3.88	H	Stockport Co.	D	0-0	0-0	14	2193
36	15.3.88	A	Darlington	L	1-2	1-2	15	1618
37	19.3.88	A	Torquay U.	D	0-0	0-0	15	2544
38	22.3.88	A	Wolverhampton W.	W	1-0	0-0	13	8049
39	26.3.88	H	Halifax T.	W	1-0	0-0	11	2308
40	2.4.88	A	Hartlepool U.	W	1-0	1-0	11	2315
41	4.4.88	H	Swansea C.	L	0-1	0-0	12	3360
42	9.4.88	A	Newport Co.	W	4-0	1-0	11	988
43	23.4.88	H	Exeter C.	W	2-1	1-0	11	2278
44	30.4.88	A	Burnley	W	2-1	0-1	8	6305
45	2.5.88	H	Scarborough	D	0-0	0-0	8	3244
46	7.5.88	A	Crewe Alex.	W	1-0	1-0	7	1533

Players: League Record, 1987-88 (Division 4)

Match Number	1	2	3	4	5	6	7	8	9	10	11	12	13	14	15	16	17	18	19	20	21	22	23	24	25	26	27	28	29	30	31	32	33	34	35	36	37	38	39	40	41	42	43	44	45	46	Apps	Subs	Goals
Benning																	★	★																									3	10		2	0	0
Butterworth				7																									11	11	11	★									★	★	10	10			6	5	0
Carr					7								★	10	10	10	5	7		7	7						★		★	★	★																8	5	0
Collins		5			8	8	8	8	11	11	11	11	11	11	11	11	3	3¹	3	3	3	3	3	3	3	3	3	3	3	3	3		3	3	3	3	3	3	3				3	3	3		39	0	1
Corner																												3	6	10	10	10	10	10	10	10											9	0	0
Fife																																	★														0	1	0
Genovese																																			10												1	0	0
Gooding	4¹	4	4	4	4	4	4¹	4	4	4	4¹	4	4¹	4³	4	4	4	4²			4¹	4	4	4	4	4	4	4	4¹	4¹	4	4	4¹	4	4¹	4	4¹	4¹	4	4	4	4²	4	4	4		44	0	18
Gunn	3	3	3	3	3	3	3	3	3	3	3	3	3	3	3	3	5	5	5	5	5	5	5	5	5	5	5	5	5	5	5	5	5	5	5	5	5	5	5	5	5	5	5	5	5	5	46	0	0
Halsall	10	10	10	10	10	10	10	10	10	8	8	8	8	8	8	8	8¹	8	8	8¹	8	8	8	8	8	8	8	8	8	8	8	8¹	8		8	8	8	8	8	8¹	8	8					45	0	4
Kelly	7	7	7												10	★	7¹		★		★						★¹	10	10	10		9	10	★	★	★	★	9									10	8	2
Kerr																		10	10	7	7	10	10	10	10¹	10																					10	0	0
Lawrence		★		★	★		7¹	7	7¹	7	7	9	9¹	9¹	9	9	9	9	★	9	9																										16	5	4
Luke	11	11	11	11	11	11	11	11	11	11	7	7	7²	7	7	7	11	11	11¹	11	11	11	11¹	11¹	11	11	11	11				11	11	11	11	11	11	11	11	11¹	11	11¹	11	11¹		43	0	8
Neenan	1	1	1	1	1	1	1			1	1	1	1	1	1	1	1	1	1	1	1	1	1	1	1	1	1	1					1	1	1	1	1	1	1	1	1	1	1	1	1	1	40	0	0
Nightingale		★		★			★		★		★		★	5	5	5		10	10	4	4	★	6	7	7	7	7	7	7	7	7	7	7	7	7	7	7	7	7	7	7	7	7	7	7	7	31	7	0
Nuttell													10											★			★		10	10	9	9	8			★	★	★									6	5	0
Paris	2	2	2	2	2	2	2	2	2	2¹	2	2	2	2	2	2	2	2	2	2¹	2	2	2	2	2	2	2	2	2	2	2	2	2	2	2	2	2	2	2	2	2	2	2	2	2	2	46	0	5
Phillips	8	8	8¹	8	8	8										★		★																		9	9	9	9¹	9	9³	9	9	9	9		16	2	5
Philpott																																			★												0	1	0
Pollard	5	5	5		5	5	5	5	5	5	5	5	5																																		12	0	0
Price	6	6	6	6	6	6	6	6	6	6	6	6	6	6	6	6	6	6	6	6	6		6	6	6	6	6	6	6	6	6		6	6	6	6	6	6	6	6	6	6	6	6	6		44	0	0
Riley	9	9¹	9	9	9	9¹	9	9	9	9	9	10	10																																		12	0	2
Shoemake													1																																		6	0	0
White																		9	9	10	10	9	9¹	9¹	9¹	9	9	9¹	9¹	9¹	9	9	9														14	0	4
Own Goals																			1																														1

FA Cup: 1987-88: 1st Round: Cardiff C. (H) 2-1; 2nd Round: Sutton U. (H) 1-3.

Littlewoods Cup: 1987-88: 1st Round: Chesterfield (A) 1-2 (H) 2-0; 2nd Round: Plymouth Arg. (H) 4-1 (A) 1-1; 3rd Round: Reading (H) 0-0 Replay (A) 0-1.

PLYMOUTH ARGYLE (Division 2)

Team Manager Dave Smith.
Club Address Home Park, Plymouth, Devon PL2 3DQ. Tel: (0752) 562561/2/3.
Current Ground Capacity 26,000.
Record Attendance 43,596 v Aston Villa, Div. 2, 10 October 1936.
Year Formed 1886. Turned professional 1903.
Previous Names Argyle Athletic Club.
Club Nickname "The Pilgrims".
Club Colours Green shirts with black trim, black shorts and white stockings.
Club Honours Football League: Div. 3(S) Champions 1929-30, 1951-52; Div. 3 Champions 1958-59.
League History 1920-30 Div. 3(S); 1930-50 Div. 2; 1950-52 Div. 3(S); 1952-56 Div. 2; 1956-58 Div. 3(S); 1958-59 Div. 3; 1959-68 Div. 2; 1968-75 Div. 3; 1975-77 Div. 2; 1977-86 Div. 3; 1986- Div. 2.
Most League Points in a Season (2 for a win) 68 in Div. 3(S), 1929-30. (3 for a win) 87 in Div. 3, 1985-86.
Most League Goals in a Season 107 in Div. 3(S), 1925-26 and 1951-52.

Record Victory 8-1 v Millwall in Div. 2, 16 January 1932.
Record Defeat 0-9 v Stoke C. in Div. 2, 17 December 1960.
Consecutive League Wins 9 in 1930 and 1986.
Consecutive League Defeats 9 in 1947.
Record League Appearances Sammy Black, 470 between 1924-38.
Record League Goalscorer—Career Sammy Black, 180 between 1924-38.
Record League Goalscorer—Season Jack Cock, 32 in Div. 3(S), 1925-26.

Plymouth Argyle: League Record, 1987-88 (Division 2)

Match Number	Date	Venue	Opponents	Result	H/T	Lge Posn	Attend
1	15.8.87	A	Manchester C.	L 1-2	1-0		20046
2	18.8.87	H	Ipswich T.	D 0-0	0-0		11901
3	22.8.87	H	Huddersfield T.	W 6-1	2-0	5	8811
4	29.8.87	A	Reading	W 1-0	1-0	1	6658
5	31.8.87	H	Sheffield U.	W 1-0	1-0	1	14504
6	5.9.87	A	Barnsley	L 1-2	0-2	2	6976
7	12.9.87	H	West Bromwich A.	D 3-3	0-1	5	10578
8	16.9.87	A	Bradford C.	L 1-3	0-1	7	11009
9	19.9.87	A	Leicester C.	L 0-4	0-3	12	8872
10	26.9.87	H	Birmingham C.	D 1-1	1-1	14	8912
11	29.9.87	H	Bournemouth	D 2-2	1-1	11	6491
12	3.10.87	H	Aston Villa	L 1-3	1-3	17	10515
13	10.10.87	A	Stoke C.	L 0-1	0-1	19	8275
14	17.10.87	H	Leeds U.	W 9-3	2-2	13	9358
15	20.10.87	H	Millwall	L 1-2	1-1	14	8958
16	24.10.87	A	Blackburn Rov.	D 1-1	0-0	17	6014
17	31.10.87	H	Hull C.	W 3-1	3-1	13	8550
18	3.11.87	A	Crystal Palace	L 1-5	0-1	17	7424
19	14.11.87	A	Swindon T.	D 1-1	1-1	16	9616
20	21.11.87	H	Middlesbrough	L 0-1	0-1	17	9428
21	28.11.87	A	Oldham Ath.	W 1-0	0-0	15	4516
22	5.12.87	H	Shrewsbury T.	W 2-0	0-0	14	7603
23	12.12.87	A	Huddersfield T.	L 1-2	0-1	15	5747
24	20.12.87	H	Bradford C.	W 2-1	2-0	14	11350
25	26.12.87	A	Birmingham C.	W 1-0	0-0	13	9166
26	28.12.87	H	Leicester C.	W 4-0	0-0	13	15581
27	1.1.88	H	Reading	L 1-3	0-0	13	13290
28	2.1.88	A	West Bromwich A.	L 0-1	0-1	13	8445
29	16.1.88	H	Manchester C.	W 3-2	0-2	13	13291
30	13.2.88	A	Ipswich T.	W 2-1	1-1	13	10476
31	27.2.88	A	Aston Villa	L 2-5	1-3	13	16142
32	5.3.88	A	Leeds U.	L 0-1	0-1	14	18115
33	12.3.88	H	Stoke C.	W 3-0	2-0	14	8749
34	19.3.88	A	Hull C.	D 1-1	1-0	14	5172
35	26.3.88	H	Blackburn Rov.	W 3-0	1-0	13	12359
36	4.4.88	H	Swindon T.	W 1-0	1-0	13	13299
37	9.4.88	A	Millwall	L 2-3	2-3	14	11052
38	15.4.88	H	Barnsley	D 0-0	0-0	14	8059
39	19.4.88	A	Sheffield U.	L 0-1	0-0	14	9052
40	23.4.88	H	Crystal Palace	L 1-3	1-0	15	8370
41	26.4.88	H	Bournemouth	L 1-2	0-1	15	6310
42	30.4.88	A	Middlesbrough	L 1-3	0-1	15	16615
43	2.5.88	H	Oldham Ath.	W 1-0	0-0	14	6084
44	7.5.88	A	Shrewsbury T.	L 1-2	0-1	16	4510

Players: League Record, 1987-88 (Division 2)

Match Number	Apps	Subs	Goals
Anderson	17	2	1
Brimacombe	42	0	1
Burrows	23	0	1
Cherry	37	0	0
Clayton	12	8	7
Cooper, L.	33	4	0
Cooper, S.	14	9	3
Coughlin	7	1	0
Crudgington	7	0	0
Evans	31	6	10
Furphy	6	0	1
Hodges	35	2	6
Law	25	1	3
McElhinney	6	0	0
Marker	26	0	1
Matthews	34	1	1
Morrison	0	1	0
Rowbotham, D.	5	4	0
Rowbotham, J.	3	1	0
Smith	41	0	6
Summerfield	32	5	5
Tynan	42	0	16
Uzzell	6	4	1
Own Goals			2

FA Cup: 1987-88: 3rd Round: Colchester U. (H) 2-0; 4th Round: Shrewsbury T. (H) 1-0; 5th Round: Manchester C. (A) 1-3.
Littlewoods Cup: 1987-88: 2nd Round: Peterborough U. (A) 1-4 (H) 1-1.

111

PORTSMOUTH (Division 2)

Team Manager Alan Ball.
Club Address Fratton Park, Frogmore Road, Portsmouth PO4 8RA. Tel: (0705) 731204.
Current Ground Capacity 36,000.
Record Attendance 51,385 v Derby Co., FA Cup 6th Round, 26 February 1949.
Year Formed 1898. Turned professional 1898.
Previous Names None.
Club Nickname "Pompey".
Club Colours Royal blue shirts with white collar and cuffs, white shorts and red stockings.
Club Honours Football League: Div. 1 Champions 1948-49, 1949-50; Div. 3(S) Champions 1923-24; Div. 3 Champions 1961-62, 1982-83. FA Cup: Winners 1939.
League History 1920-24 Div. 3(S); 1924-27 Div. 2; 1927-59 Div. 1; 1959-61 Div. 2; 1961-62 Div. 3; 1962-76 Div. 2; 1976-78 Div. 3; 1978-80 Div. 4; 1980-83 Div. 3; 1983-87 Div. 2; 1987-88 Div. 1; 1988- Div. 2.
Most League Points in a Season (2 for a win) 65 in Div. 3, 1961-62. (3 for a win) 91 in Div. 3, 1982-83.

Most League Goals in a Season 91 in Div. 4, 1979-80.
Record Victory 9-1 v Notts. Co. in Div. 2, 9 April 1927.
Record Defeat 0-10 v Leicester C. in Div. 1, 20 October 1928.
Consecutive League Wins 7 in 1980 and 1983.
Consecutive League Defeats 9 in 1959-60, 1960, 1963 and 1975.
Record League Appearances Jimmy Dickinson, 764 between 1946-65.
Record League Goalscorer—Career Peter Harris, 194 between 1946-60.
Record League Goalscorer—Season Billy Haines, 40 in Div. 2, 1926-27.

Portsmouth: League Record, 1987-88 (Division 1)

Match Number	Date	Venue	Opponents	Result	H/T	Lge Posn	Attend
1	15.8.87	A	Oxford U.	L 2-4	0-1		9174
2	18.8.87	H	Chelsea	L 0-3	0-1		16917
3	22.8.87	H	Southampton	D 2-2	1-1	20	20161
4	29.8.87	A	Arsenal	L 0-6	0-4	20	30865
5	31.8.87	H	West Ham U.	W 2-1	1-1	16	16104
6	5.9.87	A	Derby Co.	D 0-0	0-0	17	15071
7	12.9.87	H	Charlton Ath.	D 1-1	0-1	17	13136
8	19.9.87	A	Watford	D 0-0	0-0	17	13277
9	26.9.87	H	Wimbledon	W 2-1	1-1	12	13088
10	3.10.87	A	Liverpool	L 0-4	0-1	13	43665
11	10.10.87	H	Luton T.	W 3-1	0-0	12	12391
12	24.10.87	A	Q.P.R.	L 1-2	0-1	14	13171
13	31.10.87	H	Sheffield Wed.	L 1-2	1-1	16	13582
14	4.11.87	H	Tottenham H.	D 0-0	0-0	17	15302
15	14.11.87	A	Nottingham F.	L 0-5	0-3	18	15851
16	21.11.87	H	Everton	L 0-1	0-1	18	17724
17	28.11.87	A	Norwich C.	W 1-0	1-0	18	13099
18	5.12.87	H	Coventry C.	D 0-0	0-0	18	13002
19	12.12.87	A	Newcastle U.	D 1-1	1-0	18	20455
20	19.12.87	H	Manchester U.	L 1-2	0-1	18	22207
21	26.12.87	A	Charlton Ath.	L 1-2	1-1	18	6686
22	28.12.87	H	Watford	D 1-1	0-0	19	15003
23	1.1.88	H	Arsenal	D 1-1	1-0	19	17366
24	3.1.88	A	Southampton	W 2-0	2-0	18	17002
25	16.1.88	H	Oxford U.	D 2-2	0-1	16	13417
26	23.1.88	A	Chelsea	D 0-0	0-0	15	15856
27	6.2.88	H	Derby Co.	W 2-1	1-0	15	14790
28	13.2.88	A	West Ham U.	D 1-1	0-0	15	18639
29	27.2.88	H	Liverpool	L 0-2	0-1	17	28197
30	19.3.88	A	Sheffield Wed.	L 0-1	0-1	19	13731
31	26.3.88	H	Q.P.R.	L 0-1	0-1	19	13041
32	29.3.88	A	Luton T.	L 1-4	0-1	19	6740
33	2.4.88	A	Tottenham H.	W 1-0	1-0	18	18616
34	4.4.88	H	Nottingham F.	L 0-1	0-0	19	17528
35	9.4.88	A	Everton	L 1-2	1-1	19	21292
36	19.4.88	A	Wimbledon	D 2-2	0-1	19	9009
37	23.4.88	H	Norwich C.	D 2-2	0-1	19	12762
38	30.4.88	A	Coventry C.	L 0-1	0-1	19	14296
39	2.5.88	H	Newcastle U.	L 1-2	0-1	19	12496
40	7.5.88	A	Manchester U.	L 1-4	0-3	19	35105

Players: League Record, 1987-88 (Division 1)

Match Number	1	2	3	4	5	6	7	8	9	10	11	12	13	14	15	16	17	18	19	20	21	22	23	24	25	26	27	28	29	30	31	32	33	34	35	36	37	38	39	40	Apps	Subs	Goals
Baird			9	9	9	9	9	**9**		9	9¹	9	9	9	9	9	9	9	**9**	9	**9**				9		9														20	0	1
Ball					★		★		6		6	6	6	5	5	5	5	5	5	6	6	6	6¹	6	6	6	6	6			6	6	6	6	6	6				27	2	1
Blake																	5	5	5		5	5	5	5	5	5	5	5	5	5	5	**5**	5	5	5	5	5			19	0	0
Connor											10	10	10			8	8	10	4	4¹	10¹	10¹			10	10¹	10	10	**10**			10	10				10	10		19	0	4
Darby																					8																				1	0	0
Dillon	4		★		4²	4	4	4		★	4²	4	4¹	4		4	4		4	4¹			4	4	4	4	**4**	**4**	4	4¹	4	4	4¹	★¹	4	4	4			29	3	9
Fillery	11	11	7	7	7	7		4	4		8				4			★			10	8	8		8	**8**	8	8												17	1	0
Gilbert	6	6	6	6	6	6	**6**	6	6	**6**				★		★	3				★	2	2	2	6	6		★	4											17	4	0
Gosney																																	1	1	1	1				4	0	0
Hardyman	3	3	3						3	3	3	3	3	3	3	3	3	3¹	3	**3**		3	3				3	★	3										3	19	1	1
Hilaire			11¹	11	11	11	11	11	11	11	11	11	11	11	11	11	11	11	11	11	11	11	11	11	11¹	11	11	11	11	11	11	11	11	11	11	11	11	11	**11**	38	0	2
Horne	★	★		★	3	3	7	7	7	7	7	7	7	7	7	7	7	7¹	7	7	7	7	7	7	7	7	7	7	7	7¹	7	7	7	7	7	7	7	7	8	36	3	3
Kelly																												★		★									7	1	2	0
Kennedy	8	8	8	8	8	8	8		8		8	8		8	8	8	8		8	8		8	8		8															18	0	0
Kerr	9	9					★																			★														2	2	0
Knight	1	1	1	1	1	1	1	1	1	1	1	1	1	1	1	1	1	1	1	1	1	1	1	1	1	1	1	1	1	1	1	1	1	1	**1**	1	1	1	1	36	0	0
Mariner	5¹	5	5	10	10	10	**10**		9	9	★¹	★	★		5					★	★				★		9	9	9		★		9¹	9¹	9					16	7	4
Perry																				★					10					★		★							1	3	0
Quinn	10	10	10			★¹	10	10¹	10	10	10			★	10	10	10	**10**	★		10¹	10	9	9	9¹	10	9¹		9	9		10	9	9	10	10¹	**10**	9¹	9¹	29	3	8
Sandford			7	★	3			3	3	3¹	3														3	**8**	3	★	3	3	3	3	3	3	3	3	4			19	2	1
Shotton				5	5	5	5	5	5	5	5	5	5																											10	0	0
Stewart	★																																							0	1	0
Swain	2	2	2	2	2	2	2	2	2	2	2	2	2	2	2	2	2	2	2	2		3	3				2	2	2	2	2	2	2	2						32	0	0
Whitehead	7¹	4	4¹	4			★	8	★	8		6	★	5	4	6	6	6	6	6	8	2	2	2	2	2				8	8	8	8	8	8	8	2			30	3	2

FA Cup: 1987-88: 3rd Round: Blackburn Rov. (A) 2-1; 4th Round: Sheffield U. (H) 2-1; 5th Round: Bradford C. (H) 3-0; 6th Round: Luton T. (A) 1-3.
Littlewoods Cup: 1987-88: 2nd Round: Swindon T. (A) 1-3 (H) 1-3.

PORT VALE (Division 3)

Team Manager   John Rudge.
Club Address   Vale Park, Burslem, Stoke on Trent. Tel: (0782) 814134.
Current Ground Capacity   16,800.
Record Attendance   50,000 v Aston Villa, FA Cup 5th Round, 20 February 1960.
Year Formed   1876. Turned professional 1885.
Previous Names   Burslem Port Vale.
Club Nickname   "The Valiants".
Club Colours   White shirts with black trim, black shorts and white stockings.
Club Honours   Football League: Div 3(N) Champions 1929-30, 1953-54; Div. 4 Champions 1958-59.
League History   1892-96 Div. 2; 1896 Failed re-election; 1898-1907 Div. 2; 1907 Resigned; 1919-29 Div. 2; 1929-30 Div. 3(N); 1930-36 Div. 2; 1936-38 Div. 3(N); 1938-52 Div. 3(S); 1952-54 Div. 3(N); 1954-57 Div. 2; 1957-58 Div. 3(S); 1958-59 Div. 4; 1959-65 Div. 3; 1965-70 Div. 4; 1970-78 Div. 3; 1978-83 Div. 4; 1983-84 Div. 3; 1984-86 Div. 4; 1986- Div. 3.

Most League Points in a Season   (2 for a win) 69 in Div. 3(N), 1953-54. (3 for a win) 88 in Div. 4, 1982-83.
Most League Goals in a Season   110 in Div. 4, 1958-59.
Record Victory   9-1 v Chesterfield in Div. 2, 24 September 1932.
Record Defeat   0-10 v Sheffield U. in Div. 2, 10 December 1892 and v Notts. Co. Div. 2, 26 February 1895.
Consecutive League Wins   8 in 1893.
Consecutive League Defeats   9 in 1957.
Record League Appearances   Roy Sproson, 761 between 1950-72.
Record League Goalscorer—Career   Wilf Kirkham, 154 between 1923-33.
Record League Goalscorer—Season   Wilf Kirkham, 38 in Div. 2, 1926-27.

Port Vale: League Record, 1987-88 (Division 3)

Match Number	Date	Venue	Opponents	Result		H/T	Lge Posn	Attend
1	15.8.87	H	Aldershot	W	4-2	1-1		3160
2	29.8.87	H	Rotherham U.	D	0-0	0-0		2895
3	31.8.87	A	Bristol C.	L	0-1	0-0	15	8716
4	5.9.87	H	York C.	W	2-1	0-0	13	2711
5	12.9.87	A	Chesterfield	W	3-1	1-1	9	2406
6	14.9.87	H	Southend U.	W	4-1	1-0	1	3670
7	19.9.87	H	Fulham	D	1-1	0-1	7	3894
8	26.9.87	A	Northampton T.	L	0-1	0-0	11	5072
9	28.9.87	H	Brighton & H.A.	W	2-0	0-0	2	3789
10	3.10.87	A	Brentford	L	0-1	0-0	10	4013
11	10.10.87	A	Preston N.E.	L	2-3	1-0	12	6274
12	17.10.87	H	Bury	W	1-0	1-0	9	3235
13	19.10.87	H	Bristol Rov.	W	2-1	1-1	6	3598
14	24.10.87	A	Walsall	L	1-2	1-1	9	6083
15	31.10.87	H	Gillingham	D	0-0	0-0	9	3495
16	4.11.87	A	Chester C.	L	0-1	0-0	13	2789
17	7.11.87	A	Doncaster Rov.	D	1-1	0-1	13	1365
18	22.11.87	H	Blackpool	D	0-0	0-0	13	3594
19	28.11.87	A	Sunderland	L	1-2	0-2	14	15655
20	12.12.87	H	Notts Co.	L	1-3	0-0	16	3358
21	20.12.87	A	Mansfield T.	L	0-4	0-2	17	3173
22	26.12.87	H	Northampton T.	D	1-1	1-0	17	4446
23	28.12.87	A	Grimsby T.	L	1-3	1-1	19	2941
24	1.1.88	A	Rotherham U.	L	0-1	0-0	19	3913
25	2.1.88	H	Chesterfield	L	0-1	0-0	20	3495
26	16.1.88	A	Fulham	W	2-1	0-1	19	3748
27	22.1.88	A	Southend U.	D	3-3	1-2	18	3038
28	6.2.88	A	York C.	W	3-2	1-2	19	2420
29	13.2.88	H	Grimsby T.	W	2-0	0-0	16	3417
30	27.2.88	H	Brentford	W	1-0	0-0	16	3876
31	2.3.88	A	Brighton & H.A.	L	0-2	0-0	17	7296
32	5.3.88	A	Bury	W	1-0	0-0	15	2635
33	12.3.88	H	Preston N.E.	W	3-2	1-1	14	4647
34	19.3.88	A	Gillingham	D	0-0	0-0	13	3459
35	26.3.88	H	Walsall	W	2-1	1-0	13	6347
36	2.4.88	H	Doncaster Rov.	W	5-0	2-0	12	3680
37	4.4.88	A	Blackpool	W	2-1	2-0	10	5516
38	9.4.88	H	Chester C.	D	1-1	1-1	10	4278
39	12.4.88	A	Wigan Ath.	L	0-2	0-1	10	3750
40	15.4.88	A	Aldershot	L	0-3	0-2	11	2257
41	18.4.88	H	Bristol C.	D	1-1	0-0	11	2671
42	23.4.88	A	Bristol Rov.	L	0-1	0-0	13	3780
43	25.4.88	H	Wigan Ath.	W	2-1	1-1	11	3044
44	30.4.88	H	Sunderland	L	0-1	0-0	12	7569
45	2.5.88	A	Notts Co.	W	2-1	1-0	11	7702
46	7.5.88	H	Mansfield T.	D	1-1	0-0	11	3617

Players: League Record, 1987-88 (Division 3)

Match Number	1	2	3	4	5	6	7	8	9	10	11	12	13	14	15	16	17	18	19	20	21	22	23	24	25	26	27	28	29	30	31	32	33	34	35	36	37	38	39	40	41	42	43	44	45	46	Apps	Subs	Goals
Banks	2		4	10								11			★			★	★	6	★			2	5	5		★																			8	5	0
Barnes																			7			11	11																								3	0	0
Beckford	10	10	10		★	★	10	10	10¹	10	10	10¹	10		10	10	10	★	★	8	8	8	8	8	8	10¹	10	10¹	10	10	10	10³	10¹	10		10	10	10	10	10¹	10						36	4	9
Cole																								11	11	11¹	11																				4	0	1
Davies																											★	★	★	★		★	11														1	5	0
Earle	8	8	8		8¹	8	8																	8	8²	8	8	8	8	8	8	8	8	8	8	8	8	8	8	8	8	8¹	8				25	0	4
Finney		★									★		8	8	8	8	8	8	8	8				8		★				10	★									4							11	4	0
Ford																								7	7	7	7¹	7	7	7	7	7	7	7	7	7¹	7	7	7	7	7¹	7	7				23	0	3
Grew			1	1	1	1	1	1	1	1	1	1	1	1	1		1	1	1	1	1	1	1	1	1	1	1	1	1	1	1	1	1	1	1	1	1	1	1	1	1	1	1	1	1	1	41	0	0
Hamson			11					11		★	★			7	11		11	11	11	11	11¹	11¹																									9	2	2
Harper	11	11	★	11¹	11	11¹	11	★	11	11	11	11		11	11	★	11		★		7	7	★																								16	5	2
Hazell		5	5	5	5	5	5	5	5	5	5	5	5	5	5	5	5	5	5	5	5	5	5		5	5	5	5	5	5	5	5	5	5	5	5	5	5	5	5	5	5	5	5	5	5	43	0	0
Holdsworth																															11	11¹	11	11	11	11¹	11										6	0	2
Hughes			3	3	3	3	3	3	3¹	3	3	3	3	3	3	3	3	3	3	3	3	3	3	3	3	3	3	3	3	3	3	3	3	3	3	3	3	3	3	3	3	3	3	3	3	3	43	0	1
Jones	9⁴	9	9	9¹	9¹	9																																									6	0	6
Maguire	★	7	7	7	7²	7¹	7	7	7	7	7	7	7¹	7	7	★	7	7	7	7	★	★	★		★		★		11	11									★		★		★				19	9	4
Mills																								10	10	10	10	6¹	8¹	10¹	10	4	4	11	11					10	11¹	11	11	11	11	11¹	19	0	5
O'Kelly				8	10¹	10	9	9	9	9	9	9		10	★		★	10	10	10	10																										14	2	1
Pearson	3	3	3																																												3	0	0
Porter								8	8	8	8												★				★																				4	2	0
Riley												9¹	9¹	9	9	9	9	9	9¹	9¹	9	9	9	9	9	9¹	9¹	9	9	9	9	9	9	9	9	9¹	9¹	9	9	9	9	9	9	9	9	9	34	0	8
Simons													1																																		1	0	0
Smith	7	7																																													2	0	0
Sproson	6	6	6	6	6	6	6	6	6	6	6	6	6	6	6¹	6	6	6		6	6	6		6	6¹	6	6	6	6¹	6	6	6	6	6	6	6	6	6	6	6	6	6	6	6	6	6	44	0	3
Steggles																		2	2	2	2	2		2	2	2	2	2	2	2	2	2	2	2	2	2											20	0	0
Walker	4	4			4	4	4¹	4	4	4	4	4²	4	4	4	4	4	4	4	4	4	4	4	4	4		4	4¹	4	4	4¹	4	4	4	4	4¹	4	4	4	4¹	4	4					42	0	6
Webb	5	2	2	2	2	2	2	2	2	2	2	2	2	2	2	2	2	2	2											★					2	2	2	2	2	2							25	1	0
Williams	1	1	1	1																																											4	0	0
Own Goals																														1																			1

FA Cup: 1987-88: 1st Round: Tranmere Rov. (A) 2-2 Replay (H) 3-1; 2nd Round: Notts. Co. (H) 2-0; 3rd Round: Macclesfield (H) 1-0; 4th Round: Tottenham H. (H) 2-1; 5th Round: Watford (H) 0-0 Replay (A) 0-2.

Littlewoods Cup: 1987-88: 1st Round: Northampton T. (H) 0-1 (A) 0-4.

PRESTON NORTH END (Division 3)

Team Manager John McGrath.
Club Address Deepdale, Preston, PR1 6RU. Tel: (0772) 795919.
Current Ground Capacity 19,500.
Record Attendance 42,684 v Arsenal, Div. 1, 23 April 1938.
Year Formed 1881. Turned professional 1885.
Previous Names None.
Club Nickname "The Lilywhites" or "North End".
Club Colours White shirts with Navy blue collars and cuffs, navy blue shorts with white trim and white stockings with navy blue rings.
Club Honours Football League: Div. 1 Champions 1888-89, 1889-90; Div. 2 Champions 1903-04, 1912-13, 1950-51; Div. 3 Champions 1970-71. FA Cup: Winners 1889, 1938.
League History 1888-1901 Div. 1; 1901-04 Div. 2; 1904-12 Div. 1; 1912-13 Div. 2; 1913-14 Div. 1; 1914-15 Div. 2; 1919-25 Div. 1; 1925-34 Div. 2; 1934-49 Div. 1; 1949-51 Div. 2; 1951-61 Div. 1; 1961-70 Div. 2; 1970-71 Div. 3; 1971-74 Div. 2; 1974-78 Div. 3; 1978-81 Div. 2; 1981-85 Div. 3; 1985-87 Div. 4; 1987- Div. 3.

Most League Points in a Season (2 for a win) 61 in Div. 3, 1970-71. (3 for a win) 90 in Div. 4, 1986-87.
Most League Goals in a Season 100 in Div. 2, 1927-28 and Div. 1, 1957-58.
Record Victory 26-0 v Hyde in FA Cup 1st Series, 1st Round, 15 October 1887.
Record Defeat 0-7 v Blackpool in Div. 1, 1 May 1948.
Consecutive League Wins 14 in 1950-51.
Consecutive League Defeats 8 in 1983.
Record League Appearances Alan Kelly, 447 between 1961-74.
Record League Goalscorer—Career Tom Finney, 187 between 1946-60.
Record League Goalscorer—Season Ted Harper, 37 in Div. 2, 1932-33.

Preston North End: League Record, 1987-88 (Division 3)

Match Number	Date	Venue	Opponents	Result		H/T	Lge Posn	Attend
1	15.8.87	H	Chesterfield	L	0-1	0-0		6509
2	22.8.87	A	Bristol C.	L	1-3	0-1		7655
3	29.8.87	H	Wigan Ath.	L	0-1	0-0	24	7057
4	1.9.87	A	Southend U.	W	2-1	1-0	21	2600
5	5.9.87	H	Grimsby T.	L	1-3	0-2	20	5522
6	12.9.87	H	York C.	D	1-1	0-0	20	3237
7	15.9.87	H	Northampton T.	D	0-0	0-0	21	5179
8	19.9.87	H	Rotherham U.	D	0-0	0-0	21	5124
9	26.9.87	A	Blackpool	L	0-3	0-2	22	8406
10	29.9.87	H	Brentford	L	1-2	1-0	22	4241
11	3.10.87	A	Walsall	L	0-1	0-1	23	5467
12	10.10.87	H	Port Vale	W	3-2	0-1	22	6274
13	17.10.87	A	Brighton & H.A.	D	0-0	0-0	22	6043
14	20.10.87	H	Gillingham	D	1-1	1-1	22	5676
15	24.10.87	A	Bury	L	0-4	0-1	21	4316
16	31.10.87	H	Chester C.	D	1-1	1-0	21	5657
17	4.11.87	A	Bristol Rov.	W	2-1	1-0	21	2804
18	7.11.87	A	Mansfield T.	D	0-0	0-0	21	3631
19	21.11.87	H	Doncaster Rov.	L	1-2	0-2	21	5178
20	28.11.87	A	Fulham	W	1-0	1-0	21	5324
21	12.12.87	H	Aldershot	L	0-2	0-2	21	4519
22	19.12.87	A	Notts Co.	L	2-4	1-2	21	5730
23	26.12.87	H	Blackpool	W	2-1	0-1	20	11155
24	28.12.87	A	Sunderland	D	1-1	0-0	20	24814
25	1.1.88	A	Wigan Ath.	L	0-2	0-2	21	6872
26	2.1.88	H	York C.	W	3-0	2-0	20	6302
27	9.1.88	H	Bristol C.	W	2-0	1-0	19	5729
28	16.1.88	A	Rotherham U.	D	2-2	2-1	20	4011
29	27.1.88	A	Northampton T.	W	1-0	1-0	16	5052
30	30.1.88	H	Southend U.	D	1-1	1-1	16	6180
31	6.2.88	A	Grimsby T.	W	1-0	1-0	13	2907
32	13.2.88	H	Sunderland	D	2-2	2-2	15	10852
33	20.2.88	A	Chesterfield	D	0-0	0-0	15	2864
34	27.2.88	H	Walsall	W	1-0	1-0	13	6479
35	1.3.88	A	Brentford	L	0-2	0-1	14	3505
36	5.3.88	H	Brighton & H.A.	W	3-0	3-0	13	5834
37	12.3.88	A	Port Vale	L	2-3	1-1	15	4647
38	19.3.88	A	Chester C.	L	0-1	0-1	16	3724
39	26.3.88	H	Bury	W	1-0	1-0	15	6456
40	2.4.88	H	Mansfield T.	W	1-0	0-0	14	6254
41	4.4.88	A	Doncaster Rov.	L	2-3	1-0	14	2167
42	8.4.88	H	Bristol Rov.	W	3-1	2-1	13	5386
43	23.4.88	A	Gillingham	L	0-4	0-1	14	2721
44	30.4.88	H	Fulham	W	2-1	1-0	14	4192
45	2.5.88	A	Aldershot	D	0-0	0-0	15	3465
46	7.5.88	H	Notts. Co.	L	1-2	0-0	16	5822

Players: League Record, 1987-88 (Division 3)

Match Number	1	2	3	4	5	6	7	8	9	10	11	12	13	14	15	16	17	18	19	20	21	22	23	24	25	26	27	28	29	30	31	32	33	34	35	36	37	38	39	40	41	42	43	44	45	46	Apps	Subs	Goals
Allardyce	6	6	6	6	6	6	6	6	6	6	6	6	6	6	6	6	6	6	6	6	6	6	6	6	6	6	6	6	6							6	6	★	6	6		6	6				38	1	0
Atkins	4	4	4¹	4	4	4	4	4	4	4	4	4	4	4	4	4	4	4	4	4	4	4	4	4	4	4	4	4	4	4	4	4		4		4	4	4	4	4	4	4	4	4			45	1	0
Bennett		3	3	3	3		3	3	3	3	3	3	3	3	3	3	3	3	3	3	3	3	3	3	3	3	3	3	3	3	3	3	3	3													34	0	1
Branagan	2	2			11																																										3	0	0
Brazil	10	10¹	10	10	10	10¹		10				10²	10					10	10	10	10	10	10¹	10	10	10¹	10¹	10²	10	10	10¹	10	10	10¹	10	10	10	10	10	10	10¹	10	10¹	10			36	0	14
Brown		1	1	1	1						1	1	1											1	1		1	1	1	1	1	1	1	1	1	1	1	1	1	1	1	1	1	1	1	1	27	0	0
Chapman	5		5	5	5				★	7													★	5	5	5				6	6	6	6		4			3		6							15	2	0
Ellis									9¹	9	9	9	9	9¹	9		★			9	9	9		9	9				★		★			9	9	9	9	9¹	9	9	★		9¹				20	4	4
Hildersley	11		11	11	11	★	11	11	11	11			11	11	11	11	11	11		★	11	11															11	11	11	11¹	11	★	★				21	4	1
Hughes																																														6	1	0
Jeffels												11																																			1	0	0
Jemson			9	9	9	★	9		10	10	10		★			10	10¹	10	9	9¹	9	9¹			★	9				9¹	9	9	9	9	9	★	9	9¹	9								24	3	5
Jones		5										5	5	5	5	5	5	5	5	5	5	5	5	5¹	5										5	5	5	5	5¹	5		5					22	0	2
Joyce								7	8	8									11	11			11	11	11	11	11	11	11	11	11	11	11	11							★		3	11	11	11	21	1	0
Kelly	1				1	1	1	1	1			1	1	1	1	1	1	1	1	1	1	1	1			1																					19	0	0
Lowey	9	9								9¹	9																																				4	0	1
Miller	7	7	2	2	2		2	7	7	7					2	★¹		★			2	2¹	★										★	★	2	2	2	2	2	2			2	2	2	23	5	2
Mooney										8	8	10	10	7			7	7	7	7	7	7	7¹	7	7	7¹	7	7	7¹	7	7	7	7	7	7		7	7	7	7			7	7			34	0	3
Rathbone	3	11			3	2	2	2	2	2	2	2	2		2	2	2	2	2		2¹	2	2	2	2	2	2	2						3	3			3	3	3	3						36	0	3
Swann	8	8	8	8	8¹	8	8	8	8	8	8	★	11	11	11	8¹	8	8	8	8	8	8¹	8¹	8	8	8	8	8	8	8	8¹	8	8	8	8	8²	8¹	8	8	8¹	8²	8¹	8	8	8	8	45	0	12
Wilkes									★																																				1	1	0
Williams			7	7¹	7	7										7¹																							2								1	2	0
Worthington	★	★	★		★	9	10	9	9	★	★	★			★																							11			★	7	9	10			9	1	2
Wrightson		★		5	5	5	5	5	5	11	★		7																	5	5	5	5	5		3	3	6	6	5	5			5	5	5	23	2	0

FA Cup: 1987-88: 1st Round: Mansfield T. (H) 1-1 Replay (A) 2-4.
Littlewoods Cup: 1987-88: 1st Round: Bury (A) 2-2 (H) 2-3.

QUEENS PARK RANGERS (Division 1)

Team Manager Jim Smith.
Club Address South Africa Road, London W12 7PA. Tel: 01-743 0262/3/4/5.
Current Ground Capacity 27,500.
Record Attendance 35,353 v Leeds U., Div. 1, 27 April 1974.
Year Formed 1885. Turned professional 1898.
Previous Names St Jude's.
Club Nickname "Rangers" or "The R's".
Club Colours Blue and white hooped shirts, white shorts and white stockings with three blue bands at top.
Club Honours Football League: Div. 2 Champions 1982-83; Div 3(S) Champions 1947-48; Div. 3 Champions 1966-67. Football League Cup: Winners 1967.
League History 1920-48 Div. 3(S); 1948-52 Div. 2; 1952-58 Div. 3(S); 1958-67 Div. 3; 1967-68 Div. 2; 1968-69 Div. 1; 1969-73 Div. 2; 1973-79 Div. 1; 1979-83 Div. 2; 1983- Div. 1.
Most League Points in a Season (2 for a win) 67 in Div. 3, 1966-67. (3 for a win) 85 in Div. 2, 1982-83.
Most League Goals in a Season 111 in Div. 3, 1961-62.

Record Victory 9-2 v Tranmere Rov. in Div. 3, 3 December 1960.
Record Defeat 1-8 v Mansfield T. in Div. 3, 15 March 1965 and v Manchester U. in Div. 1, 19 March 1969.
Consecutive League Wins 8 in 1931.
Consecutive League Defeats 9 in 1969.
Record League Appearances Tony Ingham, 514 between 1950-63.
Record League Goalscorer—Career George Goddard, 172 between 1926-34.
Record League Goalscorer—Season George Goddard, 37 in Div. 3(S), 1929-30.

Queens Park Rangers: League Record, 1987-88 (Division 1)

Match Number	Date	Venue	Opponents	Result		H/T	Lge Posn	Attend
1	15.8.87	A	West Ham U.	W	3-0	3-0		22881
2	19.8.87	H	Derby Co.	D	1-1	1-1		11651
3	22.8.87	H	Arsenal	W	2-0	1-0	1	18981
4	29.8.87	A	Southampton	W	1-0	0-0	1	15532
5	2.9.87	A	Everton	W	1-0	1-0	1	15380
6	5.9.87	A	Charlton Ath.	W	1-0	1-0	1	7726
7	12.9.87	H	Chelsea	W	3-1	0-0	1	22583
8	19.9.87	A	Oxford U.	L	0-2	0-2	1	9800
9	26.9.87	H	Luton T.	W	2-0	0-0	1	11175
10	3.10.87	A	Wimbledon	W	2-1	0-0	1	8552
11	17.10.87	A	Liverpool	L	0-4	0-1	2	43735
12	24.10.87	H	Portsmouth	W	2-1	1-0	2	13171
13	31.10.87	A	Norwich C.	D	1-1	0-0	2	14522
14	7.11.87	H	Watford	D	0-0	0-0	3	12101
15	14.11.87	A	Tottenham H.	D	1-1	1-1	3	28113
16	21.11.87	H	Newcastle U.	D	1-1	1-0	3	11794
17	28.11.87	A	Sheffield Wed.	L	1-3	0-2	3	16933
18	5.12.87	H	Manchester U.	L	0-2	0-1	5	20632
19	13.12.87	A	Nottingham F.	L	0-4	0-1	6	18130
20	18.12.87	H	Coventry C.	L	1-2	1-0	6	7299
21	26.12.87	A	Chelsea	D	1-1	0-0	6	18020
22	28.12.87	H	Oxford U.	W	3-2	2-0	6	9125
23	1.1.88	H	Southampton	W	3-0	0-0	5	8631
24	2.1.88	A	Arsenal	D	0-0	0-0	7	28271
25	16.1.88	H	West Ham U.	L	0-1	0-0	7	14909
26	6.2.88	H	Charlton Ath.	W	2-0	1-0	5	11512
27	13.2.88	A	Everton	L	0-2	0-1	6	24724
28	27.2.88	H	Wimbledon	W	1-0	0-0	6	9080
29	5.3.88	H	Liverpool	L	0-1	0-1	6	23171
30	16.3.88	H	Nottingham F.	W	2-1	1-0	6	8316
31	19.3.88	H	Norwich C.	W	3-0	1-0	4	9033
32	26.3.88	A	Portsmouth	W	1-0	1-0	4	13041
33	1.4.88	A	Watford	W	1-0	0-0	5	16083
34	4.4.88	H	Tottenham H.	W	2-0	0-0	5	14783
35	9.4.88	A	Newcastle U.	D	1-1	1-1	5	18403
36	13.4.88	H	Derby Co.	W	2-0	1-0	3	14214
37	19.4.88	A	Luton T.	L	1-2	0-1	4	6735
38	23.4.88	H	Sheffield Wed.	D	1-1	0-1	4	12531
39	30.4.88	A	Manchester U.	L	1-2	0-1	4	35733
40	7.5.88	A	Coventry C.	D	0-0	0-0	5	16089

Players: League Record, 1987-88 (Division 1)

Match Number	1	2	3	4	5	6	7	8	9	10	11	12	13	14	15	16	17	18	19	20	21	22	23	24	25	26	27	28	29	30	31	32	33	34	35	36	37	38	39	40	Apps	Subs	Goals
Allen	7	7	7	7¹	7	7	7	7	7	7	7	7	7¹	7	7	7	7	7	7	7	7	7¹	7	7	7	7	7		7	7	7	7	7	7¹	7	7	7				38	0	4
Bannister	10¹	10¹	9	9	9	9	9³	9	9	9¹	9	9			9	9¹	9	9	9	9	9	9¹	9	9	9																24	0	8
Brock	11¹	11	11	11¹	11	11	11	11	11	11	11		11	11	11	11	11	11	11	11	11	11	11	11	11	11	11														26	0	2
Byrne	8	8	10¹	10	10	10	10	10	10	10	10	10¹	10	10	10	10	★	10	10	10			★	★¹		9¹	8	★													22	5	4
Channing											11	9	9	★	10						★				11¹	11	★	★			6			★	★					7	7	1
Coney	9	9	8	8	8	8	8¹	8	8	8¹	8	8	8	8	8¹	8	★	8	★		★		★	9¹	9¹	9¹	9	★	★		★	9¹	9	9							25	7	7
Dawes			3	3	3	3	3	3	3	3	3	3		3	3		3	3		3	2	2	2	2	2	3	2	3	3	3	3	3	3	3	3	3					33	0	0
Dennis	3	3	3										3	3		3	3		3	3	3		★																		10	1	0
Falco													8	★	8¹	8	8²	8¹	8	8	8¹		8	8		★		9	9	9	9	★	6	★						15	4	5
Fenwick	6	6	6	6	6	6	6	6¹	6¹	6	6¹	6	6	6	6	6	6	6	6																						22	0	3
Ferdinand																		8																							1	0	0
Fereday	2	2	2	2	2	2	2²	2		★	9	★	2	2	2²	2	2		★	★¹	10	10	10	10	10	10¹	10¹	10	10	10	10	10¹	10	10	10¹	10					33	4	4
Fleming																								★	★																0	2	0
Francis																										★	11	11	11	11	11	11	11	11							8	1	0
Johns													1	1	1	1	1	1	1																						7	0	0
Kerslake													10¹	10	10		★	★			11	11	7	8	8	8	8²	8¹	8	8¹	8	8	8								16	2	5
Law																															★										0	1	0
McDonald	5	5	5¹	5	5	5	5	5	5	5		5	5	5		5	5	5	5	5	5	5	5		5	5	5	5	5¹	5	5	5	5	5¹	5						36	0	3
Maddix														★					5	★		5	7	11	6	6		★	★		6										6	3	0
Maguire						★	★		★					5	★		★			6	6	6	6	6	6	6		6	6	6	6										13	5	0
Neill					★	★	2	2	2	2								2	2				★	3	3	2	2	2	2	2	2	2	2	2							20	3	0
O'Neill											5					5																									2	0	0
Parker	4	4	4	4	4	4	4	4	4	4	4	4	4	4	4	4	4	4	4	4	4	4	4	4	4	4	4	4	4	4	4	4	4	4	4	4	4				40	0	0
Peacock		★		★		★									★	★																									0	5	0
Pizanti														★		★					3	3									★		★	6							3	1	0
Roberts																			1																						1	0	0
Seaman	1	1	1	1	1	1	1	1	1	1	1	1			1	1	1	1	1	1			1	1	1	1	1	1	1	1	1	1	1	1	1						32	0	0
Own Goals		1												1																													2

FA Cup: 1987-88: 3rd Round: Yeovil T. (A) 3-0; 4th Round: West Ham U. (H) 3-1; 5th Round: Luton T. (H) 1-1 Replay (A) 0-1.
Littlewoods Cup: 1987-88: 2nd Round: Millwall (H) 2-1 (A) 0-0; 3rd Round: Bury (A) 0-1.

READING (Division 3)

Team Manager   Ian Branfoot.
Club Address   Elm Park, Norfolk Road, Reading. Tel: (0734) 507878/9/0.
Current Ground Capacity   17,500.
Record Attendance   33,042 v Brentford, FA Cup 5th Round, 19 February 1927.
Year Formed   1871. Turned professional 1895.
Previous Names   None.
Club Nickname   "The Royals".
Club Colours   Sky blue shirts with white centre panel, sky blue shorts and navy stockings.
Club Honours   Football League: Div. 3 Champions 1985-86; Div. 3(S) Champions 1925-26; Div. 4 Champions 1978-79.
League History   1920-26 Div. 3(S); 1926-31 Div. 2; 1931-58 Div. 3(S); 1958-71 Div. 3; 1971-76 Div. 4; 1976-77 Div. 3; 1977-79 Div. 4; 1979-83 Div. 3; 1983-84 Div. 4; 1984-86 Div. 3; 1986-88 Div. 2; 1988- Div. 3.
Most League Points in a Season   (2 for a win) 65 in Div. 4, 1978-79. (3 for a win) 94 in Div. 3, 1985-86.

Most League Goals in a Season   112 in Div. 3(S), 1951-52.
Record Victory   10-2 v Crystal Palace in Div. 3(S), 4 September 1946.
Record Defeat   0-18 v Preston N.E. in FA Cup 1st Round, 1893-94.
Consecutive League Wins   13 in 1985.
Consecutive League Defeats   6 in 1971.
Record League Appearances   Steve Death, 471 between 1969-82.
Record League Goalscorer—Career   Ronnie Blackman, 158 between 1947-54.
Record League Goalscorer—Season   Ronnie Blackman, 39 in Div. 3(S), 1951-52.

Reading: League Record, 1987-88 (Division 2)

Match Number	Date	Venue	Opponents	Result		H/T	Lge Posn	Attend
1	22.8.87	A	Leeds U.	D	0-0	0-0		19286
2	29.8.87	H	Plymouth Arg.	L	0-1	0-1		6658
3	1.9.87	A	Shrewsbury T.	W	1-0	1-0	17	3223
4	5.9.87	H	Oldham Ath.	W	3-0	1-0	11	4798
5	12.9.87	A	Bournemouth	L	0-3	0-1	15	7597
6	16.9.87	H	Stoke C.	L	0-1	0-0	18	5349
7	19.9.87	H	Crystal Palace	L	2-3	1-0	21	6819
8	26.9.87	A	Swindon T.	L	0-4	0-2	21	10073
9	29.9.87	A	Middlesbrough	D	0-0	0-0	21	10903
10	3.10.87	H	West Bromwich A.	L	1-2	1-1	22	5543
11	10.10.87	A	Birmingham C.	D	2-2	0-0	22	6142
12	17.10.87	H	Huddersfield T.	W	3-2	2-0	21	4678
13	20.10.87	A	Barnsley	L	2-5	2-1	22	4396
14	24.10.87	H	Bradford C.	D	1-1	0-1	22	5920
15	31.10.87	A	Aston Villa	L	1-2	0-0	22	13413
16	7.11.87	H	Ipswich T.	L	1-2	1-0	21	11508
17	14.11.87	H	Manchester C.	L	0-2	0-0	22	10052
18	21.11.87	A	Sheffield U.	L	1-4	1-3	22	6977
19	28.11.87	H	Blackburn Rov.	D	0-0	0-0	23	4535
20	1.12.87	A	Millwall	L	0-3	0-2	23	6762
21	5.12.87	A	Hull C.	D	2-2	1-0	23	5797
22	12.12.87	H	Leeds U.	L	0-1	0-0	23	6505
23	19.12.87	A	Stoke C.	L	2-4	0-0	23	6968
24	26.12.87	H	Swindon T.	L	0-1	0-0	23	8939
25	28.12.87	A	Crystal Palace	W	3-2	1-1	23	12449
26	1.1.88	A	Plymouth Arg.	W	3-1	0-0	22	13290
27	23.1.88	H	Shrewsbury T.	W	1-0	0-0	22	5170
28	30.1.88	H	Leicester C.	L	1-2	1-1	22	6645
29	6.2.88	A	Oldham Ath.	L	2-4	1-0	22	5388
30	13.2.88	H	Millwall	L	2-3	2-1	22	6050
31	20.2.88	H	Middlesbrough	D	0-0	0-0	22	6446
32	27.2.88	A	West Bromwich A.	W	1-0	0-0	22	8509
33	5.3.88	A	Huddersfield T.	W	2-0	2-0	22	6094
34	12.3.88	H	Birmingham C.	D	1-1	1-1	22	6285
35	19.3.88	H	Aston Villa	L	0-2	0-0	22	10033
36	2.4.88	H	Ipswich T.	D	1-1	0-0	22	9953
37	4.4.88	A	Manchester C.	L	0-2	0-0	22	15172
38	9.4.88	H	Barnsley	W	2-1	1-0	22	4849
39	13.4.88	H	Bournemouth	D	0-0	0-0	22	10037
40	20.4.88	A	Bradford C.	L	0-3	0-3	22	13608
41	23.4.88	A	Leicester C.	L	0-1	0-1	22	9603
42	30.4.88	H	Sheffield U.	W	2-1	2-0	22	6680
43	2.5.88	A	Blackburn Rov.	D	1-1	0-0	22	11373
44	7.5.88	H	Hull C.	D	0-0	0-0	22	6710

Players: League Record, 1987-88 (Division 2)

Match Number	1	2	3	4	5	6	7	8	9	10	11	12	13	14	15	16	17	18	19	20	21	22	23	24	25	26	27	28	29	30	31	32	33	34	35	36	37	38	39	40	41	42	43	44	Apps	Subs	Goals
Bailie							11	11	11										11	9	2	2	2	2		2	2	2	2	2	2	2	**2**	2	2	2									21	0	0
Beavon	4	4	★	4			4	★		4						4	4	4	4	4	4	4	4	4¹	4	4¹	4	4		4	4	4	4	4	4	4	4	4	4	4	4	4	4	4	32	2	2
Canoville			11¹	11	11	11					11	11	11																																7	0	1
Cowling																						11	11											★	11¹	11	11	11	11	11	11			9	1	1
Curle						6	6	6	6	6	6	6	6	6	6	6	6	6	6	6	6	6	6	6	6	6	6	6	6	6	6	6	6	6	6	6	6		6	6	6	6			30	0	0
Francis	1	1	1	1	1	1	1	1	1							1	1	1	1	1	1	1	1	1	1	1	1	1	1	1	1	1	1	1	1	1	1	1	1	1				1	34	0	0
Franklin												6	6																			★				6									3	1	0
Gilkes					★	★¹	10	10	10	10¹	**10**	10	10¹	10	2	3	3	3	3	3	3	3	3	3	3	3	3¹	3	3	3	3	3	3	3	★	10	11	3	3	3	3	3	3	3	36	3	4
Gordon	9	9	9	9¹	9	9	9			9	9	9²	9¹	9²	9¹	9	9¹	9	9	9			9			9																			20	0	8
Hicks	5	5	5	5	5	5	5	5	5	5	5	5	5	5	5	5	5	5	5	5	5	5	5	5	5	5	5	5¹	5	5	5	5	5	5	5	5	5	5	5	5	5	5	5	5	44	0	1
Horrix	10	10						9			★				10	10¹	10				★	★				9	★	10¹																	8	5	2
Jones	2	2	2	2	2	2	2	2	2	2	2	2	2			2	2	2	2	2	2				7¹	7¹				7¹	7	7		7	7	★		7							27	1	3
Joseph	★	★	10¹	10¹	10		10	10	★		★							★	★																										5	6	2
Madden																		★	8	8	8¹	8	8	8		★	4																		7	2	1
Moran														10	10¹	10	10	10¹	10	10¹	10	10¹	10	10¹	10	10	★¹	10	10	10	10	**10**	★	**10**	★	★		10	10	10²	10	10			24	4	7
Peters	6	6	6	6	6		6	6	6	6	6	★¹				★																			★	7			★						12	4	1
Richardson	3	3	3	3	3	3	3	3	3	3	3	3	3	3	★				11				2								3	3	2	2	2	2	2	2	2	2					26	1	0
Robson																																			7	7	★	7	7	7					5	2	0
Smillie	11	11	7	7	7	7	7		7	7		7		11		11					★		11	11	11	11	11	11	11	11	11														22	1	0
Tait		7	4		4	4	4		4	7	4	4	4	4	4		7	9	9¹	11	9	9		9	8¹	8	8	8	8	8	8	8	8	**10**	10		8	8	8	8					35	0	2
Taylor	8	8	8	8	8	8	8¹	8	8	8	8	8	8	8	8	8	8	8	8¹	8		★		8					★		★	8	8	8		★									26	4	2
Westwood												1	1	1	1	1	1	1	1																					1	1				10	0	0
White	★	★	11	★		★	7	4			★	11		11		11				11	11	11																							9	5	0
Whitehurst																										9	9	9	9²	9¹	9	9¹	9	9¹	9		9	9	9	9¹	9				15	0	6
Williams	7							7		7	7	7	7			7	★	7	7	7			★	7	7¹	7	7	7		★	7				7			★							17	4	1

FA Cup: 1987-88: 3rd Round: Southampton (H) 0-1.

Littlewoods Cup: 1987-88: 2nd Round: Chelsea (H) 3-1 (A) 2-3; 3rd Round: Peterborough U. (A) 0-0 Replay (H) 1-0; 4th Round: Bradford C. (H) 0-0 Replay (A) 0-1.

ROCHDALE (Division 4)

Team Manager Eddie Gray.
Club Address Spotland, Wilbutts Lane, Rochdale OL11 5DS. Tel: (0706) 44648/9.
Current Ground Capacity 12,000.
Record Attendance 24,231 v Notts. Co., FA Cup 2nd Round, 10 December 1949.
Year Formed 1907. Turned professional 1907.
Previous Names None.
Club Nickname "The Dale".
Club Colours White shirts, navy shorts and white stockings.
Club Honours None.
League History 1921-58 Div. 3(N); 1958-59 Div. 3; 1959-60 Div. 4; 1969-74 Div. 3; 1974- Div. 4.
Most League Points in a Season (2 for a win) 65 in Div. 4, 1978-79. (3 for a win) 55 in Div. 4, 1985-86.
Most League Goals in a Season 105 in Div. 3(N), 1926-27.
Record Victory 8-1 v Chesterfield in Div. 3(N), 18 December 1926.
Record Defeat 0-8 v Wrexham in Div. 3(N), 28 December 1929 and 1-9 v Tranmere Rov. in Div. 3(N), 25 December 1931.
Consecutive League Wins 8 in 1969.
Consecutive League Defeats 17 in 1931-32.
Record League Appearances Graham Smith, 317 between 1966-74.
Record League Goalscorer—Career Reg Jenkins, 119 between 1964-73.
Record League Goalscorer—Season Albert Whitehurst, 44 in Div. 3(N), 1926-27.

Rochdale: League Record, 1987-88 (Division 4)

Match Number	Date	Venue	Opponents	Result		H/T	Lge Posn	Attend
1	15.8.87	A	Hereford U.	D	0-0	0-0		2652
2	22.8.87	H	Peterborough U.	D	1-1	1-1		1808
3	28.8.87	A	Halifax T.	W	2-1	0-1	6	2275
4	31.8.87	H	Crewe Alex.	D	2-2	1-2	8	2346
5	5.9.87	A	Scunthorpe U.	L	0-1	0-1	15	1959
6	12.9.87	H	Stockport Co.	L	0-1	0-1	19	2700
7	15.9.87	A	Torquay U.	L	0-5	0-3	21	1895
8	19.9.87	A	Exeter C.	D	1-1	1-0	22	2628
9	26.9.87	H	Burnley	W	2-1	1-0	20	4426
10	29.9.87	H	Wolverhampton W.	L	0-2	0-1	20	5553
11	3.10.87	H	Carlisle U.	L	1-2	0-0	22	1940
12	9.10.87	A	Tranmere Rov.	L	1-6	1-2	23	2303
13	17.10.87	H	Darlington	L	1-3	1-1	23	1417
14	20.10.87	A	Leyton Orient	L	0-8	0-4	23	2995
15	24.10.87	H	Bolton W.	D	2-2	1-0	23	4294
16	31.10.87	A	Cardiff C.	L	0-1	0-0	23	3046
17	3.11.87	H	Colchester U.	L	1-4	1-2	23	1399
18	7.11.87	H	Swansea C.	L	2-3	0-0	24	1243
19	20.11.87	A	Cambridge U.	W	2-1	2-1	23	2104
20	28.11.87	H	Scarborough	D	1-1	0-0	23	1838
21	12.12.87	A	Wrexham	W	3-2	2-2	23	1409
22	19.12.87	H	Newport Co.	W	3-0	2-0	23	1491
23	26.12.87	A	Burnley	L	0-4	0-3	23	7013
24	28.12.87	H	Hartlepool U.	L	0-2	0-1	23	1851
25	1.1.88	H	Halifax T.	D	0-0	0-0	23	2050
26	2.1.88	A	Stockport Co.	D	1-1	1-1	23	2441
27	9.1.88	A	Peterborough U.	D	1-1	1-1	23	3212
28	16.1.88	H	Exeter C.	D	0-0	0-0	23	1431
29	26.1.88	H	Torquay U.	D	1-1	0-1	23	1254
30	29.1.88	A	Crewe Alex.	W	1-0	1-0	22	2107
31	6.2.88	H	Scunthorpe U.	W	2-1	0-0	21	1455
32	13.2.88	A	Hartlepool U.	D	1-1	0-0	20	2186
33	20.2.88	A	Hereford U.	W	3-1	2-0	19	1568
34	27.2.88	A	Carlisle U.	L	0-2	0-2	19	1983
35	1.3.88	H	Wolverhampton W.	L	0-1	0-1	20	2805
36	5.3.88	A	Darlington	L	1-2	1-1	21	1773
37	12.3.88	H	Tranmere Rov.	D	0-0	0-0	21	1621
38	26.3.88	A	Bolton W.	D	0-0	0-0	22	4875
39	29.3.88	H	Cardiff C.	D	2-2	1-0	22	1435
40	2.4.88	A	Swansea C.	W	3-0	1-0	21	5367
41	4.4.88	H	Cambridge U.	W	2-1	0-0	20	1596
42	8.4.88	A	Colchester U.	L	0-1	0-0	20	1864
43	23.4.88	H	Leyton Orient	L	1-3	1-1	21	1390
44	30.4.88	A	Scarborough	L	1-2	1-2	22	1852
45	2.5.88	H	Wrexham	L	1-2	0-0	22	1539
46	7.5.88	A	Newport Co.	W	1-0	0-0	21	2560

Players: League Record, 1987-88 (Division 4)

Match Number	Apps	Subs	Goals
Bramhall	40	0	4
Coyle	23	1	1
Crerand	3	0	0
Duggan	3	0	0
Gavin	23	0	6
Hampton	19	0	1
Hancox	0	2	0
Harris	15	0	2
Holden	15	10	2
Hughes	2	0	0
Hunt	1	0	1
Lomax	44	0	0
Mellish	12	0	0
Moore	10	0	2
Moss	10	0	2
Mycock	9	2	0
Parker	6	1	1
Parlane	19	0	3
Reid	28	0	0
Seasman	32	1	1
Simmonds	43	0	12
Smart	36	0	3
Stanton	25	7	1
Thompson	3	2	0
Walling	8	4	2
Warren	31	0	1
Welch	46	0	0
Own Goals			2

FA Cup: 1987-88: 1st Round: Wrexham (H) 0-2.
Littlewoods Cup: 1987-88: 1st Round: Tranmere Rov. (H) 3-1 (A) 0-1; 2nd Round: Wimbledon (H) 1-1 (A) 1-2.

ROTHERHAM UNITED (Division 4)

Team Manager   Billy McEwan.
Club Address   Millmoor Ground, Rotherham. Tel: (0709) 562434.
Current Ground Capacity   18,500.
Record Attendance   25,000 v Sheffield U., Div. 2, 13 December 1952 and v Sheffield Wed., Div. 2, 26 January 1952.
Year Formed   1884. Turned professional 1905.
Previous Names   Thornhill United, Rotherham County.
Club Nickname   "The Merry Millers".
Club Colours   Red shirts, white collar and sleeves, white shorts and red stockings.
Club Honours   Football League: Div. 3 Champions 1980-81; Div. 3(N) Champions 1950-51.
League History   1893-96 Div. 2; 1896 Failed re-election; 1919-23 Div. 2; 1923-51 Div. 3(N); 1951-68 Div. 2; 1968-73 Div. 3; 1973-75 Div. 4; 1975-81 Div. 3; 1981-83 Div. 2; 1983-88 Div. 3; 1988- Div. 4.
Most League Points in a Season   (2 for a win) 71 in Div. 3(N), 1950-51. (3 for a win) 67 in Div. 3, 1981-82.

Most League Goals in a Season   114 in Div. 3(N), 1946-47.
Record Victory   8-0 v Oldham Ath. in Div. 3(N), 26 May 1947.
Record Defeat   1-11 v Bradford C. in Div. 3(N), 25 August 1928.
Consecutive League Wins   9 in 1982.
Consecutive League Defeats   8 in 1956.
Record League Appearances   Danny Williams, 459 between 1946-60.
Record League Goalscorer—Career   Gladstone Guest, 130 between 1946-56.
Record League Goalscorer—Season   Wally Ardron, 38 in Div. 3(N), 1946-47.

Rotherham United: League Record, 1987-88 (Division 3)

Match Number	Date	Venue	Opponents	Result		H/T	Lge Posn	Attend
1	15.8.87	A	Bristol Rov.	L	1-3	0-2		3399
2	22.8.87	H	Bury	L	0-1	0-0		3017
3	29.8.87	A	Port Vale	D	0-0	0-0	20	2895
4	31.8.87	H	Chester C.	W	5-2	1-0	13	2551
5	5.9.87	A	Brentford	D	1-1	0-0	17	3604
6	12.9.87	H	Walsall	L	0-1	0-0	19	3325
7	16.9.87	A	Brighton & H.A	D	1-1	1-0	18	6945
8	19.9.87	A	Preston N.E.	D	0-0	0-0	19	5124
9	26.9.87	H	Mansfield T.	W	2-1	1-1	17	3839
10	29.9.87	H	Grimsby T.	D	0-0	0-0	17	3375
11	3.10.87	A	Chesterfield	L	2-3	2-1	19	2993
12	11.10.87	H	Northampton T.	D	2-2	0-2	20	5244
13	16.10.87	A	Southend U.	D	1-1	1-1	19	2217
14	20.10.87	A	York C.	W	2-1	1-0	16	1932
15	24.10.87	H	Bristol C.	W	4-1	3-1	15	3397
16	31.10.87	A	Wigan Ath.	L	0-3	0-1	17	3004
17	3.11.87	H	Notts Co.	D	1-1	1-1	17	4157
18	7.11.87	A	Blackpool	L	0-3	0-1	17	3447
19	21.11.87	H	Fulham	L	0-2	0-1	18	3427
20	28.11.87	A	Aldershot	W	3-1	2-0	17	2549
21	12.12.87	H	Gillingham	L	1-2	0-2	19	2557
22	20.12.87	A	Sunderland	L	0-3	0-2	19	20168
23	26.12.87	A	Mansfield T.	W	1-0	1-0	18	4763
24	28.12.87	H	Doncaster Rov.	W	1-0	0-0	16	5840
25	1.1.88	H	Port Vale	W	1-0	0-0	14	3913
26	2.1.88	A	Walsall	L	2-5	1-3	15	5051
27	9.1.88	A	Bury	D	2-2	0-0	15	2230
28	16.1.88	H	Preston N.E.	D	2-2	1-2	15	4011
29	30.1.88	A	Chester C.	L	0-1	0-0	15	2059
30	13.2.88	A	Doncaster Rov.	D	2-2	1-1	18	2769
31	17.2.88	H	Brentford	W	2-0	1-0	14	2572
32	20.2.88	H	Bristol Rov.	D	1-1	0-0	14	2966
33	27.2.88	H	Chesterfield	D	1-1	0-0	17	3440
34	5.3.88	H	Southend U.	D	1-1	0-0	17	2531
35	8.3.88	A	Grimsby T.	L	1-2	0-1	18	3423
36	11.3.88	A	Northampton T.	D	0-0	0-0	18	5432
37	16.3.88	H	Brighton & H.A	W	1-0	0-0	15	2562
38	19.4.88	H	Wigan Ath.	D	1-1	1-0	15	3288
39	26.3.88	A	Bristol C.	L	0-2	0-0	18	7517
40	2.3.88	H	Blackpool	L	0-1	0-0	18	3001
41	4.4.88	A	Fulham	L	1-3	0-2	18	4402
42	8.4.88	H	York C.	L	0-1	0-0	19	2942
43	23.4.88	A	Notts Co.	L	0-4	0-0	20	7021
44	30.4.88	H	Aldershot	W	1-0	0-0	20	2818
45	2.5.88	A	Gillingham	W	2-0	1-0	19	3015
46	7.5.88	H	Sunderland	L	1-4	1-0	21	9374

Players: League Record, 1987-88 (Division 3)

Match Number	1	2	3	4	5	6	7	8	9	10	11	12	13	14	15	16	17	18	19	20	21	22	23	24	25	26	27	28	29	30	31	32	33	34	35	36	37	38	39	40	41	42	43	44	45	46	Apps	Subs	Goals
Airey	9	10	10	10⁴	10¹	10	10	10	10	10	10	10¹	10	10	10²	10	10		10	10¹	10	10			★	★¹		★	9	9		★¹	9			★	★		9								25	6	11
Ash																									★																			★			0	2	0
Buckley																	7	7	7	7	7	7	7	7	7	7	7	7	7	7			7	7	7	7	7	7	7	7	7	★		★			24	2	0
Campbell	4¹		11	11¹	11	11¹		★	4	11	11	11¹	11	11	11	11		11¹	11	11	11	11	11	11	11	11		★	11									11	11	8	11	11					31	2	5
Crichton																														1	1	1	1	1	1												6	0	0
Crosby										★		3	3	3			3	3	3	3	3	3	3	3	3	3	3	3	3	3	3	3	3	3	3	3	3	3	3	3	3	3					27	1	0
Cusack																					6	6	6	6	6	6	6	6	6	6	6	6	6	6			6	6									18	0	0
Douglas	2	2	2	2	2	2	2	2	2	2			2	2	2	2	2	2	2	2	2	2	2			2	2	2	2	2	2	2	2	2	2	2	2	2¹	2	2							40	0	1
Dungworth	5	5	5	5	5	5		★	2	2	5	5	5	5	4	5		5	5		★	2	2	2	2			9	9	9		★		11				8	6	8	8	8					29	3	0
Evans	10	9	9	9	9	9	9	9	9	9	9	9¹	9	★		9¹	9¹	9	9	9	9	9	9	9	9	9	9	9	9¹	9	9																28	1	4
Goodwin																																									★	4	4	★			2	1	0
Grealish		4	4	4	4	4	4	4	4¹		4¹	4¹	4	4	4	4			4	4	4	4	4	4	4	4			4	4	4	4	4	4	4	4	4	4	4	4	4			4			38	0	3
Green	6	6	6	6	6	6	6	6	6	6	6	6	6	6	6	6	6¹	6	6	6	6¹	6	5	5	5	5	5	5	5				★			6	6	6		5	5	6	6				36	1	2
Haycock	★			★		★	★	11		9		★		★	10	★		★		10	10¹	10¹	10¹	10¹	10¹	10¹	10¹	10	10²	10¹	10¹	10	10¹	10	10¹	10	10	10	10	10	10	10	9¹	9			27	8	12
Johnson						5	5	5	5	5	5					5		5		5											5	5	5	5	5	5	5	5	5	5	5	5	5	5			23	0	0
Mendonca																																						★	★	★¹	★	9	9	10¹	10		4	4	2
O'Hanlon	1	1	1	1	1	1	1	1	1	1		1	1	1	1	1	1	1	1	1	1	1	1	1	1	1	1	1	1									1	1	1	1	1		1			40	0	0
Pepper						7	7	11										4			3									4	4		★	11	8	8	8	8	8	8							14	1	0
Pugh	11	11	7	7	7	7	7		7	11	7	7	★	7	7	7	7	7	11							11	11¹	11	7	11	11					11	11		★		11	11			7	7	27	2	1
Scott	3	3	3	3	3	3	3	3	3	3	3	3	3	3	3	3	3	3																											11			19	0	0
Tomlinson	7	7						7		★	7						★	★																			11	11									6	3	0
Williams	8	8	8	8	8	8	8	8	8	8¹	8	8	8	8	8¹	8	8	8	8	8	8	8¹	8	8	8	8	8	8	8	8	8¹	8	8	8	8	8	8¹	8	8	8							36	0	6
Wylde																																						9	9	9¹	9	9	9				6	0	1
Own Goals																			1																											1		2

FA Cup: 1987-88: 1st Round: Doncaster Rov. (A) 1-1 Replay (H) 2-0; 2nd Round Macclesfield (A) 0-4.
Littlewoods Cup: 1987-88: 1st Round: Huddersfield T. (H) 4-4 (A) 3-1; 2nd Round: Everton (A) 2-3 (H) 0-0.

SCARBOROUGH (Division 4)

Team Manager Neil Warnock.
Club Address The Athletic Ground, Seamer Road, Scarborough YO12 4HF. Tel: (0723) 375094.
Current Ground Capacity 9,950.
Record Attendance 11,130 v Luton T., FA Cup 3rd Round, 1938.
Year Formed 1879. Turned professional 1926.
Previous Names None.
Club Nickname "The Boro".
Club Colours All red.
Club Honours None.
League History 1987- Div. 4.
Most League Points in a Season (3 for a win) 65 in Div. 4, 1987-88.
Most League Goals in a Season 56 in Div. 4, 1987-88.
Record Victory 16-1 v Leeds Amateurs in FA Amateur Cup, 9 November 1907.
Record Defeat 1-16 v Southbank in Northern League, 15 November 1919.
Consecutive League Wins 3 in August-September 1987 and September-October 1987.

Consecutive League Defeats 4 in December 1987-January 1988.
Record League Appearances Tommy Graham, 44 between 1987-88.
Record League Goalscorer—Career Stewart Mell, 8 between 1987-88.
Record League Goalscorer—Season Stewart Mell, 8 in Div. 4, 1987-88.

Scarborough: League Record, 1987-88 (Division 4)

Match Number	Date	Venue	Opponents	Result		H/T	Lge Posn	Attend
1	15.8.87	H	Wolverhampton W.	D	2-2	1-2		7314
2	22.8.87	A	Leyton Orient	L	1-3	1-0		3540
3	29.8.87	H	Bolton W.	W	4-0	2-0	8	4462
4	31.8.87	A	Colchester U.	W	3-1	0-1	3	1525
5	5.9.87	H	Tranmere Rov.	W	2-0	0-0	2	2882
6	12.9.87	A	Darlington	L	1-2	0-1	6	3187
7	16.9.87	H	Newport Co.	W	3-1	1-1	4	2345
8	19.9.87	H	Swansea C.	W	2-0	0-0	1	3033
9	26.9.87	A	Carlisle U.	L	0-4	0-1	5	2693
10	29.9.87	A	Torquay U.	W	1-0	0-0	5	3255
11	3.10.87	H	Burnley	W	1-0	1-0	2	4782
12	10.10.87	H	Exeter C.	W	3-1	1-1	1	2472
13	17.10.87	A	Crewe Alex.	L	0-1	0-1	1	2723
14	21.10.87	A	Hereford U.	D	1-1	0-0	1	2359
15	24.10.87	H	Hartlepool U.	D	1-1	0-0	1	3909
16	31.10.87	A	Wrexham	L	0-1	0-1	4	1860
17	4.11.87	H	Cardiff C.	D	1-1	1-1	7	2599
18	7.11.87	A	Scunthorpe U.	W	1-0	0-0	4	4506
19	21.11.87	H	Halifax T.	D	1-1	1-0	6	2892
20	28.11.87	A	Rochdale	D	1-1	0-0	6	1838
21	12.12.87	H	Peterborough U.	D	1-1	1-0	6	2535
22	19.12.87	A	Stockport Co.	D	1-1	1-1	6	1779
23	26.12.87	H	Carlisle U.	W	3-1	1-0	5	3261
24	28.12.87	A	Cambridge U.	L	0-1	0-0	7	3243
25	1.1.88	A	Bolton W.	L	1-3	0-1	8	6295
26	2.1.88	H	Darlington	L	0-1	0-1	10	3377
27	16.1.88	A	Swansea C.	L	0-3	0-2	12	4366
28	30.1.88	H	Colchester U.	W	3-1	0-0	10	2155
29	6.2.88	A	Tranmere Rov.	L	0-1	0-0	12	4175
30	13.2.88	H	Cambridge U.	D	0-0	0-0	13	1879
31	19.2.88	A	Wolverhampton W.	D	0-0	0-0	14	11391
32	24.2.88	H	Leyton Orient	W	3-1	1-0	12	2116
33	27.2.88	A	Burnley	W	1-0	1-0	10	7845
34	2.3.88	H	Torquay U.	L	1-2	0-1	11	2182
35	5.3.88	H	Crewe Alex.	W	2-0	1-0	9	2260
36	12.3.88	A	Exeter C.	L	0-1	0-0	11	1738
37	19.3.88	H	Wrexham	L	0-2	0-2	11	2090
38	26.3.88	A	Hartlepool U.	L	0-1	0-1	13	2443
39	2.4.88	H	Scunthorpe U.	D	0-0	0-0	15	4677
40	4.4.88	A	Halifax T.	D	2-2	0-1	14	1747
41	9.4.88	H	Hereford U.	W	2-1	2-0	14	2154
42	12.4.88	A	Newport Co.	W	4-0	1-0	11	1025
43	23.4.88	A	Cardiff C.	L	0-2	0-1	13	5751
44	30.4.88	H	Rochdale	W	2-1	2-1	13	1852
45	2.5.88	A	Peterborough U.	D	0-0	0-0	12	3244
46	7.5.88	H	Stockport Co.	D	1-1	0-0	12	2236

Players: League Record, 1987-88 (Division 4)

Match Number	1	2	3	4	5	6	7	8	9	10	11	12	13	14	15	16	17	18	19	20	21	22	23	24	25	26	27	28	29	30	31	32	33	34	35	36	37	38	39	40	41	42	43	44	45	46	Apps	Subs	Goals
Adams						★[1]		★	★	7	★		7				★		7		10	10	7	7	7	★	7	7		7			★	★[1]	★		10			★		7	7	★	7	7	17	11	2
Beasley																																1	1	1	1											4	0	0
Bennyworth	4	4	4	4	4	4	4	4	4	4	4[1]	4	4	4	4	4	4	4	4	4	4	4	4	4		2	2	2	2	2	4	4	6	6			★										38	1	1
Blackwell	1	1	1	1	1	1	1	1	1	1	1	1	1	1	1	1	1	1																								1	1	1			21	0	0
Bowman							10[1]	10		11[1]		11																																			4	0	2
Brook																																			9	9	9	9	9								5	0	0
Cook	★	★	★	★	★	★		★	10	10	10	10	11	8	10	★	11			8			★	3[1]	3	9	9[2]	9	9	9	9	9	9	9	9	8	8	8[1]	★[1]	8		2	8				28	10	5
Downes																												7	11																		2	0	0
Graham	11	11	11	11	11[1]	11	11	11[1]	11	6	6	6	6	6	6	8	8	8		11	11	11	11	11	11	11[1]	11	11	11[1]	11	11	11		11	11	11[1]	11[2]	11	11	11	11	11	44	0	7
Hamill	7	7	7[1]	7	7	7	7	7		7[1]		7	9	11	★	11		10		★	★	★	★	7			7		★		7	7				★				★[1]					19	9	3
Harrison	★								2											2	2																								3	1	0
Ironside																																1	1	1	1	1	1								6	0	0
Kamara								6	2	6	6	6	6	6	6	6	3	3	3	2	7	7	7	7	2	2	4	4	4	4	4	4	4	4	29	0	0
Kendall	6	6	6	6	6	6	6	6		8	★	11	6	★	6			★	★	6	6	6	6	6	6[1]	6		8								22	5	1
Lowe, K.																						6	10	10											4	0	0
Lowe, S.															11[1]	11[1]	11[1]	★		8	10			★		8	8	8	8	8				9	9	9	14	2	3
McDonagh															1	1	1	1	1	1	1	1	1											9	0	0
McHale	9[1]	9	9	9	9	9	9	9	9	9	9	9		9	9	9	9[1]	9	9	9	9	9[1]	9	9								25	0	3
McJannet	2	2	2	2	2	2	2	2	2	2	2	2	2	2	2	2	2	2	2		2	2					★	2	2	2	2	2	★	2	29	5	4
Mell	10[1]	10	10[1]	10[1]	10	10			10	★	11	11[1]	★	10	10		10[1]	10		10	10[1]	10	★	10	★		★	10	10[2]	10	10	10	10	10		10	10	10	22	1	8
Moss	8	8	8	8[1]	8	8	8	8	8[1]	8	8	8[1]	8			8			★	8	8[1]	8		8	8	8	8	8						22	1	4
Neenan																							1	1	1	1	1	1						6	0	0
Newton																															8	8		8	8	★	4	1	0
Outhart																											★		★		10[1]	7		10	3	2	1
Podd																						2	2	2									3	0	0
Preston																													★	★	★	9			1	0	0
Richards	5	5	5	5[1]	5	5	5	5	5	5	5	5	5	5	5	5	5	5[1]	5	5	5	5		5	5	5	5	5	5[1]	5	5	5		5	5[1]	5	5[1]	5	5	42	0	5
Russell						7[1]	7[1]	7	7				7	7	7		★	7										5	4	4	4	4	4	6	6	5	6	6[1]	6	6[1]	6	6	12	1	2
Short													★																													20	1	0
Thompson	3	3[1]	3	3[1]	3[1]	3	3[2]	3	3	3	3	3	3	3	3	3	3	3	3	3	3		3	3	3	3[1]	3	3	3	3	3	3	3	3	3	3	3	3	41	0	6
Walker		★																																			0	1	0
Own Goals			1																																														1

FA Cup: 1987-88: 1st Round: Grimsby T. (H) 1-2.
Littlewoods Cup: 1987-88: 1st Round: Doncaster Rov. (H) 1-0 (A) 1-3.

SCUNTHORPE UNITED (Division 4)

Team Manager Mike Buxton.
Club Address Old Show Ground, Scunthorpe, South Humberside. Tel: (0724) 848077.
Current Ground Capacity 27,000.
Record Attendance 23,935 v Portsmouth, FA Cup 4th Round, 30 January 1954.
Year Formed 1904. Turned professional 1912.
Previous Names Scunthorpe and Lindsey United.
Club Nickname "The Iron".
Club Colours All claret and blue.
Club Honours Football League: Div. 3(N) Champions 1957-58.
League History 1950-58 Div. 3(N); 1958-64 Div. 2; 1964-68 Div. 3; 1968-72 Div 4; 1972-73 Div. 3; 1973-83 Div. 4; 1983-84 Div. 3; 1984- Div. 4.
Most League Points in a Season (2 for a win) 66 in Div. 3(N), 1957-58. (3 for a win) 83 in Div. 4, 1982-83.
Most League Goals in a Season 88 in Div. 3(N), 1957-58.
Record Victory 9-0 v Boston U. in FA Cup 1st Round, 21 November 1953.

Record Defeat 0-8 v Carlisle U. in Div. 3(N), 25 December 1952.
Consecutive League Wins 6 in 1954 and 1965.
Consecutive League Defeats 7 in 1973.
Record League Appearances Jack Brownsword, 595 between 1950-65.
Record League Goalscorer—Career Steve Cammack, 110 between 1979-86.
Record League Goalscorer—Season Barrie Thomas, 31 in Div. 2, 1961-62.

Scunthorpe United: League Record, 1987-88 (Division 4)

Match Number	Date	Venue	Opponents	Result		H/T	Lge Posn	Attend
1	15.8.87	H	Tranmere Rov.	W	3-0	0-0		2277
2	22.8.87	A	Carlisle U.	L	1-3	0-0		2074
3	29.8.87	H	Colchester U.	D	2-2	1-0	10	2003
4	31.8.87	A	Wolverhampton W.	L	1-4	1-2	19	6672
5	5.9.87	H	Rochdale	W	1-0	1-0	12	1959
6	12.9.87	A	Cambridge U.	D	3-3	2-1	11	1830
7	15.9.87	H	Bolton W.	D	1-1	0-1	11	2501
8	19.9.87	H	Newport Co.	W	3-1	2-1	10	2004
9	26.9.87	A	Darlington	W	4-1	1-1	6	1638
10	29.9.87	H	Stockport Co.	D	0-0	0-0	6	2181
11	3.10.87	A	Peterborough U.	D	1-1	0-1	8	3594
12	10.10.87	H	Halifax T.	W	1-0	0-0	5	2105
13	17.10.87	A	Hereford U.	W	3-2	2-0	3	2092
14	20.10.87	A	Burnley	D	1-1	0-0	3	6323
15	24.10.87	H	Cardiff C.	W	2-1	2-0	2	2872
16	31.10.87	A	Hartlepool U.	L	0-1	0-1	5	2763
17	3.11.87	H	Wrexham	W	3-1	1-1	4	2348
18	7.11.87	A	Scarborough	L	0-1	0-0	8	4506
19	21.11.87	A	Crewe Alex.	D	2-2	1-0	8	2045
20	28.11.87	H	Swansea C.	L	1-2	0-0	8	2309
21	12.12.87	A	Exeter C.	D	1-1	0-0	7	1831
22	18.12.87	H	Torquay U.	L	2-3	1-3	10	2261
23	26.12.87	H	Darlington	W	1-0	1-0	8	3140
24	28.12.87	A	Leyton Orient	D	1-1	1-1	9	5542
25	1.1.88	A	Colchester U.	W	3-0	0-0	7	2287
26	2.1.88	H	Cambridge U.	W	3-2	3-2	5	3253
27	16.1.88	A	Newport Co.	D	1-1	0-1	7	1760
28	30.1.88	H	Wolverhampton W.	L	0-1	0-0	8	5476
29	6.2.88	A	Rochdale	L	1-2	0-0	11	1455
30	13.2.88	H	Leyton Orient	W	3-2	0-1	7	2951
31	20.2.88	A	Tranmere Rov.	W	3-1	1-1	7	2803
32	27.2.88	H	Peterborough U.	W	5-0	1-0	4	3378
33	1.3.88	A	Stockport Co.	D	1-1	0-1	6	1854
34	5.3.88	H	Hereford U.	W	3-0	1-0	5	3413
35	12.3.88	A	Halifax T.	D	2-2	0-2	4	1807
36	19.3.88	H	Hartlepool U.	W	3-0	3-0	3	3784
37	26.3.88	A	Cardiff C.	W	1-0	0-0	2	4527
38	2.4.88	A	Scarborough	D	0-0	0-0	3	4677
39	4.4.88	H	Crewe Alex.	W	2-1	0-1	3	4091
40	9.4.88	A	Wrexham	L	1-2	1-0	3	2589
41	12.4.88	H	Carlisle U.	W	1-0	0-0	3	3514
42	19.4.88	A	Bolton W.	D	0-0	0-0	3	6669
43	23.4.88	H	Burnley	D	1-1	0-0	3	5347
44	30.4.88	A	Swansea C.	D	1-1	0-1	4	3482
45	2.5.88	H	Exeter C.	D	1-1	0-0	5	6736
46	7.5.88	A	Torquay U.	W	2-1	1-0	4	4989

Players: League Record, 1987-88 (Division 4)

Match Number	Apps	Subs	Goals
Atkins	21	1	2
Birch	0	2	0
Broddle	5	2	0
Brown	17	5	0
Cowling	1	0	0
Daws	8	2	0
Dixon	37	4	4
Flounders	45	0	24
Green	35	0	0
Harle	45	0	6
Heyes	3	0	0
Hill	26	0	3
Johnson	19	13	6
Lister	39	0	6
Longden	44	0	0
McLean	4	0	0
Money	32	0	0
Nicol	25	0	0
Reeves	6	0	4
Richardson	1	0	0
Russell	34	0	1
Shearer	15	0	7
Stevenson	1	7	0
Taylor, K.	35	0	5
Taylor, M.	8	0	0
Own Goals			3

FA Cup: 1987-88: 1st Round: Bury (H) 3-1; 2nd Round: Sunderland (H) 2-1; 3rd Round: Blackpool (H) 0-0 Replay (A) 0-1.

Littlewoods Cup: 1987-88: 1st Round: Hartlepool U. (H) 3-1 (A) 1-0; 2nd Round: Leicester C. (A) 1-2 (H) 1-2.

SHEFFIELD UNITED (Division 2)

Team Manager Dave Bassett.
Club Address Bramall Lane Ground, Sheffield S2 4SU.
Tel: (0742) 738955/6/7.
Current Ground Capacity 49,000.
Record Attendance 68,287 v Leeds U., FA Cup 5th Round, 15 February 1936.
Year Formed 1889. Turned professional 1889.
Previous Names None.
Club Nickname "The Blades".
Club Colours Red and white striped shirts, black shorts and red stockings.
Club Honours Football League: Div. 1 Champions 1897-98; Div. 2 Champions 1952-53; Div. 4 Champions 1981-82. FA Cup: Winners 1899, 1902, 1915, 1925.
League History 1892-93 Div. 2; 1893-1934 Div. 1; 1934-39 Div. 2; 1946-49 Div. 1; 1949-53 Div. 2; 1953-56 Div. 1; 1956-61 Div. 2; 1961-68 Div. 1; 1968-71 Div. 2; 1971-76 Div. 1; 1976-79 Div. 2; 1979-81 Div. 3; 1981-82 Div 4; 1982-84 Div. 3; 1984-88 Div. 2; 1988- Div. 3.
Most League Points in a Season (2 for a win) 60 in Div. 2, 1952-53. (3 for a win) 96 in Div. 4, 1981-82.

Most League Goals in a Season 102 in Div. 1, 1925-26.
Record Victory 10-0 v Port Vale in Div. 2, 10 December 1892 and v Burley in Div. 1, 19 January 1929.
Record Defeat 0-13 v Bolton W., FA Cup 2nd Round, 1 February 1890.
Consecutive League Wins 8 in 1893, 1903, 1958 and 1960.
Consecutive League Defeats 7 in 1975.
Record League Appearances Joe Shaw, 629 between 1948-66.
Record League Goalscorer—Career Harry Johnson, 205 between 1919-30.
Record League Goalscorer—Season Jimmy Dunne, 41 in Div. 1, 1930-31.

Sheffield United: League Record, 1987-88 (Division 2)

Match Number	Date	Venue	Opponents	Result		H/T	Lge Posn	Attend
1	15.8.87	H	Bournemouth	L	0-1	0-0		9757
2	22.8.87	A	Swindon T.	L	0-2	0-2		8637
3	29.8.87	H	Blackburn Rov.	W	3-1	2-0	16	8540
4	31.8.87	A	Plymouth Arg.	L	0-1	0-1	17	14504
5	5.9.87	H	Stoke C.	D	0-0	0-0	19	10086
6	12.9.87	A	Oldham Ath.	L	2-3	2-2	21	5730
7	15.9.87	H	Crystal Palace	D	1-1	0-0	21	7767
8	19.9.87	H	Millwall	L	1-2	0-1	22	8048
9	26.9.87	A	Aston Villa	D	1-1	0-1	22	14761
10	29.9.87	A	Barnsley	W	2-1	0-1	20	10203
11	3.10.87	H	Hull C.	W	2-1	1-1	19	10446
12	10.10.87	A	Manchester C.	W	3-2	1-2	12	18377
13	17.10.87	H	Leicester C.	W	2-1	2-0	11	10593
14	20.10.87	H	Birmingham C.	L	0-2	0-1	11	9287
15	24.10.87	A	Ipswich T.	L	0-1	0-0	16	11949
16	31.10.87	H	Leeds U.	D	2-2	1-0	16	12095
17	4.11.87	A	West Bromwich A.	L	0-4	0-2	18	8072
18	7.11.87	H	Middlesbrough	L	0-2	0-0	19	11278
19	14.11.87	H	Bradford C.	L	0-2	0-1	19	13694
20	17.11.87	A	Shrewsbury T.	L	0-2	0-1	19	2555
21	21.11.87	H	Reading	W	4-1	3-1	16	6977
22	28.11.87	H	Huddersfield T.	D	2-2	1-1	17	9269

Match Number	Date	Venue	Opponents	Result		H/T	Lge Posn	Attend
23	13.12.87	A	Crystal Palace	L	1-2	1-0	17	8174
24	20.12.87	H	Swindon T.	W	1-0	0-0	16	7248
25	26.12.87	H	Aston Villa	D	1-1	0-0	16	15809
26	28.12.87	A	Millwall	L	1-3	0-3	17	7255
27	1.1.88	A	Blackburn Rov.	L	1-4	0-3	18	10493
28	2.1.88	H	Oldham Ath.	L	0-5	0-3	18	9574
29	16.1.88	A	Bournemouth	W	2-1	1-0	18	6466
30	6.2.88	A	Stoke C.	L	0-1	0-0	18	9344
31	13.2.88	H	Shrewsbury T.	L	0-1	0-1	20	8227
32	20.2.88	H	Barnsley	W	1-0	0-0	19	11861
33	27.2.88	A	Hull C.	W	2-1	0-1	18	8832
34	5.3.88	A	Leicester C.	L	0-1	0-0	19	12256
35	8.3.88	H	Manchester C.	L	1-2	1-0	20	13906
36	19.3.88	A	Leeds U.	L	0-5	0-1	21	22376
37	26.3.88	H	Ipswich T.	W	4-1	2-1	20	8753
38	2.4.88	A	Middlesbrough	L	0-6	0-3	21	17340
39	4.4.88	H	Bradford C.	L	1-2	0-1	21	13888
40	9.4.88	A	Birmingham C.	L	0-1	0-1	21	7046
41	19.4.88	H	Plymouth Arg.	W	1-0	0-0	20	9052
42	23.4.88	A	West Bromwich A.	D	0-0	0-0	20	12091
43	30.4.88	A	Reading	L	1-2	0-2	21	6680
44	7.5.88	A	Huddersfield T.	W	2-0	0-0	21	8644

Players: League Record, 1987-88 (Division 2)

Match Number	1	2	3	4	5	6	7	8	9	10	11	12	13	14	15	16	17	18	19	20	21	22	23	24	25	26	27	28	29	30	31	32	33	34	35	36	37	38	39	40	41	42	43	44	Apps	Subs	Goals
Agana																																8[1]	8	8	9[1]	9		★	11	8	8	8	9	7	11	1	2
Barnsley	6	2	2	2	2							★	6	6	6	6	6	6	6	2	2	2	2	2			2	2	2	2	2				2	2	2	2	4	4	6	6			31	1	0
Beagrie	11	11	11	11	11	11	11	11	★	8	9	9	9	9	9	9	9	9	9	11	11		11	11	11	11	11	★	11	11	11	11	11[1]	11	11	11	11	4[1]	11	11	11	11			41	2	2
Benstead																																													8	0	0
Cadette	9	9	9[1]	9	9	9	9	9[1]	9	9										9[1]	9	9	9			9	9		9	9[1]	9		★	9[2]	9	9	9	9	9	★		8[1]			26	2	7
Carr																																						2	3	3					3	0	0
Dempsey	10	10	10[1]	10	10	10	10	10	10	10	10	10	10	10		10	7	10[1]	10	10	10[1]	10	10	10		10	10	10	10		★	4													32	1	3
Downes											★			★		★	8		9[1]	8		8	8	★		7	7			★ ★		★	10	10[1]		10	10			10	10				6	3	1
Eckhardt		6	6	6	6	6	6	6	6	6					★			5					★																						7	4	1
Frain	7	★			★	★	11	11	11	11[1]	11	11	11		★	11	6					★	7	11		10																			11	1	0
Hansbury											1	1	1	1	1																														13	5	1
Hetherston																																													5	0	0
Kuhl	4	4	4	4	4	4	4	4	4	4	4	4	4	4[1]	4	4	4	4[1]	4	4	4[1]	4	4	4	4	4			7	7	7	7	7	7	7	7	7	7	7	11					11	0	0
Leaning	1	1	1	1	1	1	1	1	1	1	1	1	1					1	1	1				1	1				1	1	1	1													28	0	3
Marsden			7[1]	7	7	7	7						★		10	10	11	6	10	11																									21	0	0
Mendonca										★[1]					11	11	★		9	9[1]		9			★[1]	8[1]	9				9														13	3	1
Morris	8	7					7[1]	7[1]	7[1]	7	7	7	7	7	7	7		7	7	7	7		7				7	★	7		★ ★ ★			8[1]	7	7									23	5	4
Philliskirk	★			★	★		8[1]	8	★	8[1]	8[1]	8[2]	8	8	8[1]	8	8	8	★		8				8	8[1]	8	8			8					★	10				★[1]	7	7	19	7	9
Pike	3	3	3	3	3	3	3	3	3	3	3	3	3	3	3	3	★	3	3	3	3	3	3	3	3	3	3	3	3	3		3	3	3	3	3	3						★[1]		38	1	0
Powell																																	★					3	3	2	2	3			5	1	0
Segers														1	1	1	1	1	1			1	1	1	1																				10	0	0
Smith																	3	6	6	6		6	6	6	6	6	6		6	6	6	6	10	6	6	6	6								23	0	0
Stancliffe	5	5	5	5	5	5[2]	5	5	5	5	5	5	5	5	5	5	5		5	5	5	5	5	5	5	5	5[1]	5	5	5	5			5	5	5	5	5[1]	5						41	0	4
Todd																	★	2	4	4	4	4	4	4	4	4	4	4																	11	0	1
Webster																																	5	5[1]	5					4	4				5	1	1
Wilder	2			★	★	2	2	2	2	2	2	2	2	2[1]	2	2	2				2	2	2	2[1]	★																				21	4	0
Williams																												2	2						2	2					2				5	1	0
Withe		8	8	8	8	8																												8	8	8	8					★	8		8	1	0
Wood																			8[2]	8																						★	9		8	1	2
																																												★		0	1	0

FA Cup: 1987-88: 3rd Round: Maidstone U. (H) 1-0; 4th Round: Portsmouth (A) 1-2.
Littlewoods Cup: 1987-88: 2nd Round: Bury (A) 1-2 (H) 1-1.

121

SHEFFIELD WEDNESDAY (Division 1)

Team Manager Howard Wilkinson.
Club Address Hillsborough, Sheffield S6 1SW. Tel: (0742) 343122.
Current Ground Capacity 54,181.
Record Attendance 72,841 v Manchester C., FA Cup 5th Round, 17 February 1934.
Year Formed 1867. Turned professional 1887.
Previous Names None.
Club Nickname "The Owls".
Club Colours Blue and white striped shirts, white shorts and stockings.
Club Honours Football League: Div. 1 Champions 1902-03, 1903-04, 1928-29, 1929-30; Div. 2 Champions 1899-1900, 1925-26, 1951-52, 1955-56, 1958-59. FA Cup: Winners 1896, 1907, 1935.
League History 1892-99 Div. 1; 1899-1900 Div. 2; 1900-20 Div. 1; 1920-26 Div. 2; 1926-37 Div. 1; 1937-50 Div. 2; 1950-51 Div. 1; 1951-52 Div. 2; 1952-55 Div. 1; 1955-56 Div. 2; 1956-58 Div. 1; 1958-59 Div. 2; 1959-70 Div. 1; 1970-75 Div. 2; 1975-80 Div. 3; 1980-84 Div. 2; 1984- Div. 1.

Most League Points in a Season (2 for a win) 62 in Div. 2, 1958-59. (3 for a win) 88 in Div. 2, 1983-84.
Most League Goals in a Season 106 in Div. 2, 1958-59.
Record Victory 12-0 v Halliwell in FA Cup 1st Round, 17 January 1891.
Record Defeat 0-10 v Aston Villa in Div. 1, 5 October 1912.
Consecutive League Wins 9 in 1904.
Consecutive League Defeats 7 in 1893.
Record League Appearances Andy Wilson, 502 between 1900-20.
Record League Goalscorer—Career Andy Wilson, 200 between 1900-20.
Record League Goalscorer—Season Derek Dooley, 46 in Div. 2, 1951-52.

Sheffield Wednesday: League Record, 1987-88 (Division 1)

Match Number	Date	Venue	Opponents	Result		H/T	Lge Posn	Attend
1	15.8.87	A	Chelsea	L	1-2	0-1		21929
2	18.8.87	H	Oxford U.	D	1-1	1-1		17868
3	22.8.87	H	Newcastle U.	L	0-1	0-1	17	22031
4	29.8.87	A	Everton	L	0-4	0-1	19	29649
5	31.8.87	H	Coventry C.	L	0-3	0-2	20	17171
6	5.9.87	A	Southampton	D	1-1	1-0	20	12526
7	12.9.87	H	Watford	L	2-3	1-2	20	16144
8	19.9.87	A	Derby Co.	D	2-2	0-2	21	15869
9	26.9.87	H	Charlton Ath.	W	2-0	2-0	20	16850
10	3.10.87	A	Tottenham H.	L	0-2	0-0	20	24311
11	10.10.87	H	Manchester U.	L	2-4	1-1	20	32779
12	17.10.87	A	Nottingham F.	L	0-3	0-1	20	17685
13	24.10.87	H	Norwich C.	W	1-0	1-0	19	15861
14	31.10.87	A	Portsmouth	W	2-1	1-1	18	13852
15	7.11.87	A	West Ham U.	W	1-0	1-0	16	16277
16	14.11.87	H	Luton T.	L	0-2	0-1	16	16960
17	28.11.87	H	Q.P.R.	W	3-1	2-0	17	16933
18	5.12.87	A	Arsenal	L	1-3	1-0	17	23670
19	12.12.87	H	Wimbledon	W	1-0	0-0	16	14289
20	19.12.87	A	Liverpool	L	0-1	0-0	17	35383
21	26.12.87	A	Watford	W	3-1	3-1	16	12026
22	28.12.87	H	Derby Co.	W	2-1	2-0	12	26191
23	1.1.88	H	Everton	W	1-0	1-0	10	26433
24	2.1.88	A	Newcastle U.	D	2-2	0-0	10	25503
25	16.1.88	H	Chelsea	W	3-0	1-0	9	19859
26	6.2.88	H	Southampton	W	2-1	0-1	9	14769
27	13.2.88	A	Coventry C.	L	0-3	0-1	9	14382
28	20.2.88	A	Charlton Ath.	L	1-3	0-3	9	4517
29	27.2.88	H	Tottenham H.	L	0-3	0-1	10	18046
30	5.3.88	H	Nottingham F.	L	0-1	0-1	12	19509
31	12.3.88	A	Manchester U.	L	1-4	0-2	12	33318
32	19.3.88	H	Portsmouth	W	1-0	1-0	9	13731
33	26.3.88	A	Norwich C.	W	3-0	1-0	9	13280
34	2.4.88	H	West Ham U.	W	2-1	1-0	8	18435
35	5.4.88	A	Luton T.	D	2-2	0-0	9	7337
36	13.4.88	A	Oxford U.	W	3-0	2-0	8	5727
37	23.4.88	A	Q.P.R.	D	1-1	1-0	8	12531
38	30.4.88	H	Arsenal	D	3-3	3-1	8	16681
39	3.5.88	A	Wimbledon	D	1-1	0-1	8	7854
40	7.5.88	H	Liverpool	L	1-5	0-2	11	35893

Players: League Record, 1987-88 (Division 1)

Match Number	1	2	3	4	5	6	7	8	9	10	11	12	13	14	15	16	17	18	19	20	21	22	23	24	25	26	27	28	29	30	31	32	33	34	35	36	37	38	39	40	Apps	Subs	Goals
Bradshaw	★	★	11		★	10		10	★	★		★	★		10¹				★			★	11	9¹	★		★			★	★	★									6	14	2
Chamberlain	11							7		7	7	8	7	7	7	11	11	★	★	★	★		10		★	7	7	7	7¹												15	6	1
Chapman	9¹	9¹	9	9	9	9	9¹	9¹	9	9²	9	9	9		9	9	9	9¹	9	9¹	9¹	9	9¹		9¹	9	9¹	9	9	9¹	9	9¹	9	9¹	9²	9	9¹	9			37	0	19
Cranson																											5	5	5	5											4	0	0
Fee				5		5	5	5				★	★	★			★			★			4			★	5		★			★	3								7	9	0
Galvin				11	11	11	11	11	11	★	11	11	11	11								★	★						★	11	★		★								12	6	0
Hazel			7	7	7	7	7																						★												5	1	0
Hirst	10	10	10	10	10	★	★			★	7		10			★						★			10	10	10	10¹	10	10	10	10¹	10	10¹							19	5	3
Hodge	1	1	1	1	1			1	1	1	1	1	1	1	1	1	1	1	1	1	1	1	1	1	1	1	1	1	1	1	1	1	1	1							29	0	0
Jacobs			11					★	7		11				2	2																									5	1	0
Jonsson						11	★	★																				11	11	11¹	11	11	7	11	11	11	11				11	2	1
McCall	3	3	3	3	3																																				5	0	0
Madden	4	4	4	4	4	4	4	4	4	4		4	4	5	5	4	4	4	4	4	4	4	4		4	4	4	4	4	4	4	4	4	4	4	4	4	4	4	4	38	0	0
Marwood	7	7					7								★	11	7	7	7	7	7	7¹	7¹	7	7	7	7	★													16	2	2
May	5	5	5		5				7	5	5	5	5				★	11	11¹		5		11									7		5	5	5	5				17	1	1
Megson	8	8	8	8	8	8	8	8	8¹	8	8	8	8	8	6	8	8¹		10	8	8	8		8	8	8	8		8	8	8	8	8	8	8	8	8	8	8	8	37	0	2
Owen		★												★		11	8	8	8	11	11		8	11	11	11	11							3							12	2	0
Pearson								4	5¹	5	4	4	5	5	5	5	5	5¹	5	5	5	5		5	5	5	5														19	0	2
Pressman			1	1																									1	1	1	1	1	1	1	1	1	1			11	0	0
Proctor			6	6	6	6	6	6	6	6	6	6	6	7	6	6¹	6	6	6	6	6	6	6¹	6	6	6	6	6	6	6	6	6	6	6	6	6	6	6			35	0	2
Shutt							7																																		1	0	0
Sterland	2	2	2	2	2	2	2	2¹	2	2	2¹	2	2		2	2	2	2	2	2	2	2	2	2¹	2	2	2	2	2¹	2¹	2	2¹	2¹	2	2¹	2					38	0	8
West						10¹		10	10	10	10	10	9²	9	10	10	10¹	10	★	10¹	10¹	10	10	10	10¹	10							★	7¹	7	7	7				23	2	7
Worthington	6	6	6	6	6	3	3	3	3	3	3	3	3	3	3	3	3	3	3	3	3	3	3	3	3	3	3	3	3	3	3	3	3	3	3	3			3		38	0	0
Own Goals										1									1																								2

FA Cup: 1987-88: 3rd Round: Everton (H) 1-1 Replay (A) 1-1 2nd Replay (A) 1-1 3rd Replay (H) 0-5.
Littlewoods Cup: 1987-88: 2nd Round: Shrewsbury T. (A) 1-1 (H) 2-1; 3rd Round: Barnsley (A) 2-1; 4th Round: Aston Villa (A) 2-1; Quarter Final: Arsenal (H) 0-1.

SHREWSBURY TOWN (Division 2)

Team Manager Ian McNeill.
Club Address Gay Meadow, Shrewsbury. Tel: (0743) 60111.
Current Ground Capacity 16,000.
Record Attendance 18,917 v Walsall, Div. 3, 26 April 1961.
Year Formed 1886. Turned professional 1905.
Previous Names None.
Club Nickname "Town".
Club Colours Gold shirts with blue shorts and gold and blue hooped stockings.
Club Honours Football League: Div. 3 Champions 1978-79.
League History 1950-51 Div. 3(N); 1951-58 Div. 3(S); 1958-59 Div. 4; 1959-74 Div. 3; 1974-75 Div. 4; 1975-79 Div. 3; 1979- Div. 2.
Most League Points in a Season (2 for a win) 62 in Div. 4, 1974-75. (3 for a win) 70 in Div. 2, 1981-82.
Most League Goals in a Season 101 in Div. 4, 1958-59.
Record Victory 7-0 v Swindon T. in Div. 3(S), 6 May 1955.

Record Defeat 1-8 v Norwich C. in Div. 3(S), 1952-53 and v Coventry C. in Div. 3, 22 October 1963.
Consecutive League Wins 7 in 1950 and 1955.
Consecutive League Defeats 7 in 1951-52.
Record League Appearances Colin Griffin, 405 between 1975-88.
Record League Goalscorer—Career Arthur Rowley, 152 between 1958-65.
Record League Goalscorer—Season Arthur Rowley, 38 in Div. 4, 1958-59.

Shrewsbury Town: League Record, 1987-88 (Division 2)

Match Number	Date	Venue	Opponents	Result		H/T	Lge Posn	Attend
1	15.8.87	A	Leicester C.	W	1-0	0-0		8469
2	22.8.87	H	Ipswich T.	D	0-0	0-0		3610
3	29.8.87	A	Huddersfield T.	D	0-0	0-0	10	4478
4	1.9.87	H	Reading	L	0-1	0-1	15	3223
5	5.9.87	A	West Bromwich A.	L	1-2	0-0	17	8560
6	12.9.87	H	Manchester C.	D	0-0	0-0	18	6280
7	15.9.87	A	Hull City	D	1-1	0-0	17	7939
8	19.9.87	A	Birmingham C.	D	0-0	0-0	18	7183
9	26.9.87	H	Bradford C.	D	2-2	0-0	19	4247
10	29.9.87	A	Swindon T.	D	1-1	0-0	19	8261
11	3.10.87	H	Crystal Palace	W	2-0	1-0	16	3999
12	17.10.87	A	Millwall	L	1-4	1-2	19	5202
13	20.10.87	A	Bournemouth	L	0-2	0-2	20	5587
14	24.10.87	H	Oldham Ath.	L	2-3	2-0	21	3337
15	31.10.87	A	Middlesbrough	L	0-4	0-1	21	10183
16	3.11.87	H	Aston Villa	L	1-2	1-1	22	7089
17	7.11.87	A	Leeds U.	L	1-2	0-1	22	13760
18	14.11.87	H	Blackburn Rov.	L	1-2	0-0	21	3164
19	17.11.87	H	Sheffield U.	W	2-0	1-0	20	2555
20	21.11.87	A	Barnsley	L	1-2	0-2	20	5364
21	28.11.87	H	Stoke C.	L	0-3	0-3	20	5158
22	5.12.87	A	Plymouth Arg.	L	0-2	0-0	21	7603
23	12.12.87	H	Hull C.	D	2-2	1-2	22	2588
24	18.12.87	A	Ipswich T.	L	0-2	0-0	22	9930
25	26.12.87	A	Bradford C.	D	1-1	0-0	22	12474
26	28.12.87	H	Birmingham C.	D	0-0	0-0	22	6397
27	1.1.88	H	Huddersfield T.	W	3-1	1-0	21	5448
28	2.1.88	A	Manchester C.	W	3-1	0-1	20	21455
29	16.1.88	H	Leicester C.	D	0-0	0-0	18	5025
30	23.1.88	A	Reading	L	0-1	0-0	18	5170
31	6.2.88	H	West Bromwich A.	L	0-1	0-0	21	6360
32	13.2.88	A	Sheffield U.	W	1-0	0-0	20	8227
33	20.2.88	H	Swindon T.	W	2-1	2-1	20	5649
34	27.2.88	A	Crystal Palace	W	2-1	1-1	20	8210
35	5.3.88	H	Millwall	D	0-0	0-0	18	5408
36	19.3.88	H	Middlesbrough	L	0-1	0-0	19	5603
37	26.3.88	A	Oldham Ath.	D	2-2	1-0	21	5379
38	2.4.88	H	Leeds U.	W	1-0	0-0	19	7369
39	4.4.88	A	Blackburn Rov.	D	2-2	0-2	19	13741
40	8.4.88	H	Bournemouth	W	2-1	1-0	18	7106
41	23.4.88	A	Aston Villa	L	0-1	0-1	19	18396
42	30.4.88	H	Barnsley	D	1-1	0-0	20	4712
43	2.5.88	A	Stoke C.	D	1-1	1-0	19	7452
44	7.5.88	H	Plymouth Arg.	W	2-1	1-0	18	4510

Players: League Record, 1987-88 (Division 2)

Match Number	1	2	3	4	5	6	7	8	9	10	11	12	13	14	15	16	17	18	19	20	21	22	23	24	25	26	27	28	29	30	31	32	33	34	35	36	37	38	39	40	41	42	43	44	Apps	Subs	Goals
Bell																					★	11^1	11^1	11	11	7		★	4	4	4	11			11			11	11	11					13	2	2
Brown	★		9	9	9	9		★	★	10	10	10	9	9	9	9	★	★	9^1	9^1	9^1	9	9	9	9	9	9^1	9	9	9	★	11		10	11	10	10	10	10		10^1	10			35	6	5
Cooper						9	9	9	9^2	9	9																																		6	0	2
Geddis	9^1																										★	10	10	10			9	9	9	9	9	9^1	9	9^1	9	9^2			14	1	5
Green				★								5	5	5	★	2	2		2	2	2	2	2	2	2^1	2	2	2	2		2	2	2	2	5	5^1	2	2	2	2					29	2	2
Griffin						6	6	6																										★											3	1	0
Hughes																	1	1																											2	0	0
Irvine																											★	★	9^1	10						★	10								3	3	1
Kasule																						★	10	11	7	7^1	7	7	7	7	7^1	7^1				7	7	7	7						13	1	3
Leonard			7			★			★			★	★	4	11	11	★	8	4	★	4	4	★																						8	7	0
Leworthy												10^1	10	10^1	10	9^1	9																												6	0	3
Linighan	6	6	6	6	6	6	6	6	6	6	6^1			6	6	6	6	6	6	6	6	6	6	6	6	6	6	6	6	6	6	6	6	6	6	6	6	6	6	6	6	6	6		41	0	1
McNally	4		8	8	8	8	8	8	8	8	8	8	8	8	8	8	8		8	8	8	8^1	8	8	8	8	8	8	8	8	8	8^1	8	8	8	8	8	8	8	8	8	8	8	8	43	0	2
Melrose																											9	9	9					★	7	7^1	11		★	★					6	3	1
Moyes												5	5	5	5	5	5	5	5	5	5	5	5	5	5^2	5	5	5													★				17	0	2
Narbett	8		4	4	4^1	4	4	4	4	4	4	4	4		4	4^1	4	4^1		11	★	★	★		★		★															★			19	6	3
Pearson	5	5	5	5	5	5	5	5	5	5																																			11	0	0
Perks	1	1	1	1	1	1	1	1	1	1	1	1	1	1	1	1	1	1	1		1	1	1	1	1	1	1	1	1	1	1	1	1	1	1	1	1	1	1	1	1	1	1	1	42	0	0
Pratley																												5	5	5	5	5				5	5	5	5	5					11	0	0
Priest																		4	7	11	4	4	4	4	4	4	4	4^1	4				4^1	4	4	4	4	4	4	4					21	0	2
Robinson	10	10	10	10	10	10	10	10		★	★	★	★		7	10	10	10	10	10	10	10	10	10	10	10	10^1	10	10																23	4	1
Smith																	★																												0	1	0
Steele	7	7		7	7	7	7^1	7	7	7^1	7^1	7	7	★	7	7	7	7	7	7		7	7	7	7	7^1	7	7				★	★	11	11	★		★							28	5	3
Tester	11	11	11	11	11	11	11	11	11	11	11	11	11	11	11		11	11	11	11	★	$★^1$	11	11	11	★		7			★	★	11												24	5	1
Williams, B.	3	3	3	3	3	3	3	3	3	3	3	3	3	3	3	3	3	3	3	3	3	3	3	3	3	3	3	3	3	3	3				3	3	3	3	3	3	3	3			42	0	0
Williams, W.	2	2	2	2	2	2	2	2	2	2	2	2	2	2^1	2		2					★	★		★	★	2	2	11	11		3	3	2	2^1	★	★								24	7	2
Own Goals																												1																			1

FA Cup: 1987-88: 3rd Round: Bristol Rov. (H) 2-1; 4th Round: Plymouth Arg. (A) 0-1.
Littlewoods Cup: 1987-88: 1st Round: Crewe Alex. (A) 3-3 (H) 4-1; 2nd Round: Sheffield Wed. (H) 1-1 (A) 1-2.

SOUTHAMPTON (Division 1)

Team Manager Chris Nicholl.
Club Address The Dell, Milton Road, Southampton SO9 4XX. Tel: (0703) 220505.
Current Ground Capacity 25,175.
Record Attendance 31,044 v Manchester U., Div. 1, 8 October 1969.
Year Formed 1885. Turned professional 1894.
Previous Names Southampton St Mary's.
Club Nickname "The Saints".
Club Colours Red shirts with black trim and white vertical band on chest, black shorts and white stockings with two red hoops on turnovers.
Club Honours Football League: Div. 3(S) Champions 1921-22; Div. 3 Champions 1959-60. FA Cup: Winners 1976.
League History 1920-22 Div. 3(S); 1922-53 Div. 2; 1953-58 Div. 3(S); 1958-60 Div. 3; 1960-66 Div. 2; 1966-74 Div. 1; 1974-78 Div. 2; 1978- Div. 1.
Most League Points in a Season (2 for a win) 61 in Div. 3(S), 1921-22 and Div. 3, 1959-60. (3 for a win) 77 in Div. 1, 1983-84.

Most League Goals in a Season 112 in Div. 3(S), 1957-58.
Record Victory 14-0 v Newbury in F A Cup 1st qual. Round, 10 September 1894.
Record Defeat 0-8 v Tottenham H. in Div. 2, 28 March 1936 and v Everton in Div. 1, 20 November 1971.
Consecutive League Wins 6 in 1964.
Consecutive League Defeats 5 in 1927, 1957 and 1967-68.
Record League Appearances Terry Paine, 713 between 1956-74.
Record League Goalscorer—Career Mike Channon, 182 between 1966-82.
Record League Goalscorer—Season Derek Reeves, 39 in Div. 3, 1959-60.

Southampton: League Record, 1987-88 (Division 1)

Match Number	Date	Venue	Opponents	Result		H/T	Lge Posn	Attend
1	15.8.87	H	Manchester U.	D	2-2	1-2		21214
2	19.8.87	A	Norwich C.	W	1-0	0-0		14429
3	22.8.87	A	Portsmouth	D	2-2	1-1	8	20161
4	29.8.87	H	Q.P.R.	L	0-1	0-0	10	15532
5	2.9.87	A	Nottingham F.	D	3-3	1-2	10	14173
6	5.9.87	H	Sheffield Wed.	D	1-1	0-1	10	12526
7	12.9.87	H	Tottenham H.	L	1-2	1-1	15	24728
8	26.9.87	A	Newcastle U.	L	1-2	0-0	17	18093
9	3.10.87	H	Everton	L	0-4	0-3	18	15719
10	17.10.87	H	Watford	W	1-0	0-0	17	11933
11	20.10.87	A	Coventry C.	W	3-2	1-2	11	14552
12	24.10.87	H	Chelsea	W	3-0	0-0	10	11890
13	31.10.87	A	Charlton Ath.	D	1-1	1-0	9	5158
14	7.11.87	A	Wimbledon	L	0-2	0-1	11	5014
15	14.11.87	H	Oxford U.	W	3-0	1-0	10	12095
16	21.11.87	A	Arsenal	W	1-0	0-0	9	32477
17	28.11.87	H	Derby Co.	L	1-2	0-0	9	15201
18	5.12.87	A	West Ham U.	L	1-2	1-1	10	15375
19	12.12.87	H	Liverpool	D	2-2	1-2	10	19502
20	18.12.87	A	Luton T.	D	2-2	1-1	11	6618
21	26.12.87	H	Tottenham H.	W	2-1	2-0	9	18456
22	1.1.88	A	Q.P.R.	L	0-3	0-0	13	8631
23	3.1.88	H	Portsmouth	L	0-2	0-2	13	17002
24	16.1.88	A	Manchester U.	W	2-0	1-0	11	35716
25	23.1.88	H	Norwich C.	D	0-0	0-0	11	12002
26	6.2.88	A	Sheffield Wed.	L	1-2	1-0	12	14769
27	13.2.88	H	Nottingham F.	D	1-1	1-1	11	13314
28	27.2.88	A	Everton	L	0-1	0-1	12	20754
29	1.3.88	H	Newcastle U.	D	1-1	0-0	12	13380
30	5.3.88	A	Watford	W	1-0	1-0	10	11824
31	12.3.88	H	Coventry C.	L	1-2	1-0	10	12914
32	19.3.88	H	Charlton Ath.	L	0-1	0-0	14	12103
33	26.3.88	A	Chelsea	W	1-0	0-0	10	15380
34	2.4.88	H	Wimbledon	D	2-2	0-1	14	13036
35	4.4.88	A	Oxford U.	D	0-0	0-0	12	7657
36	9.4.88	H	Arsenal	W	4-2	3-1	10	14521
37	23.4.88	A	Derby Co.	L	0-2	0-2	12	14291
38	30.4.88	H	West Ham U.	W	2-1	0-0	11	15652
39	2.5.88	A	Liverpool	D	1-1	0-1	12	37610
40	7.5.88	H	Luton T.	D	1-1	0-1	12	12722

Players: League Record, 1987-88 (Division 1)

Match Number	1	2	3	4	5	6	7	8	9	10	11	12	13	14	15	16	17	18	19	20	21	22	23	24	25	26	27	28	29	30	31	32	33	34	35	36	37	38	39	40	Apps	Subs	Goals
Baker, G.	4	11	11	11	11		11 ^{1}	10	10	10	10 ^{1}	10 ^{1}	10	**10**	10	10	**10**	10	**10**	10	10	10	**10**	10	10	4	4			★	2	7 ^{1}	7 ^{1}	7	7	7	8	8	8		35	1	5
Baker, S.			★				★													2	2																				2	2	0
Blake																					6					5	5	5	5	5 ^{1}											6	0	1
Bond	6	6	6	6	6	6	6	6	6	6	6 ^{1}	6	6	6	6	6	6	6	6	6	6	6		6	6	6	6	6	6	6	6	6	6	6	6 ^{2}	6	6				39	0	3
Burridge								1	1	1	1	1	1	1	1	1	1	1	1	1	1	1	1	1	1	1	1	1	1	1	1	1	1	1	1	1	1				31	0	0
Case	★	4	4	4	4	4	4	4	4	4	4	4	4	4	4	4	4	4	4	4	**4**	4	4		4	4	4	4	4	4	4	4	4	4	4	4	4	4	4		37	1	0
Clarke	9	9	9 ^{2}	9	9 ^{1}	9 ^{1}	9	9 ^{1}	9	9	9	9	9 ^{1}	9	9	9	9	9	9 ^{1}	9	9 ^{2}	9	9 ^{1}	9	9 ^{1}	9	9	9	9	9	9	9	9	9	9	9	9	9	9 ^{1}		40	0	16
Cockerill	8	8	8	8	8	**8**	8	**8**	8	8	8	8	8	8	8 ^{1}	8	**8**	8	8	8	8	8	8	★	★	8	8	8	8	8	8	8	8	8 ^{1}	8	8	**8**		★	★	35	4	2
Cook	3	3																																							2	0	0
Flowers	1	1	1	1	1	1	1	1	1																																9	0	0
Forrest	2	2	2	2	2	2	2	2	2	2	2	2	2	2	2	2	2	2			2	2	2	2	2	2	2		2	2	2	2	2	2	2	2					37	0	0
Hobson	10	10	10	**10**	10 ^{1}	10	10							★						11	11			7	7	7															12	1	1
Le Tissier			★		★			★	7	7	7	7			★	★		★	★	8	8				7	7	7	7					★		★						10	9	1
Moore	5	5 ^{1}	5	5	5	5	5	5	5	5	5	5	5	5	5	5	5	5	5	5	5 ^{1}	5	5	5	5	5	5	5	5	5 ^{1}	5					5	5	5	5		35	0	3
Shearer																							★		★	11 ^{3}	11	11													3	2	3
Statham			3	3	3	3	3	3	3	3	3	3	3	3	3	3	3	3	3	3	3	3	3	3	3	3	3	3	3	3	3	3	3	3	3	3	3	3	3	3	38	0	0
Townsend	7	7	7	7	7 ^{1}	7	7	7			★		7	7	7	7 ^{1}	7	7 ^{1}	7	7	7	7	7	10	10	10	10	**10**	10	10	10	10	10	10	10	**10**	10				36	1	3
Wallace, D.	11 ^{2}		★		11	★	11	11	11 ^{1}	11 ^{1}	11 ^{1}	11 ^{1}	11 ^{2}	11 ^{1}	11	11 ^{1}	11	11				11	11	11	11	11	11	11	11	11	11 ^{1}	11	**11**	11	11	★		11	11		30	3	11
Wallace, R.					★						★		★	★	★		★		★		★									★	★				★	★	7	7 ^{1}	7		3	12	1

FA Cup: 1987-88: 3rd Round: Reading (A) 1-0; 4th Round: Luton T. (A) 1-2.
Littlewoods Cup: 1987-88: 2nd Round: Bournemouth (A) 0-1 (H) 2-2.

SOUTHEND UNITED (Division 3)

Team Manager Paul Clark.
Club Address Roots Hall Ground, Victoria Avenue, Southend-on-Sea. Tel: (0702) 340707.
Current Ground Capacity 13,429.
Record Attendance 31,090 v Liverpool, FA Cup 3rd Round, 10 January 1979.
Year Formed 1906. Turned professional 1906.
Previous Names None.
Club Nickname "The Shrimpers".
Club Colours Blue shirts, white shorts and blue stockings.
Club Honours Football League: Div. 4 Champions 1980-81.
League History 1920-58 Div. 3(S); 1958-66 Div. 3; 1966-72 Div. 4; 1972-76 Div. 3; 1976-78 Div. 4; 1978-80 Div. 3; 1980-81 Div. 4; 1981-84 Div. 3; 1984-87 Div. 4; 1987- Div. 3.
Most League Points in a Season (2 for a win) 67 in Div. 4, 1980-81. (3 for a win) 80 in Div. 4, 1986-87.
Most League Goals in a Season 92 in Div. 3(S), 1950-51.
Record Victory 10-1 v Golders Green in FA Cup 1st Round, 24 November 1934 and v Brentwood in FA Cup 2nd Round, 7 December 1968.
Record Defeat 1-9 v Brighton & H.A. in Div. 3, 27 November 1965.
Consecutive League Wins 6 in 1932, 1972, 1978 and 1980.
Consecutive League Defeats 6 in 1931-32 and 1955.
Record League Appearances Sandy Anderson, 451 between 1950-63.
Record League Goalscorer—Career Roy Hollis, 122 between 1953-60.
Record League Goalscorer—Season Jim Shankly, 31 in Div. 3(S), 1928-29 and Sammy McCrory 31 in Div. 3(S), 1957-58.

Southend United: League Record, 1987-88 (Division 3)

Match Number	Date	Venue	Opponents	Result		H/T	Lge Posn	Attend
1	15.8.87	A	Bury	D	2-2	0-1		1937
2	22.8.87	H	Chester C.	D	2-2	1-1		2369
3	29.8.87	A	Gillingham	L	1-8	0-4	18	4154
4	1.9.87	H	Preston N.E.	L	1-2	0-1	23	2600
5	5.9.87	A	Notts Co.	L	2-6	2-3	23	4166
6	12.9.87	H	Brentford	L	2-3	1-3	23	2335
7	14.9.87	A	Port Vale	L	1-4	0-1	23	3670
8	19.9.87	A	Mansfield T.	L	0-1	0-1	23	2854
9	26.9.87	H	Brighton & H.A.	W	2-1	0-0	23	3789
10	29.9.87	H	Northampton T.	D	1-1	1-1	23	3407
11	3.10.87	A	Grimsby T.	W	3-1	0-2	22	2900
12	10.10.87	A	Bristol C.	L	2-3	1-1	23	8606
13	16.10.87	H	Rotherham U.	D	1-1	1-1	23	2217
14	20.10.87	H	Fulham	L	0-2	0-1	23	3419
15	24.10.87	A	Chesterfield	L	1-3	0-2	23	1726
16	30.10.87	H	Walsall	D	1-1	0-1	23	2692
17	3.11.87	A	Sunderland	L	0-7	0-3	23	15754
18	7.11.87	A	Wigan Ath.	L	0-1	0-0	23	3081
19	21.11.87	H	Aldershot	L	0-1	0-1	23	2362
20	28.11.87	A	York C.	W	3-0	1-0	23	2225
21	11.12.87	H	Doncaster Rov.	W	4-1	1-1	23	2268
22	19.12.87	A	Blackpool	D	1-1	0-1	22	3277
23	26.12.87	A	Brighton & H.A.	D	0-0	0-0	23	11147
24	28.12.87	H	Bristol Rov.	W	4-2	2-1	22	4094
25	1.1.88	H	Gillingham	L	1-3	0-2	22	5254
26	2.1.88	A	Brentford	L	0-1	0-0	22	5752
27	9.1.88	A	Chester C.	D	1-1	1-0	22	2065
28	15.1.88	H	Mansfield T.	W	2-1	1-1	21	3091
29	22.1.88	H	Port Vale	D	3-3	2-1	21	3038
30	30.1.88	A	Preston N.E.	D	1-1	1-1	22	6180
31	5.2.88	H	Notts Co.	L	1-2	1-0	22	3904
32	13.2.88	A	Bristol Rov.	D	0-0	0-0	22	3092
33	20.2.88	H	Bury	W	1-0	1-0	21	3003
34	26.2.88	H	Grimsby T.	D	0-0	0-0	22	3409
35	2.3.88	A	Northampton T.	L	0-4	0-1	22	4249
36	5.3.88	A	Rotherham U.	D	1-1	0-0	22	2531
37	11.3.88	H	Bristol C.	W	2-0	1-0	22	3664
38	19.3.88	A	Walsall	L	1-2	1-1	22	4479
39	25.3.88	H	Chesterfield	W	3-0	2-0	22	3315
40	1.4.88	H	Wigan Ath.	W	3-2	0-1	20	5003
41	4.4.88	A	Aldershot	W	1-0	0-0	19	3436
42	9.4.88	H	Sunderland	L	1-4	1-3	19	8109
43	23.4.88	A	Fulham	L	1-3	0-1	21	5043
44	29.4.88	H	York C.	W	3-1	2-1	21	3768
45	2.5.88	A	Doncaster Rov.	W	1-0	0-0	20	1306
46	7.5.88	H	Blackpool	W	4-0	1-0	17	5541

Players: League Record, 1987-88 (Division 3)

Match Number	1	2	3	4	5	6	7	8	9	10	11	12	13	14	15	16	17	18	19	20	21	22	23	24	25	26	27	28	29	30	31	32	33	34	35	36	37	38	39	40	41	42	43	44	45	46	Apps	Subs	Goals
Brush																				7	7¹	7							★		7	3	6	6	6	6	6	2	2	2							13	1	1
Burrows					4	4	4	4	4	4																																					6	0	0
Butler																																															0	0	0
Clark	7	7	7	7	7	7		★			★	7	7	7	7	7	7	7	7	7	7	7		7	7							6	6	6	6	6¹	6	6	7¹	7	7	7	7	7	7	7¹	15	0	3
Crown																																7									4	4	4	6	6	6	4	2	0
Hall	6	3	3	3	3	6	6	6	6¹	6	6	6	6	6	6	6	6	6	6	6¹	6	6	6	6	6	6¹	6	6	6		★	8	8	7	8	2	2	2	2		9	9	9¹	9	9	9¹	28	0	17
Johnson	3					3	3	3	3	3	3	3	3	3	3	3	3	3	3	3	3	3	3	3	3	3	3	3		3	3	3	3	3	3		3	3	3	3¹	3	3	3				39	1	3
Ling				★	★	11		★	11	11	11	11¹	11	11		4	4	4	4	4	4	4¹	4	4	4	4	4	10	10	7	7	7	7	★	★	★¹	11	11	11	11²	11	11²					35	7	1
McDonough	11	10	10	10	10¹	10	10¹	10	10	10	10	10¹	10¹	10	10	10¹	10	10	10	★	10	10²	10	10	10¹	10	10	★	10	10				★	★	10	11	10	10		★¹	10	10	10	10	10	37	5	9
Martin	5	6	6	6		6			2	2	2	2	2	2	2	2	2	5	2	5	5	5	5	5	5	5	5		5	5	5	5	5	5	5	5	5	5	5	5		5	4	4	4		41	0	0
Neal	10	★	9	9		★	9							9	9																																10	2	0
Newell																			1	1	1	1	1	1	1	1	1	1	1	1	1									11	11	11	11				10	0	0
Nogan				9	9	9	9¹	9	9																																			1	1		13	0	1
O'Shea																																															6	0	1
Pennyfather		★	8	8	8²	8	8	8	8¹	8	8	8	8	8	8	8	8	8	2	2	2	2	2	2	2	2	2	2	2	2	2	2	2	2	2	2	2	2	2								22	0	0
Ramsey	2	2	2	2	2	2					★	★	2											★			★		★																		16	1	3
Robinson	11²	11	11	11¹	11		9	11	7	7	7	7¹	7¹	11	9	9	9					★	★	11	10	11	11¹	11	11	11	11	11	11			★	10²	10	★	★	★						31	6	8
Rogers	4	4	4	4	4¹	4	4	★				★	★	★	11	11	11	11	11	11	11	11	11	11																							17	4	1
Sansome																																																	
Smith	8	8¹	8	★	9	6							★¹	★			★	8¹	8	8	8	8¹	8	8	8	11	8	8	8	8¹	8	8	8					8	★	8	8	8	8	8	8	8	29	5	5
Steele	1	1	1	1	1	1	1	1	1	1	1	1	1	1	1	1	1	1															1	1	1	1	1	1	1	1	1						27	0	0
Westley		5¹	5	5	5	5	5	5	5¹	5	5	5	5	5	5		5								★¹	3	7	8	5		4	4	4	4	4	4	4	4¹	4	4	4	5	5	5¹	5		35	1	5
Young		9																									★	★	10	10	10		10														5	2	0
Own Goals			1																																												5		

FA Cup: 1987-88: 1st Round: Walsall (H) 0-0 Replay (A) 1-2.
Littlewoods Cup: 1987-88: 1st Round: Brentford (A) 1-2 (H) 4-2; 2nd Round: Derby Co. (H) 1-0 (A) 0-0; 3rd Round: Ipswich T (A) 0-1.

STOCKPORT COUNTY (Division 4)

Team Manager Asa Hartford.
Club Address Edgeley Park, Hardcastle Road, Stockport, Cheshire SK3 9DD. Tel: 061-480 8888.
Current Ground Capacity 6,000.
Record Attendance 27,833 v Liverpool, FA Cup 5th Round, 11 February 1950.
Year Formed 1883. Turned professional 1891.
Previous Names Heaton Norris Rovers, Heaton Norris.
Club Nickname "County" or "The Hatters".
Club Colours Blue and white striped shirts, blue shorts and stockings.
Club Honours Football League: Div. 3(N) Champions 1921-22, 1936-37; Div. 4 Champions 1966-67.
League History 1900-04 Div. 2; 1904 Failed re-election; 1905-21 Div. 2; 1921-22 Div. 3(N); 1922-26 Div. 2; 1926-37 Div. 3(N); 1937-38 Div. 2; 1938-58 Div. 3(N); 1958-59 Div. 3; 1959-67 Div. 4; 1967-70 Div. 3; 1970- Div. 4.
Most League Points in a Season (2 for a win) 64 in Div. 4, 1966-67. (3 for a win) 64 in Div. 4, 1985-86.
Most League Goals in a Season 115 in Div. 3(N), 1933-34.

Record Victory 13-0 v Halifax T. in Div. 3(N), 6 January 1934.
Record Defeat 1-8 v Chesterfield in Div. 2, 19 April 1902 and 0-7 v Sheffield Wed. in League Cup 2nd Round 2nd leg, 6 October 1986.
Consecutive League Wins 8 in 1927-28.
Consecutive League Defeats 9 in 1908-09.
Record League Appearances Bob Murray, 465 between 1952-63.
Record League Goalscorer—Career Jack Connor, 132 between 1951-56.
Record League Goalscorer—Season Alf Lythgoe, 46 in Div. 3(N), 1933-34.

Stockport County: League Record, 1987-88 (Division 4)

Match Number	Date	Venue	Opponents	Result		H/T	Lge Posn	Attend
1	15.8.87	H	Swansea C.	L	0-2	0-0		2482
2	22.8.87	A	Darlington	W	2-1	0-1		1744
3	28.8.87	H	Tranmere Rov.	L	1-2	1-1	20	2229
4	31.8.87	H	Newport Co.	W	2-1	0-1	9	1626
5	4.9.87	H	Carlisle U.	W	3-0	1-0	5	2257
6	12.9.87	A	Rochdale	W	1-0	1-0	3	2700
7	15.9.87	H	Leyton Orient	L	1-2	1-2	5	2560
8	19.9.87	H	Wolverhampton W.	L	0-2	0-2	11	2233
9	26.9.87	A	Wrexham	L	1-2	1-2	14	1841
10	29.9.87	A	Scunthorpe U.	D	0-0	0-0	15	2181
11	2.10.87	A	Cardiff C.	L	0-1	0-1	19	2332
12	10.10.87	H	Peterborough U.	L	0-1	0-0	20	1594
13	16.10.87	A	Halifax T.	L	0-2	0-2	21	1696
14	20.10.87	A	Crewe Alex.	L	1-3	0-2	21	2251
15	23.10.87	H	Hereford U.	L	0-2	0-1	21	1566
16	31.10.87	A	Burnley	D	1-1	1-1	21	6645
17	3.11.87	H	Hartlepool U.	W	1-0	0-0	20	1408
18	6.11.87	H	Torquay U.	W	2-1	1-0	19	1697
19	21.11.87	A	Exeter C.	L	1-2	0-1	20	2217
20	27.11.87	H	Colchester U.	D	1-1	1-0	20	1703
21	11.12.87	A	Cambridge U.	L	0-2	0-2	20	1475
22	19.12.87	H	Scarborough	D	1-1	1-1	21	1779
23	26.12.87	H	Wrexham	D	1-1	0-1	21	2504
24	28.12.87	A	Bolton W.	L	1-2	0-1	22	6607
25	1.1.88	A	Tranmere Rov.	L	0-4	0-2	22	3670
26	2.1.88	H	Rochdale	D	1-1	1-1	22	2441
27	16.1.88	A	Wolverhampton W.	D	1-1	0-0	22	8872
28	23.1.88	A	Leyton Orient	D	1-1	1-0	22	4205
29	29.1.88	H	Newport Co.	W	5-1	1-1	21	2509
30	6.2.88	A	Carlisle U.	L	0-2	0-1	23	1852
31	12.2.88	H	Bolton W.	L	1-2	0-1	23	4814
32	19.2.88	A	Swansea C.	D	1-1	1-0	22	4405
33	27.2.88	A	Cardiff C.	D	0-0	0-0	23	4008
34	1.3.88	H	Scunthorpe U.	D	1-1	1-0	23	1854
35	4.3.88	H	Halifax T.	W	1-0	1-0	22	2171
36	12.3.88	A	Peterborough U.	D	0-0	0-0	22	2193
37	19.3.88	H	Burnley	W	2-0	1-0	21	4423
38	26.3.88	A	Hereford U.	W	1-0	1-0	20	1695
39	2.4.88	A	Torquay U.	L	0-3	0-1	20	2919
40	4.4.88	H	Exeter C.	W	2-1	0-1	18	2161
41	9.4.88	A	Hartlepool U.	W	3-1	2-1	18	1317
42	19.4.88	A	Darlington	D	1-1	1-0	18	1625
43	21.4.88	H	Crewe Alex.	D	1-1	0-0	19	1520
44	29.4.88	A	Colchester U.	L	0-2	0-0	19	1607
45	2.5.88	H	Cambridge U.	L	0-2	0-0	20	1842
46	7.5.88	A	Scarborough	D	1-1	0-0	20	2236

Players: League Record, 1987-88 (Division 4)

Match Number	1	2	3	4	5	6	7	8	9	10	11	12	13	14	15	16	17	18	19	20	21	22	23	24	25	26	27	28	29	30	31	32	33	34	35	36	37	38	39	40	41	42	43	44	45	46	Apps	Subs	Goals
Bailey	3			3	3	3	7	3	3	3	3	3	3	3	3	3	3	3	3	3	3	3	3			3	3	3	3								3	3	3	3	3				3	3	34	0	0
Birch											11	11	11	11	11	11	11¹	11	11¹	11	11	11	11	11		11	11	11	11¹	11											★		★				18	2	3
Bullock	7	10	5	5	5	5	5	5	5	5	5	5	5	5	2	2	2	2	2	2	2	2	2	2	2	2	2	2	2	2	2	2							2	2	5	5	5	5	5	5	41	0	0
Burke												11		10	10	10	8																														5	0	0
Chandler			9	9	9		★		8																																						4	1	0
Colville										9	9	9¹	9	8	8	8	8	8¹	9	8	8	8	8	8	8	8	8	8	8¹	8	8	8	8¹	8²	8	8	8	8¹	8¹	8	8¹	8	8¹	8	8	8	40	0	13
Crompton																																													1	1	2	0	0
Cronin	8	8	8	8	8¹					9	9	9																				8					★			★		6	9	7			11	4	1
Edwards	11	11	11	11	11	11¹	11	11	11		11	★	★		★		★		★		★		★																10¹	10							12	7	2
Entwistle	9				9			★						★	9¹		9¹	9¹	9			★	★	★		★	★	★	10	9	9	9	9	9	9¹				9	★		9					15	10	1
Evans	2	2²	2	2¹	2¹																																										5	0	4
Farnaby								8	10	2	★		2	★		★			10¹			★	10	11	3					11						2	2	2	2	2		4	2	2		★	17	5	1
Hartford	10			10	10	10	10	10						10	10	10	10	10			10	10		★	10			10	10	10		10	10	10	10	10	10	10	10			10	10	10	10		30	1	0
Hendrie																									★	★	10		10	★	7	7	7¹	7	7	7	★	★		11	11	11	11	11	11	11¹	11	17	5	1
Hodkinson		7	7¹	7¹	7¹	7	7¹	7		7	7	7	7	7	7	7	7	7	7	7	7	7	7¹	7	7	7		★		★	★	7	7	7	7	7	7¹	7	7¹	7			7	7	7		36	3	6
Howard																																													2	2	2	0	0
McKenzie			3	3	3							3																			3	3	3	3	3	3								3	3		12	0	0
Marples	1	1	1	1	1	1	1	1	1	1	1	1	1	1	1	1	1	1	1	1	1	1	1	1	1	1	1	1	1	1	1	1	1	1	1	1	1	1	1	1	1	1	1	1	1	1	44	0	0
Mills						9	8	8	★	10	10		★																																		5	2	0
Pickering																5	5	5	5	5	5																			4	4	4					8	0	0
Robinson	4	4	4	4	4	4	4	4	4	4	4	4	4	4	4	4	4	4¹	4	4	4	4	4	4	4	4	4	4¹	4	4	4	4	4	4	4												37	0	2
Scott				2	2	2	2	2		2	9					★			5	5	5	5	5													7		2									15	1	0
Sertori	★																																														0	1	0
Sword	5	5							8											★																											3	1	0
Thorpe																								5	5	5	5	5		5	5	5	5		5	5	5	5	5	5	5	4	4	4	4¹	4	20	0	0
Williams	6	6	6	6	6	6	6	6	6	6	6	6	6	6	6	6	6	6	6	6	6	6	6	6	6	6	6	6	6	6	6	6	6	6	6	6	6	6	6	6	6			6	6¹		45	0	1
Willis																								5	5	10	10				11	11	11	11	11	11											10	0	0
Worthington																	9	9	9¹	9	9¹	9	9¹	9	9¹	9¹	9	9	9	9¹	9¹						★		9	9	9	9	9				18	1	6
Own Goals																																								1									1

FA Cup: 1987-88: 1st Round: Telford (A) 1-1 Replay (H) 2-0; 2nd Round: Runcorn (A) 1-0; 3rd Round: Leyton Orient (H) 1-2.
Littlewoods Cup: 1987-88: 1st Round: Carlisle U. (H) 0-1 (A) 0-3.

STOKE CITY (Division 2)

Team Manager   Mick Mills.
Club Address   Victoria Ground, Stoke on Trent. Tel: (0782) 413511.
Current Ground Capacity   31,718.
Record Attendance   51,380 v Arsenal, Div.1, 29 March 1937.
Year Formed   1863. Turned professional 1885.
Previous Names   None.
Club Nickname   "The Potters".
Club Colours   Red and white striped shirts, white shorts and stockings.
Club Honours   Football League: Div. 2 Champions 1932-33, 1962-63; Div. 3(N) Champions 1926-27. Football League Cup: Winners 1972.
League History   1888-90 Div. 1; 1890 Not re-elected; 1891-1907 Div. 1; 1907-08 Div. 2; 1908 Resigned; 1919-22 Div. 2; 1922-23 Div. 1; 1923-26 Div. 2; 1926-27 Div. 3(N); 1927-33 Div. 2; 1933-53 Div. 1; 1953-63 Div. 2; 1963-77 Div. 1; 1977-79 Div. 2; 1979-85 Div. 1; 1985- Div. 2.
Most League Points in a Season   (2 for a win) 63 in Div. 3(N), 1926-27. (3 for a win) 58 in Div. 2, 1986-87.

Most League Goals in a Season   92 in Div. 3(N), 1926-27.
Record Victory   10-3 v West Bromwich A. in Div. 1, 14 September 1889.
Record Defeat   0-10 v Preston N.E. in Div. 1, 14 September 1889.
Consecutive League Wins   7 in 1905 and 1947.
Consecutive League Defeats   11 in 1985.
Record League Appearances   Eric Skeels, 506 between 1959-76.
Record League Goalscorer—Career   Freddie Steele, 142 between 1934-49.
Record League Goalscorer—Season   Freddie Steele, 33 in Div. 1, 1936-37.

Stoke City: League Record, 1987-88 (Division 2)

Match Number	Date	Venue	Opponents	Result		H/T	Lge Posn	Attend
1	15.8.87	A	Birmingham C.	L	0-2	0-1		13137
2	18.8.87	H	Hull C.	D	1-1	0-1		9139
3	22.8.87	H	Middlesbrough	W	1-0	0-0	11	9345
4	29.8.87	A	Ipswich T.	L	0-2	0-1	15	11149
5	31.8.87	H	Leicester C.	W	2-1	2-1	9	9948
6	5.9.87	A	Sheffield U.	D	0-0	0-0	10	10086
7	12.9.87	H	Bradford C.	L	1-2	0-1	13	9571
8	16.9.87	A	Reading	W	1-0	0-0	9	5349
9	19.9.87	A	Manchester C.	L	0-3	0-2	14	19322
10	26.9.87	H	Huddersfield T.	D	1-1	0-1	15	8665
11	30.9.87	A	Leeds U.	D	0-0	0-0	14	17208
12	3.10.87	H	Bournemouth	W	1-0	0-0	10	8104
13	10.10.87	H	Plymouth Arg.	W	1-0	1-0	9	8275
14	17.10.87	A	Blackburn Rov.	L	0-2	0-1	10	7280
15	20.10.87	A	Swindon T.	L	0-3	0-1	10	9160
16	24.10.87	H	Aston Villa	D	0-0	0-0	10	13494
17	31.10.87	A	Barnsley	L	2-5	0-2	15	5908
18	7.11.87	H	West Bromwich A.	W	3-0	2-0	14	9992
19	14.11.87	A	Crystal Palace	L	0-2	0-0	14	8309
20	21.11.87	H	Millwall	L	1-2	1-0	14	7998
21	28.11.87	A	Shrewsbury T.	W	3-0	3-0	14	5158
22	8.12.87	H	Oldham Ath.	D	2-2	1-1	15	6740
23	12.12.87	A	Middlesbrough	L	0-2	0-0	15	12289
24	19.12.87	H	Reading	W	4-2	0-0	14	6968
25	26.12.87	A	Huddersfield T.	W	3-0	0-0	14	9500
26	28.12.87	H	Manchester C.	L	1-3	0-2	15	18020
27	1.1.88	A	Ipswich T.	L	1-2	1-1	15	9976
28	2.1.88	A	Bradford C.	W	4-1	3-0	14	12223
29	16.1.88	H	Birmingham C.	W	3-1	1-1	14	10076
30	6.2.88	H	Sheffield U.	W	1-0	0-0	12	9344
31	13.2.88	A	Hull C.	D	0-0	0-0	12	6424
32	23.2.88	H	Leeds U.	W	2-1	1-0	10	10129
33	27.2.88	A	Bournemouth	D	0-0	0-0	10	6871
34	5.3.88	H	Blackburn Rov.	W	2-1	1-0	9	14100
35	12.3.88	A	Plymouth Arg.	L	0-3	0-2	10	8749
36	16.3.88	A	Leicester C.	D	1-1	0-1	10	10502
37	19.3.88	H	Barnsley	W	3-1	0-0	9	8029
38	26.3.88	A	Aston Villa	W	1-0	0-0	8	20392
39	2.4.88	A	West Bromwich A.	L	0-2	0-1	8	12144
40	4.4.88	H	Crystal Palace	D	1-1	1-0	9	9613
41	9.4.88	A	Oldham Ath.	L	1-5	1-2	9	6505
42	23.4.88	H	Swindon T.	W	1-0	1-0	8	6293
43	30.4.88	A	Millwall	L	0-2	0-0	10	12636
44	2.5.88	H	Shrewsbury T.	D	1-1	0-1	11	7452

Players: League Record, 1987-88 (Division 2)

Match Number	1	2	3	4	5	6	7	8	9	10	11	12	13	14	15	16	17	18	19	20	21	22	23	24	25	26	27	28	29	30	31	32	33	34	35	36	37	38	39	40	41	42	43	44	Apps	Subs	Goals
Allinson	11	11	11	11			9		11★		★	★																																	6	3	0
Barrett					1	1	1											1	1		1	1	1	1	1	1	1	1	1	1	1	1	1	1	1	1	1	1	1	1	1	1	1	1	27	0	0
Beeston																							6	6	2	2	2	10	6	4	4														12	0	0
Berry	6	6	6¹	6	6	6	6¹	6	6	6	6	6	6★		6	6	6¹	6		6	6	6	6	6¹	6	6		6¹	6	6	6	6			6	6									35	1	5
Bould						5	5	5	5	5	5	5				5	5	5	5	5	5	5	5	5	5¹	5	5	5	5	5	5	5	5	5	5	5	5	5	5	5	5	5	5	5	30	0	0
Carr		★	3	3	3	3	3	3	3	3	3	3	3	11	3		3	3	★	3	3	3	3	3	3	3	3	3	3	3	3	3	3	3	3	3	3	3	3	3	3	3	3	3	39	2	0
Daly	8	8	8		★	10	10	4		★	8		10	10	8	4	6	8	8							★	★									★¹	4								16	5	1
Dixon	2	2	2	2	2	2	2	2	2	2	2	2	2	2	2	2	2	2	2	2	2¹	2	2	2	2	2	2¹	2																	29	0	2
Ford	7	7¹	7	7	7	7	7	7	7	7	7¹	7	7¹	7	7	7	7	7¹	7	7	7	7¹	7	7	7	7¹	7	7	7	7	7	7	7	7	7	7	7	7	7	7	7	7	7	7	44	0	7
Fowler																																						★							0	1	0
Fox	1	1	1	1	1				1	1	1	1	1	1	1	1	1	1	1		1																								17	0	0
Gibbons																																			★										0	1	0
Hackett																															11														1	0	0
Heath	★	★		★	11¹	11	11	11		11	11	11	11¹	11	★	11	11	11¹	11	11¹		★¹	★	11	11	11			11	11	11	11	11¹	11	★	11	11	11¹	11	11	11¹	11	11	11	32	7	8
Hemming	5	5	5	5	5	5				★	9	6	5	5	5	5	5	5												★	2	2¹	★	6		★	6	3							20	4	1
Henry												8	8¹	8	8	8	8¹	8²	8	8	8	8	8	8	8	8¹	8	8	8	8	8	8	6												22	0	5
Holmes														★	5																														1	1	0
Lewis																																				★									0	1	0
Mills														3																															1	0	0
Morgan	9	9	9	9	9	9		9	9	9	9	9					9	9	9	9	9	9	9	9¹	9¹	9	9¹	9¹	9		★	9	9¹	9											27	1	5
Parkin	3	3	★	8	8	8	8	8¹	8	4	4	8	4		8	3	4¹	8	3	11	11	11		4¹	4	4	11		2	2	4	4	4	4	2	2	2	2	2	2	2				42	1	3
Puckett																																		10	4	10	10	4	4	8				7	0	0
Saunders	10	10	10	10	10¹	10	10			8	8	9				★	10	8	10¹		★					4¹	4																		15	2	3
Shaw							★	10	10	10	10	10	9	9	9	10¹	10		10¹	10	10	10¹	10	10	10¹	10		★	9	9	9	★	10¹	10	9¹	9	9	10	9¹	9	9	9	9	9	30	3	6
Stainrod																							10	10	10	10	10	10	10					★	9			10¹	10	10¹					11	1	2
Talbot	4	4	4	4	4	4	4	4	4						4	4	4		★	4	4	4	4	4★¹		★	4	4¹																	19	3	2
Ware																																									4				1	0	0

FA Cup: 1987-88: 3rd Round: Liverpool (H) 0-0 Replay (A) 0-1.
Littlewoods Cup: 1987-88: 2nd Round: Gillingham (H) 2-0 (A) 1-0; 3rd Round: Norwich C. (H) 2-1; 4th Round: Arsenal (A) 0-3.

SUNDERLAND (Division 2)

Team Manager Denis Smith.
Club Address Roker Park Ground, Sunderland. Tel: (0783) 5140332).
Current Ground Capacity 37,875.
Record Attendance 75,118 v Derby Co., FA Cup 6th Round replay, 8 March 1933.
Year Formed 1879. Turned professional 1886.
Previous Names Sunderland and District Teachers AFC.
Club Nickname "The Rokerites".
Club Colours Red and white striped shirts, black shorts and white stockings.
Club Honours Football League: Div. 1 Champions 1891-92, 1892-93, 1894-95, 1901-02, 1912-13, 1935-36; Div. 2 Champions 1975-76; Div. 3 Champions 1987-88. FA Cup: Winners 1937, 1973.
League History 1890-58 Div. 1; 1958-64 Div. 2; 1964-70 Div. 1; 1970-76 Div. 2; 1976-77 Div. 1; 1977-80 Div. 2; 1980-85 Div. 1; 1985-87 Div. 2; 1987-88 Div. 3; 1988- Div. 2.
Most League Points in a Season (2 for a win) 63 in Div. 3(N), 1926-27. (3 for a win) 93 in Div. 3, 1987-88.

Most League Goals in a Season 109 in Div. 1, 1935-36.
Record Victory 11-1 v Fairfield in FA Cup 1st Round, 1894-95.
Record Defeat 0-8 v West Ham U. in Div. 1, 19 October 1968 and v Watford in Div. 1, 25 September 1982.
Consecutive League Wins 13 in 1891-92.
Consecutive League Defeats 9 in 1976-77.
Record League Appearances Jim Montgomery, 537 between 1962-77.
Record League Goalscorer—Career Charlie Buchan, 209 between 1911-25.
Record League Goalscorer—Season Dave Halliday, 43 in Div. 1, 1928-29.

Sunderland: League Record, 1987-88 (Division 3)

Match Number	Date	Venue	Opponents	Result		H/T	Lge Posn	Attend
1	15.8.87	A	Brentford.	W	1-0	0-0		7509
2	22.8.87	H	Bristol Rov.	D	1-1	0-0		13059
3	29.8.87	A	Doncaster Rov.	W	2-0	1-0	3	2740
4	31.8.87	H	Mansfield T.	W	4-1	0-1	1	13994
5	5.9.87	A	Walsall	D	2-2	1-1	1	6909
6	12.9.87	H	Bury	D	1-1	1-1	3	13227
7	15.9.87	A	Gillingham	D	0-0	0-0	5	9184
8	19.9.87	A	Brighton & H.A.	L	1-3	0-2	10	8949
9	26.9.87	H	Chester C.	L	0-2	0-1	12	12760
10	29.9.87	A	Fulham	W	1-0	1-0	9	6996
11	3.10.87	H	Aldershot	W	3-1	1-1	4	12542
12	10.10.87	H	Wigan Ath.	W	4-1	3-1	1	13974
13	17.10.87	A	Blackpool	W	2-0	0-0	2	8476
14	20.10.87	A	Bristol C.	W	1-0	1-0	1	15109
15	24.10.87	H	York C.	W	4-2	3-1	1	19314
16	31.10.87	A	Notts Co.	L	1-2	1-1	1	8854
17	3.11.87	H	Southend U.	W	7-0	3-0	1	15754
18	7.11.87	H	Grimsby T.	D	1-1	0-1	1	18197
19	21.11.87	A	Chesterfield	D	1-1	0-0	1	5700
20	28.11.88	H	Port Vale	W	2-1	2-0	1	15655
21	12.12.87	A	Northampton T.	W	2-0	0-0	2	7279
22	20.12.87	H	Rotherham U.	W	3-0	0-0	1	20168
23	26.12.87	A	Chester C.	W	2-1	2-0	1	6663
24	28.12.87	H	Preston N.E.	D	1-1	0-0	1	24814
25	1.1.88	H	Doncaster Rov.	W	3-1	3-1	1	19419
26	2.1.88	A	Bury	W	3-2	1-1	1	4883
27	16.1.88	H	Brighton & H.A.	W	1-0	1-0	1	17404
28	30.1.88	H	Gillingham	W	2-1	0-0	1	16195
29	6.2.88	H	Walsall	D	1-1	0-1	1	18311
30	13.2.88	A	Preston N.E.	D	2-2	2-2	1	10852
31	20.2.88	H	Brentford	W	2-0	2-0	1	15458
32	24.2.88	A	Bristol Rov.	L	0-4	0-1	1	4501
33	27.2.88	A	Aldershot	L	2-3	2-2	2	5010
34	1.3.88	H	Fulham	W	2-0	2-0	1	11379
35	5.3.88	H	Blackpool	D	2-2	2-1	2	15513
36	12.3.88	A	Wigan Ath.	D	2-2	0-1	2	6949
37	19.3.88	H	Notts Co.	D	1-1	1-0	2	24071
38	26.3.88	A	York C.	L	1-2	0-1	2	8878
39	2.4.88	A	Grimsby T.	W	1-0	1-0	1	7001
40	4.4.88	H	Chesterfield	W	3-2	2-2	1	21886
41	9.4.88	A	Southend U.	W	4-1	3-1	1	8109
42	23.4.88	H	Bristol C.	L	0-1	0-1	1	18225
43	26.4.88	A	Mansfield T.	W	4-0	2-0	1	6930
44	30.4.88	H	Port Vale	W	1-0	0-0	1	7569
45	2.5.88	H	Northampton T.	W	3-1	1-1	1	29454
46	7.5.88	A	Rotherham U.	W	4-1	2-0	1	9374

Players: League Record, 1987-88 (Division 3)

Match Number	1	2	3	4	5	6	7	8	9	10	11	12	13	14	15	16	17	18	19	20	21	22	23	24	25	26	27	28	29	30	31	32	33	34	35	36	37	38	39	40	41	42	43	44	45	46	Apps	Subs	Goals
Agboola	3	3	3	3	3	3	3	**3**	3	3	3	3	3	3	3	**3**		3	3	3	3	3	3	3	**3**	3	3	3	3	3	3	3	3	3	3	3	**3**						★				37	1	0
Armstrong	6	6	6	6¹	6	6	6	**6**									★	8	7¹	7		11	11	11	11	**11**	11	11	11	11	11	11	11	11	11¹	11¹	11		11	11	11	11	**11**	11	11	11¹	36	1	5
Atkinson			11¹						★	11	11	11	11	11	11	11	11²	11	11	11				6			6	6	6	**6**	**6**	6			11												21	1	3
Bennett	4	4	4		4	4	4	4	4	4	4	**4**	4						4	4	4	4	4	⁴4	4	4¹	4¹	4	4	4	4	4	4	4	4	4	4	4			4	4	4				38	0	2
Bertschin	9¹	9	9	9	9²	9	9	9	9								★	10	★			★	9	★	★	★			10¹	10			★	★				★								★¹	14	11	5
Buchanan							10																																								1	0	0
Carter																												1																			1	0	0
Corner									4	4	4	4																																			4	0	0
Cornforth							7	7	7	7²	7	7							8	8	8		8					8	8	8	8¹	8	8	8	★		8	★		6	6		★				8	4	2
Doyle			8	8	8	8	8	8	8	8	8	8	8	8			8	8	8		8	8	8	8	8¹	8	8	8	8			6	6		★		6	6	6	6					31	1	1
Gabbiadini									10	10²	10²	10²	10	10	10¹	10	10¹	**10**		10	10¹	10	10	10	10¹	10	10				10¹	10¹	10	**10¹**	**10¹**	10	10¹	10¹	10	10¹	10	10	10	10	10	10²	35	0	21
Gates	**10**	**10**	10	10	**10**		10	10		9	9²	9	9	9¹	9	9⁴	9	9	9¹	9	9³	9		9	9¹	9	9	9	9	9¹	9	9	9	9	9¹	9¹	9	9	9	9	**9**	9²	9¹	9¹	9	42	0	19
Gray	★	★	★		★	★		★	★	★	★	★	★	★	★	★	3	3				★	★		★			★	★	★		6	6	6		★	★	3	3	3	3	3	3	3	12	22	0
Hardwick	1	1	1	1	1	1		1																																						6	0	0
Heathcote																★																															0	1	0
Hesford						1	1	1	1	1	1	1	1	1	1	1	1	1	1	1	1	1	1	1	1	1	1	1	1	1	1	1	1	1	1	1	1	1		1	1	1	1	39	0	0
Kay	2	2	2	2	2	2	2	2	2	2	2	2	2	2	2	2	2	2	2	2	2	2	2	2	2	2	2	2	2	2	2	2	2	2	2	2	2	2	2	2	2	2	2	2	2	2	46	0	0
Lemon	7	7¹	7¹	7	7	7		7	7	7	7		★	★		8	★	★	★	7	7¹	7	7¹	7	7²	7	7¹	7	7		★	8	8	8	8				7¹	7¹	7	7	7	7	35	6	9
McGuire																																		8												1	0	0
MacPhail	5	5	5	5²	5	5	5	5¹	5	5	5¹	5	5²	5	5	5¹	5	5	5¹	5¹	5	5	5¹	5¹	5	5	5	5	5	5¹	5	5	5¹	5	5	5	5	5	5	5	5¹	5	5	5	5¹	5¹	46	0	16
Moore	★	★	★		★	★		★	★												★					★							★														0	9	0
Ord											4	4	4														★					★	★	4				★							4	4	4	0
Owers	11	11	11¹		11	11¹	11	11	6	6	6	6	6	6	6¹	6	6	6	**6**	6	6	6	6	6		6	6			7¹	7	7	7	7	7	**7**	6	6	6	6							37	0	4
Pascoe																																	★¹	8	8¹	8¹	8	8¹	8	8	8	8					8	1	4
Proctor	8	8	8	8																																											4	0	0
Own Goals																				1																														1

FA Cup: 1987-88: 1st Round: Darlington (H) 2-0; 2nd Round: Scunthorpe U. (A) 1-2.
Littlewoods Cup: 1987-88: 1st Round: Middlesbrough (H) 1-0 (A) 0-2.

SWANSEA CITY (Division 4)

Team Manager   Terry Yorath.
Club Address   Vetch Field, Swansea. Tel: (0792) 51311.
Current Ground Capacity   26,237.
Record Attendance   32,796 v Arsenal, FA Cup 4th Round, 17 February 1968.
Year Formed   1900. Turned professional 1912.
Previous Names   Swansea Town.
Club Nickname   "The Swans".
Club Colours   White shirts and stockings with black trim and black shorts.
Club Honours   Football League: Div. 3(S) Champions 1924-25, 1948-49.
League History   1920-25 Div. 3(S); 1925-47 Div. 2; 1947-49 Div. 3(S); 1949-65 Div. 2; 1965-67 Div. 3; 1967-70 Div. 4; 1970-73 Div. 3; 1973-78 Div. 4; 1978-79 Div. 3; 1979-81 Div. 2; 1981-83 Div. 1; 1983-84 Div. 2; 1984-86 Div. 3; 1986-88 Div. 4; 1988- Div. 3.
Most League Points in a Season   (2 for a win) 62 in Div. 3(S), 1948-49. (3 for a win) 70 in Div. 4, 1987-88.
Most League Goals in a Season   90 in Div. 2, 1956-57.

Record Victory   12-0 v Sliema Wanderers in European Cup-winners Cup 1st Round, 1st leg, 15 September 1982.
Record Defeat   1-8 v Fulham in Div. 2, 22 January 1938.
Consecutive League Wins   8 in 1961.
Consecutive League Defeats   6 in 1935 and 1957.
Record League Appearances   Wilfred Milne, 585 between 1919-37.
Record League Goalscorer—Career   Ivor Allchurch, 166 between 1949-68.
Record League Goalscorer—Season   Cyril Pearce, 35 in Div. 2, 1931-32.

Swansea City: League Record, 1987-88 (Division 4)

Match Number	Date	Venue	Opponents	Result	H/T	Lge Posn	Attend
1	15.8.87	A	Stockport Co.	W 2-0	0-0		2482
2	22.8.87	H	Exeter C.	L 0-2	0-1		5557
3	29.8.87	A	Cardiff C.	L 0-1	0-0	19	6010
4	31.8.87	H	Hartlepool U.	W 2-1	0-1	21	3569
5	5.9.87	A	Burnley	L 0-1	0-0	18	4778
6	12.9.87	H	Hereford U.	W 3-0	0-0	8	3794
7	16.9.87	H	Halifax T.	L 1-3	0-2	12	1236
8	19.9.87	A	Scarborough	L 0-2	0-0	18	3033
9	26.9.87	H	Crewe Alex.	L 2-4	0-2	21	3832
10	29.9.87	A	Colchester U.	L 1-2	0-1	22	1140
11	3.10.87	H	Cambridge U.	D 1-1	0-1	21	3378
12	10.10.87	H	Wrexham	W 2-1	0-0	21	3741
13	17.10.87	H	Newport Co.	L 1-2	0-1	20	3739
14	20.10.87	A	Tranmere Rov.	W 2-1	2-1	18	2210
15	24.10.87	H	Leyton Orient	W 3-0	1-0	17	3895
16	31.10.87	A	Bolton W.	D 1-1	1-0	17	4607
17	3.11.87	H	Wolverhampton W.	L 1-2	0-1	18	5293
18	7.11.87	A	Rochdale	W 3-2	0-0	16	1243
19	21.11.87	H	Peterborough U.	W 2-1	1-1	13	4033
20	28.11.88	A	Scunthorpe U.	W 2-1	0-0	11	2309
21	12.12.87	H	Carlisle U.	W 3-1	1-0	12	3876
22	19.12.87	A	Darlington	L 0-2	0-1	11	1726
23	26.12.87	A	Crewe Alex.	D 2-2	0-1	11	2976
24	28.12.87	H	Torquay U.	D 1-1	0-0	13	6108
25	1.1.88	H	Cardiff C.	D 2-2	0-0	14	10300
26	2.1.88	A	Hereford U.	D 0-0	0-0	13	3504
27	9.1.88	A	Exeter C.	L 1-3	0-1	13	2225
28	16.1.88	H	Scarborough	W 3-0	2-0	10	4366
29	23.1.88	H	Halifax T.	D 1-1	1-1	10	5064
30	30.1.88	A	Hartlepool U.	W 2-0	2-0	9	2092
31	6.2.88	H	Burnley	D 0-0	0-0	9	3498
32	19.2.88	H	Stockport Co.	D 1-1	0-1	12	4405
33	27.2.88	A	Cambridge U.	W 3-0	2-0	11	2080
34	1.3.88	A	Colchester U.	L 1-2	0-0	12	4011
35	5.3.88	A	Newport Co.	W 2-1	0-1	11	2235
36	12.3.88	A	Wrexham	W 2-1	1-0	9	1916
37	19.3.88	H	Bolton W.	W 1-0	0-0	7	3980
38	26.3.88	A	Leyton Orient	L 0-3	0-1	10	3390
39	29.3.88	A	Torquay U.	W 1-0	0-0	10	3037
40	2.4.88	H	Rochdale	L 0-3	0-1	6	5367
41	4.4.88	A	Peterborough U.	W 1-0	0-0	5	3360
42	9.4.88	H	Tranmere Rov.	L 1-2	0-2	7	4104
43	23.4.88	A	Wolverhampton W.	L 0-2	0-1	9	12344
44	30.4.88	H	Scunthorpe U.	D 1-1	1-0	10	3482
45	2.5.88	A	Carlisle U.	W 1-0	1-0	7	1854
46	7.5.88	H	Darlington	W 3-0	1-0	6	4071

Players: League Record, 1987-88 (Division 4)

Match Number	1	2	3	4	5	6	7	8	9	10	11	12	13	14	15	16	17	18	19	20	21	22	23	24	25	26	27	28	29	30	31	32	33	34	35	36	37	38	39	40	41	42	43	44	45	46	Apps	Subs	Goals
Allon		11	8	8			★	8		★	9¹	9¹	9¹	9¹	9¹	9¹	9	9		9¹	9²	9	9	9	9¹	9	9¹		★		10	9	9				★		★	9¹	9	9					26	6	12
Andrews		★	11	11	11		★	11		★	11	11	11		11				11		★		8	11	11	11	11¹	11	★			★	9														16	6	1
Bodak																																			10	10	10	10	10	11	11	11	11	11		9	0	0
Coleman	3	3	3	3	3	3	3			3	3	3	3	3	3	3	3	3	3	3	3	3	3	★	3	3		11	11									3	3	3							29	1	0
D'Auria			★							★	★	★																																			0	4	0
Davey																								9	9	9	9																				4	0	0
Davies	6	6	6	6	6	6	6	7		6		7	7¹	7	7	7	7	7	7	7	7	7	7	7	7	7	7	7	7	7	7	7	7	7	7	7	7	7¹	7	7	7	7	7	7	7	7¹	42	0	3
Emmanuel			11	11	6	6	6		6	6	6	6	6	6	6	6	6	6	6	6	6	6	6		11	★			★			★			★	★	★										22	5	0
Guthrie																										1	1	1	1	1	1	1	1	1	1	1	1	1	1								14	0	0
Harrison	2			2	2	2	2	2	2	2	2¹	2								★		2	2	2	2	2	2	2	2	2	2	2	2¹	2	2	2	2	2	2	2	2	2	2	2	2	2	34	1	2
Hough	★	2	2	2	★		★	★		★	8	8	★	2	2	2	2	2	2	2	2																										14	6	0
Hughes	1	1	1	1	1	1	1	1	1	1	1	1	1	1	1	1	1	1	1	1	1	1	1									1	1	1	1	1	1	1			★	10	8	8		32	1	0
Hutchison	11											7	11																																		6	1	0
James																								6	6	6¹	6	6	6	6	6	6¹	6	6	6	6	6	6¹	6	6	6	6	6¹	6	6	6	19	0	3
Knill	5	5	5	5	5	5	5	5		5	5	5	5	5	5	5	5	5	5	5	5	5	5	5	5	5	5	5	5	5	5	5	5	5	5	5	5	5	5	5	5	5	5¹	5			46	0	1
Lewis, D.												3	11												4	4	4	4	4	4	4	4	4	4	4	4	4	4	4	10							18	0	0
Lewis, J.															11	11	11	11¹	11		11	11	11¹	3				3	3	3	3¹	3	3	3	3	3	3	3	3	3	3¹	3					25	0	0
Love																								10¹	★		11²	11¹	11	11¹	11¹	11¹	11	11	11												11	1	6
McCarthy	8¹	8	★	★¹	8	8¹	8	8	★	8						★¹											10	★	9	★¹	9	9	9	9	9		★	★	9¹	9	9²						17	8	8
Marsh												11																																			1	0	0
Melville	4	4	4	4	4	4	4	4	4	4	4	4	4	4	4	4	4¹	4	4	4¹	4	4¹	4	4		★¹		★		★	★		★		★		4	4	4	4							31	6	4
Pascoe	10	10	10	10¹	10	10²	10	10¹	10	10	10	10	10	10	10¹	10	10	10²	10	10¹	10	10	10	10	10	10	10¹	10¹			10	10	10¹	10	10												34	0	13
Raynor	9¹	9	9	9	9	9	9¹	9	9	9¹	9¹		8¹	8	8	8	8	8	8¹	8	8	8	★	8¹	8	8	8¹	8	8	8	8	8	8	8	8	8	8	8	8	8	8	8	8	10	10		43	1	8
Williams	7	7	7	7	7	7	7	3	7¹	7	7	7	8			★	★		★					★				★																			13	5	1

FA Cup: 1987-88: 1st Round: Hayes (A) 1-0; 2nd Round: Leyton Orient (A) 0-2.
Littlewoods Cup: 1987-88: 1st Round: Torquay U. (A) 1-2 (H) 1-1.

SWINDON TOWN (Division 2)

Team Manager   Lou Macari.
Club Address   County Ground, Swindon, Wiltshire. Tel: (0793) 642984.
Current Ground Capacity   14,520.
Record Attendance   32,000 v Arsenal, FA Cup 3rd Round, 15 January 1972.
Year Formed   1881. Turned professional 1894.
Previous Names   None.
Club Nickname   "The Robins".
Club Colours   Red shirts with white pinstripe, white shorts and red stockings.
Club Honours   Football League: Div. 4 Champions 1985-86. Football League Cup: Winners 1969.
League History   1920-58 Div. 3(S); 1958-63 Div. 3; 1963-65 Div. 2; 1965-69 Div. 3; 1969-74 Div. 2; 1974-82 Div. 3; 1982-86 Div. 4; 1986-87 Div. 3; 1987- Div. 2.
Most League Points in a Season   (2 for a win) 64 in Div. 3, 1968-69. (3 for a win) 102 in Div. 4, 1985-86.
Most League Goals in a Season   100 in Div. 3(S), 1926-27.
Record Victory   10-1 v Farnham United in Breweries FA Cup 1st Round, 28 November 1925.

Record Defeat   1-10 v Manchester C. in FA Cup 4th Round replay, 25 January 1930.
Consecutive League Wins   8 in 1926 and 1986.
Consecutive League Defeats   6 in 1967 and 1980.
Record League Appearances   John Trollope, 770 between 1960-80.
Record League Goalscorer—Career   Harry Morris, 216 between 1926-33.
Record League Goalscorer—Season   Harry Morris, 47 in Div. 3(S), 1926-27.

Swindon Town: League Record, 1987-88 (Division 2)

Match Number	Date	Venue	Opponents	Result		H/T	Lge Posn	Attend
1	15.8.87	A	Bradford C.	L	0-2	0-0		10553
2	22.8.87	H	Sheffield U.	W	2-0	2-0		8637
3	29.8.87	A	West Bromwich A.	W	2-1	1-1	8	7503
4	31.8.87	H	Hull C.	D	0-0	0-0	8	9600
5	5.9.87	A	Middlesbrough	W	3-2	2-1	10	9324
6	12.9.87	H	Birmingham C.	L	0-2	0-0	9	9128
7	15.9.87	A	Barnsley	W	1-0	0-0	5	7773
8	19.9.87	A	Ipswich T.	L	2-3	1-3	7	10460
9	26.9.87	H	Reading	W	4-0	2-0	5	10073
10	29.9.87	H	Shrewsbury T.	D	1-1	0-0	5	8261
11	3.10.87	A	Millwall	D	2-2	0-1	5	7018
12	10.10.87	H	Oldham Ath.	W	2-0	0-0	6	8160
13	20.10.87	H	Stoke C.	W	3-0	1-0	4	9160
14	24.10.87	A	Crystal Palace	L	1-2	1-1	7	9077
15	31.10.87	H	Manchester C.	L	3-4	1-2	7	11536
16	7.11.87	A	Leicester C.	L	2-3	1-0	11	8346
17	14.11.87	H	Plymouth Arg.	D	1-1	1-1	9	9616
18	21.11.87	A	Leeds U.	L	2-4	1-3	13	15457
19	28.11.87	H	Bournemouth	W	4-2	2-1	12	7934
20	1.12.87	H	Huddersfield T.	W	4-1	2-0	10	6963
21	5.12.87	A	Aston Villa	L	1-2	0-0	13	16127
22	20.12.87	A	Sheffield U.	L	0-1	0-0	13	7248
23	26.12.87	A	Reading	W	1-0	0-0	12	8939
24	28.12.87	H	Ipswich T.	W	4-2	2-0	11	12429
25	1.1.88	H	West Bromwich A.	W	2-0	0-0	11	12155
26	2.1.88	A	Birmingham C.	D	1-1	0-0	11	7829
27	6.2.88	H	Middlesbrough	D	1-1	1-1	11	9941
28	13.2.88	H	Huddersfield T.	W	3-0	1-0	11	5458
29	20.2.88	A	Shrewsbury T.	L	1-2	1-2	11	5649
30	27.2.88	H	Millwall	L	0-1	0-1	11	9570
31	12.3.88	A	Oldham Ath.	L	3-4	1-0	12	5193
32	15.3.88	H	Barnsley	W	3-0	1-0	13	7558
33	19.3.88	A	Manchester C.	D	1-1	0-0	12	17022
34	27.3.88	H	Crystal Palace	D	2-2	0-0	12	12915
35	30.3.88	H	Bradford C.	D	2-2	0-0	11	8203
36	2.4.88	H	Leicester C.	W	3-2	1-1	11	9450
37	4.4.88	A	Plymouth Arg.	L	0-1	0-1	10	13299
38	9.4.88	H	Blackburn Rov.	L	1-2	1-0	10	9373
39	12.4.88	A	Hull C.	W	4-1	2-1	12	4583
40	23.4.88	A	Stoke C.	L	0-1	0-1	10	6293
41	25.4.88	A	Blackburn Rov.	D	0-0	0-0	12	13536
42	30.4.88	H	Leeds U.	L	1-2	1-2	12	8299
43	2.5.88	A	Bournemouth	L	0-2	0-2	12	5212
44	7.5.88	H	Aston Villa	D	0-0	0-0	12	10959

Players: League Record, 1987-88 (Division 2)

Match Number	1	2	3	4	5	6	7	8	9	10	11	12	13	14	15	16	17	18	19	20	21	22	23	24	25	26	27	28	29	30	31	32	33	34	35	36	37	38	39	40	41	42	43	44	Apps	Subs	Goals
Bamber	9	7	7	7	7[1]	7	7[1]	7	7	7	7	7[1]	7	7	7[1]	7	7	7	7	7	8	8	7[1]	7	8	7[1]	7[2]	7[1]	7			8[1]	8	8[1]	8	8		8[2]	8	9	7	7	7		41	0	13
Barnard			11	11	11	11[1]	11	11	11[1]	11	11	11	11	★	10	4	4	8	8																										16	1	2
Bames														11	11	11[1]	11[1]	11[1]	11[2]	11[1]	11[1]	11		7	7	11	11		7[1]	★	11		11	7	7	★		11[1]	11	7[1]	11	7	7	11	8	26	2	10
Berry		10	10	8																																									3	0	0
Bodin																															11[1]	11	11						★			★			3	2	1
Calderwood	6	6[1]	6	6	6	6	6	6	**6**	6	6	6	6	6	6	6	6	6	6	6	6	6	6	6	6	6	6								★				4	6	4	6		33	1	1
Coyne	4		★	★		★													4																										2	3	0
Crichton																								1	1	1	1																	4	0	0
Digby	1	1	1	1	1	1	1	1	1	1	1	1	1	1									1	1	1	1	1	1	1	1	1	1	1	1	1		1	1	1	1	1		31	0	0
Flowers																		1	1	1	1	1																						5	0	0
Foley				10	10	10	**10**	10	10	10	10[1]	10	10		10[1]	10	**10**		10	10[2]	**10**	10	10	10	10	10		10	4		7	11	10	10	10	10	10	10	10	10	10	10	35	0	4
Gittens	7								★	★				9					5	5	5	5	5	5	5	8	5	8	8	8	6	6		6	6	6	6	6	6	6	8	**6**	8	27	2	0
Hammond													1	1							1															1							4	0	0
Henry	★					★			8	8	9		★	★	★		★							★			★	★[1]	6	6		★											5	10	1
Hockaday	2		2	2	2	2	2	2	2	2	2	2	2	2	2	2	2	2	2	2	2	2	2	2	2	2	2	2	2	2	2	2	2	2	2	2	2	2	2	2	2	2	43	0	0
Kamara	11	4	4	4	4	4	4	4	4[2]	4	4	4		8	4			4	4	4	4	4	**4**	4	4																		25	0	0
Kelly	8	8	8[1]		★	★	★		★																																			3	4	1
King	3	3	3	3	3	**3**	3	3	3	3	3	3	**3**	3	3	3	3	3	3	3	3[1]	3	3	3	3	**3**	3	3	3	3	3	3	3	3	**3**	`3	3	3	3	44	0	1
McLoughlin																											4	8		11		★	4	4	11	4							7	1	0
O'Regan		2			8	8	8	8		8		4	★		★	10	4			★	10	10[1]	11	8	8	4	4	4	4	4	**4**				11	4		23	3	1
Parkin	5	5	5	5	5	5	5	5[1]	5	5	5	5	**5**	5	5	5	5		★		11	8	5	11	5	5	5	5	5[1]	5	5	5	5	5	5	5	5	5	39	1	2
Quinn	10	9[1]	9[1]	9	9	9	**9**	9	9[1]	9[1]	9[1]	★[1]	9	9[1]		9	9[1]	9	9[1]	9[1]	**9**[1]	9	9[1]	9	9	9	9	9	9	**9**	9[1]	9	9	9	9	9[2]	9	9	9[2]	9	9[1]	9	9	41	1	21
Wade																★	★											★														0	3	0
Wegerle																											7	7[1]	7	**7**	7	11	7	11								7	0	1
White					★			8[1]		8[2]	8[1]	8		★			8[2]	8	8	11			★[2]	★	11		★	10	**10**	10[2]	10	10[1]		★	8		★	8		★	11	17	8	11
Own Goals																1																													1

FA Cup: 1987-88: 3rd Round: Norwich C. (H) 0-0 Replay (A) 2-0; 4th Round: Newcastle U. (A) 0-5.
Littlewoods Cup: 1987-88: 1st Round: Bristol C. (H) 3-0 (A) 2-3; 2nd Round: Portsmouth (H) 3-1 (A) 3-1; 3rd Round: Watford (H) 1-1 Replay (A) 2-4.

TORQUAY UNITED (Division 4)

Team Manager   Cyril Knowles.
Club Address   Plainmoor Ground, Torquay, Devon TQ1 3PS. Tel: (0803) 38666.
Current Ground Capacity   4,999.
Record Attendance   21,908 v Huddersfield T., FA Cup 4th Round, 29 January 1955.
Year Formed   1898. Turned professional 1921.
Previous Names   Torquay Town.
Club Nickname   "The Gulls".
Club Colours   Yellow shirts, royal blue shorts and stockings.
Club Honours   None.
League History   1927-58 Div. 3(S); 1958-60 Div. 4; 1960-62 Div. 3; 1962-66 Div. 4; 1966-72 Div. 3; 1972- Div. 4.
Most League Points in a Season   (2 for a win) 60 in Div. 4, 1959-60. (3 for a win) 77 in Div. 4, 1987-88.
Most League Goals in a Season   89 in Div. 3(S), 1956-57.
Record Victory   9-0 v Swindon T. in Div. 3(S), 8 March 1952.
Record Defeat   2-10 v Fulham in Div. 3(S), 7 September 1931 and v Luton T. in Div. 3(S), 2 September 1933.

Consecutive League Wins   6 in 1953.
Consecutive League Defeats   8 in 1948 and 1971.
Record League Appearances   Dennis Lewis, 443 between 1947-59.
Record League Goalscorer—Career   Sammy Collins, 203 between 1948-58.
Record League Goalscorer—Season   Sammy Collins, 40 in Div. 3(S), 1955-56.

Torquay United: League Record, 1987-88 (Division 4)

Match Number	Date	Venue	Opponents	Result	H/T	Lge Posn	Attend
1	15.8.87	H	Wrexham	W 6-1	2-1		1731
2	21.8.87	A	Colchester U.	W 1-0	0-0		1372
3	29.8.87	H	Leyton Orient	D 1-1	0-0	2	2705
4	31.8.87	A	Darlington	D 1-1	0-0	2	2251
5	5.9.87	H	Cambridge U.	L 0-1	0-0	7	2676
6	12.9.87	A	Newport Co.	L 1-3	1-2	10	1368
7	15.9.87	H	Rochdale	W 5-0	3-0	7	1895
8	19.9.87	H	Bolton W.	W 2-1	2-0	4	2211
9	26.9.87	A	Wolverhampton W.	W 2-1	0-0	2	7349
10	29.9.87	H	Scarborough	L 0-1	0-0	5	3255
11	3.10.87	A	Exeter City	W 1-0	1-0	4	6281
12	10.10.87	H	Crewe Alex.	W 1-0	1-0	2	2499
13	17.10.87	A	Hartlepool U.	D 0-0	0-0	2	2870
14	20.10.87	A	Cardiff C.	L 1-2	1-0	4	3503
15	24.10.87	H	Burnley	L 1-3	0-1	7	2740
16	31.10.87	A	Peterborough U.	W 2-0	0-0	3	3500
17	3.11.87	H	Tranmere Rov.	W 1-0	1-0	3	2512
18	6.11.87	A	Stockport Co.	L 1-2	0-1	7	1697
19	21.11.87	H	Hereford U.	W 1-0	1-0	4	2305
20	28.11.87	A	Carlisle U.	D 3-3	2-3	4	2017
21	12.12.87	H	Halifax T.	L 1-2	1-1	5	2422
22	18.12.87	A	Scunthorpe U.	W 3-2	3-1	6	2261
23	28.12.87	A	Swansea C.	D 1-1	0-0	6	6108
24	1.1.88	A	Leyton Orient	W 2-0	1-0	8	4589
25	16.1.88	A	Bolton W.	W 2-1	1-1	5	5996
26	26.1.88	A	Rochdale	D 1-1	1-0	6	1254
27	6.2.88	A	Cambridge U.	L 0-1	0-0	7	1948
28	20.2.88	A	Wrexham	W 3-2	2-0	8	1488
29	23.2.88	H	Wolverhampton W.	D 0-0	0-0	8	3803
30	30.2.88	H	Exeter C.	D 1-1	1-0	8	3383
31	2.3.88	A	Scarborough	W 2-1	1-0	7	2182
32	5.3.88	H	Hartlepool U.	D 1-1	1-1	7	2867
33	11.3.88	A	Crewe Alex.	W 1-0	1-0	5	1858
34	19.3.88	H	Peterborough U.	D 0-0	0-0	6	2544
35	29.3.88	H	Swansea C.	L 0-1	0-0	8	3037
36	2.4.88	H	Stockport Co.	W 3-0	1-0	5	2919
37	4.4.88	A	Hereford U.	D 0-0	0-0	6	2425
38	9.4.88	H	Cardiff C.	W 2-0	2-0	5	3082
39	15.4.88	H	Colchester U.	D 0-0	0-0	5	3508
40	19.4.88	H	Newport Co.	W 6-1	2-1	4	3416
41	22.4.88	A	Tranmere Rov.	D 1-1	0-0	5	6189
42	27.4.88	H	Darlington	D 0-0	0-0	3	3939
43	30.4.88	H	Carlisle U.	W 1-0	1-0	3	3537
44	2.5.88	A	Halifax T.	W 3-2	1-1	3	1218
45	4.5.88	A	Burnley	L 0-1	0-1	3	5075
46	7.5.88	H	Scunthorpe U.	L 1-2	0-1	5	4989

Players: League Record, 1987-88 (Division 4)

Match Number	1	2	3	4	5	6	7	8	9	10	11	12	13	14	15	16	17	18	19	20	21	22	23	24	25	26	27	28	29	30	31	32	33	34	35	36	37	38	39	40	41	42	43	44	45	46	Apps	Subs	Goals
Allen	1	1	1	1	1	1	1	1	1	1	1	1	1	1	1	1	1	1	1	1	1	1	1	1	1	1	1	1	1	1	1	1	1	1	1	1	1	1	1	1	1	1	1	1	1	1	46	0	0
Caldwell									9	9^1	9					9	9^2		9	9	9	9		9			9	9	9^1	9	9	9	9	9	9	9	9	9	9	9							24	0	4
Cann						6	★																																									1	1	0
Cole	5^1	5	5	5	5	5	5^1	5	5^1	5	5	5	5	5	5	5	5	5	5	5	5^1	5	5	5	5	5	5^1	5	5	5	5	5	5	5	5	5	5	5	5	5	5	5	5	5	5	5	46	0	5
Dawkins						7	7	7	7			3	7	7	7^1	7	7	★		7	7	7	7	7^1	7	7	7	7	7	7		★	★	★	★	★	7	4	4	7^1	7	4					30	8	3
Dobson	11^3	11^1	11^1	11	11	11	11	11^2	11^1	11^1	11	11	11	11	11	11^1	11^1	11	11	11^1	11	11^2					11^2	11	11	11^1	11	11	11	★			★	★	$★^2$	★	10^1	10^1	10^1	10	10^1		33	5	22
Gardiner	7	7	7	7	7	★		★	★	7	★	★	10	9	9	9	7	3			★	★	★	6	★			9	★			★	★		3												15	12	1
Gibbins																																	11	11^1	11	11	11	11^1	11	11	11	11	11	11	11	11	12	0	2
Haslegrave	4	4	4	4	4	4	4	4	4	4	4	4	4	4	4	4	4	4	4	4	4	4	4	4	★		★		7		★			4^1			4	4									31	3	1
Impey	6	6	6	6		6		6	6	6	6	6	6		6	6			6	6	6	6						6	6	6	6	6	6	6	6	6	6	6	6^1	6	6						34	0	1
Kelly	3	3	3	3	3	3	3	3	3		3	3	3						3	3	3	3	3	3	3	3	3	3	3	3	3	3	3		3	3	3	3	3	3	3						38	0	0
Lloyd	8	8	8	8	8	8	8	8	8	8	8	8	8	8	8	8	8	8	8	8^1	8	8	8	8	8	8^1	8	8	8	8	8	8	8	8	8	8	8	8	8	8	8	8	8	8	8	8	46	0	2
Loram	10	10	10	10^1	10	10^1	10	10^1	10	10	10	10^1		10	10^1	10	10^1	10	10	10^1	10	10	10^1	10	10	10	10	10	10	★	10	10^1	10	10	10	10	10	10	10^1	10	10	★	★	★			40	5	8
McLoughlin	9^2	9	9	9	9	★	$★^1$	★																																							5	3	3
McNichol	2	2	2	2	2	2	2	2	2	2	2^1	2	2	2	2	2	2	2	2^1	2	2	2	2	2	2	2	2	2	2^1	2	2	2	2	2^1	2	2^1	2	2^1	2	2	2	2	2	2	2	2	46	0	6
Milton																															4	4^1	4	7													4	0	1
Musker	★	★	★	★	★		6	★	★	7						6	7				9	11	11	11	11	11		4	4	4	4																14	7	0
Nardiello	★				★	★				★				★	★			★	★		9					9^1	★	★																			2	7	1
Pearce			★	★			★			★				$★^1$	3	3	3	6	3	3			★	★			6	6	6	6	6^1	9	7	4	4	4	4	4		★							20	7	1
Riley					9	9^1	9	9	9	9																																					6	0	1
Sharpe								★									★								10	★					7	7	7^1	7	7^2	★	7	7		★	7						9	5	3
Smith			★																																												0	1	0
Walker												9	9	9																																	3	0	0
Wright																★	6																														1	1	0

FA Cup: 1987-88: 1st Round: Bognor (A) 3-0; 2nd Round: (A) 1-0; 3rd Round: Coventry C. (A) 0-2.
Littlewoods Cup: 1987-88: 1st Round: Swansea C. (H) 2-1 (A) 1-1; 2nd Round: Tottenham H. (H) 1-0 (A) 0-3.

TOTTENHAM HOTSPUR (Division 1)

Team Manager Terry Venables.
Club Address 748 High Road, Tottenham, London N17.
Tel: 01-801 3411.
Current Ground Capacity 48,200.
Record Attendance 75,038 v Sunderland, FA Cup 6th Round, 5 March 1938.
Year Formed 1882. Turned professional 1895.
Previous Names Hotspur Football Club .
Club Nickname "The Spurs".
Club Colours White Shirts, navy blue shorts and white stockings.
Club Honours Football League: Div. 1 Champions 1950-51, 1960-61; Div. 2 Champions 1919-20, 1949-50. FA Cup: Winners 1901, 1921, 1961, 1962, 1967, 1981, 1982. Football League Cup: Winners 1971, 1973. European Cup-winners Cup: Winners 1962-63. UEFA Cup: Winners 1971-72, 1983-84.
League History 1908-09 Div. 2; 1909-15 Div. 1; 1919-20 Div. 2; 1920-28 Div. 1; 1928-33 Div. 2; 1933-35 Div. 1; 1935-50 Div. 2; 1950-77 Div. 1; 1977-78 Div. 2; 1978- Div. 1.

Most League Points in a Season (2 for a win) 70 in Div. 2, 1919-20. (3 for a win) 77 in Div. 1, 1984-85.
Most League Goals in a Season 115 in Div. 1, 1960-61.
Record Victory 13-2 v Crewe Alex. in FA Cup 4th Round Replay, 3 February 1960.
Record Defeat 0-7 v Liverpool in Div. 1, 2 September 1978.
Consecutive League Wins 13 in 1960.
Consecutive League Defeats 5 in 1912, 1955 and 1975.
Record League Appearances Steve Perryman, 655 between 1969-86.
Record League Goalscorer—Career Jimmy Greaves, 220 between 1961-70.
Record League Goalscorer—Season Jimmy Greaves, 37 in Div. 1, 1962-63.

Tottenham Hotspur: League Record, 1987-88 (Division 1)

Match Number	Date	Venue	Opponents	Result		H/T	Lge Posn	Attend
1	15.8.87	A	Coventry C.	L	1-2	0-2		23947
2	19.8.87	H	Newcastle U.	W	3-1	3-0		26261
3	22.8.87	H	Chelsea	W	1-0	0-0	4	37079
4	29.8.87	A	Watford	D	1-1	0-0	6	19073
5	1.9.87	H	Oxford U.	W	3-0	2-0	2	21811
6	5.9.87	A	Everton	D	0-0	0-0	4	32389
7	12.9.87	H	Southampton	W	2-1	1-1	2	24728
8	19.9.87	A	West Ham U.	W	1-0	1-0	2	27750
9	26.9.87	A	Manchester U.	L	0-1	0-1	4	47601
10	3.10.87	H	Sheffield Wed.	W	2-0	0-0	3	24311
11	10.10.87	A	Norwich C.	L	1-2	1-1	7	18669
12	18.10.87	H	Arsenal	L	1-2	1-2	7	36680
13	24.10.87	A	Nottingham F.	L	0-3	0-1	8	23543
14	31.10.87	H	Wimbledon	L	0-3	0-1	8	22200
15	4.11.87	A	Portsmouth	D	0-0	0-0	8	15302
16	7.11.87	H	Q.P.R.	D	1-1	1-1	8	28113
17	21.11.87	A	Luton T.	L	0-2	0-1	10	10091
18	28.11.87	H	Liverpool	L	0-2	0-0	11	47362
19	13.12.87	H	Charlton Ath.	L	0-1	0-0	14	20392
20	20.12.87	A	Derby Co.	W	2-1	0-1	12	17593

Match Number	Date	Venue	Opponents	Result		H/T	Lge Posn	Attend
21	26.12.87	A	Southampton	L	1-2	0-2	13	18456
22	28.12.87	H	West Ham U.	W	2-1	1-0	11	39461
23	1.1.88	H	Watford	W	2-1	0-0	9	25471
24	2.1.88	A	Chelsea	D	0-0	0-0	9	29317
25	16.1.88	H	Coventry C.	D	2-2	1-0	10	25650
26	23.1.88	A	Newcastle U.	L	0-2	0-1	10	24616
27	13.2.88	A	Oxford U.	D	0-0	0-0	10	9906
28	23.2.88	H	Manchester U.	D	1-1	1-0	10	25731
29	27.2.88	A	Sheffield Wed.	W	3-0	1-0	9	18046
30	1.3.88	H	Derby Co.	D	0-0	0-0	8	15986
31	6.3.88	A	Arsenal	L	1-2	0-1	8	37143
32	9.3.88	H	Everton	W	2-1	1-0	8	18262
33	12.3.88	H	Norwich C.	L	1-3	0-1	8	19322
34	19.3.88	A	Wimbledon	L	0-3	0-1	8	8616
35	26.3.88	H	Nottingham F.	D	1-1	1-0	8	25306
36	2.4.88	H	Portsmouth	L	0-1	0-1	10	18616
37	4.4.88	A	Q.P.R.	L	0-2	0-0	10	14783
38	23.4.88	A	Liverpool	L	0-1	0-1	14	44798
39	2.5.88	A	Charlton Ath.	D	1-1	0-0	14	13977
40	4.5.88	H	Luton T.	W	2-1	1-1	13	15437

Players: League Record, 1987-88 (Division 1)

Match Number	1	2	3	4	5	6	7	8	9	10	11	12	13	14	15	16	17	18	19	20	21	22	23	24	25	26	27	28	29	30	31	32	33	34	35	36	37	38	39	40	Apps	Subs	Goals
Allen, C.	7	7¹	7	7¹	7¹	7	7¹	7		7		★	7	7	★		7	7	7	7	7¹	7		7¹	7	7²	7	7	7¹	7¹	7	7¹	7	7				★	7	7	31	3	11
Allen, P.	8	8	8	8	8	8	8	8	8	8¹	8	8	8	8	8	8¹	8	8	8		8	8	8	8	8	8	8¹	8	8	8	8	8	8	8	8	8	8	8	8	8	39	0	3
Ardiles	★		2	2	2	2	9	9	9	9	4	9	9	9	9	9			10	10	10	10		10	10		10		★	9	9	9	9								26	2	0
Claesen	11		★¹	11	11²	11	11¹	11	11	11¹	11¹	11	11	11	11	11	★	11	11¹				11		★¹			★¹		11	11			★¹							19	5	0
Clemence	1	1	1	1	1	1	1	1	1	1	1																														11	0	0
Close										★	7	7	★	★				★					★																		2	5	0
Fairclough	5	5	5	5	5	5	5	5¹	5	5	5	5	5	5	5	5	5	5	5	5¹	5¹	5	5	5	5	5	5	5	5	5¹	5	5	5	5	5	5	5	5	5	5	40	0	4
Fenwick																					2	4	4	4	4	4	4	4	4	4	4	4	4	4					4	4	17	0	0
Gough				4	4	4	4	4	4	4	4																														9	0	0
Gray																																									0	1	0
Hodge		10	10¹	10	10	10	10	10	10	10	10	10					10	10	10				8	4	4	10						★	9	9	9	11	11¹	11¹			25	1	3
Howells													★						11				★	11	★	★	★					★	★	11							3	8	0
Hughton															2	2	3	3	3	2	2	★	2	2			2	2	2												12	1	0
Mabbutt	6¹	6	6	6	6	6			6	6	6	6	6	6	6	6	6	6	6	6		6	6	6	6	6	6	6	6	6	6	6	6	6	6	6	6	6	6	6¹	37	0	2
Metgod	★	11	11		★	★	★	★																									3	4	★	10					5	7	0
Mimms																											1	1	1	1	1	1	1	1	1	1	1	1	1	1	13	0	0
Moncur															★									9	9	★				3											3	2	0
Moran							6	7						7					★	11	7	11¹	11	11	11				★	★	★										9	4	1
O'Shea																	★																								0	1	0
Parks												1	1	1	1	1	1	1	1	1	1	1	1	1	1	1															16	0	0
Polston		★			★																																				0	2	0
Ruddock													4	4		4										★															3	2	0
Samways					★	★	4	4	★	4	4	10	★	4		4	4	4						10		10	10	10	10	10	10	10	10	10	10	10	10	★			21	5	0
Statham															★	★			★	★			2	2	2	2	2	2	2	2	2	2	2	2	2	2	2	2			14	4	0
Stevens	2	2				2	2	2	2	2	2	10	10	2	2	2	11	10	2	6	6																				18	0	0
Thomas	3	3	3	3	3	3	3	3	3	3	3	3		★	3	3	3	3	3	3	3	3	3	3	3	3	3	3	3	3	3			3	3	3					35	0	0
Waddle	9	9¹	9	9	9	9			9								9	9	9	9	9¹	9	9	9	9	9							★			9	9	9			21	1	2
Walsh																						11	11	11	11	11¹	11	11	11	7	7	7	7								11	0	1
Own Goals																														1													1

FA Cup: 1987-88: 3rd Round: Oldham Ath. (A) 4-2; 4th Round: Port Vale (A) 1-2.
Littlewoods Cup: 1987-88: 2nd Round: Torquay U. (A) 0-1 (H) 3-0; 3rd Round: Aston Villa (A) 1-2.

TRANMERE ROVERS (Division 4)

Team Manager John King.
Club Address Prenton Park, Prenton Road West, Birkenhead. Tel: 051-608 3677/4194.
Current Ground Capacity 8,000
Record Attendance 24,424 v Stoke C., FA Cup 4th Round, 5 February 1972.
Year Formed 1883. Turned professional 1912.
Previous Names Belmont AFC.
Club Nickname "Rovers".
Club Colours Blue shirts, white shorts and stockings.
Club Honours Football League: Div. 3(N) Champions 1937-38.
League History 1921-38 Div. 3(N); 1938-39 Div. 2; 1946-58 Div. 3(N); 1958-61 Div. 3; 1961-67 Div. 4; 1967-75 Div. 3; 1975-76 Div. 4; 1976-79 Div. 3; 1979- Div. 4.
Most League Points in a Season (2 for a win) 60 in Div. 4, 1964-65. (3 for a win) 75 in Div. 4, 1984-85.
Most League Goals in a Season 111 in Div. 3(N), 1930-31.
Record Victory 13-4 v Oldham Ath. in Div. 3(N), 26 December 1935.

Record Defeat 1-9 v Tottenham H. in FA Cup 3rd Round replay, 14 January 1953.
Consecutive League Wins 8 in 1964.
Consecutive League Defeats 8 in 1938.
Record League Appearances Harold Bell, 595 between 1946-59.
Record League Goalscorer—Career Bunny Bell, 104 between 1931-36.
Record League Goalscorer—Season Bunny Bell, 35 in Div. 3(N), 1933-34.

Tranmere Rovers: League Record, 1987-88 (Division 4)

Match Number	Date	Venue	Opponents	Result		H/T	Lge Posn	Attend
1	15.8.87	A	Scunthorpe U.	L	0-3	0-0		2277
2	21.8.87	H	Hereford U.	L	0-1	0-0		2824
3	28.8.87	A	Stockport Co.	W	2-1	1-1	21	2229
4	31.8.87	H	Exeter C.	W	2-1	1-0	11	3107
5	5.9.87	A	Scarborough	L	0-2	0-0	19	2882
6	11.9.87	H	Burnley	L	0-1	0-0	21	4209
7	15.9.87	A	Crewe Alex.	D	0-0	0-0	19	1839
8	18.9.87	A	Halifax T.	L	1-2	0-0	23	1754
9	25.9.87	H	Cardiff C.	L	0-1	0-0	23	2543
10	3.10.87	A	Darlington	D	0-0	0-0	23	1612
11	9.10.87	H	Rochdale	W	6-1	2-1	22	2303
12	17.10.87	A	Wolverhampton W.	L	0-3	0-3	22	6608
13	20.10.87	H	Swansea C.	L	1-2	1-2	22	2210
14	24.10.87	A	Carlisle U.	L	2-3	1-0	24	2160
15	30.10.87	H	Cambridge U.	L	0-1	0-0	24	2240
16	3.11.87	A	Torquay U.	L	0-1	0-1	24	2512
17	6.11.87	H	Wrexham	W	1-0	0-0	22	3271
18	21.11.87	A	Hartlepool U.	W	2-1	1-1	22	2507
19	27.11.87	H	Newport Co.	W	4-0	3-0	22	3252
20	12.12.87	A	Leyton Orient	L	1-3	0-1	22	3684
21	15.12.87	H	Bolton W.	W	2-0	0-0	20	3064
22	18.12.87	H	Colchester U.	L	0-2	0-1	22	2642
23	26.12.87	A	Cardiff C.	L	0-3	0-1	22	5233
24	28.12.87	H	Peterborough U.	W	3-1	1-0	20	3193
25	1.1.88	H	Stockport Co.	W	4-0	2-0	19	3670
26	2.1.88	A	Burnley	D	1-1	1-0	19	7317
27	9.1.88	A	Hereford U.	D	1-1	0-1	19	2209
28	15.1.88	H	Halifax T.	W	2-0	0-0	18	3317
29	30.1.88	A	Exeter C.	W	1-0	0-0	17	2261
30	6.2.88	H	Scarborough	W	1-0	0-0	15	4175
31	13.2.88	A	Peterborough U.	L	1-2	1-1	16	2230
32	20.2.88	H	Scunthorpe U.	L	1-3	1-1	16	2803
33	26.2.88	H	Darlington	W	2-1	1-0	16	2756
34	1.3.88	A	Bolton W.	L	0-2	0-0	17	3979
35	4.3.88	H	Wolverhampton W.	W	3-0	1-0	15	5007
36	12.3.88	A	Rochdale	D	0-0	0-0	16	1621
37	19.3.88	A	Cambridge U.	D	1-1	0-1	16	1514
38	25.3.88	H	Carlisle U.	W	3-0	2-0	17	3093
39	2.4.88	A	Wrexham	L	0-3	0-2	17	3134
40	4.4.88	H	Hartlepool U.	W	3-1	1-0	16	3921
41	9.4.88	A	Swansea C.	W	2-1	2-0	15	4104
42	22.4.88	H	Torquay U.	D	1-1	0-0	17	6189
43	25.4.88	H	Crewe Alex.	D	2-2	2-1	16	2962
44	30.4.88	A	Newport Co.	W	3-0	1-0	14	1110
45	2.5.88	H	Leyton Orient	W	2-1	1-0	14	3604
46	6.5.88	A	Colchester U.	D	0-0	0-0	14	1660

Players: League Record, 1987-88 (Division 4)

Match Number	1	2	3	4	5	6	7	8	9	10	11	12	13	14	15	16	17	18	19	20	21	22	23	24	25	26	27	28	29	30	31	32	33	34	35	36	37	38	39	40	41	42	43	44	45	46	Apps	Subs	Goals
Aspinall				★		7	11	11	11	11	11	11	11	11	11¹	11				8																											11	1	1
Bishop																																									★		★	8¹	★	8	2	3	1
Chamberlain												1	1	1	1	1	1	1	1	1	1	1	1	1	1	1	1	1																			15	0	0
Craven	8	8	8	8	8	8				★	★	★			★	★				★	★																										6	7	0
Garnett																																						★									0	1	0
Gorton																																														1	1	0	0
Hall						★																																									0	1	0
Harvey											8¹	8	8	8	8	8		8	8	8	8¹	8	8	8	8	8	8	8	8	8	8	8¹	8	8	8	8	8	8	8	8	8		8		8		33	0	3
Higgins										2		★		★	2	2	2	2	2	2	2	2	2	2	2	2	2	2	2	2	★	2	2	2	2		2	2	2	2	2	2¹	2				31	2	1
Hughes	4	4	4	4	4	4	4	4	4	4	4	4	4	5	5															★			2					5	5							19	1	0
McCarrick	2	2	2	2¹			3	3	3				3	3	3	3	3	3	3	3	3	3¹	3	3	3	3	3	3	3	3	3	3	3¹	3	3	3¹	3	3	3¹	3	3	3	3				40	0	5
McKenna	★	9	9¹	9	9	9	9	9	9¹	9			9	9					10¹	10	10																										13	1	3
Malkin				★	★					9	9	9																																			3	2	0
Martindale	7								8				4	4	4¹	4¹	4	4	4	4	4	4¹	4	4¹	4	4	4	4	4	4	4	4	4	4	4	4	4	4	4	4	4	4	4	4	34	0	4
Moore											9	9	5	5	5	5	5	5	5	5	5	5	5	5	5	5	5	5	5	5	5	5	5	5	5											30	0	0
Morrissey	11	11				7	7	7	7	7	7	7¹	7	7	7¹		★		★	★	★	11	7¹	7	7	7	7¹	7	7		7	7	7	7	7	7	7	7	7	7	7	7	7	7	7	7	35	4	4
Muir	10	10	10¹	10	10	10	10	10	10	10	10³	10	10	10¹	10	10	10	10	10²		10	10¹	10²	10	10¹	10¹	10¹	10¹	10¹	10	10	10¹	10	10¹	10	10	10¹	10	10²	10¹	10¹	10²	10²	10	10		43	0	27
Mungall	9	7	7	7	2	2	2	2	2		2	2	2	2	2	7	7	7	7	7	7	7	11	11	11	11	11	11	11	11	11	11	11	11	11	11	11	11	11	11	11	11	11	11	11	11	45	0	1
Murray		★	11	11	11			★	★				11	11	11	11¹	11	11	11						★		7	★	★											★	★		★				11	9	0
Nixon																															1	1	1	1	1					1	1	1	1	1	.1	8	0	0
O'Rourke	1	1	1	1	1	1	1	1	1	1	1	1	1	1	1	1	1																														22	0	0
Steel																			9	9¹	9	9¹	9	9	9	9	9¹	9	9	9	9	9	9	9¹	9	9	9	9¹	9	9	9	9	9	9¹	9		29	0	7
Thorpe	5	5	5	5	5	5	5	5	5	5	5	5		★																																	13	1	0
Vickers	6	6	6	6	6	6	6	6	6	6	6¹	6	6	6	6	6	6	6	6	6	6	6	6	6	6	6	6	6	6	6	6	6	6	6	6	6	6	6	6	6	6	6	6	6	6	6	46	0	1
Williams	3	3	3	3	3	3	8	8	8	3	3	3	3	5	11	★	5					★	★					★			6		★		★	★	★										16	8	0
Own Goals				1													1													1																				3

FA Cup: 1987-88: 1st Round: Port Vale (H) 2-2 Replay (A) 1-3.
Littlewoods Cup: 1987-88: 1st Round: Rochdale (A) 1-3 (H) 1-0.

WALSALL (Division 2)

Team Manager Tommy Coakley.
Club Address Fellows Park, Walsall. Tel: (0922) 22791.
Current Ground Capacity 16,018.
Record Attendance 24,453 v Newcastle U., Div. 2, 29 August 1961.
Year Formed 1888. Turned professional 1888.
Previous Names Walsall Swifts, Walsall Town, Walsall Town Swifts.
Club Nickname "The Saddlers".
Club Colours White shirts with red trim, red shorts and white stockings.
Club Honours Football League: Div. 4 Champions 1959-60.
League History 1892-95 Div. 2; 1895 Failed to be re-elected; 1921-27 Div. 3(N); 1927-31 Div. 3(S); 1931-36 Div. 3(N); 1936-58 Div. 3(S); 1958-60 Div. 4; 1960-61 Div. 3; 1961-63 Div. 2; 1963-79 Div. 3; 1979-80 Div. 4; 1980-88 Div. 3; 1988- Div. 2.
Most League Points in a Season (2 for a win) 65 in Div. 4, 1959-60. (3 for a win) 82 in Div. 3, 1987-88.

Most League Goals in a Season 102 in Div. 4, 1959-60.
Record Victory 10-0 v Darwen in Div. 2, 4 March 1899.
Record Defeat 0-12 v Small Heath, 17 December 1892 and v Darwen, 26 December 1896, both Div. 2.
Consecutive League Wins 7 in 1933 and 1959.
Consecutive League Defeats 9 in 1894-95.
Record League Appearances Colin Harrison, 467 between 1964-82.
Record League Goalscorer—Career Tony Richards, 184 between 1954-63.
Record League Goalscorer—Season Gilbert Alsop, 40 in Div. 3(N), 1933-34 and 1934-35.

Walsall: League Record, 1987-88 (Division 3)

Match Number	Date	Venue	Opponents	Result		H/T	Lge Posn	Attend
1	15.8.87	H	Fulham	L	0-1	0-0		4691
2	22.8.87	A	Blackpool	W	2-1	1-0		4614
3	29.8.87	H	Northampton T.	W	1-0	1-0	8	5993
4	31.8.87	A	York C.	W	3-1	1-0	4	2661
5	5.9.87	H	Sunderland	D	2-2	1-1	3	6909
6	12.9.87	A	Rotherham U.	W	1-0	0-0	1	3325
7	15.9.87	H	Bristol C.	D	1-1	0-0	3	6425
8	19.9.87	H	Wigan Ath	L	1-2	0-1	9	5353
9	26.9.87	A	Grimsby T.	W	2-0	1-0	3	3311
10	29.9.87	A	Bury	D	2-2	2-1	4	2449
11	3.10.87	H	Preston N.E.	W	1-0	1-0	2	5467
12	10.10.87	H	Brighton & H.A.	D	1-1	1-0	2	5020
13	17.10.87	A	Brentford	D	0-0	0-0	6	5056
14	20.10.87	A	Doncaster Rov.	W	4-0	3-0	3	1387
15	24.10.87	H	Port Vale	W	2-1	1-1	2	6083
16	30.10.87	H	Southend U.	D	1-1	1-0	2	2692
17	3.11.87	H	Aldershot	W	2-0	1-0	2	4816
18	7.11.87	A	Chester C.	D	1-1	0-0	2	3269
19	21.11.87	A	Notts Co.	L	1-3	1-2	4	7211
20	28.11.87	H	Mansfield T.	W	2-1	1-0	3	4227
21	12.12.87	H	Bristol Rov.	D	0-0	0-0	3	4234
22	18.12.87	A	Gillingham	W	1-0	1-0	3	4020
23	26.12.87	H	Grimsby T.	W	3-2	0-1	3	6272
24	28.12.87	A	Chesterfield	L	1-2	0-1	3	3916
25	1.1.88	A	Northampton T.	D	2-2	2-0	3	5832
26	2.1.88	H	Rotherham U.	W	5-2	3-1	3	5051
27	9.1.88	A	Aldershot	W	1-0	1-0	3	3270
28	16.1.88	A	Wigan Ath.	L	1-3	0-2	4	5063
29	30.1.88	H	York C.	W	2-1	1-1	3	4371
30	6.2.88	A	Sunderland	D	1-1	1-0	4	18311
31	9.2.88	A	Bristol C.	D	0-0	0-0	3	8454
32	13.2.88	H	Chesterfield	D	0-0	0-0	3	4162
33	20.2.88	A	Fulham	L	0-2	0-0	4	3718
34	23.2.88	H	Blackpool	W	3-2	0-0	3	4252
35	27.2.88	A	Preston N.E.	L	0-1	0-1	3	6479
36	1.3.88	H	Bury	W	2-1	1-1	3	3920
37	5.3.88	H	Brentford	W	4-2	2-1	3	4494
38	12.3.88	A	Brighton & H.A.	L	1-2	0-1	3	8345
39	19.3.88	H	Southend U.	W	2-1	1-1	3	4479
40	26.3.88	A	Port Vale	L	1-2	0-1	3	6347
41	2.4.88	H	Chester C.	W	1-0	1-0	3	4978
42	5.4.88	A	Mansfield T.	W	3-1	2-1	2	4900
43	9.4.88	H	Doncaster Rov.	W	2-1	0-0	2	6631
44	30.4.88	H	Notts Co.	W	2-1	0-1	2	11913
45	2.5.88	A	Bristol Rov.	L	0-3	0-3	3	6328
46	7.5.88	H	Gillingham	D	0-0	0-0	3	8850

Players: League Record, 1987-88 (Division 3)

Match Number	1	2	3	4	5	6	7	8	9	10	11	12	13	14	15	16	17	18	19	20	21	22	23	24	25	26	27	28	29	30	31	32	33	34	35	36	37	38	39	40	41	42	43	44	45	46	Apps	Subs	Goals
Barber	1	1	1	1	1	1	1	1	1	1	1	1	1	1	1	1	1	1	1	1	1	1	1	1	1	1	1	1	1	1	1	1	1	1	1	1	1	1	1	1	1	1	1	1	1	1	46	0	0
Christie			★	10	10	10		10	10¹	10			10¹	10	10	10	**10**	10	10	★		★	9	★	★		★	9¹	9	9		9	9¹	9	9	9¹	9¹	**9**		9	9	9¹	9	9	9	9	30	6	7
Cross	8	8²	8	8¹	8	8	8	8	8	8	8	8	8	8	**8**	8	★	8		8	8	8¹	8	8¹	8³	8	8			★																	25	1	8
Doman	2	2	2	2	2	2	2	2	2	2	2	2	2	2	2	2	2	2		2	2	2	2					★	2	2	2	2	2														30	1	0
Forbes	5	5	5	5¹	5	5	5	5	5	5¹	**5**	5	5	5	5	5	5	5	5	**5**	5	5	5	5	5	5	5	5	5	5			5	5¹	5	5	5	**5**	5	5	5						44	0	3
Goodwin	7	7	7	7	7	7	7	7	7	7		7	★¹	11	7			★	★		★		10	10	10	10	**8**	8¹	**8**	8	8	8		★	8			★	★	6	6						29	7	2
Hart	6	6	6	6	6	6	6	6	6	6	6	6	**6**		6	6	6	6¹	6	6	6	6	6	6	6	6	6	6	6					8	8	8	8	8	8	8							37	0	1
Hawker						★			★				10	11	6				11	**11**	**10**	10	10	10	★	3	3¹	3	3	7		★		5	7	7	7	7	7¹	7	7	7	7	7			26	3	2
Hutchinson			★		★																																										0	1	0
Jones, M.																												2	2	2	7	7		★			9										6	2	0
Jones, P.	10	10	10¹	10	10	11	11	11	11	11¹	11	11	**11**		★	11	8	8¹	7	7	7	7¹	7	7¹	7¹	7	7	7	**7**		7	6²	6	6¹	6¹	6	6	6	**6**								41	2	11
Kelly	9	9	9		9¹	9	9¹	9¹		9	9	9¹	9²	9	9²	9	9	9	9	9	9²		9	9¹	9	9¹	10¹	10	10	10	10		10	10	10²		10	10³	10¹	10¹	10	10					39	0	20
Marsh																					★		★	★																							0	3	0
Mower	3	3						9	3		3	3	3	3	3		3	3	3					3	3	3	3	3								2	2	2	2	2	2	2				26	0	0
Naughton	11	11	11	11¹	11		10¹		9	7		★	★	★	11	11			8	11	11	11	11	**11**	11	11	11	11	11	11	**11**	11	11	11	11	11¹	11	11	11	11¹	11	11					38	3	3
O'Kelly																					★	★	9		5	★	10	8¹	8	8	10			★		★											7	5	1
Palgrave	★																																														0	1	0
Rees					★	9																								★																	1	2	0
Sanderson																																		★							★	★				0	3	0
Shakespeare	4		4	4	4¹	4¹	4	4	4	3¹	4	4	4	4¹	4	4¹	4	4	4	4²	4	4	4	4	4	4	4	4¹	4	4	4	4	4	4	4	4	4	4	4	4	4¹	4	4	4	4	4	45	0	8
Taylor		4	3	3	3	3	3	3	3¹		★	3	★	**7**	7	★	7	7	3	2	★		3	3	3	2	2	2	2		7		3	3	3	3	3	3	3	3	3	3	3	3			36	4	1
Own Goals													1																																					1

FA Cup: 1st Round: Southend U. (A) 0-0 Replay (H) 2-1; 2nd Round: Gillingham (A) 1-2.
Littlewoods Cup: 1987-88: 1st Round: West Bromwich A. (A) 3-2 (H) 0-0; 2nd Round: Charlton Ath. (A) 0-3 (H) 2-0.

WATFORD (Division 2)

Team Manager Steve Harrison.
Club Address Vicarage Road Stadium, Watford WD1 8ER. Tel: (0923) 30933.
Current Ground Capacity 26,996.
Record Attendance 34,099 v Manchester U., FA Cup 4th Round, 3 February 1969.
Year Formed 1891. Turned professional 1897.
Previous Names West Herts, Watford St Mary's.
Club Nickname "The Hornets".
Club Colours Yellow shirts with black and red facings, red shorts and red stockings with black and yellow tops.
Club Honours Football League: Div. 3 Champions 1968-69; Div. 4 Champions 1977-78.
League History 1920-58 Div. 3(S); 1958-60 Div. 4; 1960-69 Div. 3; 1969-72 Div. 2; 1972-75 Div. 3; 1975-78 Div. 4; 1978-79 Div. 3; 1979-82 Div. 2; 1982-88 Div. 1; 1988- Div. 2.
Most League Points in a Season (2 for a win) 71 in Div. 4, 1977-78. (3 for a win) 80 in Div. 2, 1981-82.
Most League Goals in a Season 92 in Div. 4, 1959-60.

Record Victory 10-1 v Lowestoft T. in FA Cup 1st Round, 27 November 1926.
Record Defeat 0-10 v Wolverhampton W. in FA Cup 1st Round replay, 13 January 1912.
Consecutive League Wins 7 in 1934 and 1977-78.
Consecutive League Defeats 9 in 1972-73.
Record League Appearances Duncan Welbourne, 411 between 1963-74.
Record League Goalscorer—Career Luther Blissett, 148 between 1975-88.
Record League Goalscorer—Season Cliff Holton, 42 in Div. 4, 1959-60.

Watford: League Record, 1987-88 (Division 1)

Match Number	Date	Venue	Opponents	Result		H/T	Lge Posn	Attend
1	15.8.87	H	Wimbledon	W	1-0	1-0		15344
2	19.8.87	A	Nottingham F.	L	0-1	0-1		14527
3	22.8.87	A	Manchester U.	L	0-2	0-2	14	38582
4	29.8.87	H	Tottenham H.	D	1-1	0-0	15	19073
5	5.9.87	H	Norwich C.	L	0-1	0-0	19	11724
6	12.9.87	A	Sheffield Wed.	W	3-2	2-1	15	16144
7	19.9.87	H	Portsmouth	D	0-0	0-0	13	13277
8	26.9.87	H	Chelsea	L	0-3	0-1	16	16213
9	3.10.87	A	Coventry C.	L	0-1	0-0	16	16111
10	17.10.87	A	Southampton	L	0-1	0-0	19	11933
11	24.10.87	A	Everton	L	0-2	0-1	20	28501
12	31.10.87	H	West Ham U.	L	1-2	0-1	20	14427
13	7.11.87	A	Q.P.R.	D	0-0	0-0	20	12101
14	14.11.87	H	Charlton Ath.	W	2-1	1-0	19	12093
15	21.11.87	A	Oxford U.	D	1-1	1-0	19	7811
16	24.11.87	A	Liverpool	L	0-4	0-0	19	32396
17	28.11.87	H	Arsenal	W	2-0	1-0	19	19598
18	5.12.87	A	Derby Co.	D	1-1	0-1	19	14516
19	12.12.87	H	Luton T.	L	0-1	0-1	19	12152
20	26.12.87	H	Sheffield Wed.	L	1-3	1-3	21	12026
21	28.12.87	A	Portsmouth	D	1-1	0-0	21	15003
22	1.1.88	A	Tottenham H.	L	1-2	0-0	21	25471
23	2.1.88	H	Manchester U.	L	0-1	0-1	21	18038
24	16.1.88	A	Wimbledon	W	2-1	0-0	20	6848
25	23.1.88	H	Nottingham F.	D	0-0	0-0	20	13158
26	6.2.88	A	Norwich C.	D	0-0	0-0	19	13316
27	13.2.88	H	Liverpool	L	1-4	0-1	20	23838
28	27.2.88	H	Coventry C.	L	0-1	0-1	21	12052
29	5.3.88	A	Southampton	L	0-1	0-1	21	11824
30	19.3.88	A	West Ham U.	L	0-1	0-0	21	16015
31	26.3.88	H	Everton	L	1-2	0-1	21	13503
32	29.3.88	A	Chelsea	D	1-1	1-0	21	11240
33	1.4.88	H	Q.P.R.	L	0-1	0-0	21	16083
34	4.4.88	A	Charlton Ath.	L	0-1	0-1	21	6196
35	9.4.88	H	Oxford U.	W	3-0	2-0	21	10045
36	12.4.88	A	Newcastle U.	L	0-3	0-1	21	16318
37	15.4.88	A	Arsenal	W	1-0	0-0	20	19541
38	19.4.88	H	Newcastle U.	D	1-1	1-0	20	12075
39	30.4.88	H	Derby Co.	D	1-1	1-1	20	14181
40	2.5.88	A	Luton T.	L	1-2	0-2	20	10409

Players: League Record, 1987-88 (Division 1)

Match Number	1	2	3	4	5	6	7	8	9	10	11	12	13	14	15	16	17	18	19	20	21	22	23	24	25	26	27	28	29	30	31	32	33	34	35	36	37	38	39	40	Apps	Subs	Goals
Agana	11	11	11	11	11	★		8	★	7	7						★		11	8¹	8	8														★					12	3	1
Allen		★							8¹	8	8¹	8	8	8	8	8	8	★	★	★	8¹	8	8	8	8	★	8	8				★									16	6	3
Bardsley	7	7		7	7																																				4	0	0
Blissett	8¹	8	8	8	8		★	★		8			7¹	7	7¹	7	7	7			9	9	★¹	★	★	9	9	★	★	9											17	8	4
Chivers						7	7	7				4			2	2	2	2	2		2	2	2	2	2																14	0	0
Coton	1	1	1	1	1	1	1	1	1	1	1	1	1	1	1		1	1	1	1	1	1	1	1	1	1	1	1	1	1	1	1	1	1	1	1	1	1	1	1	37	0	0
Gibbs	2	2	2	2	2	2	2	2	2	2	2	2	2				2			2	2	2	2	2	2	2	2	2	2	2	2	2	2	2	2	2	2	2	2	2	30	0	0
Hetherston							★		7								★		★	7																					2	3	0
Hill		★	★	4	4																																				2	2	0
Hodges											11	11	11	11	11	11	11	11	11	11¹	11			7	11	11	11	11			11				★		7²	7	7	7	★	22	2	3
Holden																													11	11	11	11	11¹	11	11¹	11	11	11	11		10	0	2
Holdsworth													★																									★			0	2	0
Jackett	4	4	4	3	3					★	★	4	4	3	4	3	3	4¹	3	4	4	4	4		4	4	4	4	11	4	4	4	3			4	4¹	4	4		32	1	2
Kuhl																								11							4	4	4								4	0	0
McClelland	6	6	6	6	6	6	6	6	6	6	6	6	6	6	6	6	6	6	6	6	6	6	6	6	6	6	6	6	6¹	6	6	6	6	6	6	6	6	6	6	6	40	0	0
Morris	5	5	5	5	5	4	4	4	4	5	5	5	5	5	5	5	5	5	5	5	5¹	5	5	5	5	5		5	5	5	5	5	5	5	5	5	5	5	5	5	39	0	1
Porter	10	10	10	10¹	10	10¹	10	10	10	**10**	★	10	10	10	10	10	10	10	10	10	**10**	10	10	10	10	10	10	10	10	10¹	10	10	10	10	10	10	10	10	10	**10**	39	1	3
Pullan												4			7					★																					2	2	0
Rees																			1	1	1																				3	0	0
Rimmer																									8¹	8	8	8	8	8	8	8	8								9	0	1
Roberts	★		★	★	★	8	8	8	★	9	8		9	9¹	9			9						8	★	★	9	9		9	9	9	9	9	9¹	9					18	7	2
Rostron	3	3	3	★	★	3	3	3	3	3	3		3		★	3	3	3	3	3	3	3	3	3	3	★	3	3	3	3	3										33	4	1
Senior	9	9	9	9	9	9¹	9	9	9					★	9	9	9	9	9★	9	9	9		9	9	9															22	2	1
Sherwood						★				10	★	7	7	4	4				★	4		11			4			7						★							9	4	0
Sterling			7				11¹	11	11	7				★	★	★		★		11	11		7¹	7	7	7	7	7	7	7	7	7									17	4	2
Terry				5	5	5	5	5																					5												6	1	0
Thomas																																		★	★	★	7				1	3	0
Own Goals																			1															1									2

FA Cup: 1987-88: 3rd Round: Hull C. (H) 1-1 Replay (A) 2-2 2nd Replay (H) 1-0; 4th Round: Coventry C. (A) 1-0; 5th Round: Port Vale (A) 0-0 Replay (H) 2-0; 6th Round: Wimbledon (A) 1-2.
Littlewoods Cup: 1987-88: 2nd Round: Darlington (A) 3-0 (H) 8-0; 3rd Round: Swindon T. (A) 1-1 Replay (H) 4-2; 4th Round: Manchester C. (A) 1-3.

WEST BROMWICH ALBION (Division 2)

Team Manager Ron Atkinson.
Club Address The Hawthorns, West Bromwich B71 4LF. Tel: 021-525 8888.
Current Ground Capacity 39,159.
Record Attendance 64,815 v Arsenal, FA Cup 6th Round, 6 March 1937.
Year Formed 1879. Turned professional 1885.
Previous Names None.
Club Nicknames "The Throstles", "Baggies" or "Albion".
Club Colours Navy blue and white striped shirts, navy shorts and white stockings.
Club Honours Football League: Div. 1 Champions 1919-20; Div. 2 Champions 1901-02, 1910-11. FA Cup: Winners 1888, 1892, 1931, 1954, 1968. Football League Cup: Winners 1966.
League History 1888-1901 Div. 1; 1901-02 Div. 2; 1902-04 Div. 1; 1904-11 Div. 2; 1911-27 Div. 1; 1927-31 Div. 2; 1931-38 Div. 1; 1938-49 Div. 2; 1949-73 Div. 1; 1973-76 Div. 2; 1976-86 Div. 1; 1986- Div. 2.

Most League Points in a Season (2 for a win) 60 in Div. 1, 1919-20. (3 for a win) 57 in Div. 1, 1982-83.
Most League Goals in a Season 105 in Div. 2, 1929-30.
Record Victory 12-0 v Darwen in Div. 1, 4 April 1892.
Record Defeat 3-10 v Stoke C. in Div. 1, 4 February 1937.
Consecutive League Wins 11 in 1930.
Consecutive League Defeats 9 in 1985.
Record League Appearances Tony Brown, 574 between 1963-80.
Record League Goalscorer—Career Tony Brown, 218 between 1963-80.
Record League Goalscorer—Season William Richardson, 39 in Div. 1, 1935-36.

West Bromwich Albion: League Record, 1987-88 (Division 2)

Match Number	Date	Venue	Opponents	Result		H/T	Lge Posn	Attend
1	15.8.87	H	Oldham Ath.	D	0-0	0-0		8873
2	22.8.87	A	Blackburn Rov.	L	1-3	1-2		5619
3	29.8.87	H	Swindon T.	L	1-2	1-1	23	7503
4	31.8.87	A	Leeds U.	L	0-1	0-0	23	19847
5	5.9.87	H	Shrewsbury T.	W	2-1	0-0	21	8560
6	8.9.87	A	Crystal Palace	L	1-4	0-1	21	8554
7	12.9.87	A	Plymouth Arg.	D	3-3	1-0	20	10578
8	16.9.87	H	Aston Villa	L	0-2	0-1	22	22072
9	19.9.87	H	Bournemouth	W	3-0	1-0	19	7749
10	26.9.87	A	Millwall	L	0-2	0-1	20	6564
11	30.9.87	H	Birmingham C.	W	3-1	1-0	18	15399
12	3.10.87	A	Reading	W	2-1	1-1	14	5543
13	10.10.87	H	Bradford C.	L	0-1	0-1	18	12241
14	17.10.87	A	Middlesbrough	L	1-2	0-0	18	10684
15	21.10.87	A	Leicester C.	L	0-3	0-1	19	9262
16	24.10.87	H	Huddersfield T.	W	3-2	2-2	19	8450
17	4.11.87	H	Sheffield U.	W	4-0	2-0	17	8072
18	7.11.87	A	Stoke C.	L	0-3	0-2	18	9992
19	14.11.87	H	Ipswich T.	D	2-2	0-1	17	8457
20	21.11.87	A	Hull C.	L	0-1	0-0	18	7654
21	28.11.87	H	Manchester C.	D	1-1	1-0	17	15425
22	5.12.87	A	Barnsley	L	1-3	0-1	18	5395
23	12.12.87	H	Blackburn Rov.	L	0-1	0-1	18	7303
24	18.12.88	A	Aston Villa	D	0-0	0-0	18	24437
25	26.12.87	H	Millwall	L	1-4	1-2	20	9291
26	28.12.87	A	Bournemouth	L	2-3	0-1	20	8969
27	1.1.88	A	Swindon T.	L	0-2	0-0	20	12155
28	2.1.88	H	Plymouth Arg.	W	1-0	1-0	19	8445
29	16.1.88	A	Oldham Ath.	L	1-2	0-0	20	5557
30	30.1.88	H	Leeds U.	L	1-4	0-2	21	9008
31	6.2.88	A	Shrewsbury T.	W	1-0	0-0	19	6360
32	13.2.88	H	Crystal Palace	W	1-0	0-0	18	8944
33	27.2.88	H	Reading	L	0-1	0-0	21	8509
34	5.3.88	A	Middlesbrough	D	0-0	0-0	21	8316
35	8.3.88	A	Birmingham C.	W	1-0	0-0	19	12331
36	12.3.88	A	Bradford C.	L	1-4	0-1	19	12502
37	26.3.88	A	Huddersfield T.	W	3-1	0-1	19	4503
38	2.4.88	H	Stoke C.	W	2-0	1-0	18	12144
39	4.4.88	A	Ipswich T.	D	1-1	1-0	17	10665
40	9.4.88	H	Leicester C.	D	1-1	1-1	17	11031
41	23.4.88	A	Sheffield U.	D	0-0	0-0	18	12091
42	30.4.88	H	Hull C.	D	1-1	1-0	19	8004
43	2.5.88	A	Manchester C.	L	2-4	1-2	20	16490
44	7.5.88	H	Barnsley	D	2-2	1-0	20	8483

Players: League Record, 1987-88 (Division 2)

Match Number	1	2	3	4	5	6	7	8	9	10	11	12	13	14	15	16	17	18	19	20	21	22	23	24	25	26	27	28	29	30	31	32	33	34	35	36	37	38	39	40	41	42	43	44	Apps	Subs	Goals
Anderson										11	11					★	★	★	10	10		3		10	10						11[1]	11		11	11	11	10	11	11	11	11	11	**11**	11	20	3	1
Bennett	4	4	4[1]			4	4	4																																					6	0	1
Bradley	10	2	★	2	★	★	6	6	10	10	2	2	2	2	2	2	**10**	10																								★			15	4	0
Burrows	★	3	3	3					5	5	5	5	5	3	3	3	3	3		3	2	2	★			★		★																	17	4	0
Cowdrill					3	3	3	3	3	3	3	3	3	3	**3**								3	3	3	3	3	3	3	3	3	3	3	3	3	3	3	3	3	3	3	3	3	3	32	0	0
Dickinson	5	5	**5**	5	5	5	★		★	4									5	5			7	2	2	2		★[1]																	13	3	1
Dobbins		★	2											★	★				10	11	10					★	7																		5	5	0
Dyson																															6	6	6	6	6	6[1]	6[1]	6							8	0	2
Goodman	8	**8**	8	8	8[1]	8	**8**	8	8	8	8	8	8	8	★		8[1]		8[1]	8	8[1]	8	8	8	8[1]	8	8[1]	★	8	8	8[1]	8	8	8	8	**8**	★	★	★	★	9				34	6	7
Gray					9[2]		9	9	**9**	9[1]	9[1]	9	9	9	9	9[1]	9	9[1]	9	9	9		★	9[1]	9	9	9	9	9			★	9[2]	9[1]	9	9	9	**9**		9					30	2	10
Hodson																																						2	2	2	2	2	2	2	7	0	0
Hogg																	4	4	4	4	4	4	4																						7	0	0
Hopkins	7	7				★	7	7	7	7	7	7	7	7						7	7	7	7			7	7	2	2	7	7		7[1]	7	7	7	7			7	7	7[1]			28	1	2
Hucker																															1	1	1	1	1	1	1								7	0	0
Kelly	6	6	6	6	6	6				6	6	6	6	6	6[1]	6	6	6	6	6			5	5	5	6	6	**6**	10																26	0	1
Lynex																	7	7	7	7	7	**7**	6	**6**	**6**	6	6	7		★	7			7			7[1]	7		★[1]	★				16	3	2
Morley	11	11	**11**	11	11	11	11	11	11[2]			11	11		11	11[3]	11[1]	11	11	11	11	★	11	11	11[1]	**11**		11	**11**	11		11			11			1	1		★[1]	★			27	1	7
Naylor	1	1	1	1	1	1	1	1	1	1	1	1	1	1	1	1	1	1	1	1	1	1	1	1	1	1		1							1		1	1	1	1	1	1	1	1	35	0	0
North																								5	5	5	5	5	5	5	5	5	5	5	5	5	5	5	5	5	5	5	5	5	18	0	0
Palmer	★	★	7	7	2	2	2	2[1]	2	2[1]	**2**	4[1]	4	4	4	2	4	2	5	2	2	2	2	4	4	4	4	4	4	6	6	6	6	6	6	10	10								36	2	3
Phillips																													9	9	9			8	8[1]	8	8	8	8	8[1]					10	0	1
Powell																					1	1																							2	0	0
Reilly			9			5	5	5	5						5	5	5		5		★	9	9	**9**	5																				13	1	0
Robson	2	10	9	9	7	7						10	10		★		★		10	★	★	★	10	10	**10**	10[1]	7	10	10	10	10	**10**	10		★		10	**10**	10	10	10				25	6	1
Singleton			10	10	10	10	10	10	★	★	10[1]	10	**10**	10																															10	2	0
Statham	3																																												1	0	0
Steggles				4	4	4																2																							4	0	0
Swain																															2	2	2	2	2	2	2[1]								7	0	1
Talbot																													4	4	4	4	4	4	4[1]	4	4[1]	4	4[1]	4	4	4	4	4	15	0	2
Williamson	9	★	★	9	9[1]	★	★		★	★	★	★[1]	★	11	8	8	★[1]	8			★				★	11	★	8			9														10	12	3
Own Goals		1			1																			1																								3

FA Cup: 1987-88: 3rd Round: Wimbledon (A) 1-4.
Littlewoods Cup: 1987-88: 1st Round: Walsall (H) 2-3 (A) 0-0.

136

WEST HAM UNITED (Division 1)

Team Manager John Lyall.
Club Address Boleyn Ground, Green Street, Upton Park, London E13. Tel: 01-472 2740.
Current Ground Capacity 35,510.
Record Attendance 42,322 v Tottenham H., Div. 1, 17 October 1970.
Year Formed 1895. Turned professional 1900.
Previous Names Thames Ironworks FC.
Club Nickname "The Hammers".
Club Colours Claret shirts with single blue hoop, white shorts and stockings.
Club Honours Football League: Div. 2 Champions 1957-58, 1980-81. FA Cup: Winners 1964, 1975, 1980. European Cup-winners Cup: Winners 1964-65.
League History 1919-23 Div. 2; 1923-32 Div. 1; 1932-58 Div. 2; 1958-78 Div. 1; 1978-81 Div. 2; 1981- Div. 1.
Most League Points in a Season (2 for a win) 66 in Div. 2, 1980-81. (3 for a win) 84 in Div. 1, 1985-86.
Most League Goals in a Season 101 in Div. 2, 1957-58.
Record Victory 10-0 v Bury in Milk Cup 2nd Round 2nd Leg, 25 October 1983.

Record Defeat 2-8 v Blackburn Rov. in Div. 1, 26 December 1963.
Consecutive League Wins 9 in 1985.
Consecutive League Defeats 9 in 1932.
Record League Appearances Billy Bonds, 663 between 1967-88.
Record League Goalscorer—Career Vic Watson, 306 between 1920-35.
Record League Goalscorer—Season Vic Watson, 41 in Div. 1, 1929-30.

West Ham United: League Record, 1987-88 (Division 1)

Match Number	Date	Venue	Opponents	Result		H/T	Lge Posn	Attend
1	15.8.87	H	Q.P.R.	L	0-3	0-3		22881
2	22.8.87	A	Luton T.	D	2-2	2-1		8073
3	29.8.87	H	Norwich C.	W	2-0	0-0	14	16394
4	31.8.87	A	Portsmouth	L	1-2	1-1	14	16104
5	5.9.88	H	Liverpool	D	1-1	0-0	15	29865
6	12.9.87	A	Wimbledon	D	1-1	0-1	16	8507
7	19.9.87	H	Tottenham H.	L	0-1	0-1	18	27750
8	26.9.87	A	Arsenal	L	0-1	0-0	19	40127
9	3.10.87	H	Derby Co.	D	1-1	1-0	19	17226
10	10.10.87	H	Charlton Ath.	D	1-1	1-1	17	15757
11	17.10.87	A	Oxford U.	W	2-1	2-1	15	9092
12	25.10.87	H	Manchester U.	D	1-1	0-1	16	19863
13	3.11.87	A	Watford	W	2-1	1-0	14	14427
14	7.11.87	H	Sheffield Wed.	L	0-1	0-1	15	16277
15	14.11.87	A	Everton	L	1-3	0-3	15	29405
16	21.11.87	H	Nottingham F.	W	3-2	1-1	13	17216
17	28.11.87	A	Coventry C.	D	0-0	0-0	14	16740
18	5.12.87	H	Southampton	W	2-1	1-1	11	15375
19	12.12.87	A	Chelsea	D	1-1	1-0	12	22850
20	19.12.87	H	Newcastle U.	W	2-1	0-0	9	18679
21	26.12.87	H	Wimbledon	L	1-2	0-2	10	18605
22	28.12.87	A	Tottenham H.	L	1-2	0-1	13	39461
23	1.1.88	A	Norwich C.	L	1-4	1-0	14	20059
24	2.1.88	H	Luton T.	D	1-1	0-0	14	16716
25	16.1.88	A	Q.P.R.	W	1-0	0-0	12	14909
26	6.2.88	A	Liverpool	D	0-0	0-0	13	42049
27	13.2.88	H	Portsmouth	D	1-1	0-0	13	18639
28	27.2.88	A	Derby Co.	L	0-1	0-0	13	16301
29	5.3.88	H	Oxford U.	D	1-1	0-0	13	14980
30	12.3.88	A	Charlton Ath.	L	0-3	0-2	15	8118
31	19.3.88	H	Watford	W	1-0	0-0	15	16015
32	26.3.88	A	Manchester U.	L	1-3	0-0	15	37269
33	2.4.88	A	Sheffield Wed.	L	1-2	0-1	15	18435
34	4.4.88	H	Everton	D	0-0	0-0	16	21195
35	12.4.88	H	Arsenal	L	0-1	0-0	17	26746
36	20.4.88	A	Nottingham F.	D	0-0	0-0	17	15775
37	23.4.88	H	Coventry C.	D	1-1	0-0	17	17733
38	30.4.88	A	Southampton	L	1-2	0-0	18	15652
39	2.5.88	H	Chelsea	W	4-1	2-0	16	28521
40	7.5.88	A	Newcastle U.	L	1-2	1-0	16	23731

Players: League Record, 1987-88 (Division 1)

Match Number	1	2	3	4	5	6	7	8	9	10	11	12	13	14	15	16	17	18	19	20	21	22	23	24	25	26	27	28	29	30	31	32	33	34	35	36	37	38	39	40	Apps	Subs	Goals
Bonds														2	2	2	2	2	**2**	2	2	2	2	4	4	4	4	4	4	4	**4**		4	4	4						22	0	0
Brady	9	6	6	6	6	6	6	6	6¹	6	6	6	6	6				7	★	8			8	8	8	**8**															21	1	1
Cottee	10	10	10²	10	10¹	10¹	10	10	10	10	10	10¹	10	10	10¹	10	10²	10	10	10	10	10	10	10¹	10	10	10	10¹	10	10	10	10	10	10	10	10	10¹	10¹	10¹	10	40	0	13
Devonshire	6																																								1	0	0
Dickens	★							8	8	8	8¹	8	8	8	8	8¹	8	8	**8**		8		9¹	9	9	9		8	★	11	★	8		8	8	8	8	8			25	3	3
Dicks																													3	3	3	3	3	3	3	3					8	0	0
Dolan												★						★					★	9																	1	3	0
Gale																			8	6	6	6	6	6	6	6	6	6	6	6	6	6	6	6							17	1	0
Hilton						★		★			4¹	4	4		9	★	★	4¹	4	9												★			5¹	5					9	5	3
Ince		9	9	9	9	9	9	9	9	9¹	9	9	9	9	9	9	9	9¹	9	9	9	9	★¹	3	3	3	9			★		9									26	2	3
Keen								7	7	4	4	4	4	**4**	★	6	6	6¹	6	6	6	6	**6**			★	8	★	8	8		★		4							19	4	1
McAlister	1	1	1	1	1	1	1	1	1	1	1	1	1	1	1	1	1	1	1	1	1	1	1	1	1	1	1	1	1	1	1	1	1		1	1	1	1	1	1	39	0	0
McAvennie	8	8	8	8	8	8	8	8																																	8	0	0
McQueen	3	3	3	3	**3**			3		11													3	★		★	3	3													10	2	0
Martin	5	5	5	5	5	5	5	5	5	5	5	5	5	**5**																											15	0	0
Orr	4																																								1	0	0
Parkes																															1										1	0	0
Parris				★	★	3	3	3	8	3	3	3	3	3	3	3	3	3¹	3	3	3	3	**3**							★		8	4	8	2	11	2	2			27	3	1
Potts																							6					3	3	★		2			2		4	4			7	1	0
Robson	11	11	11	11	11	11	11	11	11	11		11	11	11	11	11	11	11¹	11	11	11	11	11	11	11	11	11	11	**11**		11	11	11	11	11		11	11¹			37	0	2
Rosenior																												9¹	9¹	9¹	9	9	9		9	9²	9				9	0	5
Slater													★																						★						0	2	0
Stewart	2	2¹	2	**2**	2	2	2	2	**2**	2	2	2¹	2	2		5¹	5	5	5	5	5¹	5	5	2	2	2	2	2	2	2	2	**2**									33	0	4
Strodder	★	4	4	4¹	4	4	4	4						★		4	4	4	4	★		4	5	5	5	5	5	5	5	**5**	5	5	5	5							27	3	1
Ward	7	7	7	7	7	7		7	7	7	7	7	7	7	7	7		7	**7**	7	7	7	7	7	7	**7**	7¹	7	7	7	7	7	7	7	7	7	7	7	7	7	37	0	1
Own Goals		1											1																														2

FA Cup: 1987-88: 3rd Round: Charlton Ath. (H) 2-0; 4th Round: Q.P.R. (A) 1-3.
Littlewoods Cup: 1987-88: 2nd Round: Barnsley (A) 0-0 (H) 2-5.

WIGAN ATHLETIC (Division 3)

Team Manager Ray Mathias.
Club Address Springfield Park, Wigan. Tel: (0942) 44433.
Current Ground Capacity 25,000.
Record Attendance 27,500 v Hereford U., FA Cup, 12 December 1953.
Year Formed 1932. Turned Professional 1932.
Previous Names None.
Club Nickname "The Latics".
Club Colours Royal blue shirts and shorts and white stockings.
Club Honours None.
League History 1978-82 Div. 4; 1982- Div.3.
Most League Points in a Season (2 for a win) 55 in Div 4, 1978-79 and 1979-80. (3 for a win) 91 in Div. 4, 1981-82.
Most League Goals in a Season 80 in Div. 4, 1981-82.
Record Victory 7-2 v Scunthorpe U. in Div. 4, 12 March 1982.
Record Defeat 0-5 v Bristol Rov. in Div. 3, 26 February 1983 and 0-5 v Chelsea in FA Cup 3rd Round replay, 26 January 1985.

Consecutive League Wins 6 in 1985 and 1986-87.
Consecutive League Defeats 5 in 1983.
Record League Appearances Colin Methven, 296 between 1979-86.
Record League Goalscorer—Career Peter Houghton, 62 between 1978-84.
Record League Goalscorer—Season Les Bradd, 19 in Div. 4, 1981-82.

Wigan Athletic: League Record, 1987-88 (Division 3)

Match Number	Date	Venue	Opponents	Result		H/T	Lge Posn	Attend
1	15.8.87	A	Notts Co.	D	4-4	3-2		6344
2	29.8.87	A	Preston N.E.	W	1-0	0-0		7057
3	31.8.87	H	Gillingham	D	1-1	0-1	11	3412
4	5.9.87	A	Bristol Rov.	W	3-2	2-2	8	3168
5	12.9.87	H	Doncaster Rov.	W	2-1	1-1	6	2764
6	15.9.87	H	Mansfield T.	W	1-0	0-0	2	3261
7	19.9.87	A	Walsall	W	2-1	1-0	1	5353
8	26.9.87	H	Bury	L	0-2	0-1	4	3664
9	29.9.87	A	Aldershot	L	2-3	1-2	7	2259
10	3.10.87	H	York C.	D	1-1	0-0	9	2878
11	10.10.87	A	Sunderland	L	1-4	1-3	11	13974
12	17.10.87	H	Fulham	L	1-3	0-2	12	2806
13	20.10.87	H	Brighton & H.A.	D	3-3	1-0	12	2392
14	24.10.87	A	Blackpool	D	0-0	0-0	14	4821
15	31.10.87	H	Rotherham U.	W	3-0	1-0	11	3004
16	3.11.87	A	Chesterfield	W	1-0	1-0	8	1725
17	7.11.87	H	Southend U.	W	1-0	0-0	7	3081
18	21.11.87	A	Brentford	L	1-2	0-1	8	3625
19	28.11.87	H	Bristol C.	D	1-1	0-1	9	2879
20	12.12.87	A	Grimsby T.	W	2-0	1-0	7	2127
21	19.12.87	H	Northampton T.	D	2-2	1-1	8	2692
22	26.12.87	A	Bury	W	2-0	1-0	6	4555
23	28.12.87	H	Chester C.	W	1-0	0-0	6	4394
24	1.1.88	H	Preston N.E.	W	2-0	2-0	4	6872
25	2.1.88	A	Doncaster Rov.	W	4-3	1-2	4	2464
26	16.1.88	H	Walsall	W	3-1	2-0	4	5063
27	23.1.88	A	Gillingham	W	1-0	1-0	3	4256
28	30.1.88	A	Northampton T.	D	1-1	1-0	4	4825
29	6.2.88	H	Bristol Rov.	W	1-0	0-0	3	3827
30	13.2.88	A	Chester C.	L	0-1	0-0	4	3088
31	20.2.88	H	Notts Co.	W	2-1	1-1	3	5182
32	27.2.88	A	York C.	L	1-3	0-1	4	2360
33	1.3.88	H	Aldershot	W	4-0	0-0	4	3017
34	5.3.88	A	Fulham	L	2-3	2-3	4	3860
35	12.3.88	H	Sunderland	D	2-2	1-0	4	6949
36	19.3.88	A	Rotherham U.	D	1-1	0-1	4	3288
37	25.3.88	H	Blackpool	D	0-0	0-0	4	4505
38	28.3.88	H	Mansfield T.	W	2-1	1-1	4	3217
39	1.4.88	A	Southend U.	L	2-3	1-0	4	5003
40	4.4.88	H	Brentford	D	1-1	1-1	4	3597
41	9.4.88	A	Brighton & H.A.	L	0-1*	0-0	5	9423
42	12.4.88	H	Port Vale	W	2-0	1-0	5	3750
43	23.4.88	H	Chesterfield	L	1-2	1-1	6	3303
44	25.4.88	A	Port Vale	L	1-2	1-1	6	3044
45	30.4.88	A	Bristol C.	L	1-4	1-2	6	7340
46	2.5.88	H	Grimsby T.	L	0-1	0-0	7	2705

Players: League Record, 1987-88 (Division 3)

Match Number	1	2	3	4	5	6	7	8	9	10	11	12	13	14	15	16	17	18	19	20	21	22	23	24	25	26	27	28	29	30	31	32	33	34	35	36	37	38	39	40	41	42	43	44	45	46	Apps	Subs	Goals
Adkins													1	1																																	2	0	0
Ainscow				★[1]								★	★	11	★					★	★		9	9	9	9	9	9[1]	9[2]	9																	9	6	4
Atherton							7				6				3			★	2	2	2	2	2	2	2	2	2	2											2								15	1	0
Beesley	6	6	6	6[1]	6	6	6	6	3	3	5	5	5	5	5	5	5	5	★	6	6	6	6	6	6	6	6	6	6	6		6	6	6	6	6	6	6	6	6	6	6	6	6	6	6	41	1	1
Butler	2	2	2	2	2	2	2	2	2[1]	2	2	2	2	2	2	2	2														★	★	2	2							11	2				23	3	1
Campbell	9[1]	9	9	9[1]	9[1]	9	9	9	9[1]	9		9[1]	9	9	9[2]	9	9	9	9		★						★	★	★	9	★	9	9	9	9[1]	9[1]	9	9[1]	9[1]	9	★	9					28	6	11
Cook	11	11[1]	11	11	11	11	11	★	11				★	10[1]	10[1]	11	11	11	11	11	11	11	11[1]	11	11	11	11	11[1]	11	11	11	11	11	11	11[1]	11	11	11	11[1]	11	11	11	★	11			38	3	8
Cribley	5[1]	5	5[1]	5	5	5[1]	5	5	5	5																																					11	0	3
Griffiths											11	★	11	11					8														★	★		★	★[1]		4	★		★					5	8	1
Hamilton	4	4	4	4	4[1]	4	4	4	4	4	4	4	4	4	4	4	4	4	4	4	4	4	4	4[1]	4	4	4	4	4	4	4	4	4	4	4	4	4	4		4	4	4	4	4	4	4	45	0	2
Hilditch	★	7	7	★	★	8	8	8	8[1]	8	9	7	11[2]	11	11	11	11		2				10[2]	10[1]		★	9	9	9	9	9	9[1]	9[1]		9												25	4	8
Holden									★	6	6	6	6	6	6	6		6[1]	6		6[1]	6	6	6																							14	1	2
Hughes																	1	1	1	1	1	1	1	1	1	1	1	1	1	1	1	1	1	1	1	1	1	1	1	1	1	1	1	1	1	1	31	0	0
Jewell	10	10	10	10	10	10	10[2]	10	10	10	10[1]	10	10	10	10[1]		★	10	10	10	10	10		10[1]	10	10	10	10	10[1]	10[1]	10[3]	10	10	10	10	10	10	10	10	10	10	10[1]	10				42	1	11
Kennedy																							3	3	3	3	3	3	3	3	3	3	3	3	3	3	3	3	3	3	3	3					22	0	0
Knowles	3[1]	3	3	3	3	3	3	3	3	★	★	3	3	3	3	3	3	3	3																								3	3	3		21	2	1
McEwan																		5[1]	5	5	5	5[1]	5	5	5	5					5	5	5[1]	5	5[1]	5	5	5	5	5	5	5	5				23	0	4
Pilling																		★[1]	8	8	8[1]	8	8	8	8	8	8	8[1]	8	8	8					★	★				★	9	8				16	4	3
Redfern													1	1			1																															3	0	0
Senior																		7	7	7	7	7	7	7	2	2					★	5	5		2[1]	2		6	2	2	2	2		2	2	★	20	2	1
Smith																				★																											0	1	0
Storer	7		★	7	7	7	7	7	7	7	7	★	★																																		9	3	0
Thompson, C.	8[1]	8	8	8	8		★			8	8	8[1]	8	8	8	8											★	★	★	★	8	8	8	8	8	8	8	8[1]	8	8	8	★					25	6	3
Thompson, D.													7							6[1]	7	7	7	7[1]	7	7	7	7	7	7[1]	7	7	7	7	7	7	7	7	7	7	7	8[1]	7	7	7	7	27	0	3
Tunks	1	1	1	1	1	1	1	1	1	1				1																																	10	0	0
Wilson																				2																											1	0	0
Own Goals																			1												1												1						3

FA Cup: 1987-88: 1st Round: Altrincham (A) 2-0; 2nd Round: Wolverhampton W. (A) 1-3.
Littlewoods Cup: 1987-88: 1st Round: Bolton W. (H) 2-3 (A) 3-1; 2nd Round: Luton T. (H) 0-1 (A) 2-4.

WIMBLEDON (Division 1)

Team Manager Bobby Gould.
Club Address Plough Lane Ground, Durnsford Road, Wimbledon, London SW19. Tel: 01-946 6311.
Current Ground Capacity 16,000
Record Attendance 18,000 v HMS Victory, FA Amateur Cup 3rd Round, 1934-35.
Year Formed 1889. Turned professional 1964.
Previous Names Wimbledon Old Centrals.
Club Nickname "The Dons".
Club Colours Royal blue shirts with yellow trim, blue shorts with yellow trim and blue stockings.
Club Honours Football League: Div. 4 Champions 1982-83. FA Cup: Winners 1988.
League History 1977-79 Div. 4; 1979-80 Div. 3; 1980-81 Div. 4; 1981-82 Div. 3; 1982-83 Div. 4; 1983-84 Div. 3; 1984-86 Div. 2; 1986- Div. 1.
Most League Points in a Season (2 for a win) 61 in Div. 4, 1978-79. (3 for a win) 98 in Div. 4, 1982-83.
Most League Goals in a Season 97 in Div. 3, 1983-84.
Record Victory 15-2 v Polytechnic in FA Cup Preliminary Round, 7 February 1929.

Record Defeat 0-8 v Everton in League Cup 2nd Round, 29 August 1978.
Consecutive League Wins 7 in 1983.
Consecutive League Defeats 4 in 1982.
Record League Appearances Alan Cork, 316 between 1978-88.
Record League Goalscorer—Career Alan Cork, 131 between 1978-88.
Record League Goalscorer—Season Alan Cork, 29 in Div. 3, 1983-84.

Wimbledon: League Record, 1987-88 (Division 1)

Match Number	Date	Venue	Opponents	Result		H/T	Lge Posn	Attend
1	15.8.87	A	Watford	L	0-1	0-1		15344
2	18.8.87	H	Everton	D	1-1	1-0		7763
3	22.8.87	H	Oxford U.	D	1-1	0-1	15	4229
4	29.8.87	A	Derby Co.	W	1-0	0-0	11	15165
5	1.9.87	H	Charlton Ath.	W	4-1	1-1	6	5184
6	5.9.87	A	Newcastle U.	W	2-1	2-0	5	22684
7	12.9.87	H	West Ham U.	D	1-1	1-0	4	8507
8	19.9.87	A	Arsenal	L	0-3	0-3	8	27752
9	26.9.87	A	Portsmouth	L	1-2	1-1	10	13088
10	3.10.87	H	Q.P.R.	L	1-2	0-0	11	8552
11	17.10.87	A	Luton T.	L	0-2	0-1	15	7018
12	31.10.87	A	Tottenham H.	W	3-0	1-0	13	22200
13	4.11.87	H	Liverpool	D	1-1	0-1	13	13454
14	7.11.87	H	Southampton	W	2-0	1-0	10	5014
15	14.11.87	A	Coventry C.	D	3-3	0-1	9	14966
16	21.11.87	H	Manchester U.	W	2-1	0-0	8	11532
17	28.11.87	A	Chelsea	D	1-1	0-0	8	15608
18	5.12.87	H	Nottingham F.	D	1-1	0-1	8	5170
19	12.12.87	A	Sheffield Wed.	L	0-1	0-0	8	14289
20	18.12.87	H	Norwich C.	W	1-0	1-0	7	4026
21	26.12.87	A	West Ham U.	W	2-1	2-0	7	18605
22	28.12.87	H	Arsenal	W	3-1	0-1	7	12473
23	1.1.88	H	Derby Co.	W	2-1	1-1	7	5479
24	2.1.88	A	Oxford U.	W	5-2	3-0	6	6926
25	16.1.88	H	Watford	L	1-2	0-0	6	6848
26	6.2.88	H	Newcastle U.	D	0-0	0-0	7	10505
27	13.2.88	A	Charlton Ath.	D	1-1	0-1	7	5520
28	27.2.88	A	Q.P.R.	L	0-1	0-0	7	9080
29	5.3.88	H	Luton T.	W	2-0	1-0	7	5058
30	19.3.88	H	Tottenham H.	W	3-0	0-0	7	8616
31	26.3.88	A	Liverpool	L	1-2	0-1	7	36464
32	29.3.88	A	Everton	D	2-2	2-2	7	20351
33	2.4.88	A	Southampton	D	2-2	1-0	7	13036
34	5.4.88	H	Coventry C.	L	1-2	1-2	7	5920
35	19.4.88	H	Portsmouth	D	2-2	1-0	7	9009
36	23.4.88	H	Chelsea	D	2-2	1-0	7	15128
37	30.4.88	A	Nottingham F.	D	0-0	0-0	7	14341
38	3.5.88	H	Sheffield Wed.	D	1-1	1-0	7	7854
39	7.5.88	A	Norwich C.	W	1-0	0-0	7	11782
40	9.5.88	A	Manchester U.	L	1-2	1-0	7	28040

Players: League Record, 1987-88 (Division 1)

Match Number	1	2	3	4	5	6	7	8	9	10	11	12	13	14	15	16	17	18	19	20	21	22	23	24	25	26	27	28	29	30	31	32	33	34	35	36	37	38	39	40	Apps	Subs	Goals
Beasant	1	1	1	1	1	1	1	1	1	1	1	1	1	1	1	1	1	1	1	1	1	1	1	1	1	1	1	1	1	1	1	1	1	1	1	1	1	1	1	1	40	0	0
Bedford												3	3	3	3																										4	0	0
Clement						★		★			★											★	★	8	★			★	★	7		★									2	9	0
Cork	4	7¹	11¹	11	11¹	11¹	11			7	8	★	★	★¹	★	8	8	8	★	8	8	8¹	8¹	8¹	8²	8	★	8	8	8	8	8		8		8	8				28	6	9
Cunningham																				11				7	7¹	7¹						11		11							6	0	2
Fairweather	11	11		★	★		11	11	11	11	11	7¹	7¹	7	7¹	7	7		7	7	7	7	7¹	7																	19	2	4
Fashanu	9	9	9	9¹	9²	9	9	9	9	9¹	9	9	9¹	9	9	9²	9	9	9	9	9¹	9¹	9	9¹	9¹	9	9	9	9	9	9¹	9¹	9	9	9		9	9	9		38	0	13
Galliers	7																																								1	0	0
Gannon		★	★								7	7¹	11	11	11			7					11							★	7	7				8					10	3	1
Gayle			2		★	★	2	6		5	5	5	5	5	5	5	5				6	6	5	5	5	5		★¹	★	6	★	★			5	6					20	6	1
Gibson			8	8		★	8	8	8		8¹	8								7	7¹	7	7¹	7					7				7¹	7¹	7¹						16	1	6
Goodyear			★					2	2	2	2		2	2	2	2	2	2	2	2	2	2	2	2	2										2	2	2				21	1	0
Hazel								★	★	4				8																	10					★					3	3	0
Jones					4	4	4				4	4	4	4	4	4	4¹	4	4	4	4	4	4	4	4¹		4			4				4	4	4	4			24	0	2
Miller	★					★																									10		8	8							3	2	0
Phelan	3	3	3	3	3	3	3	3	3	3					★			★	3	3	3	3	3	3	3	3	3	3	3	3	3	3	3	3	3						28	2	0
Ryan	★	4	4	4	4¹	4	4	4	★	★	2	4	4	4					★	★				4	2	4	8	4	4		4										17	5	1
Sanchez	10	10	10	10	10	10	10	10	10¹	10	10	10	10	10	10	10	10	10	10¹	10	10	10¹	10	10	10	10	10	10	10	10¹	10	10	10	10							38	0	4
Sayer	8	8	8			8	8											★											★		★				★						5	4	0
Scales	2	2	2		2	2			2	2				★	3¹	3	3	3	3	3	3				11	★	2		2	2	2	2	2								23	2	1
Swindlehurst																													9	9											2	0	0
Thorn	6	6	6	6	6	6	6	6		6	6	6	6		6	6	6	6	6	6	6	6	6		6	6	6	6	6	6	6	6	6		6	6	6	6			35	0	0
Turner															★	★			★					11										★							0	4	0
Wise		7	7	7	7	7¹	7	7			8	8¹	11	11¹	11¹	11	11	11	11¹	11	11		11	11					11¹	11	11¹	11	11	11²	11¹	11	★	11			29	1	10
Young	5	5	5	5	5	5	5	5	5	5		2	★	5	5	5	5	5	5	5¹					5	5¹	5	5	5¹	5	5	5		5							28	1	3
Own Goals						1																																					1

FA Cup: 1987-88: 3rd Round: West Bromwich A. (H) 4-1; 4th Round: Mansfield T. (A) 2-1; 5th Round: Newcastle U. (A) 3-1; 6th Round: Watford (H) 2-1; Semi Final: Luton T. 2-1; Final: Liverpool 1-0.
Littlewoods Cup: 1987-88: 2nd Round: Rochdale (A) 1-1 (H) 2-1; 3rd Round: Newcastle U. (H) 2-1; 4th Round: Oxford U. (A) 1-2.

WOLVERHAMPTON WANDERERS (Division 3)

Team Manager Graham Turner.
Club Address Molineux Grounds, Wolverhampton WV1 4QR. Tel: (0902) 712181.
Current Ground Capacity 28,051.
Record Attendance 61,315 v Liverpool, FA Cup 5th Round, 11 February 1939.
Year Formed 1877. Turned professional 1888.
Previous Names St Luke's, Blakenhall.
Club Nickname "Wolves".
Club Colours Old gold shirts, black collar, cuffs and shorts and old gold stockings.
Club Honours Football League: Div. 1 Champions 1953-54, 1957-58, 1958-59; Div. 2 Champions 1931-32, 1976-77; Div. 3(N) Champions 1923-24; Div. 4 Champions 1987-88. FA Cup: Winners 1893, 1908, 1949, 1960. Football League Cup: Winners 1974, 1980.
League History 1888-1906 Div. 1; 1906-23 Div. 2; 1923-24 Div. 3(N); 1924-32 Div. 2; 1932-65 Div. 1; 1965-67 Div. 2; 1967-76 Div.1; 1976-77 Div. 2; 1977-82 Div.1; 1982-83 Div. 2; 1983-84 Div. 1; 1984-85 Div. 2; 1985-86 Div. 3; 1986-88 Div. 4; 1988- Div. 3.

Most League Points in a Season (2 for a win) 64 in Div. 1, 1957-58. (3 for a win) 90 in Div. 4, 1987-88.
Most League Goals in a Season 115 in Div. 2, 1931-32.
Record Victory 14-0 v Crosswell's Brewery in FA Cup 2nd Round, 1886-87.
Record Defeat 1-10 v Newton Heath in Div. 1, 15 October 1892.
Consecutive League Wins 8 in 1915, 1967 and 1987.
Consecutive League Defeats 8 in 1981-82.
Record League Appearances Derek Parkin, 501 between 1967-82.
Record League Goalscorer—Career Bill Hartill, 164 between 1928-35.
Record League Goalscorer—Season Dennis Westcott, 37 in Div. 1, 1946-47.

Wolverhampton Wanderers: League Record, 1987-88 (Division 4)

Match Number	Date	Venue	Opponents	Result		H/T	Lge Posn	Attend
1	15.8.87	A	Scarborough	D	2-2	2-1		7314
2	22.8.87	H	Halifax T.	L	0-1	0-0		7223
3	29.8.87	A	Hereford U.	W	2-1	0-0	12	2730
4	31.8.87	H	Scunthorpe U.	W	4-1	2-0	4	2628
5	5.9.87	A	Cardiff C.	L	2-3	1-1	11	2258
6	12.9.87	H	Crewe Alex.	D	2-2	1-1	11	6285
7	16.9.87	A	Peterborough U.	D	1-1	1-0	11	3089
8	19.9.87	A	Stockport Co.	W	2-0	2-0	9	2233
9	26.9.87	H	Torquay U.	L	1-2	0-0	12	7349
10	29.9.87	H	Rochdale	W	2-0	1-0	8	5553
11	3.10.87	A	Bolton W.	L	0-1	0-0	11	3833
12	10.10.87	A	Carlisle U.	W	1-0	1-0	8	2620
13	17.10.87	H	Tranmere Rov.	W	3-0	3-0	6	6608
14	20.10.87	H	Cambridge U.	W	3-0	3-0	3	6492
15	24.10.87	A	Darlington	D	2-2	2-2	4	2282
16	31.10.87	H	Newport Co.	W	2-1	0-0	1	6467
17	3.11.87	A	Swansea C.	W	2-1	1-0	1	5293
18	7.11.87	H	Burnley	W	3-0	0-0	1	10002
19	21.11.87	A	Colchester U.	W	1-0	0-0	1	2413
20	28.11.87	H	Wrexham	L	0-2	0-1	1	8541
21	12.12.87	A	Hartlepool U.	D	0-0	0-0	2	2760
22	19.12.87	H	Leyton Orient	W	2-0	0-0	1	12051
23	26.12.87	H	Exeter C.	W	3-0	1-0	2	15588

Match Number	Date	Venue	Opponents	Result		H/T	Lge Posn	Attend
24	1.1.88	H	Hereford U.	W	2-0	1-0	1	14577
25	2.1.88	A	Crewe Alex.	W	2-0	1-0	1	4629
26	16.1.88	H	Stockport Co.	D	1-1	0-0	1	8872
27	30.1.88	A	Scunthorpe U.	W	1-0	0-0	1	5476
28	6.2.88	H	Cardiff C.	L	1-4	0-0	1	9077
29	13.2.88	A	Exeter C.	W	4-2	2-0	1	3483
30	16.2.88	A	Halifax T.	L	1-2	1-1	1	2281
31	19.2.88	H	Scarborough	D	0-0	0-0	1	11391
32	23.2.88	A	Torquay U.	D	0-0	0-0	1	3803
33	27.2.88	H	Bolton W.	W	4-0	4-0	1	12430
34	1.3.88	A	Rochdale	W	1-0	1-0	1	2805
35	4.3.88	A	Tranmere Rov.	L	0-3	0-1	1	5007
36	12.3.88	H	Carlisle U.	W	3-1	1-0	1	9262
37	22.3.88	H	Peterborough U.	L	0-1	0-0	1	8049
38	26.3.88	H	Darlington	W	5-3	2-0	1	9349
39	2.4.88	A	Burnley	W	3-0	1-0	1	10341
40	4.4.88	H	Colchester U.	W	2-0	1-0	1	13443
41	10.4.88	A	Cambridge U.	D	1-1	0-0	1	5107
42	23.4.88	H	Swansea C.	W	2-0	1-0	1	12344
43	26.4.88	A	Newport Co.	W	3-1	2-0	1	3409
44	30.4.88	A	Wrexham	L	2-4	2-3	1	6898
45	2.5.88	H	Hartlepool U.	W	2-0	1-0	1	17895
46	7.5.88	A	Leyton Orient	W	2-0	1-0	1	7738

Players: League Record, 1987-88 (Division 4)

Match Number	1	2	3	4	5	6	7	8	9	10	11	12	13	14	15	16	17	18	19	20	21	22	23	24	25	26	27	28	29	30	31	32	33	34	35	36	37	38	39	40	41	42	43	44	45	46	Apps	Subs	Goals
Barnes	3																																														1	0	0
Bellamy					2	5	2	2	2	2	2													2	2	2	2¹					5	2¹	4	2	2	2	2	2	2	2	2	2	2			24	0	2
Bull	9¹	9	9¹	9²	9¹	9¹	9¹	9	9¹	9¹	9	9¹	9¹	9¹	9		9¹	9	9	9		9²	9	9²	9	9	9	9¹	9³	9	9	9	9²	9	9	9	9	9³	9¹	9²	9	9¹	9²	9²	9		44	0	34
Chard																																			8¹	8	8	8	8	11	8	8¹	8	★			8	1	2
Clarke			3	3	3	3											5	★		5						4																					7	1	0
Dennison	8	7	7	7	8	7	7	7	7	7	7	7	7	7	7	7	7	7	7	7	7	7¹	7	7	7	7	7		7	7	7¹	7	7	7	7	7	7	7	7			7		7	7	7¹	43	0	3
Downing	★	11	11	11	11					★		11	11	11	11		11	11¹	11		11	11	11	11	11	11	11	11	11	11	11	11	11	11		★	★	★		★		6	8	11	★	11	11	27	7	1
Edwards																				11																											1	0	0
Gallagher		★		★	★	★¹		★		★	★	★	★		9	6¹	6¹	6	11	9					★				★	★			★	★			★										6	13	3
Holmes	11							6	6						★					★						★			11	11	11¹	11	11	11	11¹	11	★	7	11				8				16	4	2
Kendall	1	1	1	1	1	1	1	1	1	1	1	1	1	1	1	1	1	1	1	1	1	1	1	1	1	1	1	1	1	1	1	1	1	1	1	1	1	1	1	1	1	1	1	1	1	1	46	0	0
McDonald																													3	3	3	3	3	3													6	0	0
Mutch	10	10	10¹	10²	10	10	10	10¹	10	10¹	10	10¹	10	10¹	10²	10¹	10	10	10	10	10	10	10¹	10	10²	10¹	10	10	10	10	10	10	10	10	10	10¹	10	10	10¹	10	10¹	10	10¹	10¹	10	10	46	0	19
Powell																		★																													0	1	0
Purdie				11	11	11	11	11¹	11	11	11																	★¹	7							★											7	2	1
Robertson	5	5	5	5	5	5		5	5	5	5	5	5	5	5	5	5		5	5	5			5	5	5	5	5	5	5	5	5	5	5	5		5	5	5	5	5	5		5	5	5	41	0	0
Robinson	6	6	6	6	6	6	6¹	6	6	6	6	6				★		6	6	6	6	6	6	6	6	6	6	6	6¹	6	6	6	6	6¹	6	6		6¹	6	6	6	6¹					40	1	5
Stoutt	2¹	2	2	2	2	★	2								2	2	2	2	2	2	2	2	2	2	2	2	2		2							2						5					21	1	1
Streete	4	4	4	4	4	4		4	4	4	4	4	4	4	4	4	4	4	4	4	4	4	4	4		4		4	4	4	4	4	4	4		4	4	4	4	4	4	4	4	4	4	4	44	0	0
Thompson	7	8	8	8	7	3	3	3	3	3	3	3	3	3	3	3	3	3	3	3¹	3	3	3	3¹	3	3	3	3	3	3	3	3	2	2	2	2	2		★		3	3	3	3	3	3	41	1	2
Vaughan				★¹	8	8	8	8	8	8	8	8	8	8¹	8¹	8	8	8¹	8	8¹	8	8	8	8	8	8	8	8¹	8	8	8	8	8	8	8	8	8	8		★	7				★		33	3	6
Venus																																	3	3	3	3											4	0	0
Own Goals																																			1															1

FA Cup: 1987-88: 1st Round: Cheltenham T. (H) 5-1; 2nd Round: Wigan Ath. (A) 3-1; 3rd Round: Bradford C. (A) 1-2.
Littlewoods Cup: 1987-88: 1st Round: Notts. Co. (H) 3-0 (A) 2-1; 2nd Round: Manchester C. (A) 2-1 (H) 0-2.

140

WREXHAM (Division 4)

Team Manager Dixie McNeil.
Club Address Racecourse Ground, Mold Road, Wrexham. Tel: (0978) 262129.
Current Ground Capacity 28,500.
Record Attendance 34,445 v Manchester U., FA Cup 4th Round, 26 January 1957.
Year Formed 1873. Turned professional 1912.
Previous Names None.
Club Nickname "The Robins".
Club Colours Red shirts with white trim, white shorts with red trim and red stockings with white hoops on turnovers.
Club Honours Football League: Div. 3 Champions 1977-78.
League History 1921-58 Div. 3(N); 1958-60 Div. 3; 1960-62 Div. 4; 1962-64 Div. 3; 1964-70 Div. 4; 1970-78 Div. 3; 1978-82 Div. 2; 1982-83 Div. 3; 1983- Div. 4.
Most League Points in a Season (2 for a win) 61 in Div. 4, 1969-70 and Div. 3, 1977-78. (3 for a win) 65 in Div. 4, 1986-87.

Most League Goals in a Season 106 in Div. 3(N), 1932-33.
Record Victory 10-1 v Hartlepools U. in Div. 4, 3 March 1962.
Record Defeat 0-9 v Brentford in Div. 3, 15 October 1963.
Consecutive League Wins 7 in 1961 and 1978.
Consecutive League Defeats 9 in 1963.
Record League Appearances Arfon Griffiths, 592 between 1959-79.
Record League Goalscorer—Career Tom Bamford, 175 between 1928-34.
Record League Goalscorer—Season Tom Bamford, 44 in Div. 3(N), 1933-34.

Wrexham: League Record, 1987-88 (Division 4)

Match Number	Date	Venue	Opponents	Result		H/T	Lge Posn	Attend
1	15.8.87	A	Torquay U.	L	1-6	1-2		1731
2	22.8.87	H	Hartlepool U.	W	2-1	0-0		1816
3	29.8.87	A	Crewe Alex.	L	0-2	0-1	12	2210
4	31.8.87	H	Halifax T.	D	2-2	1-0	21	1661
5	5.9.87	A	Exeter C.	D	1-1	0-0	21	2719
6	12.9.87	H	Cardiff C.	W	3-0	0-0	16	2212
7	15.9.87	A	Burnley	L	0-1	0-0	20	5642
8	19.9.87	A	Peterborough U.	L	0-1	0-1	20	2805
9	26.9.87	H	Stockport Co.	W	2-1	2-1	16	1841
10	29.9.87	H	Cambridge U.	W	1-0	0-0	13	2257
11	3.10.87	H	Leyton Orient	D	2-2	1-1	13	2123
12	10.10.87	A	Swansea C.	L	1-2	0-0	16	3741
13	17.10.87	H	Colchester U.	L	0-1	0-1	15	1493
14	20.10.87	A	Darlington	L	0-1	0-0	17	1278
15	24.10.87	A	Newport Co.	L	0-2	0-1	18	1470
16	31.10.87	H	Scarborough	W	1-0	1-0	19	1860
17	3.11.87	A	Scunthorpe U.	L	1-3	1-1	19	2348
18	6.11.87	A	Tranmere Rov.	L	0-1	0-0	21	3271
19	21.11.87	H	Carlisle U.	W	4-0	1-0	19	1485
20	28.11.88	A	Wolverhampton W.	W	2-0	1-0	18	8541
21	12.12.87	H	Rochdale	L	2-3	2-2	18	1409
22	19.12.87	A	Bolton W.	L	0-2	0-1	19	3701
23	26.12.87	A	Stockport Co.	D	1-1	1-0	19	2504
24	28.12.87	H	Hereford U.	D	0-0	0-0	19	2443
25	1.1.88	H	Crewe Alex.	W	2-1	0-0	20	2939
26	16.1.88	H	Peterborough U.	W	3-1	1-0	20	1506
27	26.1.88	A	Hartlepool U.	L	0-1	0-0	20	1692
28	6.2.88	H	Burnley	L	1-3	0-0	20	1821
29	13.2.88	A	Hereford U.	W	2-0	2-0	19	2002
30	20.2.88	H	Torquay U.	L	2-3	0-2	20	1488
31	23.2.88	A	Halifax T.	L	0-2	0-1	20	1284
32	27.2.88	A	Leyton Orient	L	1-2	0-2	20	3448
33	1.3.88	H	Cambridge U.	W	3-0	2-0	20	1025
34	4.3.88	A	Colchester U.	W	2-1	2-1	19	1797
35	12.3.88	H	Swansea C.	L	1-2	0-1	19	1916
36	16.3.88	A	Cardiff C.	D	1-1	1-0	16	4083
37	19.3.88	A	Scarborough	W	2-0	2-0	17	2090
38	22.3.88	H	Exeter C.	W	3-0	0-0	16	963
39	26.3.88	H	Newport Co.	W	4-1	1-1	14	1627
40	2.4.88	H	Tranmere Rov.	W	3-0	2-0	13	3134
41	4.4.88	A	Carlisle U.	W	4-0	2-0	11	2284
42	9.4.88	A	Scunthorpe U.	W	2-1	0-1	9	2589
43	23.4.88	A	Darlington	L	1-2	0-1	12	1711
44	30.4.88	H	Wolverhampton W.	W	4-2	3-2	12	6898
45	2.5.88	A	Rochdale	W	2-1	0-1	9	1539
46	7.5.88	H	Bolton W.	L	0-1	0-0	11	5977

Players: League Record, 1987-88 (Division 4)

Match Number	1	2	3	4	5	6	7	8	9	10	11	12	13	14	15	16	17	18	19	20	21	22	23	24	25	26	27	28	29	30	31	32	33	34	35	36	37	38	39	40	41	42	43	44	45	46	Apps	Subs	Goals
Alleyne																7	★	10	10	9¹	9¹	9	9	★																							7	3	2
Bowden		6	6	6	6		4	4		8	8								8	8¹	6	6	6	6	6	6				★		8	★		★		★		11	11	★	★					20	6	1
Buxton	★	★	7	7	7	7¹	7	7	7¹	7		7¹	7	7		7	7¹	7	7	7	7	7	7		11	★		★	9	9	9¹	9			★	★	★	7¹	7		★						27	6	8
Carter	7¹	7							★	10						11¹	11					★																									8	2	6
Cooke	5	5	5	5																★	★	5	5	5					5	5	5			11	11	11¹	11¹	11	11	11	11	11¹	11¹		11	11	11	19	2	6
Cunnington	11	11	11	11¹	11	11	11	11	11	6	3	6	6	6					11¹	3	3	3	11	11¹	8	8	8																				11	2	0
Emson											11	11	★	11¹	11¹	11			★	11	11	11			11¹	11	11																				24	0	3
Fairbrother											10	10	6	6	6	6																															12	2	0
Flynn																																															7	0	0
Harvey				6	6	6	6	6													6		6	6	6	6	6	6		6	6	6	6	6	6	6	6	6¹	6	6							17	0	1
Hencher											★	★	★																																		6	0	0
Hinnigan	3	★	4	4	4	4			4	4	4		4	4	4	4	4	4	4	4	4	4	4	4	4	4	4	4¹	4																		28	1	1
Hunter	8	8		★	8¹	8	8	★	11	8	8	8	8	8	8	★	8	8¹		8	8	8	8			6	8	8	8	8¹		8	8	8	8	8	8	8	8¹	8	8						37	2	4
Jones	6	3	3	3	3	3	3	3	3		3	3	3	3	6									3	3	3	3	3	4	4	4	4	4	4	4	4	4	4	4	4	4						35	0	4
Kearns																		9	9	9	9	9	9	9²	9	10		★	9	9	9	9³	9¹	9²	9												16	1	8
Massey																											★¹	★	9				7	7	7		9	9	9	9							8	2	1
Morris																	1	1	1														1	1	1												6	0	0
Preece		2	8	8	8	★	★	★	★	7¹	10	2	10	2	2	2	2	2	2	2	★	7	7	7	7	7	7	7	7	7	7	7	7	7¹	7¹	7			★	★	7	7¹	7				33	7	4
Russell	10	10	10	10	10	10¹	10	10	10	10	10											10	10¹	10	10	10¹	10	10²	10²	10	10	10	10¹	10	10¹	10³	10¹	10¹	10¹	10¹	10¹	10					38	0	21
Salathiel	2			2	2	2	2	2	2	2																			2	2	2	2	2	2	2	2	2	2	2	2	2	2	2	2	2	2	24	0	0
Salmon	1	1	1	1	1	1	1	1	1	1	1	1	1	1	1	1		1	1	1		1	1		1	1	1	1	1	1	1						1	1	1	1	1	1	1	1			40	0	0
Scott																★	★																														0	2	0
Slater												★						★	★																												0	3	0
Steel	9	9²	9	9¹	9¹	9	9	9	9¹	9	9¹	9	9	9	9	9	9																														18	0	5
Williams	4	4		2	5	5	5	5	5	5¹	5	5	5	5	5	5	5	5	5	2	2	2	2	2	5	5			5	5	5	5	5	5	5	5	5	5	5	5¹	5	5					42	0	2
Wright		2	★	★				★		★	2	11	3	3	3	3	3			3	3	5	2	2	2	3	3	3	3	3	3	3	3	3	3	3	3	3	3	3	3	3					31	4	0
Own Goals																	1																																1

FA Cup: 1987-88: 1st Round: Rochdale (A) 2-0; 2nd Round: Bolton W. (H) 1-2.
Littlewoods Cup: 1987-88: 1st Round: Burnley (H) 1-0 (A) 0-3.

YORK CITY (Division 4)

YORK CITY FC

Team Manager Bobby Saxton.
Club Address Bootham Crescent, York. Tel: (0904) 24447.
Current Ground Capacity 14,109.
Record Attendance 28,123 v Huddersfield T., FA Cup 6th Round, 5 March 1938.
Year Formed 1922. Turned professional 1922.
Previous Names None.
Club Nickname "The Minstermen".
Club Colours Red shirts, navy blue shorts and white stockings.
Club Honours Football League: Div. 4 Champions 1983-84.
League History 1929-58 Div. 3(N); 1958-59 Div. 4; 1959-60 Div. 3; 1960-65 Div. 4; 1965-66 Div. 3; 1966-71 Div. 4; 1971-74 Div. 3; 1974-76 Div. 2; 1976-77 Div. 3; 1977-84 Div. 4; 1984-88 Div. 3; 1988- Div. 4.
Most League Points in a Season (2 for a win) 62 in Div. 4, 1964-65. (3 for a win) 101 in Div. 4, 1983-84.
Most League Goals in a Season 96 in Div. 4, 1983-84.

Record Victory 9-1 v Southport in Div. 3(N), 2 February 1957.
Record Defeat 0-12 v Chester C. in Div. 3(N), 1 February 1936.
Consecutive League Wins 7 in 1964.
Consecutive League Defeats 6 in 1966.
Record League Appearances Barry Jackson, 482 between 1958-70.
Record League Goalscorer—Career Norman Wilkinson, 125 betwen 1954-66.
Record League Goalscorer—Season Bill Fenton, 31 in Div. 3(N), 1951-52; Arthur Bottom, 31 in Div. 3(N), 1954-55 and 1955-56.

York City: League Record, 1987-88 (Division 3)

Match Number	Date	Venue	Opponents	Result		H/T	Lge Posn	Attend
1	15.8.87	A	Brighton & H.A.	L	0-1	0-0		6068
2	22.8.87	H	Notts Co.	L	3-5	2-4		2878
3	29.8.87	A	Chester C.	L	0-1	0-0	23	2010
4	31.8.87	H	Walsall	L	1-3	0-1	24	2661
5	5.9.87	A	Port Vale	L	1-2	0-0	24	2711
6	12.9.87	H	Preston N.E.	D	1-1	0-0	24	3237
7	16.9.87	A	Bristol Rov.	L	1-2	0-1	24	3177
8	19.9.87	A	Gillingham	L	1-3	1-0	24	5507
9	26.9.87	H	Doncaster Rov.	D	1-1	0-0	24	2702
10	29.9.87	H	Blackpool	L	1-3	1-2	24	2559
11	3.10.87	A	Wigan Ath.	D	1-1	0-0	24	2878
12	10.10.87	A	Fulham	L	1-3	1-2	24	4057
13	17.10.87	H	Aldershot	D	2-2	1-0	24	1984
14	20.10.87	H	Rotherham U.	L	1-2	0-1	24	1932
15	24.10.87	A	Sunderland	L	2-4	1-3	24	19314
16	31.10.87	H	Chesterfield	W	1-0	1-0	24	2316
17	4.11.87	A	Northampton T.	D	0-0	0-0	24	4950
18	7.11.87	H	Bury	D	1-1	0-1	24	2641
19	21.11.87	A	Grimsby T.	L	1-5	1-2	24	2200
20	28.11.87	H	Southend U.	L	0-3	0-1	24	2225
21	12.12.87	A	Bristol C.	L	2-3	1-2	24	6238
22	18.12.87	H	Brentford	D	1-1	1-0	24	1801
23	26.12.87	A	Doncaster Rov.	L	0-2	0-0	24	2409
24	28.12.87	H	Mansfield T.	D	2-2	1-2	24	2781
25	1.1.88	H	Chester C.	W	2-0	1-0	24	2686
26	2.1.88	A	Preston N.E.	L	0-3	0-2	24	6302
27	9.1.88	A	Notts Co.	L	0-3	0-1	24	5924
28	16.1.88	H	Gillingham	L	0-2	0-0	24	2129
29	30.1.88	A	Walsall	L	1-2	1-1	24	4371
30	6.2.88	H	Port Vale	L	2-3	2-1	24	2420
31	13.2.88	A	Mansfield T.	L	1-2	1-0	24	2749
32	20.2.88	H	Brighton & H.A.	L	0-2	0-1	24	2576
33	27.2.88	H	Wigan Ath.	W	3-1	1-0	24	2360
34	1.3.88	A	Blackpool	L	1-2	1-1	24	2249
35	5.3.88	A	Aldershot	W	2-1	1-0	24	2672
36	12.3.88	H	Fulham	L	1-3	1-2	24	2560
37	19.3.88	A	Chesterfield	L	1-2	1-0	24	1966
38	26.3.88	H	Sunderland	W	2-1	1-0	24	8878
39	2.4.88	A	Bury	W	1-0	0-0	24	2277
40	4.4.88	H	Grimsby T.	L	0-2	0-1	24	3215
41	8.4.88	A	Rotherham U.	W	1-0	0-0	24	2942
42	15.4.88	H	Bristol Rov.	L	0-4	0-2	24	1834
43	23.4.88	H	Northampton T.	D	2-2	1-0	24	2048
44	29.4.88	A	Southend U.	L	1-3	1-2	24	3768
45	2.5.88	H	Bristol C.	L	0-1	0-0	24	2616
46	7.5.88	A	Brentford	W	2-1	2-0	23	4180

Players: League Record, 1987-88 (Division 3)

Match Number	1	2	3	4	5	6	7	8	9	10	11	12	13	14	15	16	17	18	19	20	21	22	23	24	25	26	27	28	29	30	31	32	33	34	35	36	37	38	39	40	41	42	43	44	45	46	Apps	Subs	Goals
Banton	★	10¹	10	10¹	10	10	10¹	10	10			10¹	10	10²	10¹	10¹	10¹		10	10	10	10²	10	10	10¹			10		10¹	10¹	10	10	10²	10	10	10	10	10¹								32	1	16
Bradshaw																		★	7	8	2	8		8	8	8	8	8			8	8	8¹	8	8	8	8	8	8	8	8	8	8	8	8	8	24	1	1
Branagan				2	2	2	2	2	2	2	2							2	3		★	2	2	2	2				6	3	6	6	6	6	6	6	6¹	6	2								27	1	1
Brough																							★																								0	1	0
Buchanan									9	10¹	9	9¹	9	9		10																															7	0	2
Butler	10	7	7	7								★																																			4	1	0
Canham	11	11¹	11	11	11¹	11	★											11	11						11	11¹	11	★	★	★				4	4	4	4	4¹	4	4	4	4	4	4	4	13	5	2
Clegg	6	6	6	6	6	6	6	6		6	6	6	6	6	6	6	6	★	6¹	6	6	6¹	6	★	6																						35	2	3
Cook					8	8	8	8	8	7¹																																					1	2	1
Costello																	7								★		★																				1	0	0
Downing																		7														1	1	1	1	1	1	1	1	1	1	1	1	1	1	1	34	0	0
Endersby	1	1	1				1	1	1	1	1	1	1	1	1	1	1	1	1	1	1	1	1																								8	0	1
Gabbiadini, M.	9	9	9	9	9	9	9	9	9¹																																						0	1	0
Gabbiadini, R.												9	9	9	9¹	9	9	9	9	9	9	9¹	9	9	9	9	9	9¹	9	9¹	9	9¹	9	9	9	9	9	9	9¹	9	9¹						32	0	8
Helliwell																					11	★	★		7	7	7	7	7	7	8¹	11	11	11	11	11¹	11	11	11	11	11	11	11	11	11	11	28	3	2
Himsworth	7							★	11	11															5		5	5	5¹	5¹	5		★	5	5	★	6										24	4	4
Hood	8	8	8	★	2	2¹	2	2		8				5¹	★		2	2	3	2	2		3					6	7	7	7	7	7	7	7	7	7	7²	7	7	7						18	0	2
Howlett																													3	3	3	3	3	4	3	3	3	3	3	3	3	3	3	3	3	3	39	0	0
Johnson	3	3	3	3	3	3	3	3	3	3	3	3	3	3	3	3			3	3			★	8	10	10		10	★																		7	6	0
Kitching	★	★						4		★	8										4															★							6	6	12	1	0
McKenzie	2	2	2	2	7		7	11	★		9							7	7																								6	2	20	2	0
McMillan																									★	★		5	6	2	2	2	2	2	2	2	2	2	2	2	2	2				17	1	2
Mills				★	7	11	7	8	7	7	8	8	8	8¹	8	8	8	8¹	8	7	8			3	3	3	★	6	6	★																	5	2	2
Rogers																				1	1							1	1																		6	0	0
Smallwood				1	1																						6	3																			3	0	0
Spofforth																	3																			6	3						2	10	10	10¹	15	4	1
Staniforth													★	7	7	7	7	★		7	11	11	11	11	11	11	★	★																			6	0	1
Stowell																									1	1	1	1	1													5	5	5	5	5	20	1	0
Tutill		★					6	6	11	11	11	11	11	11	11	6	6																						★								29	1	1
Whitehead	5	5¹	5	5	5	5	5	5	5	5	5		5	5	5	5	5	5	5	5	5	4¹	4	4	4	4	4	4	4	4	4					★		★	★	10	10	10					33	3	1
Wilson	4	4	4	4	4	4	4		4	4	4	4	4	4	4	4	4	4	4	4		4	4	4	4	4	4	4¹	4	4	4	4	4																

FA Cup: 1987-88: 1st Round: Burton A. (H) 0-0 Replay (A) 2-1; 2nd Round: Hartlepool U. (H) 1-1 Replay (A) 1-3.
Littlewoods Cup: 1987-88: 1st Round: Halifax T. (A) 1-1 (H) 1-0; 2nd Round: Leeds U. (A) 1-1 (H) 0-4.

A–Z of English Football League Players

The Career Record of Every Footballer who Played in the Barclays League During 1987–88.

The criteria for inclusion is as follows: Every player who played in the Football League during 1987–88. All players registered with Football League clubs at the close of 1987–88 who did not appear last season but played in 1986–87. Also includes specially selected players currently playing abroad or in the Scottish League, plus the players of Lincoln City, who appeared in the Vauxhall Conference during 1987–88, but will re-appear in 1988–89.

Key to Reading the Entries

Players' Names: Surname shown first, followed by leading Christian name plus any initials.

Birthplace: For players born outside the British Isles and Ireland only the name of the country is given.

Date: Birthdate by day, month and year.

Source: This column indicates a player's origins, whether from outside the F.L. or within the ranks of the League. For the latter the following code is used:

Jnrs = Junior players signed from school/college without serving an apprenticeship or trainee period.

App = Apprentice signing prior to 1986.

YTS = Trainee. This rank was introduced in 1986 and includes players sponsored by the Government's Youth Training Scheme.

Tr = Transfers (including free transfers).

L = Loan signing, or temporary transfer, shown only when the player made an appearance.

League Club: All clubs who have been members of the Football League. Where the club name is followed by the following codes: (Am) = Amateur; (App) = Apprentice; (N/C) = Non-contract; (Sch) = Schoolboy — indicates that the player did not, or has not, signed a professional contract with the club.

Date Sign'd: The date given by month/year is when the player signed professional forms. In the case of non-contract players and apprentices who did not turn professional, the date of signing is that of the status indicated. N/L denotes that the player was signed while the club in question was outside the League. For players signed first on loan before a permanent transfer was arranged, the date of signing is that of the loan transfer, except when the player returned to his former club and made further appearances.

Seasons Played: The years that are shown indicate the first year of a season.

Career Record: Only Football League matches are shown and do not include the "play-offs". Figures for substitutes are only given when the player took part in the match and does not include non-playing subs.

Pos.: Position. As many players fill more than one position during their career, only their principal role is shown here. Since 1970 most teams adopted a 4-3-3 or 4-4-2 formation. In the late 1980s many clubs played with a fifth defender known as a "Sweeper", but as few players can claim to be a specialist, the term is not used.

(CD) = Central Defender.
(M) = Midfield (central).
(RM/LM) = Right or Left Midfield, primarily defensive.
(RW/LW) = Right or Left Wing, auxiliary forwards.

Misc: The miscellaneous column records other information including: International honours at Schoolboy (Sch), Youth (Yth), Under 21/23 and Full, plus Semi-Professional (Semi-Pro). For the four home countries: England (E), Northern Ireland (NI), Scotland (S) and Wales (W), plus the Irish Republic (IR), international appearances are updated to the end of May, 1988. Playing substitutes are used in the totals.

General Note: Player's records shown span Football League careers only.

Players Names	Birthplace	Date	Source	League Club	Date Sign'd	Seasons Played	Apps	Sub	Gls	Pos.	Misc
ABBOTT, Greg S.	Coventry	14.12.63	App	Coventry C.	12.81					(M)	
			Tr	Bradford C.	09.82	1982-87	177	15	31		
ABEL, Graham	Runcorn	17.09.60	Northwich Vic.	Chester C.	10.85	1985-87	109	0	5	(D)	
ABLETT, Gary I.	Liverpool	19.11.65	App	Liverpool	11.83	1986-87	20	2	1	(D)	E U21-1
			L	Derby Co.	01.85	1984	3	3	0		
			L	Hull C.	09.86	1986	5	0	0		
ABRAHAM, Gareth J.	Merthyr Tydfil	13.02.69	YTS	Cardiff C.	07.87	1987	2	0	1	(D)	
ABRUZZESE, David	Aberdare	08.10.69	YTS	Newport Co. (YTS)	08.86	1986-87	24	1	0	(D)	
ACHAMPONG, Kenny	Kilburn	26.06.66	App	Fulham	06.84	1984-87	68	13	15	(F)	
ADAMS, Micky R.	Sheffield	08.11.61	App	Gillingham	11.79	1979-82	85	7	5	(W)	E Yth Int
			Tr	Coventry C.	07.83	1983-86	85	5	9		
			Tr	Leeds U.	01.87	1986-87	57	0	1		
ADAMS, Neil J.	Stoke	23.11.65		Stoke C.	06.85	1985	31	1	4	(M)	E U21-1
			Tr	Everton	06.86	1986-87	17	3	0		
ADAMS, Steve	Sheffield	07.09.59	Worksop T.	Scarborough	09.87	1987	17	11	2	(W)	
ADAMS, Tony A.	Romford	10.10.66	App	Arsenal	01.84	1983-87	109	1	9	(CD)	E Yth Int/E U21-5 E-11
ADCOCK, A.C. (Tony)	Bethnal Green	27.02.63	App	Colchester U.	02.81	1980-86	192	18	98	(F)	
			Tr	Manchester C.	06.87	1987	12	3	5		
			Tr	Northampton T.	01.88	1987	18	0	10		
ADKINS, Nigel H.	Birkenhead	11.03.65	App	Tranmere Rov.	03.83	1982-85	86	0	0	(G)	E Sch Int
			Tr	Wigan Ath.	07.86	1986-87	10	0	0		
AGANA, P.A. (Tony)	Bromley	02.10.63	Weymouth	Watford	08.87	1987	12	3	1	(W)	E Semi-Pro Int 1986
			Tr	Sheffield U.	02.88	1987	11	1	2		
AGBOOLA, Reuben O.F.	Camden	30.05.62	App	Southampton	04.80	1980-84	89	1	0	(D)	
			Tr	Sunderland	01.85	1984-87	68	1	0		
			L	Charlton Ath.	10.86	1986	1	0	0		
AGNEW, Paul	Lisburn (NI)	15.08.65	Cliftonville	Grimsby T.	02.84	1983-87	94	2	1	(LB)	NI Yth Int
AGNEW, Steve M.	Shipley	09.11.65	App	Barnsley	11.83	1983-87	67	4	7	(M)	
AINSCOW, Alan	Bolton	15.07.53	App	Blackpool	07.71	1971-77	178	14	28	(M)	
			Tr	Birmingham C.	07.78	1978-80	104	4	16		
			Tr	Everton	08.81	1981-82	24	4	3		
			L	Barnsley	11.82	1982	2	0	0		
			Hong Kong	Wolverhampton W.	08.84	1984-85	56	2	5		
			Tr	Blackburn Rov.	12.85	1985-87	36	14	5		
AINSCOW, Andrew P.	Orrell	01.10.68	App	Wigan Ath.	10.86	1987	9	6	4	(M)	E Yth Int
AIREY, Carl	Wakefield	06.02.65	App	Barnsley	02.83	1982-83	30	8	5	(F)	
			L	Bradford C.	10.83	1983	4	1	0		
			Tr	Darlington	08.84	1984-85	72	3	28		
			Charleroi (Bel.)	Chesterfield	12.86	1986	24	2	4		
			Tr	Rotherham U.	08.87	1987	25	6	11		
AIZLEWOOD, Mark	Newport	01.10.59	App	Newport Co.	10.77	1975-77	35	3	1	(M)	W Sch Int/ W U21-2/W-8
			Tr	Luton T.	04.78	1978-81	90	8	3		
			Tr	Charlton Ath.	11.82	1982-86	152	0	9		
			Tr	Leeds U.	02.87	1986-87	31	1	0		
ALBISTON, Arthur R.	Edinburgh	14.07.57	App	Manchester U.	07.74	1974-87	364	15	6	(LB)	S Sch Int/ S U21-5/S-14
ALDRIDGE, John W.	Liverpool	18.09.58	South Liverpool	Newport Co.	04.79	1979-83	159	11	69	(F)	IR-14
			Tr	Oxford U.	03.84	1983-86	111	3	72		
			Tr	Liverpool	01.87	1986-87	38	8	28		
ALEXANDER, Ian	Glasgow	26.01.63	Leicester Juv.	Rotherham U.	10.81	1981-82	5	6	0	(RB)	
			Cyprus	Bristol Rov.	08.86	1986-87	65	2	2		
ALLARDYCE, Sam	Dudley	19.10.54	App	Bolton W.	11.71	1973-79	180	4	21	(CD)	
			Tr	Sunderland	07.80	1980	24	1	2		
			Tr	Millwall	09.81	1981-82	63	0	2		
			Tr	Coventry C.	09.83	1983	28	0	1		
			Tr	Huddersfield T.	07.84	1984	37	0	0		
			Tr	Bolton W.	07.85	1985	14	0	0		
			Tr	Preston N.E.	08.86	1986-87	75	1	2		
ALLATT, Vernon	Hednesford	28.05.59	Hednesford T.	Halifax T.	11.79	1979-82	93	5	14	(F)	
			Tr	Rochdale	08.83	1983	40	0	8		
			Tr	Crewe Alex.	06.84	1984-85	36	3	8		
			Tr	Preston N.E.	11.85	1985	17	2	3		
			Tr	Stockport Co.	10.86	1986	23	1	10		
			Hednesford T.	Crewe Alex.(N/C)	12.87	1987	4	1	2		
ALLEN, Clive D.	Stepney	20.05.61	App	Q.P.R.	09.78	1978-79	43	6	32	(F)	Son of Les E Sch Int/E Yth Int/E U21-3/E-5 FWA & PFA Footballer of Year 1986-87
			Tr	Arsenal	06.80						
			Tr	Crystal Palace	08.80	1980	25	0	9		
			Tr	Q.P.R.	06.81	1981-83	83	4	40		
			Tr	Tottenham H.	08.84	1984-87	97	8	60		
ALLEN, Kenny R.	Thornaby	12.01.52	Jnrs	Hartlepool U. (Am)	08.68	1968	7	0	0	(G)	
			South Africa	West Bromwich A.	12.72						
			Bath City	Bournemouth	08.78	1978-82	152	0	0		
			Bury (trial)	Peterborough U.(N/C)	12.83						
			Tr	Torquay U.	03.84	1983-85	58	0	0		
			Tr	Swindon T.	09.85	1985-86	45	0	0		
			Tr	Torquay U.	12.86	1986-87	74	0	0		
ALLEN, Malcolm	Caernarfon	21.03.67	App	Watford	03.85	1985-87	27	12	5	(F)	W-3
			L	Aston Villa	09.87	1987	4	0	0		
ALLEN, Martin J.	Reading	14.08.65	App	Q.P.R.	05.83	1984-87	100	6	12	(M)	E Yth Int/E U21-2
ALLEN, Paul K.	Aveley	28.08.62	App	West Ham U.	08.79	1979-84	149	3	6	(M)	E Yth Int/E U21-3
			Tr	Tottenham H.	06.85	1985-87	102	7	7		
ALLEYNE, Robert A.	Dudley	27.09.68		Leicester C.	01.87	1986	1	2	0	(F)	
			L	Wrexham	10.87	1987	7	3	2		
			Tr	Chesterfield	03.88	1987	10	0	2		

Clive Allen (Tottenham Hotspur) Scorer of over 100 League goals, now with his fifth London club.

Match Magazine

Osvaldo Ardiles (Blackburn Rovers) Another former Tottenham star of world-wide repute.

Match Magazine

Paul Allen (Tottenham Hotspur) Only missed one game in the "Spurs" midfield last season.

Match Magazine

Steve Archibald (Blackburn Rovers) Seen here playing for the "Spurs" prior to going to Barcelona at the end of 1983-84 season.

Match Magazine

Players Names	Birthplace	Date	Source	League Club	Date Sign'd	Seasons Played	Career Record Apps	Sub	Gls	Pos.	Misc
ALLINSON, Ian J.R.	Hitchin	01.10.57	App	Colchester U.	10.75	1974-82	291	17	69	(W)	
			Tr	Arsenal	10.83	1983-86	60	23	16		
			Tr	Stoke C.	06.87	1987	6	3	0		
			Tr	Luton T.	10.87	1987	23	4	3		
ALLISON, Wayne	Huddersfield	16.10.68	YTS	Halifax T.	06.87	1986-87	33	10	7	(F)	
ALLON, Joe B.	Gateshead	12.11.66	YTS	Newcastle U.	11.84	1984-86	9	0	2	(F)	E Yth Int
			Tr	Swansea C.	07.87	1987	26	6	12		
ANDERSON, Colin R.	Newcastle	26.04.62	App	Burnley	04.80	1980-81	3	3	0	(W)	
			North Shields	Torquay U.	09.82	1982-84	107	2	11		
			Tr	West Bromwich A.	03.85	1985-87	54	8	2		
ANDERSON, Dale	Darlington	23.08.70	YTS	Darlington (YTS)	09.86	1986-87	0	5	0		
ANDERSON, Darren I.	Merton	06.09.66	Coventry C.(App)	Charlton Ath.	03.84	1983-84	10	0	1	(CD)	E Yth Int
			L	Crewe Alex.	10.85	1985	5	0	0		
			Tr	Aldershot	07.86	1986-87	37	12	1		
ANDERSON, Doug E.	Hong Kong	29.08.63	Port Glasgow	Oldham Ath.	09.80	1981-83	4	5	0	(W)	
			Tr	Tranmere Rov.	08.84	1984-86	125	1	15		
			Tr	Plymouth A.	08.87	1987	17	2	1		
ANDERSON, John C.P.	Dublin	07.11.59	App	West Bromwich A.	11.77					(RB)	IR U21-1/IR-15
			Tr	Preston N.E.	08.79	1979-81	47	4	0		
			Tr	Newcastle U.	09.82	1982-87	206	8	8		
ANDERSON, Nick J.	Lincoln	29.03.69	YTS	Mansfield T.	01.87	1986-87	8	10	0	(M)	
ANDERSON, Viv A.	Nottingham	29.08.56	App	Nottingham F.	08.74	1974-83	323	5	15	(RB)	E U21-1/E-30/
			Tr	Arsenal	07.84	1984-86	120	0	9		E F L Rep
			Tr	Manchester U.	05.87	1987	30	1	2		
ANDREWS, Ian E.	Nottingham	01.12.64	App	Leicester C.	12.82	1983-87	126	0	0	(G)	E Yth Int/
			L	Swindon T.	01.84	1983	1	0	0		E U21-1
ANDREWS, Keri A.	Swansea	28.04.68	App	Swansea C.	04.86	1984-87	32	9	3	(W)	W Yth Int
ANGELL, Darren J.	Newbury	19.01.67	Newbury T.	Portsmouth	06.85					(D)	
			L	Colchester U.	12.87	1987	1	0	0		
ANTHROBUS, Stephen A.	Lewisham	10.11.68	YTS	Millwall	08.86	1987	3	0	0	(W)	
ARCHIBALD, Steve	Glasgow	27.09.56	Aberdeen	Tottenham H.	05.80	1980-83	128	3	58	(F)	S-27/S U21-5
			Barcelona (Sp)	Blackburn Rov.	12.87	1987	20	0	6		
ARDILES, Osvaldo C.	Argentina	03.08.52	Huracan (Arg)	Tottenham H.	07.78	1978-87	222	16	16	(M)	Argentine Int
			L	Blackburn Rov.	03.88	1987	5	0	0		
ARMSTRONG, David	Durham	26.12.54	App	Middlesbrough	01.72	1971-80	357	2	59	(M)	E U23-4/E-3/
			Tr	Southampton	08.81	1981-86	222	0	59		E 'B'
			Tr	Bournemouth	07.87	1987	6	3	2		
ARMSTRONG, Gerry J.	Belfast	23.05.54	Bangor (NI)	Tottenham H.	11.75	1976-80	65	19	10	(F)	NI-63
			Tr	Watford	11.80	1980-82	50	26	12		
			Real Mallorca (Sp)	West Bromwich A.	08.85	1985	7	1	0		
			L	Chesterfield	01.86	1985	12	0	1		
			Tr	Brighton & H.A.	07.86	1986-87	27	15	5		
			L	Millwall	01.87	1987	7	0	0		
ARMSTRONG, Gordon I.	Newcastle	15.07.67	App	Sunderland	07.85	1984-87	92	4	12	(M)	
ARNOTT, Kevin W.	Gateshead	28.09.58	App	Sunderland	09.76	1976-81	132	1	16	(M)	
			L	Blackburn Rov.	11.81	1981	17	0	2		
			Tr	Sheffield U.	06.82	1982-86	120	1	11		
			L	Blackburn Rov.	11.82	1982	11	1	1		
			L	Rotherham U.	03.83	1982	9	0	2		
			Vasalund (Swe)	Chesterfield(N/C)	11.87	1987	19	0	1		
ASH, Mark C.	Sheffield	22.01.68	App	Rotherham U.	01.86	1986-87	13	6	0	(RB)	
ASHLEY, Kevin M.	Birmingham	31.12.68	App	Birmingham C.	12.86	1986-87	7	1	0	(FB)	
ASHURST, Jack	Coatbridge	12.10.54	App	Sunderland	10.71	1972-79	129	11	4	(CD)	
			Tr	Blackpool	10.79	1979-80	53	0	3		
			Tr	Carlisle U.	08.81	1981-85	194	0	2		
			Tr	Leeds U.	07.86	1986-87	82	0	1		
ASKEW, W. (Billy)	Lumley	02.10.59	App	Middlesbrough	10.77	1979-81	10	2	0	(M)	
			Gateshead	Hull C.	09.82	1982-87	199	6	18		
ASPIN, Neil	Gateshead	12.04.65	App	Leeds U.	10.82	1981-87	172	2	5	(D)	
ASPINALL, John J.	Birkenhead	15.03.59		Tranmere Rov.	10.82	1982-84	100	7	25	(W)	
			Bangor C.	Tranmere Rov.	07.87	1987	11	1	1		
ASPINALL, Warren	Wigan	13.09.67	App	Wigan Ath.	08.85	1984-85	39	12	22	(F)	E Yth Int
			Tr	Everton	05.86	1985-86	0	7	0		
			Tr	Aston Villa	02.87	1986-87	40	4	14		
ASTBURY, Mike J.	Leeds	22.01.64	App	York C.	01.82	1980-85	48	0	0	(G)	
			L	Peterborough U.	01.86	1985	4	0	0		
			Tr	Darlington	03.86	1985-86	38	0	0		
			Tr	Chester C.	07.87	1987	5	0	0		
ATHERTON, Peter	Orrell	06.04.70	YTS	Wigan Ath.	02.88	1987	15	1	0	(D)	
ATKINS, Ian L.	Birmingham	16.01.57	App	Shrewsbury T.	01.75	1975-81	273	5	58	(M)	
			Tr	Sunderland	08.82	1982-83	76	1	6		
			Tr	Everton	11.84	1984-85	6	1	1		
			Tr	Ipswich T.	09.85	1985-87	73	4	4		
			Tr	Birmingham C.	03.88	1987	8	0	1		
ATKINS, Mark N.	Doncaster	14.08.68	Jnrs	Scunthorpe U.	07.86	1984-87	45	5	2	(CD)	
ATKINS, Robert G.	Leicester	16.10.62	Enderby T.	Sheffield U.	07.82	1982-84	36	4	3	(CD)	
			Tr	Preston N.E.	02.85	1984-87	132	1	4		
ATKINSON, Dalian R.	Shrewsbury	21.03.68	App	Ipswich T.	06.85	1985-87	16	10	8	(F)	
ATKINSON, Paul	Chester le Street	19.01.66	App	Sunderland	11.83	1983-87	46	14	5	(W)	E Yth Int
ATKINSON, Paul G.	Otley	14.08.61	App	Oldham Ath.	08.79	1979-82	139	4	11	(W)	
			Tr	Watford	07.83	1983	8	3	0		
			Tr	Oldham Ath.	08.85	1985-87	29	4	1		
			L	Swansea C.	12.86	1986	6	0	1		
			L	Bolton W.	02.87	1986	2	1	0		
			L	Swansea C.	03.87	1986	12	0	2		

Players Names	Birthplace	Date	Source	League Club	Date Sign'd	Seasons Played	Apps	Sub	Gls	Pos.	Misc
AYLOTT, Trevor K.C.	Bermondsey	26.11.57	App	Chelsea	07.76	1977-79	26	3	2	(F)	
			Tr	Barnsley	11.79	1979-81	93	3	26		
			Tr	Millwall	08.82	1982	32	0	5		
			Tr	Luton T.	03.83	1982-83	32	0	10		
			Tr	Crystal Palace	07.84	1984-85	50	3	12		
			L	Barnsley	02.86	1985	9	0	0		
			Tr	Bournemouth	08.86	1986-87	80	0	19		
BAILEY, Dennis	Lambeth	13.11.65	Barking	Fulham(N/C)	11.86					(F)	
			Farnborough T.	Crystal Palace	12.87	1987	0	5	1		
BAILEY, John A.	Liverpool	01.04.57	App	Blackburn Rov.	04.75	1975-78	115	5	1	(LB)	
			Tr	Everton	07.79	1979-85	171	0	3		
			Tr	Newcastle U.	10.85	1985-87	39	1	0		
BAILEY, Neil	Billinge	26.09.58	App	Burnley	07.76					(LM)	
			Tr	Newport Co.	09.78	1978-83	129	5	7		
			Tr	Wigan Ath.	10.83	1983-85	31	10	2		
			Tr	Stockport Co.	07.86	1986-87	50	1	0		
BAILIE, Colin J.	Belfast	31.03.64	App	Swindon T.	03.82	1981-84	105	2	4	(FB)	
			Tr	Reading	07.85	1985-87	83	1	1		
BAIRD, Ian J.	Rotherham	01.04.64	App	Southampton	04.82	1982-84	20	2	5	(F)	E Sch Int
			L	Cardiff C.	11.83	1983	12	0	6		
			L	Newcastle U.	12.84	1984	4	1	1		
			Tr	Leeds U.	03.85	1984-86	84	1	33		
			Tr	Portsmouth	06.87	1987	20	0	1		
			Tr	Leeds U.	03.88	1987	10	0	3		
BAKER, Clive E.	North Walsham	14.03.59	Jnrs	Norwich C.	07.77	1977-80	14	0	0	(G)	
			Tr	Barnsley	08.84	1984-87	162	0	0		
BAKER, D. Paul	Newcastle	05.01.63	Bishop Auckland	Southampton	06.84					(F)	
			Tr	Carlisle U.	06.85	1985-86	66	5	11		
			Tr	Hartlepool U.	07.87	1987	38	1	19		
BAKER, Graham E.	Southampton	03.12.58	App	Southampton	12.76	1977-81	111	2	22	(M)	E U21-2
			Tr	Manchester C.	08.82	1982-86	114	3	19		
			Tr	Southampton	06.87	1987	35	1	5		
BAKER, Steve	Newcastle	02.12.61	App	Southampton	12.79	1980-87	61	12	0	(FB)	
			L	Burnley	02.84	1983	10	0	0		
			Tr	Leyton Orient	03.88	1987	9	0	2		
BAKER, Terry B.	Rochford	13.11.65	App	West Ham U.	11.83					(CD)	
			Billericay T.	Colchester U.	11.85	1985-87	55	0	2		
BALL, Kevin A.	Hastings	12.11.64	Coventry C.(App)	Portsmouth	10.82	1983-87	46	9	1	(D)	
BAMBER, J. Dave	St. Helens	01.02.59	Manchester Univ.	Blackpool	09.79	1979-82	81	5	29	(F)	
			Tr	Coventry C.	06.83	1983	18	1	3		
			Tr	Walsall	03.84	1983-84	17	3	7		
			Tr	Portsmouth	12.84	1984	4	0	1		
			Tr	Swindon T.	11.85	1985-87	103	3	31		
BANKS, Chris	Stone	12.11.65	Jnrs	Port Vale	12.82	1984-87	50	14	1	(FB)	
BANKS, Ian F.	Mexborough	09.01.61	App	Barnsley	01.79	1978-82	158	6	37	(M)	
			Tr	Leicester C.	06.83	1983-86	78	15	14		
			Tr	Huddersfield T.	09.86	1986-87	78	0	17		
BANKS, Jason M.	Farnworth	16.11.68	App	Wigan Ath.	11.86					(D)	
				Chester C.	10.87	1987	1	1	0		
BANNISTER, Gary	Warrington	22.07.60	App	Coventry C.	05.78	1978-80	17	5	3	(F)	E U21-1
			Tr	Sheffield Wed.	08.81	1981-83	117	1	55		
			Tr	Q.P.R.	08.84	1984-87	136	0	56		
			Tr	Coventry C.	03.88	1987	7	1	1		
BANTON, Dale C.	Kensington	15.05.61	App	West Ham U.	05.79	1979-81	2	3	0	(F)	
			Tr	Aldershot	08.82	1982-84	105	1	47		
			Tr	York C.	11.84	1984-87	118	9	45		
BARBER, Fred	Ferryhill	26.08.63	App	Darlington	08.81	1982-85	135	0	0	(G)	
			Tr	Everton	03.86						
			Tr	Walsall	10.86	1986-87	82	0	0		
BARBER, Philip A.	Tring	10.06.65	Aylesbury U.	Crystal Palace	02.84	1983-87	125	14	27	(M)	
BARDSLEY, David J.	Manchester	11.09.64	App	Blackpool	09.82	1981-83	45	0	0	(RB)	E Yth Int
			Tr	Watford	11.83	1983-87	97	3	7		
			Tr	Oxford U.	09.87	1987	34	0	1		
BARHAM, Mark F.	Folkestone	12.07.62	App	Norwich C.	04.80	1979-86	169	8	23	(W)	E Yth Int/ E-2
			Tr	Huddersfield T.	07.87	1987	24	2	1		
BARKER, Simon	Farnworth	04.11.64	App	Blackburn Rov.	11.82	1983-87	180	2	35	(M)	E U21-4
BARLOW, Andrew J.	Oldham	24.11.65	Jnrs	Oldham Ath.	07.84	1984-87	103	11	2	(D)	
BARNARD, Leigh K.	Worsley	29.10.58	App	Portsmouth	10.76	1977-81	71	8	8	(W)	
			L	Peterborough U.	03.82	1981	1	3	0		
			Tr	Swindon T.	07.82	1982-87	206	4	21		
			L	Exeter C.	02.85	1984	6	0	2		
BARNES, David	Paddington	16.11.61	App	Coventry C.	05.79	1979-81	9	0	0	(LB)	E Yth Int
			Tr	Ipswich T.	05.82	1982-83	16	1	0		
			Tr	Wolverhampton W.	10.84	1984-87	86	2	4		
			Tr	Aldershot	08.87	1987	29	1	0		
BARNES, David O. (Bobby)	Kingston	17.12.62	App	West Ham U.	09.80	1980-85	31	12	5	(W)	
			L	Scunthorpe U.	11.85	1985	6	0	0		
			Tr	Aldershot	03.86	1985-87	49	0	26		
			Tr	Swindon T.	10.87	1987	26	2	10		
BARNES, John C.B.	Jamaica	07.11.63	Sudbury Court	Watford	07.81	1981-86	232	1	65	(F)	E U21-2/E-38
			Tr	Liverpool	06.87	1987	38	0	15		FWA/PFA Player of Year 1987-88
BARNES, Paul L.	Leicester	16.11.67	App	Notts Co.	11.85	1985-87	15	10	6	(F)	

Players Names	Birthplace	Date	Source	League Club	Date Sign'd	Seasons Played	Apps	Sub	Gls	Pos.	Misc
BARNES, Peter S.	Manchester	10.06.57	App	Manchester C.	08.74	1974-78	108	7	15	(W)	E Yth Int/
			Tr	West Bromwich A.	07.79	1979-80	76	1	23		E U21-9/E-22
			Tr	Leeds U.	08.81	1981	31	0	1		F L Rep
			Real Betis (Sp.)	Leeds U.	08.83	1983	25	2	4		
			Tr	Coventry	10.84	1984	18	0	2		
			Tr	Manchester U.	07.85	1985-86	19	1	2		
			Tr	Manchester C.	01.87	1986	8	0	0		
			L	Bolton W.	10.87	1987	2	0	0		
			L	Port Vale	12.87	1987	3	0	0		
			Tr	Hull C.	03.88	1987	11	0	0		
BARNETT, Gary L.	Stratford	11.03.63	App	Coventry C.	01.81					(W)	
			Tr	Oxford U.	07.82	1982-85	37	8	9		
			L	Wimbledon	02.83	1982	5	0	1		
			L	Fulham	12.84	1984	0	2	1		
			Tr	Fulham	09.85	1985-87	115	5	24		
BARNSLEY, Andy	Sheffield	09.06.22	Denaby U.	Rotherham U.	06.85	1985	28	0	0	(D)	
			Tr	Sheffield U.	07.86	1986-87	72	2	0		
BARR, Robert A.	Halifax	05.12.69	YTS	Halifax T. (YTS)	08.86	1986	0	1	0	(F)	
BARR, W.J. (Billy)	Halifax	21.01.69	YTS	Halifax T.	07.87	1987	25	5	0	(D)	
BARRATT, A. (Tony)	Salford	18.10.65	Billingham T.	Grimsby T.	08.85	1985	20	2	0	(RB)	
			Billingham T.	Hartlepool U.	12.86	1986-87	62	4	3		
BARRETT, Earl D.	Rochdale	28.04.67	App	Manchester C.	04.84	1985-86	2	1	0	(D)	
			L	Chester C.	03.86	1985	12	0	0		
			Tr	Oldham Ath.	11.87	1987	16	2	0		
BARRETT, Scott	Ilkeston	02.04.63	Ilkeston T.	Wolverhampton W.	09.84	1984-86	30	0	0	(G)	
			Tr	Stoke C.	07.87	1987	27	0	0		
BARROW, Graham	Chorley	13.06.54	Altrincham	Wigan Ath.	07.81	1981-85	173	6	36	(M)	
			Tr	Chester C.	07.86	1986-87	79	0	9		
BARTLETT, Kevin F.	Portsmouth	12.10.62	App	Portsmouth	10.80	1980-81	0	3	0	(F)	
			Fareham T.	Cardiff C.	09.86	1986-87	42	18	16		
BARTRAM, Vince L.	Birmingham	07.08.68	SCH	Wolverhampton W.	08.85	1986	1	0	0	(G)	
BASTOCK, Paul A.	Leamington	19.05.70	Coventry C. (YTS)	Cambridge U.	03.88	1987	10	0	0	(G)	
BATCH, Nigel A.	Huddersfield	09.11.57	Derby Co.(App)	Grimsby T.	07.76	1976-86	348	0	0	(G)	
			Tr	Lincoln C.	(N/L)						
BATER, Phil T.	Cardiff	26.10.55	App	Bristol Rov.	10.73	1974-80	211	1	2	(FB)	W U21-2
			Tr	Wrexham	09.81	1981-82	73	0	1		
			Tr	Bristol Rov.	09.83	1983-85	90	8	1		
			Tr	Brentford	05.86	1986	19	0	2		
			Tr	Cardiff C.	07.87	1987	40	0	0		
BATES, Jamie A.	Croydon	24.02.68	YTS	Brentford	08.86	1986-87	40	7	2	(CD)	
BATTY, David	Leeds	02.12.68	YTS	Leeds U.	07.87	1987	22	1	1	(M)	E U21-1
BATTY, Lawrence W.	Westminster	15.02.64	Maidenhead U.	Fulham	08.84	1985	4	0	0	(G)	
BATTY, Paul W.	Doncaster	09.01.64	App	Swindon T.	01.82	1982-84	102	6	7	(M)	
			Tr	Chesterfield	07.85	1985	24	2	0		
			Tr	Exeter C.	07.86	1986-87	59	6	8		
BEAGRIE, Peter S.	Middlesbrough	28.11.65	Jnrs	Middlesbrough	09.83	1984-85	24	9	2	(W)	E U21-2
			Tr	Sheffield U.	08.86	1986-87	81	3	11		
BEARDSLEY, Peter A.	Newcastle	18.01.61	Wallsend B.C.	Carlisle U.	08.79	1979-81	93	11	22	(F)	E-24
			Vancouver W. (Can.)	Manchester U.	09.82						
			Vancouver W. (Can.)	Newcastle U.	09.83	1983-86	146	1	61		
			Tr	Liverpool	07.87	1987	36	2	15		
BEASANT, Dave	Willesden	20.03.59	Edgware T.	Wimbledon	08.79	1979-87	340	0	0	(G)	
BEASLEY, Andy	Sedgley	05.02.64	App	Luton T.	02.82					(G)	
			Tr	Mansfield T.	07.84	1984-87	11	0	0		
			L	Peterborough U.	07.86	1986	7	0	0		
			L	Scarborough	03.88	1987	4	0	0		
BEATTIE, Andy H.	Liverpool	09.02.64	App	Cambridge U.	02.82	1983-87	94	3	2	(CD)	
BEATTIE, Stuart R.	Stevenston	10.07.67	Glasgow Rangers	Doncaster Rov.	01.87	1986-87	9	0	0	(CD)	
BEAUMONT, Nigel	Hemsworth	11.02.67	YTS	Bradford C.	07.85	1985	2	0	0	(FB)	
BEAVON, M. Stuart	Wolverhampton	30.11.58	App	Tottenham H.	07.76	1978-79	3	1	0	(M)	Son of Cyril
			L	Notts. Co.	12.79	1979	6	0	0		
			Tr	Reading	07.80	1980-87	314	11	32		
BECK, John A.	Edmonton	25.05.54	App	Q.P.R.	05.72	1972-75	32	8	1	(M)	
			Tr	Coventry C.	06.76	1976-78	60	9	6		
			Tr	Fulham	10.78	1978-81	113	1	12		
			Tr	Bournemouth	09.82	1982-85	132	5	13		
			Tr	Cambridge U.	07.86	1986-87	68	2	7		
BECKFORD, Darren R.	Manchester	12.05.67	App	Manchester C.	08.84	1984-86	7	4	0	(F)	E Yth Int
			L	Bury	10.85	1985	12	0	5		
			Tr	Port Vale	03.87	1986-87	45	6	13		
BECKFORD, Jason N.	Manchester	14.02.70	YTS	Manchester C.	08.87	1987	5	0	0	(F)	Brother of Darren
BEDFORD, Kevin E.	Carshalton	26.12.68	App	Wimbledon	11.86	1987	4	0	0	(LB)	
			L	Aldershot	02.88	1987	16	0	0		
BEESLEY, Paul	Liverpool	21.07.65	Altrincham	Wigan Ath.	09.84	1984-87	98	2	1	(CD)	
BEESTON, Carl F.	Stoke	30.06.67	App	Stoke C.	06.85	1984-87	15	3	0	(M)	
BEGLIN, Jim M.	Waterford	29.07.63	Shamrock Rov.	Liverpool	05.83	1984-86	64	0	2	(LB)	IR-15
BELFORD, Dale	Burton on Trent	11.07.67	App	Aston Villa	07.85					(G)	
			Sutton Coldfield	Notts. Co.	03.87	1987	1	0	0		
BELL, Doug	Paisley	05.09.59	Hibernian	Shrewsbury T.	12.87	1987	13	2	2	(M)	S U21-2
BELL, Steve	Middlesbrough	13.03.65	App	Middlesbrough	05.82	1981-84	79	6	12	(LW)	E Yth Int
			Whitby T.	Darlington	03.87	1986-87	28	12	3		
BELLAMY, Gary	Worksop	04.07.62	App	Chesterfield	06.80	1980-86	181	3	7	(CD)	
			Tr	Wolverhampton W.	07.87	1987	24	0	2		
BENBOW, Ian R.	Hereford	09.01.69	YTS	Hereford U.	07.87	1987	12	9	2	(M)	

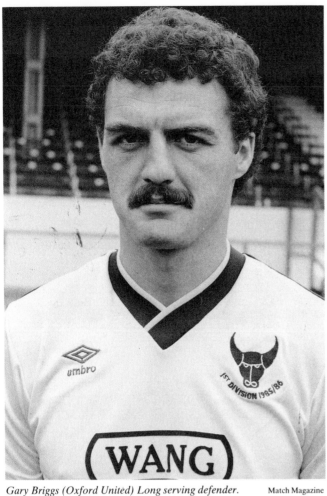

Gary Briggs (Oxford United) Long serving defender.   Match Magazine

Gary Bannister (Coventry City) Pictured in Q.P.R.'s colours, prior to joining the "Sky Blues" last March.   Match Magazine

David Bardsley (Oxford United) In action (left) for Watford at Arsenal in 1986-87.   Match Magazine

Players Names	Birthplace	Date	Source	League Club	Date Sign'd	Seasons Played	Apps	Sub	Gls	Pos.	Misc
BENJAMIN, Ian T.	Nottingham	11.12.61	App	Sheffield U.	05.79	1978-79	4	1	3	(F)	Brother of Triston
			Tr	West Bromwich A.	08.79	1980	1	1	0		E Yth Int
			Tr	Notts. Co.	02.82						
			Tr	Peterborough U.	08.82	1982-83	77	3	14		
			Tr	Northampton T.	08.84	1984-87	147	3	58		
			Tr	Cambridge U.	10.87	1987	20	5	2		
BENJAMIN, Triston L.	St. Kitts (WI)	01.04.57	App	Notts. Co.	03.75	1974-86	296	15	4	(D)	Brother of Ian
			Tr	Chesterfield	07.87	1987	32	2	0		
BENNETT, David A.	Manchester	11.07.59	Jnrs	Manchester C.	06.77	1978-80	43	9	9	(W)	Brother of Gary E.
			Tr	Cardiff C.	09.81	1981-82	75	2	18		
			Tr	Coventry C.	07.83	1983-87	152	13	25		
BENNETT, Gary E.	Manchester	04.12.61	Ashton U.	Manchester C.	09.79					(CD)	Brother of
			Tr	Cardiff C.	09.81	1981-83	85	2	11		David A.
			Tr	Sunderland	07.84	1984-87	144	0	12		
BENNETT, Gary M.	Kirkby	20.09.62		Wigan Ath.	10.84	1984	10	10	3	(F)	
			Tr	Chester C.	08.85	1985-87	107	12	36		
BENNETT, Martyn	Birmingham	04.08.61	App	West Bromwich A.	08.78	1978-87	180	1	9	(CD)	E Sch Int
BENNETT, Michael	Bolton	24.12.62	App	Bolton W.	01.80	1979-82	62	3	1	(LB)	E Yth Int
			Tr	Wolverhampton W.	06.83	1983	6	0	0		
			Tr	Cambridge U.	03.84	1983-85	76	0	0		
			Tr	Preston N.E.	09.86	1986-87	75	1	1		
BENNETT, Michael R.	Lambeth	27.07.69	App	Charlton Ath.	04.87	1986-87	11	7	1	(W)	
BENNETT, Sean	Newport	03.09.70	Leeds U. (YTS)	Newport Co. (YTS)	01.88	1987	4	1	0	(LB)	
BENNING, Paul M.	Watford	07.06.63	Australia	Peterborough U.(N/C)	12.87	1987	2	0	0	(D)	Son of Mike
BENNYWORTH, Ian R.	Hull	15.01.62	App	Hull C.	01.80	1979	1	0	0	(CD)	
			Nuneaton Bor.	Scarborough	(N/L)	1987	38	1	1		
BENSTEAD, Graham M.	Aldershot	20.08.63	App	Q.P.R.	07.81					(G)	E Yth Int
			Tr	Norwich C.	03.85	1984-87	16	0	0		
			L	Colchester U.	08.87	1987	18	0	0		
			L	Sheffield U.	03.88	1987	8	0	0		
BENT, Junior A.	Huddersfield	01.03.70	YTS	Huddersfield T.	12.87	1987	5	2	0	(W)	
BERESFORD, John	Sheffield	04.09.66	App	Manchester C.	09.83					(M)	E Sch Int/
			Tr	Barnsley	07.86	1986-87	52	9	4		E Yth Int
BERNAL, Andrew	Australia	16.05.66	Sporting Gijon (Sp)	Ipswich T.	09.87	1987	4	5	0	(D)	
BERRY, George F.	West Germany	19.11.57	App	Wolverhampton W.	11.75	1976-81	124	0	4	(CD)	W-5
			Tr	Stoke C.	08.82	1982-87	182	6	22		
			L	Doncaster Rov.	08.84	1984	1	0	0		
BERRY, Les D.	Plumstead	04.05.56	App	Charlton Ath.	03.74	1975-85	352	6	11	(CD)	
			Tr	Brighton & H.A.	08.86	1986	22	1	0		
			Tr	Gillingham	03.87	1986-87	26	5	0		
BERRY, Steve A.	Gosport	04.04.63	App	Portsmouth	01.81	1981-82	26	2	2	(M)	
			L	Aldershot	03.84	1983	5	2	0		
			Tr	Sunderland	07.84	1984-85	32	3	2		
			Tr	Newport Co.	12.85	1985-86	60	0	6		
			Tr	Swindon T.	03.87	1986-87	4	0	0		
			Tr	Aldershot	10.87	1987	36	0	6		
BERTSCHIN, Keith E.	Enfield	25.08.56	Barnet	Ipswich T.	10.73	1975-76	19	13	8	(F)	E Yth Int/E U21-3
			Tr	Birmingham C.	07.77	1977-80	113	5	29		
			Tr	Norwich C.	08.81	1981-84	112	2	29		
			Tr	Stoke C.	11.84	1984-86	82	6	29		
			Tr	Sunderland	03.87	1986-87	25	11	7		
BIGGINS, Wayne	Sheffield	20.11.61	App	Lincoln C.	11.79	1980	8	0	1	(F)	
			Matlock T.	Burnley	02.84	1983-85	78	0	29		
			Tr	Norwich C.	10.85	1985-87	66	3	16		
BILLING, Peter G.	Liverpool	24.10.64	South Liverpool	Everton	01.86	1985	1	0	0	(CD)	
				Crewe Alex.	12.86	1986-87	47	4	0		
BIRCH, Alan	West Bromwich	12.08.56	App	Walsall	08.73	1972-78	158	13	23	(W)	Brother of Paul
			Tr	Chesterfield	07.79	1979-80	90	0	35		
			Tr	Wolverhampton W.	08.81	1981	13	2	0		
			Tr	Barnsley	02.82	1981-82	43	1	11		
			Tr	Chesterfield	08.83	1983	30	2	5		
			Tr	Rotherham U.	03.84	1983-85	99	2	28		
			Tr	Scunthorpe U.	06.86	1986-87	19	4	2		
			Tr	Stockport Co.	10.87	1987	18	2	3		
BIRCH, Paul	Birmingham	20.11.62	App	Aston Villa	07.80	1983-87	135	6	16	(M)	Brother of Alan
BIRCH, Paul A.	Reading	03.12.68	Arsenal (App)	Portsmouth	01.87					(F)	
				Brentford	12.87	1987	13	3	2		
BIRD, Adrian L.	Bristol	08.07.69	App	Birmingham C.	07.87	1986-87	12	3	0	(CD)	
BIRTLES, Garry	Nottingham	27.07.56	Long Eaton U.	Nottingham F.	12.76	1976-80	87	0	32	(F)	E U21-2/
			Tr	Manchester U.	10.80	1980-81	57	1	11		E-3/E 'B'
			Tr	Nottingham F.	09.82	1982-86	122	3	38		
			Tr	Notts. Co.	06.87	1987	43	0	7		
BISHOP, D. Charlie	Nottingham	16.02.68	Stoke C. (App)	Watford	04.86					(D)	
			Tr	Bury	08.87	1987	13	4	0		
BISHOP, Eddie M.	Liverpool	28.11.62	Runcorn	Tranmere Rov.	03.88	1987	2	3	1	(F)	
BISHOP, Ian W.	Liverpool	29.05.65	App	Everton	05.83	1983	0	1	0	(M)	
			L	Crewe Alex.	03.84	1983	4	0	0		
			Tr	Carlisle U.	10.84	1984-87	131	1	14		
BLACK, Kingsley	Luton	22.06.68	Jnrs	Luton T.	07.86	1987	10	3	0	(W)	NI-1
BLACK, Russell P.	Dumfries	29.07.60	Gretna	Sheffield U.	08.84	1984-85	10	4	0	(F)	
			Tr	Halifax T.	08.86	1986-87	63	9	14		
BLACKMORE, Clayton G.	Neath	23.09.64	App	Manchester U.	09.82	1983-87	39	9	7	(M)	W U21-3/W-15/
											W Yth Int
BLACKWELL, Kevin P.	Luton	21.12.58	Barnet	Scarborough	(N/L)	1987	21	0	0	(G)	
BLADES, Paul A.	Peterborough	05.01.65	App	Derby Co.	12.82	1982-87	101	8	0	(D)	E Yth Int
BLAIN, Colin A.	Urmston	07.03.70	YTS	Halifax T.	06.88	1987	2	1	0	(M)	

John Barnes (Liverpool) The Player of the Year is tackled from behind during last season's 3-0 victory at Oxford. Action Images Ltd

Steve Bull (Wolverhampton Wanderers) Has the goalscoring touch envied by many clubs. Match Magazine

John Byrne (Q.P.R.) Irish international striker who was signed from York City in October 1984. Match Magazine

Players Names	Birthplace	Date	Source	League Club	Date Sign'd	Seasons Played	Apps	Sub	Gls	Pos.	Misc
BLAIR, Andy	Kirkcaldy	18.12.59	App	Coventry C.	10.77	1978-80	90	3	6	(M)	S U21-5
			Tr	Aston Villa	08.81	1981-83	24	10	4		
			L	Wolverhampton W.	10.83	1983	10	0	0		
			Tr	Sheffield Wed.	08.84	1984-85	58	0	3		
			Tr	Aston Villa	03.86	1985-87	19	2	1		
			L	Barnsley	03.88	1987	6	0	0		
BLAKE, Mark C.	Portsmouth	17.12.67	App	Southampton	12.85	1985-87	15	0	2	(CD)	E Yth Int
BLAKE, Noel L.G.	Jamaica	12.01.62	Sutton Coldfield	Aston Villa	08.79	1979-81	4	0	0	(CD)	
			L	Shrewsbury T.	03.82	1981	6	0	0		
			Tr	Birmingham C.	09.82	1982-83	76	0	5		
			Tr	Portsmouth	08.84	1984-87	144	0	10		
BLISSETT, Gary P.	Manchester	29.06.64	Altrincham	Crewe Alex.	08.83	1983-86	112	10	38	(F)	
			Tr	Brentford	03.87	1986-87	50	1	14		
BLISSETT, Luther L.	Jamaica	01.02.58	Jnrs	Watford	07.75	1975-82	222	24	95	(F)	E U21-4/
			A.C. Milan (It)	Watford	08.84	1984-87	110	14	43		E-14
BLOOMER, R. (Bob)	Sheffield	21.06.66	Jnrs	Chesterfield	08.85	1985-87	64	11	4	(FB)	
BLUNDELL, Chris K.	Wigan	07.12.69	YTS	Oldham Ath.	07.88	1987	0	1	0	(M)	
BODAK, Peter J.	Birmingham	12.08.61	App	Coventry C.	05.79	1980-81	30	2	5	(W)	
			Tr	Manchester U.	08.82						
			Tr	Manchester C.	12.82	1982	12	2	1		
			Antwerp (Bel.)	Crewe Alex.	12.86	1986-87	49	4	7		
			Tr	Swansea C.	03.88	1987	9	0	0		
BODIN, Paul J.	Cardiff	13.09.64	Newport Co.(N/C)	Cardiff C.	08.82	1982-84	68	7	4	(M)	
			Bath C.	Newport Co.	01.88	1987	6	0	1		
			Tr	Swindon T.	03.88	1987	3	2	1		
BODLEY, Mike J.	Hayes	14.09.67	App	Chelsea	09.85	1987	6	0	1	(CD)	
BOGIE, Ian	Newcastle	06.12.67	App	Newcastle U.	12.85	1986-87	4	4	0	(W)	E Sch Int
BOLDER, R.J. (Bob)	Dover	02.10.58	Dover T.	Sheffield Wed.	03.77	1977-82	196	0	0	(G)	
			Tr	Liverpool	08.83						
			Tr	Sunderland	09.85	1985	22	0	0		
			Tr	Charlton Ath.	08.86	1986-87	61	0	0		
BOND, Kevin J.	West Ham	22.06.67	Bournemouth(App)	Norwich C.	07.74	1975-80	137	5	12	(CD)	Son of John
			Seattle S. (USA)	Manchester C.	09.81	1981-84	108	2	11		
			Tr	Southampton	09.84	1984-87	139	1	6		
BONDS, W.A. (Billy)	Woolwich	17.09.46	App	Charlton Ath.	09.64	1964-66	95	1	1	(CD)	E U23-2
			Tr	West Ham U.	05.67	1967-87	655	8	48		
BONNYMAN, Phil	Glasgow	06.02.54	Hamilton Ac.	Carlisle U.	03.76	1975-79	149	3	26	(M)	
			Tr	Chesterfield	03.80	1979-81	98	1	25		
			Tr	Grimsby T.	08.82	1982-86	146	5	15		
			L	Stoke C.	03.86	1985	7	0	0		
			Tr	Darlington	07.87	1987	38	0	3		
BOOKER, R. (Bob)	Watford	25.01.58	Bedmond S.C.	Brentford	10.78	1978-87	202	41	42	(M)	
BORROWS, Brian	Liverpool	20.12.60	Jnrs	Everton	04.80	1981-82	27	0	0	(RB)	
			Tr	Bolton W.	03.83	1982-84	95	0	0		
			Tr	Coventry C.	06.85	1985-87	114	1	1		
BORTHWICK, John R.	Hartlepool	24.03.64	Owton MSC	Hartlepool U.	12.82	1982-87	82	16	14	(F)	
BOUGHEN, Dean	Hemsworth	25.07.71	YTS	Newport Co. (YTS)	08.87	1987	1	0	0	(M)	
BOULD, Stephen A.	Stoke	16.11.62	App	Stoke C.	11.80	1981-87	179	4	6	(CD)	
			L	Torquay U.	10.82	1982	9	0	0		
BOWDEN, Jon	Stockport	21.01.63	Jnrs	Oldham Ath.	01.80	1981-84	73	9	5	(M)	
			Tr	Port Vale	09.85	1985-86	64	6	7		
			Tr	Wrexham	07.87	1987	20	6	1		
BOWEN, R. Mark	Neath	07.12.63	App	Tottenham H.	12.81	1983-86	14	3	2	(M)	W Sch/Yth Int/
			Tr	Norwich C.	07.87	1987	23	1	1		W U21-3/W-3
BOWMAN, David M.	Scarborough	16.12.60	Bridlington T.	Scarborough	08.87	1987	4	0	2	(F)	
BOWYER, Ian	Ellesmere Port	06.06.51	App	Manchester C.	08.68	1968-70	42	8	13	(M)	
			Tr	Leyton Orient	06.71	1971-72	75	3	18		
			Tr	Nottingham F.	10.73	1973-80	222	17	49		
			Tr	Sunderland	01.81	1980-81	15	0	1		
			Tr	Nottingham F.	01.82	1981-86	203	3	19		
			Tr	Hereford U.	07.87	1987	28	1	1		
BOYLE, Terry D.J.	Ammanford	29.10.58	App	Tottenham H.	11.75					(CD)	W Sch Int/
			Tr	Crystal Palace	01.78	1977-80	24	2	1		W U21-1/
			L	Wimbledon	09.81	1981	5	0	1		W-2
			Tr	Bristol City	10.81	1981-82	36	1	0		
			Tr	Newport Co.	11.82	1982-85	165	1	11		
			Tr	Cardiff C.	08.86	1986-87	92	0	5		
BRACEWELL, Paul W.	Heswall	19.07.62	App	Stoke C.	02.80	1979-82	123	6	5	(M)	E U21-13/
			Tr	Sunderland	07.83	1983	38	0	4		E-3
			Tr	Everton	05.84	1984-86	75	0	5		
BRADLEY, Darren M.	Birmingham	24.11.65	App	Aston Villa	11.83	1984-85	16	4	0	(M)	E Yth Int
			Tr	West Bromwich A.	03.86	1985-87	39	4	1		
BRADSHAW, Carl	Sheffield	02.10.68	App	Sheffield Wed.	08.86	1986-87	15	14	4	(F)	E Yth Int
			L	Barnsley	08.86	1986	6	0	1		
BRADSHAW, Darren S.	Sheffield	19.03.67	Matlock T.	Chesterfield	08.87	1987	18	0	0	(M)	E Yth Int
			Matlock T.	York C.	11.87	1987	24	1	1		
BRADSHAW, Mark	Ashton-u-Lyne	07.06.69	YTS	Blackpool	12.87	1986-87	16	4	0	(D)	
BRADSHAW, Paul W.	Altrincham	28.04.56	App	Blackburn Rov.	07.73	1973-77	78	0	0	(G)	E Yth Int/
			Tr	Wolverhampton W.	09.77	1977-83	200	0	0		E U21-4
			Vancouver W. (Can)	West Bromwich A.	04.85	1985	8	0	0		
				Bristol Rov (N/C)	03.87	1986	5	0	0		
			Tr	Newport Co. (N/C)	07.87	1987	23	0	0		
BRADY, W. Liam	Dublin	13.02.56	App	Arsenal	08.73	1973-79	227	8	43	(M)	IR-67/PFA
			Ascoli (It.)	West Ham U.	03.87	1986-87	33	1	3		Footballer of Year 1979
BRAITHWAITE, J. Rod	Isleworth	19.12.65	Jnrs	Fulham	07.84	1985-86	7	5	2	(F)	

152

Mark Bright (Crystal Palace) Averaged well over a goal a game last season.   Match Magazine

Kevin Brock (Q.P.R.) Former Oxford United midfield star.   Match Magazine

Tommy Caton (Oxford United) Former Manchester City and Arsenal defender, now starring in the heart of the "U's" defence.   Match Magazine

Nico Claesen (Tottenham Hotspur) Joined the "Spurs" from Standard Liege in October 1986 for a fee of £600,000.   Match Magazine

153

Players Names	Birthplace	Date	Source	League Club	Date Sign'd	Seasons Played	Apps	Sub	Gls	Pos.	Misc
BRAMHALL, John	Warrington	20.11.56	Stockton Heath	Tranmere Rov.	07.76	1976-81	164	6	7	(CD)	
			Tr	Bury	03.82	1981-85	165	2	17		
			L	Chester C.	11.85	1985	4	0	0		
			Tr	Rochdale	08.86	1986-87	86	0	13		
BRANAGAN, Jim P.S.	Urmston	03.07.55	Jnrs	Oldham Ath.	07.73	1974-76	24	3	0	(FB)	Son of Ken
			Cape Town C.(SA)	Huddersfield T.	11.77	1977-78	37	1	0		
			Tr	Blackburn Rov.	10.79	1979-86	290	4	5		
			Tr	Preston N.E.	05.87	1987	3	0	0		
			Tr	York C.	10.87	1987	27	1	1		
BRANAGAN, Keith G.	Fulham	10.07.66	Jnrs	Cambridge U.	08.83	1983-87	110	0	0	(G)	
			Tr	Millwall	03.88						
BRANNIGAN, Kenny	Glasgow	08.06.65	Queens Park	Sheffield Wed.	08.86	1986	1	0	0	(CD)	
			L	Stockport Co.	08.86	1986	8	0	0		
			L	Doncaster Rov.	12.87	1987	15	0	1		
BRATTAN, Gary	Hull	01.01.60	App	Hull C.	01.78					(M)	
			North Ferriby U.	Cambridge U. (N/C)	08.87	1987	7	1	0		
BRAY, Ian M.	Neath	06.12.62	App	Hereford U.	12.80	1981-84	105	3	4	(LB)	
			Tr	Huddersfield T.	07.85	1985-87	74	1	1		
BRAZIL, Gary N.	Tunbridge Wells	19.09.62	Crystal Palace(App)	Sheffield U.	08.80	1980-84	39	23	9	(F)	
			L	Port Vale	08.84	1984	6	0	3		
			Tr	Preston N.E.	02.85	1984-87	140	1	48		
BREACKER, Tim S.	Bicester	02.07.65	App	Luton T.	05.83	1983-87	139	3	2	(RB)	E U21-2
BREMNER, Des G.	Banff	07.09.52	Hibernian	Aston Villa	09.79	1979-84	170	4	9	(M)	S U23-9/ S-1
			Tr	Birmingham C.	09.84	1984-87	139	0	4		
BREMNER, Kevin J.	Banff	07.10.57	Keith	Colchester U.	10.80	1980-82	89	6	31	(F)	Brother of Des
			L	Birmingham C.	10.82	1982	3	1	1		
			L	Wrexham	12.82	1982	4	0	1		
			L	Plymouth Arg.	01.83	1982	5	0	1		
			Tr	Millwall	02.83	1982-84	87	9	33		
			Tr	Reading	08.85	1985-86	60	4	21		
			Tr	Brighton & H.A.	07.87	1987	42	2	8		
BRENNAN, Mark R.	Rossendale	04.10.65	App	Ipswich T.	04.83	1983-87	165	3	19	(M)	E Yth Int/E U21-5
BREVETT, Rufus E.	Derby	24.09.69	YTS	Doncaster Rov.	06.88	1987	16	1	0	(LB)	
BRIEN, A.J. (Tony)	Dublin	10.02.69	App	Leicester C.	02.87	1987	11	4	1	(CD)	
BRIGGS, Gary	Leeds	08.05.59	App	Middlesbrough	05.77					(CD)	
			Tr	Oxford U.	01.78	1977-87	403	2	17		
BRIGHT, Mark A.	Stoke	06.06.62	Leek T.	Port Vale	10.81	1981-83	18	11	10	(F)	
			Tr	Leicester C.	07.84	1984-86	26	16	6		
			Tr	Crystal Palace	11.86	1986-87	66	0	31		
BRIGHTWELL, Ian R.	Lutterworth	09.04.68	YTS	Manchester C.	05.86	1986-87	44	5	6	(M)	E Yth Int
BRIGNULL, Phil A.	Stratford	02.12.60	App	West Ham U.	09.78	1978	0	1	0	(CD)	E Sch Int
			Tr	Bournemouth	08.81	1981-84	128	1	11		
			L	Wrexham	12.85	1985	5	0	1		
			Tr	Cardiff C.	02.86	1985-86	49	0	0		
			Tr	Newport Co.	08.87	1987	3	0	0		
BRILEY, Les	Lambeth	02.10.56	App	Chelsea	06.74					(M)	
			Tr	Hereford U.	05.76	1976-77	60	1	2		
			Tr	Wimbledon	02.78	1977-79	59	2	2		
			Tr	Aldershot	03.80	1979-83	157	0	3		
			Tr	Millwall	05.84	1984-87	148	1	8		
BRIMACOMBE, John	Plymouth	25.11.58	Saltash U.	Plymouth Arg.	08.85	1985-87	51	3	2	(RB)	
BRINDLEY, Chris P.	Stoke	05.07.69	Hednesford T.	Wolverhampton W.	11.86	1986	7	0	0	(CD)	
BRITTON, Ian	Dundee	19.05.54	App	Chelsea	07.71	1972-81	253	10	33	(W)	
			Dundee U.	Blackpool	12.83	1983-85	100	6	15		
			Tr	Burnley	08.86	1986-87	66	5	7		
BROCK, Kevin S.	Bicester	09.09.62	App	Oxford U.	09.79	1979-86	229	17	26	(W)	E Sch Int/ E U21-4
			Tr	Q.P.R.	08.87	1987	26	0	2		
BROCKIE, Vincent	Greenock	02.02.69	YTS	Leeds U.	07.87	1987	2	0	0	(RB)	
BRODDLE, Julian R.	Laughton	01.11.64	App	Sheffield U.	11.82	1981	1	0	0	(W)	
			Tr	Scunthorpe U.	08.83	1983-87	126	18	32		
			Tr	Barnsley	09.87	1987	9	10	1		
BROMAGE, Russell	Stoke	09.11.59	App	Port Vale	11.77	1977-86	339	8	13	(LB)	
			L	Oldham Ath.	10.83	1983	2	0	0		
			Tr	Bristol C.	08.87	1987	28	2	0		
BROOK, Gary	Dewsbury	09.05.64	Frickley Ath.	Newport Co.	12.87	1987	14	0	2	(F)	
			Tr	Scarborough	03.88	1987	5	0	0		
BROOKMAN, Nicky A.	Manchester	28.10.68	YTS	Bolton W.	11.86	1986-87	27	3	6	(M)	
BROOKS, Shaun	Reading	09.10.62	App	Crystal Palace	10.79	1979-83	47	7	4	(M)	E Sch Int/ E Yth Int/ Son of John
			Tr	Leyton Orient	10.83	1983-86	140	8	26		
			Tr	Bournemouth	06.87	1987	33	4	6		
BROTHERSTON, Noel	Belfast	18.11.56	App	Tottenham H.	04.74	1975	1	0	0	(W)	NI U21-1/ NI-27
			Tr	Blackburn Rov.	07.77	1977-86	307	10	40		
			Tr	Bury	06.87	1987	30	6	4		
BROUGH, Paul P.	York	24.01.65		York C. (N/C)	08.87	1987	0	1	0		
BROWN, A.J. (Tony)	Bradford	17.09.58	Thackley	Leeds U.	03.83	1982-84	24	0	1	(CD)	
			L	Doncaster Rov.	11.84	1984	5	0	0		
			Tr	Doncaster Rov.	03.85	1984-86	80	2	2		
			Tr	Scunthorpe U.	07.87	1987	17	5	0		
BROWN, David J.	Hartlepool	28.01.57	Horden CW	Middlesbrough	02.77	1977	10	0	0	(G)	
			L	Plymouth Arg.	08.79	1979	5	0	0		
			Tr	Oxford U.	10.79	1979-80	21	0	0		
			Tr	Bury	09.81	1981-84	146	0	0		
			Tr	Preston N.E.	06.86	1986-87	51	0	0		
BROWN, Grant A.	Sunderland	19.11.69	YTS	Leicester C.	07.88	1987	2	0	0	(CD)	
BROWN, Jim G.	Coatbridge	11.05.52	Albion Rovers	Chesterfield	12.72	1972-73	47	0	0	(G)	S U23-4/ S-1
			Tr	Sheffield U.	03.74	1973-77	170	0	0		
			Washington Dip.(USA)	Cardiff C.	12.82	1982	3	0	0		
			Kettering T.	Chesterfield	07.83	1983-87	123	0	1		

Steve Clarke (Chelsea) Excellent full-back acquisition from St Mirren in January 1987.
Match Magazine

Nigel Clough (Nottingham Forest) Pictured on the right trying to get the better of Chelsea's Steve Wicks.
Action Images Ltd

Dean Coney (Q.P.R.) Joined from nearby Fulham in the close season, playing in 25 matches and scoring 7 goals.
Match Magazine

Tony Cottee (West Ham United) Goalscoring forward who is the local pride and joy.
Match Magazine

Carson, T — Charles, S

Players Names	Birthplace	Date	Source	League Club	Date Sign'd	Seasons Played	Apps	Sub	Gls	Pos.	Misc
CARSON, Tom	Dumbarton	26.03.59	Dundee	Ipswich T.	01.88	1987	1	0	0	(G)	
CARTER, Jimmy W.C.	Hammersmith	09.11.65	App	Crystal Palace	11.83					(W)	
			Tr	Q.P.R.	09.85						
			Tr	Millwall	03.87	1986-87	37	1	1		
CARTER, Lee R.	Dartford	22.03.70	YTS	Northampton T.	06.88	1987	0	1	0	(CD)	
CARTER, Mike	Warrington	18.04.60	App	Bolton W.	07.77	1979-81	37	12	8	(W)	
			L	Mansfield T.	03.79	1978	18	0	4		
			L	Swindon T.	03.82	1981	4	1	0		
			Tr	Plymouth Arg.	08.82	1982	6	6	1		
			Tr	Hereford U.	03.83	1982-86	91	6	11		
			Tr	Wrexham	07.87	1987	19	2	6		
CARTER, Roy W.	Torpoint	19.02.54	Falmouth	Hereford U.	04.75	1974-77	64	7	9	(M)	
			Tr	Swindon T.	12.77	1977-82	193	7	34		
			Tr	Torquay U.	10.82	1982-83	27	0	8		
			L	Bristol Rov.	12.82	1982	4	0	1		
			Tr	Newport Co.	09.83	1983-86	150	2	22		
			Tr	Exeter C.	06.87	1987	37	4	2		
CARTER, Tim D.	Bristol	05.10.67	App	Bristol Rov.	10.85	1985-87	47	0	0	(G)	E Yth Int
				Newport Co.	12.87	1987	1	0	0		
			Tr	Sunderland	12.87	1987	1	0	0		
			L	Carlisle U.	03.88	1987	4	0	0		
CASCARINO, A.G. (Tony)	Orpington	01.09.62	Crockenhill	Gillingham	01.82	1981-86	209	10	77	(F)	IR-4
			Tr	Millwall	06.87	1987	39	0	20		
CASE, Jimmy R.	Liverpool	18.05.54	South Liverpool	Liverpool	05.73	1974-80	170	16	23	(M)	E U23-1
			Tr	Brighton & H.A.	08.81	1981-84	124	3	10		
			Tr	Southampton	03.85	1984-87	122	1	6		
CASEY, Paul	Great Yarmouth	29.07.69	YTS	Cambridge U. (N/C)	07.87	1987	1	0	0	(G)	
CASS, David W.	Forest Gate	27.03.62	Billericay T.	Leyton Orient (N/C)	03.87	1986	7	0	0	(G)	
CASSELLS, Keith B.	Islington	10.07.57	Wembley	Watford	11.77	1978-80	6	6	0	(F)	
			L	Peterborough U.	01.80	1979	8	0	0		
			Tr	Oxford U.	11.80	1980-81	43	2	13		
			Tr	Southampton	03.82	1981-82	13	6	4		
			Tr	Brentford	02.83	1982-84	80	6	28		
			Tr	Mansfield T.	08.85	1985-87	126	0	38		
CASTLE, Stephen C.	Barkingside	17.05.66	App	Leyton Orient	05.84	1984-87	103	7	20	(W)	
CATON, Tommy	Liverpool	06.10.62	App	Manchester C.	10.79	1979-83	164	1	8	(CD)	E Sch Int/
			Tr	Arsenal	12.83	1983-85	81	0	2		E Yth Int/
			Tr	Oxford U.	02.87	1986-87	50	3	3		E U21-14
CAWLEY, Peter	Middlesbrough	15.09.65	Chertsey T.	Wimbledon	01.87					(CD)	
				Bristol Rov.	02.87	1986	9	1	0		
CECERE, Michele J.	Chester	04.01.68	App	Oldham Ath.	01.86	1986-87	26	13	6	(M)	
CHAMBERLAIN, Alec F.R.	March	20.06.64	Ramsey T.	Ipswich T.	07.81					(G)	
			Tr	Colchester U.	08.82	1982-86	188	0	0		
			Tr	Everton	07.87						
			L	Tranmere Rov.	11.87	1987	15	0	0		
CHAMBERLAIN, Mark V.	Stoke	19.11.61	App	Port Vale	04.79	1978-81	90	6	17	(W)	E Sch Int/
			Tr	Stoke C.	08.82	1982-85	110	2	17		E U21-3/E-8
			Tr	Sheffield Wed.	09.85	1985-87	32	34	8		Brother of Neville
CHAMBERLAIN, Neville P.	Stoke	22.01.60	App	Port Vale	01.78	1977-82	133	8	33	(F)	Brother of Mark
			Tr	Stoke C.	09.82	1982-83	6	0	0		
			L	Newport Co.	11.83	1983	6	0	2		
			L	Plymouth Arg.	03.84	1983	7	4	3		
			Tr	Newport Co.	07.84	1984	39	2	13		
			Tr	Mansfield T.	07.85	1985-86	56	5	19		
			Tr	Doncaster Rov.	08.87	1987	22	7	4		
CHAMBERS, Stephen	Worksop	27.07.68	Sheffield Wed(App)	Mansfield T.	11.86	1986-87	5	8	0	(M)	
CHANDLER, Ian	Sunderland	20.03.68	Sch	Barnsley	08.86	1986	8	4	4	(F)	E Sch Int
			L	Stockport Co.	08.87	1987	4	1	0		
CHANDLER, Jeff G.	Hammersmith	19.06.59	App	Blackpool	08.76	1977-78	31	6	7	(W)	IR U21-1/
			Tr	Leeds U.	09.79	1979-80	21	5	2		
			Tr	Bolton W.	10.81	1981-84	152	5	36		
			Tr	Derby Co.	07.85	1985-86	45	1	9		
			L	Mansfield T.	11.86	1986	6	0	0		
			Tr	Bolton W.	07.87	1987	2	1	2		
CHANNING, Justin A.	Reading	19.11.68	App	Q.P.R.	08.86	1986-87	9	7	1	(D)	E Yth Int
CHAPMAN, Ian R.	Brighton	31.05.70	YTS	Brighton & H.A.	06.87	1986	5	0	0	(LB)	
CHAPMAN, Lee R.	Lincoln	05.12.59	Jnrs	Stoke C.	06.78	1979-81	95	4	34	(F)	Son of Roy/
			L	Plymouth Arg	12.78	1978	3	1	0		E U21-1
			Tr	Arsenal	08.82	1982-83	15	8	4		
			Tr	Sunderland	12.83	1983	14	1	3		
			Tr	Sheffield Wed	08.84	1984-87	147	2	63		
CHAPMAN, Les	Oldham	27.09.48		Oldham Ath.	01.67	1966-69	75	1	9	(M)	
			Tr	Huddersfield T.	09.69	1969-74	120	13	8		
			Tr	Oldham Ath.	12.74	1974-78	186	1	11		
			Tr	Stockport Co.	05.79	1979	32	0	1		
			Tr	Bradford C.	02.80	1979-82	137	2	3		
			Tr	Rochdale	06.83	1983-84	87	1	0		
			Tr	Stockport Co.	07.85	1985	38	0	3		
			Tr	Preston N.E.	07.86	1986-87	50	3	1		
CHAPMAN, Vincent J.	Newcastle	05.12.67	Tow Law T.	Huddersfield T.	01.88	1987	4	2	0	(D)	
CHAPPLE, Philip R.	Norwich	26.11.66	YTS	Norwich C.	07.85					(CD)	
			Tr	Cambridge U.	03.88	1987	4	2	1		
CHARD, Philip, J.	Corby	16.10.60	Corby T.	Peterborough U.	01.79	1978-84	153	19	18	(M)	
			Tr	Northampton T.	08.85	1985-87	113	2	27		
			Tr	Wolverhampton W.	03.88	1987	8	1	2		
CHARLES, Steve	Sheffield	10.05.60	Sheffield Univ.	Sheffield U.	01.80	1979-84	112	11	10	(M)	
			Tr	Wrexham	10.84	1984-86	111	2	37		
			Tr	Mansfield T.	07.87	1987	46	0	12		

158

Alan Cork (Wimbledon) Long serving forward.   Match Magazine

Nicky Cross (Leicester City) Another player who knows where the net is, signed for the "Filberts" from Walsall last January.   Match Magazine

Tony Cunningham (Blackpool) Now with his sixth club having been signed from Newcastle United during the close season.   Match Magazine

Ian Dawes (Q.P.R.) Former England schoolboy international full-back who came through the junior ranks.   Match Magazine

159

Players Names	Birthplace	Date	Source	League Club	Date Sign'd	Seasons Played	Career Record Apps	Sub	Gls	Pos.	Misc
CHATTERTON, Nick J.	Norwood	18.05.54	Jnrs	Crystal Palace	03.72	1973-78	142	9	31	(M)	
			Tr	Millwall	11.78	1978-85	258	6	56		
			Tr	Colchester U.	09.86	1986-87	46	1	8		
CHERRY, Steve R.	Nottingham	05.08.60	App	Derby Co.	03.78	1979-83	77	0	0	(G)	E Yth Int
			L	Port Vale	11.80	1980	4	0	0		
			Tr	Walsall	08.84	1984-85	71	0	0		
			Tr	Plymouth Arg.	10.86	1986-87	58	0	0		
CHETTLE, Stephen	Nottingham	27.09.68	App	Nottingham F.	08.86	1987	28	1	0	(RB)	
CHIEDOZIE, John O.	Nigeria	18.04.60	App	Leyton Orient	04.77	1976-80	131	14	20	(W)	Nigerian Int
			Tr	Notts Co.	08.81	1981-83	110	1	15		
			Tr	Tottenham H.	08.84	1984-86	45	8	12		
CHILDS, Gary P.C.	Birmingham	19.04.64	App	West Bromwich A.	02.82	1981-83	2	1	0	(W)	E Yth Int
			Tr	Walsall	10.83	1983-86	120	11	17		
			Tr	Birmingham C.	07.87	1987	23	9	1		
CHIVERS, Gary P.S.	Stockwell	15.05.60	App	Chelsea	07.78	1978-82	128	5	4	(CD)	
			Tr	Swansea C.	08.83	1983	10	0	0		
			Tr	Q.P.R.	02.84	1984-86	58	2	0		
			Tr	Watford	09.87	1987	14	0	0		
			Tr	Brighton & H.A.	03.88	1987	10	0	0		
CHRISTIE, Trevor	Newcastle	28.02.59	App	Leicester C.	12.76	1977-78	28	3	8	(F)	
			Tr	Notts Co.	06.79	1979-83	158	29	64		
			Tr	Nottingham F.	07.84	1984	14	0	5		
			Tr	Derby Co.	02.85	1984-85	65	0	22		
			Tr	Manchester C.	08.86	1986	9	0	3		
			Tr	Walsall	10.86	1986-87	65	6	20		
CLAESEN, Nico P.J.	Belgium	01.10.62	Standard Liége	TottenhamH.	10.86	1986-87	37	13	18	(F)	Belgian Int
CLARK, Jonathan	Swansea	12.11.58	App	Manchester C.	11.75	1976	0	1	0	(M)	W Sch Int/ W U21--2
			Tr	Derby Co.	09.78	1978-80	48	5	3		
			Tr	Preston N.E.	08.81	1981-86	107	3	10		
			Tr	Bury	12.86	1986	13	1	1		
			Tr	Carlisle U.	08.87	1987	40	1	1		
CLARK, Paul P.	Benfleet	14.09.58	App	Southend U.	07.76	1976-77	29	4	1	(D)	E Sch Int/ E Yth Int
			Tr	Brighton & H.A.	11.77	1977-80	69	10	9		
			L	Reading	10.81	1981	2	0	0		
			Tr	Southend U.	08.82	1982-87	189	6	3		
CLARK, W.R. (Billy)	Christchurch	19.05.67	YTS	Bournemouth	09.84	1984-87	4	0	0	(CD)	
			Tr	Bristol Rov.	10.87	1987	31	0	1		
CLARKE, Colin J.	Newry (NI)	30.10.62	App	Ipswich T.	10.80						(F)	NI-15
			Tr	Peterborough U.	07.81	1981-83	76	6	18		
			L	Gillingham	03.84	1983	8	0	1		
			Tr	Tranmere Rov.	07.84	1984	45	0	22		
			Tr	Bournemouth	06.85	1985	46	0	26		
			Tr	Southampton	06.86	1986-87	73	0	36		
CLARKE, David A.	Nottingham	03.12.64	App	Notts Co.	12.82	1982-86	113	10	7	(LW)	E Yth Int
			Tr	Lincoln C.	N/L							
CLARKE, Michael D.	Birmingham	22.12.67	Birmingham C.(App)	Barnsley	11.86	1986-87	34	3	3	(LW)	
CLARKE, Nick J.	Walsall	20.08.67	Jnrs	Wolverhampton W.	02.85	1985-87	51	4	1	(D)	
CLARKE, Stephen	Saltcoats	29.08.63	St Mirren	Chelsea	01.87	1986-87	53	1	1	(D)	S U21-8/S-5
CLARKE, Wayne	Wolverhampton	28.02.61	App	Wolverhampton W.	03.78	1977-83	129	19	30	(F)	E Sch Int/E Yth Int/Brother of Allan and Derek
			Tr	Birmingham C.	08.84	1984-86	92	0	38		
			Tr	Everton	03.87	1986-87	34	3	14		
CLAYTON, Gary	Sheffield	02.02.63	Burton Albion	Doncaster Rov.	08.86	1986	34	1	5	(M)	E Semi-pro Int 1986
			Tr	Cambridge U.	06.87	1987	45	0	5		
CLAYTON, John	Elgin	20.08.61	App	Derby Co.	12.78	1978-81	21	3	4	(F)	
			Hong Kong	Chesterfield	06.83	1983	25	8	5		
			Tr	Tranmere Rov.	07.84	1984-85	47	0	35		
			Tr	Plymouth Arg.	08.85	1985-87	68	9	22		
CLAYTON, Paul S.	Dunstable	04.01.65	App	Norwich C.	01.83	1983-85	8	5	0	(F)	
			Tr	Darlington	03.88	1987	11	1	3		
CLEGG, A. (Tony)	Keighley	08.11.65	App	Bradford C.	11.83	1983-86	41	7	2	(D)	
			Tr	York C.	08.87	1987	35	2	3		
CLEMENCE, Ray N.	Skegness	05.08.48	Notts Co. (Jnr)	Scunthorpe U.	08.65	1965-66	48	0	0	(G)	E U23-4/E-61/ F Lge Rep
			Tr	Liverpool	06.67	1969-80	470	0	0		
			Tr	Tottenham H.	08.81	1981-87	240	0	0		
CLEMENT, Andy D.	Cardiff	12.11.67	App	Wimbledon	10.85	1986-87	5	10	0	(D)	W Yth Int
			L	Bristol Rov.	03.87	1986	5	1	0		
			L	Newport Co.	12.87	1987	5	0	1		
CLEMENTS, Kenny H.	Manchester	09.04.55	Groundstaff	Manchester C.	07.75	1975-78	116	3	0	(CD)	
			Tr	Oldham Ath.	09.79	1979-84	204	2	2		
			Tr	Manchester C.	03.85	1984-87	104	2	1		
			Tr	Bury	03.88	1987	9	0	1		
CLOSE, Shaun C.	Islington	08.09.66	YTS	Tottenham H.	08.84	1986-87	3	6	0	(F)	
			Tr	Bournemouth	01.88	1987	15	1	6		
CLOUGH, Nigel H.	Sunderland	19.03.66	Jnrs	Nottingham F.	09.84	1984-87	121	3	49	(F)	Son of Brian/ E U21-11
COADY, John	Dublin	25.08.60	Shamrock Rov.	Chelsea	12.86	1986-87	9	7	2	(M)	
COATSWORTH, Gary	Sunderland	07.10.68	Jnrs	Barnsley	02.87	1987	3	3	0	(FB)	
COBB, Gary E.	Luton	06.08.68	App	Luton T.	08.86	1986-87	6	3	0	(M)	
COCKERILL, Glenn	Grimsby	25.08.59	Louth U.	Lincoln C.	11.76	1976-79	65	6	10	(M)	Son of Ron
			Tr	Swindon T.	12.79	1979-80	23	3	1		
			Tr	Lincoln C.	08.81	1981-83	114	1	25		
			Tr	Sheffield U.	03.84	1983-85	62	0	10		
			Tr	Southampton	10.85	1985-87	107	4	16		
COCKRAM, Allan C.	Kensington	08.10.63	App	Tottenham H.	01.81	1983	2	0	0	(M)	
			Tr	Bristol Rov.	08.85	1985	1	0	0		
			St Albans C.	Brentford (N/C)	03.88	1987	7	0	2		

Players Names	Birthplace	Date	Source	League Club	Date Sign'd	Seasons Played	Career Record Apps	Sub	Gls	Pos.	Misc
COLE, David A.	Barnsley	28.09.62		Sunderland	10.83					(CD)	
			Tr	Swansea C.	09.84	1984	7	1	0		
			Tr	Swindon T.	02.85	1984-86	69	0	3		
			Tr	Torquay U.	11.86	1986-87	75	0	5		
COLE, Michael W.	Stepney	03.09.66	App	Ipswich T.	11.83	1984-87	24	14	3	(F)	
			L	Port Vale	01.88	1987	4	0	1		
			Tr	Fulham	03.88	1987	9	0	1		
COLEMAN, Christopher	Swansea	10.06.70	Manchester C. (Jnr)	Swansea C.	08.87	1987	29	1	0	(LB)	
COLEMAN, David H.	Salisbury	08.04.67	Jnrs	Bournemouth	09.84	1985-87	5	2	0	(CD)	
			L	Colchester U.	02.88	1987	6	0	1		
COLEMAN, Nicky	Crayford	06.05.66	App	Millwall	01.84	1984-87	84	1	0	(LB)	
			L	Swindon T.	09.85	1985	13	0	4		
COLEMAN, Philip	Woolwich	08.09.60	App	Millwall	08.78	1978-80	23	13	1	(D)	
			Tr	Colchester U.	02.81	1980-83	82	4	6		
			L	Wrexham	09.83	1983	17	0	2		
			Chelmsford C.	Exeter C.	12.84	1984	6	0	0		
			Tr	Aldershot	02.85	1984-85	45	0	5		
			Dulwich Hamlet	Millwall	09.86	1986	8	2	0		
COLEMAN, Simon	Worksop	13.03.68	Jnrs	Mansfield T.	07.85	1986-87	46	0	2	(CD)	
COLES, David A.	Wandsworth	15.06.64	App	Birmingham C.	04.82					(G)	
			Tr	Mansfield T.	03.83	1982	3	0	0		
			Tr	Aldershot	08.83	1983-87	120	0	0		
			L	Newport Co.	01.88	1987	14	0	0		
COLLINS, Eamonn A.S.	Dublin	22.10.65	App	Southampton	10.83	1984	1	2	0	(M)	IR Yth Int
			Tr	Portsmouth	05.86	1986	4	1	0		
			L	Exeter C.	11.87	1987	8	1	0		
COLLINS, Jimmy P.	Urmston	27.12.66	YTS	Oldham Ath.	08.84	1983	0	1	0	(RB)	
			Tr	Bury	10.86	1986-87	10	1	0		
COLLINS, Roderick	Dublin	07.08.62	Dundalk	Mansfield T.	12.85	1985-86	11	5	1	(F)	
			Tr	Newport Co.	08.87	1987	5	2	1		
COLLINS, Steve M.	Stamford	21.03.62	App	Peterborough U.	08.79	1978-82	92	2	1	(LB)	
			Tr	Southend U.	08.83	1983-84	51	0	0		
			Tr	Lincoln C.	03.85	1984-85	24	0	0		
			Tr	Peterborough U.	12.85	1985-87	86	2	1		
COLVILLE, Robert J.	Nuneaton	27.04.63	Rhos U.	Oldham Ath.	02.84	1983-86	22	10	4	(F)	
			Tr	Bury	10.86	1986-87	5	6	1		
			Tr	Stockport Co.	09.87	1987	40	0	13		
COMFORT, Alan	Aldershot	08.12.64	App	Q.P.R.	10.82					(W)	E Yth Int
			Tr	Cambridge U.	09.84	1984-85	61	2	5		
			Tr	Leyton Orient	03.86	1985-87	101	5	27		
COMSTIVE, Paul T.	Southport	25.11.61	Jnrs	Blackburn Rov.	10.79	1980-82	3	3	0	(M)	
			L	Rochdale	09.82	1982	9	0	2		
			Tr	Wigan Ath.	08.83	1983-84	35	0	2		
			Tr	Wrexham	11.84	1984-86	95	4	8		
			Tr	Burnley	07.87	1987	44	0	8		
CONEY, Dean H.	Dagenham	18.09.63	App	Fulham	05.81	1980-86	209	2	56	(F)	E U21-9
			Tr	Q.P.R.	06.87	1987	25	7	7		
CONNOR, Terry F.	Leeds	09.11.62	App	Leeds U.	11.79	1979-82	83	13	19	(F)	E Yth Int/
			Tr	Brighton & H.A.	03.83	1982-86	153	3	51		E U21-1
			Tr	Portsmouth	06.87	1987	19	0	4		
CONROY, Mike G.	Johnstone	31.07.57	Hibernian	Blackpool	08.84	1984-85	66	0	2	(M)	
			Tr	Wrexham	07.86	1986	23	2	2		
			Tr	Leyton Orient	07.87	1987	2	1	0		
COOK, Andy C.	Romsey	10.08.69	App	Southampton	06.87	1987	2	0	0	(LB)	
COOK, Michael J.	Stroud	18.10.68	YTS	Coventry C.	03.87					(M)	
			L	York C.	08.87	1987	6	0	1		
COOK, Mitchell C.	Scarborough	15.10.61	Scarborough	Darlington	08.84	1984-85	34	0	4	(M)	
			Tr	Middlesbrough	09.85	1985	3	3	0		
			Tr	Scarborough	08.86	1987	28	10	5		
COOK, Paul	Liverpool	22.02.67	Jnrs	Wigan Ath.	07.84	1984-87	77	6	14	(M)	
COOKE, Joe	Dominica (WI)	15.02.55	App	Bradford C.	05.72	1971-78	184	20	62	(CD)	
			Tr	Peterborough U.	01.79	1978	18	0	5		
			Tr	Oxford U.	08.79	1979-80	71	1	13		
			Tr	Exeter C.	06.81	1981	17	0	3		
			Tr	Bradford C.	01.82	1981-83	61	1	6		
			Tr	Rochdale	07.84	1984-85	75	0	4		
			Tr	Wrexham	07.86	1986-87	49	2	4		
COOKE, John	Salford	25.04.62	App	Sunderland	11.79	1979-84	42	13	4	(W)	E Yth Int
			L	Carlisle U.	11.84	1984	5	1	2		
			Tr	Sheffield Wed.	06.85							
			Tr	Carlisle U.	10.85	1985-87	105	1	11		
COOKE, Richard E.	Islington	04.09.65	App	Tottenham H.	05.83	1983-85	9	2	2	(W)	E Yth Int/
			L	Birmingham C.	09.86	1986	5	0	0		E U21-1
			Tr	Bournemouth	01.87	1986-87	52	5	12		
COOKE, Robbie L.	Rotherham	16.02.57	App	Mansfield T.	02.75	1976-77	7	8	1	(F)	
			Grantham	Peterborough U.	05.80	1980-82	115	2	51		
			Tr	Cambridge U.	02.83	1982-84	62	3	14		
			Tr	Brentford	12.84	1984-87	122	1	53		
			Tr	Millwall	12.87	1987	4	0	1		
COOPER, Colin T.	Hartlepool	28.02.67	Jnrs	Middlesbrough	06.84	1985-87	98	2	2	(LB)	E U21-1
COOPER, Geoff V.	Kingston	27.12.60	Bognor Regis T.	Brighton & H.A.	12.87	1987	0	2	0	(F)	
COOPER, Graham	Huddersfield	22.05.62	Emley	Huddersfield T.	03.84	1983-87	61	13	13	(F)	
COOPER, Leigh V.	Reading	07.05.61	App	Plymouth Arg.	05.79	1979-87	299	7	17	(LB)	
COOPER, Mark D.	Watford	05.04.67	App	Cambridge U.	10.84	1983-86	62	9	17	(F)	
			Tr	Tottenham H.	03.87							
			L	Shrewsbury T.	09.87	1987	6	0	2		
			Tr	Gillingham	10.87	1987	24	7	8		
COOPER, Neale J.	India	24.11.63	Aberdeen	Aston Villa	07.86	1986-87	19	1	0	(M)	S Yth Int/S U 21-13

Players Names	Birthplace	Date	Source	League Club	Date Sign'd	Seasons Played	Apps	Sub	Gls	Pos.	Misc
COOPER, Paul D.	Brierley Hill	21.12.53	App	Birmingham C.	07.71	1971-73	17	0	0	(G)	
			Tr	Ipswich T.	03.74	1973-86	447	0	0		
			Tr	Leicester C.	06.87	1987	32	0	0		
COOPER, Richard D.	Brent	07.05.65	App	Sheffield U.	05.83	1982-84	2	4	0	(M)	
			Tr	Lincoln C.	08.85	1985-86	57	4	2		
			Tr	Exeter C.	07.87	1987	30	3	1		
COOPER, Steve B.	Birmingham	22.06.64	Moor Green	Birmingham C.	11.83					(F)	
			L	Halifax T.	12.83	1983	7	0	1		
			Tr	Newport Co.	09.84	1984	38	0	11		
			Tr	Plymouth Arg.	08.85	1985-87	58	15	15		
CORK, Alan G.	Derby	04.03.59	Jnrs	Derby Co.	07.77					(F)	
			L	Lincoln C.	09.77	1977	5	0	0		
			Tr	Wimbledon	02.78	1978-87	310	20	131		
CORK, David	Doncaster	28.10.62	App	Arsenal	06.80	1983	5	2	1	(F)	
			Tr	Huddersfield T.	07.85	1985-87	104	6	25		
CORKAIN, Steve	Stockton	25.02.67	Jnrs	Hull C.	06.85	1986	5	0	1	(M)	
CORNER, David E.	Sunderland	15.05.66	App	Sunderland	04.84	1984-87	33	0	1	(CD)	E Yth Int
			L	Cardiff C.	09.85	1985	6	0	0		
			L	Peterborough U.	03.88	1987	9	0	0		
CORNFORTH, John M.	Whitley Bay	07.10.67	App	Sunderland	10.85	1984-87	9	4	2	(M)	
			L	Doncaster Rov.	11.86	1986	6	1	0		
CORNWELL, John A.	Bethnal Green	13.10.64	App	Leyton Orient	10.82	1981-86	193	9	35	(M)	
			Tr	Newcastle U.	07.87	1987	20	4	1		
COSTELLO, Nigel G.	Catterick	22.11.68	YTS	York C. (N/C)	07.87	1986-87	2	2	0	(W)	
COTON, A.P. (Tony)	Tamworth	19.05.61	Mile Oak Rov.	Birmingham C.	10.78	1980-84	94	0	0	(G)	
			Tr	Watford	09.84	1984-87	141	0	0		
COTTEE, A.R. (Tony)	West Ham	11.07.65	App	West Ham U.	09.82	1982-87	203	9	92	(F)	E Yth Int/ E U21-8/E-3
COUGHLIN, Russell	Swansea	15.02.60	App	Manchester C.	02.78					(M)	
			Tr	Blackburn Rov.	03.79	1978-80	22	2	0		
			Tr	Carlisle U.	10.80	1980-83	114	16	13		
			Tr	Plymouth Arg.	07.84	1984-87	128	2	18		
			Tr	Blackpool	12.87	1987	24	0	2		
COWANS, Gordon S.	Cornforth (Dm.)	27.10.58	App	Aston Villa	09.76	1975-84	276	10	42	(M)	E Yth Int/E U21-5/ E-9/to Bari (It) 7.85
COWDRILL, Barry L.	Birmingham	03.01.57	Sutton Coldfield T.	West Bromwich A.	04.79	1979-87	127	4	0	(FB)	
			L	Rotherham U.	10.85	1985	2	0	0		
COWLING, David R.	Doncaster	27.11.58	App	Mansfield T.	11.76					(LW)	
			Tr	Huddersfield T.	08.77	1978-87	331	9	43		
			L	Scunthorpe U.	11.87	1987	1	0	0		
			L	Reading	12.87	1987	1	0	0		
			Tr	Reading	03.88	1987	8	1	1		
COX, Brian R.	Sheffield	07.05.61	App	Sheffield Wed.	02.79	1978-80	22	0	0	(G)	
			Tr	Huddersfield T.	03.82	1981-87	213	0	0		
COYLE, A. (Tony)	Glasgow	17.01.60	Albion Rovers	Stockport Co.	12.79	1979-85	215	4	28	(W)	
			Tr	Chesterfield	06.86	1986-87	71	5	4		
COYLE, Ronnie P.	Glasgow	19.08.61	Glasgow Celtic	Middlesbrough	12.86	1986	1	2	0	(M)	
			Tr	Rochdale	08.87	1987	23	1	1		
COYNE, Peter D.	Hartlepool	13.11.58	App	Manchester U.	11.75	1975	1	1	1	(F)	
			Ashton U.	Crewe Alex.	08.77	1977-80	113	21	47		
			Hyde U.	Swindon T.	08.84	1984-87	99	10	30		
CRAIG, Albert H.	Glasgow	03.01.62	Hamilton Acad.	Newcastle U.	02.87	1986-87	6	3	0	(W)	
CRANSON, Ian	Easington	02.07.64	App	Ipswich T.	07.82	1983-87	130	1	4	(CD)	E U21-5
			Tr	Sheffield Wed.	03.88	1987	4	0	0		
CRAVEN, Steve J.	Birkenhead	17.09.57		Tranmere Rov.	03.78	1977-81	106	8	17	(M)	
			Tr	Crewe Alex.	08.82	1982	26	3	3		
			Caernarfon T.	Tranmere Rov.	07.87	1987	6	7	0		
CRERAND, Danny P.	Manchester	05.05.69	Chapel Villa	Rochdale (N/C)	02.88	1987	3	0	0	(M)	Son of Pat
CRIBLEY, Alex	Liverpool	01.04.57		Liverpool	06.78					(CD)	
			Tr	Wigan Ath.	10.80	1980-87	268	3	16		
CRICHTON, Paul A.	Pontefract	03.10.65	Jnrs	Nottingham F.	05.86					(G)	
			L	Notts. Co.	09.86	1987	5	0	0		
			L	Darlington	01.87	1986	5	0	0		
			L	Peterborough U.	03.87	1986	4	0	0		
			L	Darlington	09.87	1987	3	0	0		
			L	Swindon T.	12.87	1987	4	0	0		
			L	Rotherham U.	03.88	1987	6	0	0		
CROFT, Brian G.A.	Chester	27.09.67	YTS	Chester C.	07.86	1985-87	36	23	3	(W)	
CROMBIE, Dean M.	Lincoln	09.08.57	Ruston Sports	Lincoln C.	02.77	1976-77	33	0	0	(D)	
			Tr	Grimsby T.	08.78	1978-86	316	4	3		
			Tr	Bolton W.	08.87	1987	24	0	0		
CROMPTON, Steve G.	Partington	20.04.68	Jnrs	Manchester C.	05.86					(G)	
			Tr	Carlisle U.	07.87	1987	10	0	0		
			Tr	Stockport Co. (N/C)	02.88	1987	2	0	0		
CRONIN, Dennis	Manchester	30.10.67	App	Manchester U.	10.85					(F)	
			Tr	Stockport Co.	08.87	1987	11	4	1		
CROOK, Ian S.	Romford	18.01.63	App	Tottenham H.	08.80	1981-85	10	10	1	(W)	
			Tr	Norwich C.	06.86	1986-87	47	9	6		
CROOKS, Garth A.	Stoke	10.03.58	App	Stoke C.	03.76	1975-79	141	6	48	(F)	E U21-4
			Tr	Tottenham H.	07.80	1980-84	121	4	48		
			L	Manchester U.	11.83	1983	6	1	2		
			Tr	West Bromwich A.	08.85	1985-86	39	1	16		
			Tr	Charlton Ath.	03.87	1986-87	29	6	12		
CROSBY, Gary	Sleaford	08.05.64	Lincoln Utd.	Lincoln C. (N/C)	08.86	1986	6	1	0	(W)	
			Grantham	Nottingham F.	12.87	1987	12	2	1		
CROSBY, Philip A.	Leeds	09.11.62	App	Grimsby T.	09.80	1979-82	34	5	1	(LB)	E Yth Int
			Tr	Rotherham U.	08.83	1983-87	145	1	0		

Players Names	Birthplace	Date	Source	League Club	Date Sign'd	Seasons Played	Career Record Apps	Sub	Gls	Pos.	Misc
CROSS, Nicky J.R.	Birmingham	07.02.61	App	West Bromwich A.	02.79	1980-84	68	37	15	(F)	
			Tr	Walsall	08.85	1985-87	107	2	45		
			Tr	Leicester C.	01.88	1987	17	0	6		
CROSS, Paul	Barnsley	31.10.65	App	Barnsley	10.83	1982-87	76	2	0	(LB)	
CROSS, Steve C.	Wolverhampton	22.12.59	App	Shrewsbury T.	12.77	1976-85	240	22	34	(M)	
			Tr	Derby Co.	06.86	1986-87	14	7	3		
CROWE, Mark A.	Southwold	21.01.65	App	Norwich C.	01.83	1982	0	1	0	(CD)	
			Tr	Torquay U.	07.85	1985-86	57	0	2		
			Tr	Cambridge U.	12.86	1986-87	51	0	0		
CROWN, David I.	Enfield	16.02.58	Walthamstow Ave.	Brentford	07.80	1980-81	44	2	8	(F)	
			Tr	Portsmouth	10.81	1981-82	25	3	2		
			L	Exeter C.	03.83	1982	6	1	3		
			Tr	Reading	08.83	1983-84	87	1	15		
			Tr	Cambridge U.	07.85	1985-87	106	0	44		
			Tr	Southend U.	11.87	1987	28	0	17		
CRUDGINGTON, Geoff	Wolverhampton	14.02.52	Wolves (Jnr)	Aston Villa	09.69	1970-71	4	0	0	(G)	E Sch Int
			L	Bradford C.	03.71	1970	1	0	0		
			Tr	Crewe Alex.	03.72	1971-77	250	0	0		
			Tr	Swansea C.	07.78	1978-79	52	0	0		
			Tr	Plymouth Arg.	10.79	1979-87	326	0	0		
CRUMPLIN, John L.	Bath	26.05.67	Bognor Regis T.	Brighton & H.A.	02.87	1986-87	24	7	2	(W)	
CULPIN, Paul	Kirkby Muxloe	08.02.62		Leicester C.	05.81					(F)	E Semi-pro Int 1984-85
			Nuneaton Bor.	Coventry C.	06.85	1985-86	5	4	2		
			Tr	Northampton T.	10.87	1987	18	2	10		
CULVERHOUSE, Ian B.	Bishop's Stortford	22.09.64	App	Tottenham H.	09.82	1983	1	1	0	(RB)	E Yth Int
			Tr	Norwich C.	10.85	1985-87	88	0	0		
CUMMING, R. (Bobby)	Airdrie	07.12.55	Baillieston Jnrs	Grimsby T.	03.74	1974-86	338	27	56	(W/FB)	
			Tr	Lincoln C.	N/L						
CUNNINGHAM, A.E. (Tony)	Jamaica	12.11.59	Stourbridge	Lincoln C.	05.79	1979-82	111	12	32	(F)	
			Tr	Barnsley	09.82	1982-83	40	2	11		
			Tr	Sheffield Wed.	11.83	1983	26	2	5		
			Tr	Manchester C.	07.84	1984	16	2	1		
			Tr	Newcastle U.	02.85	1984-86	37	10	4		
			Tr	Blackpool	07.87	1987	40	0	10		
CUNNINGHAM, Laurie P.	Holloway	08.03.56	App	Leyton Orient	07.74	1974-76	72	3	15	(W)	E U21-6/ E-6
			Tr	West Bromwich A.	03.77	1976-78	81	5	21		
			Real Madrid (Sp)	Manchester U.	03.83	1982	3	2	1		
			Marseille (Fr)	Leicester C. (N/C)	10.85	1985	13	2	0		
			Charleroi (Bel.)	Wimbledon (N/C)	02.88	1987	6	0	2		
CUNNINGTON, Shaun G.	Bourne	04.01.66	Jnrs	Wrexham	01.84	1982-87	196	3	12	(D)	
			Tr	Grimsby T.	02.88	1987	15	0	2		
CURBISHLEY L.C. (Alan)	Forest Gate	08.11.57	App	West Ham U.	07.75	1974-78	78	7	5	(M)	E Sch Int/ E Yth Int/ E U21-1
			Tr	Birmingham C.	07.79	1979-82	128	2	11		
			Tr	Aston Villa	03.83	1982-84	34	2	1		
			Tr	Charlton Ath.	12.84	1984-86	62	1	6		
			Tr	Brighton & H.A.	08.87	1987	34	0	6		
CURLE, Keith	Bristol	14.11.63	App	Bristol Rov.	11.81	1981-82	21	11	4	(CD)	
			Tr	Torquay U.	11.83	1983	16	0	5		
			Tr	Bristol C.	03.84	1983-87	113	8	1		
			Tr	Reading	10.87	1987	30	0	0		
CURRAN, E. (Terry)	Kinsley	20.03.55	Jnrs	Doncaster Rov.	07.73	1973-75	67	1	11	(W)	
			Tr	Nottingham F.	08.75	1975-76	46	2	12		
			L	Bury	10.77	1977	2	0	0		
			Tr	Derby Co.	11.77	1977	26	0	2		
			Tr	Southampton	08.78	1978	25	1	0		
			Tr	Sheffield Wed.	03.79	1978-81	122	3	35		
			Tr	Sheffield U.	08.82	1982	31	2	3		
			L	Everton	12.82	1982	7	0	1		
			Tr	Everton	09.83	1983-84	12	5	0		
			Tr	Huddersfield T.	07.85	1985	33	1	7		
			Panionis (Greece)	Hull C.	10.86	1986	4	0	0		
			Tr	Sunderland	11.86	1986	9	0	1		
			Grantham	Grimsby T.	11.87	1987	10	2	0		
			Tr	Chesterfield (N/C)	03.88	1987	0	1	0		
CURRIE, David N.	Stockton	27.11.62		Middlesbrough	02.82	1981-85	94	19	31	(F)	
			Tr	Darlington	06.86	1986-87	76	0	33		
			Tr	Barnsley	02.88	1987	15	0	7		
CURRY, Sean P.	Liverpool	13.11.66	App	Liverpool	07.84					(F)	
			Tr	Blackburn Rov.	01.87	1986-87	24	7	7		
CURTIS, Alan T.	Rhondda	16.04.54	Jnrs	Swansea C.	07.72	1972-78	244	4	72	(F)	W U23-1/ W U21-1/ W-35
			Tr	Leeds U.	06.79	1979-80	28	0	5		
			Tr	Swansea C.	12.80	1980-83	82	8	21		
			Tr	Southampton	11.83	1983-85	43	7	5		
			L	Stoke C.	03.86	1985	3	0	0		
			Tr	Cardiff C.	07.86	1986-87	80	2	6		
CUSACK, David S.	Thurcroft	06.06.56	App	Sheffield Wed.	06.74	1975-77	92	3	1	(CD)	
			Tr	Southend U.	09.78	1978-82	186	0	17		
			Tr	Millwall	03.83	1982-84	98	0	9		
			Tr	Doncaster Rov.	07.85	1985-87	100	0	4		
			Tr	Rotherham U.	12.87	1987	18	0	0		
CUSACK, Nicky J.	Maltby	24.12.65	Alvechurch	Leicester C.	06.87	1987	5	11	1	(F)	
CUTLER, Chris P.	Manchester	07.04.64	Jnrs	Bury	08.81	1981-84	8	15	3	(M)	
			Tr	Crewe Alex.	08.85	1985-87	90	9	17		
DAISH, Liam S.	Portsmouth	23.09.68	App	Portsmouth	09.86	1986	1	0	0	(CD)	
DALEY, A.M. (Tony)	Birmingham	18.10.67	App	Aston Villa	05.85	1984-87	55	20	8	(W)	E Yth Int
DALGLISH, Kenny M.	Glasgow	04.03.51	Glasgow Celtic	Liverpool	08.77	1977-87	342	12	118	(F)	S U23-4/S-102/ Footballer of Year 1979 & 1983

Players Names	Birthplace	Date	Previous Club	League Club	Date Sign'd	Seasons Played	Apps	Sub	Gls	Pos.	Misc
DALY, Gerry	Dublin	30.04.54	Bohemians	Manchester U.	04.73	1973-76	107	4	23	(M)	IR U21-1/
			Tr	Derby Co.	03.77	1976-79	111	1	31		IR-46
			Tr	Coventry C.	08.80	1980-83	82	2	15		
			L	Leicester C.	01.83	1982	17	0	1		
			Tr	Birmingham C.	08.84	1984-85	31	1	1		
			Tr	Shrewsbury T.	10.85	1985-86	55	0	8		
			Tr	Stoke C.	03.87	1986-87	17	5	1		
DALZIEL, Ian	South Shields	24.10.62	App	Derby Co.	10.79	1981-82	22	0	4	(FB)	
			Tr	Hereford U.	05.83	1983-87	137	13	8		
DANIEL, Peter W.	Hull	12.12.55	Jnrs	Hull C.	09.73	1974-77	113	0	9	(M)	E U23-3/
			Tr	Wolverhampton W.	05.78	1978-83	157	0	13		E U21-7
			Tr	Sunderland	08.84	1984-85	33	1	0		
			Tr	Lincoln C.	11.85	1985-86	55	0	2		
			Tr	Burnley	07.87	1987	26	1	0		
DANIEL, Ray C.	Luton	10.12.64	App	Luton T.	09.82	1982-85	14	8	4	(M)	
			L	Gillingham	09.83	1983	5	0	0		
			Tr	Hull C.	06.86	1986-87	32	3	2		
DANIELS, Scott	Benfleet	22.11.69	YTS	Colchester U.	06.88	1987	0	1	0		
DANSKIN, Jason	Winsford	28.12.67	YTS	Everton	07.85	1984	1	0	0	(M)	
			Tr	Mansfield T.	03.87	1986	10	0	0		
			L	Hartlepool U.	01.88	1987	3	0	0		
DARBY, Julian T.	Bolton	03.10.67	YTS	Bolton W.	07.86	1985-87	60	5	2	(D)	E Sch Int
DARBY, Lee A.	Salford	20.09.69	YTS	Portsmouth	10.86	1987	1	0	0	(M)	
D'AURIA, David A.	Swansea	26.03.70	YTS	Swansea C. (YTS)	01.87	1987	0	4	0		
DAVENPORT, Peter	Birkenhead	24.03.61	Cammell Laird	Nottingham F.	01.82	1981-85	114	4	54	(F)	E-'B'/E-1
			Tr	Manchester U.	03.86	1985-87	66	18	20		
DAVEY, Simon	Swansea	01.10.70	YTS	Swansea C. (YTS)	08.87	1986-87	4	1	0	(F)	
DAVIES, Alan	Manchester	05.12.61	App	Manchester U.	12.78	1981-83	6	1	0	(W)	W U21-3/
			Tr	Newcastle U.	08.85	1985-86	20	1	1		W-6
			L	Charlton Ath.	03.86	1985	1	0	0		
			L	Carlisle U.	11.86	1986	4	0	1		
			Tr	Swansea C.	07.87	1987	42	0	3		
DAVIES, Gordon J.	Merthyr Tydfil	08.08.55	Merthyr Tydfil	Fulham	03.78	1977-84	244	3	114	(F)	W Sch Int/
			Tr	Chelsea	11.84	1984-85	11	2	6		W-18
			Tr	Manchester C.	10.85	1985-86	31	0	9		
			Tr	Fulham	10.86	1986-87	53	7	19		
DAVIES, Michael J.	Stretford	19.01.66	App	Blackpool	01.84	1983-87	126	10	11	(RB)	
DAVIES, Roy M.	Cardiff	19.08.71	YTS	Newport Co. (YTS)	08.87	1987	0	2	0		
DAVIES, Steven E.	Liverpool	16.07.60	Congleton T.	Port Vale	12.87	1987	1	5	0	(W)	
DAVIS, Darren J.	Sutton in Ashfield	05.02.67	App	Notts Co.	02.85	1983-87	90	2	1	(LB)	E Yth Int
DAVIS, Mark R.	Wallsend	12.10.69	YTS	Darlington (YTS)	08.86	1986	0	2	0		
DAVIS, Paul E.	Newham	31.01.68	App	Q.P.R.	12.85					(D)	
			Tr	Aldershot	08.87	1987	1	0	0		
DAVIS, Paul V.	Camberwell	09.12.61	App	Arsenal	07.79	1979-87	234	13	24	(M)	E U21-11
DAVIS, Steve P.	Birmingham	26.07.65	Stoke C.(App)	Crewe Alex.	08.83	1983-87	140	5	1	(CD)	E Yth Int.
			Tr	Burnley	10.87	1987	33	0	5		
DAVISON, R. (Bobby)	South Shields	17.07.59	Seaham CW	Huddersfield T.	07.80	1980	1	1	0	(F)	
			Tr	Halifax T.	08.81	1981-82	63	0	29		
			Tr	Derby Co.	12.82	1982-87	203	3	83		
			Tr	Leeds U.	11.87	1987	15	1	6		
D'AVRAY, J. Mich	South Africa	19.02.62	App	Ipswich T.	05.79	1979-87	138	29	33	(F)	E U21-2
			L	Leicester C.	02.87	1986	3	0	0		
DAWES, Ian R.	Croydon	22.02.63	App	Q.P.R.	12.80	1981-87	229	0	3	(LB)	E Sch Int
DAWKINS, Derek A.	Edmonton	29.11.59	App	Leicester C.	11.77	1977	3	0	0	(FB)	
			Tr	Mansfield T.	12.78	1978-80	73	0	0		
			Tr	Bournemouth	08.81	1981-82	4	4	0		
				Torquay U.	02.84	1983-87	147	16	7		
DAWS, A. (Tony)	Sheffield	10.09.66	App	Notts Co.	09.84	1984-85	6	2	1	(F)	E Yth Int
			Tr	Sheffield U.	08.86	1986	7	4	3		
			Tr	Scunthorpe U.	06.87	1987	8	2	3		
DAWSON, Alistair	Glasgow	25.02.58	Glasgow Rangers	Blackburn Rov.	08.87	1987	20	2	0	(CD)	S Yth Int/ S U21-8/S-5
DAY, Keith	Grays	29.11.62	Aveley	Colchester U.	08.84	1984-86	113	0	12	(CD)	
			Tr	Leyton Orient	07.87	1987	41	0	3		
DAY, Mervyn R.	Chelmsford	26.06.55	App	West Ham U.	03.73	1973-78	194	0	0	(G)	E Yth Int/
			Tr	Leyton Orient	07.79	1979-82	170	0	0		E U23-5
			Tr	Aston Villa	08.83	1983-84	30	0	0		
			Tr	Leeds U.	01.85	1984-87	136	0	0		
DE MANGE, Ken J.P.	Dublin	03.09.64	Home Farm	Liverpool	08.83					(M)	IR Youth Int/
			L	Scunthorpe U.	12.86	1986	3	0	2		IR-1
			Tr	Leeds U.	09.87	1987	14	1	1		
			Tr	Hull C.	03.88	1987	8	1	0		
DEAKIN, Ray J.	Liverpool	19.06.59	App	Everton	06.77					(D)	
			Tr	Port Vale	08.81	1981	21	2	6		
			Tr	Bolton W.	08.82	1982-84	104	1	2		
			Tr	Burnley	07.85	1985-87	129	0	6		
DEANE, Brian C.	Leeds	07.02.68	Jnrs	Doncaster Rov.	12.85	1985-87	59	7	12	(F)	
DEARY, John S.	Ormskirk	18.10.62	App	Blackpool	03.80	1980-87	250	16	38	(M)	
DEEHAN, John M.	Birmingham	06.08.57	App	Aston Villa	04.75	1975-79	107	3	42	(F)	E Yth Int/
			Tr	West Bromwich A.	09.79	1979-81	44	3	5		E U21-7
			Tr	Norwich C.	12.81	1981-85	158	4	62		
			Tr	Ipswich T.	06.86	1986-87	45	4	11		
DELVE, John F.	Isleworth	27.09.53	App	Q.P.R.	07.71	1972-73	9	6	0	(M)	
			Tr	Plymouth Arg.	07.74	1974-77	127	5	6		
			Tr	Exeter C.	03.78	1977-82	215	0	20		
			Tr	Hereford U.	06.83	1983-86	116	2	11		
				Exeter C. (N/C)	10.87	1987	12	1	1		

Alan Dickens (West Ham United) Another of the "Hammers'" bright young stars. Match Magazine

Alan Devonshire (West Ham United) Now in his 13th season with the "Hammers" after signing from non-leaguers, Southall. Match Magazine

Andy Dibble (Luton Town) Pictured diving at the feet of Wimbledon's Gibson during last season's FA Cup semi-final. Action Images Ltd

Players Names	Birthplace	Date	Source	League Club	Date Sign'd	Seasons Played	Apps	Sub	Gls	Pos.	Misc
DEMPSEY, Mark J.	Manchester	14.01.64	App	Manchester U.	01.82	1985	1	0	0	(M)	
			L	Swindon T.	01.85	1984	5	0	0		
			Tr	Sheffield U.	08.86	1986-87	60	3	8		
DENNIS, Mark E.	Streatham	02.05.61	App	Birmingham C.	08.78	1978-82	130	0	1	(LB)	E Yth Int/
			Tr	Southampton	11.83	1983-86	95	0	2		E U23-3
			Tr	Q.P.R.	05.87	1987	10	1	0		
DENNISON, Robbie	Banbridge (NI)	30.04.63	Glenavon	West Bromwich A.	09.85	1985-86	9	7	1	(M)	NI-2
			Tr	Wolverhampton W.	03.87	1986-87	53	0	6		
DENTON, Edward J.	Oxford	18.05.70	YTS	Oxford U.	07.88	1987	0	2	0	(M)	
DEVANEY, Philip C.	Huyton	12.02.69	App	Burnley	02.87	1986-87	8	5	1	(F)	
DEVINE, Steve B.	Strabane (NI)	11.12.64	App	Wolverhampton W.	12.82					(D)	
			Tr	Derby Co.	03.83	1983-84	10	1	0		
			Tr	Stockport Co.	08.85	1985	2	0	0		
			Tr	Hereford U.	10.85	1985-87	91	4	2		
DEVONSHIRE, Alan E.	Park Royal	13.04.56	Southall	West Ham U.	10.76	1976-87	328	3	29	(M)	Son of Les/E-8
DIAMOND, Anthony J.	Rochdale	23.08.68	YTS	Blackburn Rov.	06.86	1986-87	8	7	2	(F)	
DIBBLE, Andy G.	Cwmbran	08.05.65	App	Cardiff C.	08.82	1981-83	62	0	0	(G)	W Yth Int/
			Tr	Luton T.	07.84	1984-87	30	0	0		W U21-2/
			L	Sunderland	02.86	1985	12	0	0		W-2
			L	Huddersfield T.	03.87	1986	5	0	0		
DICK, Alistair J.	Stirling	25.04.65	App	Tottenham H.	05.82	1981-85	16	1	2	(F)	S Sch Int/S Yth Int
DICKENS, Alan W.	Plaistow	03.09.64	App	West Ham U.	08.82	1982-87	139	16	18	(M)	E Yth Int/E U21-1
DICKENSON, Kevin J.	Hackney	24.11.62	Tottenham H.(App)	Charlton Ath.	04.80	1979-84	72	3	1	(LB)	
			Tr	Leyton Orient	07.85	1985-87	107	0	2		
DICKINSON, Martin J.	Leeds	14.03.63	App	Leeds U.	05.80	1979-85	100	3	2	(CD)	
			Tr	West Bromwich A.	02.86	1985-87	46	4	2		
DICKS, Julian A.	Bristol	08.08.68	App	Birmingham C.	03.86	1985-87	83	6	1	(LB)	Son of Alan/
			Tr	West Ham U.	03.88	1987	8	0	0		E U21-1
DIGBY, Fraser C.	Sheffield	23.04.67	App	Manchester U.	04.85					(G)	E Yth Int/
			Tr	Swindon T.	09.86	1986-87	70	0	0		E U21-4
DIGWEED, Perry M.	Westminster	26.10.59	App	Fulham	08.77	1976-80	15	0	0	(G)	
			Tr	Brighton & H.A.	01.81	1980-86	101	0	0		
			L	Chelsea	02.88	1987	3	0	0		
DILLON, Andrew	Caerphilly	20.01.69	YTS	Newport Co.	07.87	1986-87	15	0	0	(G)	
DILLON, Kevin P.	Sunderland	18.12.59	App	Birmingham C.	07.77	1977-82	181	5	15	(M)	E Yth Int/
			Tr	Portsmouth	03.83	1982-87	182	4	45		E U21-1
DIXON, Andrew	Louth	19.04.68	YTS	Grimsby T.	05.86	1986-87	31	2	0	(FB)	
DIXON, Andrew P.	Hartlepool	05.08.68	Jnrs	Hartlepool U.	07.87	1986-87	7	7	1	(F)	
DIXON, Kerry M.	Luton	24.07.61	Chesham U.	Tottenham H.	07.78					(F)	Son of Mike
			Dunstable T.	Reading	07.80	1980-82	110	6	51		E U21-1/
			Tr	Chelsea	08.83	1983-87	189	1	87		E-8
DIXON, Kevin L.	Consett	27.07.60	Tow Law T.	Carlisle U.	08.83	1983	5	4	0	(W)	
			L	Hartlepool U.	10.83	1983	6	0	3		
			Tr	Hartlepool U.	08.84	1984-86	103	4	26		
			L	Scunthorpe U.	01.86	1985	14	0	2		
			Tr	Scunthorpe U.	08.87	1987	37	4	4		
DIXON, Lee M.	Manchester	17.03.64	Jnrs	Burnley	07.82	1982-83	4	0	0	(FB)	
			Tr	Chester C.	02.84	1983-84	56	1	1		
			Tr	Bury	07.85	1985	45	0	6		
			Tr	Stoke C.	07.86	1986-87	71	0	5		
			Tr	Arsenal	01.88	1987	6	0	0		
DOBBIN, Jim	Dunfermline	17.09.63	Glasgow Celtic	Doncaster Rov.	03.84	1983-86	56	8	9	(M)	
				Barnsley	09.86	1986-87	44	2	6		
DOBBINS, L. Wayne	Bromsgrove	30.08.68	App	West Bromwich A.	08.86	1986-87	8	8	0	(M)	
DOBSON, A.J. (Tony)	Coventry	02.02.69	App	Coventry C.	07.86	1986-87	2	0	0	(D)	
DOBSON, Paul	Hartlepool	17.12.62	Newcastle U. (Jnr)	Hartlepool U.	11.81	1981-82	23	8	8	(F)	
			Horden Colliery	Hartlepool U.	12.83	1983-85	60	20	24		
			Tr	Torquay U.	07.86	1986-87	63	14	38		
DOCKER, Ian	Gravesend	12.09.69	YTS	Gillingham	09.87	1987	0	1	0	(LB)	
DOIG, Russell	Millport	17.01.64	East Stirling	Leeds U.	07.86	1986-87	3	3	0	(W)	
			L	Peterborough U.	10.86	1986	7	0	0		
			Tr	Hartlepool U.	03.88	1987	9	0	0		
DOLAN, Eamonn J.	Dagenham	20.09.67	App	West Ham U.	03.85	1986-87	1	4	0	(F)	IR Yth Int
DOLAN, Pat D.	Dagenham	20.09.67	App	Arsenal	07.85					(D)	IR Yth Int
			Tr	Walsall	08.86	1986	1	0	0		
DONACHIE, Willie	Glasgow	05.10.51	Jnrs	Manchester C.	12.68	1969-79	347	4	2	(LB)	S U23-2/S-35
			Portland Timb. (USA)	Norwich C.	09.81	1981	11	0	0		
			Portland Timb. (USA)	Burnley	11.82	1982-84	60	0	3		
			Tr	Oldham Ath.	07.84	1984-87	135	1	3		
DONAGHY, Mal	Belfast	13.09.57	Larne T.	Luton T.	06.78	1978-87	404	0	16	(CD)	NI U21-1/NI-56
DONALD, Warren R.	Hillingdon	07.10.64	App	West Ham U.	10.82	1983	1	1	0	(M)	E Sch Int
			L	Northampton T.	03.85	1984	11	0	2		
			Tr	Northampton T.	10.85	1985-87	112	1	8		
DONEGAL, Glenville	Northampton	20.06.69	YTS	Northampton T.	08.87	1987	2	8	1	(F)	
DONNELLAN, Leo J.	Brent	19.01.65	App	Chelsea	08.82					(M)	IR U21-1/
			L	Leyton Orient	12.84	1984	6	0	0		Brother of Gary
			Tr	Fulham	08.85	1985-87	46	18	4		
DONOWA, B. Louie	Ipswich	24.09.64	App	Norwich C.	09.82	1982-85	56	6	11	(W)	E U21-3
			L	Stoke C.	12.85	1985	4	0	1		
DORIGO, A.R. (Tony)	Australia	31.12.65	App	Aston Villa	07.83	1983-86	106	5	1	(LB)	E U21-11
			Tr	Chelsea	05.87	1987	40	0	0		
DORNAN, Andy	Aberdeen	19.08.61	Motherwell	Walsall	08.86	1986-87	73	1	0	(RB)	
DOUGLAS, Colin F.	Kilmarnock	09.09.62	Glasgow Celtic(Jnr)	Doncaster Rov.	11.81	1981-85	202	10	48	(FB)	
			Tr	Rotherham U.	07.86	1986-87	82	1	4		

Players Names	Birthplace	Date	Source	League Club	Date Sign'd	Seasons Played	Career Record Apps	Sub	Gls	Pos.	Misc
DOWNES, Chris B.	Sheffield	17.01.69	YTS	Sheffield U.	06.87					(FB)	
			L	Scarborough	03.88	1987	2	0	0		
DOWNES, Wally J.	Hammersmith	09.06.61	App	Wimbledon	01.79	1978-86	194	14	14	(M)	
			L	Newport Co.	12.87	1987	4	0	2		
			Tr	Sheffield U. (N/C)	02.88	1987	6	3	1		
DOWNING, David W.	Bideford	06.10.69	YTS	York C.	06.88	1987	1	0	0	(W)	
DOWNING, Keith G.	Oldbury	23.07.65	Mile Oak Rovers	Notts. Co.	05.84	1984-86	23	0	1	(W)	
			Tr	Wolverhampton W.	07.87	1987	27	7	1		
DOWNS, Greg	Nottingham	13.12.58	App	Norwich C.	12.76	1977-84	162	7	7	(LB)	
			L	Torquay U.	11.77	1977	1	0	1		
			Tr	Coventry C.	07.85	1985-87	106	1	4		
DOYLE, Maurice	Ellesmere Port	17.10.69	YTS	Crewe Alex.	07.88	1987	3	1	0	(M)	
DOYLE, Steve C.	Neath	02.06.58	App	Preston N.E.	06.75	1974-81	178	19	8	(M)	W U21-2
			Tr	Huddersfield T.	09.82	1982-86	158	3	6		
			Tr	Sunderland	09.86	1986-87	64	1	1		
DOZZELL, Jason A.W.	Ipswich	09.12.67	App	Ipswich T.	12.84	1983-87	124	17	9	(M)	EYthInt/E U21-6
DREYER, John B.	Alnwick	11.06.63	Wallingford T.	Oxford U.	01.85	1986-87	57	3	2	(D)	
			L	Torquay U.	12.85	1985	5	0	0		
			L	Fulham	03.86	1985	12	0	2		
DRINKELL, Kevin S.	Grimsby	18.06.60	App	Grimsby T.	06.78	1976-84	242	28	89	(F)	
			Tr	Norwich C.	08.85	1985-87	121	0	50		
DRYDEN, Richard A.	Stroud	14.06.69	YTS	Bristol Rov.	07.87	1986-87	12	0	0	(LB)	
DUBLIN, Keith B.L.	High Wycombe	29.01.66	App	Chelsea	01.84	1983-86	50	1	0	(LB)	E Yth Int
			Tr	Brighton & H.A.	08.87	1987	46	0	5		
DUFFIELD, Peter	Middlesbrough	04.02.69	App	Middlesbrough	11.86					(W)	
			Tr	Sheffield U.	08.87	1987	7	4	1		
			L	Halifax T.	03.88	1987	12	0	6		
DUGGAN, Andrew J.	Bradford	19.09.67	YTS	Barnsley	07.85	1986	1	1	0	(D)	
			L	Rochdale	11.87	1987	3	0	0		
DUNGWORTH, John H.	Rotherham	30.03.55	App	Huddersfield T.	04.72	1972-74	18	5	1	(F)	
			L	Barnsley	10.74	1974	2	1	1		
			Tr	Oldham Ath.	03.75	1975	2	2	0		
			L	Rochdale	03.77	1976	14	0	3		
			Tr	Aldershot	09.77	1977-79	105	0	58		
			Tr	Shrewsbury T.	11.79	1979-81	81	5	17		
			L	Hereford U.	10.81	1981	7	0	3		
			Tr	Mansfield T.	08.82	1982-83	50	6	16		
			Tr	Rotherham U.	02.84	1983-87	177	11	16		
DURIE, Gordon S.	Paisley	06.12.65	Hibernian	Chelsea	04.86	1985-87	45	7	17	(F)	S U21-3/S-1
DUXBURY, Mike	Accrington	01.09.59	App	Manchester U.	10.76	1980-87	246	16	6	(D)	E U21-7/E-10
DYER, Alex C.	West Ham	14.11.65	Watford(App)	Blackpool	10.83	1983-86	101	7	19	(W)	
			Tr	Hull C.	02.87	1986-87	44	1	12		
DYSON, Paul	Birmingham	27.12.59	App	Coventry C.	06.77	1978-82	140	0	5	(CD)	E U21-4
			Tr	Stoke C.	07.83	1983-85	106	0	5		
			Tr	West Bromwich A.	03.86	1985-87	61	0	4		
EARLE, Robbie	Newcastle-u-Lyme	27.01.65	School	Port Vale	07.82	1982-87	163	9	41	(M)	
EATON, Jason C.	Bristol	29.01.69	Jnrs	Bristol Rov.	06.87	1987	0	3	0	(D)	
EBANKS, M. Wayne A.	Birmingham	02.10.64	App	West Bromwich A.	04.82	1983	6	1	0	(D)	
			L	Stoke C.	08.84	1984	10	0	0		
			Tr	Port Vale	03.85	1984-86	36	3	0		
			Tr	Cambridge U.(N/C)	08.87	1987	3	1	0		
ECKHARDT, Jeff E.	Sheffield	07.10.65	Jnrs	Sheffield U.	08.84	1984-87	73	1	2	(D)	
			Tr	Fulham	11.87	1987	29	0	1		
EDMONDS, Neil A.	Accrington	18.10.68	YTS	Oldham Ath.	06.86	1986-87	3	2	0	(LB)	
EDWARDS, Dean S.	Wolverhampton	25.02.62	App	Shrewsbury T.	02.80	1979-81	7	6	1	(F)	
			Telford U.	Wolverhampton W.	10.85	1985-86	28	3	9		
			Tr	Exeter C.	03.87	1986-87	51	3	17		
EDWARDS, Keith	Stockton	16.07.57	Sch	Sheffield U.	08.75	1975-77	64	6	29	(F)	
			Tr	Hull C.	08.78	1978-81	130	2	57		
			Tr	Sheffield U.	09.81	1981-85	183	8	114		
			Tr	Leeds U.	08.86	1986-87	28	10	6		
			Aberdeen	Hull C.	03.88	1987	9	0	3		
EDWARDS, Levi W.	St. Lucia (WI)	10.09.61		Crewe Alex.	08.85	1985	10	3	0	(M)	
				Altrincham	09.86	1986-87	40	9	5		
EDWARDS, Neil A.	Rowley Regis	14.03.66	Oldswinford	Wolverhampton W.	08.85	1985-87	26	3	7	(M)	
EDWARDS, Paul R.	Birkenhead	23.12.63	Altrincham	Crewe Alex.	01.88	1987	10	3	1	(FB)	
EDWARDS, Robert	Manchester	23.02.70	YTS	Crewe Alex.	07.88	1987	4	2	1	(M)	
ELEY, Kevin	Mexborough	04.03.68	App	Rotherham U.	03.86	1983-86	3	10	0	(W)	
			Tr	Chesterfield	08.87	1987	30	6	2		
ELI, Roger	Bradford	11.09.65	App	Leeds U.	09.83	1984-85	1	1	0	(M)	
			Tr	Wolverhampton W.	01.86	1985-86	16	2	0		
			Cambridge U.(N/C)	Crewe Alex.(N/C)	09.87	1987	20	7	1		
ELKINS, Gary	Wallingford	04.05.66	App	Fulham	12.83	1984-87	71	1	0	(D)	E Yth Int
ELLIOTT, Paul M.	Lewisham	18.03.64	App	Charlton Ath.	03.81	1981-82	61	2	1	(CD)	E Yth Int/E U21-3/
			Tr	Luton T.	03.83	1982-85	63	3	4		to Pisa (It.) 7.87
			Tr	Aston Villa	12.85	1985-86	56	1	7		
ELLIOTT, Shaun	Haydon Bridge	26.01.57	App	Sunderland	01.75	1976-85	316	5	11	(CD)	E 'B'-
			Tr	Norwich C.	08.86	1986-87	29	2	2		
ELLIOTT, Steve B.	Haltwhistle	15.09.58	App	Nottingham F.	09.76	1978	4	0	0	(F)	
			Tr	Preston N.E.	03.79	1978-83	202	6	70		
			Tr	Luton T.	07.84	1984	12	0	3		
			Tr	Walsall	12.84	1984-85	68	1	21		
			Tr	Bolton W.	07.86	1986-87	54	3	10		
ELLIS, A.J. (Tony)	Salford	20.10.64	Horwich RMI	Oldham Ath.	08.86	1986-87	5	3	0	(F)	
			Tr	Preston N.E.	10.87	1987	20	4	4		
ELLIS, Mark E.	Bradford	06.01.62	Jnrs	Bradford C.	08.80	1980-87	183	24	29	(W)	

Players Names	Birthplace	Date	Source	League Club	Date Sign'd	Seasons Played	Apps	Sub	Gls	Pos.	Misc
ELSEY, Karl W.	Swansea	20.11.58	Pembroke Bor	Q.P.R.	01.79	1978-79	6	1	0	(M)	
			Tr	Newport Co.	07.80	1980-83	114	9	15		
			Tr	Cardiff C.	09.83	1983-84	59	0	5		
			Tr	Gillingham	08.85	1985-87	126	2	13		
EMERSON, Dean	Salford	27.12.62		Stockport Co.	02.82	1981-84	156	0	7	(M)	
			Tr	Rotherham U.	07.85	1985-86	55	0	8		
			Tr	Coventry C.	10.86	1986-87	38	1	0		
EMMANUEL, J. Gary	Swansea	01.02.54	App	Birmingham C.	07.71	1974-78	61	10	6	(M)	W U23-1
			Tr	Bristol Rov.	12.78	1978-80	59	6	2		
			Tr	Swindon T.	07.81	1981-83	109	2	8		
			Tr	Newport Co.	07.84	1984	12	0	0		
			Tr	Bristol C.(N/C)	08.85	1985	2	0	0		
			Tr	Swansea C.	08.85	1985-87	104	7	5		
EMSON, Paul D.	Lincoln	22.10.58	Brigg T.	Derby Co.	09.78	1978-82	112	15	13	(W)	
			Tr	Grimsby T.	08.83	1983-85	90	7	15		
			Tr	Wrexham	07.86	1986-87	42	7	5		
ENDERSBY, Scott A.G.	Lewisham	20.02.62	App	Ipswich T.	03.79					(G)	E Yth Int
			Tr	Tranmere Rov.	07.81	1981-82	79	0	0		
			Tr	Swindon T.	08.83	1983-85	85	0	0		
			Tr	Carlisle U.	11.85	1985-86	52	0	0		
			Tr	York C.	07.87	1987	34	0	0		
			L	Cardiff C.	12.87	1987	4	0	0		
ENGLISH, A.K.(Tony)	Luton	19.10.66	Coventry C.(App)	Colchester U.	12.84	1984-87	140	2	22	(M)	Brother of Tom/ E Yth Int
ENTWISTLE, Wayne P.	Bury	06.08.58	App	Bury	08.76	1976-77	25	6	7	(F)	E Yth Int
			Tr	Sunderland	11.77	1977-79	43	2	13		
			Tr	Leeds U.	10.79	1979	7	1	2		
			Tr	Blackpool	11.80	1980-81	27	5	6		
			Tr	Crewe Alex.	03.82	1981	11	0	0		
			Tr	Wimbledon	07.82	1982	4	5	3		
			Grays Ath.	Bury	08.83	1983-84	80	3	32		
			Tr	Carlisle U.	06.85	1985	8	1	2		
			Tr	Bolton W.	10.85	1985	5	3	0		
			L	Burnley	08.86	1986	6	2	2		
			Tr	Stockport Co.	10.86	1986-87	38	11	8		
EVANS, Allan	Dunfermline	12.10.56	Dunfermline Ath.	Aston Villa	05.77	1977-87	348	5	51	(CD)	S-4
EVANS, A. Clive	Birkenhead	01.05.57	App	Tranmere Rov.	05.75	1976-80	176	3	27	(W)	
			Tr	Wigan Ath.	07.81	1981	29	3	2		
			Tr	Crewe Alex.	08.82	1982	26	2	7		
			Tr	Stockport Co.	08.83	1983-87	158	2	23		
			Tr	Lincoln C.	N/L						
EVANS, David G.	West Bromwich	20.05.58	App	Aston Villa	02.76	1978	2	0	0	(CD)	
			Tr	Halifax T.	06.79	1979-83	218	0	9		
			Tr	Bradford C.	06.84	1984-87	165	0	3		
EVANS, Gareth J.	Coventry	14.01.67	App	Coventry C.	01.85	1985-86	5	2	0	(F)	to Hibernian 2.88
			Tr	Rotherham U.	10.86	1986-87	62	1	13		
EVANS, Paul A.	Brentwood	14.09.64	Jnrs	Cardiff C.	09.82	1983	0	2	0	(F)	
			Brecon Cor.	Newport Co.(N/C)	07.87	1987	9	1	2		
EVANS, Stewart J.	Maltby	15.11.60	App	Rotherham U.	11.78					(F)	
			Gainsborough Trin	Sheffield U.	11.80						
			Tr	Wimbledon	03.82	1981-85	165	10	50		
			Tr	West Bromwich A.	08.86	1986	13	1	1		
			Tr	Plymouth Arg.	03.87	1986-87	35	7	10		
EVANS, Terry W.	Hammersmith	12.04.65	Hillingdon Bor	Brentford	07.85	1985-87	48	1	5	(CD)	
EVES, Mel J.	Wednesbury	10.09.56		Wolverhampton W.	07.75	1977-83	169	11	44	(F)	E 'B'
			L	Huddersfield T.	03.84	1983	7	0	4		
				Sheffield U.	12.84	1984-85	25	1	10		
			Tr	Gillingham	08.86	1986-87	19	8	9		
			L	Mansfield T.	10.87	1987	3	0	0		
FAIRBROTHER, Ian A.	Bootle	02.10.66	App	Liverpool	07.84					(M)	
			Tr	Bury	02.87	1986-87	16	10	3		
			L	Wrexham	10.87	1987	7	0	0		
FAIRCLOUGH, Chris H.	Nottingham	12.04.64	App	Nottingham F.	10.81	1982-86	102	5	1	(CD)	E U21-7
			Tr	Tottenham H.	08.87	1987	40	0	4		
FAIRCLOUGH, Wayne R.	Nottingham	27.04.68	App	Notts. Co.	04.86	1985-87	20	23	0	(D)	Brother of Chris
FAIRWEATHER, Carlton	Camberwell	22.09.61	Tooting & Mitcham	Wimbledon	12.84	1984-87	66	14	21	(W)	
FALCO, Mark P.	Hackney	22.10.60	App	Tottenham H.	07.78	1978-86	162	12	68	(F)	E Yth Int
			L	Chelsea	11.82	1982	3	0	0		
			Tr	Watford	10.86	1986	33	0	14		
			Glasgow Rangers	Q.P.R.	12.87	1987	15	4	5		
FARNABY, Craig	Hartlepool	08.08.67	Jnrs	Hartlepool U.(N/C)	10.84	1984	5	0	0	(M)	
			Tr	Middlesbrough	11.85						
			Tr	Halifax T.	09.86	1986	7	3	1		
			Shotton Com.	Stockport Co.	09.87	1987	17	5	1		
FARNWORTH, Simon	Chorley	28.10.63	App	Bolton W.	09.81	1983-85	113	0	0	(G)	
			L	Stockport Co.	09.86	1986	10	0	0		
			L	Tranmere Rov.	01.87	1986	7	0	0		
			Tr	Bury	03.87	1986-87	53	0	0		
FARRELL, Andrew J.	Colchester	07.10.65	App	Colchester U.	09.83	1983-86	98	7	5	(W)	
			Tr	Burnley	08.87	1987	45	0	3		
FARRELL, Sean P.	Watford	28.02.69	App	Luton T.	02.87					(F)	
			L	Colchester U.	03.88	1987	4	5	1		
FASHANU, John	Kensington	18.09.62	Cambridge U.(Jnr)	Norwich C.	10.79	1981-82	6	1	1	(F)	Brother of Justin
			L	Crystal Palace	08.83	1983	1	0	0		
			Tr	Lincoln C.	09.83	1983-84	31	5	11		
			Tr	Millwall	11.84	1984-85	50	0	12		
			Tr	Wimbledon	03.86	1985-87	83	1	28		
FAZACKERLEY, Derek W.	Preston	05.11.51	App	Blackburn Rov.	10.69	1970-86	593	3	24	(CD)	
			Tr	Chester C.	01.87	1986-87	66	0	0		
FEARON, Ron T.	Romford	19.11.60	Dover T.	Reading	02.80	1980-82	61	0	0	(G)	
			Sutton U.	Ipswich T.	08.87	1987	10	0	0		

Mel Donaghy (Luton Town) Solid "Hatters" defender. Match Magazine

Mark Falco (Q.P.R.) After a brief stint with Glasgow Rangers, he came back to London to score his goals, this time with the "R's". Match Magazine

Kerry Dixon (Chelsea) Has yet to recapture the goalscoring touch of a season or two ago. Match Magazine

Tony Dorigo (Chelsea) Australian born full-back signed from Aston Villa before last season got under way. Match Magazine

Players Names	Birthplace	Date	Previous Club	League Club	Date Sign'd	Seasons Played	Apps	Sub	Gls	Pos	Misc
FEE, Greg P.	Halifax	24.06.64	YTS	Bradford C.	05.83	1982-83	6	1	0	(CD)	
			Boston U.	Sheffield Wed.	08.87	1987	7	9	0		
FEELEY, Andy J.	Hereford	30.09.61	App	Hereford U.	08.79	1978-79	50	1	3	(FB)	
			Trowbridge T.	Leicester C.	02.84	1983-86	74	2	0		
			Tr	Brentford	08.87	1987	27	7	0		
FELGATE, David W.	Blaenau Ffestiniog	04.03.60	Jnrs	Bolton W.	08.78					(G)	W Sch int/W-1
			L	Rochdale	10.78	1978	35	0	0		
			L	Crewe Alex	09.79	1979	14	0	0		
			L	Rochdale	03.80	1979	12	0	0		
			Tr	Lincoln C.	09.80	1980-84	198	0	0		
			L	Cardiff C.	11.84	1984	4	0	0		
			Tr	Grimsby T.	02.85	1984-86	36	0	0		
			L	Bolton W.	02.86	1985	15	0	0		
			Tr	Bolton W.	02.87	1986-87	66	0	0		
FENWICK, Terry W.	Seaham	17.11.59	App	Crystal Palace	12.76	1977-80	62	8	0	(D)	E Yth Int/
			Tr	Q.P.R.	12.80	1980-87	256	0	33		E U21-11/E-20
			Tr	Tottenham H.	12.87	1987	17	0	0		
FERDINAND, Leslie	Paddington	18.12.66	Hayes	Q.P.R.	04.87	1986-87	1	2	0	(F)	
			L	Brentford	03.88	1987	3	0	0		
FEREBEE, Stewart R.	Carshalton	06.09.60	Harrogate T.	York C.	07.79	1979-80	7	6	0	(F)	
			Whitley Bay	Darlington(N/C)	03.87	1986	9	0	0		
			Tr	Halifax T.	07.87	1987	6	6	0		
FEREDAY, Wayne	Warley	16.06.63	App	Q.P.R.	09.80	1980-87	138	28	21	(W)	E U21-5
FIFE, Adrian	Peterborough	13.09.69	YTS	Peterborough U.(YTS)	08.86	1986-87	1	1	0	(F)	
FILLERY, Mike C.	Mitcham	17.09.60	App	Chelsea	08.78	1978-82	156	5	32	(M)	E Sch Int/E Yth Int
			Tr	Q.P.R.	08.83	1983-86	95	2	9		
			Tr	Portsmouth	07.87	1987	17	1	0		
FINDLAY, Jake W.	Blairgowrie	13.07.54	App	Aston Villa	06.72	1973-76	14	0	0	(G)	
			Tr	Luton T.	11.78	1978-84	167	0	0		
			L	Barnsley	09.83	1983	6	0	0		
			L	Derby Co.	01.84	1983	1	0	0		
			L	Swindon T.	07.85	1985	4	0	0		
			Tr	Portsmouth	01.86							
			Tr	Coventry C.	08.86							
FINNEY, Kevin	Newcastle-u-Lyme	19.10.69	YTS	Port Vale	06.87	1987	11	4	0	(M)	
FINNIGAN, A. (Tony)	Wimbledon	17.10.62	App	Fulham	10.80					(M)	E Yth Int
			Corinthian Casuals	Crystal Palace	02.85	1984-87	94	11	10		
FISHENDEN, Paul	Hillingdon	02.08.63	App	Wimbledon	10.81	1981-85	57	18	25	(F)	
			L	Fulham	12.85	1985	3	0	0		
			L	Millwall	09.86	1986	3	0	1		
			L	Leyton Orient	10.86	1986	4	0	0		
			Tr	Crewe Alex.	02.88	1987	15	0	3		
FITZPATRICK, Paul J.	Oxford	05.10.65	Tranmere Rov. (YTS)	Bolton W.	03.85	1984-85	13	1	0	(M)	
			Tr	Bristol C.	08.86	1986-87	40	3	7		
FLECK, Robert	Glasgow	11.08.65	Glasgow Rangers	Norwich C.	12.87	1987	18	0	7	(F)	S Yth Int/S U21-6
FLEMING, J. Gary	Derry (NI)	17.02.67	App	Nottingham F.	11.84	1984-87	71	3	0	(RB)	NI-7
FLEMING, Mark J.	Hammersmith	11.08.69	YTS	Q.P.R.	01.88	1987	0	2	0		
FLEMING, Paul	Halifax	06.09.67	YTS	Halifax T.	09.85	1985-87	34	3	0	(LB)	
FLOUNDERS, Andy J.	Hull	13.12.63	App	Hull C.	12.81	1980-86	126	33	54	(F)	
			Tr	Scunthorpe U.	03.87	1986-87	60	0	30		
FLOWERS, Tim D.	Kenilworth	03.02.67	App	Wolverhampton W.	08.84	1984-85	63	0	0	(G)	Son of Ron/
			Tr	Southampton	06.86	1986-87	18	0	0		E Yth Int/E U21-3
			L	Swindon T.	03.87	1986	2	0	0		
			L	Swindon T.	11.87	1987	5	0	0		
FLYNN, Brian	Port Talbot	12.10.55	App	Burnley	10.72	1973-77	115	5	8	(M)	W Sch Int/
			Tr	Leeds U.	11.77	1977-82	152	2	11		W U23-2/W-66
			L	Burnley	03.82	1981	2	0	0		
			Tr	Burnley	11.82	1982-84	76	4	11		
			Tr	Cardiff C.	11.84	1984-85	32	0	0		
			Tr	Doncaster Rov.	11.85	1985	27	0	0		
			Tr	Bury	07.86	1986	19	0	0		
			Limerick C.(IR)	Doncaster Rov. (N/C)	08.87	1987	18	6	1		
			Tr	Wrexham(N/C)	02.88	1987	17	0	1		
FLYNN, Michael A.	Oldham	23.02.69	App	Oldham Ath.	02.87	1987	29	2	1	(CD)	
FOLEY, Steve	Liverpool	04.10.62	App	Liverpool	09.80					(M)	
			L	Fulham	12.83	1983	2	1	0		
			Tr	Grimsby T.	08.84	1984	31	0	2		
			Tr	Sheffield U.	08.85	1985-86	56	10	14		
			Tr	Swindon T.	06.87	1987	35	0	4		
FORBES, Graeme S.A.	Forfar	29.07.58	Motherwell	Walsall	09.86	1986-87	84	0	6	(CD)	
FORD, Gary	York	08.02.61	App	York C.	02.79	1978-86	359	7	52	(W)	
			Tr	Leicester C.	06.87	1987	15	1	2		
			Tr	Port Vale	12.87	1987	23	0	3		
FORD, Michael P.	Bristol	09.02.66	App	Leicester C.	02.84					(D)	Son of Anthony
			Devizes T.	Cardiff C.	09.84	1984-87	144	1	13		
FORD, Tony	Grimsby	14.05.59	App	Grimsby T.	05.77	1975-85	321	33	54	(W)	
			L	Sunderland	03.86	1985	8	1	1		
			Tr	Stoke C.	07.86	1986-87	85	0	13		
FOREMAN, Darren	Southampton	12.02.68	Sch	Barnsley	08.86	1986-87	22	3	5	(F)	E Sch Int
FORMAN, Matthew C.	Evesham	08.09.67	App	Aston Villa	09.85					(M)	
			Tr	Wolverhampton W.	08.86	1986	24	1	4		
FORREST, Craig L.	Canada	30.09.67	App	Ipswich T.	08.85					(G)	
			L	Colchester U.	03.88	1987	11	0	0		
FORREST, Gerry	Stockton	21.01.57	South Bank	Rotherham U.	02.77	1977-85	357	0	8	(RB)	
			Tr	Southampton	12.85	1985-87	96	1	0		
FORSYTH, Mike E.	Liverpool	20.03.66	App	West Bromwich A.	11.83	1983-85	28	1	0	(LB)	E Yth Int/E U21-1
			Tr	Derby Co.	03.86	1986-87	80	0	4		
FOSTER, Colin J.	Chislehurst	16.07.64	App	Leyton Orient	02.82	1981-86	173	1	10	(CD)	
			Tr	Nottingham F.	02.87	1986-87	45	3	3		

Terry Fenwick (Tottenham Hotspur) Pictured in Q.P.R.'s colours before moving across London last December.
Match Magazine

Steve Foster (Luton Town) Key player in the heart of the Town's defence.
Match Magazine

Ron Futcher (Bradford City) Still takes goals regularly and was the club's leading scorer last season.
Match Magazine

Wayne Fereday (Q.P.R.) A regular whether it be in defence or up front.
Match Magazine

Players Names	Birthplace	Date	Source	League Club	Date Sign'd	Seasons Played	Career Record Apps	Sub	Gls	Pos.	Misc
FOSTER, George W.	Plymouth	26.09.56	App	Plymouth Arg.	09.74	1973-81	201	11	6	(CD)	
			L	Torquay U.	10.76	1976	6	0	3		
			L	Exeter C.	12.81	1981	28	0	0		
			Tr	Derby Co.	06.82	1982	30	0	0		
			Tr	Mansfield T.	08.83	1983-87	221	0	0		
FOSTER, Steve B.	Portsmouth	24.09.57	App	Portsmouth	09.75	1975-78	101	8	6	(CD)	E U21-1/E-3
			Tr	Brighton & H.A.	07.79	1979-83	171	1	6		
			Tr	Aston Villa	03.84	1983-84	15	0	3		
			Tr	Luton T.	11.84	1984-87	127	0	8		
FOSTER, Wayne P.	Leigh	11.09.63	App	Bolton W.	08.81	1981-84	92	13	13	(M)	E Yth Int
			Tr	Preston N.E.	06.85	1985	25	6	3		
FOWLER, Lee E.	Nottingham	26.01.69	YTS	Stoke C.	07.88	1987	0	1	0	(FB)	
FOX, Peter D.	Scunthorpe	05.07.57	App	Sheffield Wed.	06.75	1972-76	49	0	0	(G)	
			L	Barnsley	12.77	1977	1	0	0		
			Tr	Stoke C.	03.78	1978-87	288	0	0		
FOX, Ruel A.	Ipswich	14.01.68	App	Norwich C.	01.86	1986-87	34	3	2	(W)	
FOYLE, Martin J.	Salisbury	02.05.63	App	Southampton	08.80	1982-83	6	6	1	(F)	
			Tr	Aldershot	07.84	1984-86	98	0	35		
			Tr	Oxford U.	03.87	1986-87	33	4	10		
FRAIN, David	Sheffield	11.10.62	Dronfield U.	Sheffield U.	09.85	1985-87	35	9	6	(W)	
FRAIN, John W.	Birmingham	08.10.68	App	Birmingham C.	10.86	1985-87	15	5	3	(M)	
FRANCE, M. Paul	Holmfirth	10.09.68	YTS	Huddersfield T.	06.87	1987	5	3	0	(CD)	
FRANCIS, Gerry C.J.	Chiswick	06.12.51	App	Q.P.R.	06.69	1969-78	289	4	53	(M)	Son of George
			Tr	Crystal Palace	07.79	1979-80	59	0	7		E U23-6/E-12
			Tr	Q.P.R.	02.81	1980-81	17	0	4		
			Tr	Coventry C.	02.82	1981-82	50	0	2		
			Tr	Exeter C.	08.83	1983	28	0	3		
			Tr	Cardiff C. (N/C)	09.84	1984	7	0	0		
			Tr	Swansea C. (N/C)	10.84	1984	3	0	0		
			Tr	Portsmouth (N/C)	11.84	1984	3	0	0		
			Tr	Bristol Rov. (N/C)	09.85	1985-87	33	0	0		
FRANCIS, Steve S.	Billericay	29.05.64	App	Chelsea	04.82	1981-85	71	0	0	(G)	E Yth Int
			Tr	Reading	02.87	1986-87	48	0	0		
FRANCIS, Trevor J.	Plymouth	19.04.54	App	Birmingham C.	05.71	1970-78	278	2	118	(F)	E-43/E U23-5/
			Tr	Nottingham F.	02.79	1978-81	69	1	28		E Yth Int
			Tr	Manchester C.	09.81	1981	26	0	12		
			Glasgow Rangers	Q.P.R.	03.88	1987	8	1	0		
FRANKLIN, Neil J.	Lincoln	10.03.69	YTS	Lincoln C. (YTS)	09.86	1986	15	0	0	(FB)	
FRANKLIN, Paul L.	Hainault	05.10.63	App	Watford	08.81	1982-86	32	0	0	(CD)	
			L	Shrewsbury T.	10.86	1986	6	0	0		
			L	Swindon T.	11.86	1986	5	0	1		
			Tr	Reading	06.87	1987	3	1	0		
FREESTONE, Roger	Caerleon	19.08.68	YTS	Newport Co.	04.86	1986	13	0	0	(G)	
			Tr	Chelsea	04.87	1986-87	21	0	0		
FUCCILLO, P. ('Lil')	Bedford	02.05.56	App	Luton T.	07.74	1974-82	153	7	24	(M)	
			Tulsa R. (USA)	Southend U.	12.83	1983-84	40	5	5		
			Tr	Peterborough U.(N/C)	08.85	1985-86	82	0	3		
			Malta	Cambridge U.(N/C)	01.88	1987	18	1	2		
FULBROOK, Gary	Bath	04.05.66	YTS	Swindon T.	09.84	1984	0	1	0	(D)	
			Bath C.	Carlisle U.	09.87	1987	6	0	0		
FURPHY, Keith	Stockton	30.07.58	Sheffield U. (App)	Q.P.R.	10.76					(LW)	Son of Ken
			Baltimore (USA)	Plymouth Arg. (N/C)	08.87	1987	6	0	1		
FUTCHER, Paul	Chester	25.09.56	App	Chester C.	01.74	1972-73	20	0	0	(CD)	Twin Brother of Ron
			Tr	Luton T.	06.74	1974-77	131	0	1		E U21-11
			Tr	Manchester C.	06.78	1978-79	36	1	0		
			Tr	Oldham Ath	08.80	1980-82	98	0	1		
			Tr	Derby Co.	01.83	1982-83	35	0	0		
			Tr	Barnsley	03.84	1983-87	160	0	0		
FUTCHER, Ron	Chester	25.09.56	App	Chester C.	01.74	1973	4	0	0	(F)	Twin brother of Paul
			Tr	Luton T.	06.74	1974-77	116	4	40		
			Tr	Manchester C.	08.78	1978	10	7	7		
			NAC Breda (Neth)	Barnsley	12.84	1984	18	1	6		
			Tr	Oldham Ath	07.85	1985-86	65	0	30		
			Tr	Bradford C.	03.87	1986-87	35	7	18		
FYFE, Tony	Carlisle	23.02.62	Penrith	Carlisle U.(N/C)	09.87	1987	5	5	4	(F)	
GABBIADINI, Marco	Nottingham	20.01.68	App	York C.	09.85	1984-87	42	18	14	(F)	
			Tr	Sunderland	09.87	1987	35	0	21		
GABBIADINI, Ricardo	Newport	11.03.70	YTS	York C.	06.88	1987	0	1	0	(F)	Brother of Marco
GAGE, Kevin W.	Chiswick	21.04.64	App	Wimbledon	01.82	1980-86	135	33	15	(RB)	E Yth Int
			Tr	Aston Villa	07.87	1987	44	0	2		
GAGE, Wakely A.J.	Northampton	05.05.58	Desborough T.	Northampton T.	10.79	1979-84	215	3	17	(CD)	
			Tr	Chester C.	08.85	1985	17	0	1		
			Tr	Peterborough U.	11.85	1985-86	73	0	1		
			Tr	Crewe Alex.	06.87	1987	39	1	1		
GALE, A.P. (Tony)	Westminster	19.11.59	App	Fulham	08.77	1977-83	277	0	19	(CD)	E Yth Int/
			Tr	West Ham U.	07.84	1984-87	127	2	2		E U21-1
GALLACHER, Bernard	Johnstone	22.03.67	App	Aston Villa	03.85	1986-87	44	0	0	(LB)	
GALLAGHER, Jackie C.	Wisbech	06.04.58	March T.	Lincoln C.	02.76	1976	1	0	0	(F)	
			Kings Lynn	Peterborough U.	04.80	1979-80	11	2	1		
			Hong Kong	Torquay U(N/C)	08.82	1982	38	4	7		
			Wisbech T.	Peterborough U.	08.85	1985-86	78	4	19		
			Tr	Wolverhampton W.	06.87	1987	6	13	3		
GALLIERS, Steve	Preston	21.08.57	Chorley	Wimbledon	06.77	1977-81	148	7	10	(M)	
			Tr	Crystal Palace	10.81	1981	8	5	0		
			Tr	Wimbledon	08.82	1982-87	145	1	5		
			L	Bristol C.	02.87	1986	9	0	0		
			Tr	Bristol C.	09.87	1987	35	0	6		
GALLOWAY, Mike	Oswestry	30.05.65		Mansfield T.	09.83	1983-85	39	15	3	(CD)	S Yth Int/
			Tr	Halifax T.	02.86	1985-87	79	0	5		to Hearts 11.87

Players Names	Birthplace	Date	Source	League Club	Date Sign'd	Seasons Played	Apps	Sub	Gls	Pos.	Misc
GALVIN, A. (Tony)	Huddersfield	12.07.56	Goole T.	Tottenham H.	01.78	1978-86	194	7	20	(W)	Brother of Chris/
			Tr	Sheffield Wed.	08.87	1987	12	6	0		IR-23
GANNON, John S.	Wimbledon	18.12.66	App	Wimbledon	12.84	1985-87	13	3	2	(M)	
			L	Crewe Alex.	12.86	1986	14	1	0		
GARDINER, Mark C.	Cirencester	25.12.66	App	Swindon T.	09.84	1983-86	7	3	1	(W)	
			Tr	Torquay U.	02.87	1986-87	37	12	4		
GARDNER, Stephen G.	Middlesbrough	03.07.68	App	Manchester U.	07.86					(D)	
			Tr	Burnley	07.87	1987	41	1	0		
GARNER, Andy	Stonebroom (Dy.)	08.03.66	App	Derby Co.	12.83	1983-87	48	23	17	(F)	
GARNER, Paul	Doncaster	01.12.55	App	Huddersfield T.	12.72	1972-75	96	0	2	(LB)	E Yth Int
			Tr	Sheffield U.	11.75	1975-83	248	3	7		
			L	Gillingham	09.83	1983	5	0	0		
			Tr	Mansfield T.	09.84	1984-87	101	7	8		
GARNER, Simon	Boston	23.11.59	App	Blackburn Rov.	11.77	1978-87	346	14	124	(F)	
GARNETT, Shaun M.	Wallasey	22.11.69	YTS	Tranmere Rov.	06.88	1987	0	1	0	(D)	
GARTON, W.F.(Billy)	Salford	15.03.65	App	Manchester U.	03.83	1984-87	26	1	0	(D)	
			L	Birmingham C.	03.86	1985	5	0	0		
GASCOIGNE, Paul J.	Gateshead	27.05.67	App	Newcastle U.	05.85	1984-87	83	9	20	(M)	E U21-9
GATES, Eric L.	Ferryhill	28.06.55	App	Ipswich T.	10.72	1973-74	267	29	73	(F)	Brother of Bill/
			Tr	Sunderland	08.85	1985-87	102	6	33		E-2
GATTING, Steve P.	Willesden	29.05.59	App	Arsenal	03.77	1978-80	50	8	5	(CD)	Brother of Mike
			Tr	Brighton & H.A.	09.81	1981-87	222	3	15		(Cricketer)
GAUGHAN, Steve E.	Doncaster	14.04.70	Hatfield Main	Doncaster Rov.	09.87	1987	0	4	0	(W)	
GAVIN, Mark W.	Baillieston	10.12.63	App	Leeds U.	12.81	1982-84	20	10	3	(LW)	
			L	Hartlepool U.	03.85	1984	7	0	0		
			Tr	Carlisle U.	07.85	1985	12	1	1		
			Tr	Bolton W.	03.86	1985-86	48	1	3		
			Tr	Rochdale	08.87	1987	23	0	6		to Hearts 1.88
GAYLE, Brian W.	Kingston	06.03.65	Tooting & Mitcham	Wimbledon	10.84	1984-87	76	7	3	(CD)	
GAYLE, Howard	Liverpool	18.05.58		Liverpool	11.77	1980	3	1	1	(W)	E U21-3
			L	Fulham	01.80	1979	14	0	0		
			L	Newcastle U.	11.82	1982	8	0	2		
			Tr	Birmingham C.	01.83	1982-83	45	1	9		
			Tr	Sunderland	08.84	1984-85	39	9	4		
			Dallas (USA)	Stoke C.	03.87	1986	4	2	2		
			Tr	Blackburn Rov.	07.87	1987	10	3	1		
GAYNOR, Tom	Limerick	29.01.63	Limerick C.	Doncaster Rov.	12.86	1986-87	28	4	7	(F)	
			Tr	Nottingham F.	10.87	1987	10	2	3		
GEDDIS, David	Carlisle	12.03.58	App	Ipswich T.	08.75	1976-78	26	17	5	(F)	E Yth Int
			L	Luton T.	02.77	1976	9	4	4		
			Tr	Aston Villa	09.79	1979-82	43	4	12		
			L	Luton T.	12.82	1982	4	0	0		
			Tr	Barnsley	09.83	1983-84	45	0	24		
			Tr	Birmingham C.	12.84	1984-86	45	1	18		
			L	Brentford	11.86	1986	4	0	0		
			Tr	Shrewsbury T.	02.87	1986-87	29	1	9		
GEE, Philip J.	Pelsall	19.12.64	Gresley Rov.	Derby Co.	09.85	1985-87	77	6	23	(F)	
GENNOE, Terry W.	Shrewsbury	16.03.53	Bricklayers Spts	Bury	06.73	1972-73	3	0	0	(G)	
			Tr	Halifax T.	05.75	1975-77	78	0	0		
			Tr	Southampton	02.78	1978-79	36	0	0		
			L	Crystal Palace	01.81	1980	3	0	0		
			Tr	Blackburn Rov.	08.81	1981-87	217	0	0		
GENOVESE, Domenico	Peterborough	02.02.61	Cambridge C.	Peterborough U.(N/C)	03.88	1987	1	0	0	(F)	
GERNON, F.A.J.(Irvin)	Birmingham	30.12.62	App	Ipswich T.	01.80	1981-86	76	0	0	(FB)	E Yth Int/E U21-1
			L	Northampton T.	11.86	1986	9	0	0		
			Tr	Gillingham	03.87	1986-87	33	2	1		
GIBB, Dean A.	Newcastle	26.10.66	Brandon U.	Hartlepool U.	07.86	1986-87	32	16	3	(M)	
GIBBINS, Roger G.	Enfield	06.09.55	App	Tottenham H.	12.72					(M)	Son of Eddie
			Tr	Oxford U.	08.75	1975	16	3	2		E Sch Int
			Tr	Norwich C.	06.76	1976-77	47	1	12		
			New England(USA)	Cambridge U.	09.79	1979-81	97	3	12		
			Tr	Cardiff C.	08.82	1982-85	135	4	17		
			Tr	Swansea C.	10.85	1985	35	0	6		
			Tr	Newport Co.	08.86	1986-87	79	0	8		
			Tr	Torquay U.	03.88	1987	12	0	2		
GIBBONS, Ian K.	Stoke	08.02.70	YTS	Stoke C.	07.88	1987	0	1	0		
GIBBS, Nigel J.	St Albans	20.11.65	App	Watford	11.83	1983-87	97	3	1	(RB)	E U21-5/E Yth Int
GIBSON, Colin J.	Bridport	06.04.60	App	Aston Villa	04.78	1978-85	181	4	10	(LB/M)	E Sch Int/E U21-1
			Tr	Manchester U.	11.85	1985-87	68	3	8		
GIBSON, Terry B.	Walthamstow	23.12.62	App	Tottenham H.	01.80	1979-82	16	2	4	(F)	E Sch Int/E Yth Int
			Tr	Coventry C.	08.83	1983-85	97	1	43		
			Tr	Manchester U.	01.86	1985-86	14	9	1		
			Tr	Wimbledon	08.87	1987	16	1	6		
GIDMAN, John	Liverpool	10.01.54	Liverpool(App)	Aston Villa	08.71	1972-79	196	1	9	(RB)	E Yth Int/
			Tr	Everton	10.79	1979-80	64	0	2		E U23-4/E-1
			Tr	Manchester U.	08.81	1981-85	94	1	4		
			Tr	Manchester C.	10.86	1986-87	52	1	1		
GILBERT, David J.	Lincoln	22.06.63	App	Lincoln C.	06.81	1980-81	15	15	1	(M)	
			Tr	Scunthorpe U.	08.82	1982	1	0	0		
			Boston U.	Northampton T.	07.86	1986-87	86	0	14		
GILBERT, W.A. (Billy)	Lewisham	10.11.59	App	Crystal Palace	12.76	1977-83	235	2	3	(CD)	E Sch Int/
			Tr	Portsmouth	06.84	1984-87	124	4	0		E Yth Int/E U21-11
GILES, Paul A.	Cardiff	21.02.61	Jnrs	Cardiff C.	06.79	1980-82	17	7	1	(W)	Brother of David
			L	Exeter C.	03.82	1981	9	0	1		W U21-3
			Netherlands	Newport Co.(N/C)	12.84	1984	0	1	0		
			Merthyr Tydfil	Newport Co.	03.87	1986-87	28	1	2		
GILKES, Michael E.	Hackney	20.07.65	Leicester C.(Jnrs)	Reading	07.84	1984-87	57	14	8	(F)	
GILL, A.G.D. (Tony)	Bradford	06.03.68	App	Manchester U.	03.86	1986	1	0	0	(FB)	

Players Names	Birthplace	Date	Source	League Club	Date Sign'd	Seasons Played	Apps	Sub	Gls	Pos.	Misc
GILL, Gary	Middlesbrough	28.11.64	App	Middlesbrough	11.82	1983-87	62	6	2	(W)	
			L	Hull C.	12.83	1983	0	1	0		
GILLESPIE, Gary T.	Bonnybridge	05.07.60	Falkirk	Coventry C.	03.78	1978-82	171	1	6	(CD)	S U21-8/S-3
			Tr	Liverpool	07.83	1983-87	96	2	8		
GILLIGAN, Jimmy M.	Hammersmith	24.01.64	App	Watford	08.81	1981-84	18	9	6	(F)	E Yth Int
			L	Lincoln C.	10.82	1982	0	3	0		
			Tr	Grimsby T.	08.85	1985	19	6	4		
			Tr	Swindon T.	06.86	1986	13	4	5		
			L	Newport Co.	02.87	1986	4	1	1		
			Tr	Lincoln C.	03.87	1986	11	0	1		
			Tr	Cardiff C.	07.87	1987	46	0	19		
GIPP, David T.	Stratford	13.07.69	App	Brighton & H.A.	07.86	1986-87	1	4	0	(F)	
GITTENS, Jon	Birmingham	22.01.64	Paget Rangers	Southampton	10.85	1985-86	18	0	0	(CD)	
			Tr	Swindon T.	07.87	1987	27	2	0		
GLEASURE, Peter	Luton	08.10.60	App	Millwall	08.78	1980-82	55	0	0	(G)	
			Tr	Northampton T.	03.83	1982-87	236	0	0		
GLEGHORN, Nigel W.	Seaham	12.08.62	Seaham Red Star	Ipswich T.	08.85	1985-87	54	12	11	(W)	
GLENN, David A.	Wigan	30.11.62	App	Wigan Ath.	11.80	1980-82	68	4	4	(RB)	
			Tr	Blackburn Rov.	08.83	1983-84	24	0	0		
			Tr	Chester C.	07.85	1985-87	53	2	1		
GLOVER, Dean V.	West Bromwich	29.12.63	App	Aston Villa	12.81	1984-86	25	3	0	(CD)	
			L	Sheffield U.	10.86	1986	5	0	0		
			Tr	Middlesbrough	06.87	1987	36	2	4		
GLOVER, E. Lee	Kettering	24.04.70	YTS	Nottingham F.	04.87	1987	17	1	3	(F)	S Yth Int
GOBLE, Steve R.	Aylsham	05.09.60	App	Norwich C.	09.78	1979-80	30	0	2	(LW)	
			Groningen (Neth.)	Norwich C.	08.84	1984					
			Utrecht (Neth)	Cambridge C.(N/C)	02.88	1987	1	1	0		
GODDARD, Karl E.	Leeds	29.12.67	App	Manchester U.	12.85					(LB)	E Sch Int
			Tr	Bradford C.	06.86	1986-87	49	0	0		
GODDARD, Paul	Harlington	12.10.59	App	Q.P.R.	07.77	1977-79	63	7	23	(F)	E U21-8/E-1
			Tr	West Ham U.	08.80	1980-86	159	11	54		
			Tr	Newcastle U.	11.86	1986-87	61	0	19		
GODDEN, A.L. (Tony)	Gillingham	02.08.55	Ashford T.	West Bromwich A.	08.75	1976-85	267	0	0	(G)	
			L	Luton T.	03.83	1982	12	0	0		
			L	Walsall	10.83	1983	19	0	0		
			Tr	Chelsea	03.86	1985-86	34	0	0		
			Tr	Birmingham C.	07.87	1987	22	0	0		
GODFREY, Kevin	Kennington	24.02.60	App	Leyton Orient	03.77	1977-87	255	30	62	(W)	
			L	Plymouth Arg.	02.86	1985	7	0	1		
GOODING, Mick C.	Newcastle	12.04.59	Bishop Auckland	Rotherham U.	07.79	1979-82	90	12	10	(M)	
			Tr	Chesterfield	12.82	1982	12	0	0		
			Tr	Rotherham U.	09.83	1983-86	149	7	32		
			Tr	Peterborough U.	08.87	1987	44	0	18		
GOODISON, C. Wayne	Wakefield	23.09.64	App	Barnsley	09.82	1982-85	31	5	0	(FB)	
			Tr	Crewe Alex.	09.86	1986-87	66	3	0		
GOODMAN, Don R.	Leeds	09.05.66	Jnrs	Bradford C.	07.84	1983-86	65	5	14	(F)	
			Tr	West Bromwich A.	03.87	1986-87	44	6	9		
GOODWIN, Mark A.	Sheffield	23.02.60	App	Leicester C.	11.77	1977-80	69	22	8	(M)	
			Tr	Notts. Co.	03.81	1980-86	226	11	24		
			Tr	Walsall	07.87	1987	29	7	2		
GOODWIN, Shaun L.	Rotherham	14.06.69	YTS	Rotherham U.	06.87	1987	2	1	0	(M)	
GOODYEAR, Clive	Lincoln	15.01.61	Lincoln Utd.	Luton T.	10.78	1979-83	85	5	4	(CD)	
			Tr	Plymouth Arg.	08.84	1984-86	99	7	5		
			Tr	Wimbledon	07.87	1987	21	1	0		
GORAM, Andy L.	Bury	13.04.64	West Bromwich (App)	Oldham Ath.	08.81	1981-87	195	0	0	(G)	S U21-1/S-4/ to Hibernian 10.87
GORDON, Colin K.	Stourbridge	17.01.63	Oldbury U.	Swindon T.	10.84	1984-85	70	2	34	(F)	
			Tr	Wimbledon	06.86	1986	2	1	0		
			L	Gillingham	02.87	1986	4	0	2		
			Tr	Reading	07.87	1987	20	0	8		
			L	Bristol C.	03.88	1987	8	0	4		
GORDON, Dale A.	Great Yarmouth	09.01.67	App	Norwich C.	01.84	1984-87	80	11	12	(W)	E Sch Int/E Yth Int/ E U21-4
GORE, Shaun M.	West Ham	21.09.68	YTS	Fulham	06.86	1985-87	19	1	0	(D)	
GORMAN, Paul A.	Dublin	06.08.63	App	Arsenal	10.80	1981-83	5	1	0	(M)	
			Tr	Birmingham C.	06.84	1984	6	0	0		
			Tr	Carlisle U.	03.85	1984-87	92	11	1		
GORMAN, Paul M.	Macclesfield	18.09.68	YTS	Doncaster Rov.	07.87	1987	1	6	1	(F)	
GORTON, Andy W.	Salford	23.09.66	YTS	Oldham Ath.	07.84	1985-87	26	0	0	(G)	
			L	Stockport Co.	12.86	1986	14	0	0		
			Tr	Tranmere Rov.	04.88	1987	1	0	0		
GOSNEY, Andrew R.	Southampton	08.11.63	App	Portsmouth	11.81	1981-87	9	0	0	(G)	E Yth Int
GOSS, Jeremy	Cyprus	11.05.65	YTS	Norwich C.	03.83	1983-87	22	7	2	(M)	
GOUGH, Richard C.	Stockholm(Swed.)	05.04.62	Dundee U.	Tottenham H.	08.86	1986-87	49	0	2	(CD)	S U21-5/S-38 to Rangers 10.87
GOULET, Brent	USA	19.06.64	Seattle S.(USA)	Bournemouth	11.87	1987	2	4	0	(F)	
			L	Crewe Alex.	01.88	1987	2	1	3		
GRAHAM, Deiniol W.J.	Cannock	04.10.69	YTS	Manchester U.	10.87	1987	1	0	0	(F)	W Yth Int
GRAHAM, Mike A.	Lancaster	24.02.59	App	Bolton W.	02.77	1977-80	43	3	0	(D)	
			Tr	Swindon T.	07.81	1981-84	141	0	1		
			Tr	Mansfield T.	07.85	1985-87	131	1	1		
GRAHAM, Milton M.	Tottenham	02.11.62	Jnrs	Bournemouth	05.81	1981-84	54	19	12	(M)	
			Tr	Chester C.	08.85	1985-87	103	2	9		

Eric Gates (Sunderland) Joined the club after 13 years at Ipswich and was a decisive factor in the promotion battle.

Marco Gabbiadini (Sunderland) Young striker who scored well over a goal a game in the surge to Division 2.

Simon Garner (Blackburn Rovers) A regular name on the score sheet for the "Blue and Whites".

Players Names	Birthplace	Date	Source	League Club	Date Sign'd	Seasons Played	Career Record Apps	Sub	Gls	Pos.	Misc
GRAHAM, Tommy	Glasgow	3.03.58	Arthurlie	Aston Villa	04.78					(M)	
			Tr	Barnsley	12.78	1978-79	36	2	13		
			Tr	Halifax T.	10.80	1980-81	68	3	17		
			Tr	Doncaster Rov.(N/C)	08.82	1982	9	2	2		
			Tr	Scunthorpe U.	03.83	1982-85	102	7	21		
			Tr	Scarborough	(N/L)	1987	44	0	7		
GRANGER, Keith W.	Southampton	05.10.68	App	Southampton	10.86	1985	2	0	0	(G)	
			Tr	Darlington	12.87	1987	23	0	0		
GRAVETTE, Warren	Thetford	13.09.68	App	Tottenham H.	08.86					(M)	
			Tr	Brentford	07.87	1987	1	4	0		
GRAY, Andy	Lambeth	22.02.64	Dulwich Hamlet	Crystal Palace	11.84	1984-87	91	7	27	(M)	E U21-2
			Tr	Aston Villa	11.87	1987	19	0	1		
GRAY, Andy M.	Glasgow	30.11.55	Dundee U.	Aston Villa	10.75	1975-78	112	1	54	(F)	SU23-4/S-20
			Tr	Wolverhampton W.	09.79	1979-3	130	3	38		
			Tr	Everton	11.83	1983-84	44	5	14		
			Tr	Aston Villa	07.85	1985-86	53	1	5		
			Tr	Notts Co.	08.87	1987	3	1	0		
			Tr	West Bromwich A.	09.87	1987	30	2	10		
GRAY, Frank T.	Glasgow	27.10.54	App	Leeds U.	11.71	1972-78	188	5	17	(LB)	S Sch Int/
			Tr	Nottingham F.	08.79	1979-80	81	0	5		S U23-2/S-32
			Tr	Leeds U.	05.81	1981-84	139	0	10		Brother of Eddie
			Tr	Sunderland	07.85	1985-87	82	24	8		
GRAY, Philip	Belfast	02.10.68	App	Tottenham H.	08.86	1986-87	1	1	0	(M)	
GRAY, Stuart	Withernsea	19.04.60	Withernsea YC	Nottingham F.	03.78	1980-82	48	1	3	(M)	
			L	Bolton W.	03.83	1982	10	0	0		
			Tr	Barnsley	08.83	1983-87	117	3	23		
			Tr	Aston Villa	11.87	1987	19	1	5		
GRAYSON, Simon D.	Sheffield	21.10.68	App	Sheffield U.	10.86					(F)	
			L	Chesterfield	11.87	1987	7	1	0		
			Tr	Hartlepool U.	04.88	1987	1	0	0		
GRAYSON, Simon N.	Ripon	16.12.69	YTS	Leeds U.	07.88	1987	2	0	0	(M)	
GREALISH, A.P. (Tony)	Paddington	21.09.56	App	Leyton Orient	07.74	1974-78	169	2	10	(M	IR-44
			Tr	Luton T.	08.79	1979-80	78	0	2		
			Tr	Brighton & H.A.	07.81	1981-83	95	5	6		
			Tr	West Bromwich A.	03.84	1983-85	55	10	5		
			Tr	Manchester C.	10.86	1986	11	0	0		
			Tr	Rotherham U.	08.87	1987	38	0	3		
GREAVES, Steven R.	London	17.01.70	YTS	Fulham	07.88	1987	0	1	0	(FB)	
GREEN, John R.	Rotherham	07.08.58	App	Rotherham U.	03.76	1975-83	247	1	8	(CD)	
			Tr	Scunthorpe U.	09.83	1983-85	100	0	4		
			Tr	Darlington	10.85	1985-86	45	0	2		
			Tr	Rotherham U.	12.86	1986-87	63	1	2		
GREEN, Richard E.	Wolverhampton	22.11.67	YTS	Shrewsbury T.	07.86	1986-87	43	3	2	(CD)	
GREEN, Ron R.	Birmingham	03.10.56	Alvechurch	Walsall	06.77	1977-83	163	0	0	(G)	
			Tr	Shrewsbury T.	06.84	1984	19	0	0		
			Tr	Bristol Rov.	02.85	1984-85	56	0	0		
			Tr	Scunthorpe U.	08.86	1986-87	78	0	0		
GREENALL, Colin A.	Wigan	30.12.63	App	Blackpool	01.81	1980-86	179	4	9	(CD)	E Yth Int
			Tr	Gillingham	09.86	1986-87	62	0	4		
			Tr	Oxford U.	02.88	1987	12	0	0		
GREENOUGH, Ricky A.	Mexborough	30.05.61	Alfreton T.	Chester C.	01.85	1984-87	123	9	15	(D)	
GREENWOOD, Nigel P.	Preston	27.11.66	App	Preston N.E.	09.84	1984-85	36	9	14	(F)	
			Tr	Bury	08.86	1986-87	55	12	18		
GREGORY, A.G.(Tony)	Doncaster	21.03.68	App	Sheffield Wed	01.86	1985-86	13	2	1	(M)	E Sch Int/E Yth Int
GREGORY, John C.	Scunthorpe	11.05.54	App	Northampton T.	05.72	1972-76	187	0	8	(M)	Son of John E./
			Tr	Aston Villa	06.77	1977-78	59	6	10		E-6
			Tr	Brighton & H.A.	07.79	1979-80	72	0	7		
			Tr	Q.P.R.	06.81	1981-85	159	2	36		
			Tr	Derby Co.	11.85	1985-87	103	0	22		
GRENFELL, Stephen J.	Enfield	27.10.66	App	Tottenham H.	08.84					(M)	
			Tr	Colchester U.	10.86	1986-87	62	2	1		
GREW, Mark	Bilston	15.02.58	Jnrs	West Bromwich A.	06.76	1981-82	33	0	0	(G)	
			L	Wigan Ath	12.78	1978	4	0	0		
			Tr	Leicester C.	07.83	1983	5	0	0		
			L	Oldham Ath.	10.63	1983	5	0	0		
			Tr	Ipswich T.	03.84	1984	6	0	0		
			L	Fulham	09.85	1985	4	0	0		
			L	West Bromwich A.	01.86	1985	1	0	0		
			Tr	Port Vale	06.86	1986-87	44	0	0		
GREWCOCK, Neil	Leicester	26.04.62	App	Leicester C.	07.79	1979-80	7	1	1	(W)	
			Tr	Gillingham	03.82	1981-82	30	4	4		
			Shepshed Charterh.	Burnley	06.84	1984-87	143	9	22		
GREYGOOSE, Dean	Thetford	18.12.64	App	Cambridge U.	11.82	1983-84	26	0	0	(G)	E Yth Int
			L	Lincoln C.	09.85	1985	6	0	0		
			Tr	Leyton Orient	12.85	1985	1	0	0		
			Tr	Crystal Palace	08.86							
			Tr	Crewe Alex.	08.87	1987	43	0	0		
GRIFFIN, Colin R.	Dudley	08.01.56	App	Derby Co.	01.74					(CD)	
			Tr	Shrewsbury T.	01.76	1975-87	402	3	7		
GRIFFITHS, David J.	Newport	20.05.62	Cwmbran T.	Newport Co.(N/C)	03.88	1987	0	1	0		
GRIFFITHS, Ian J.	Birkenhead	17.04.60	Jnrs	Tranmere Rov	02.79	1978-82	110	6	5	(LW)	
			Tr	Rochdale	08.83	1983-84	40	2	5		
			Tr	Port Vale(N/C)	09.84	1984	9	3	0		
			Tr	Wigan Ath	07.85	1985-87	73	9	7		
GRIMES, A. Ashley	Dublin	02.08.57	Bohemians	Manchester U.	03.77	1977-82	62	28	10	(LB)	IR 21-2/IR-17
			Tr	Coventry C.	08.83	1983	29	3	1		
			Tr	Luton T.	08.84	1984-87	73	2	3		
GRITT, Steve J.	Bournemouth	31.10.57	App	Bournemouth	10.75	1976	4	2	3	(M)	
			Tr	Charlton Ath.	07.77	1977-87	298	27	22		

Terry Gibson (Wimbledon) Signed from Manchester United last season and was unlucky to miss the FA Cup final.

John Gregory (Derby County) Holder of six England caps, he is still in fine form for the "Rams".

Ashley Grimes (Luton Town) Former midfielder who now plays in the number three shirt.

Gary Gillespie (Liverpool) An excellent utility player.

Players Names	Birthplace	Date	Source	League Club	Date Sign'd	Seasons Played	Career Record Apps	Sub	Gls	Pos.	Misc
GROBBELAAR, Bruce D.	Durban (SA)	06.10.57	Vancouver W. (Can)	Crewe. Alex.(N/C)	12.79	1979	24	0	1	(G)	Zimbabwe Int
			Vancouver W. (Can)	Liverpool	03.81	1981-87	279	0	0		
GROCOCK, Chris R.	Grimsby	30.10.68	Sch	Grimsby T.	06.87	1985-87	14	18	1	(W)	
GROVES, Paul	Derby	28.02.66	Burton A.	Leicester C.	04.88	1987	0	1	0	(M)	
GROVES, Perry	City of London	19.04.65	App	Colchester U.	06.82	1981-86	142	14	26	(F)	
			Tr	Arsenal	09.86	1986-87	47	12	9		
GUMMER, Jason C.	Tredegar	27.10.67	YTS	Cardiff C.	07.85	1985-87	19	3	4	(M)	W Yth Int
GUNN, Bryan	Thurso	22.12.63	Aberdeen	Norwich C.	10.86	1986-87	67	0	0	(G)	S Sch Int/S Yth Int/S U21-8
GUNN, Bryn C.	Kettering	21.08.58	App	Nottingham F.	08.75	1975-84	129	2	1	(D)	
			L	Shrewsbury T.	11.85	1985	9	0	0		
			L	Walsall	01.86	1985	6	0	0		
			L	Mansfield T.	03.86	1985	5	0	0		
			Tr	Peterborough U.	08.86	1986-87	84	1	7		
GUTHRIE, Peter J.	Newcastle	10.10.61	Weymouth	Tottenham H.	01.88					(G)	
			L	Swansea C.	02.88	1987	14	0	0		
GWINNETT, Mel L.	Worcester	14.05.63	Stourbridge	Peterborough U.	05.81					(G)	
			Tr	Hereford U.(N/C)	09.82	1982	1	0	0		
			Gloucester C.	Bradford C.	06.84						
			Tr	Exeter C.	08.85	1985-87	29	0	0		
GYMER, John P.	Romford	11.11.66	App	Southend U.	08.84	1983-86	30	25	12	(M)	
			Tr	Crewe Alex.	07.87	1987	10	5	5		
GYNN, Micky	Peterborough	19.08.61	App	Peterborough U.	04.79	1978-82	152	4	33	(M)	
			Tr	Coventry C.	08.83	1983-87	93	28	15		
HACKETT, Gary S.	Stourbridge	11.10.62	Bromsgrove Rov.	Shrewsbury T.	07.83	1983-86	142	8	17	(M)	
			Aberdeen	Stoke C.	03.88	1987	1	0	0		
HADDOCK, Peter M.	Newcastle	09.12.61	App	Newcastle U.	12.79	1981-85	53	4	0	(D)	
			L	Burnley	03.86	1985	7	0	0		
			Tr	Leeds U.	07.86	1986-87	48	3	1		
HAIGH, Paul	Scarborough	04.05.58	App	Hull C.	06.75	1974-80	179	1	8	(D)	E U21-1
			Tr	Carlisle U.	11.80	1980-86	228	5	4		
			Tr	Hartlepool U.	07.87	1987	39	0	0		
HAINES, Ivan G.	Chatham	14.09.68	YTS	Gillingham	06.87	1987	0	1	0	(D)	
HALES, Kevin P.	Dartford	13.01.61	App	Chelsea	01.79	1979-82	18	2	2	(D)	
			Tr	Leyton Orient	08.83	1983-87	176	6	11		
HALL, A.D. (Tony)	Billingham	17.01.69	Billingham T.	Tranmere Rov.	08.87	1987	0	1	0		
				Hartlepool U.	10.87	1987	0	1	0		
HALL, Derek R.	Ashton-u-Lyne	05.01.65	App	Coventry C.	10.82	1982	1	0	0	(M)	
			Tr	Torquay U.	03.84	1983-84	55	0	6		
			Tr	Swindon T.	07.85	1985	9	0	0		
			Tr	Southend U.	08.86	1986-87	82	1	12		
HALL, Gareth D.	Croydon	20.03.69	App	Chelsea	05.86	1986-87	8	6	0	(D)	W-1
HALL, Mark	Doncaster	11.05.70	YTS	Doncaster Rov.	06.88	1987	0	1	0	(RB)	
HALLWORTH, Jonathan	Stockport	26.10.65	App	Ipswich T.	05.83	1985-87	45	0	0	(G)	
			L	Bristol Rov.	01.85	1984	2	0	0		
HALPIN, John	Broxburn	15.11.61	Glasgow Celtic	Carlisle U.	10.84	1984-87	80	2	9	(LW)	
HALSALL, Mike	Bootle	21.07.61	App	Liverpool	05.79					(M)	
			Tr	Birmingham C.	03.83	1982-84	35	1	3		
			Tr	Carlisle U.	10.84	1984-86	92	0	11		
			Tr	Grimsby T.	02.87	1986	12	0	0		
			Tr	Peterborough U.	07.87	1987	45	0	4		
HAMER, Kevin J.	Merthyr Tydfil	02.02.69	YTS	Newport Co.	07.87	1985-87	15	2	1	(D)	
HAMILL, Stewart P.	Glasgow	22.01.60	Pollok Jnrs	Leicester C.	09.80	1980-81	10	0	2	(W)	
			L	Scunthorpe U.	03.82	1981	4	0	0		
			Nuneaton Bor.	Northampton T.	03.86	1985	3	0	1		
			Altrincham	Scarborough	03.87	1987	19	9	3		
HAMILTON, David	South Shield	07.11.60	App	Sunderland	09.78					(M)	E Yth Int
			Tr	Blackburn Rov.	01.81	1980-85	104	10	7		
			L	Cardiff C.	03.85	1984	10	0	0		
			Tr	Wigan Ath.	07.86	1986-87	84	2	5		
HAMILTON, Gary J.	Glasgow	27.12.65	App	Middlesbrough	06.83	1982-87	182	11	22	(M)	S Yth Int
HAMILTON, Ian R.	Stevenage	14.12.67	App	Southampton	12.85					(W)	
			Tr	Cambridge U.	03.88	1987	9	0	1		
HAMMOND, Nicky D.	Hornchurch	07.09.67	App	Arsenal	09.85					(G)	
			L	Bristol Rov.	08.86	1986	3	0	0		
			Tr	Swindon T.	06.87	1987	4	0	0		
HAMPTON, Peter J.	Oldham	12.09.54	App	Leeds U.	09.71	1972-79	63	5	2	(LB)	E Yth Int
			Tr	Stoke C.	08.80	1980-83	134	4	4		
			Tr	Burnley	08.84	1984-86	116	2	2		
			Tr	Rochdale	08.87	1987	19	0	1		
			Tr	Carlisle U.	12.87	1987	12	0	0		
HAMSON, Gary	Nottingham	24.08.59	App	Sheffield U.	11.76	1976-78	107	1	8	(LW)	
			Tr	Leeds U.	07.79	1979-85	126	8	3		
			Tr	Bristol C.	07.86	1986	12	0	2		
			Tr	Port Vale	12.86	1986-87	36	2	3		
HANCOX, Paul A.	Manchester	22.07.70	YTS	Rochdale (YTS)	12.87	1987	0	2	0		
HANDYSIDES Ian R.	Jarrow	14.12.62	App	Birmingham C.	01.80	1980-83	44	18	2	(W)	E Yth Int
			Tr	Walsall	01.84	1983-85	58	8	11		
			Tr	Birmingham C.	03.86	1985-87	53	3	5		
				Wolverhampton W.	09.86	1986	11	0	2		
HANSBURY, Roger	Barnsley	26.01.55	App	Norwich C.	01.73	1974-80	78	0	0	(G)	
			L	Cambridge U.	11.77	1977	11	0	0		
			Eastern (HK)	Burnley	08.83	1983-84	83	0	0		
			Tr	Cambridge U.	07.85	1985	37	0	0		
			Tr	Birmingham C.	03.86	1986-87	53	0	0		
			L	Sheffield U.	10.87	1987	5	0	0		
HANSEN, Alan D.	Alloa	13.06.55	Partick Thistle	Liverpool	04.77	1977-87	397	0	8	(CD)	S U23-3/S-26

Players Names	Birthplace	Date	Source	League Club	Date Sign'd	Seasons Played	Apps	Sub	Gls	Pos.	Misc
HARBACH, Peter C.	Carlisle	30.04.67	App	Newcastle U.	04.85					(F)	
			Tr	Carlisle U.	08.87	1987	0	7	0		
HARBEY, Graham K.	Chesterfield	29.08.64	App	Derby Co.	08.82	1983-86	35	5	1	(LB)	
			Tr	Ipswich T.	07.87	1987	34	1	1		
HARBOTTLE, Mark S.	Nottingham	26.09.68	App	Notts Co.	09.86	1985	1	3	1	(M)	E Yth Int
			L	Doncaster Rov.	01.88	1987	4	0	0		
HARDWICK, Steve	Mansfield	06.09.56	Jnrs	Chesterfield	07.74	1974-76	38	0	0	(G)	E Yth Int
			Tr	Newcastle U.	12.76	1977-82	92	0	0		
			Tr	Oxford U.	02.83	1982-87	156	0	0		
			L	Crystal Palace	03.86	1985	3	0	0		
			L	Sunderland	08.87	1987	6	0	0		
HARDY, Jason P.	Manchester	14.12.69	YTS	Burnley	07.88	1986	0	1	0	(FB)	
HARDYMAN, Paul G.	Portsmouth	11.03.64	Waterlooville	Portsmouth	07.83	1983-87	90	2	2	(LB)	E U 21-2
HARFORD, Mick G.	Sunderland	12.02.59	Sunderland B.C.	Lincoln C.	07.77	1977-80	109	6	41	(F)	E-1/E 'B'
			Tr	Newcastle U.	12.80	1980	18	1	4		
			Tr	Bristol C.	08.81	1981	30	0	11		
			Tr	Birmingham C.	03.82	1981-84	92	0	25		
			Tr	Luton T.	12.84	1984-87	101	0	50		
HARLE, David	Denaby	15.08.63	App	Doncaster Rov.	11.80	1979-81	48	13	3	(M)	E Yth Int
			Tr	Exeter C.	07.82	1982-83	42	1	6		
			Tr	Doncaster Rov.	09.83	1983-85	80	3	17		
			Tr	Leeds U.	12.85	1985	3	0	0		
			Tr	Bristol C.	03.86	1985-86	23	0	2		
			Tr	Scunthorpe U.	11.86	1986-87	70	1	8		
HARPER, Alan	Liverpool	01.11.60	App	Liverpool	04.78					(M)	E Yth Int
			Tr	Everton	06.83	1983-87	103	24	4		
HARPER, Stephen J.	Newcastle-u-Lyme	03.02.69	YTS	Port Vale	06.87	1987	16	5	2	(W)	
HARRIS, Carl S.	Neath	03.11.56	App	Leeds U.	11.73	1974-81	123	30	26	(W)	W Sch Int/
			Tr	Charlton Ath.	07.82	1982-84	73	3	7		W U23-1/W-24
			Leeds U. (N/C)	Bury	12.85	1985-86	33	5	4		
			Cardiff C.(N/C)	Rochdale(N/C)	01.88	1987	15	0	2		
HARRIS, Jamie	Exeter	04.06.69	YTS	Exeter C.	08.86	1987	5	4	1	(F)	
HARRIS, Jason M.	Rochdale	26.12.69	YTS	Burnley(YTS)	07.86	1986	4	0	0	(M)	
HARRIS, Neil J.	Manchester	07.11.69	YTS	Crewe Alex.	07.88	1987	3	0	0	(W)	
HARRISON, Andrew F.	Long Eaton	13.09.57	Kettering Town	Scarborough	(N/L)	1987	3	1	0	(FB)	
HARRISON, Chris C.	Launceston	17.10.56	App	Plymouth Arg.	10.74	1975-84	315	9	7	(D)	
			Tr	Swansea C.	09.85	1985-87	114	3	14		
HARRISON, Frank N.	Eston	19.09.63	Guisborough T.	Middlesbrough	09.82					(LB)	
				Lincoln C.(N/C)	11.85	1985	0	1	0		
				Halifax T.	03.87	1986-87	32	0	1		
HARRISON, Wayne	Stockport	15.11.67	App	Oldham Ath.	12.84	1984	5	1	1	(F)	
			Tr	Liverpool	03.85						
HARRISON, Wayne M.	Whitehaven	16.10.57	Everton (Jnr)	Workington (N/C)	08.75	1975	1	3	0	(M)	
			Sheffield Wed.(N/C)	Blackpool	09.79	1979-81	81	5	6		
			Workington	Carlisle U. (N/C)	08.87	1987	1	1	0		
HARROWER, Steven G.	Exeter	09.10.61	Dawlish	Exeter C.	01.84	1983-87	144	18	10	(W)	
HART, Nigel	Golborne	01.10.58		Wigan Ath.	08.78	1979	1	0	0	(CD)	Brother of Paul
			Tr	Leicester C.	10.79						
			Tr	Blackpool	08.81	1981-82	36	1	0		
			Tr	Crewe Alex.	11.82	1982-86	139	3	10		
			Tr	Bury	02.87	1986-87	33	12	2		
HART, Paul A.	Golborne	04.05.53	Jnrs	Stockport Co.	09.70	1970-72	88	0	5	(CD)	Brother of Nigel/
			Tr	Blackpool	06.73	1973-77	143	0	17		Son of John
			Tr	Leeds U.	03.78	1977-82	191	0	16		
			Tr	Nottingham F.	05.83	1983-84	70	0	1		
			Tr	Sheffield Wed.	08.85	1985-86	52	0	2		
			Tr	Birmingham C.	12.86	1986	1	0	0		
			Tr	Notts Co.	06.87	1987	23	0	0		
HART, Peter O.	Mexborough	14.08.57	App	Huddersfield T.	08.74	1973-79	208	2	7	(CD)	
			Tr	Walsall	08.80	1980-87	353	0	12		
HARTFORD, R. Asa	Clydebank	24.10.50	Jnrs	West Bromwich A.	11.67	1967-73	206	8	18	(M)	S U23-5/
			Tr	Manchester C.	08.74	1974-78	184	1	22		S U21-1/S-50
			Tr	Nottingham F.	07.79	1979	3	0	0		
			Tr	Everton	08.79	1979-81	81	0	6		
			Tr	Manchester C.	10.81	1981-83	75	0	7		
			Ft Lauderdale(USA)	Norwich C.	10.84	1984	28	0	2		
			Tr	Bolton W.	07.85	1985-86	81	0	8		
			Tr	Stockport Co.	06.87	1987	30	1	0		
HARVEY, Jimmy	Lurgan (NI)	02.05.58	Glenavon	Arsenal	08.77	1977-78	2	1	0	(M)	
			Tr	Hereford U.	03.80	1979-86	276	2	39		
			Tr	Bristol C.	03.87	1986-87	2	1	0		
			L	Wrexham	09.87	1987	6	0	0		
			Tr	Tranmere Rov.	10.87	1987	33	0	3		
HARVEY, Lee D.	Harlow	21.12.66	App	Leyton Orient	12.84	1983-87	29	29	4	(M)	E Yth Int
HARVEY, Richard G.	Letchworth	19.04.69	App	Luton T.	01.87	1986	5	0	0	(LB)	E Yth Int
HASLEGRAVE, Sean M.	Stoke	07.06.51	Jnrs	Stoke C.	11.68	1970-75	106	7	5	(M)	
			Tr	Nottingham F.	07.76	1976	5	2	1		
			Tr	Preston N.E.	09.77	1977-80	111	2	2		
			Tr	Crewe Alex.	08.81	1981-82	78	4	1		
			Tr	York C.	07.83	1983-86	137	5	0		
			Tr	Torquay U.	08.87	1987	31	3	1		
HATELEY, Mark W.	Liverpool	07.11.61	App	Coventry C.	12.78	1978-82	86	7	25	(F)	E Yth Int/E U21-10/
			Tr	Portsmouth	06.83	1983	38	0	22		E-27/Son of Tony/ to A.C. Milan (It.) 6.84
HAWKER, Phil N.	Solihull	07.12.62	App	Birmingham C.	06.80	1980-82	34	1	1	(D)	E Yth Int
			Tr	Walsall	12.82	1982-87	114	7	7		
HAWKINS, Nigel S.	Bristol	07.09.68	YTS	Bristol C.	02.87	1987	1	0	0	(M)	
HAWTIN, Craig S.	Buxton	29.03.70	Port Vale (YTS)	Chester C.(YTS)	05.87	1987	3	1	0	(RB)	

Players Names	Birthplace	Date	Source	League Club	Date Sign'd	Seasons Played	Career Record			Pos.	Misc
							Apps	Sub	Gls		
HAYCOCK, T. Paul	Sheffield	08.07.62	Burton A.	Rotherham U.	08.86	1986-87	48	13	18	(F)	
HAYES, Martin	Walthamstow	21.03.66	App	Arsenal	11.83	1985-87	59	14	22	(W)	E U21-2
HAYLOCK, Paul	Lowestoft	24.03.63	App	Norwich C.	01.81	1981-85	154	1	3	(RB)	
			Tr	Gillingham	08.86	1986-87	77	0	0		
HAZARD, Mike	Sunderland	05.02.60	App	Tottenham H.	02.78	1979-85	75	16	13	(M)	
			Tr	Chelsea	09.85	1985-87	61	3	9		
HAZEL, Desmond L.	Bradford	15.07.67	App	Sheffield Wed.	07.85	1987	5	1	0	(W)	
			L	Grimsby T.	10.86	1986	9	0	2		
HAZEL, Ian	Merton	01.12.67	App	Wimbledon	12.85	1987	3	3	0	(M)	
HAZELL, R.J. (Bob)	Jamaica	14.06.59	App	Wolverhampton W.	05.77	1977-78	32	1	1	(CD)	E Yth Int/
			Tr	Q.P.R.	09.79	1979-83	100	6	8		E U21-1/E 'B'
			Tr	Leicester C.	09.83	1983-84	41	0	2		
			L	Wolverhampton W.	09.85	1985	1	0	0		
			Tr	Luton T.	08.86						
			Tr	Reading	11.86	1986	4	0	0		
			Tr	Port Vale	12.86	1986-87	64	0	1		
HEALEY, Jonathan P.	Morecambe	30.12.66	YTS	Oldham Ath.	06.85					(M)	
			Alsager College	Crewe Alex.	12.87	1987	7	3	2		
HEARD, T. Pat	Hull	17.03.60	App	Everton	03.78	1978-79	10	1	0	(LB)	E Yth Int
			Tr	Aston Villa	10.79	1979-82	20	4	2		
			Tr	Sheffield Wed.	01.83	1982-84	22	3	3		
			Tr	Newcastle U.	09.84	1984	34	0	2		
			Tr	Middlesbrough	08.85	1985	25	0	2		
			Tr	Hull C.	03.86	1985-87	79	1	5		
HEATH, Adrian P.	Stoke	11.01.61	App	Stoke C.	01.79	1978-81	94	1	16	(F)	E U21-8/
			Tr	Everton	01.82	1981-87	200	19	69		Brother of Philip
HEATH, Philip A.	Stoke	24.11.64	App	Stoke C.	10.82	1982-87	144	12	17	(LW)	Brother of Adrian
HEATHCOTE, Michael	Durham	10.09.65	Spennymoor U.	Sunderland	08.87	1987	0	1	0	(CD)	
			L	Halifax T.	12.87	1987	7	0	1		
HEBBERD, Trevor N.	Winchester	19.06.58	App	Southampton	06.76	1976-81	69	28	7	(M)	
			L	Bolton W.	09.81	1981	6	0	0		
			L	Leicester C.	11.81	1981	4	0	1		
			Tr	Oxford U.	03.82	1981-87	260	0	37		
HEDMAN, Rudi G.	Lambeth	16.11.64	Jnrs	Colchester U.	02.84	1983-87	149	10	9	(D)	
HEDWORTH, Chris	Wallsend	05.01.64	App	Newcastle U.	01.82	1982-85	8	1	0	(D)	
			Tr	Barnsley	08.86	1986-87	19	6	0		
HEFFERNAN, Tom P.	Dublin	30.04.55	Dunleary Celtic	Tottenham H.	10.77					(RB)	
			Tr	Bournemouth	05.79	1979-82	152	2	21		
			Tr	Sheffield U.	08.83	1983-84	82	0	5		
			Tr	Bournemouth	06.85	1985-87	58	5	6		
HELLIWELL, Ian	Rotherham	07.11.62	Matlock T.	York C.	10.87	1987	32	0	8	(F)	
HEMMING, Chris A.J.	Newcastle-u-Lyme	13.04.66	Jnrs	Stoke C.	04.84	1983-87	81	8	2	(D)	
HENCHER, Nicky H.	Wrexham	24.08.61	Lex	Wrexham(N/C)	08.85	1985-87	26	6	5	(W)	
HENDERSON, Mick R.	Newcastle	31.03.56	App	Sunderland	03.74	1975-78	81	3	2	(M)	
			Tr	Watford	11.79	1979-81	50	1	0		
			Tr	Cardiff C.	03.82	1981	11	0	0		
			Tr	Sheffield U.	08.82	1982-84	65	2	0		
			Tr	Chesterfield	01.85	1984-87	125	0	10		
HENDRIE, John G.	Lennoxtown	24.10.63	App	Coventry C.	05.81	1981-83	15	6	2	(RW)	
			L	Hereford U.	01.84	1983	6	0	0		
			Tr	Bradford C.	06.84	1984-87	173	0	46		
HENDRIE, Paul F.	Glasgow	27.03.54	Kirkintilloch Rob Roy	Birmingham C.	03.72	1972-75	19	4	1	(W)	
			Portland T. (USA)	Bristol Rov.	09.77	1977-78	17	13	1		
			Tr	Halifax T.	07.79	1979-83	187	0	12		
			Tr	Stockport Co.	08.84	1984-87	103	7	6		
HENDRY, E. Colin J.	Keith	07.12.65	Dundee	Blackburn Rov.	03.87	1986-87	56	1	15	(CD)	
HENRY, A (Tony)	Houghton le Spring	26.11.57	App	Manchester C.	12.74	1976-81	68	11	6	(M)	
			Tr	Bolton W.	09.81	1981-82	70	0	22		
			Tr	Oldham Ath.	03.83	1982-87	185	5	25		
			Tr	Stoke C.	11.87	1987	22	0	5		
HENRY, Charlie A.	Acton	13.02.62	App	Swindon T.	02.80	1980-87	187	14	23	(M)	
			L	Torquay U.	02.87	1986	6	0	1		
			L	Northampton T.	03.87	1986	4	0	1		
HENRY, Nicky I.	Liverpool	21.02.69	YTS	Oldham Ath.	06.87	1987	3	2	0	(F)	
HENSHAW, Gary	Leeds	18.02.65	App	Grimsby T.	02.83	1983-86	46	4	9	(W)	
			Tr	Bolton W.	06.87	1987	23	8	2		
HESFORD, Iain	Kenya	04.03.60	App	Blackpool	08.77	1977-82	202	0	0	(G)	E Yth Int/E U21-7
			Tr	Sheffield Wed.	08.83							
			L	Fulham	01.85	1984	3	0	0		
			L	Notts. Co.	11.85	1985	10	0	0		
			Tr	Sunderland	08.86	1986-87	77	0	0		
HETHERINGTON, R. Brent	Carlisle	06.12.61	Workington	Carlisle U.	08.87	1987	31	6	10	(F)	
HETHERSTON, Peter	Bellshill	06.11.64	Falkirk	Watford	07.87	1987	2	3	0	(W)	
			Tr	Sheffield U.	02.88	1987	11	0	0		
HETZKE, Steve E.R.	Marlborough	03.06.55	App	Reading	06.73	1971-81	254	7	23	(CD)	
			Tr	Blackpool	07.82	1982-85	140	0	18		
			Tr	Sunderland	03.86	1985-86	31	0	0		
			Tr	Chester C.	06.87	1987	14	0	0		
			Tr	Colchester U.	03.88	1987	5	0	0		
HEWITT, Jamie R.	Chesterfield	17.05.68	YTS	Chesterfield	04.86	1985-87	80	7	4	(RB)	
HEYES, Darren L.	Swansea	11.01.67	App	Nottingham F.	01.84					(G)	E Sch Int/
			L	Wrexham	01.87	1986	2	0	0		E Yth Int/
			Tr	Scunthorpe U.(N/C)	07.87	1987	3	0	0		Son of George
HIBBITT, Kenny	Bradford	03.01.51	App	Bradford P.A.	11.68	1967-68	13	2	0	(M)	Brother of Terry/
			Tr	Wolverhampton W.	11.68	1968-83	446	19	88		E U23-1
			Tr	Coventry C.	08.84	1984-85	42	5	4		
			Tr	Bristol Rov.	08.86	1986-87	51	1	5		

Bruce Grobbelaar (Liverpool) Extrovert goalkeeper.

Players Names	Birthplace	Date	Source	League Club	Date Sign'd	Seasons Played	Apps	Sub	Gls	Pos.	Misc
HICKS, Jim M.	Ipswich	16.09.60	St. Lukes College	Exeter C. (N/C)	09.83	1983	3	0	0	(D)	
			Tr	Oxford U.	08.84						
			Tr	Fulham	08.85	1985-87	39	1	1		
HICKS, Martin	Stratford on Avon	27.02.57	Stratford T.	Charlton Ath.	02.77					(CD)	
			Tr	Reading	02.78	1977-87	366	1	18		
HICKS, Stuart J.	Peterborough	30.05.67	YTS	Peterborough U.	07.84					(CD)	
			Wisbech T.	Colchester U.	03.88	1987	7	0	0		
HIGGINS, David A.	Liverpool	19.08.61	Eagle F.C.	Tranmere Rov.	08.83	1983-84	27	1	0	(D)	
			Caernarfon T.	Tranmere Rov.	07.87	1987	31	2	1		
HIGGINS, Mark N.	Buxton	29.09.58	App	Everton	08.76	1976-83	150	2	6	(CD)	Son of John/
			Retired	Manchester U.	12.85	1985	6	0	0		E Sch Int/
			Tr	Bury	01.87	1986-87	62	1	0		E Yth Int
HILAIRE, Vince M.	Forest Hill	10.10.59	App	Crystal Palace	10.76	1976-83	239	16	29	(LW)	E Yth Int/
			Tr	Luton T.	07.84	1984	5	1	0		E U21-9/E 'B'
			Tr	Portsmouth	11.84	1984-87	144	2	25		
HILDERSLEY, Ron	Kirkcaldy	06.04.65	App	Manchester C.	04.83	1982	1	0	0	(W)	
			L	Chester C.	01.84	1983	9	0	0		
			Tr	Chester C.	07.84	1984	5	4	0		
			Tr	Rochdale (N/C)	08.85	1985	12	4	0		
			Tr	Preston N.E.	06.86	1986-87	54	4	3		
			L	Cambridge U.	02.88	1987	9	0	3		
HILDITCH, Mark W.	Royton	20.08.60	Jnrs	Rochdale	11.78	1977-82	184	13	40	(F)	
			Tr	Tranmere Rov.	08.83	1983-85	47	2	12		
			Altrincham	Wigan Ath.	09.86	1986-87	46	11	16		
HILEY, Scott P.	Plymouth	27.09.68	YTS	Exeter C.	08.86	1987	12	3	1	(M)	
HILL, Andy R.	Maltby	20.01.65	App	Manchester U.	01.83					(RB)	E Yth Int
			Tr	Bury	07.84	1984-87	163	0	8		
HILL, Colin F.	Uxbridge	12.11.63	App	Arsenal	08.81	1982-84	46	0	1	(D)	
			Maritimo (Port.)	Colchester U.	10.87	1987	22	3	0		
HILL, David M.	Nottingham	06.06.66	YTS	Scunthorpe U.	02.85	1983-87	139	1	10	(LW)	
HILL, Keith J.	Bolton	17.05.69	Jnrs	Blackburn Rov.	05.87	1987	1	0	0	(D)	
HILL, Richard W.	Hinckley	20.09.63	Jnrs	Leicester C.	11.81					(W)	
			Nuneaton Bor.	Northampton T.	06.85	1985-86	86	0	46		
			Tr	Watford	05.87	1987	2	2	0		
			Tr	Oxford U.	09.87	1987	15	9	4		
HILL, Ricky A.	Paddington	05.03.59	App	Luton T.	05.76	1975-87	396	7	51	(M)	E Yth Int/E-3
HILLYARD, Ron W.	Rotherham	31.03.52	Jnrs	York C.	12.69	1969-73	61	0	0	(G)	
			L	Hartlepool U.	01.72	1971	23	0	0		
			Tr	Gillingham	07.74	1974-87	498	0	0		
HILTON, Paul	Oldham	08.10.59	Chadderton	Bury	07.78	1978-83	136	12	39	(CD)	
			Tr	West Ham U.	02.84	1983-87	38	11	7		
HIMSWORTH, Gary P.	Pickering	19.12.69	YTS	York C.	01.88	1987	28	3	2	(W)	
HINCHCLIFFE, Andy G.	Manchester	05.02.69	App	Manchester C.	08.86	1987	42	0	1	(LB)	E Yth Int
HINCHLEY, Gary	Guisborough	14.11.68	Jnrs	Darlington	08.86	1986-87	13	1	0	(RB)	
HINDMARCH, Rob	Morpeth	27.04.61	App	Sunderland	04.78	1977-83	114	1	2	(CD)	E Yth Int
			L	Portsmouth	12.83	1983	2	0	0		
			Tr	Derby Co.	07.84	1984-87	113	0	9		
HINE, Mark	Middlesbrough	18.05.64	Whitby T.	Grimsby T.	10.83	1984-85	20	2	1	(M)	
				Darlington	06.86	1986-87	88	0	6		
HINNIGAN, Joe P.	Liverpool	03.12.55	South Liverpool	Wigan Ath.	(N/L)	1978-79	66	0	10	(D)	
			Tr	Sunderland	02.80	1979-82	63	0	4		
			Tr	Preston N.E.	12.82	1982-83	51	1	8		
			Tr	Gillingham	08.84	1984-86	99	4	7		
			Tr	Wrexham	07.87	1987	28	1	1		
HINSHELWOOD, Paul A.	Bristol	14.08.56	App	Crystal Palace	08.73	1973-82	271	5	23	(RB)	Son of Wally/
			Tr	Oxford U.	08.83	1983-84	45	0	0		Brother of Martin/
			Tr	Millwall	01.85	1984-86	59	2	2		E U21-2
			Tr	Colchester U.	09.86	1986-87	81	0	6		
HIRST, David E.	Cudworth	07.12.67	App	Barnsley	11.85	1985	26	2	9	(F)	E Yth Int
			Tr	Sheffield Wed.	08.86	1986-87	32	13	9		
HITCHCOCK, Kevin	Canning Town	05.10.62	Barking	Nottingham F.	08.83					(G)	
			Tr	Mansfield T.	02.84	1983-87	182	0	0		
			Tr	Chelsea	03.88	1987	8	0	0		
HOBSON, Gordon	Sheffield	27.11.57	Sheffield Rangers	Lincoln C.	12.77	1977-84	260	12	73	(F)	
			Tr	Grimsby T.	06.85	1985-86	50	2	18		
			Tr	Southampton	11.86	1986-87	32	1	8		
HOCKADAY, David	Billingham	09.11.57	Billingham Synth.	Blackpool	06.75	1976-82	131	16	24	(FB)	
			Tr	Swindon T.	08.83	1983-87	171	7	7		
HODDLE, Glenn	Hayes	27.10.57	App	Tottenham H.	04.57	1975-86	370	7	88	(M)	E Yth Int/E U21-12/ E-49/to Monaco (Fr.) 7.87
HODDY, Kevin R.	Romford	06.01.68	App	Fulham	01.86	1986-87	13	7	1	(M)	
HODGE, Martin J.	Southport	04.02.59	App	Plymouth Arg.	02.77	1977-78	45	0	0	(G)	
			Tr	Everton	07.79	1979-80	25	0	0		
			L	Preston N.E.	12.81	1981	28	0	0		
			L	Oldham Ath.	07.82	1982	4	0	0		
			L	Gillingham	01.83	1982	4	0	0		
			L	Preston N.E.	02.83	1982	16	0	0		
			Tr	Sheffield Wed.	08.83	1983-87	197	0	0		
HODGE, Steve B.	Nottingham	25.10.62	App	Nottingham F.	10.80	1981-85	122	1	30	(M)	E U21-8/E-15
			Tr	Aston Villa	08.85	1985-86	53	0	12		
			Tr	Tottenham H.	12.86	1986-87	44	1	7		
HODGES, David	Hereford	17.01.70	Jnrs	Mansfield T.	08.87	1986-87	22	3	2	(M)	
HODGES, Glyn P.	Streatham	30.04.63	App	Wimbledon	02.81	1980-86	200	32	49	(W)	W U21-3/W-8
			Tr	Newcastle U.	07.87	1987	7	0	0		
			Tr	Watford	10.87	1987	22	2	3		
HODGES, Kevin	Bridport	12.06.60	App	Plymouth Arg.	03.78	1978-87	383	12	73	(M)	

Perry Groves (Arsenal) Seen in front of Viv Anderson during last season's home game against Manchester United.

Alan Hansen (Liverpool) Missed only one game in the "Reds" number six shirt last season as the club strode to their 17th Championship win.

Players Names	Birthplace	Date	Source	League Club	Date Sign'd	Seasons Played	Career Record Apps	Career Record Sub	Career Record Gls	Pos.	Misc
HODGSON, David J.	Gateshead	01.11.60	Jnrs	Middlesbrough	08.78	1978-81	116	9	16	(F)	E U21-6
			Tr	Liverpool	08.82	1982-83	21	7	4		
			Tr	Sunderland	08.84	1984-85	32	8	5		
			Tr	Norwich C.	07.86	1986	3	3	1		
HODKINSON, Andy J.	Ashton-u-Lyne	04.11.65	Bolton W.(App)	Oldham Ath.	08.83	1983-84	4	1	1	(W)	E Sch Int
			Tr	Stockport Co.	08.85	1985-87	114	4	18		
HODSON, Simeon P.	Lincoln	05.03.66	App	Notts Co.	03.84	1983-84	27	0	0	(RB)	
			Tr	Charlton Ath.	03.85	1984	5	0	0		
			Tr	Lincoln C.	01.86	1985-86	54	2	0		
			Tr	Newport Co.	08.87	1987	34	0	1		
			Tr	West Bromwich A.	03.88	1987	7	0	0		
HOGG, Graeme J.	Aberdeen	17.06.64	App	Manchester U.	06.82	1983-87	82	1	1	(CD)	S U21-4
			L	West Bromwich A.	11.87	1987	7	0	0		
HOLDEN, Andy I.	Flint	14.09.62	Rhyl	Chester C.	08.83	1983-86	100	0	17	(CD)	W U21-1/W-1
			Tr	Wigan Ath.	10.86	1986-87	25	1	3		
HOLDEN, Richard W.	Skipton	09.09.64		Burnley(N/C)	03.86	1985	0	1	0	(LW)	
			Tr	Halifax T.	09.86	1986-87	66	1	12		
			Tr	Watford	03.88	1987	10	0	2		
HOLDEN, Simon J.	Littleborough	09.03.68	Jnrs	Rochdale	07.85					(M)	
				Rochdale	01.87	1986-87	35	14	4		
HOLDSWORTH, Dean C.	Walthamstow	08.11.68	App	Watford	11.86	1987	0	2	0	(F)	
			L	Carlisle U.	02.88	1987	4	0	1		
			L	Port Vale	03.88	1987	6	0	2		
HOLLIS, Andy	Huntingdon	16.09.63	Ramsey T.	Cambridge U.(N/C)	04.87	1986-87	3	1	0	(F)	
HOLLOWAY, Ian S.	Kingswood	12.03.63	App	Bristol Rov.	03.81	1980-84	104	7	14	(W)	
			Tr	Wimbledon	07.85	1985	19	0	2		
			Tr	Brentford	03.86	1985-87	27	3	2		
			L	Torquay U.	01.87	1986	5	0	0		
			Tr	Bristol Rov.	08.87	1987	43	0	5		
HOLMES, Andrew J.	Stoke	07.01.69	App	Stoke C.	01.87	1987	1	1	0	(D)	
HOLMES, Micky A.	Bradford	09.09.65	Jnrs	Bradford C.(N/C)	07.84	1984	0	5	0	(M)	
			Burnley (N/C)	Wolverhampton W.	11.85	1985-87	74	9	13		
HOLMES, Paul	Chapeltown	18.02.68	App	Doncaster Rov.	02.86	1985-87	42	5	1	(FB)	Son of Albert
HOLSGROVE, Paul	Wellington	26.08.69	YTS	Aldershot	02.87	1987	0	2	0	(D)	
HOLTHAM, Dean M.	Pontypridd	30.09.63	App	Cardiff C.	09.81					(D)	
			Tr	Swansea C.	08.82	1982	6	0	0		
			Ebbw Vale	Newport Co.(N/C)	09.87	1987	4	2	0		
HONE, Mark J.	Croydon	31.03.68	Jnrs	Crystal Palace	07.85	1987	3	0	0	(D)	
HONOR, Christian R.	Bristol	05.06.68	App	Bristol C.	06.86	1985-87	16	4	0	(CD)	
			L	Torquay U.	11.86	1986	3	0	0		
HONOUR, Brian	Horden	16.02.64	App	Darlington	02.82	1981-83	59	15	4	(M)	
			Peterlee	Hartlepool U.	02.85	1984-87	130	9	10		
HOOD, Derek	Washington	17.12.58	App	West Bromwich A.	12.76					(M)	
			Tr	Hull C.	08.77	1977-79	20	4	0		
			Tr	York C.	02.80	1979-87	287	13	32		
HOOLICKIN, Gary J.	Middleton	29.10.57	App	Oldham Ath.	07.75	1976-86	209	2	2	(D)	
HOOPER, Michael D.	Bristol	10.02.64		Bristol C.	01.84	1984	1	0	0	(G)	
			Tr	Wrexham	02.85	1984-85	34	0	0		
			Tr	Liverpool	10.85	1986-87	13	0	0		
HOPKINS, Anthony	Pontypool	17.02.71	YTS	Newport Co.(YTS)	08.87	1987	2	4	0	(W)	
HOPKINS, Jeff	Swansea	14.04.64	App	Fulham	09.81	1980-87	213	6	4	(CD)	W U21-2/W-14
HOPKINS, Robert	Birmingham	25.10.61	App	Aston Villa	07.79	1979-82	1	2	1	(W)	
			Tr	Birmingham C.	03.83	1982-86	123	0	21		
			Tr	Manchester C.	08.86	1986	7	0	1		
			Tr	West Bromwich A.	10.86	1986-87	53	1	6		
HORNE, Barry	St Asaph	18.05.62	Rhyl	Wrexham	06.84	1984-86	136	0	17	(M)	W-3
			Tr	Portsmouth	07.87	1987	36	3	3		
HORNE, Brian S.	Billericay	05.10.67	App	Millwall	10.85	1986-87	75	0	0	(G)	E Yth Int
HORNER, Philip M.	Leeds	10.11.66	App	Leicester C.	11.84	1986-87	7	3	0	(CD)	E Yth Int
			L	Rotherham U.	03.86	1985	3	1	0		
HORRIX, Dean V.	Maidenhead	21.11.61	App	Millwall	04.79	1980-82	65	7	19	(F)	
			Tr	Gillingham	03.83	1982	7	7	0		
			Tr	Reading	08.83	1983-87	135	23	35		
			L	Cardiff C.	02.87	1986	9	0	3		
			Tr	Millwall	03.88	1987	0	2	1		
HORSCROFT, Grant	Fletching (E.Sx)	30.07.61	Lewes	Brighton & H.A.	03.87	1987	2	0	0	(CD)	
HORWOOD, Neil K.	Peterhead	04.08.64	Kings Lynn	Grimsby T.	08.86	1986	0	1	0	(F)	
			L	Halifax T.	12.86	1986	3	0	0		
			L	Tranmere Rov.	03.87	1986	4	0	1		
			Tr	Cambridge U.(N/C)	08.87	1987	4	10	2		
HOSKIN, J. Ashley	Accrington	27.03.68	App	Burnley	12.85	1985-87	70	13	11	(LW)	
HOTTE, Tim A.	Bradford	04.10.63	Arsenal (App)	Huddersfield T.	09.81	1981-82	14	2	4	(F)	
			Harrogate T.	Halifax T.(N/C)	08.85	1985	2	2	0		
			Frickley Ath.	Hull C.	10.87	1987	1	3	0		
HOUCHEN, Keith M.	Middlesbrough	25.07.60	Chesterfield (Jnr.)	Hartlepool U.	02.78	1977-81	160	10	65	(F)	
			Tr	Leyton Orient	03.82	1981-83	74	2	20		
			Tr	York C.	03.84	1983-85	56	11	19		
			Tr	Scunthorpe U.	03.86	1985	9	0	2		
			Tr	Coventry C.	06.86	1986-87	33	8	5		
HOUGH, David J.	Crewe	20.02.66	App	Swansea C.	02.84	1983-87	96	13	8	(W)	W Yth Int
HOUGHTON, Peter	Liverpool	30.11.54	South Liverpool	Wigan Ath.	(N/L)	1978-83	169	16	62	(F)	
			Tr	Preston N.E.	10.83	1983-84	52	4	16		
			L	Wrexham	11.84	1984	5	0	2		
			Tr	Chester C.	08.85	1985-87	78	7	13		

Players Names	Birthplace	Date	Source	League Club	Date Sign'd	Seasons Played	Career Record Apps	Sub	Gls	Pos.	Misc
HOUGHTON, Ray J.	Glasgow	09.01.62	Jnrs	West Ham U.	07.79	1981	0	1	0	(M)	IR-14
			Tr	Fulham,	07.82	1982-85	129	0	16		
			Tr	Oxford U.	09.85	1985-87	83	0	10		
			Tr	Liverpool	10.87	1987	26	2	5		
HOUSTON, Graham R.	Gibraltar	24.02.60	Jnrs	Preston N.E.	03.78	1979-84	90	38	11	(W)	
			Tr	Burnley (N/C)	09.85						
			Tr	Wigan Ath.	06.86	1986	16	1	4		
			Northwich Vic.	Carlisle U.(N/C)	10.87	1987	8	8	1		
HOWARD, Mark	Kings Lynn	25.10.64	Kings Lynn	Stockport Co.(N/C)	04.88	1987	2	0	0	(RB)	
HOWARD, Matthew J.	Watford	05.12.70	YTS	Brentford (YTS)	07.87	1987	0	1	0	(D)	
HOWARD, Terry	Stepney	26.02.66	App	Chelsea	02.84	1984-86	6	0	0	(CD)	E Yth Int
			L	Crystal Palace	01.86	1985	4	0	0		
			L	Chester C.	01.87	1986	2	0	0		
			Tr	Leyton Orient	03.87	1986-87	53	0	4		
HOWELLS, David G.	Guildford	15.12.67	YTS	Tottenham H.	01.85	1985-87	5	8	1	(F)	E Yth Int
HOWLETT, Gary P.	Dublin	02.04.63	Home Farm	Coventry C.	11.80					(M)	IR Yth Int/IR-1
			Tr	Brighton & H.A.	08.82	1982-84	30	2	2		
			Tr	Bournemouth	12.84	1984-86	56	4	7		
			L	Aldershot	08.87	1987	1	0	0		
			L	Chester C.	12.87	1987	6	0	1		
			Tr	York C.	01.88	1987	18	0	2		
HOYLAND, Jamie W.	Sheffield	23.01.66	App	Manchester C.	11.83	1983-84	2	0	0	(M)	Son of Tommy/
			Tr	Bury	07.86	1986-87	77	3	10		E Yth Int
HUCKER, Peter I.	Hampstead	28.10.59	App	Q.P.R.	07.77	1980-85	160	0	0	(G)	E U21-2
			Tr	Oxford U.	02.87	1986-87	32	0	0		
			L	West Bromwich A.	01.88	1987	7	0	0		
HUGHES, Adrian F.S.	Billinge	19.12.70	YTS	Preston N.E.(YTS)	08.87	1987	1	0	0	(CD)	
HUGHES, Darren J.	Prescot	06.10.65	App	Everton	10.83	1983-84	3	0	0	(LB)	
			Tr	Shrewsbury T.	06.85	1985-86	34	3	1		
			Tr	Brighton & H.A.	09.86	1986	26	0	2		
			Tr	Port Vale	09.87	1987	43	0	1		
HUGHES, Ken D.	Barmouth	09.01.66	Jnrs	Crystal Palace	08.85					(G)	
			Tr	Shrewsbury T.	07.86	1986-87	8	0	0		
HUGHES, L. Mark	Wrexham	01.11.63	App	Manchester U.	11.80	1983-85	85	4	37	(F)	W Sch Int/W U21-3 to Barcelona (Sp.) 7.86
HUGHES, Mark	Port Talbot	03.02.62	App	Bristol Rov.	02.80	1979-83	73	1	3	(CD)	Brother of Wayne/
			L	Torquay U.	12.82	1982	9	0	1		W Yth Int
			Tr	Swansea C.	07.84	1984	12	0	0		
			Tr	Bristol C.	02.85	1984-85	21	1	0		
			Tr	Tranmere Rov.	09.85	1985-87	87	3	1		
HUGHES, Mike R.	Bridgend	19.08.64	App	Swansea C.	08.82	1983-87	139	0	0	(G)	W Yth Int
HUGHES, Paul	Ashton-u-Lyne	19.12.68	YTS	Bolton W.	07.87	1987	99	0	0	(FB)	
HUGHES, Zacari D.	Australia	06.06.71	YTS	Rochdale (YTS)	07.87	1987	2	0	0	(CD)	
HUGHTON, Chris W.G.	Stratford	11.12.58	Jnrs	Tottenham H.	06.77	1979-87	265	3	12	(FB)	Brother of Henry IR U21-1/IR-35
HUGHTON, Henry T.	Stratford	18.11.59	App	Leyton Orient	12.76	1978-81	104	7	2	(D)	
			Tr	Crystal Palace	07.82	1982-85	113	5	1		
			Tr	Brentford	09.86	1986	5	3	0		
			Tr	Leyton Orient	12.86	1986-87	16	2	0		
HULL, Alan E.	Southend	04.09.62	Barking	Leyton Orient	05.87	1987	27	9	5	(M)	Brother of Jeff
HUMES, A. (Tony)	Blyth	19.03.66	App	Ipswich T.	05.83	1986-87	44	5	2	(CD)	
HUMPHREY, John	Paddington	31.01.61	App	Wolverhampton W.	01.79	1979-84	149	0	3	(RB)	
			Tr	Charlton Ath.	07.85	1985-87	118	0	2		
HUMPHRIES, Glenn	Hull	11.08.64	App	Doncaster Rov.	08.82	1980-87	174	6	8	(CD)	E Yth Int
			L	Lincoln C.	03.87	1986	9	0	0		
			Tr	Bristol C.	10.87	1987	24	0	0		
HUNT, David	Leicester	17.04.59	App	Derby Co.	04.77	1977	5	0	0	(M)	
			Tr	Notts. Co.	03.78	1977-86	331	5	28		
			Tr	Aston Villa	06.87	1987	11	1	0		
HUNT, Mark G.	Farnworth	05.10.69	YTS	Rochdale (YTS)	08.86	1986-87	1	1	1	(F)	
HUNT, Steve K.	Birmingham	04.08.56	App	Aston Villa	01.74	1974-76	4	3	1	(M)	E-2
			New York Cos.(USA)	Coventry C.	08.78	1978-83	178	7	26		
			Tr	West Bromwich A.	03.84	1983-85	68	0	15		
			Tr	Aston Villa	03.86	1985-87	61	1	6		
HUNTER, Geoff	Hull	27.10.59	App	Manchester U.	11.76					(M)	
			Tr	Crewe Alex.	08.79	1979-80	86	1	8		
			Tr	Port Vale	08.81	1981-86	218	3	15		
			Tr	Wrexham	08.87	1987	37	2	4		
HUNTER, Lee	Oldham	05.10.69	YTS	Colchester U.	06.88	1987	1	0	0	(D)	Son of Alan
HUNTER, Les	Middlesbrough	15.01.58	App	Chesterfield	08.75	1975-81	156	9	8	(CD)	
			Tr	Scunthorpe U.	07.82	1982-83	61	0	8		
			Tr	Chesterfield	01.84	1983-85	99	0	9		
			Tr	Scunthorpe U.	03.86	1985-86	49	0	5		
			Lincoln C.	Chesterfield	12.87	1987	25	0	3		
HURLOCK, Terry A.	Hackney	22.09.58	Leytonstone & Ilford	Brentford	08.80	1980-85	220	0	18	(M)	
			Tr	Reading	02.86	1985-86	29	0	0		
			Tr	Millwall	02.87	1986-87	40	1	5		
HUTCHINGS, Chris	Winchester	05.07.57	Harrow Bor.	Chelsea	07.80	1980-83	83	4	3	(FB)	
			Tr	Brighton & H.A.	11.83	1983-87	153	0	4		
			Tr	Huddersfield T.	12.87	1987	23	0	0		
HUTCHINSON, R.(Bobby)	Glasgow	19.06.53	Hibernian	Wigan Ath.	07.80	1980	34	1	3	(M)	
			Tr	Tranmere Rov.	08.81	1981-82	32	3	6		
			Tr	Mansfield T.	10.82	1982-83	35	0	3		
			Tr	Tranmere Rov.	01.84	1983	21	0	4		
			Tr	Bristol C.	07.84	1984-86	89	3	10		
			Tr	Walsall	02.87	1986-87	8	8	0		
			L	Blackpool	09.87	1987	3	3	0		
			L	Carlisle U.	01.88	1987	12	1	2		

Players Names	Birthplace	Date	Previous Club	League Club	Date Sign'd	Seasons Played	Apps	Sub	Gls	Pos.	Misc
HUTCHISON, Tommy	Cardenden	22.09.47	Alloa Ath.	Blackpool	02.68	1967-72	163	2	10	(LW)	S-17
			Tr	Coventry C.	10.72	1972-80	312	2	24		
			Tr	Manchester C.	10.80	1980-81	44	2	4		
			Hong Kong	Burnley	08.83	1983-84	92	0	4		
			Tr	Swansea C.	07.85	1985-87	84	5	4		
HYDE, Gary S.	Wolverhampton	28.12.69	YTS	Darlington	07.88	1987	0	2	0	(F)	
IMPEY, John E.	Exeter	11.08.54	App	Cardiff C.	08.72	1972-74	13	8	0	(CD)	E Sch Int/
			Tr	Bournemouth	07.75	1975-82	280	4	7		E Yth Int
			Tr	Torquay U.	08.83	1983-84	72	0	0		
			Tr	Exeter C.	08.85	1985	26	0	0		
			Tr	Torquay U.	07.86	1986-87	58	0	2		
INCE, Paul E.C.	Ilford	21.10.67	YTS	West Ham U.	07.85	1986-87	33	5	4	(M)	E Yth Int
IRONSIDE, Ian	Sheffield	08.03.64	Jnrs	Barnsley	09.82					(G)	Son of Roy
			North Ferriby U.	Scarborough (N/C)	03.88	1987	6	0	0		
IRVINE, Alan J.	Broxburn	29.11.62	Falkirk	Liverpool	11.86	1986	0	2	0	(F)	
			Dundee U.	Shrewsbury T.	02.88	1987	3	3	1		
IRWIN, Dennis J.	Cork	31.10.65	App	Leeds U.	10.83	1983-85	72	0	1	(RB)	IR Yth Int
			Tr	Oldham Ath.	05.86	1986-87	84	0	1		
ISAAC, Robert C.	Hackney	30.11.65	App	Chelsea	11.83	1984-86	9	0	0	(CD)	E Yth Int
			Tr	Brighton & H.A.	02.87	1986-87	21	0	0		
JACKETT, Kenny F.	Watford	05.01.62	App	Watford	01.80	1979-87	273	3	26	(M)	Son of Frank/W Yth Int/W U21-2/W-31
JACKSON, Craig	Newark	15.09.68	YTS	Notts Co.	08.86	1985-86	3	2	0	(CD)	
JACKSON, Darren	Edinburgh	25.07.66	Meadowbank Th.	Newcastle U.	10.86	1986-87	40	14	5	(W)	
JACKSON, Peter A.	Bradford	06.04.61	App	Bradford C.	04.79	1978-86	267	11	24	(CD)	
			Tr	Newcastle U.	10.86	1986-87	59	0	3		
JACOBS, Wayne G.	Sheffield	03.02.69	App	Sheffield Wed.	01.87	1987	5	1	0	(M)	
			Tr	Hull C.	03.88	1987	6	0	0		
JAMES, Julian C.	Tring	22.03.70	YTS	Luton T.	06.88	1987	0	3	0	(CD)	
JAMES, Leighton	Loughor	16.02.53	App	Burnley	02.70	1970-75	180	1	44	(LW)	W Sch Int/
			Tr	Derby Co.	10.75	1975-77	67	1	15		W U23-7/W-54
			Tr	Q.P.R.	10.77	1977-78	27	1	4		
			Tr	Burnley	09.78	1978-79	76	0	9		
			Tr	Swansea C.	04.80	1979-82	88	10	27		
			Tr	Sunderland	01.83	1982-83	50	2	4		
			Tr	Bury	08.84	1984	46	0	5		
			Tr	Newport Co.	08.85	1985	21	7	2		
			Tr	Burnley	08.86	1986-87	61	0	10		
JAMES, Paul J.	Cardiff	11.11.63	Hamilton(Can.)	Doncaster Rov.	11.87	1987	7	1	0	(M)	Canadian Int
JAMES, Robbie M.	Swansea	23.03.57	App	Swansea C.	04.74	1972-82	386	8	99	(M)	W U21-3/W-47
			Tr	Stoke C.	07.83	1983-84	48	0	6		
			Tr	Q.P.R.	10.84	1984-86	78	9	5		
			Tr	Leicester C.	06.87	1987	21	2	0		
			Tr	Swansea C.	01.88	1987	19	0	3		
JASPER, Dale W.	Croydon	14.01.64	App	Chelsea	01.82	1983-84	10	0	0	(M)	
			Tr	Brighton & H.A.	05.86	1986-87	44	5	6		
JEFFELS, Simon	Darton	18.01.66	App	Barnsley	01.84	1983-87	39	3	0	(CD)	E Yth Int
			L	Preston N.E.	10.87	1987	1	0	0		
JEMSON, Nigel B.	Preston	10.08.69	YTS	Preston N.E.	06.87	1985-87	28	4	8	(F)	
			Tr	Nottingham F.	03.88						
JENKINSON, Leigh	Thorne	09.07.69	YTS	Hull C.	06.87	1987	2	1	1	(W)	
JEWELL, Paul	Liverpool	28.09.64	App	Liverpool	09.82					(F)	
			Tr	Wigan Ath.	12.84	1984-87	117	20	35		
JOBLING, Kevin A.	Sunderland	01.01.68	App	Leicester C.	01.86	1986-87	4	5	0	(M)	
			Tr	Grimsby T.	02.88	1987	15	0	1		
JOBSON, Richard I.	Holderness	09.05.63	Burton A.	Watford	11.82	1982-84	26	2	4	(D)	
			Tr	Hull C.	02.85	1984-87	126	2	14		
JOHN, Stephen P.	Brentwood	22.12.66	App	Leyton Orient	12.84	1985-86	23	0	0	(D)	
JOHNROSE, Leonard	Preston	29.11.69	YTS	Blackburn Rov.	06.88	1987	0	1	0		
JOHNS, Nicky P.	Bristol	08.06.57	Minehead	Millwall	02.76	1976-77	50	0	0	(G)	
			Tampa Bay (USA)	Sheffield U.	09.78	1978	1	0	0		
			Tr	Charlton Ath.	12.78	1978-87	288	0	0		
			Tr	Q.P.R.	12.87	1987	7	0	0		
JOHNSON, Gary J.	Peckham	14.09.59	App	Chelsea	08.78	1978-80	16	3	9	(F)	
			Tr	Brentford	12.80	1980-82	55	5	13		
			South Africa	Aldershot	08.85	1985-87	73	2	20		
JOHNSON, Marvin A.	Wembley	29.10.68	App	Luton T.	10.86	1986-87	7	2	0	(CD)	
JOHNSON, Nigel M.	Rotherham	23.06.64	App	Rotherham U.	06.82	1982-84	89	0	1	(CD)	
			Tr	Manchester C.	06.85	1985	4	0	0		
			Tr	Rotherham U.	07.87	1987	23	0	0		
JOHNSON, Paul	Stoke	25.05.59	App	Stoke C.	05.77	1978-80	33	1	0	(LB)	
			Tr	Shrewsbury T.	05.81	1981-86	178	2	3		
			Tr	York C.	07.87	1987	39	0	0		
JOHNSON, Peter E.	Harrogate	05.10.58	App	Middlesbrough	10.76	1977-79	42	1	0	(LB)	
			Tr	Newcastle U.	10.80	1980	16	0	0		
			L	Bristol C.	09.82	1982	20	0	0		
			Tr	Doncaster Rov.	03.83	1982	12	0	0		
			Tr	Darlington	08.83	1983-84	89	0	2		
			Whitby T.	Crewe Alex.(N/C)	10.85	1985	8	0	0		
			Whitby T.	Exeter C.(N/C)	03.86	1985	5	0	0		
			Tr	Southend U.	08.86	1986-87	83	0	3		
JOHNSON, Robert S.	Bedford	22.02.62	App	Luton T.	08.79	1983-87	72	4	0	(FB)	
			L	Lincoln C.	08.83	1983	4	0	0		

Steve Hardwick (Oxford United) One of the many fine keepers to have started with Chesterfield.
Match Magazine

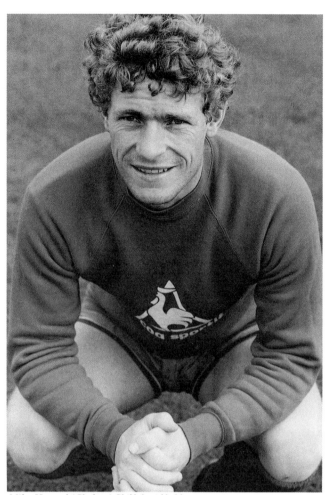

Mike Hazard (Chelsea) Skilful midfield man.
Match Magazine

Paul Hart (Notts County) Rugged central defender seen here in action on the right for Sheffield Wednesday.
Match Magazine

Trevor Hebberd (Oxford United) Midfield player who has hardly missed a match since signing from Southampton in 1982.
Match Magazine

Players Names	Birthplace	Date	Source	League Club	Date Sign'd	Seasons Played	Career Record Apps	Career Record Sub	Career Record Gls	Pos.	Misc
JOHNSON, Steve A.	Liverpool	23.06.57	Altrincham	Bury	11.77	1977-82	139	15	52	(F)	
			Tr	Rochdale	08.83	1983	17	2	7		
			Tr	Wigan Ath.	02.84	1983-84	50	1	18		
			Tr	Bristol C.	03.85	1984-85	14	7	3		
			L	Rochdale	12.85	1985	3	3	1		
			L	Chester C.	03.86	1985	10	0	6		
			Tr	Scunthorpe U.	07.86	1986-87	59	13	20		
JOHNSTON, Craig P.	South Africa	08.12.60	Australia/App	Middlesbrough	02.78	1977-80	61	3	16	(W)	E U21-2
				Liverpool	04.81	1981-87	165	25	30		
JONES, Alex	Blackburn	27.11.64	App	Oldham Ath.	12.82	1982-84	8	1	0	(CD)	
			L	Stockport Co.	10.84	1984	3	0	0		
			Tr	Preston N.E.	06.86	1986-87	68	0	3		
JONES, Andy M.	Wrexham	09.01.63	Rhyl	Port Vale	06.85	1985-87	87	3	47	(F)	W-5
			Tr	Charlton Ath.	09.87	1987	21	4	6		
JONES, Joey P.	Llandudno	04.03.55	Jnrs	Wrexham	01.73	1972-74	98	0	2	(D)	Brother of Frank
			Tr	Liverpool	07.75	1975-77	72	0	3		W U23-4/W-72
			Tr	Wrexham	10.78	1978-82	145	1	6		
			Tr	Chelsea	10.82	1982-84	76	2	2		
			Tr	Huddersfield T.	08.85	1985-86	67	1	3		
			Tr	Wrexham	08.87	1987	35	0	0		
JONES, Keith A.	Dulwich	14.10.65	App	Chelsea	08.83	1982-86	43	9	7	(M)	E Sch Int/E Yth Int
			Tr	Brentford	09.87	1987	34	2	1		
JONES, Linden	Tredegar	05.03.61	App	Cardiff C.	03.79	1978-83	142	3	2	(RB)	W U21-3
			Tr	Newport Co.	09.83	1983-86	141	0	5		
			Tr	Reading	07.87	1987	27	1	3		
JONES, Mark	Brownhills	04.01.68	App	Walsall	01.86	1987	6	2	0	(RB)	
JONES, Mark	Berinsfield	26.09.61	App	Oxford U.	09.79	1979-85	101	28	7	(M)	
			Tr	Swindon T.	09.86	1986	39	1	9		
JONES, Mark A.W.	Warley	22.10.61	App	Aston Villa	07.79	1981-83	24	0	0	(RB)	
			Tr	Brighton & H.A.	03.84	1983-84	9	0	0		
			Tr	Birmingham C.	10.84	1984-86	33	1	0		
			Tr	Shrewsbury T.	03.87						
			Tr	Hereford U.	06.87	1987	27	1	0		
JONES, Paul A.	Walsall	06.09.65	App	Walsall	09.83	1982-87	109	15	15	(M)	
JONES, Paul B.	Ellesmere Port	13.05.53	App	Bolton W.	06.70	1970-82	440	4	37	(CD)	
			Tr	Huddersfield T.	07.83	1983-85	73	0	8		
			Tr	Oldham Ath.	12.85	1985-86	32	0	1		
			Tr	Blackpool	03.87	1986-87	31	6	0		
JONES, Philip A.	Liverpool	01.12.69	YTS	Everton	06.88	1987	0	1	0	(D)	
JONES, Richard J.	Pontypool	26.04.69	YTS	Newport Co.	07.87	1986-87	31	10	1	(M)	
JONES, Rob	Wrexham	05.11.71	Jnrs	Crewe Alex.(Sch.)		1987	4	1	0	(D)	
JONES, Vaughan	Tonyrefail	02.09.59	App	Bristol Rov.	09.77	1976-81	93	8	3	(D)	W Yth Int/
			Tr	Newport Co.	08.82	1982-83	67	1	4		W U21-2
			Tr	Cardiff C.	07.84	1984	11	0	0		
			Tr	Bristol Rov.	12.84	1984-87	129	3	4		
JONES, Vince	Watford	05.01.65	Wealdstone	Wimbledon	11.86	1986-87	46	0	6	(M)	
JONSSON, Siggi	Iceland	27.09.66	Akranes(Ice.)	Sheffield Wed.	02.85	1984-87	34	5	3	(M)	Iceland Int
			L	Barnsley	01.86	1985	5	0	0		
JORDAN, Joe	Carluke	15.12.51	Morton	Leeds U.	10.70	1971-77	139	30	35	(F)	S-52/S U23-1/
			Tr	Manchester U.	01.78	1977-80	109	0	37		A.C. Milan (It)
			Verona (It.)	Southampton	08.84	1984-86	48	0	12		1980-83
			Tr	Bristol C.	02.87	1986-87	36	11	7		
JOSEPH, Francis	Kilburn	06.03.60	Hillingdon Bor.	Wimbledon	11.80	1980-81	42	9	14	(F)	Brother of Roger
			Tr	Brentford	07.82	1982-86	103	7	44		
			L	Wimbledon	03.87	1986	2	3	1		
			Tr	Reading	07.87	1987	5	6	2		
			L	Bristol Rov.	01.88	1987	3	0	0		
			L	Aldershot	03.88	1987	9	1	2		
JOSEPH, Roger	Paddington	24.12.65	Southall	Brentford	10.84	1984-87	103	1	2	(RB)	Brother of Francis
JOYCE, Joe P.	Consett	18.03.61	School	Barnsley	11.79	1979-87	284	2	4	(RB)	
JOYCE, Sean W.	Doncaster	15.02.67	YTS	Doncaster Rov.	09.86	1985-87	39	2	2	(M)	
			L	Exeter C.	11.86	1986	1	0	0		
JOYCE, Warren G.	Oldham	20.01.65	Jnrs	Bolton W.	06.82	1982-87	180	4	17	(M)	Son of Walter
			Tr	Preston N.E.	10.87	1987	21	1	0		
JUDGE, Alan G.	Kingsbury	14.05.60	Jnrs	Luton T.	01.78	1979-82	11	0	0	(G)	
			Tr	Reading	09.82	1982-84	77	0	0		
			Tr	Oxford U.	12.84	1985-87	37	0	0		
			L	Lincoln C.	11.85	1985	2	0	0		
			L	Cardiff C.	10.87	1987	8	0	0		
JURYEFF, Ian M.	Gosport	24.11.62	App	Southampton	11.80	1983	0	2	0	(F)	
			L	Mansfield T.	03.84	1983	12	0	5		
			L	Reading	11.84	1984	7	0	1		
			Tr	Leyton Orient	02.85	1984-87	78	4	35		
KAMARA, Alan	Sheffield	15.07.58	Kiveton Park	York C.	07.79	1979	10	0	0	(FB)	
			Tr	Darlington	06.80	1980-82	134	0	1		
			Burton Albion	Scarborough	11.87	1987	29	0	0		
KAMARA, Chris	Middlesbrough	25.12.57	App	Portsmouth	12.75	1975-76	56	7	7	(M)	
			Tr	Swindon T.	08.77	1977-80	133	14	21		
			Tr	Portsmouth	08.81	1981	11	0	0		
			Tr	Brentford	10.81	1981-84	150	2	28		
			Tr	Swindon T.	08.85	1985-87	86	1	6		
KASULE, Victor P.A.	Glasgow	28.05.65	Meadowbank Th.	Shrewsbury T.	01.88	1987	13	1	3	(W)	
KAY, John	Sunderland	29.01.64	App	Arsenal	08.81	1982-83	13	1	0	(RB)	
			Tr	Wimbledon	07.84	1984-86	63	0	2		
			L	Middlesbrough	01.85	1984	8	0	0		
			Tr	Sunderland	07.87	1987	46	0	0		
KEANE, Tommy J.	Galway	16.09.68	App	Bournemouth	09.86	1985-87	1	2	0	(F)	IR Yth Int
			Tr	Colchester U.	12.87	1987	9	7	0		

Ricky Hill (Luton Town) A grand clubman who has been at Kenilworth Road since leaving school.
Match Magazine

Ray Houghton (Liverpool) Midfield acquisition from Oxford United last October.
Match Magazine

Peter Hucker (West Bromiwch Albion) A former Q.P.R. goalkeeping hero.
Match Magazine

Craig Johnston (Liverpool) South African born midfielder. Match Magazine

Players Names	Birthplace	Date	Source	League Club	Date Sign'd	Seasons Played	Apps	Sub	Gls	Pos.	Misc
KEARNEY, Mark J.	Ormskirk	12.06.62	Marine	Everton	10.81					(W)	
			Tr	Mansfield T.	03.83	1982-87	143	1	24		
KEARNS, Ollie A.	Banbury	12.06.56	Banbury U.	Reading	03.77	1976-79	75	11	40	(F)	Brother of Mike
			Tr	Oxford U.	08.81	1981	9	9	4		
			Tr	Walsall	08.82	1982	31	7	11		
			Tr	Hereford U.	06.83	1983-87	166	4	58		
			Tr	Wrexham	12.87	1987	16	1	8		
KEELEY, Glenn M.	Barking	01.09.54	App	Ipswich T.	08.72	1972-73	4	0	0	(CD)	E Yth Int
			Tr	Newcastle U.	07.74	1974-75	43	1	2		
			Tr	Blackburn Rov.	08.76	1976-86	365	5	23		
			L	Everton	10.82	1982	1	0	0		
			Tr	Oldham Ath.	08.87	1987	10	1	0		
			L	Colchester U.	02.88	1987	4	0	0		
KEELEY, John H.	Plaistow	27.07.61	App	Southend U.	07.79	1979-84	63	0	0	(G)	
			Chelmsford C.	Brighton & H.A.	08.86	1986-87	66	0	0		
KEEN, Kevin I.	Amersham	25.02.67	App	West Ham U.	03.84	1986-87	26	10	1	(M)	Son of Mike/ E Yth Int/E Sch Int
KELLOW, Tony	Falmouth	01.05.52	Falmouth	Exeter C.	07.76	1976-78	107	0	40	(F)	
			Tr	Blackpool	11.78	1978-79	57	0	23		
			Tr	Exeter C.	03.80	1979-83	140	3	61		
			Tr	Plymouth Arg.	11.83	1983	8	2	2		
			Tr	Swansea C.(N/C)	10.84	1984	0	1	0		
			Tr	Newport Co.(N/C)	11.84	1984	18	2	8		
			Tr	Exeter C.	07.85	1985-87	51	31	27		
KELLY, Alan T.	Preston	11.08.68	YTS	Preston N.E.	09.85	1985-87	54	0	0	(G)	Son of Alan J./ IR Yth Int
KELLY, A.G. (Tony)	Prescot	01.10.64	App	Liverpool	09.82					(M)	
			Prescot Cables	Wigan Ath.	01.84	1983-85	98	3	15		
			Tr	Stoke C.	04.86	1985-86	33	3	4		
			Tr	West Bromwich A.	07.87	1987	26	0	1		
KELLY, David T.	Birmingham	25.11.65	Alvechurch	Walsall	12.83	1983-87	115	32	63	(F)	IR-3
KELLY, Errington E.	St. Vincent (WI)	08.04.58	Ledbury T.	Bristol Rov.	09.81	1981-82	12	6	3	(W)	
			Tr	Lincoln C.(N/C)	01.83	1982	0	2	0		
			Tr	Bristol C.	02.83	1982	4	1	1		
			Tr	Coventry C.	08.83							
			Tr	Peterborough U.	03.84	1983-85	59	13	22		
				Peterborough U.	12.86	1986-87	36	10	6		
KELLY, Gary A.	Preston	03.08.66	App	Newcastle U.	06.84	1986-87	40	0	0	(G)	Son of Alan J.
KELLY, John	Bebington	20.10.60	Cammell Laird	Tranmere Rov.	09.79	1979-81	55	9	9	(W)	
			Tr	Preston N.E.	10.81	1981-84	120	10	27		
			Tr	Chester C.	08.85	1985-86	85	0	17		
			Tr	Swindon T.	06.87	1987	3	4	1		
			Tr	Oldham Ath.	11.87	1987	10	0	0		
KELLY, Mark D.	Blackpool	07.10.66		Shrewsbury T.	12.85						(LW)	
			Tr	Cardiff C.	06.87	1987	28	8	1		
KELLY, Mark J.	Sutton	27.11.69	YTS	Portsmouth	11.86	1987	1	2	0	(W)	IR-1
KELLY, Norman	Belfast	10.10.70	YTS	Oldham Ath.(YTS)	07.87	1987	0	1	0		
KELLY, Robert A.	Birmingham	21.12.64	App	Leicester C.	12.82	1983-86	17	7	1	(M)	
			L	Tranmere Rov.	12.84	1984	5	0	2		
			Tr	Wolverhampton W.	03.87	1986	13	1	2		
KELLY, Tom J.	Bellshill	28.03.64	Queen of South	Hartlepool U.	08.85	1985	14	1	0	(LB)	
			Tr	Torquay U.	07.86	1986-87	73	3	0		
KENDALL, Mark	Blackwood	20.09.58	App	Tottenham H.	07.76	1978-80	29	0	0	(G)	W Sch Int/ W U21-1
			L	Chesterfield	11.79	1979	9	0	0		
			Tr	Newport Co.	09.80	1980-86	272	0	0		
			Tr	Wolverhampton W.	12.86	1986-87	70	0	0		
KENDALL, Paul S.	Halifax	19.10.64	App	Halifax T.	10.82	1981-85	91	15	4	(CD)	
			Tr	Scarborough	(N/L)	1987	22	5	1		
			Tr	Halifax T.	03.88	1987	9	1	0		
KENNEDY, Alan P.	Sunderland	31.08.54	App	Newcastle U.	08.72	1972-77	155	3	9	(LB)	E U23-6/E-2
			Tr	Liverpool	08.78	1978-85	249	2	15		
			Tr	Sunderland	09.85	1985-86	54	0	2		
			Sweden	Hartlepool U.(N/C)	10.87	1987	4	1	0		
			Grantham	Wigan Ath.	12.87	1987	22	0	0		
KENNEDY, Andy J.	Stirling	08.10.64	Hong Kong	Birmingham C.	03.85	1984-87	51	25	18	(F)	ex Glasgow Rangers
			L	Sheffield U.	03.87	1986	8	1	1		
KENNEDY, Mick F.	Salford	09.04.61	App	Halifax T.	01.79	1978-79	74	2	4	(M)	IR-2
			Tr	Huddersfield T.	08.80	1980-81	80	1	9		
			Tr	Middlesbrough	08.82	1982-83	68	0	5		
			Tr	Portsmouth	06.84	1984-87	129	0	4		
			Tr	Bradford C.	01.88	1987	15	0	1		
KENT, Kevin J.	Stoke	19.03.65	App	West Bromwich A.	12.82	1983	1	1	0	(W)	
			Tr	Newport Co.	07.84	1984	23	10	1		
			Tr	Mansfield T.	08.85	1985-87	122	3	24		
KENWORTHY, A.D.(Tony)	Leeds	30.10.58	App	Sheffield U.	07.76	1975-85	281	5	34	(CD)	E Yth Int
			Tr	Mansfield T.	03.86	1985-87	78	1	0		
KEOWN, Martin R.	Oxford	24.07.66	App	Arsenal	01.84	1985	22	0	0	(CD)	E Yth Int/E U21-8
			L	Brighton & H.A.	02.85	1984-85	21	2	1		
			Tr	Aston Villa	06.86	1986-87	77	1	3		
KERNAGHAN, Alan N.	Otley	25.04.67	App	Middlesbrough	03.85	1984-87	44	18	7	(F)	
KERR, John J.	Scarborough	06.03.65	Harrow Bor.	Portsmouth	08.87	1987	2	2	0	(F)	USA Int
			L	Peterborough U.	12.87	1987	10	0	1		
KERR, Paul A.	Portsmouth	09.06.64	App	Aston Villa	05.82	1983-86	16	8	3	(M)	
			Tr	Middlesbrough	01.87	1986-87	63	1	5		
KERRINS, Wayne M.	Brentwood	05.08.65	App	Fulham	08.83	1984-87	48	14	1	(M)	Son of Pat
			L	Port Vale	03.85	1984	6	2	0		
KERSLAKE, David	Stepney	19.06.66	App	Q.P.R.	06.83	1984-87	27	9	6	(W)	E Sch Int/E Yth Int/ E U21-1

Players Names	Birthplace	Date	Source	League Club	Date Sign'd	Seasons Played	Apps	Sub	Gls	Pos.	Misc
KETTERIDGE, Steve J.	Stevenage	07.11.59	Derby Co.(App)	Wimbledon	04.78	1978-84	229	8	32	(M)	
			Tr	Crystal Palace	08.85	1985-86	58	1	6		
			Tr	Leyton Orient	07.87	1987	21	5	1		
KEVAN, David J.	Stranraer	31.08.68	App	Notts Co.	08.86	1985-87	65	3	1	(M)	
KILCLINE, Brian	Nottingham	07.05.62	App	Notts Co.	05.80	1979-83	156	2	9	(CD)	E U21-2
			Tr	Coventry C.	06.84	1984-87	115	0	20		
KIMBLE, Alan F.	Dagenham	06.08.66	Jnrs	Charlton Ath.	08.84	1984	6	0	0	(LB)	Twin brother of
			L	Exeter C.	08.85	1985	1	0	0		Garry
			Tr	Cambridge U.	08.86	1986-87	72	4	2		
KIMBLE, Garry L.	Dagenham	06.08.66	Jnrs	Charlton Ath.	08.84	1984	7	2	1	(LW)	Twin brother of
			L	Exeter C.	08.85	1985	1	0	0		Alan
			Tr	Cambridge U.	08.86	1986-87	39	2	2		
			Tr	Doncaster Rov.	10.87	1987	34	0	1		
KING, Andy E.	Luton	14.08.56	App	Luton T.	07.74	1974-75	30	3	9	(M)	E U21-2
			Tr	Everton	04.76	1975-79	150	1	38		
			Tr	Q.P.R.	09.80	1980-81	28	2	9		
			Tr	West Bromwich A.	09.81	1981	21	4	4		
			Tr	Everton	07.82	1982-83	43	1	11		
			Cambuur (Neth.)	Wolverhampton W.	01.85	1984-85	28	0	10		
			Tr	Luton T.	12.85	1985	3	0	0		
			Tr	Aldershot	08.86	1986	36	0	11		
KING, Philip G.	Bristol	28.12.67	App	Exeter C.	01.85	1984-85	24	3	0	(FB)	
			Tr	Torquay U.	07.86	1986	24	0	3		
			Tr	Swindon T.	02.87	1986-87	64	1	1		
KINSELLA, A.S. (Tony)	Grays	30.10.61	App	Millwall	11.78	1978-80	55	6	1	(LW)	IR U21-2
			Tampa Bay (USA)	Ipswich T.	04.82	1982-83	7	2	0		
			Tr	Millwall	06.84	1984-85	20	2	1		
			Enfield	Doncaster Rov.	02.78	1986-87	29	1	4		
KIRKHAM, Paul	Manchester	05.07.69	Manchester U.(YTS)	Huddersfield T.	09.87	1987	0	1	0	(F)	
KITCHING, Philip J.	Lewisham	30.09.67	Bradford C.(YTS)	York C.(N/C)	08.87	1987	7	6	0	(M)	
KITE, Phil D.	Bristol	26.10.62	App	Bristol Rov.	10.80	1980-83	96	0	0	(G)	E Yth Int
			Tr	Southampton	08.84	1984-85	4	0	0		
			L	Middlesbrough	03.86	1985	2	0	0		
			Tr	Gillingham	02.87	1986-87	43	0	0		
KIWOMYA, Andy D.	Huddersfield	01.10.67	YTS	Barnsley	07.85	1985	1	0	0	(W)	E Yth Int
			Tr	Sheffield Wed.	10.86						
KNIGHT, Alan E.	Balham	03.07.61	App	Portsmouth	03.79	1977-87	301	0	0	(G)	E Yth Int/E U21-2
KNIGHT, Ian J.	Hartlepool	26.10.66	App	Barnsley	10.84					(CD)	E U21-2
			Tr	Sheffield Wed.	08.85	1985-86	19	0	0		
KNILL, Alan R.	Slough	08.10.64	App	Southampton	10.82					(CD)	W Yth Int
			Tr	Halifax T.	07.84	1984-86	118	0	6		
			Tr	Swansea C.	08.87	1987	46	0	1		
KNOWLES, J. Barry	Wigan	25.04.59	Barrow	Wigan Ath.	10.84	1984-87	124	3	3	(LB)	
KUHL, Martin	Frimley	10.01.65	App	Birmingham C.	01.83	1982-86	103	8	5	(M)	
			Tr	Sheffield U.	03.87	1986-87	38	0	4		
			Tr	Watford	02.88	1987	4	0	0		
LAKE, Paul A.	Denton	28.10.68	YTS	Manchester C.	05.87	1986-87	33	3	3	(M)	
LANCASHIRE, Carl P.	Blackpool	17.01.09	YTS	Blackpool	06.87	1987	2	5	0	(M)	
LANE, Martin J.	Altrincham	12.04.61	Jnrs	Manchester U.	05.79					(LB)	
			Tr	Chester C.	08.82	1982-86	175	0	3		
			Tr	Coventry C.	01.87	1986-87	0	3	0		
LANGAN, David F.	Dublin	15.02.57	App	Derby Co.	02.75	1976-79	143	0	1	(RB)	IR-25
			Tr	Birmingham C.	07.80	1980-82	92	0	3		
			Tr	Oxford U.	08.84	1984-87	112	2	2		
			L	Leicester C.	10.87	1987	5	0	0		
			Tr	Bournemouth	12.87	1987	19	1	0		
LANGE, A.S. (Tony)	West Ham	10.12.64	App	Charlton Ath.	12.82	1983-85	12	0	0	(G)	
			L	Aldershot	08.85	1985	7	0	0		
			Tr	Aldershot	07.86	1986-87	80	0	0		
LANGLEY, Kevin J.	St. Helens	24.05.64	App	Wigan Ath.	05.82	1981-85	156	4	6	(M)	
			Tr	Everton	07.86	1986	16	0	2		
			Tr	Manchester C.	03.87	1986	9	0	0		
			L	Chester C.	01.88	1987	9	0	0		
			Tr	Birmingham C.	03.88	1987	7	0	0		
LANGLEY, Richard J.	Lambeth	20.03.65	Corinthian Casuals	Fulham	11.86	1986-87	16	0	0	(D)	
LANGLEY, Tommy W.	Lambeth	08.02.58	App	Chelsea	04.75	1974-79	129	13	40	(F)	E Sch Int/E Yth Int/
			Tr	Q.P.R.	08.80	1980	24	1	8		E U21-1
			Tr	Crystal Palace	03.81	1980-82	54	5	9		
			AEK Athens (Gr.)	Coventry C.	03.84	1983	2	0	0		
			Tr	Wolverhampton W.	07.84	1984	22	1	4		
			L	Aldershot	03.85	1984	16	0	4		
			Hong Kong	Aldershot	08.86	1986-87	80	1	21		
LAW, Brian J.	Merthyr Tydfil	01.01.70	App	Q.P.R.	08.87	1987	0	1	0	(D)	
LAW, Nicky	Greenwich	08.09.61	App	Arsenal	07.79					(D)	E Sch Int
			Tr	Barnsley	08.81	1981-85	113	1	1		
			Tr	Blackpool	08.85	1985-86	64	2	1		
			Tr	Plymouth Arg.	03.87	1986-87	37	1	5		
LAWRENCE, George R.	Kensington	14.09.62	App	Southampton	09.80	1981-82	7	3	1	(W)	
			L	Oxford U.	03.82	1981	15	0	4		
			Tr	Oxford U.	11.82	1982-84	63	0	21		
			Tr	Southampton	01.85	1984-86	58	12	11		
			Tr	Millwall	07.87	1987	16	1	4		
LAWRENCE, Les O.	Wolverhampton	18.05.57	Stourbridge	Shrewsbury T.	02.75	1975-76	10	4	2	(F)	
			Telford U.	Torquay U.	07.77	1977-81	170	19	45		
			Tr	Port Vale	08.82	1982	5	3	0		
			Tr	Aldershot	07.83	1983	39	0	22		
			Tr	Rochdale	08.84	1984	15	0	4		
			Tr	Burnley	11.84	1984-85	22	9	8		
			Tr	Peterborough U.	07.86	1986-87	28	5	8		
			Tr	Cambridge U.	02.88	1987	11	2	0		

Players Names	Birthplace	Date	Source	League Club	Date Sign'd	Seasons Played	Apps	Sub	Gls	Pos.	Misc
LAWRENSON, Mark T.	Preston	02.06.57	Jnrs	Preston N.E.	08.74	1974-76	73	0	2	(D)	Son of Tom
			Tr	Brighton & H.A.	07.77	1977-80	152	0	5		IR-38
			Tr	Liverpool	08.81	1981-87	233	8	11		
LAWS, Brian	Wallsend	14.10.61	App	Burnley	10.79	1979-82	125	0	12	(M)	
			Tr	Huddersfield T.	08.83	1983-84	56	0	1		
			Tr	Middlesbrough	03.85	1984-87	103	4	12		
LEABURN, Carl W.	Lewisham	30.03.69	App	Charlton Ath.	03.87	1986-87	11	4	1	(F)	
LEADBITTER, Chris J.	Middlesbrough	17.10.67	App	Grimsby T.	09.85					(W)	
				Hereford U.	08.86	1986-87	32	4	1		
LEANING, Andy J.	Howden	18.05.63	Rowntree-Mackintosh	York C.	06.85	1985-86	69	0	0	(G)	
			Tr	Sheffield U.	05.87	1987	21	0	0		
LEE, Colin	Torquay	12.06.56	App	Bristol C.	06.74					(F/CD)	
			L	Hereford U.	11.74	1974	7	2	0		
			Tr	Torquay U.	01.77	1976-77	35	0	14		
			Tr	Tottenham H.	10.77	1977-79	57	5	18		
			Tr	Chelsea	01.80	1979-86	167	18	36		
			Tr	Brentford	07.87	1987	19	3	1		
LEE, Robert M.	West Ham	01.02.66	Jnrs	Charlton Ath.	07.83	1983-87	123	18	27	(W)	E U21-2
LEE, Sammy	Liverpool	07.02.59	App	Liverpool	04.76	1977-85	190	7	13	(M)	E Yth Int/E U21-6/
			Tr	Q.P.R.	08.86	1986	29	1	0		E-14
LEEBROOK, Peter D.	Saltburn	18.09.68	YTS	Burnley	05.87	1986-87	52	0	0	(RB)	
LEMON, Paul A.	Middlesbrough	03.06.66	App	Sunderland	05.84	1984-87	79	10	14	(W)	
			L	Carlisle U.	12.84	1984	2	0	0		
LENNON, Neil F.	Lurgan (NI)	25.06.71	YTS	Manchester C.(YTS)	11.87	1987	1	0	0	(RB)	
LEONARD, Gary	Newcastle	28.11.65	App	West Bromwich A.	11.83					(M)	
			Tr	Shrewsbury T.	07.85	1985-87	48	19	1		
			L	Hereford U.	03.88	1987	11	0	1		
LEONARD, Mark A.	St. Helens	27.09.62	Witton Albion	Everton	02.82					(F)	
			L	Tranmere Rov.	03.83	1982	6	1	0		
			Tr	Crewe Alex.	06.83	1983-84	51	3	15		
			Tr	Stockport Co.	02.85	1984-86	73	0	23		
			Tr	Bradford C.	09.86	1986-87	32	20	13		
LEONARD, Mike C.	Carshalton	09.05.59	Epsom & Ewell	Halifax T.	07.76	1976-79	69	0	0	(G)	
			Tr	Notts Co.	09.79	1979-87	177	0	0		
LESTER, Mike J.	Manchester	04.08.54	App	Oldham Ath.	08.72	1972-73	26	1	1	(M)	
			Tr	Manchester C.	11.73	1973-76	1	1	0		
			L	Stockport Co.	08.75	1975	8	1	1		
			Washington D.(USA)	Grimsby T.	11.77	1977-79	45	3	10		
			Tr	Barnsley	10.79	1979-80	64	0	11		
			Tr	Exeter C.	08.81	1981	18	1	6		
			Tr	Bradford C.	02.82	1981-82	46	3	2		
			Tr	Scunthorpe U.	03.83	1982-85	106	0	9		
			L	Hartlepool U.	01.86	1985	11	0	1		
			Tr	Stockport Co.	09.86	1986	11	0	0		
			Sweden	Blackpool	12.87	1987	11	0	1		
LE TISSIER, Matt P.	Guernsey	14.10.68	App	Southampton	10.86	1986-87	22	21	6	(W)	E Yth Int
LEVER, Mark	Beverley	29.03.70	YTS	Grimsby T.	06.88	1987	0	1	0		
LEWINGTON, Ray	Lambeth	07.09.56	App	Chelsea	02.74	1975-78	80	5	4	(M)	
			Vancouver W.(Can.)	Wimbledon	09.79	1979	23	0	0		
			Tr	Fulham	03.80	1979-84	172	2	20		
			Tr	Sheffield U.	07.85	1985	36	0	0		
			Tr	Fulham	07.86	1986-87	56	0	1		
LEWIS, Dudley K.	Swansea	17.11.62	App	Swansea C.	11.79	1980-87	188	2	2	(CD)	W Sch Int/ W U21-9/W-1
LEWIS, John	Tredegar	15.10.55	Pontllanfraith	Cardiff C.	08.78	1978-83	135	5	9	(M)	W U21-1
			Tr	Newport Co.	09.83	1983-87	153	0	8		
			Tr	Swansea C.	10.87	1987	25	0	0		
LEWIS, Kevin	Hull	17.10.70	YTS	Stoke C.(YTS)	07.87	1987	0	1	0	(D)	
LEWIS, Micky	Birmingham	15.02.65	App	West Bromwich A.	02.82	1981-83	22	2	0	(M)	E Yth Int
			Tr	Derby Co.	11.84	1984-87	37	6	1		
LEWORTHY, David J.	Portsmouth	22.10.62	App	Portsmouth	09.80	1981	0	1	0	(F)	
			Fareham T.	Tottenham H.	08.84	1984-85	8	3	3		
			Tr	Oxford U.	12.85	1985-86	22	3	7		
			L	Shrewsbury T.	10.87	1987	6	0	3		
LIGHTFOOT, Chris I.	Warrington	01.04.70	YTS	Chester C.	07.88	1987	15	1	1	(CD)	
LILLIS, Jason W.	Chatham	01.10.69	YTS	Gillingham	10.87	1987	3	4	0	(F)	
LILLIS, Mark A.	Manchester	17.01.60	Manchester C.(Jnr)	Huddersfield T.	07.78	1978-84	199	7	56	(F)	
			Tr	Manchester C.	06.85	1985	39	0	11		
			Tr	Derby Co.	08.86	1986-87	6	9	1		
			Tr	Aston Villa	09.87	1987	28	1	4		
LINEKER, Gary W.	Leicester	30.11.60	App	Leicester C.	11.78	1978-84	187	7	95	(F)	E-32/Footballer of
			Tr	Everton	07.85	1985	41	0	30		Year 1986/to Barcelona(Sp.)7.86
LING, Martin	West Ham	15.07.66	App	Exeter C.	01.84	1982-85	109	7	14	(W)	
			Tr	Swindon T.	07.86	1986	2	0	0		
			Tr	Southend U.	10.86	1986-87	59	7	14		
LINIGHAN, Andy	Hartlepool	18.06.62		Hartlepool U.	09.80	1980-83	110	0	4	(CD)	Brother of David
			Tr	Leeds U.	05.84	1984-85	66	0	3		
			Tr	Oldham Ath.	01.86	1985-87	87	0	6		
			Tr	Norwich C.	03.88	1987	12	0	2		
LINIGHAN, David	Hartlepool	09.01.65	Jnrs	Hartlepool U.	03.82	1981-85	84	7	5	(CD)	Brother of Andy
			Tr	Derby Co.	08.86						
			Tr	Shrewsbury T.	12.86	1986-87	65	0	2		
LISTER, Steve H.	Doncaster	18.11.61	App	Doncaster Rov.	05.79	1978-84	229	8	30	(M)	
			Tr	Scunthorpe U.	07.85	1985-87	114	2	19		
LITCHFIELD, Peter	Manchester	27.07.56	Droylsden	Preston N.E.	01.79	1980-84	107	0	0	(G)	
			Tr	Bradford C.	07.85	1985-87	83	0	0		
LIVINGSTONE, Stephen	Middlesbrough	08.09.68	YTS	Coventry C.	07.86	1986-87	4	3	0	(F)	

David Langan (Bournemouth) Joined the "Cherries" from Oxford United last December.
Match Magazine

Martin Keown (Aston Villa) Clearing his lines against the challenge of Crystal Palace's Ian Wright.
Action Images Ltd

Carl Leaburn (Charlton Athletic) Pictured here being outjumped by Oxford United's Colin Greenall.
Action Images Ltd

Players Names	Birthplace	Date	Source	League Club	Date Sign'd	Seasons Played	Apps	Sub	Gls	Pos.	Misc
LLEWELLYN, Andy D.	Bristol	26.02.66	App	Bristol C.	02.84	1982-87	131	9	2	(FB)	E Yth Int
LLOYD, Philip R.	Hemsworth	26.12.64	App	Middlesbrough	12.82					(CD)	
			Tr	Barnsley(N/C)	09.83						
			Tr	Darlington	03.84	1983-86	127	0	3		
			Tr	Torquay U.	08.87	1987	46	0	2		
LOGAN, David	Middlesbrough	05.12.63	Whitby T.	Mansfield T.	06.84	1984-86	67	0	1	(LB)	
			Tr	Northampton T.	02.87	1986-87	39	2	1		
LOMAX, Geoff W.	Droylsden	06.07.64	Jnrs	Manchester C.	07.81	1982-84	23	2	1	(D)	
			L	Wolverhampton W.	10.85	1985	5	0	0		
			Tr	Carlisle U.	12.85	1985-86	37	0	0		
			Tr	Rochdale	07.87	1987	44	0	0		
LONGDEN, D. Paul	Wakefield	28.09.62	App	Barnsley	09.80	1981-82	5	0	0	(LB)	
			Tr	Scunthorpe U.	08.83	1983-87	174	0	0		
LONGHURST, David J.	Northampton	15.01.65	App	Nottingham F.	01.83					(F)	
			Tr	Halifax T.	07.85	1985-86	85	0	24		
			Tr	Northampton T.	06.87	1987	33	2	7		
LORAM, Mark J.	Paignton	13.08.67	Brixham Villa	Torquay U.	01.85	1984-85	50	2	8	(F)	
			Tr	Q.P.R.	05.86						
			Tr	Torquay U.	03.87	1986-87	52	6	12		
LORMOR, Anthony	Ashington	29.10.70	YTS	Newcastle U.	02.88	1987	3	2	2	(F)	
LOVE, Ian J.	Cardiff	01.03.58	Hong Kong	Swansea C.	08.86	1986-87	26	1	9	(F)	
LOVELL, Steve J.	Swansea	16.07.60	App	Crystal Palace	08.77	1980-82	68	6	3	(F)	W Sch Int/W-6
			L	Stockport Co.	10.79	1979	12	0	0		
			Tr	Millwall	03.83	1982-85	143	3	44		
			L	Swansea C.	02.87	1986	2	0	1		
			Tr	Gillingham	02.87	1986-87	51	1	26		
LOWE, David A.	Liverpool	30.08.65	App	Wigan Ath.	06.83	1982-86	179	9	40	(RW)	E Yth Int/ E U21-2
			Tr	Ipswich T.	06.87	1987	41	0	17		
LOWE, Kenny	Sedgefield	06.11.61	App	Hartlepool U.	11.78	1981-83	50	4	3	(M)	
			Barrow	Scarborough	01.88	1987	4	0	0		
LOWE, Simon J.	Westminster	26.12.62	Ossett T.	Barnsley	12.83	1983	2	0	0	(F)	
			Tr	Halifax T.	07.84	1984-85	74	3	19		
			Tr	Hartlepool U.	08.86	1986	12	2	1		
			Tr	Colchester U.	12.86	1986-87	32	4	8		
			Tr	Scarborough	11.87	1987	14	2	3		
LOWERY, A.W. (Tony)	Wallsend	06.07.61	Ashington	West Bromwich A.	03.81	1981	1	0	0	(M)	
			L	Walsall	02.82	1981	4	2	1		
			Tr	Mansfield T.	04.83	1982-87	219	0	19		
LOWEY, John A.	Manchester	07.03.58	App	Manchester U.	03.75					(M)	
			Chicago S.(USA)	Blackburn Rov.	07.77						
			Tr	Port Vale	12.77						
			California S.(USA)	Sheffield Wed.	10.78	1978-79	35	7	4		
			Tr	Blackburn Rov.	11.80	1980-85	136	5	14		
			Tr	Wigan Ath.	07.86	1986	1	2	0		
			L	Chesterfield	11.86	1986	2	0	0		
			L	York C.	03.87	1986	3	3	0		
			Tr	Preston N.E.	08.87	1987	4	0	1		
			Tr	Chester C.	03.88	1987	9	0	0		
LOWNDES, Steve R.	Cwmbran	17.06.60	Jnrs	Newport Co.	10.77	1977-82	200	8	39	(W)	W U21-4/W-9
			Tr	Millwall	08.83	1983-85	95	1	16		
			Tr	Barnsley	08.86	1986-87	58	1	10		
LUFF, Neil	Bletchley	09.04.69	Jnrs	Gillingham	06.87	1987	0	1	0	(M)	
LUKE, Noel E.	Birmingham	28.12.64	App	West Bromwich A.	04.82	1982-83	8	1	1	(W)	
			Tr	Mansfield T.	07.84	1984-85	41	9	9		
			Tr	Peterborough U.	08.86	1986-87	73	0	18		
LUKIC, John	Chesterfield	11.12.60	App	Leeds U.	12.78	1979-82	146	0	0	(G)	E Yth Int/E U21-7
			Tr	Arsenal	07.83	1983-87	147	0	0		
LUND, Gary J.	Grimsby	13.09.64	Sch	Grimsby T.	07.83	1983-85	47	13	24	(F)	E Yth Int/E U21-3
			Tr	Lincoln C.	08.86	1986	41	3	13		
			Tr	Notts. Co.	06.87	1987	32	8	20		
LUNDON, Sean	Liverpool	07.03.69	YTS	Chester C.	12.86	1986-87	34	0	2	(D)	
LYNEX, Steve C.	West Bromwich	23.01.58	App	West Bromwich A.	01.76					(W)	
			Shamrock Rov.	Birmingham C.	04.79	1978-80	28	18	10		
			Tr	Leicester C.	02.81	1980-86	200	13	57		
			L	Birmingham C.	10.86	1986	10	0	2		
			Tr	West Bromwich A.	03.87	1986-87	26	3	3		
McALISTER, Tom G.	Clydebank	10.12.52	App	Sheffield U.	05.70	1971-75	63	0	0	(G)	
			Tr	Rotherham U.	01.76	1975-78	159	0	0		
			Tr	Blackpool	07.79	1979	16	0	0		
			Tr	Swindon T.	05.80	1980	1	0	0		
			L	Bristol Rov.	02.81	1980	13	0	0		
			Tr	West Ham U.	05.81	1981-87	83	0	0		
McALLISTER, Gary	Motherwell	25.12.64	Motherwell	Leicester C.	08.85	1985-87	110	2	25	(M)	
McALLISTER, Kevin	Falkirk	08.11.62	Falkirk	Chelsea	05.85	1985-87	24	9	0	(W)	
McATEER, Andy W.	Preston	24.04.61	App	Preston N.E.	04.79	1979-86	236	2	8	(LB)	
			Tr	Blackpool	12.86	1986-87	37	4	0		
McAUGHTRIE, David	Cumnock	30.01.63	App	Stoke C.	01.81	1980-83	48	3	1	(CD)	
			Tr	Carlisle U.	07.84	1984	28	0	1		
			Tr	York C.	06.85	1985-86	64	0	1		
			Tr	Darlington	07.87	1987	17	2	0		
McAVENNIE, Frank	Glasgow	22.11.59	St Mirren	West Ham U.	06.85	1985-87	85	0	33	(F)	S U21-5/S-5/to Glasgow Celtic 10.87
McCAFFERY, Aiden	Newcastle	30.08.57	App	Newcastle U.	01.75	1974-77	57	2	4	(CD)	E Yth Int
			Tr	Derby Co.	08.78	1978-79	31	6	4		
			Tr	Bristol Rov.	08.80	1980-84	183	1	11		
			L	Bristol C.	02.82	1981	6	0	1		
			L	Torquay U.	03.85	1984	6	0	0		
			Tr	Exeter C.	07.85	1985-86	55	3	0		
			Tr	Hartlepool U.	02.87	1986	6	0	1		
			Whitley Bay	Carlisle U.	01.88	1987	14	0	0		

Players Names	Birthplace	Date	Source	League Club	Date Sign'd	Seasons Played	Apps	Sub	Gls	Pos.	Misc
McCALL, Steve H.	Carlisle	15.10.60	App	Ipswich T.	10.78	1979-86	249	8	7	(LB)	E Yth Int/E U21-6
			Tr	Sheffield Wed.	06.87	1987	5	0	0		
McCALL, Stuart M.	Leeds	10.06.64	App	Bradford C.	06.82	1982-87	235	3	37	(M)	E Yth Int/S U21-1/ Son of Andy
McCARRICK, Mark B.	Liverpool	04.02.62	Witton Albion	Birmingham C.	05.83	1983	12	3	0	(FB)	
			Tr	Lincoln C.	07.84	1984-85	42	2	0		
			Tr	Crewe Alex (N/C)	02.86	1985	10	1	0		
			Runcorn	Tranmere Rov.	08.87	1987	40	0	5		
McCARTHY, Jonathan D.	Middlesbrough	18.08.70	Jnrs	Hartlepool U. (N/C)	11.87	1987	0	1	0	(F)	
McCARTHY, Mike J.	Barnsley	07.02.59	App	Barnsley	07.77	1977-83	272	0	7	(CD)	IR-26/to Glasgow Celtic 5.87
			Tr	Manchester C.	12.83	1983-86	140	0	2		
McCARTHY, Sean C.	Bridgend	12.09.65	Bridgend T.	Swansea C.	10.85	1985-87	76	15	25	(F)	
McCLAIR, Brian J.	Bellshill	08.12.63	Glasgow Celtic	Manchester U.	07.87	1987	40	0	24	(F)	S U21-8/S-7
McCLAREN, Steve	York	03.05.61	App	Hull C.	04.79	1979-84	171	7	16	(M)	
			Tr	Derby Co.	08.85	1985-87	23	2	0		
			L	Lincoln C.	02.87	1986	8	0	0		
			Tr	Bristol C.	02.88	1987	16	0	1		
McCLEAN, Christian A.	Colchester	17.10.63	Clacton T.	Bristol Rov.	03.88	1987	2	4	0	(F)	
McCLELLAND, John	Belfast	07.12.55	Portadown	Cardiff C.	02.74	1974	1	3	1	(CD)	NI-47
			Bangor City	Mansfield T.	05.78	1978-80	122	3	8		
			Glasgow Rangers	Watford	11.84	1984-87	141	0	3		
McCORD, Brian J.	Derby	24.08.68	App	Derby Co.	06.87	1987	1	0	0	(M)	
McCREERY, David	Belfast	16.09.57	App	Manchester U.	10.74	1974-78	48	38	7	(M)	NI Sch Int/ NI U21-1/NI-60
			Tr	Q.P.R.	08.79	1979-80	56	1	4		
			Tulsa R. (USA)	Newcastle U.	10.82	1982-87	201	6	2		
McDERMOTT, Brian J.	Slough	08.04.61	App	Arsenal	02.79	1978-83	38	23	12	(F)	E Yth Int
			L	Fulham	03.83	1982	0	3	0		
			Tr	Oxford U.	12.84	1984-86	16	8	2		
			L	Huddersfield T.	10.86	1986	4	0	1		
			Tr	Cardiff C.	08.87	1987	45	0	7		
McDERMOTT, John	Middlesbrough	03.02.69	YTS	Grimsby T.	06.87	1986-87	34	7	0	(RB)	
McDONAGH, Jim M. (Seamus)	Rotherham	06.10.52	App	Rotherham U.	10.70	1970-75	121	0	0	(G)	E Yth Int/IR-24
			Tr	Bolton W.	08.76	1976-79	161	0	0		
			Tr	Everton	07.80	1980	40	0	0		
			Tr	Bolton W.	08.81	1981-82	81	0	1		
			Tr	Notts. Co.	07.83	1983-84	35	0	0		
			L	Birmingham C.	09.84	1984	1	0	0		
			L	Gillingham	03.85	1984	10	0	0		
			L	Sunderland	08.85	1985	7	0	0		
			USA	Scarborough	11.87	1987	9	0	0		
			L	Huddersfield T.	01.88	1987	6	0	0		
			Tr	Charlton Ath.	03.88						
McDONALD, Alan	Belfast	12.10.63	App	Q.P.R.	08.81	1983-87	137	1	8	(CD)	NI Yth Int/NI-18
			L	Charlton Ath.	03.83	1982	9	0	0		
MacDONALD, Gary	Middlesbrough	26.03.62	App	Middlesbrough	03.80	1980-83	40	13	5	(F)	
			Tr	Carlisle U.	07.84	1984	7	2	0		
			Tr	Darlington	10.84	1984-87	118	3	30		
McDONALD, Ian C.	Barrow	10.05.53	App	Barrow	05.71	1970-71	30	5	2	(M)	
			Tr	Workington	02.73	1972-73	42	0	4		
			Tr	Liverpool	01.74						
			L	Colchester U.	02.75	1974	5	0	2		
			Tr	Mansfield T.	07.75	1975-76	47	9	4		
			Tr	York C.	11.77	1977-81	175	0	29		
			Tr	Aldershot	11.81	1981-87	297	0	43		
MacDONALD, John	Glasgow	15.04.61	Glasgow Rangers	Charlton Ath.	09.86	1986	2	0	0	(F)	S Sch Int/S Yth Int/ S U21-8
			Tr	Barnsley	11.86	1986-87	56	2	14		
MacDONALD, Kevin D.	Inverness	22.12.60	Inverness Caled.	Leicester C.	05.80	1980-84	133	5	8	(M)	
			Tr	Liverpool	11.84	1984-87	26	11	1		
			L	Leicester C.	12.87	1987	3	0	0		
McDONALD, Neil R.	Wallsend	02.11.65	App	Newcastle U.	02.83	1982-87	163	17	24	(M)	E Sch Int/E Yth Int/ E U21-5
McDONALD, R.W. (Bobby)	Aberdeen	13.04.55	App	Aston Villa	09.72	1972-75	33	6	3	(LB)	
			Tr	Coventry C.	08.76	1976-80	161	0	14		
			Tr	Manchester C.	10.80	1980-82	96	0	11		
			Tr	Oxford U.	09.83	1983-86	93	1	14		
			Tr	Leeds U.	02.87	1986-87	18	0	1		
			L	Wolverhampton W.	02.88	1987	6	0	0		
McDONOUGH, Darren K.	Belgium	07.11.62	App	Oldham Ath.	01.80	1980-86	178	5	14	(M)	
			Tr	Luton T.	09.86	1986-87	34	11	5		
McDONOUGH, Roy	Solihull	16.10.58	App	Birmingham C.	10.76	1976	2	0	1	(F)	
			Tr	Walsall	09.78	1978-80	76	6	15		
			Tr	Chelsea	10.80						
			Tr	Colchester U.	02.81	1980-82	89	4	24		
			Tr	Southend U.	08.83	1983	22	0	4		
			Tr	Exeter C.	01.84	1983-84	19	1	1		
			Tr	Cambridge U.	10.84	1984	30	2	5		
			Tr	Southend U.	08.85	1985-87	100	13	20		
McELHINNEY, Gerry A.	Derry (NI)	19.09.56	Distillery	Bolton W.	09.80	1980-84	107	2	2	(CD)	
			L	Rochdale	11.82	1982	20	0	1		
			L	Plymouth Arg.	01.85	1984-87	90	1	2		
McEVOY, Richard P.	Gibraltar	06.08.67	App	Luton T.	08.85	1986	0	1	0	(M)	IR Yth Int
			L	Cambridge U.	02.87	1986	10	1	1		
McEWAN, Stan	Wishaw	08.06.57	App	Blackpool	07.74	1974-81	204	10	24	(CD)	Brother of Billy
			Tr	Exeter C.	07.82	1982-83	65	0	15		
			Tr	Hull C.	03.84	1983-87	113	0	25		
			Tr	Wigan Ath.	12.87	1987	23	0	4		

Players Names	Birthplace	Date	Source	League Club	Date Sign'd	Seasons Played	Career Record Apps	Sub	Gls	Pos.	Misc
McGARVEY, Scott T.	Glasgow	22.04.63	App	Manchester U.	04.80	1980-82	13	12	3	(F)	S-U21-4
			L	Wolverhampton W.	03.84	1983	13	0	2		
			Tr	Portsmouth	07.84	1984-85	17	6	6		
			L	Carlisle U.	01.86	1985	10	0	3		
			Tr	Carlisle U.	07.86	1986	25	0	8		
			Tr	Grimsby T.	03.87	1986-87	49	1	7		
McGEENEY, Pat M.	Sheffield	31.10.66	App	Sheffield U.	10.84	1984-85	15	1	0	(M)	
			L	Rochdale	11.86	1986	3	0	0		
			Tr	Chesterfield	08.87	1987	35	3	1		
McGINLEY, John	Rowlands Gill	11.06.59	Gateshead	Sunderland	01.82	1981	3	0	0	(LW)	
			Charleroi (Bel.)	Lincoln C.	09.84	1984-86	69	2	11		
			Tr	Rotherham U.	09.86	1986	1	2	0		
			L	Hartlepool U.	01.87	1986	2	0	0		
			Tr	Lincoln C.	01.87	1986	21	0	5		
McGOLDRICK, Eddie J.P.	Corby	30.04.65	Nuneaton Bor.	Northampton T.	08.86	1986-87	75	10	7	(W)	
McGRATH, Lloyd A.	Birmingham	24.02.65	App	Coventry C.	12.82	1983-87	102	1	3	(M)	E Yth Int/E U21-1
McGRATH, Paul	Ealing	04.12.59	St Patricks Ath	Manchester U.	04.82	1982-87	141	2	11	(CD)	IR-22
McGRORY, Shaun P.	Coventry	29.02.68	YTS	Coventry C.	07.86					(D)	
			Tr	Burnley	07.87	1987	16	0	1		
McGUGAN, Paul	Glasgow	17.07.64	Glasgow Celtic	Barnsley	10.87	1987	28	1	1	(CD)	
McGUIRE, Doug	Bathgate	06.09.67	Glasgow Celtic	Sunderland	03.88	1987	1	0	0	(M)	
McHALE, Ray	Sheffield	12.08.50		Chesterfield	08.70	1971-74	123	1	27	(M)	
			Tr	Halifax T.	10.74	1974-76	86	0	21		
			Tr	Swindon T.	09.76	1976-79	171	2	32		
			Tr	Brighton & H.A.	05.80	1980	9	2	0		
			Tr	Barnsley	03.81	1980-81	52	1	1		
			Tr	Sheffield U.	08.82	1982-84	66	1	2		
			L	Bury	02.83	1982	6	0	0		
			Tr	Swansea C.	01.85	1984-85	45	2	1		
			Tr	Rochdale(N/C)	08.86	1986	6	1	0		
			Tr	Scarborough	(N/L)	1987	25	0	3		
McILROY, Sammy B.	Belfast	02.08.54	App	Manchester U.	08.71	1971-81	320	22	57	(M)	NI-88
			Tr	Stoke C.	02.82	1981-84	132	1	14		
			Tr	Manchester C.	08.85	1985	12	0	1		
			Orgryte(Swe.)	Manchester C.	11.86	1986	1	0	0		
			Tr	Bury	03.87	1986-87	43	0	6		
McINALLY, Alan	Ayr	10.02.63	Glasgow Celtic	Aston Villa	07.87	1987	18	7	4	(F)	
McJANNET, W. Les	Cumnock	02.08.61		Mansfield T.	08.79	1979-81	73	1	0	(RB)	
			Matlock T.	Scarborough	08.87	1987	29	2	0		
McKENNA, Ken M.	Birkenhead	02.07.60		Tranmere Rov.(N/C)	08.82	1982	2	2	0	(F)	
			Telford U.	Tranmere Rov.	08.87	1987	13	1	3		
McKENZIE, Ian E.	Wallsend	22.08.66	Newcastle U.(App)	Barnsley(N/C)	08.85	1985	1	0	0	(LB)	
			Tr	Stockport Co.	09.86	1986-87	41	1	0		
MACKENZIE, Steve	Romford	23.11.61	App	Crystal Palace	07.79					(M)	E Yth Int/E U21-3
			Tr	Manchester C.	07.79	1979-80	56	2	8		
			Tr	West Bromwich A.	08.81	1981-86	153	3	23		
			Tr	Charlton Ath.	06.87	1987	31	1	2		
McKENZIE, Stuart R.	Hull	19.09.67	YTS	York C.	12.85	1985-87	30	2	0	(FB)	
McKERNON, Craig A.	Gloucester	23.02.68	App	Mansfield T.	02.86	1984-87	30	15	0	(M)	
McKINNON, Robert	Glasgow	31.07.66	Rutherglen Glencairn	Newcastle U.	11.84	1985	1	0	0	(LB)	
			Tr	Hartlepool U.	07.86	1986-87	86	1	2		
MacLAREN, Ross	Edinburgh	14.04.62	Glasgow Rgrs (Jnrs)	Shrewsbury T.	08.80	1980-84	158	3	18	(CD)	
			Tr	Derby Co.	07.85	1985-87	113	9	4		
McLAUGHLIN, Joe	Greenock	02.06.60	Morton	Chelsea	06.83	1983-87	189	0	5	(CD)	S U21-10
McLEAN, David J.	Newcastle	24.11.57	App	Newcastle U.	11.75	1975-77	7	2	0	(M)	E Sch Int
			Tr	Carlisle U.	03.78	1977-78	9	6	0		
			Tr	Darlington	08.79	1979-85	289	5	46		
			Tr	Scunthorpe U.	07.86	1986-87	23	1	3		
			L	Hartlepool U.	03.87	1986	6	0	0		
McLEARY, Alan T.	Lambeth	06.10.64	App	Millwall	10.81	1982-87	148	14	4	(CD)	E Yth Int/E U21-1
McLOUGHLIN, Alan F.	Manchester	20.04.67	App	Manchester U.	04.85					(M)	
			Tr	Swindon T.	08.86	1986-87	15	2	0		
			L	Torquay U.	03.87	1986-87	21	3	4		
McLOUGHLIN, Paul B.	Bristol	23.12.63	Gisborne C.(NZ)	Cardiff C.	12.84	1984-85	40	9	4	(W)	
			Bristol C.(N/C)	Hereford U.	06.87	1987	28	1	1		
McMAHON, Steve	Liverpool	20.08.61	App	Everton	08.79	1980-82	99	1	11	(M)	E U21-6/E-3
			Tr	Aston Villa	05.83	1983-85	74	1	7		
			Tr	Liverpool	09.85	1985-87	100	0	20		
McMILLAN, L. Andy	South Africa	22.06.68	Hull C.(N/C)	York C.	10.87	1987	20	2	0	(FB)	
McMINN, Kevin (Ted)	Castle Douglas	28.09.62	Seville (Sp.)	Derby Co.	02.88	1987	7	0	1	(W)	ex Rangers
McNAB, Neil	Greenock	04.06.57	Morton	Tottenham H.	02.74	1973-78	63	9	3	(M)	S Sch Int/S U21-1
			Tr	Bolton W.	11.78	1978-79	33	2	4		
			Tr	Brighton & H.A.	02.80	1979-82	100	3	4		
			L	Leeds U.	12.82	1982	5	0	0		
			Tr	Manchester C.	07.83	1983-87	163	4	11		
McNALLY, Bernard A.	Shrewsbury	17.02.63	App	Shrewsbury T.	02.81	1980-87	257	3	21	(M)	NI-4
McNAUGHT, John	Glasgow	19.06.64	Hamilton Acad.	Chelsea	04.86	1985-87	9	1	2	(M)	
McNEIL, R.M. (Bobby)	Hamilton	01.11.62	App	Hull C.	11.80	1980-84	135	3	3	(RB)	
			Blackpool (Trial)	Lincoln C.	10.85	1985	4	0	0		
			Tr	Preston N.E.	12.85	1985-86	43	0	0		
			Tr	Carlisle U.	08.87	1987	18	1	0		
McNICHOL, Jim A.	Glasgow	09.06.58	Ipswich T.(App)	Luton T.	07.76	1976-78	13	2	0	(CD)	S U21-7
			Tr	Brentford	10.78	1978-83	151	4	22		
			Tr	Exeter C.	07.84	1984-85	87	0	10		
			Tr	Torquay U.	07.86	1986-87	88	0	9		
McPARLAND, Ian J.	Edinburgh	04.10.61	Ormiston Primrose	Notts. Co.	12.80	1980-87	171	27	63	(F)	

Players Names	Birthplace	Date	Source	League Club	Date Sign'd	Seasons Played	Apps	Sub	Gls	Pos.	Misc
MacPHAIL, John	Dundee	07.12.55	Dundee	**Sheffield U.**	01.79	1979-82	135	0	7	(CD)	
			Tr	**York C.**	02.83	1982-85	141	1	24		
			Tr	**Bristol C.**	07.86	1986	26	0	1		
			Tr	**Sunderland**	07.87	1987	46	0	16		
McPHERSON, Keith A.	Greenwich	11.09.63	App	**West Ham U.**	09.81	1984	1	0	0	(CD)	
			L	**Cambridge U.**	09.85	1985	11	0	1		
			Tr	**Northampton T.**	01.86	1985-87	98	0	5		
McPHILLIPS, Terry	Manchester	01.10.68	Liverpool(YTS)	**Halifax T.**	09.87	1987	11	14	3	(F)	
McQUEEN, Tommy F.	Bellshill	01.04.63	Aberdeen	**West Ham U.**	03.87	1986-87	19	2	0	(LB)	
McSTAY, Willie	Hamilton	26.11.61	Glasgow Celtic	**Huddersfield T.**	03.87	1986-87	4	5	0	(D)	
			Tr	**Notts Co.**	02.88	1987	6	3	0		
MABBUTT, Gary V.	Bristol	23.08.61	App	**Bristol Rov.**	01.79	1978-81	122	9	10	(CD)	E Yth Int/E-13
			Tr	**Tottenham H.**	08.82	1982-87	177	13	20		E U21-5/Son of Ray
MACOWAT, Ian S.	Oxford	19.11.65	App	**Everton**	11.83					(LB)	E Sch Int/E Yth Int
			Tr	**Gillingham**	01.85	1984-85	4	1	0		
			Tr	**Crewe Alex.**	07.86	1986-87	39	3	0		
MADDEN, Craig	Manchester	25.09.58	Northern Nomads	**Bury**	03.78	1977-85	278	19	129	(F)	
			Tr	**West Bromwich A.**	03.86	1985-86	10	2	3		
			Tr	**Blackpool**	02.87	1986-87	44	9	16		
MADDEN, David J.	Stepney	06.01.63	App	**Southampton**	01.81					(M)	
			L	**Bournemouth**	01.83	1982	5	0	0		
			Tr	**Arsenal**	08.83	1983	2	0	0		
			Tr	**Charlton Ath.**	06.84	1984	19	1	1		
			Los Angeles(USA)	**Reading**	11.87	1987	7	2	1		
MADDEN, Lawrie D.	Hackney	28.09.55	Arsenal (N/C)	**Mansfield T.(N/C)**	03.75	1974-75	9	1	0	(CD)	
			Manchester Univ.	**Charlton Ath.**	03.78	1977-81	109	4	7		
			Tr	**Millwall**	03.82	1981-82	44	3	2		
			Tr	**Sheffield Wed.**	08.83	1983-87	154	1	2		
MADDIX, Danny S.	Ashford	11.10.67	App	**Tottenham H.**	07.85					(M)	
			Tr	**Southend U.**	10.86	1986	2	0	0		
			Tr	**Q.P.R.**	07.87	1987	6	2	0		
MADDY, Paul M.	Cwmcarn	17.08.62	App	**Cardiff C.**	08.80	1980-82	35	8	3	(LM)	W U21-1
			L	**Hereford U.**	03.83	1982	9	0	1		
			Tr	**Swansea C.**	08.83	1983	18	2	3		
			Tr	**Hereford U.**	03.84	1983-85	75	2	16		
			Tr	**Brentford**	07.86	1986	29	2	5		
			Tr	**Chester C.**	07.87	1987	17	1	1		
			Tr	**Hereford U.**	03.88	1987	6	2	0		
MADRICK, Carl J.	Bolton	20.09.68	YTS	**Huddersfield T.**	06.87	1987	3	5	1	(F)	
MAGUIRE, Gavin T.	Hammersmith	24.11.67	App	**Q.P.R.**	10.85	1986-87	26	6	0	(CD)	
MAGUIRE, Paul B.	Glasgow	21.08.56	Kilbirnie Ladeside	**Shrewsbury T.**	08.76	1976-79	143	8	35	(W)	
			Tr	**Stoke C.**	09.80	1980-83	93	14	24		
			Tacoma T.(USA)	**Port Vale**	07.85	1985-87	101	14	22		
MAGUIRE, Peter J.	Holmfirth	11.09.69	YTS	**Leeds U.**	07.88	1987	2	0	0	(F)	
MAIL, David	Bristol	12.09.62	App	**Aston Villa**	07.80					(CD)	
			Tr	**Blackburn Rov.**	01.82	1982-87	135	6	2		
MALCOLM, Paul A.	Felling	11.12.64	App	**Newcastle U.**	12.82					(G)	
			Durham C.	**Rochdale**	09.84	1984	24	0	0		
			Tr	**Shrewsbury T.**	07.85						
			Tr	**Barnsley**	08.86	1986	3	0	0		
MALKIN, Chris G.	Hoylake	04.06.67	Stork	**Tranmere Rov.**	07.87	1987	3	2	0	(F)	
MALLENDER, Paul R.	Norwich	30.11.69	YTS	**Hereford U.**	07.88	1987	0	1	0	(D)	Son of Ken
MALLEY, Phil,	Felling	01.11.65	Sunderland (App)	**Hartlepool U.**	11.83	1983	0	1	0	(M)	
			Berwick R.(trial)	**Burnley**	02.84	1983-87	91	4	5		
			L	**Stockport Co.**	11.84	1984	3	0	0		
MANN, Adrian G.	Northampton	12.07.67	YTS	**Northampton T.**	05.85	1983-87	71	11	5	(M)	
			L	**Torquay U.**	03.87	1986	6	2	0		
			Tr	**Newport Co.**	11.87	1987	17	0	1		
MARDENBOROUGH, Steve A.	Birmingham	11.09.64	App	**Coventry C.**	08.82					(F)	
			Tr	**Wolverhampton W.**	09.83	1983	9	0	1		
			L	**Cambridge U.**	02.84	1983	6	0	0		
			Tr	**Swansea C.**	07.84	1984	32	4	7		
			Tr	**Newport Co.**	07.85	1985-86	50	14	11		
			Tr	**Cardiff C.**	03.87	1986-87	18	14	1		
MARDON, Paul J.	Bristol	14.09.69	YTS	**Bristol C.**	01.88	1987	8	0	0	(CD)	
MARINER, Paul	Bolton	22.05.53	Chorley	**Plymouth Arg.**	07.73	1973-76	134	1	56	(F)	E-35
			Tr	**Ipswich T.**	09.76	1976-83	260	0	96		
			Tr	**Arsenal**	02.84	1983-85	52	8	14		
			Tr	**Portsmouth**	07.86	1986-87	49	7	9		
MARKER, Nick R.T.	Budleigh Salterton	03.05.65	App	**Exeter C.**	05.83	1981-87	196	6	3	(CD)	
			Tr	**Plymouth Arg.**	10.87	1987	26	0	1		
MARKS, Michael D.	Lambeth	22.03.68	App	**Millwall**	07.86	1986	36	0	10	(F)	
			L	**Mansfield T.**	01.88	1987	0	1	0		
			Tr	**Leyton Orient**	02.88	1987	3	0	0		
MARPLES, Chris	Chesterfield	03.08.64	Goole T.	**Chesterfield**	03.84	1984-86	84	0	0	(G)	Derbyshire
			Tr	**Stockport Co.**	03.87	1986-87	57	0	0		Cricketer
MARSDEN, Chris	Sheffield	03.01.69	App	**Sheffield U.**	01.87	1987	13	3	1	(M)	
MARSH, Chris J.	Sedgley	14.01.70	YTS	**Walsall**	06.88	1987	0	3	0	(M)	
MARSH, Ian	Swansea	27.10.69	YTS	**Swansea C.(YTS)**	01.87	1987	1	0	0	(M)	
MARSHALL, Gary	Bristol	20.04.64	Shepton Mallet	**Bristol C.**	07.83	1983-87	48	20	7	(W)	
			L	**Torquay U.**	12.84	1984	7	0	1		
MARSHALL, Ian P.	Oxford	20.03.66	App	**Everton**	03.84	1985-87	9	6	0	(CD)	
			Tr	**Oldham Ath.**	03.88	1987	10	0	0		
MARSHALL, John P.	Balham	18.08.64	App	**Fulham**	08.82	1983-87	145	8	10	(W/RB)	
MARTIN, Alvin E.	Bootle	29.07.58	App	**West Ham U.**	07.76	1977-87	314	2	22	(CD)	E Yth Int/E-17/E 'B'

Players Names	Birthplace	Date	Source	League Club	Date Sign'd	Seasons Played	Career Record Apps	Sub	Gls	Pos.	Misc
MARTIN, David	East Ham	25.04.63	App	Millwall	05.80	1979-84	131	9	6	(D)	E Yth Int
			Tr	Wimbledon	09.84	1984-85	30	5	3		
			Tr	Southend U.	08.86	1986-87	69	4	3		
MARTIN, Dean	Halifax	09.09.67	App	Halifax T.	09.85	1986-87	54	2	4	(M)	
MARTIN, Lee A.	Hyde	05.02.68	YTS	Manchester U.	05.86	1987	0	1	0	(D)	
MARTIN, Lee B.	Huddersfield	09.09.68	YTS	Huddersfield T.	06.87	1987	18	0	0	(G)	
MARTINDALE, David	Liverpool	09.04.64	Caernarfon T.	Tranmere Rov.	07.87	1987	34	0	4	(M)	
MARTYN, A. Nigel	St. Austell	11.08.66	St. Blazey	Bristol Rov.	08.87	1987	39	0	0	(G)	E U21-1
MARWOOD, Brian	Seaham	05.02.60	App	Hull C.	02.78	1979-83	154	4	51	(W)	
			Tr	Sheffield Wed.	08.84	1984-87	125	3	27		
			Tr	Arsenal	03.88	1987	4	0	1		
MASKELL, Craig D.	Aldershot	10.04.68	App	Southampton	04.86	1985-86	2	4	1	(M)	
MASSEY, Richard	Wolverhampton	11.10.68	YTS	Exeter C.	07.86	1985-87	22	6	1	(D)	
MASSEY, Steve	Denton	28.03.58	App	Stockport Co.	07.75	1974-77	87	14	20	(F)	
			Tr	Bournemouth	07.78	1978-80	85	12	19		
			Tr	Peterborough U.	08.81	1981	13	5	2		
			Tr	Northampton T.	02.82	1981-82	60	0	26		
			Tr	Hull C.	07.83	1983-84	34	8	9		
			Tr	Cambridge U.	08.85	1985	28	3	11		
			Tr	Wrexham	07.86	1986-87	38	5	10		
MATTHEWS, John M.	Camden	01.11.55	App	Arsenal	08.73	1974-77	38	7	2	(M)	
			Tr	Sheffield U.	08.78	1978-81	98	5	14		
			Tr	Mansfield T.	08.82	1982-83	70	2	6		
			Tr	Chesterfield	08.84	1984	38	0	1		
			Tr	Plymouth Arg.	08.85	1985-87	102	3	4		
MATTHEWS, Mike	Hull	25.09.60	App	Wolverhampton W.	10.78	1980-83	72	4	7	(M)	
			Tr	Scunthorpe U.	02.84	1983-85	56	2	5		
			North Ferriby U.	Halifax T.	09.86	1986-87	83	1	7		
MATTHEWS, Neil	Grimsby	19.09.66	App	Grimsby T.	09.84	1984-86	9	2	1	(F)	
			L	Scunthorpe U.	11.85	1985	1	0	0		
			L	Halifax T.	10.86	1986	9	0	2		
			L	Bolton W.	03.87	1986	1	0	0		
			Tr	Halifax T.	08.87	1987	29	3	10		
MATTHEWS, Neil P.	Manchester	03.12.67	App	Blackpool	12.85	1985-87	49	1	0	(RB)	
MATTHEWSON, Trevor	Sheffield	12.02.63	App	Sheffield Wed.	02.81	1980-82	3	0	0	(CD)	Nephew of Reg
			Tr	Newport Co.	10.83	1983-84	73	2	0		
			Tr	Stockport Co.	09.85	1985-86	79	1	0		
			Tr	Lincoln C.	(N/L)						
MAUCHLEN, Alistair H.	Kilwinning	29.06.60	Motherwell	Leicester C.	08.85	1985-87	98	5	5	(M)	
MAY, Andy M.	Bury	26.01.64	App	Manchester C.	01.82	1980-86	141	9	8	(M)	E U21-1
			Tr	Huddersfield T.	07.87	1987	27	1	3		
			L	Bolton W.	03.88	1987	9	1	2		
MAY, Larry C.	Sutton Coldfield	26.12.58	App	Leicester C.	12.76	1976-82	180	7	12	(CD)	
			Tr	Barnsley	09.83	1983-86	122	0	3		
			Tr	Sheffield Wed.	02.87	1986-87	30	1	1		
MAZZON, Giorgio	Cheshunt	04.09.60	Hertford T.	Tottenham H.	04.79	1980-82	3	1	0	(D)	
			Tr	Aldershot	08.83	1983-86	166	1	5		
MEACHAM, Jeff	Bristol	06.02.62	Trowbridge T.	Bristol Rov.	03.87	1986-87	19	7	9	(F)	
MEADE, Raphael J.	Islington	22.11.62	App	Arsenal	06.80	1981-84	25	16	14	(F)	to Sp Lisbon (Port) 6.85
MEASHAM, Ian	Barnsley	14.12.64	App	Huddersfield T.	12.82	1984	17	0	0	(RB)	
			L	Lincoln C.	10.85	1985	6	0	0		
			L	Rochdale	03.86	1985	12	0	0		
			Tr	Cambridge U.	07.86	1986	46	0	0		
MEGSON, Gary J.	Manchester	02.05.59	App	Plymouth Arg.	05.77	1977-79	78	0	10	(M)	Son of Don
			Tr	Everton	12.79	1979-80	20	2	2		
			Tr	Sheffield Wed.	08.81	1981-83	123	0	13		
			Tr	Nottingham F.	08.84						
			Tr	Newcastle U.	11.84	1984-85	21	3	1		
			Tr	Sheffield Wed.	12.85	1985-87	91	1	11		
MEHEW, David S.	Camberley	29.10.67	Leeds U. (YTS)	Bristol Rov.	07.85	1985-87	37	6	18	(F)	
MEHMET, Dave	Camberwell	02.12.60	App	Millwall	12.77	1976-80	97	17	15	(M)	
			Tampa Bay R. (USA)	Charlton Ath.	01.82	1981-82	29	0	3		
			Tr	Gillingham	03.83	1982-85	128	4	39		
			Tr	Millwall	07.86	1986-87	17	1	1		
MELL, Stewart A.	Doncaster	15.10.57	Appleby Frodingham	Doncaster Rov.	02.80	1979-82	62	14	14	(F)	E Semi-pro Int 1985
			Tr	Halifax T.	07.83	1983	22	8	8		
			Burton Albion	Scarborough	(N/L)	1987	29	5	8		
MELLISH, Stuart M.	Hyde	19.11.69	YTS	Rochdale	07.88	1987	12	0	0	(M)	
MELROSE, Jim M.	Glasgow	07.10.58	Partick Thistle	Leicester C.	07.80	1980-82	57	15	21	(F)	S U21-8/ S Sch Int/ S F Lge Rep
			Tr	Coventry C.	09.82	1982	21	3	8		
			Glasgow Celtic (L)	Wolverhampton W.	09.84	1984	6	1	2		
			Glasgow Celtic	Manchester C.	11.84	1984-85	27	7	8		
			Tr	Charlton Ath.	03.86	1985-87	44	4	19		
			Tr	Leeds U.	09.87	1987	3	1	0		
			Tr	Shrewsbury T.	02.88	1987	6	3	1		
MELVILLE, Andrew R.	Swansea	29.11.68	YTS	Swansea C.	07.86	1985-87	75	9	7	(CD)	
MENDONCA, Clive P.	Sunderland	09.09.68	App	Sheffield U.	09.86	1986-87	8	5	4	(F)	
			L	Doncaster Rov.	02.88	1987	2	0	0		
			Tr	Rotherham U.	03.88	1987	4	4	2		
MERSON, Paul C.	Brent	20.03.68	App	Arsenal	11.85	1986-87	12	10	8	(F)	E Yth Int
			L	Brentford	01.87	1986	6	1	0		
METGOD, Johnny A.B.	Netherlands	27.02.58	Real Madrid (Sp.)	Nottingham F.	08.84	1984-86	113	3	15	(M)	Neth Int
			Tr	Tottenham H.	07.87	1987	5	7	0		
METHVEN, Colin J.	India	10.12.55	East Fife	Wigan Ath.	10.79	1979-85	295	1	21	(CD)	
			Tr	Blackpool	07.86	1986-87	81	5	7		
MICKLEWHITE, Gary	Southwark	21.03.61	App	Manchester U.	03.78					(RW)	
			Tr	Q.P.R.	07.79	1980-84	97	9	11		
			Tr	Derby Co.	02.85	1984-87	119	4	22		

David McCreary (Newcastle United) Northern Ireland international with 60 caps to his credit.   *Match Magazine*

Stuart McCall (Bradford City) Midfielder with a great future in the game.   *Match Magazine*

Tom McAlister (West Ham United) In action saving at the feet of Q.P.R.'s Martin Allen last season.   *Match Magazine*

Players Names	Birthplace	Date	Source	League Club	Date Sign'd	Seasons Played	Career Record Apps	Sub	Gls	Pos.	Misc
MILLAR, John	Coatbridge	08.12.66	Jnrs	Chelsea	08.84	1985-86	11	0	0	(FB)	
			L	Northampton T.	01.87	1986	1	0	0		
			Tr	Blackburn Rov.	07.87	1987	13	2	0		
MILLEN, Keith	Croydon	26.09.66	Jnrs	Brentford	08.84	1984-87	125	3	7	(CD)	
MILLER, Colin F.	Lanarkshire	04.10.64	Glasgow Rangers	Doncaster Rov.	12.86	1986-87	61	0	3	(M)	Canadian Int
MILLER, David B.	Burnley	08.01.64	App	Burnley	01.82	1982-84	27	5	3	(M)	Son of Brian
			L	Crewe Alex.	03.83	1982	3	0	0		
			Tr	Tranmere Rov.	07.85	1985	25	4	1		
			Colne Dynamoes	Preston N.E.	12.86	1986-87	38	5	2		
MILLER, Ian	Perth	13.05.55	Jnrs	Bury	08.73	1973	9	6	0	(RW)	
			Tr	Nottingham F.	08.74						
			Tr	Doncaster Rov.	08.75	1975-77	124	0	14		
			Tr	Swindon T.	07.78	1978-80	123	4	9		
			Tr	Blackburn Rov.	08.81	1981-87	231	6	15		
MILLER, Paul A.	Woking	31.01.68	Yeovil T.	Wimbledon	08.87	1987	3	2	0	(F)	
			L	Newport Co.	10.87	1987	6	0	2		
MILLER, Paul R.	Stepney	11.10.59	App	Tottenham H.	05.77	1978-86	206	2	7	(CD)	
			Tr	Charlton Ath.	02.87	1986-87	35	2	2		
MILLETT, Glynne	Crickhowell	13.10.68	YTS	Newport Co.	07.87	1986-87	23	14	2	(W)	
MILLIGAN, Michael J.	Manchester	20.02.67	YTS	Oldham Ath.	02.85	1985-87	81	1	4	(M)	Brother of Terry
MILLIGAN, Terry J.	Manchester	10.01.66	App	Manchester C.	11.83					(M)	Brother of Mike
			New Zealand	Oldham Ath.	02.86						
			Tr	Crewe Alex.	07.86	1986-87	71	6	5		
MILLS, Gary R.	Northampton	11.11.61	App	Nottingham F.	11.78	1978-81	50	8	8	(W)	E Sch Int/E Yth Int/
			Seattle S.(USA)	Derby Co.	10.82	1982	18	0	2		E U21-2/
			Seattle S.(USA)	Nottingham F.	12.83	1983-86	63	16	4		Son of Roly
			Tr	Notts. Co.	08.87	1987	46	0	5		
MILLS, Keith	Newcastle	30.12.63	North Shields	Carlisle U.(N/C)	02.88	1987	0	1	0	(M)	
MILLS, Mick D.	Godalming	04.01.49	Portsmouth (App)	Ipswich T.	02.66	1965-82	588	3	22	(FB)	E Yth Int/E U23-5/
			Tr	Southampton	11.82	1982-84	103	0	3		E-42/E F Lge Rep
			Tr	Stoke C.	07.85	1985-87	38	0	0		
MILLS, Neil	Littleborough	27.10.63	Tin Bobbin	Rochdale	08.86	1986	4	6	0	(F)	
			Tr	Stockport Co.(N/C)	08.87	1987	5	2	0		
MILLS, Simon A.	Sheffield	16.08.64	App	Sheffield Wed.	08.82	1982-84	1	4	0	(M)	E Yth Int
			Tr	York C.	06.85	1985-87	97	2	5		
			Tr	Port Vale	12.87	1987	19	0	5		
MILNE, Ralph	Dundee	13.05.61	Dundee U.	Charlton Ath.	01.87	1986-87	19	3	0	(W)	S Yth Int/S U21-3
			Tr	Bristol C.	01.88	1987	19	0	4		
MILTON, Simon C.	Fulham	23.08.63	Bury Town	Ipswich T.	07.87	1987	7	1	1	(M)	
			L	Exeter C.	11.87	1987	2	0	3		
			L	Torquay U.	03.88	1987	4	0	1		
MIMMS, R.A. (Bob)	York	12.10.63	App	Halifax T.	08.81					(G)	E U21-3
			Tr	Rotherham U.	11.81	1981-84	83	0	0		
			Tr	Everton	06.85	1985-87	29	0	0		
			L	Notts. Co.	03.86	1985	2	0	0		
			L	Sunderland	12.86	1986	4	0	0		
			L	Blackburn Rov.	01.87	1986	6	0	0		
			L	Manchester C.	09.87	1987	3	0	0		
			Tr	Tottenham H.	02.88	1987	13	0	0		
MIRANDINHA, (Da Silva, Francisco)	Brazil	02.07.59	Palmeiras (Br.)	Newcastle U.	08.87	1987	25	1	11	(F)	Brazilian Int
MITCHELL, C. Brian	Stonehaven	16.07.63	Aberdeen	Bradford C.	02.87	1986-87	58	0	6	(RB)	
MITCHELL, Graham L.	Shipley	16.02.68	YTS	Huddersfield T.	06.86	1986-87	44	2	1	(D)	
MOLBY, Jan	Denmark	04.07.63	Ajax Amsterdam	Liverpool	08.84	1984-87	93	9	22	(M)	Danish Int
MONCUR, John F.	Stepney	22.09.66	App	Tottenham H.	08.84	1986-87	4	2	0	(M)	
			L	Doncaster Rov.	09.86	1986	4	0	0		
			L	Cambridge U.	03.87	1986	3	1	0		
MONEY, Richard	Lowestoft	13.10.55	Lowestoft T.	Scunthorpe U.	07.73	1973-77	165	8	4	(CD)	E 'B'
			Tr	Fulham	12.77	1977-79	106	0	3		
			Tr	Liverpool	04.80	1980	12	2	0		
			L	Derby Co.	12.81	1981	5	0	0		
			Tr	Luton T.	03.82	1981-82	44	0	1		
			Tr	Portsmouth	08.83	1983-85	17	0	0		
			Tr	Scunthorpe U.	10.85	1985-87	99	0	0		
MOONEY, Brian J.	Dublin	02.02.66	Home Farm	Liverpool	08.83					(M)	IR Yth Int
			L	Wrexham	12.85	1985	9	0	2		
			Tr	Preston N.E.	10.87	1987	34	0	3		
MOORE, David	Grimsby	17.12.59	App	Grimsby T.	12.77	1978-82	136	0	2	(RB)	Brother of Andy/
			Tr	Carlisle U.	08.83	1983	13	0	1		Kevin
			Tr	Blackpool	12.83	1983-86	114	1	1		
			Tr	Grimsby T.	12.86	1986-87	3	1	0		
MOORE, John	Consett	01.10.66	App	Sunderland	10.84	1984-87	4	11	1	(F)	
			L	Newport Co.	12.85	1985	2	0	0		
			L	Darlington	11.86	1986	2	0	1		
			L	Mansfield T.	03.87	1986	5	0	1		
			L	Rochdale	01.88	1987	10	0	2		
MOORE, Kevin T.	Grimsby	29.04.58	Jnrs	Grimsby T.	07.76	1976-86	397	3	27	(CD)	Brother of Andy/
			Tr	Oldham Ath.	02.87	1986	13	0	1		David/E Sch Int
			Tr	Southampton	07.87	1987	35	0	3		
MOORE, Ronnie D.	Liverpool	29.01.53	Jnrs	Tranmere Rov.	05.71	1971-78	248	1	72	(F)	
			Tr	Cardiff C.	02.79	1978-79	54	2	6		
			Tr	Rotherham U.	08.80	1980-83	124	1	51		
			Tr	Charlton Ath.	09.83	1983-84	60	2	13		
			Tr	Rochdale	07.85	1985	43	0	9		
			Tr	Tranmere Rov.	07.86	1986-87	65	0	6		
MOORE, Stephen J.	Chester	17.12.69	YTS	Chester C.(YTS)	08.86	1987	0	1	0		
MORAN, Kevin B.	Dublin	29.04.56	Gaelic Football	Manchester U.	02.78	1978-87	228	3	21	(CD)	IR-34
MORAN, Paul	Enfield	22.05.68	YTS	Tottenham H.	07.85	1986-87	10	4	1	(W)	

Kevin MacDonald (Liverpool) Was signed from Leicester City in 1984 and played on loan for them last season.

Match Magazine

Steve McMahon (Liverpool) An ever present in the club's Championship winning side last season.

Match Magazine

Joe McLaughlin (Chelsea) Fine central defender of the old school.

Match Magazine

Neil McNab (Manchester City) Fiery Scottish international midfielder who started his career in England with the "Spurs".

Match Magazine

Players Names	Birthplace	Date	Source	League Club	Date Sign'd	Seasons Played	Career Record Apps	Sub	Gls	Pos.	Misc
MORAN, Steve J.	Croydon	10.01.61	Jnrs	Southampton	08.79	1979-85	173	7	78	(F)	E U21-2
			Tr	Leicester C.	09.86	1986-87	35	8	14		
			Tr	Reading	11.87	1987	24	4	7		
MORGAN, Darren J.	Camberwell	05.11.67	App	Millwall	11.85	1986-87	20	5	1	(M)	W Yth Int
MORGAN, Gary	Consett	01.04.61	Berwick Rangers	Darlington	07.85	1985-87	108	0	2	(LB)	
MORGAN, Nick	East Ham	30.10.59	App	West Ham U.	11.77	1978-82	14	7	2	(F)	
			Tr	Portsmouth	03.83	1982-86	79	16	32		
			Tr	Stoke C.	11.86	1986-87	56	1	14		
MORGAN, Simon C.	Birmingham	05.09.66	YTS	Leicester C.	11.84	1985-87	103	8	2	(FB)	E U21-2
MORGAN, Simon D.	Merthyr Tydfil	03.09.70	YTS	Newport Co.(YTS)	08.87	1987	0	2	0		
MORGAN, Stephen A.	Oldham	19.09.68	App	Blackpool	08.86	1985-87	56	6	6	(M)	
MORGAN, Stephen J.	Wrexham	28.12.70	YTS	Oldham Ath.(YTS)	07.87	1987	0	1	0	(W)	W Yth Int
MORGAN, Trevor J.	Forest Gate	30.09.56	Leytonstone	Bournemouth	09.80	1980-81	53	0	13	(F)	
			Tr	Mansfield T.	11.81	1981	12	0	6		
			Tr	Bournemouth	03.82	1981-83	88	0	33		
			Tr	Bristol C.	03.84	1983-84	32	0	8		
			Tr	Exeter C.	11.84	1984-85	30	0	9		
			Tr	Bristol Rov.	09.85	1985-86	54	1	24		
			Tr	Bristol C.	01.87	1986	19	0	7		
			Tr	Bolton W.	06.87	1987	31	7	7		
MORLEY, A.W. (Tony)	Ormskirk	26.08.54	App	Preston N.E.	08.72	1972-75	78	6	15	(LW)	E Yth Int/E U23-1/ E-6
			Tr	Burnley	02.76	1975-78	78	13	5		
			Tr	Aston Villa	06.79	1979-83	128	9	25		
			Tr	West Bromwich A.	12.83	1983-84	33	0	4		
			L	Birmingham C.	11.84	1984	4	0	3		
			Den Haag (Neth.)	West Bromwich A.	08.87	1987	27	1	7		
MORLEY, Trevor W.	Nottingham	20.03.61	Nuneaton Bor.	Northampton T.	06.85	1985-87	107	0	39	(F)	E Semi-Pro Int 1984/5
			Tr	Manchester C.	01.88	1987	13	2	4		
MORRELL, Paul D.P.	Poole	23.03.61	Weymouth	Bournemouth	06.83	1983-87	187	4	6	(LB)	
MORRIS, Andy D.	Sheffield	17.11.67	Jnrs	Rotherham U.	07.85	1984-86	0	7	0	(F)	
			Tr	Chesterfield	01.88	1987	7	3	0		
MORRIS, Chris B.	Newquay	24.12.63	Jnrs	Sheffield Wed.	10.82	1983-86	61	13	1	(FB)	E Sch Int/IR-4/ to Celtic 8.87
MORRIS, Colin	Blyth	22.08.53	App	Burnley	08.71	1974-75	9	1	0	(RW)	
			Tr	Southend U.	01.77	1976-79	133	0	25		
			Tr	Blackpool	12.79	1979-81	87	0	26		
			Tr	Sheffield U.	02.82	1981-87	235	5	68		
MORRIS, Mark	Chester	01.08.68	YTS	Wrexham	08.87	1985-87	9	0	0	(G)	
MORRIS, Mark J.	Morden	26.09.62	App	Wimbledon	09.80	1981-86	167	1	9	(CD)	
			L	Aldershot	09.85	1985	14	0	0		
			Tr	Watford	07.87	1987	39	0	1		
MORRIS, Ronnie	Birmingham	25.09.70	YTS	Birmingham C.(YTS)	07.87	1987	0	1	0		
MORRISON, Andrew C.	Inverness	30.07.70	YTS	Plymouth Arg.	07.88	1987	0	1	0		
MORRISSEY, John J.(Jnr.)	Liverpool	08.03.65	App	Everton	03.83	1984	1	0	0	(RW)	Son of John (Snr.)/ E Yth Int
			Tr	Wolverhampton W.	08.85	1985	5	5	1		
			Tr	Tranmere Rov.	10.85	1985-87	98	11	16		
MORTIMER, Paul H.	Kensington	08.05.68	Fulham (App)	Charlton Ath.	09.87	1987	11	1	0	(W)	
MORTON, Neil	Congleton	21.12.68	YTS	Crewe Alex.	09.87	1986-87	18	8	1	(M)	
MOSELEY, Graham	Manchester	16.11.53	App	Blackburn Rov.	09.71					(G)	E Yth Int
			Tr	Derby Co.	09.71	1972-76	32	0	0		
			L	Aston Villa	08.74	1974	3	0	0		
			L	Walsall	10.77	1977	3	0	0		
			Tr	Brighton & H.A.	11.77	1977-85	189	0	0		
			Tr	Cardiff C.	08.86	1986-87	38	0	0		
MOSES, Remi M.	Manchester	14.11.60	App	West Bromwich A.	11.78	1979-81	63	0	5	(M)	E U21-8
			Tr	Manchester U.	09.81	1981-87	143	7	7		
MOSS, Ernie	Chesterfield	19.10.49	Chesterfield Tube	Chesterfield	10.68	1968-75	271	0	95	(F)	
			Tr	Peterborough U.	01.76	1975-76	34	1	9		
			Tr	Mansfield T.	12.76	1976-78	56	1	21		
			Tr	Chesterfield	01.79	1978-80	105	2	33		
			Tr	Port Vale	06.81	1981-82	74	0	23		
			Tr	Lincoln C.	03.83	1982	10	1	2		
			Tr	Doncaster Rov.	06.83	1983	41	3	15		
			Tr	Chesterfield	07.84	1984-86	90	1	33		
			Tr	Stockport Co.	12.86	1986	26	0	7		
			Tr	Scarborough	08.87	1987	22	1	4		
			L	Rochdale	03.88	1987	10	0	2		
MOULDEN, Paul C.	Farnworth	06.09.67	App	Manchester C.	09.84	1985-87	19	9	5	(F)	E Yth Int
MOUNTFIELD, Derek N.	Liverpool	02.11.62	App	Tranmere Rov.	11.80	1980-81	26	0	1	(CD)	E U21-1
			Tr	Everton	06.82	1982-87	100	6	19		
MOWBRAY, A.M. (Tony)	Saltburn	22.11.63	App	Middlesbrough	11.81	1982-87	223	3	17	(CD)	
MOWER, Kenny M.	Walsall	01.12.60	App	Walsall	11.78	1978-87	337	2	8	(LB)	
MOYES, David W.	Glasgow	25.04.63	Glasgow Celtic	Cambridge U.	10.83	1983-85	79	0	1	(CD)	
			Tr	Bristol C.	10.85	1985-87	83	0	6		
			Tr	Shrewsbury T.	10.87	1987	17	0	2		
MUGGLETON, Carl D.	Leicester	13.09.68	App	Leicester C.	09.86					(G)	
			L	Chesterfield	09.87	1987	17	0	0		
			L	Blackpool	02.88	1987	2	0	0		
MUIR, Ian J.	Coventry	05.05.63	App	Q.P.R.	09.80	1980	2	0	2	(F)	E Yth Int/E Sch Int
			L	Burnley	11.82	1982	1	1	1		
			Tr	Birmingham C.	08.83	1983	1	0	0		
			Tr	Brighton & H.A.	02.84	1983-84	3	1	0		
			L	Swindon T.	01.85	1984	2	0	0		
			Tr	Tranmere Rov.	07.85	1985-87	116	5	60		
MUMBY, Peter	Bradford	22.02.69	YTS	Leeds U.	07.87	1987	3	2	0	(F)	
MUNGALL, Steve H.	Bellshill	22.05.58	Motherwell	Tranmere Rov.	07.79	1979-87	313	10	6	(D)	

Players Names	Birthplace	Date	Source	League Club	Date Sign'd	Seasons Played	Apps	Sub	Gls	Pos.	Misc
MURPHY, Aidan J.	Manchester	17.09.67	App	Manchester U.	09.84					(M)	E Sch Int/E Yth Int
			L	Lincoln C.	10.86	1986	2	0	0		
			Tr	Crewe Alex.	05.87	1987	15	5	2		
MURPHY, Jerry M.	Stepney	23.09.59	App	Crystal Palace	10.76	1976-84	214	15	20	(LM)	E Sch Int/IR-3
			Tr	Chelsea	08.85	1985-87	34	0	3		
MURRAY, Edward J.	Crosby	10.07.62	Stork	Tranmere Rov.	08.87	1987	11	9	1	(W)	
MURRAY, Jamie G.	Glasgow	27.12.58	Rivet Sp.(Aylesbury)	Cambridge U.	09.76	1976-83	213	16	3	(LB)	
			L	Sunderland	03.84	1983	0	1	0		
			Tr	Brentford	07.84	1984-87	134	0	3		
			Tr	Cambridge U.	09.87	1987	13	0	0		
MUSKER, Russell	Plymouth	10.07.62	App	Bristol C.	08.79	1980-83	44	2	1	(W)	
			L	Exeter C.	10.83	1983	6	0	0		
			Tr	Gillingham	11.83	1983-85	54	10	7		
			Tr	Torquay U.	08.86	1986-87	36	9	0		
MUSTOE, Robbie	Witney	28.08.68	Jnrs	Oxford U.	07.86	1986-87	14	6	0	(M)	
MUTCH, Andy T.	Liverpool	28.12.63	Southport	Wolverhampton W.	02.86	1985-87	99	3	37	(F)	
MYCOCK, David C.	Todmorden	18.09.69	YTS	Rochdale	06.88	1987	9	2	0	(D)	
MYERS, Chris	Yeovil	01.04.69	YTS	Torquay U.	06.87	1986	8	1	0	(M)	Son of Cliff
NARBETT, Jonathan V.	Birmingham	21.11.68	App	Shrewsbury T.	09.86	1986-87	20	6	3	(M)	
NARDIELLO, Gerry	Warley	05.05.66	App	Shrewsbury T.	05.84	1982-85	32	6	11	(F)	E Yth Int
			L	Cardiff C.	03.86	1985	7	0	4		
			Tr	Torquay U.	07.86	1986-87	28	9	11		
NAUGHTON, Willie B.S.	Catrine, (Ayrs)	20.03.62	App	Preston N.E.	03.80	1979-84	148	14	10	(LW)	
			Tr	Walsall	03.85	1984-87	108	8	9		
NAYLOR, Stuart W.	Wetherby	06.12.62	Yorkshire Amateurs	Lincoln C.	06.80	1981-85	49	0	0	(G)	E Yth Int
			L	Peterborough U.	02.83	1982	8	0	0		
			L	Crewe Alex.	10.83	1983-84	55	0	0		
			Tr	West Bromwich A.	02.86	1985-87	89	0	0		
NEAL, Dean J.	Edmonton	05.01.61	App	Q.P.R.	01.79	1979-80	20	3	8	(F)	
			Tulsa R.(USA)	Millwall	10.81	1981-84	101	19	42		
			Tr	Southend U.	01.86	1985-87	35	3	6		
			L	Cambridge U.	12.87	1987	4	0	0		
NEAL, Phil G.	Irchester	29.02.51	App	Northampton T.	12.68	1968-74	182	4	29	(RB)	E-50
			Tr	Liverpool	10.74	1974-85	453	2	41		
			Tr	Bolton W.	12.85	1985-87	53	3	3		
NEBBELING, Gavin M.	South Africa	15.05.63	Arcadia Shep(SA)	Crystal Palace	08.81	1981-87	131	6	7	(CD)	
			L	Northampton T.	10.85	1985	11	0	0		
NEENAN, Joe P.	Manchester	17.03.59	App	York C.	03.77	1976-79	56	0	0	(G)	
			Tr	Scunthorpe U.	01.80	1979-84	191	0	0		
			L	Burnley	01.85	1984	9	0	0		
			Tr	Burnley	07.85	1985-86	81	0	0		
			Tr	Peterborough U.	07.87	1987	40	0	0		
			L	Scarborough	01.88	1987	6	0	0		
NEILL, Warren A.	Acton	21.11.62	App	Q.P.R.	09.80	1980-87	177	4	3	(RB)	E Sch Int
NELSON, Gary P.	Braintree	16.01.61	Jnrs	Southend U.	07.79	1979-82	106	23	17	(W)	
			Tr	Swindon T.	08.83	1983-84	78	1	7		
			Tr	Plymouth Arg.	07.85	1985-86	71	3	20		
			Tr	Brighton & H.A.	07.87	1987	42	0	21		
NESBITT, Michael D.	Doncaster	08.01.69	App	Doncaster Rov.	01.86	1985-87	6	5	1	(F)	E Yth Int
NEVILLE, Steve F.	Walthamstow	18.09.57	App	Southampton	09.75	1977	5	1	1	(W)	
			Tr	Exeter C.	09.78	1978-80	90	3	22		
			Tr	Sheffield U.	10.80	1980-81	40	9	6		
			Tr	Exeter C.	10.82	1982-84	89	3	27		
			Tr	Bristol C.	11.84	1984-87	128	6	40		
NEVIN, Pat K.F.	Glasgow	06.09.63	Clyde	Chelsea	07.83	1983-87	190	3	36	(RW)	S Yth Int/ S U21-5/S-6
NEWCOMBE, Giles A.	Doncaster	09.07.68	YTS	Rotherham U.	06.87	1986	6	0	0	(G)	
NEWELL, Mike C.	Liverpool	27.01.65	Liverpool(Jnr)	Crewe Alex.	09.83	1983	3	0	0	(F)	E U21-4
			Tr	Wigan Ath.	10.83	1983-85	64	8	25		
			Tr	Luton T.	01.86	1985-87	62	1	18		
			Tr	Leicester C.	09.87	1987	36	0	8		
NEWELL, Paul C.	Woolwich	23.02.69	YTS	Southend U.	06.87	1987	13	0	0	(G)	
NEWHOUSE, Aiden R.	Wallasey	23.05.72	Jnrs	Chester C. (Sch)		1987	0	1	0		
NEWMAN, Rob N.	Bradford on Avon	13.12.63	App	Bristol C.	10.81	1981-87	244	12	30	(FB)	
NEWSON, Mark J.	Stepney	07.12.60	App	Charlton Ath.	12.78					(D)	E Semi-pro Int
			Maidstone U.	Bournemouth	05.85	1985-87	121	0	15		
NEWTON, S. Doug	Newcastle	16.01.59	Boston U.	Scarborough (N/C)	03.88	1987	4	1	0	(M)	
NICHOLAS, Charlie	Glasgow	30.12.61	Glasgow Celtic	Arsenal	07.83	1983-87	145	6	34	(F)	S Yth Int/S U21-6/ S-19/To Aberdeen 1.88
NICHOLAS, Peter	Newport	10.11.59	App	Crystal Palace	12.76	1977-80	127	0	7	(M)	W Sch Int/ W U21-3/ W-54 To Aberdeen 8.87
			Tr	Arsenal	03.81	1980-82	57	3	1		
			Tr	Crystal Palace	10.83	1983-84	47	0	7		
			Tr	Luton T.	01.85	1984-86	102	0	1		
NICHOLSON, Shane M.	Newark	03.06.70	YTS	Lincoln C. (YTS)	07.86	1986	6	1	0	(M)	
NICOL, Paul J.	Scunthorpe	31.10.67	YTS	Scunthorpe U.	07.86	1986-87	31	3	0	(CD)	
NICOL, Steve	Irvine	11.12.61	Ayr U.	Liverpool	10.81	1982-87	137	9	23	(FB/M)	S U21-14/S-17
NIEDZWICKI, A. Eddie	Bangor	03.05.59	Jnrs	Wrexham	07.76	1977-82	111	0	0	(G)	W Sch Int/ W-2
			Tr	Chelsea	06.83	1983-87	136	0	0		
NIGHTINGALE, Mark B.D.	Salisbury	01.02.57	App	Bournemouth	07.74	1974-75	44	5	4	(D/M)	E Yth Int
			Tr	Crystal Palace	06.76						
			Tr	Norwich C.	07.77	1977-81	28	7	0		
			Bulova (HK)	Bournemouth	11.82	1982-85	144	6	4		
			Tr	Peterborough U.	07.86	1986-87	71	7	2		

Players Names	Birthplace	Date	Source	League Club	Date Sign'd	Seasons Played	Apps	Sub	Gls	Pos.	Misc
NISBET, Gordon J.M.	Wallsend	18.09.51	Jnrs	West Bromwich A.	09.68	1969-75	136	0	0	(RB)	E U23-1
			Tr	Hull C.	09.76	1976-80	190	3	1		
			Tr	Plymouth Arg.	12.80	1980-86	281	0	14		
			Tr	Exeter C.	06.87	1987	12	0	0		
NIXON, Eric W.	Manchester	04.10.62	Curzon Ashton	Manchester C.	12.83	1985-87	58	0	0	(G)	
			L	Wolverhampton W.	08.86	1986	16	0	0		
			L	Bradford C.	11.86	1986	3	0	0		
			L	Southampton	12.86	1986	4	0	0		
			L	Carlisle U.	01.87	1986	16	0	0		
			L	Tranmere Rov.	03.88	1987	8	0	0		
NOBBS, A. Keith	Bishop Auckland	19.09.61	App	Middlesbrough	09.79	1980	1	0	0	(RB)	
			Tr	Halifax T.	08.82	1982-83	87	0	1		
			Bishop Auckland	Hartlepool U.	08.85	1985-87	119	3	1		
NOGAN, Lee M.	Cardiff	21.05.69	YTS	Oxford U.	03.87	1987	2	1	0	(F)	
			L	Brentford	03.87	1986	10	1	2		
			L	Southend U.	09.87	1987	6	0	1		
NORMAN, A.J. (Tony)	Deeside	24.02.58	Jnrs	Burnley	08.76					(G)	W-3
			Tr	Hull C.	02.80	1979-87	351	0	0		
NORMAN, Sean	Lowestoft	27.11.66	Lowestoft T.	Colchester U.	07.85	1986-87	18	3	1	(LB/LM)	
NORTH, Marc V.	Ware	29.05.66	App	Luton T.	03.84	1985-86	11	7	3	(F)	Brother of Stacey
			L	Lincoln C.	03.85	1984	4	0	0		
			L	Scunthorpe U.	01.87	1986	4	1	2		
			L	Birmingham C.	03.87	1986	4	1	1		
			Tr	Grimsby T.	08.87	1987	37	1	11		
NORTH, Stacey S.	Luton	25.11.64	App	Luton T.	08.82	1983-87	24	1	0	(CD)	Brother of Marc/ E Yth Int
			L	Wolverhampton W.	11.85	1985	3	0	0		
			Tr	West Bromwich A.	12.87	1987	18	0	0		
NORTON, David W.	Cannock	03.03.65	App	Aston Villa	03.83	1984-87	42	2	2	(RB)	E Yth Int
NOTEMAN, Kevin S.	Preston	15.10.69	YTS	Leeds U.	07.88	1987	0	1	0	(F)	
NUGENT, Kevin P.	Edmonton	10.04.69	YTS	Leyton Orient	07.87	1987	10	1	3	(F)	
NUTTELL, Michael J.	Boston	22.11.68	YTS	Peterborough U.	08.87	1985-87	12	9	0	(F)	
			L	Crewe Alex.	12.87	1987	2	1	1		
NWAJIOBI, C. (Emeka)	Nigeria	25.05.59	Dulwich Hamlet	Luton T.	12.83	1983-87	59	13	17	(F)	
O'BRIEN, Liam F.	Dublin	05.09.64	Shamrock Rov.	Manchester U.	10.86	1986-87	15	13	2	(M)	IR-6
O'CALLAGHAN, Kevin	Dagenham	19.10.61	App	Millwall	11.78	1978-79	15	5	3	(W)	IR-20
			Tr	Ipswich T.	01.80	1979-84	72	43	3		
			Tr	Portsmouth	01.85	1984-86	84	3	16		
			Tr	Millwall	06.87	1987	22	0	7		
O'CONNELL, Brendan	Lambeth	12.11.66	YTS	Portsmouth	07.85					(F)	
			Tr	Exeter C.	07.86	1986-87	73	8	20		
O'CONNOR, Mark A.	Southend	10.03.63	App	Q.P.R.	06.80	1981-82	2	1	0	(M)	
			L	Exeter C.	10.83	1983	38	0	1		
			Tr	Bristol Rov.	08.84	1984-85	79	1	10		
			Tr	Bournemouth	03.86	1985-87	81	8	10		
O'DELL, Andy	Hull	02.01.63	App	Grimsby T.	01.81	1981-82	18	2	0	(M)	
			Tr	Rotherham U.	08.83	1983-84	16	2	0		
			Tr	Torquay U.	03.85	1984	12	2	1		
			North Ferriby U.	Darlington	09.87	1987	1	2	0		
O'DOHERTY, Ken	Dublin	30.03.63	U.C. Dublin (IR)	Crystal Palace	02.85	1985-87	41	1	0	(FB)	
O'DONNELL, Chris	Newcastle	26.05.68	App	Ipswich T.	06.85	1986-87	9	3	0	(D)	
			L	Northampton T.	01.88	1987	1	0	0		
O'DRISCOLL, Sean M.	Wolverhampton	01.07.57	Alvechurch	Fulham	11.79	1979-83	141	7	3	(W)	IR-3
			Tr	Bournemouth	02.84	1983-87	194	6	16		
O'HAGAN, Patrick J.	Caerphilly	15.03.71	YTS	Newport Co. (YTS)	08.87	1987	3	0	0	(G)	
O'HANLON, Kelham G.	Saltburn	16.05.62	App	Middlesbrough	05.80	1982-84	87	0	0	(G)	IR-1
			Tr	Rotherham U.	08.85	1985-87	126	0	0		
O'KEEFE, J. Vince	Birmingham	02.04.57		Birmingham C.	07.75					(G)	
			Tr	Walsall	07.76						
			AP Leamington	Exeter C.	06.78	1978-79	53	0	0		
			Tr	Torquay U.	02.80	1979-81	108	0	0		
			Tr	Blackburn Rov.	08.82	1982-87	67	0	0		
			L	Bury	10.83	1983	2	0	0		
			L	Blackpool	12.86	1986	1	0	0		
O'KELLY, Richard F.	West Bromwich	08.01.57	Alvechurch	Walsall	10.79	1980-85	189	15	55	(F)	
			Tr	Port Vale	07.86	1986-87	26	2	4		
O'LEARY, David A.	Stoke Newington	02.05.58	App	Arsenal	07.75	1975-87	441	9	9	(CD)	IR-40
O'NEILL, John P.	Derry (NI)	11.03.58	Derry ABC	Leicester C.	03.76	1978-86	313	0	10	(CD)	NI-39
			Tr	Q.P.R.	07.87	1987	2	0	0		
			Tr	Norwich C.	12.87	1987	1	0	0		
O'NEILL, Michael A.	Portadown (NI)	05.07.69	Coleraine	Newcastle U.	10.87	1987	19	2	12	(F)	NI-4
O'REGAN, Kieran	Cork	09.11.63	Tramore Ath.	Brighton & H.A.	04.83	1982-86	69	17	2	(M/D)	IR-4
			Tr	Swindon T.	08.87	1987	23	3	1		
O'REILLY, Gary M.	Isleworth	21.03.61	Jnrs	Tottenham H.	09.79	1980-83	39	6	0	(CD)	IR Yth Int
			Tr	Brighton & H.A.	08.84	1984-86	78	1	3		
			Tr	Crystal Palace	01.87	1986-87	14	3	0		
O'RIORDAN, Donal J.	Dublin	14.05.57	App	Derby Co.	05.75	1976-77	2	4	1	(CD)	IR U21-1
			L	Doncaster Rov.	01.78	1977	2	0	0		
			Tulsa R. (USA)	Preston N.E.	10.78	1978-82	153	5	8		
			Tr	Carlisle U.	08.83	1983-84	84	0	18		
			Tr	Middlesbrough	08.85	1985	41	0	2		
			Tr	Grimsby T.	08.86	1986-87	86	0	16		
O'ROURKE, W.J. (Billy)	Nottingham	02.04.60	App	Burnley	02.78	1979-82	14	0	0	(G)	
			L	Blackpool	08.83	1983	6	0	0		
			Tr	Chester C.	03.84	1983	5	0	0		
			Tr	Blackpool	07.84	1984-85	92	0	0		
			L	Tranmere Rov.	09.86	1986	15	0	0		
			Tr	Tranmere Rov.	02.87	1986-87	38	0	0		

Gary Mabbutt (Tottenham Hotspur) Central defender who has played for England on 13 occasions.
Match Magazine

Jan Molby (Liverpool) Danish international powerhouse of a midfielder.
Match Magazine

Alvin Martin (West Ham United) Strong defender who has played 17 times for England.
Match Magazine

Bobby Mimms (Tottenham Hotspur) Signed from Everton to guard the "Spurs" goal.
Match Magazine

Players Names	Birthplace	Date	Source	League Club	Date Sign'd	Seasons Played	Apps	Sub	Gls	Pos.	Misc
O'SHAUGHNESSY, Steve	Wrexham	13.10.67	YTS	Leeds U.	10.85					(D)	W Yth Int
			Tr	Bradford C.	11.85	1987	0	1	0		
O'SHEA, Danny E.	Kennington	26.03.63	App	Arsenal	12.80	1982	6	0	0	(M)	
			L	Charlton Ath.	02.84	1983	9	0	0		
			Tr	Exeter C.	08.84	1984	45	0	2		
			Tr	Southend U.	08.85	1985-87	97	1	11		
O'SHEA, Timothy J.	Pimlico	12.11.66	App	Tottenham H.	08.84	1986-87	1	2	0	(D)	IR Yth Int
			L	Newport Co.	10.86	1986	10	0	0		
OAKES, Keith B.	Bedworth	03.07.56	App	Peterborough U.	07.73	1972-77	48	14	2	(CD)	
			Tr	Newport Co.	09.78	1978-83	232	0	27		
			Tr	Gillingham	08.84	1984-86	84	2	7		
			Tr	Fulham	09.86	1986-87	76	0	3		
OGHANI, George W.	Manchester	02.09.60	Sheffield U. (Jnrs)	Bury	02.78					(F)	
			Hyde U.	Bolton W.	10.83	1983-86	86	13	27		
			L	Wrexham	03.87	1986	6	1	0		
			Tr	Burnley	06.87	1987					
OGLEY, Mark A.	Barnsley	10.03.67	App	Barnsley	03.85	1985-86	19	0	0	(D)	Son of Alan
			L	Aldershot	12.87	1987	6	2	0		
			Tr	Carlisle U.	03.88	1987	3	0	0		
OGRIZOVIC, Steve	Mansfield	12.09.57	Mansfield YC	Chesterfield	07.77	1977	16	0	0	(G)	
			Tr	Liverpool	11.77	1977-80	4	0	0		
			Tr	Shrewsbury T.	08.82	1982-83	84	0	0		
			Tr	Coventry C.	06.84	1984-87	166	0	0		
OLDFIELD, David C.	Australia	30.05.68	App	Luton T.	05.86	1987	6	2	3	(F)	
OLIVER, A.J. (Tony)	Portsmouth	22.09.67	Portsmouth(N/C)	Brentford (N/C)	08.87	1987	11	0	0	(G)	
OLIVER, Gavin R.	Felling	06.09.62	App	Sheffield Wed.	08.80	1980-84	14	6	0	(D)	
			L	Tranmere Rov.	01.83	1982	17	0	1		
			L	Brighton & H.A.	08.85	1985	15	1	0		
			Tr	Bradford C.	11.85	1985-87	110	0	2		
OLSEN, Jesper	Denmark	20.03.61	Ajax Amsterdam	Manchester U.	07.84	1984-87	113	6	21	(LW)	Danish Int
OLSSON, Paul	Hull	24.12.65	App	Hull C.	12.83					(M)	
			Tr	Exeter C.	03.87	1986-87	38	5	2		
ORD, Richard J.	Murton	03.03.70	YTS	Sunderland	07.87	1987	4	4	0	(CD)	
ORMONDROYD, Ian	Bradford	22.09.64	Thackley	Bradford C.	09.85	1985-87	47	15	16	(F)	
			L	Oldham Ath.	03.87	1986	8	2	1		
ORMSBY, Brendan T.C.	Birmingham	01.10.60	App	Aston Villa	10.78	1978-85	115	2	4	(CD)	E Sch Int/ E Yth Int
			Tr	Leeds U.	02.86	1985-86	45	0	5		
ORR, Neil I.	Greenock	13.05.59	Morton	West Ham U.	01.82	1981-87	133	13	4	(D)	S U21-7/ to Hibernian 8.87
OSBORNE, Lawrence W.	West Ham	20.10.67	App	Arsenal	07.85					(M)	
				Newport Co.	11.87	1987	15	0	0		
OSMAN, Russell C.	Repton (Dy.)	14.02.59	App	Ipswich T.	03.76	1977-84	244	0	17	(CD)	Son of Rex/E-11/ E Yth Int/E U21-7
			Tr	Leicester C.	07.85	1985-87	108	0	8		
OSVOLD, Kjetil	Norway	05.06.61	Lillestrom (Nor.)	Nottingham F.	03.87	1986-87	5	2	0	(W)	
			L	Leicester C.	12.87	1987	3	1	0		
OUTHART, Anthony J.	Scarborough	17.09.63	Bridlington T.	Scarborough (N/C)	11.87	1987	3	2	1	(F)	
OUTTERSIDE, Mark J.	Hexham	13.01.67	App	Sunderland	01.85	1986	1	0	0	(RB)	
			Tr	Darlington	07.87	1987	37	1	0		
OVERSON, Vince D.	Kettering	15.05.62	App	Burnley	11.79	1979-85	207	4	6	(CD)	Brother of Richard
			Tr	Birmingham C.	06.86	1986-87	71	0	1		
OWEN, Gary A.	St. Helens	07.07.58	App	Manchester C.	08.75	1975-78	101	2	19	(M)	E Yth Int/ E U21-22/E 'B'
			Tr	West Bromwich A.	06.79	1979-85	185	2	21		
			Panionios (Greece)	Sheffield Wed.	08.87	1987	12	2	0		
OWEN, Gordon	Barnsley	14.06.59	Jnrs	Sheffield Wed.	11.76	1977-82	32	15	5	(RW)	
			L	Rotherham U.	03.80	1979	9	0	0		
			L	Doncaster Rov.	11.82	1982	9	0	0		
			L	Chesterfield	03.83	1982	6	0	2		
			Tr	Cardiff C.	08.83	1983	38	1	14		
			Tr	Barnsley	08.84	1984-85	68	0	25		
			Tr	Bristol C.	08.86	1986-87	51	2	11		
			L	Hull C.	12.87	1987	3	0	0		
			Tr	Mansfield T.	01.88	1987	15	2	3		
OWERS, Adrian R.	Chelmsford	26.02.65	App	Southend U.	02.83	1982-84	18	9	0	(M)	
			Chelmsford C.	Brighton & H.A.	12.87	1987	9	0	2		
OWERS, Gary	Newcastle	03.10.68	App	Sunderland	10.86	1987	37	0	4	(M)	
OWERS, Phil	Bishop Auckland	28.04.55	Jnrs	Darlington	06.73	1972-74	45	0	0	(G)	
			Tr	Gillingham	07.75	1975	2	0	0		
			Tr	Darlington	07.76	1976-79	69	0	0		
			Brandon U.	Hartlepool U. (N/C)	08.87	1987	2	0	0		
PAINTER, Peter R.	Ince	26.01.71	YTS	Chester C. (YTS)	07.87	1987	0	2	0		
PALGRAVE, Brian U.	Birmingham	12.07.66	Alvechurch	Walsall	07.84	1984-87	5	3	1	(F)	
PALIN, Leigh G.	Worcester	12.09.65	App	Aston Villa	09.83					(M)	E Yth Int/ Son of Grenville
			L	Shrewsbury T.	12.84	1984	2	0	0		
			Tr	Nottingham F.	11.85							
			Tr	Bradford C.	10.86	1986-87	37	4	6		
PALLISTER, Gary A.	Ramsgate	30.06.65	Billingham T.	Middlesbrough	11.84	1985-87	116	0	4	(CD)	E-1
			L	Darlington	10.85	1985	7	0	0		
PALMER, Carlton L.	Rowley Regis	05.12.65	YTS	West Bromwich A.	12.84	1985-87	88	7	4	(D)	
PALMER, Charlie A.	Aylesbury	10.07.63	App	Watford	07.81	1983	10	0	1	(RB)	
			Tr	Derby Co.	07.84	1984-85	51	0	2		
			Tr	Hull C.	02.87	1986-87	52	0	0		
PALMER, Lee J.	Croydon	19.09.70	YTS	Gillingham (YTS)	06.87	1987	1	0	0	(LB)	
PALMER, Roger N.	Manchester	30.01.59	App	Manchester C.	01.77	1977-80	22	9	9	(W)	
			Tr	Oldham Ath.	11.80	1980-87	300	3	98		
PARDEW, Alan S.	Wimbledon	18.07.61	Yeovil T.	Crystal Palace	03.87	1987	16	4	0	(M)	
PARIS, Alan D.	Slough	15.08.64	Slough T.	Watford	11.82					(RB)	
			Tr	Peterborough U.	08.85	1985-87	135	2	2		

Jerry Murphy (Chelsea) Left sided midfield player who was signed on a free from Crystal Palace.

Kevin Moran (Manchester United) Reliable central defender who came to United from Gaelic football.

Phil Neal (Bolton Wanderers) Former Liverpool and England star full-back, now player-manager at Burnden Park.

Remi Moses (Manchester United) Unlucky with injuries.

Players Names	Birthplace	Date	Source	League Club	Date Sign'd	Seasons Played	Career Record Apps	Sub	Gls	Pos.	Misc
PARKER, Derrick	Wallsend	07.02.57	App	Burnley	02.74	1974-75	5	1	2	(F)	
			Tr	Southend U.	02.77	1976-79	129	0	43		
			Tr	Barnsley	02.80	1979-82	104	3	32		
			Tr	Oldham Ath.	08.83	1983-84	54	3	11		
			L	Doncaster Rov.	12.84	1984	5	0	1		
			Tr	Burnley	10.85	1985-86	43	0	10		
			Finland	Rochdale (N/C)	10.87	1987	6	1	1		
PARKER, Gary S.	Oxford	07.09.65	App	Luton T.	05.83	1982-83	31	11	3	(M)	E Yth Int/E U21-3
			Tr	Hull C.	02.86	1985-87	82	2	8		
			Tr	Nottingham F.	03.88	1987	1	1	0		
PARKER, Jeffrey S.	Liverpool	23.01.69	YTS	Crewe Alex.	07.87	1987	7	3	0	(F)	
PARKER, Paul A.	West Ham	04.04.64	App	Fulham	04.82	1980-86	140	13	2	(D)	E Yth Int/E-U21-8
			Tr	Q.P.R.	06.87	1987	40	0	0		
PARKES, Phil B.F.	Sedgley	08.08.50	Jnrs	Walsall	01.68	1968-69	52	0	0	(G)	E U23-6/E U21-1/
			Tr	Q.P.R.	06.70	1970-78	344	0	0		E-1/E 'B'
			Tr	West Ham U.	02.79	1978-87	309	0	0		
PARKIN, Brian	Birkenhead	12.10.65	Jnrs	Oldham Ath.	03.83	1983-84	6	0	0	(G)	
			Tr	Crewe Alex.	11.84	1984-87	98	0	0		
PARKIN, Steve J.	Mansfield	07.11.65	App	Stoke C.	11.83	1982-87	100	9	5	(M/LB)	E Sch Int/
											E Yth Int/E U21-5
PARKIN, Tim J.	Penrith	31.12.57	App	Blackburn Rov.	03.76	1976-78	13	0	0	(CD)	
			FK Malmö (Swe.)	Bristol Rov.	08.81	1981-85	205	1	12		
			Tr	Swindon T.	07.86	1986-87	71	1	4		
PARKINSON, Gary	Middlesbrough	10.01.68	Everton (Jnr)	Middlesbrough	01.86	1986-87	81	3	0	(RB)	
PARKINSON, Philip J.	Chorley	01.12.67	App	Southampton	12.85					(W)	
			Tr	Bury	03.88	1987	8	0	1		
PARKS, A. (Tony)	Hackney	28.01.63	App	Tottenham H.	09.80	1981-87	37	0	0	(G)	
			L	Oxford U.	10.86	1986	5	0	0		
			L	Gillingham	09.87	1987	2	0	0		
PARLANE, Derek J.	Helensburgh	05.05.53	Glasgow Rangers	Leeds U.	03.80	1979-82	45	5	10	(F)	S U23-5/S U21-1/
			Hong Kong	Manchester C.	08.83	1983-84	47	1	20		S-12
			Tr	Swansea C.	01.85	1984	21	0	3		
			Hong Kong	Rochdale	12.86	1986-87	42	0	10		
PARRIS, George M.R.	Ilford	11.09.64	App	West Ham U.	09.82	1984-87	86	7	3	(LB)	E Sch Int
PARRY, Mark	Wrexham	21.05.70	YTS	Chester C. (YTS)	08.86	1987	4	1	1	(W)	
PARSELLE, Norman J.	Newport	08.01.70	YTS	Newport Co. (YTS)	08.86	1987	4	6	0	(D)	
PASCOE, Colin J.	Port Talbot	09.04.65	App	Swansea C.	04.83	1982-87	167	7	39	(F)	W Yth Int/
			Tr	Sunderland	03.88	1987	8	1	4		W U21-3/W-2
PASHLEY, Terry	Chesterfield	11.10.56	App	Burnley	10.73	1975-77	16	2	0	(LB)	E Sch Int
			Tr	Blackpool	08.78	1978-82	201	0	7		
			Tr	Bury	08.83	1983-87	182	10	4		
PATES, Colin G.	Carshalton	10.08.61	App	Chelsea	07.79	1979-87	270	1	9	(CD)	E Yth Int
PATTERSON, Mark	Leeds	13.09.68	YTS	Carlisle U.	08.87	1986-87	19	3	0	(RB)	
			Tr	Derby Co.	11.87						
PATTERSON, Mark A.	Darwen	24.05.65	App	Blackburn Rov.	05.83	1983-87	89	12	20	(W)	
PAYTON, Andrew P.	Whalley	03.10.67	YTS	Hull C.	05.86	1986-87	11	13	2	(M)	
PEACOCK, Darren	Bristol	03.02.68	YTS	Newport Co.	02.86	1985-87	24	4	0	(CD)	
PEACOCK, Gavin K.	Eltham	18.11.67	App	Q.P.R.	11.84	1986-87	7	10	1	(M)	Son of Keith/
			L	Gillingham	10.87	1987	6	0	0		E Sch Int/E Yth Int
			Tr	Gillingham	12.87	1987	20	0	2		
PEAKE, Andy M.	Market Harborough	01.11.61	App	Leicester C.	01.79	1978-84	141	6	13	(M)	E Yth Int/E U21-1
			Tr	Grimsby T.	08.85	1985-86	39	0	4		
			Tr	Charlton Ath.	09.86	1986-87	44	1	0		
PEAKE, Trevor	Nuneaton	10.02.57	Nuneaton Bor.	Lincoln C.	06.79	1979-82	171	0	7	(CD)	E Semi-Pro Int
			Tr	Coventry C.	07.83	1983-87	174	1	5		1979
PEARCE, Alan J.	Middlesbrough	25.10.65	Jnrs	York C.	10.83	1983-86	76	2	9	(LW)	
			Tr	Torquay U.	08.87	1987	20	7	2		
PEARCE, Chris L.	Newport	07.08.61	W'hampton W.(App)	Blackburn Rov.	10.79					(G)	W Sch Int
			L	Rochdale	08.80	1980	5	0	0		
			Tr	Rochdale	08.82	1982	36	0	0		
			Tr	Port Vale	06.83	1983-85	48	0	0		
			Tr	Wrexham	07.86	1986	25	0	0		
			Tr	Burnley	07.87	1987	46	0	0		
PEARCE, Graham	Hammersmith	08.07.59	Barnet	Brighton & H.A.	01.82	1982-85	87	1	2	(LB)	
			Tr	Gillingham	07.86	1986-87	65	0	0		
PEARCE, Stuart	Hammersmith	24.04.62	Wealdstone	Coventry C.	10.83	1983-84	51	0	4	(LB)	E U21-1/E-4
			Tr	Nottingham F.	06.85	1985-87	103	0	12		
PEARS, Steve	Brandon	22.01.62	App	Manchester U.	01.79	1984	4	0	0	(G)	
			L	Middlesbrough	11.83	1983	12	0	0		
			Tr	Middlesbrough	07.85	1985-87	127	0	0		
PEARSON, John S.	Sheffield	01.09.63	App	Sheffield Wed.	05.81	1980-84	64	41	24	(F)	E Yth Int
			Tr	Charlton Ath.	05.85	1985-86	52	9	15		
			Tr	Leeds U.	01.87	1986-87	39	7	10		
PEARSON, Lawrence	Wallsend	02.07.65	Gateshead	Hull C.	06.84	1984-86	58	1	0	(LB)	
			Tr	Bristol C.	06.87						
			Tr	Port Vale	08.87	1987	3	0	0		
PEARSON, Nigel G.	Nottingham	21.08.63	Heanor T.	Shrewsbury T.	11.81	1982-87	153	0	5	(CD)	
			Tr	Sheffield Wed.	10.87	1987	19	0	2		
PECKETT, Andy R.	Sheffield	19.09.69	YTS	Doncaster Rov.	06.88	1987	2	0	0	(M)	
PEER, Dean	Dudley	08.08.69	YTS	Birmingham C.	07.87	1986	1	1	0	(M)	
PEJIC, Mel	Newcastle-u-Lyme	27.04.59	Jnrs	Stoke C.	07.77	1979	1	0	0	(CD)	Brother of Mike
			Tr	Hereford U.	06.80	1980-87	293	2	4		
PEMBERTON, John M.	Oldham	18.11.64	Chadderton	Rochdale (N/C)	09.84	1984	1	0	0	(FB)	
			Tr	Crewe Alex.	03.85	1984-87	116	5	1		
			Tr	Crystal Palace	03.88	1987	0	2	0		

Players Names	Birthplace	Date	Source	League Club	Date Sign'd	Seasons Played	Apps	Sub	Gls	Pos.	Misc
PENDER, John P.	Luton	19.11.63	App	Wolverhampton W.	11.81	1981-84	115	2	3	(CD)	IR Yth Int/
			Tr	Charlton Ath.	07.85	1985-87	41	0	0		IR U21-1
			Tr	Bristol C.	10.87	1987	28	0	2		
PENNEY, David M.	Wakefield	17.08.64	Pontefract Colly.	Derby Co.	09.85	1986-87	3	7	0	(F)	
PENNEY, Steve A.	Ballymena (NI)	16.01.64	Ballymena U.	Brighton & H.A.	11.83	1983-87	116	12	14	(W)	NI-15
PENNYFATHER, Glenn J.	Billericay	11.02.63	App	Southend U.	02.81	1980-87	231	7	36	(M)	
				Crystal Palace	11.87	1987	18	1	1		
PENRICE, Gary K.	Bristol	23.03.64	Mangotsfield	Bristol Rov.	11.84	1984-87	131	2	30	(M)	
PEPPER, Nigel C.	Rotherham	25.04.68	App	Rotherham U.	04.86	1985-87	19	5	0	(M)	
PERKS, Stephen J.	Bridgnorth	19.04.63	App	Shrewsbury T.	04.81	1984-87	143	0	0	(G)	
PERRY, Andy	Dulwich	28.12.62	Dulwich Hamlet	Portsmouth	11.86	1987	1	3	0	(F)	
PERRY, David	Sheffield	17.05.67	Jnrs	Chesterfield	07.87	1985-87	12	5	0	(D)	
PERRY, Jason	Newport	02.04.70	Jnrs	Cardiff C.	08.87	1986-87	4	0	0	(D)	
PERRYMAN, Steve J.	Ealing	21.12.51	App	Tottenham H.	01.69	1969-85	653	2	31	(M)	E Sch Int/E Yth Int/
			Tr	Oxford U.	03.86	1985-86	17	0	0		E U23-17/E-1
			Tr	Brentford	11.86	1986-87	39	6	0		FWA Footballer of Year 1981-82
PETERS, Gary D.	Carshalton	03.08.54	Guildford C.	Reading	05.75	1975-78	150	6	7	(D)	
			Tr	Fulham	08.79	1979-81	57	7	2		
			Tr	Wimbledon	07.82	1982-83	83	0	7		
			Tr	Aldershot	07.84	1984	17	0	1		
			Tr	Reading	02.85	1984-87	93	7	3		
PEYTON, Gerry J.	Birmingham	20.05.56	Atherstone T.	Burnley	05.75	1975-76	30	0	0	(G)	IR-25
			Tr	Fulham	12.76	1976-85	345	0	0		
			L	Southend U.	09.83	1983	10	0	0		
			Tr	Bournemouth	07.86	1986-87	88	0	0		
PHELAN, Mike C.	Nelson	24.09.62	App	Burnley	07.80	1980-84	166	2	9	(M)	E Yth Int
			Tr	Norwich C.	07.85	1985-87	119	0	7		
PHELAN, Terry	Manchester	16.03.67	YTS	Leeds U.	08.84	1985	12	2	0	(LB)	IR Yth Int
			Tr	Swansea C.	07.86	1986	45	0	0		
			Tr	Wimbledon	07.87	1987	28	2	0		
PHILLIPS, David O.	West Germany	29.07.63	App	Plymouth Arg.	08.81	1981-83	65	8	15	(M)	W U21-3/W-20
			Tr	Manchester C.	08.84	1984-85	81	0	13		
			Tr	Coventry C.	06.86	1986-87	71	3	6		
PHILLIPS, Gary C.	St. Albans	20.09.61	Jnrs	West Bromwich A.	06.79					(G)	E Semi-Pro Int
			Barnet	Brentford	12.84	1984-87	143	0	0		1982
PHILLIPS, Ian A.	Edinburgh	23.04.59	Ipswich T. (App)	Mansfield T.	08.77	1977-78	18	5	0	(LB)	
			Tr	Peterborough U.	08.79	1979-81	97	0	3		
			Tr	Northampton T.	08.82	1982	42	0	1		
			Tr	Colchester U.	09.83	1983-86	150	0	8		
			Tr	Aldershot	08.87	1987	32	0	0		
PHILLIPS, Jimmy N.	Bolton	08.02.66	App	Bolton W.	08.83	1983-86	103	5	2	(LB)	to Glasgow Rgrs 3.87
PHILLIPS, Les M.	Lambeth	07.01.63	App	Birmingham C.	08.80	1981-83	36	8	3	(M)	
			Tr	Oxford U.	03.84	1983-87	94	8	6		
PHILLIPS, Steve E.	Edmonton	04.08.54	App	Birmingham C.	08.71	1971-75	15	5	1	(F)	E Yth int
			L	Torquay U.	12.74	1974	6	0	0		
			Tr	Northampton T.	10.75	1975-76	50	1	8		
			Tr	Brentford	02.77	1976-79	156	1	65		
			Tr	Northampton T.	08.80	1980-81	75	0	29		
			Tr	Southend U.	03.82	1981-85	157	1	66		
			Tr	Torquay U.	01.86	1985-86	32	0	11		
			Tr	Peterborough U.	11.86	1986-87	46	0	16		
			L	Exeter C.	09.87	1987	5	1	1		
			L	Chesterfield	01.88	1987	9	0	2		
PHILLIPS, Stuart G.	Halifax	30.12.61	App	Hereford U.	11.79	1977-87	285	8	83	(F)	
			Tr	West Bromwich A.	03.88	1987	10	0	2		
PHILLISKIRK, A. (Tony)	Sunderland	10.02.65	Sch	Sheffield U.	08.83	1983-87	62	18	20	(F)	E Sch Int
			L	Rotherham U.	10.86	1986	6	0	1		
PHILPOTT, Lee	Barnet	21.02.70	YTS	Peterborough U.(YTS)	07.86	1987	0	1	0		
PICKERING, Mike J.	Heckmondwike	29.09.56	Jnrs	Barnsley	10.74	1974-76	100	0	1	(CD)	
			Tr	Southampton	06.77	1977-78	44	0	0		
			Tr	Sheffield Wed.	10.78	1978-82	106	4	1		
			L	Norwich C.	09.83	1983	0	1	0		
			L	Bradford C.	11.83	1983	4	0	0		
			L	Barnsley	12.83	1983	3	0	0		
			Tr	Rotherham U.	01.84	1983-85	102	0	1		
			Tr	York C.	07.86	1986	31	1	1		
			Tr	Stockport Co.	07.87	1987	8	0	0		
PICKERING, Nick	Newcastle	04.08.63	App	Sunderland	08.81	1981-85	177	2	18	(LM)	E Yth Int/E U21-15
			Tr	Coventry C.	01.86	1985-87	76	2	9		
PIKE, Chris	Cardiff	19.10.61	Barry T.	Fulham	03.85	1985-87	32	10	4	(F)	
			L	Cardiff C.	12.86	1986	6	0	2		
PIKE, Geoff A.	Clapton	28.09.56	App	West Ham U.	09.74	1975-86	275	16	32	(M)	
			Tr	Notts Co.	07.87	1987	46	0	14		
PIKE, Martin R.	South Shields	21.10.64	App	West Bromwich A.	10.82					(LB)	
			Tr	Peterborough U.	08.83	1983-85	119	7	8		
			Tr	Sheffield U.	08.86	1986-87	80	1	0		
PILLING, Andrew J.	Wigan	30.06.69	YTS	Preston N.E. (YTS)	07.85	1985	1	0	0	(M)	
			Tr	Wigan Ath.	07.87	1987	16	4	3		
PISANTI, David	Israel	27.05.62	F.C. Köln (WG)	Q.P.R.	09.87	1987	3	4	0	(M)	
PLATNAUER, Nicky R.	Leicester	10.06.61	Bedford T.	Bristol Rov.	08.82	1982	21	3	7	(M)	
			Tr	Coventry C.	08.83	1983-84	38	6	6		
			Tr	Birmingham C.	12.84	1984-85	23	5	2		
			L	Reading	01.86	1985	7	0	0		
			Tr	Cardiff C.	09.86	1986-87	71	5	4		
PLATT, David A.	Oldham	10.06.66	Chadderton	Manchester U.	07.84					(F)	
			Tr	Crewe Alex.	01.85	1984-87	134	0	55		
			Tr	Aston Villa	02.88	1987	11	0	5		

Players Names	Birthplace	Date	Previous Club	League Club	Date Sign'd	Seasons Played	Career Record Apps	Sub	Gls	Pos.	Misc
PLUMMER, Calvin A.	Nottingham	14.02.63	App	Nottingham F.	02.81	1981-82	10	2	2	(W)	
			Tr	Chesterfield	12.82	1982	28	0	7		
			Tr	Derby Co.	08.83	1983	23	4	3		
			Tr	Barnsley	03.84	1983-86	41	13	6		
			Tr	Nottingham F.	12.86						
			Finland	Nottingham F.	10.87	1987	8	0	2		
PODD, Cyril M. (Ces)	St. Kitts(WI)	07.08.52	Jnrs	Bradford C.	08.70	1970-73	44	8	2	(FB)	
			Tr	Halifax T.	08.84	1984-85	52	2	0		
POINTON, Neil G.	Warsop	28.11.64	App	Scunthorpe U.	08.82	1981-85	159	0	2	(LB)	
			Tr	Everton	11.85	1985-87	56	4	4		
POLLARD, Gary	Staveley	30.12.59	Jnrs	Chesterfield	07.77	1977-82	83	4	1	(CD)	
			Tr	Port Vale	06.83	1983	18	0	0		
			Tr	Mansfield T.	07.84	1984-86	66	1	1		
			Tr	Peterborough U.	08.87	1987	12	0	0		
POLSTON, Jonathan D.	Walthamstow	10.06.68	App	Tottenham H.	07.85	1986-87	6	2	0	(CD)	E Yth Int
POOLE, Gary	Stratford	11.09.67	Jnrs	Tottenham H.	07.85					(RB)	
			Tr	Cambridge U.	08.87	1987	41	1	0		
POOLE, Kevin	Bromsgrove	21.07.63	App	Aston Villa	06.81	1984-86	28	0	0	(G)	
			L	Northampton T.	11.84	1984	3	0	0		
			Tr	Middlesbrough	08.87	1987	1	0	0		
PORTER, Andrew M.	Macclesfield	17.09.68	YTS	Port Vale	06.87	1986-87	4	3	0	(M)	
PORTER, Gary M.	Sunderland	06.03.66	App	Watford	03.84	1983-87	74	11	8	(M)	E Yth Int/E U21-12
POSKETT, Malcolm	Middlesbrough	19.07.53	South Bank	Middlesbrough	04.73	1973	0	1	0	(F)	
			Whitby T.	Hartlepool U.	11.76	1976-77	50	1	20		
			Tr	Brighton & H.A.	02.78	1977-79	33	12	16		
			Tr	Watford	01.80	1979-81	57	6	17		
			Tr	Carlisle U.	08.82	1982-84	108	2	40		
			Tr	Darlington	07.85	1985	18	3	4		
			Tr	Stockport Co.	01.86	1985	8	0	1		
			L	Hartlepool U.	03.86	1985	4	1	0		
			Tr	Carlisle U.	08.86	1986-87	67	9	20		
POTTS, Steven J.	USA	07.05.67	App	West Ham U.	05.84	1984-87	16	2	0	(FB)	E Yth Int
POWELL, Barry I.	Kenilworth	29.01.54	App	Wolverhampton W.	01.72	1972-74	58	6	7	(M)	E U23-4
			Tr	Coventry C.	09.75	1975-79	162	2	28		
			Tr	Derby Co.	10.79	1979-81	86	0	7		
			Hong Kong	Burnley	07.84	1984	9	2	0		
			Tr	Swansea C.	02.85	1984	8	0	0		
			Hong Kong	Wolverhampton W.	11.86	1986-87	10	4	0		
POWELL, Cliff G.	Watford	21.02.68	App	Watford	02.86					(D)	
			L	Hereford U.	12.87	1987	7	0	0		
			Tr	Sheffield U.	03.88	1987	5	1	0		
POWELL, David R.	Hednesford	24.09.67	Cherry Valley FC	West Bromwich A.	04.86	1987	2	0	0	(G)	
			L	Wrexham	02.87	1986	2	0	0		
POWELL, Richard	Chesterfield	03.09.69	YTS	Blackpool	06.88	1986-87	14	0	0	(G)	Son of Ron
POWER, Paul C.	Manchester	30.10.53	Leeds Polytechnic	Manchester C.	09.73	1975-85	358	7	26	(LM)	E-'B'
			Tr	Everton	06.86	1986-87	52	2	6		
PRATLEY, Richard G.	Banbury	12.01.63	Banbury U.	Derby Co.	07.83	1983-86	29	2	1	(CD)	
			L	Scunthorpe U.	03.84	1983	10	0	0		
			Tr	Shrewsbury T.	02.88	1987	11	0	0		
PRATT, Lee S.	Cleethorpes	31.03.70	YTS	Grimsby T.	06.88	1986	1	0	0	(G)	
PREECE, David W.	Bridgnorth	28.05.63	App	Walsall	07.80	1980-84	107	4	5	(LM)	
			Tr	Luton T.	12.84	1984-87	88	1	4		
PREECE, Roger	Much Wenlock	09.06.69	Coventry C. (YTS)	Wrexham	08.86	1986-87	39	8	6	(M)	
PREECE, Ryan	Neath	10.01.69	YTS	Newport Co. (N/C)	10.87	1987	7	3	2	(M)	
PRESSMAN, Kevin P.	Fareham	06.11.67	App	Sheffield Wed.	11.85	1987	11	0	0	(G)	E Sch Int/E Yth Int
PRESTON, Richard F.	Nottingham	10.06.67	Stanton	Scarborough	03.88	1987	1	3	0	(F)	
PRICE, Chris J.	Hereford	30.03.60	App	Hereford U.	01.78	1976-85	327	3	27	(RB)	
			Tr	Blackburn Rov.	07.86	1986-87	83	0	10		
PRICE, Paul T.	St. Albans	23.03.54	Jnrs	Luton T.	07.71	1972-80	206	1	8	(CD)	W U21-1/W-25
			Tr	Tottenham H.	06.81	1981-83	35	4	0		
			Minnesota (USA)	Swansea C.	01.85	1984-85	61	0	1		
			Tr	Peterborough U.	08.86	1986-87	86	0	0		
PRIDDLE, Sean P.	Hammersmith	14.12.65	App	Wimbledon	12.83					(M)	
			Tr	Crewe Alex.	02.85	1984	6	5	0		
			Wimbledon(N/C)	Exeter C.	07.86	1986	18	0	1		
				Brentford	07.87	1987	5	1	0		
PRIEST, Philip	Warley	09.09.66	App	Chelsea	09.83					(M)	E Sch Int/E Yth Int
			L	Blackpool	12.86	1986	1	0	0		
			L	Brentford	03.87	1986	3	2	1		
			Tr	Shrewsbury T.	07.87	1987	21	0	2		
PRINDIVILLE, Stephen	Harlow	26.12.68	App	Leicester C.	12.86	1987	0	1	0	(FB)	
PRITCHARD, Howard K.	Cardiff	18.10.58	App	Bristol C.	08.76	1978-80	31	7	2	(W)	W Yth Int/W-1
			Tr	Swindon T.	08.81	1981-82	59	6	11		
			Tr	Bristol C.	08.83	1983-85	117	2	22		
			Tr	Gillingham	08.86	1986-87	84	4	20		
PROCTOR, Mark G.	Middlesbrough	30.01.61	App	Middlesbrough	09.78	1978-80	107	2	12	(M)	E Yth Int/E U21-4
			Tr	Nottingham F.	08.81	1981-82	60	4	5		
			Tr	Sunderland	03.83	1982-87	115	2	19		
			Tr	Sheffield Wed.	09.87	1987	35	0	2		
PROUDLOCK, Paul	Hartlepool	25.10.65		Hartlepool U.	09.84	1984-85	8	7	0	(W)	
				Middlesbrough	11.86	1986-87	2	2	0		

Russell Osman (Leicester City) Former England central defender. Match Magazine

Phil Parkes (West Ham United) Long serving goalkeeper. Match Magazine

Jesper Olsen (Manchester United) Danish international star. Match Magazine

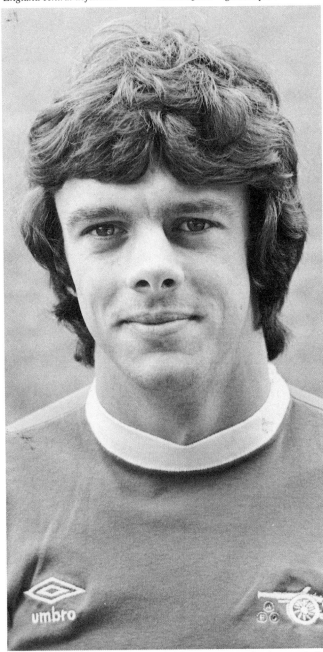

David O'Leary (Arsenal) As reliable as ever at the heart of the "Gunners" defence. Match Magazine

Les Phillips (Oxford United) Hard working midfielder who came to the club from Birmingham City. Match Magazine

Players Names	Birthplace	Date	Source	League Club	Date Sign'd	Seasons Played	Apps	Sub	Gls	Pos.	Misc
PRUDHOE, Mark	Washington	11.11.63	App	Sunderland	09.81	1982	7	0	0	(G)	
			L	Hartlepool U.	11.83	1983	3	0	0		
			Tr	Birmingham C.	09.84	1984	1	0	0		
			Tr	Walsall	02.86	1985-86	26	0	0		
			L	Doncaster Rov.	12.86	1986	5	0	0		
			L	Grimsby T.	03.87	1986	8	0	0		
			L	Hartlepool U.	08.87	1987	13	0	0		
			L	Bristol C.	11.87	1987	3	0	0		
			Tr	Carlisle U.	12.87	1987	22	0	0		
PUCKETT, David C.	Southampton	29.10.60	App	Southampton	10.78	1980-85	51	43	14	(F)	
			Tr	Bournemouth	07.86	1986-87	27	4	14		
			L	Stoke C.	03.88	1987	7	0	0		
PUGH, Daral J.	Neath	05.06.61	App	Doncaster Rov.	12.78	1978-82	136	18	15	(W)	W U21-2
			Tr	Huddersfield T.	09.82	1982-84	52	32	7		
			Tr	Rotherham U.	07.85	1985-87	106	6	6		
			L	Cambridge U.	12.87	1987	6	0	1		
PULIS, A.R. (Tony)	Newport	16.01.58	App	Bristol Rov.	09.75	1975-80	78	7	3	(D/M)	
			Hong Kong	Bristol Rov.	06.82	1982-83	44	1	2		
			Tr	Newport Co.	07.84	1984-85	75	2	0		
			Tr	Bournemouth	08.86	1986-87	58	6	3		
PULLAN, Chris J.	Durham	14.12.67	Jnrs	Watford	07.86	1986-87	2	3	0	(M)	
PURDIE, Jon	Corby	22.02.67	App	Arsenal	01.85					(W)	E Sch Int
			Tr	Wolverhampton W.	07.85	1985-87	82	7	12		
			L	Cambridge U.	10.87	1987	7	0	2		
PURNELL, Philip	Bristol	16.09.64	Mangotsfield	Bristol Rov.	09.85	1985-87	67	6	13	(W)	
PUTNEY, Trevor A.	Harold Hill	11.02.61	Brentwood & Warley	Ipswich T.	09.80	1982-85	94	9	8	(M)	
			Tr	Norwich C.	06.86	1986-87	45	4	5		
QUINN, Jimmy M.	Belfast	18.11.59	Oswestry T.	Swindon T.	12.81	1981-83	34	15	10	(F)	NI-19
			Tr	Blackburn Rov.	08.84	1984-86	58	13	17		
			Tr	Swindon T.	12.86	1986-87	61	3	30		
QUINN, Mike	Liverpool	02.05.62	Derby Co. (App)	Wigan Ath.	09.79	1979-81	56	13	19	(F)	
			Tr	Stockport Co.	07.82	1982-83	62	1	39		
			Tr	Oldham Ath.	01.84	1983-85	78	2	34		
			Tr	Portsmouth	03.86	1986-87	79	3	36		
QUINN, Nial J.	Dublin	06.10.66	Jnrs	Arsenal	11.83	1985-87	51	7	11	(F)	IR Yth Int/IR-8
QUOW, Trevor	Peterborough	28.09.60	App	Peterborough U.	09.78	1978-85	191	12	17	(M)	
			Tr	Gillingham	08.86	1986-87	48	11	2		
RADFORD, Mark	Leicester	20.12.68	Jnrs	Colchester U.	05.87	1987	12	2	0	(LB)	
RAFFELL, Stephen C.	Blyth	27.04.70	YTS	Doncaster Rov.	06.88	1987	11	3	0	(CD)	
RAMSEY, Chris L.	Birmingham	28.04.62	Bristol City (App)	Brighton & H.A.	08.80	1980-83	30	0	0	(RB)	
			Tr	Swindon T.	08.84	1984-86	99	1	5		
			Tr	Southend U.	08.87	1987	8	5	0		
RAMSEY, Paul	Derry (NI)	03.09.62	App	Leicester C.	04.80	1980-87	205	4	10	(M/RB)	NI-13
RANDALL, Adrian J.	Amesbury	10.11.68	App	Bournemouth	08.86	1985-87	3	0	0	(M)	E Yth Int
RANKINE, S. Mark	Doncaster	30.09.69	YTS	Doncaster Rov.	06.88	1987	14	4	2	(M)	
RANSON, Ray	St. Helens	12.06.60	App	Manchester C.	06.77	1978-83	181	2	1	(RB)	E Yth Int/
			Tr	Birmingham C.	11.84	1984-87	119	1	0		E U21-10
RANTANEN, Jari J.	Finland	31.12.61	Gothenburg (Swe.)	Leicester C.	09.87	1987	10	3	3	(F)	
RATCLIFFE, Kevin	Deeside	12.11.60	App	Everton	11.78	1979-87	259	1	2	(CD)	W Sch Int/ W U21-2/W-43
RATCLIFFE, Simon	Urmston	08.02.67	App	Manchester U.	02.85					(D)	E Sch Int/E Yth Int
			Tr	Norwich C.	06.87	1987	6	3	0		
RATHBONE, Mike J.	Birmingham	06.11.58	App	Birmingham C.	11.76	1976-78	17	3	0	(LB)	E Yth Int
			Tr	Blackburn Rov.	03.79	1978-86	270	3	2		
			Tr	Preston N.E.	07.87	1987	36	0	1		
RAVEN, Paul	Salisbury	28.07.70	Sch	Doncaster Rov.	06.88	1987	17	0	3	(CD)	E Sch Int
RAWCLIFFE, Peter	Cleethorpes	08.12.63	Louth U.	Grimsby T.	09.86	1986-87	9	13	1	(F)	
RAY, John W.	Newmarket	21.11.68	YTS	Colchester U.	10.87	1987	0	1	0	(CD)	
RAYNOR, Paul J.	Nottingham	29.04.66	App	Nottingham F.	04.84	1984	3	0	0	(F)	
			L	Bristol Rov.	03.85	1984	7	1	0		
			Tr	Huddersfield T.	08.85	1985-86	38	12	9		
			Tr	Swansea C.	03.87	1986-87	55	1	9		
RECK, Sean M.	Oxford	05.05.67	App	Oxford U.	04.85	1986-87	5	3	0	(M)	
			L	Newport Co.	08.85	1985	15	0	0		
			L	Reading	03.86	1985	1	0	0		
REDFEARN, Neil D.	Dewsbury	20.06.65	Nottingham F.(App)	Bolton W.	06.82	1982-83	35	0	1	(M)	
			Tr	Lincoln C.	03.84	1983-85	96	4	13		
			Tr	Doncaster Rov.	08.86	1986	46	0	14		
			Tr	Crystal Palace	07.87	1987	42	0	8		
REDFERN, David	Sheffield	08.11.62	Sch	Sheffield Wed.	06.81				(G)		
			Tr	Rochdale	03.85	1984-86	87	0	0		
			L	Wigan Ath.	10.87	1987	3	0	0		
REDMOND, Steve	Liverpool	02.11.67	App	Manchester C.	12.84	1985-87	81	2	2	(CD)	E Yth Int
REECE, Andy J.	Shrewsbury	05.09.62	Dudley T.	Bristol Rov.	08.87	1987	35	5	1	(M)	
REED, Graham	Doncaster	24.06.61	App	Barnsley	06.79	1978-79	3	0	0	(RB)	
			Frickley Ath.	Northampton T.	06.85	1985-87	97	7	2		
REES, A.A. (Tony)	Merthyr Tydfil	01.08.64	App	Aston Villa	08.82					(F)	W Sch Int/
			Tr	Birmingham C.	07.83	1983-87	75	20	12		W Yth Int/
			L	Peterborough U.	10.85	1985	5	0	2		W U21-1/W-1
			L	Shrewsbury T.	03.86	1985	1	1	0		
			Tr	Barnsley	03.88	1987	12	1	2		
REES, Mark	Smethwick	13.10.61	App	Walsall	08.79	1978-87	165	40	35	(RW)	
			L	Rochdale	10.86	1986	2	1	0		
REES, Melvyn J.	Cardiff	25.01.67	YTS	Cardiff C.	09.84	1984-86	31	0	0	(G)	W Yth Int
			Tr	Watford	07.87	1987	3	0	0		

Stuart Rimmer (Watford) Young forward signed from Chester last March seen in centre tousling with Q.P.R.'s Paul Parker. Action Images Ltd

Tony Philliskirk (Sheffield United) Appears to be pushed into the background by Kenny Clements of Manchester City. Action Images Ltd

Glen Roeder (Newcastle United) Has been a regular since signing from Q.P.R. during the 1983-84 season. Match Magazine

Stewart Robson (West Ham United) Joined the "Hammers" from Arsenal in whose colours he is pictured here. Match Magazine

Players Names	Birthplace	Date	Source	League Club	Date Sign'd	Seasons Played	Apps	Sub	Gls	Pos.	Misc
REEVES, David	Birkenhead	19.11.67	Heswall	Sheffield Wed.	08.86					(F)	
			L	Scunthorpe U.	12.86	1986	3	1	2		
			L	Scunthorpe U.	10.87	1987	6	0	4		
			L	Burnley	11.87	1987	16	0	8		
REEVES, John C.	Hackney	08.07.63	App	Fulham	06.81	1981-84	9	5	0	(LM)	
			Tr	Colchester U.	08.85	1985-87	58	3	7		
REGIS, Cyrille	French Guyana	09.02.58	Hayes	West Bromwich A.	05.77	1977-84	233	4	82	(F)	E U21-6/E-4/E 'B'
			Tr	Coventry C.	10.84	1984-87	134	1	32		
REID, A.J. (Tony)	Nottingham	09.05.63	App	Derby Co.	05.80	1980-82	27	3	1	(M)	
			L	Scunthorpe U.	02.83	1982	6	0	0		
			Tr	Newport Co.	03.83	1982-84	74	2	12		
			Tr	Chesterfield	07.85	1985-87	63	4	6		
REID, Mark	Kilwinning	15.09.61	Glasgow Celtic	Charlton Ath.	05.85	1985-87	120	0	12	(LB)	S U21-2
REID, Nicky S.	Urmston	30.10.60	App	Manchester C.	10.78	1978-86	211	5	2	(D)	E U21-6
			Tr	Blackburn Rov.	07.87	1987	49	0	1		
REID, Paul R.	Warley	19.01.68	App	Leicester C.	01.86	1986-87	28	4	5	(F)	
REID, Peter	Huyton	20.06.56	App	Bolton W.	05.74	1974-82	222	3	23	(M)	E U21-6/E-13
			Tr	Everton	12.82	1982-87	139	2	7		PFA Player of Year 1984-85
REID, Shaun	Huyton	13.10.65	YTS	Rochdale	09.83	1983-87	109	6	2	(M)	Brother of Peter
			L	Preston N.E.	12.85	1985	3	0	0		
REILLY, George G.	Bellshill	14.09.57	Corby T.	Northampton T.	06.76	1976-79	124	3	46	(F)	
			Tr	Cambridge U.	11.79	1979-82	136	2	36		
			Tr	Watford	08.83	1983-84	46	2	14		
			Tr	Newcastle U.	02.85	1984-85	31	0	10		
			Tr	West Bromwich A.	12.85	1985-87	42	1	9		
RENNIE, David	Edinburgh	29.08.64	App	Leicester C.	05.82	1983-85	21	0	1	(CD)	S Yth Int
			Tr	Leeds U.	01.86	1985-87	65	3	4		
REYNOLDS, Jamie A.	Swindon	27.10.67	App	Swindon T.	09.85	1984-86	0	2	0	(M)	E Yth Int
RHOADES-BROWN, Peter	Hampton	02.01.62	App	Chelsea	07.79	1979-83	86	10	4	(LW)	
			Tr	Oxford U.	01.84	1983-87	82	23	13		
RHODES, Andy C.	Askern	23.08.64	App	Barnsley	08.82	1983-84	36	0	0	(G)	
			Tr	Doncaster Rov.	10.85	1985-87	106	0	0		
			Tr	Oldham Ath.	03.88	1987	11	0	0		
RICE, Brian	Bellshill	11.10.63	Hibernian	Nottingham F.	08.85	1985-87	52	0	6	(LW)	S U21-1
			L	Grimsby T.	10.86	1986	4	0	0		
RICHARDS, Carl L.	Jamaica	01.12.60	Enfield	Bournemouth	07.86	1986-87	49	14	16	(F)	Semi-Pro Int 1986
RICHARDS, Gary V.	Swansea	02.08.63	App	Swansea C.	08.81	1981-84	63	3	1	(D)	
				Lincoln C. (N/C)	11.85	1985	2	5	0		
			Tr	Cambridge U. (N/C)	03.86	1985	8	0	0		
			Tr	Torquay U.	07.86	1986	24	1	1		
RICHARDS, Steve C.	Dundee	24.10.61	App	Hull C.	10.79	1979-82	55	3	2	(CD)	
			Gainsborough Trin.	York C. (N/C)	12.84	1984	6	1	0		
			Tr	Lincoln C.	08.85	1985	21	0	0		
			Tr	Cambridge U. (N/C)	03.86	1985	4	0	2		
			Tr	Scarborough	(N/L)	1987	42	0	5		
RICHARDSON, Ian P.	Ely	09.05.64	App	Watford	05.82	1983-84	5	3	2	(F)	
			L	Blackpool	12.82	1982	4	1	2		
			L	Rotherham U.	02.85	1984	5	0	2		
			Tr	Chester C.	11.85	1985-86	31	4	10		
			Tr	Scunthorpe U.	10.86	1986-87	9	0	3		
RICHARDSON, Kevin	Newcastle	04.12.62	App	Everton	12.80	1981-86	95	14	16	(LM)	
			Tr	Watford	09.86	1986	39	0	2		
			Tr	Arsenal	08.87	1987	24	5	4		
RICHARDSON, Lee J.	Halifax	12.03.69	YTS	Halifax T.	07.87	1986-87	21	10	1	(M)	
RICHARDSON, Steve E.	Slough	11.02.62	App	Southampton	02.80					(LB)	
			Tr	Reading	07.82	1982-87	211	2	2		
RIDEOUT, Paul D.	Bournemouth	14.08.64	App	Swindon T.	08.81	1980-82	90	5	38	(F)	E Sch Int/E Yth Int/ E U21-5/to Bari (It.) 7.85
			Tr	Aston Villa	06.83	1983-84	50	4	19		
RIGBY, Jonathan K.	Bury St. Edmunds	31.01.65	App	Norwich C.	08.82	1983-84	7	3	0	(F)	
			Tr	Aldershot	03.86	1985	1	0	0		
			Tr	Cambridge U.	10.86	1986-87	28	3	6		
RILEY, David S.	Northampton	08.12.60	Keyworth U.	Nottingham F.	01.84	1983-86	7	5	2	(F)	
			L	Darlington	02.87	1986	6	0	2		
			L	Peterborough U.	07.87	1987	12	0	2		
			Tr	Port Vale	10.87	1987	34	0	8		
RILEY, Glyn	Barnsley	24.07.58	App	Barnsley	07.76	1974-81	102	28	16	(F)	
			L	Doncaster Rov.	12.79	1979	7	1	2		
			Tr	Bristol C.	08.82	1982-86	184	15	61		
			L	Torquay U.	09.87	1987	6	0	1		
			Tr	Aldershot	10.87	1987	26	3	5		
RIMMER, Neill	Liverpool	13.11.67	App	Everton (App)	04.84	1984	0	1	0	(M)	E Sch Int/E Yth Int
			Tr	Ipswich T.	08.85	1985-87	19	3	3		
RIMMER, Stuart A.	Southport	12.10.64	App	Everton	10.82	1981-83	3	0	0	(F)	E Yth Int
			Tr	Chester C.	01.85	1984-87	110	4	68		
			Tr	Watford	03.88	1987	9	0	1		
RING, Mike P.	Brighton	13.02.61	App	Brighton & H.A.	02.79	1981-83	1	4	0	(W)	
			Tr	Hull C.	07.84	1984-85	17	7	2		
			L	Bolton W.	03.86	1985	1	2	0		
			Tr	Aldershot	07.86	1986-87	45	20	14		
RIPLEY, Stuart E.	Middlesbrough	20.11.67	App	Middlesbrough	11.85	1984-87	90	6	12	(W)	E Yth Int
			L	Bolton W.	02.86	1985	5	0	1		
RITCHIE, Andy T.	Manchester	28.11.60	App	Manchester U.	12.77	1977-80	26	7	13	(F)	E Yth Int/E U21-1
			Tr	Brighton & H.A.	10.80	1980-82	82	7	23		
			Tr	Leeds U.	03.83	1982-86	127	9	40		
			Tr	Oldham Ath.	08.87	1987	36	0	19		
RITCHIE, Stuart A.	Southampton	20.05.68	App	Aston Villa	05.86	1986	0	1	0	(M)	
			Tr	Crewe Alex.	06.87	1987	13	5	0		

Players Names	Birthplace	Date	Source	League Club	Date Sign'd	Seasons Played	Apps	Sub	Gls	Pos.	Misc
RIX, Graham	Doncaster	23.10.57	App L	Arsenal Brentford	01.75 12.87	1976-87 1987	338 6	13 0	41 0	(LM)	E U21-7/E-17
ROBERTS, Alan	Newcastle	08.12.64	App Tr	Middlesbrough Darlington	12.82 09.85	1982-85 1985-87	28 116	10 3	2 19	(RW)	
ROBERTS, Anthony M.	Bangor	04.08.69	YTS	Q.P.R.	07.87	1987	1	0	0	(G)	
ROBERTS, Brian L.F.	Manchester	06.11.55	App L Tr	Coventry C. Hereford U. Birmingham C.	11.73 02.75 03.84	1975-83 1974 1983-87	209 5 132	6 0 4	1 0 0	(FB)	
ROBERTS, Garreth W.	Hull	15.11.60	App	Hull C.	11.78	1978-87	330	5	44	(W)	W U21-1
ROBERTS, Graham P.	Southampton	03.07.59	Sholing Weymouth	Portsmouth (N/C) Tottenham H.	03.77 05.80	 1980-86	 200	 9	 23	(CD)	E-6/To Glasgow Rangers 12.86
ROBERTS, Iwan W.	Bangor	26.06.68	YTS	Watford	06.86	1985-87	21	11	3	(F)	W Yth Int
ROBERTS, Jeremy	Middlesbrough	24.11.66	Sch Sch Luton T. (Trial)	Hartlepool U. (N/C) Leicester C. Darlington	12.83 07.84 03.87	1983 1985 1986-87	1 3 29	0 0 0	0 0 0	(G)	E Yth Int
ROBERTS, Jonathan W.	Ferndale	30.12.68	YTS	Cardiff C.	11.87	1987	8	0	0	(G)	W Yth Int
ROBERTS, Paul	West Ham	27.04.62	App Tr Finland Tr Tr	Millwall Brentford Swindon T. (N/C) Southend U. Aldershot	04.79 09.83 09.85 07.86 08.87	1978-82 1983-84 1985 1986 1987	142 61 25 38 36	4 1 2 0 3	0 0 0 0 0	(RB)	
ROBERTSON, Alistair	Linlithgow	09.09.52	App Tr	West Bromwich A. Wolverhampton W.	09.69 09.86	1969-85 1986-87	504 72	2 0	8 0	(CD)	S Sch Int
ROBERTSON, James	Gateshead	24.11.69	YTS	Carlisle U.	07.88	1987	4	1	0	(RB)	
ROBINSON, Andy C.	Oldham	10.03.66	App L Tr Tr	Manchester U. Burnley Bury Carlisle U.	03.84 10.85 01.86 03.87	 1985 1985-86 1986-87	 5 12 43	 0 7 3	(M) 1 0 3		
ROBINSON, Colin R.	Birmingham	15.05.69	Mile Oak Rovers Tr	Shrewsbury T. Birmingham C.	11.82 01.88	1982-87 1987	176 3	18 1	41 1	(F)	
ROBINSON, David A.	Middlesbrough	14.01.65	 Tr	Hartlepool U. Halifax T.	08.83 08.86	1983-85 1986-87	64 42	2 0	1 0	(CD)	
ROBINSON, Leslie	Shirebrook	01.03.67	Chesterfield (Jnrs) Tr Tr	Mansfield T. Stockport Co. Doncaster Rov.	10.84 11.86 03.88	1984-86 1986-87 1987	11 67 7	4 0 0	0 3 1	(M)	
ROBINSON, S. Liam	Bradford	29.12.65	Nottingham F. (App) L Tr	Huddersfield T. Tranmere Rov. Bury	01.84 12.85 07.86	1983-85 1985 1986-87	17 4 69	4 0 7	2 3 32	(F)	
ROBINSON, Mark J.	Rochdale	21.11.68	App Tr	West Bromwich(N/C) Barnsley (N/C)	11.86 06.87	1985-86 1987	2 1	0 2	0 0	(M)	
ROBINSON, Martin J.	Ilford	17.07.57	App Tr L Tr Tr	Tottenham H. Charlton Ath. Reading Gillingham Southend U.	05.75 02.78 09.82 10.84 07.87	1975-77 1977-84 1982 1984-86 1987	5 218 6 91 31	1 10 0 5 6	2 58 2 24 8	(W)	
ROBINSON, Michael J.	Leicester	12.07.58	App Tr Tr Tr Tr	Preston N.E. Manchester C. Brighton & H.A. Liverpool Q.P.R.	07.76 07.79 07.80 08.83 12.84	1975-78 1979 1980-82 1983-84 1984-86	45 29 111 26 41	3 1 2 4 7	15 8 37 6 6	(F)	IR-23 To Osasuna (Sp.) 1.87
ROBINSON, Neil	Liverpool	20.04.57	App Tr Tr	Everton Swansea C. Grimsby T.	05.74 10.79 09.84	1975-78 1979-84 1984-87	13 114 109	3 9 0	1 7 6	(RB/M)	
ROBINSON, Peter	Ashington	04.09.57	Sch Blyth Spartans Tr L	Burnley Rochdale (N/C) Darlington Halifax T.	06.76 03.85 08.85 12.85	1976-79 1984 1985-87 1985	48 9 110 3	7 3 2 2	3 0 5 0	(CD)	E Semi Pro Int
ROBINSON, Philip J.	Stafford	06.01.67	App Tr	Aston Villa Wolverhampton W.	01.85 06.87	1986 1987	2 40	1 1	1 5	(M)	
ROBINSON, Ronnie	Sunderland	22.10.66	SC Vaux SC Vaux Tr	Ipswich T. Leeds U. Doncaster Rov.	10.84 11.85 02.87	 1985-86 1986-87	 27 49	 0 0	(D) 0 1		
ROBSON, Bryan	Witton Gilbert (Dm.)	11.01.57	App Tr	West Bromwich A. Manchester U.	08.74 10.81	1974-81 1981-87	194 216	4 2	39 60	(M)	E Yth Int/ E U21-7/E-67
ROBSON, Gary	Chester-le-Street	06.07.65	App	West Bromwich A.	05.83	1982-87	52	18	2	(M)	Brother of Bryan
ROBSON, Mark A.	Newham	22.05.69	App Tr	Exeter C. Tottenham H.	12.86 07.87	1986	26	0	7	(LW)	
ROBSON, Stewart I.	Billericay	06.11.64	App Tr	Arsenal West Ham U.	11.81 01.87	1981-86 1986-87	150 55	1 0	16 3	(M)	E Yth Int/E U21-8
ROCASTLE, David	Lewisham	02.05.67	App	Arsenal	12.84	1985-87	89	3	9	(RW)	E U21-10
ROCHE, Pat J.	Dublin	04.01.51	Shelbourne Tr Tr	Manchester U. Brentford Halifax T.	10.73 08.82 07.84	1974-81 1982-83 1984-87	46 71 159	0 0 0	0 0 0	(G)	IR-7
RODGER, Graham	Glasgow	01.04.67	App Tr	Wolverhmptn W. (App) Coventry C.	08.83 02.85	1983 1985-87	1 23	0 5	0 1	(CD)	E U21-4
RODGERSON, Ian	Hereford	09.04.66		Hereford U.	06.85	1985-87	95	5	6	(RB/M)	Son of Alan
ROEDER, Glenn V.	Woodford	13.12.55	App Tr L Tr	Orient Q.P.R. Notts. Co. Newcastle U.	12.73 08.78 11.83 12.83	1974-77 1978-83 1983 1983-87	107 157 4 175	8 0 0 0	4 17 0 8	(CD)	E 'B'
ROGERS, Andy	Chatteris	01.12.56	Chatteris T. Hampton Tr Tr Tr	Peterborough U. Southampton Plymouth Arg. Reading Southend U.	07.76 02.80 09.81 07.85 10.86	1975-77 1979-81 1981-84 1985-86 1986-87	25 0 159 44 40	4 5 4 0 5	1 0 14 5 2	(LW)	
ROGERS, Lee J.	Doncaster	28.10.66	YTS Tr	Doncaster Rov. (N/C) Chesterfield	07.84 08.86	 1986-87	 77	 2	(D) 0		

Players Names	Birthplace	Date	Source	League Club	Date Sign'd	Seasons Played	Apps	Sub	Gls	Pos.	Misc
ROGERS, Lee M.	Bristol	08.04.67	App	Bristol C.	12.84	1984-86	30	0	0	(CD)	
			L	Hereford U.	03.87	1986	13	0	0		
			L	York C.	12.87	1987	5	2	0		
ROLPH, Darren G.	Romford	19.11.68	Kings Lynn	Barnsley	08.87	1987	1	1	0	(D)	
ROONEY, Simon A.	Manchester	10.07.70	YTS	Blackpool	06.88	1987	4	4	0	(F)	
ROSARIO, Robert M.	Hammersmith	04.03.66	Hillingdon Bor.	Norwich C.	12.83	1983-87	52	7	9	(F)	E U21-4
			L	Wolverhampton W.	12.85	1985	2	0	1		
ROSE, Kevin P.	Evesham	23.11.60	Ledbury T.	Lincoln C.	08.79					(G)	
			Ledbury T.	Hereford U.	03.83	1982-87	245	0	0		
ROSENIOR, Leroy De G.	Clapton	24.03.64	Jnrs	Fulham	08.82	1982-84	53	1	15	(F)	E Sch Int/E Yth Int
			Tr	Fulham	06.87	1987	34	0	20		
			Tr	West Ham U.	03.88	1987	9	0	5		
ROSTRON, J. Wilf	Sunderland	29.09.56	App	Arsenal	10.73	1974-76	12	5	2	(LB)	E Sch Int
			Tr	Sunderland	07.77	1977-79	75	1	17		
			Tr	Watford	10.79	1979-87	299	11	22		
ROUGVIE, Doug	Ballingry (Fife)	24.05.56	Aberdeen	Chelsea	08.84	1984-86	74	0	3	(D)	S-1
			Tr	Brighton & H.A.	06.87	1987	35	0	2		
ROWBOTHAM, Darren	Cardiff	22.10.66	Jnrs	Plymouth Arg.	11.84	1984-87	22	24	2	(M)	Brother of Jason
			Tr	Exeter C.	10.87	1987	20	3	2		
ROWBOTHAM, Jason	Cardiff	03.01.69	YTS	Plymouth Arg.	07.87	1987	3	1	0	(D)	Brother of Darren
ROWELL, Gary	Seaham	06.06.57	App	Sunderland	07.74	1975-83	229	25	88	(W)	E U21-1
			Tr	Norwich C.	08.84	1984	2	4	1		
			Tr	Middlesbrough	08.85	1985	27	0	10		
			Tr	Brighton & H.A.	08.86	1986-87	9	3	0		
			Tr	Carlisle U.	03.88	1987	7	0	0		
RUDDOCK, Neil	Wandsworth	09.05.68	App	Millwall	03.86					(D)	E Yth Int
			Tr	Tottenham H.	04.86	1986-87	7	2	0		
RUSH, Ian J.	St. Asaph	20.10.61	App	Chester C.	09.79	1978-79	33	1	14	(F)	W Sch Int/ W U21-2/W-36/ To Juventus (It.) 7.87 FWA & PFA Player of Year 1983-84
			Tr	Liverpool	04.80	1980-86	224	0	139		
RUSSELL, Colin	Liverpool	21.01.61	App	Liverpool	04.78	1980	0	1	0	(W)	
			Tr	Huddersfield T.	09.82	1982-83	64	2	23		
			L	Stoke C.	03.84	1983	11	0	2		
			Tr	Bournemouth	08.84	1984-85	65	3	14		
			Tr	Doncaster Rov.	07.86	1986-87	43	0	5		
			Tr	Scarborough	10.87	1987	12	1	2		
RUSSELL, Guy R.	Birmingham	28.09.67	YTS	Birmingham C.	05.86	1984-87	7	4	0	(F)	
			L	Carlisle U.	03.87	1986	9	3	2		
RUSSELL, Kevin J.	Portsmouth	06.12.66	Brighton & H.A.(App)	Portsmouth	10.84	1985-86	3	1	0	(F)	E Yth Int
			Tr	Wrexham	07.87	1987	38	0	21		
RUSSELL, Martin C.	Dublin	27.04.67	App	Manchester U.	04.84					(M)	IR Yth Int
			L	Birmingham C.	10.86	1986	3	2	0		
			Tr	Leicester C.	03.87	1986-87	7	3	0		
RUSSELL, W.M. (Billy)	Glasgow	14.09.59	App	Everton	07.77					(RB)	S Yth Int
			Glasgow Celtic	Doncaster Rov.	07.79	1979-84	241	3	15		
			Tr	Scunthorpe U.	08.85	1985-87	113	4	7		
RYAN, John B.	Ashton-u-Lyne	18.02.62	App	Oldham Ath.	02.80	1981-82	77	0	8	(LB)	E U21-1
			Tr	Newcastle U.	08.83	1983-84	28	0	1		
			Tr	Sheffield Wed.	09.84	1984	5	0	1		
			Tr	Oldham Ath.	08.85	1985-86	20	3	0		
			Tr	Mansfield T.	10.87	1987	30	2	1		
RYAN, Laurie J.	Watford	15.10.63	Dunstable	Cambridge U.	04.88	1987	2	0	0	(F)	
RYAN, Vaughan W.	Westminster	02.09.68	App	Wimbledon	08.86	1986-87	18	5	1	(M)	
SADDINGTON, Nigel J.	Sunderland	09.12.65	S.C. Vaux.	Doncaster Rov.	09.84	1984	5	0	0	(CD)	
			Roker	Sunderland	01.86	1986	3	0	0		
			Tr	Carlisle U.	02.88	1987	13	0	1		
SAGE, Mel	Gillingham	24.03.64	App	Gillingham	03.82	1981-85	126	6	5	(RB)	
			Tr	Derby County	08.86	1986-87	38	1	2		
SALAKO, John A.	Nigeria	11.02.69	App	Crystal Palace	11.86	1986-87	23	12	1	(LW)	
SALATHIEL, D. Neil	Wrexham	19.11.62	Sheffield Wed. (Jnr)	Wrexham (N/C)	05.80	1980	4	0	0	(RB)	W Sch Int
			Tr	Crewe Alex.	06.81	1981-82	64	1	0		
			Arcadia Shep. (SA)	Wrexham	12.83	1983-87	176	0	3		
SALMAN, Danis M.M.	Cyprus	12.03.60	App	Brentford	08.77	1975-85	316	9	8	(D)	E Yth Int
			Tr	Millwall	08.86	1986-87	67	0	3		
SALMON, Mike B.	Leyland	14.07.64	Jnrs	Blackburn Rov.	10.81	1981	1	0	0	(G)	
			L	Chester C.	10.82	1982	16	0	0		
			Tr	Stockport Co.	08.83	1983-85	118	0	0		
			Tr	Bolton W.	07.86	1986	26	0	0		
			Tr	Wrexham	03.87	1986-87	57	0	0		
SAMWAYS, Mark	Doncaster	11.11.68	YTS	Doncaster Rov.	08.87	1987	11	0	0	(G)	
SAMWAYS, Vincent	Bethnal Green	27.10.68	App	Tottenham H.	10.85	1986-87	22	6	0	(M)	E Yth Int/E U21-1
SANCHEZ, Lawrie P.	Lambeth	22.10.59	Jnrs	Reading	09.78	1977-84	249	13	28	(M)	
			Tr	Wimbledon	12.84	1984-87	129	0	18		
SANDEMAN, Bradley	Northampton	24.02.70	YTS	Northampton T.	06.88	1987	0	2	0	(M)	
SANDERSON, Paul D.	Blackpool	16.12.66	Fleetwood T.	Manchester C.	11.83					(W)	
			Tr	Chester C.	02.84	1983	24	0	3		
			Tr	Halifax T.	08.84	1984-86	88	16	5		
			Tr	Cardiff C.	07.87	1987	8	13	1		
			Tr	Walsall	03.88	1987	0	3	0		
SANDFORD, Lee R.	Basingstoke	22.04.68	App	Portsmouth	12.85	1985-87	25	3	1	(LB)	E Yth Int
SANSOM, Kenny G.	Camberwell	26.09.58	App	Crystal Palace	12.75	1974-79	172	0	3	(LB)	E Sch Int/E Yth Int/ E U21-8/E-83
			Tr	Arsenal	08.80	1980-87	314	0	6		
SANSOME, Paul E.	New Addington	06.10.61	Crystal Palace (App)	Millwall	04.80	1981-87	156	0	0	(G)	
			Tr	Southend U.	03.88	1987	6	0	0		

Gary Shelton (Oxford United) Seen in the foreground under pressure from West Ham's Paul Ince.   Action Images Ltd

David Seaman (Q.P.R.) Reliable goalkeeper who joined the club from Birmingham City.   Match Magazine

Lawrie Sanchez (Wimbledon) One of the midfield stars in the Londoner's rise to fame.   Action Images Ltd

Kenny Samson (Arsenal) Still a regular for club and country in the left-back position.   Match Magazine

Players Names	Birthplace	Date	Source	League Club	Date Sign'd	Seasons Played	Career Record Apps	Sub	Gls	Pos.	Misc
SAUNDERS, Carl S.	Birmingham	26.11.64		Stoke C.	03.83	1982-87	91	18	20	(F/M)	
SAUNDERS, Dean N.	Swansea	21.06.64	App	Swansea C.	06.82	1983-84	42	7	12	(F)	W-7
			L	Cardiff C.	03.85	1984	3	1	0		
			Tr	Brighton & H.A.	08.85	1985-86	66	6	20		
			Tr	Oxford U.	03.87	1986-87	47	2	17		
SAUNDERS, Steve J.P.	Warrington	21.09.64	App	Bolton W.	09.82	1983	3	0	0	(F)	
			Tr	Crewe Alex.	07.85	1985	15	7	1		
			Tr	Preston N.E. (N/C)	08.86						
			Northwich Vic.	Grimsby T.	08.87	1987	34	1	3		
SAUNDERS, Wesley	Sunderland	23.02.63	Sch	Newcastle U.	06.81	1981-84	79	0	0	(CD)	
			L	Bradford C.	03.85	1984	1	3	0		
			Tr	Carlisle U.	08.85	1985-87	97	0	11		To Dundee 2.88
SAVAGE, Rob J.	Liverpool	08.01.60	App	Liverpool	01.78					(M)	
			L	Wrexham	10.82	1982	27	0	10		
			Tr	Stoke C.	07.83	1983	5	2	0		
			Tr	Bournemouth	12.83	1983-86	80	2	18		
			Tr	Bradford C.	12.86	1986-87	11	0	0		
			Tr	Bolton W.	09.87	1987	39	0	5		
SAVILLE, Andy V.	Hull	12.12.64		Hull C.	09.83	1983-87	60	20	17	(F)	
SAYER, Andy C.	Brent	06.06.66	App	Wimbledon	06.84	1983-87	46	12	15	(F)	
			L	Cambridge U.	02.88	1987	2	3	0		
SCALES, John R.	Harrogate	04.07.66	Leeds U.(YTS)	Bristol Rov.	07.85	1985-86	68	4	2	(RB)	
			Tr	Wimbledon	07.87	1987	23	2	1		
SCOTT, Derek E.	Gateshead	08.02.58	App	Burnley	02.75	1974-84	277	8	24	(RB)	E Sch Int
			Tr	Bolton W.	07.85	1985-87	119	0	0		
SCOTT, Ian	Radcliffe	20.09.67	App	Manchester C.	09.85	1987	19	4	3	(M)	E Sch Int
SCOTT, Ian R.	Otley	04.03.69	App	Manchester U.	03.87					(D)	
			Tr	Stockport Co.	09.87	1987	15	1	0		
SCOTT, Kevin W.	Easington	17.12.66	App	Newcastle U.	12.84	1986-87	7	0	2	(CD)	
SCOTT, Martin	Sheffield	07.01.68	App	Rotherham U.	01.86	1984-87	34	0	0	(LB)	
SCOTT, Peter R.	Notting Hill	01.10.63	App	Fulham	09.81	1981-87	133	4	19	(M)	
SCOTT, Stephen R.	Wrexham	05.11.66	Oswestry T.	Wrexham (N/C)	03.86	1987	0	2	0	(D)	
SEAGRAVES, Mark	Bootle	22.10.66	App	Liverpool	11.83					(CD)	Brother of Chris
			L	Norwich C.	11.86	1986	3	0	0		E Sch Int/E Yth Int
			Tr	Manchester C.	09.87	1987	13	4	0		
SEALEY, Les J.	Bethnal Green	29.09.57	App	Coventry C.	03.76	1976-82	158	0	0	(G)	Cousin of Alan
			Tr	Luton T.	08.83	1983-87	175	0	0		
			L	Plymouth Arg.	10.84	1984	6	0	0		
SEALY, A.J. (Tony)	Hackney	07.05.59	App	Southampton	05.77	1977-78	2	5	0	(F)	
			Tr	Crystal Palace	03.79	1978-80	16	8	5		
			L	Port Vale	02.80	1979	17	0	6		
			Tr	Q.P.R.	03.81	1980-83	57	6	18		
			L	Port Vale	02.82	1981	6	0	4		
			L	Fulham	12.83	1983	5	0	1		
			L	Fulham	08.84	1984	3	1	1		
			Tr	Fulham	01.85	1984-85	14	2	9		
			Tr	Leicester C.	09.85	1985-86	28	11	7		
			L	Bournemouth	03.87	1986	8	5	2		
SEAMAN, David A.	Rotherham	19.09.63	App	Leeds U.	09.81					(G)	E U21-10
			Tr	Peterborough U.	08.82	1982-84	91	0	0		
			Tr	Birmingham C.	10.84	1984-85	75	0	0		
			Tr	Q.P.R.	08.86	1986-87	73	0	0		
SEASMAN, John	Liverpool	21.02.55	App	Tranmere Rov.	02.73	1972-74	15	2	0	(M)	
			Tr	Luton T.	01.75	1974-75	7	1	2		
			Tr	Millwall	02.76	1975-79	157	1	35		
			Tr	Rotherham U.	08.80	1980-83	93	7	25		
			Tr	Cardiff C.	08.84	1984	10	2	2		
			L	Rochdale	11.84	1984	8	0	0		
			Tr	Chesterfield	01.85	1984	8	2	1		
			Tr	Rochdale	07.85	1985-87	86	1	4		
SEDGLEY, Stephen P.	Enfield	26.05.68	App	Coventry C.	05.86	1986-87	50	3	2	(CD)	E U21-4
SEGERS, J.C.A. (Hans)	Netherlands	30.10.61	PSV Eindhoven	Nottingham F.	08.84	1984-87	58	0	0	(G)	
			L	Stoke C.	02.87	1986	1	0	0		
			L	Sheffield U.	11.87	1987	10	0	0		
SELLARS, Scott	Sheffield	27.11.65	App	Leeds U.	07.83	1982-85	72	4	12	(M)	E U21-3
			Tr	Blackburn Rov.	07.86	1986-87	68	6	11		
SENDALL, Richard A.	Stamford	10.07.67	Watford(App)	Blackpool	07.85	1985-86	6	5	0	(F)	
SENIOR, Steve	Sheffield	15.05.63	App	York C.	05.81	1980-86	158	10	6	(RB)	
			L	Darlington	10.84	1984	5	0	0		
			Tr	Northampton T.	06.87	1987	1	3	0		
			Tr	Wigan Ath.	10.87	1987	20	2	1		
SENIOR, Trevor J.	Dorchester	28.11.61	Dorchester T.	Portsmouth	12.81	1981-82	11	0	2	(F)	
			L	Aldershot	03.83	1982	10	0	7		
			Tr	Reading	08.83	1983-86	164	0	102		
			Tr	Watford	07.87	1987	22	2	1		
			Tr	Middlesbrough	03.88	1987	5	1	2		
SERTORI, Mark A.	Manchester	01.09.67		Stockport Co.	02.87	1986-87	3	1	0	(F)	
			Tr	Lincoln C.	N/L						
SHAKESPEARE, Craig R.	Birmingham	26.10.63	App	Walsall	10.81	1982-87	231	8	42	(M)	
SHARP, Graeme M.	Glasgow	16.10.60	Dumbarton	Everton	04.80	1979-87	226	10	94	(F)	S U21-1/S-11
SHARPE, Lee S.	Birmingham	27.05.71	YTS	Torquay U. (YTS)	08.87	1987	9	5	3	(F)	
SHAW, Adrian	Easington	13.04.66	App	Nottingham F.	12.83					(D)	
			Tr	Halifax T.	12.84	1984-87	95	5	1		
SHAW, Gary R.	Birmingham	21.01.61	App	Aston Villa	01.79	1978-87	158	7	59	(F)	E Yth Int/
			L	Blackpool	02.87	1987	4	2	0		E U21-7
SHAW, Graham P.	Stoke	07.06.67	App	Stoke C.	06.85	1985-87	64	7	13	(F)	

Bernie Slaven (Middlesbrough) Scored 21 times in the "Boro's" climb to First Division status.   Match Magazine

Neil Slatter (Oxford United) Welsh international defender who previously played for Bristol Rovers.   Match Magazine

Nigel Spackman (Liverpool) Has fitted in well to the Champions' midfield pattern since signing from Chelsea.   Match Magazine

David Speedie (Coventry City) Seen in Chelsea's colours where he formed a formidable partnership with Kerry Dixon.   Match Magazine

Players Names	Birthplace	Date	Source	League Club	Date Sign'd	Seasons Played	Apps	Sub	Gls	Pos.	Misc
SHAW, John	Stirling	04.02.54	App	Leeds U.	02.71					(G)	
			Tr	Bristol C.	05.74	1976-84	295	0	0		
			Tr	Exeter C.	07.85	1985-87	109	0	0		
SHAW, Richard E.	Brentford	11.09.68	App	Crystal Palace	09.86	1987	2	1	0	(D)	
SHEARER, Alan	Newcastle	13.08.70	YTS	Southampton	04.88	1987	3	2	3	(F)	
SHEARER, David J.	Inverness	16.10.58	Inverness Clach.	Middlesbrough	01.78	1977-82	88	9	23	(F)	Brother of Duncan
			L	Wigan Ath.	03.80	1979	11	0	9		
			Tr	Grimsby T.	08.83	1983	1	3	0		
			Tr	Gillingham	08.84	1984-87	82	11	42		
			Tr	Bournemouth	10.87	1987	8	3	3		
			Tr	Scunthorpe U.	02.88	1987	15	0	7		
SHEARER, Duncan N.	Fort William	28.08.62	Inverness Clach.	Chelsea	11.83	1985	2	0	1	(F)	Brother of David
			Tr	Huddersfield T.	03.86	1985-87	80	3	38		
SHEEDY, Kevin M.	Builth Wells	21.10.59	App	Hereford U.	10.76	1975-77	47	4	4	(LM)	IR U21-1/IR-13
			Tr	Liverpool	07.78	1980-81	1	2	0		
			Tr	Everton	08.82	1982-87	170	3	45		
SHELTON, Gary	Nottingham	21.03.58	App	Walsall	03.76	1975-77	12	12	0	(M)	E U21-1
			Tr	Aston Villa	01.78	1978-81	24	0	7		
			L	Notts. Co.	03.80	1979	8	0	0		
			Tr	Sheffield Wed.	03.82	1981-86	195	3	18		
			Tr	Oxford U.	07.87	1987	32	0	0		
SHERIDAN, John J.	Manchester	01.10.64	Manchester C.(Jnr)	Leeds U.	03.82	1982-87	187	3	40	(M)	IR Yth Int/IR-3
SHERINGHAM, Edward P. (Teddy)	Walthamstow	02.04.66	App	Millwall	01.84	1983-87	98	12	40	(F)	E Yth Int/ E U21-1
			L	Aldershot	02.85	1984	4	1	0		
SHERLOCK, Steve E.	Birmingham	10.05.59	App	Manchester C.	05.77					(LB)	
			Tr	Luton T.	06.78	1978	2	0	0		
			Tr	Stockport Co.	08.79	1979-85	236	9	7		
			Tr	Cardiff C.	07.86	1986	14	1	0		
			L	Newport Co.	12.86	1986	5	0	0		
			Tr	Newport Co.	03.87	1986-87	42	2	2		
SHERWOOD, Steve	Selby	10.12.53	App	Chelsea	07.71	1971-75	16	0	0	(G)	
			L	Millwall	10.73	1973	1	0	0		
			L	Brentford	01.74	1973-74	62	0	0		
			Tr	Watford	11.76	1976-86	211	0	1		
			Tr	Grimsby T.	07.87	1987	46	0	0		
SHERWOOD, Timothy A.	St. Albans	06.02.69	App	Watford	02.87	1987	9	4	0	(M)	
SHILTON, Peter L.	Leicester	18.09.49	App	Leicester C.	09.66	1965-74	286	0	1	(G)	E Sch Int/E Yth Int E U23-13/E-98/ E F Lge Rep
			Tr	Stoke C.	11.74	1974-77	110	0	0		
			Tr	Nottingham F.	09.77	1977-81	202	0	0		
			Tr	Southampton	08.82	1982-86	188	0	0		
			Tr	Derby Co.	07.87	1987	40	0	0		
SHINNERS, Paul	Westminster	08.01.59	Fisher Ath.	Gillingham	10.84	1984	1	3	0	(F)	
			L	Colchester U.	03.85	1984	6	0	1		
			Tr	Leyton Orient	07.85	1985-87	69	2	32		
SHIPLEY, George M.	Newcastle	07.03.59	App	Southampton	03.77	1979	2	1	0	(M)	
			L	Reading	03.79	1978	11	1	1		
			Tr	Lincoln C.	01.80	1979-84	229	1	42		
			Tr	Charlton Ath.	07.85	1985-86	61	0	6		
			Tr	Gillingham	08.87	1987	15	0	2		
SHIRTLIFF, Peter A.	Hoyland	06.04.61	App	Sheffield Wed.	10.78	1978-85	188	0	4	(CD)	Brother of Paul
			Tr	Charlton Ath.	07.86	1986-87	69	0	5		
SHOEMAKE, Kevin P.	Wickford	28.01.65	App	Leyton Orient	01.83	1983	4	0	0	(G)	
			Welling U.	Peterborough U.	09.86	1986-87	40	0	0		
SHORT, J. Craig	Bridlington	25.06.68	Pickering T.	Scarborough	10.87	1987	20	1	2	(CD)	
SHORT, Russell D.V.	Ilford	04.09.68	YTS	Southend U.	06.87	1986	0	1	0	(D)	
SHOTTON, Malcolm	Newcastle	16.02.57	App	Leicester C.	02.75					(CD)	
			Nuneaton Bor.	Oxford U.	05.80	1980-87	262	1	12		
			Tr	Portsmouth	08.87	1987	10	0	0		
			Tr	Huddersfield T.	02.88	1987	14	0	0		
SHOULDER, Alan	Bishop Auckland	04.02.53	Blyth Spartans	Newcastle U.	12.78	1978-81	99	8	35	(F)	
			Tr	Carlisle U.	08.82	1982-84	110	2	32		
			Tr	Hartlepool U.	06.85	1985-87	66	0	24		
SHUTT, Carl S.	Sheffield	10.10.61	Spalding U.	Sheffield Wed.	05.85	1985-87	36	4	16	(F)	
			Tr	Bristol C.	10.87	1987	18	4	9		
SIDDALL, Barry	Ellesmere Port	12.09.54	App	Bolton W.	01.72	1972-76	137	0	0	(G)	E Yth Int
			Tr	Sunderland	09.76	1976-81	167	0	0		
			L	Darlington	10.80	1980	8	0	0		
			Tr	Port Vale	08.82	1982-84	81	0	0		
			L	Blackpool	10.83	1983	7	0	0		
			Tr	Stoke C.	01.85	1984-85	20	0	0		
			L	Tranmere Rov.	10.85	1985	12	0	0		
			L	Manchester C.	03.86	1985	6	0	0		
			Tr	Blackpool	08.86	1986-87	75	0	0		
SIMMONDS, R. Lyndon	Pontypool	11.11.66	App	Leeds U.	11.84	1984-85	6	3	3	(F)	W Yth Int
			L	Swansea C.	10.86	1986	7	1	1		
			Tr	Rochdale	02.87	1986-87	65	0	22		
SIMONS, Alan G.	Wrexham	02.09.68	YTS	Port Vale (N/C)	09.87	1987	1	0	0	(G)	
SIMPSON, Paul D.	Carlisle	26.07.66	App	Manchester C.	08.83	1982-87	98	22	18	(LW)	E Yth Int/E U21-5
SIMS, Steve F.	Lincoln	02.07.57	App	Leicester C.	08.74	1975-78	78	1	3	(CD)	E U21-10/E-'B'
			Tr	Watford	12.78	1978-83	150	2	4		
			Tr	Notts. Co.	09.84	1984-86	85	0	5		
			Tr	Watford	10.86	1986	19	0	1		
			Tr	Aston Villa	06.87	1987	29	0	0		
SINCLAIR, Ronnie M.	Stirling	19.11.64	App	Nottingham F.	10.82					(G)	
			L	Wrexham	03.84	1983	11	0	0		
			Tr	Leeds U.	06.86	1986	8	0	0		
			L	Halifax T.	03.87	1986	4	0	0		

Players Names	Birthplace	Date	Source	League Club	Date Sign'd	Seasons Played	Apps	Sub	Gls	Pos.	Misc
SINGLETON, Martin D.	Banbury	02.08.63	App	Coventry C.	01.81	1981-84	20	3	1	(M)	E Yth Int
			Tr	Bradford C.	12.84	1984-86	69	2	3		
			Tr	West Bromwich A.	12.86	1986-87	15	4	1		
			Tr	Northampton T.	11.87	1987	28	1	3		
SINNOTT, Lee	Pelsall	12.07.65	App	Walsall	11.82	1981-83	40	0	2	(D)	E Yth Int/E U21-1
			Tr	Watford	09.83	1983-86	71	7	2		
			Tr	Bradford C.	07.87	1987	42	0	1		
SINTON, Andy	Newcastle	19.03.66	App	Cambridge U.	04.83	1982-85	90	3	13	(M)	E Sch Int
			Tr	Brentford	12.85	1985-87	118	0	19		
SITTON, John E.	Hackney	21.10.59	App	Chelsea	10.77	1978-79	11	2	0	(D)	
			Tr	Millwall	02.80	1979-80	43	2	1		
			Tr	Gillingham	09.81	1981-84	102	5	5		
			Tr	Leyton Orient	07.85	1985-87	71	1	1		
SKINNER, Justin	Hounslow	30.01.69	App	Fulham	11.86	1986-87	29	6	5	(M)	
SKIPPER, Peter D.	Hull	11.04.58	Schultz YC	Hull C.	02.79	1978-79	22	1	2	(CD)	
			L	Scunthorpe U.	02.80	1979	0	1	0		
			Tr	Darlington	05.80	1980-81	91	0	4		
			Tr	Hull C.	08.82	1982-87	261	1	17		
SLACK, Trevor C.	Peterborough	26.09.62	App	Peterborough U.	08.80	1980-85	201	1	18	(CD)	E Yth Int
			Tr	Rotherham U.	08.86	1986	14	1	1		
			Tr	Grimsby T.	08.87	1987	21	0	0		
SLATER, Jim J.	Wrexham	27.10.68	Jnrs	Wrexham	07.87	1987	0	3	0	(F)	
SLATER, Stuart I.	Sudbury	27.03.69	App	West Ham U.	03.87	1987	0	2	0	(F)	
SLATTER, Neil J.	Cardiff	30.05.64	App	Bristol Rov.	05.82	1980-84	147	1	4	(D)	W Yth Int/
			Tr	Oxford U.	07.85	1985-87	53	3	6		W U21-6/W-19
SLAVEN, Bernie	Paisley	13.11.60	Albion Rov.	Middlesbrough	09.85	1985-87	122	0	46	(F)	
SMALLEY, Mark A.	Newark	02.01.65	App	Nottingham F.	01.83	1982-84	1	2	0	(CD)	E Yth Int
			L	Birmingham C.	03.86	1985	7	0	0		
			L	Bristol Rov.	08.86	1986	10	0	0		
			Tr	Leyton Orient	02.87	1986-87	55	2	4		
SMALLEY, Paul T.	Nottingham	17.11.66	App	Notts. Co.	11.84	1985-87	112	6	0	(RB)	E Yth Int
SMALLWOOD, Neil	York	03.12.66		York C.	06.85	1986-87	13	0	0	(G)	
SMART, Jason	Rochdale	15.02.69	YTS	Rochdale	08.86	1985-87	75	0	3	(G)	
SMEULDERS, John	Hackney	28.03.57	App	Leyton Orient	07.74					(G)	E Yth Int
			Tr	Bournemouth	07.79	1979-80	14	0	0		
			Weymouth	Bournemouth	01.84	1983-85	75	0	0		
			Tr	Torquay U.	07.86	1986	18	0	0		
			L	Peterborough U.	12.86	1986	1	0	0		
			Poole T.	Bournemouth (N/C)	08.87	1987	2	0	0		
SMILLIE, Neil	Barnsley	19.07.58	App	Crystal Palace	10.75	1976-81	71	12	7	(W)	Son of Ron
			L	Brentford	01.77	1976	3	0	0		
			Tr	Brighton & H.A.	08.82	1982-84	62	13	2		
			Tr	Watford	06.85	1985	10	6	3		
			L	Reading	12.86	1986	6	0	0		
			Tr	Reading	03.87	1986-87	32	1	0		
SMITH, Alan D.	Sheffield	07.12.66	App	Sheffield Wed.	12.84					(D)	
			Tr	Darlington	09.86	1986	16	0	1		
SMITH, Alan M.	Bromsgrove	21.11.62	Alvechurch	Leicester C.	06.82	1982-86	190	10	76	(F)	E Semi-Pro Int 1982
			Tr	Arsenal	05.87	1987	36	3	12		
SMITH, A. (Tony)	Sunderland	20.02.57	Jnrs	Newcastle U.	07.75	1977	1	1	0	(CD)	
			Tr	Peterborough U.	03.79	1978-81	68	0	5		
			Tr	Halifax T.	08.82	1982-83	81	2	3		
			Tr	Hartlepool U.	08.84	1984-87	181	0	6		
SMITH, Barry J.	Ashton Makerfield	21.09.69	YTS	Wigan Ath. (YTS)	07.86	1987	0	1	0		
SMITH, Brian	Sheffield	27.10.66	App	Sheffield U.	10.84	1984-87	47	2	0	(D)	
			L	Scunthorpe U.	03.87	1986	6	0	1		
SMITH, Colin R.	Ruddington	03.11.58	Jnrs	Nottingham F.	06.77					(CD)	
			Tr	Norwich C.	08.82	1982	2	2	0		
			Hong Kong	Cardiff C.	10.83	1983-84	50	0	3		
			Tr	Aldershot	12.84	1984-87	118	2	2		
SMITH, David	Gloucester	29.03.68	YTS	Coventry C.	07.86	1987	14	2	4	(W)	
SMITH, David A.	Sidcup	25.06.61	Welling U.	Gillingham	08.86	1986-87	50	12	8	(LW)	
SMITH, Gary N.	Harlow	03.12.68	App	Fulham	08.86	1985	0	1	0	(D)	
				Colchester U. (N/C)	09.87	1987	11	0	0		
SMITH, James	Johnstone	22.11.69	YTS	Torquay U. (YTS)	09.86	1987	0	1	0		
SMITH, Kevan	Eaglescliffe	13.12.59	Stockton	Darlington	09.79	1979-84	242	3	11	(CD)	
			Tr	Rotherham U.	07.85	1985-86	59	0	4		
			Tr	Coventry C.	12.86	1987	5	1	0		
SMITH, Lindsay J.	Enfield	18.09.54	App	Colchester U.	03.72	1970-76	185	27	16	(CD)	
			L	Charlton Ath.	08.77	1977	1	0	0		
			L	Millwall	09.77	1977	4	1	0		
			Tr	Cambridge U.	10.77	1977-82	173	1	7		
			L	Lincoln C.	09.81	1981	5	0	0		
			Tr	Plymouth Arg.	10.82	1982-83	76	0	5		
			Tr	Millwall	07.84	1984-85	54	1	5		
			Tr	Cambridge U.	07.86	1986-87	84	0	12		
SMITH, Malcolm A.	Maidstone	03.08.70	YTS	Gillingham	06.88	1987	1	1	0	(M)	
SMITH, Mark C.	Sheffield	21.03.60	App	Sheffield Wed.	03.78	1977-86	281	1	16	(CD)	E U21-5
			Tr	Plymouth Arg.	07.87	1987	41	0	6		
SMITH, Neil	Warley	10.02.70	YTS	Shrewsbury T. (YTS)	07.86	1987	0	1	0		
SMITH, Nick L.	Berkeley (Glos.)	28.01.69	YTS	Southend U.	07.87	1986-87	30	5	5	(M)	
SMITH, Paul M.	Rotherham	09.11.64	App	Sheffield U.	11.82	1982-85	29	7	1	(W)	
			L	Stockport Co.	08.85	1985	7	0	5		
			Tr	Port Vale	07.86	1986-87	43	2	7		
			Tr	Lincoln C.	(N/L)						
SMITH, Paul S.	Brent	05.10.67	App	Arsenal	10.85					(W)	
			Tr	Brentford	08.87	1987	10	7	1		

Players Names	Birthplace	Date	Source	League Club	Date Sign'd	Seasons Played	Apps	Sub	Gls	Pos.	Misc
SNODIN, Glynn	Rotherham	14.02.60	App	Doncaster Rov.	10.77	1976-84	288	21	61	(LB/LW)	Brother of Ian
			Tr	Sheffield Wed.	06.85	1985-86	51	8	1		
			Tr	Leeds U.	07.87	1987	33	2	7		
SNODIN, Ian	Rotherham	15.08.63	App	Doncaster Rov.	08.80	1979-84	181	7	25	(M)	Brother of Glynn
			Tr	Leeds U.	05.85	1985-86	51	0	6		E Yth Int/E U21-4
			Tr	Everton	01.87	1986-87	44	3	2		
SOUTHALL, Neville	Llandudno	16.09.58	Winsford U.	Bury	06.80	1980	39	0	0	(G)	W-34
			Tr	Everton	07.81	1981-87	215	0	0		
			L	Port Vale	01.83	1982	9	0	0		
SPACKMAN, Nigel J.	Romsey	02.12.60	Andover T.	Bournemouth	05.80	1980-82	118	1	10	(M)	
			Tr	Chelsea	06.83	1983-86	139	2	12		
			Tr	Liverpool	02.87	1986-87	31	8	0		
SPARHAM, Sean R.	Bexley	04.12.68	Jnrs	Millwall	05.87	1987	7	0	0	(LB)	
SPEARING, A. (Tony)	Romford	07.10.64	App	Norwich C.	10.82	1983-87	67	2	0	(LB)	E Yth Int
			L	Stoke C.	11.84	1984	9	0	0		
			L	Oxford U.	02.85	1984	5	0	0		
SPEEDIE, David R.	Glenrothes	20.02.60	Jnrs	Barnsley	10.78	1978-79	10	13	0	(F)	S U21-1/S-5
			Tr	Darlington	06.80	1980-81	88	0	21		
			Tr	Chelsea	06.82	1982-86	155	7	47		
			Tr	Coventry C.	07.87	1987	35	1	6		
SPINK, Nigel P.	Chelmsford	08.08.58	Chelmsford C.	Aston Villa	01.77	1979-87	177	0	0	(G)	E-1
SPOFFORTH, David J.	York	21.03.69	Jnrs	York C.	07.87	1987	3	0	0	(D)	
SPOONER, Steve A.	Sutton	25.01.61	App	Derby Co.	12.78	1978-81	7	1	0	(M)	
			Tr	Halifax T.	12.81	1981-82	71	1	13		
			Tr	Chesterfield	07.83	1983-85	89	4	14		
			Tr	Hereford U.	07.86	1986-87	84	0	19		
SPROSON, Phil J.	Stoke	13.10.59	Jnrs	Port Vale	12.77	1977-87	402	4	31	(CD)	Nephew of Roy
SPROSTON, Neil R.	Dudley	20.11.70	YTS	Birmingham C. (YTS)	07.87	1987	0	1	0		
STAINROD, Simon A.	Sheffield	01.02.59	App	Sheffield U.	07.76	1975-78	59	8	14	(F)	E Yth Int
			Tr	Oldham Ath.	03.79	1978-80	69	0	21		
			Tr	Q.P.R.	11.80	1980-84	143	2	48		
			Tr	Sheffield Wed.	02.85	1984-85	8	7	2		
			Tr	Aston Villa	09.85	1985-87	58	5	16		
			Tr	Stoke C.	12.87	1987	11	1	2		
STANCLIFFE, Paul I.	Sheffield	05.05.58	App	Rotherham U.	03.76	1975-82	285	0	8	(CD)	
			Tr	Sheffield U.	08.83	1983-87	193	0	9		
STANIFORTH, Gordon	Hull	23.03.57	App	Hull C.	04.74	1973-76	7	5	2	(F)	E Sch Int
			Tr	York C.	12.76	1976-79	128	0	33		
			Tr	Carlisle U.	10.79	1979-82	118	8	33		
			Tr	Plymouth Arg.	03.83	1982-84	87	4	20		
			Tr	Newport Co.	08.85	1985-86	84	3	13		
			Retired	York C. (N/C)	10.87	1987	15	4	1		
STANISLAUS, Roger E.P.	Hammersmith	02.11.68	YTS	Arsenal	07.86					(LB)	
			Tr	Brentford	09.87	1987	36	1	2		
STANNARD, Jim D.	Harold Hill	06.10.62	Ford U.	Fulham	06.80	1980-84	41	0	0	(G)	
			L	Southend U.	09.84	1984	6	0	0		
			L	Charlton Ath.	01.85	1984	1	0	0		
			Tr	Southend U.	03.85	1984-86	103	0	0		
			Tr	Fulham	08.87	1987	46	0	0		
STANT, Philip R.	Bolton	13.10.62	Army	Reading (N/C)	08.82	1982	3	1	2	(F)	
			Army	Hereford U.	11.86	1986-87	43	5	10		
STANTON, Brian	Liverpool	07.02.56	New Brighton	Bury	10.75	1976-78	72	11	14	(M)	
			Tr	Huddersfield T.	09.79	1979-85	199	10	45		
			L	Wrexham	03.86	1985	8	0	0		
			Morecambe	Rochdale	12.86	1986-87	42	7	4		
STAPLETON, Frank A.	Dublin	10.07.56	App	Arsenal	09.73	1974-80	223	2	75	(F)	IR Yth Int/IR-62
			Tr	Manchester U.	08.81	1981-86	204	19	60		
			Ajax Amsterdam	Derby Co.	03.88	1987	10	0	1		
STARBUCK, Philip M.	Nottingham	24.11.68	App	Nottingham F.	08.86	1986-87	4	11	2	(F)	
			L	Birmingham C.	03.88	1987	3	0	0		
STATHAM, Brian	Zimbabwe	21.05.69	YTS	Tottenham H.	07.87	1987	14	4	0	(FB)	E U21-1
STATHAM, Derek J.	Wolverhampton	24.03.59	App	West Bromwich A.	01.77	1976-87	298	1	8	(LB)	E Yth Int/E U21-6
			Tr	Southampton	08.87	1987	38	0	0		E 'B'/E-3
STAUNTON, Steve	Drogheda	19.01.69	Dundalk	Liverpool	09.86					(FB)	
			L	Bradford C.	11.87	1987	7	1	0		
STEAD, Micky J.	West Ham	28.02.57	App	Tottenham H.	11.74	1975-77	14	1	0	(FB)	Brother of Kevin
			L	Swansea C.	02.77	1976	5	0	1		
			Tr	Southend U.	09.78	1978-85	296	1	5		
			Tr	Doncaster Rov.	11.85	1985-87	83	2	0		
STEBBING, Gary S.	Croydon	11.08.65	App	Crystal Palace	08.83	1983-87	95	7	3	(M)	E Yth Int
			L	Southend U.	01.86	1985	5	0	0		
STEEL, W. Jim	Dumfries	04.12.59	App	Oldham Ath.	12.77	1978-82	101	7	24	(F)	
			L	Wigan Ath.	11.82	1982	2	0	2		
			L	Wrexham	01.83	1982	9	0	6		
			Tr	Port Vale	03.83	1982-83	27	1	6		
			Tr	Wrexham	01.84	1983-87	164	0	51		
			Tr	Tranmere Rov.	11.87	1987	29	0	7		
STEELE, Eric G.	Newcastle	14.05.54	Jnrs	Newcastle U.	07.72					(G)	
			Tr	Peterborough U.	12.73	1973-76	124	0	0		
			Tr	Brighton & H.A.	02.77	1976-79	87	0	0		
			Tr	Watford	10.79	1979-83	51	0	0		
			L	Cardiff C.	03.83	1982	7	0	0		
			Tr	Derby Co.	07.84	1984-86	47	0	0		
			Tr	Southend U.	07.87	1987	27	0	0		
			L	Mansfield T.	03.88	1987	5	0	0		
STEELE, Timothy W.	Coventry	01.12.67	App	Shrewsbury T.	12.85	1985-87	35	11	4	(M)	

Frank Stapleton (Derby County) Former Arsenal star who still gets among the goals.

Match Magazine

Gary Stevens (Tottenham Hotspur) Elegant defensive midfield player.

Match Magazine

Trevor Steven (Everton) Photographed tumbling over Watford's Ricky Holden during the match at Vicarage Road last season.

Action Images Ltd

Players Names	Birthplace	Date	Source	League Club	Date Sign'd	Seasons Played	Career Record Apps	Sub	Gls	Pos.	Misc
STEGGLES, Kevin P.	Bungay	19.03.61	App	Ipswich T.	12.78	1980-85	49	1	1	(D)	
			L	Southend U.	02.84	1983	3	0	0		
			L	Fulham	08.86	1986	3	0	0		
			Tr	West Bromwich A.	02.87	1986-87	14	0	0		
				Port Vale	11.87	1987	20	0	0		
STEIN, Brian	South Africa	19.10.57	Edgware T.	Luton T.	10.77	1977-87	378	10	127	(F)	E U21-3/E-1
STEIN, E. Mark S.	South Africa	28.01.66	Jnrs	Luton T.	01.84	1983-87	41	13	19	(F)	E Yth Int/
			L	Aldershot	01.86	1985	2	0	1		Brother of Brian
STEPHENS, Archie	Liverpool	19.05.54	Melksham T.	Bristol Rov.	08.81	1981-84	100	27	40	(F)	
			Tr	Middlesbrough	03.85	1984-87	87	5	24		
			Tr	Carlisle U.	12.87	1987	5	1	2		
STEPHENSON, Paul	Wallsend	02.01.68	App	Newcastle U.	12.85	1985-87	51	2	1	(RW)	E Yth Int
STERLAND, Mel	Sheffield	01.10.61	App	Sheffield Wed.	10.79	1978-87	249	8	31	(RB)	E U21-7/E 'B'
STERLING, Worrell R.	Bethnal Green	08.06.65	App	Watford	06.83	1982-87	79	12	14	(W)	
STEVEN, Trevor M.	Berwick	21.09.63	App	Burnley	09.81	1980-82	74	2	11	(RW)	E Yth Int/E-U21-2/
			Tr	Everton	07.83	1983-87	181	4	42		E-22
STEVENS, Gary A.	Hillingdon	30.03.62	App	Brighton & H.A.	10.79	1979-82	120	13	2	(RB/M)	E U21-8/E-7
			Tr	Tottenham H.	06.83	1983-87	131	4	6		
STEVENS, Gary M.	Birmingham	30.08.54	Evesham	Cardiff C.	09.78	1978-82	138	12	44	(F/CD)	
			Tr	Shrewsbury T.	09.82	1982-85	144	6	29		
			Tr	Brentford	07.86	1986	29	3	10		
			Tr	Hereford U.	03.87	1986-87	55	0	7		
STEVENS, M. Gary	Barrow	27.03.63	App	Everton	03.81	1981-87	207	1	9	(RB)	E U21-1/E-23
STEVENS, Ian D.	Malta	21.10.66	YTS	Preston N.E.	11.84	1984-85	9	2	2	(F)	
			Lancaster C.	Stockport Co. (N/C)	10.86	1986	1	1	0		
			Lancaster C.	Bolton W.	03.87	1986-87	7	10	2		
STEVENS, Keith H.	Merton	21.06.64	App	Millwall	06.81	1980-87	192	3	3	(RB)	
STEVENSON, Andrew J.	Scunthorpe	29.09.67	Jnrs	Scunthorpe U.	01.86	1985-87	6	11	0	(M)	
STEVENSON, Nigel C.A.	Swansea	02.11.58	App	Swansea C.	11.76	1975-86	247	12	15	(CD)	W U21-2/W-4
			L	Cardiff C.	10.85	1985	14	0	0		
			L	Reading	03.86	1985	3	0	0		
			Tr	Cardiff C.	08.87	1987	35	1	1		
STEWART, Ian E.	Belfast	10.09.61	Jnrs	Q.P.R.	05.80	1980-84	55	12	2	(LW)	NI Sch Int/NI-31
			L	Millwall	03.83	1982	10	1	3		
			Tr	Newcastle U.	08.85	1985-86	34	8	3		
			Tr	Portsmouth	07.87	1987	0	1	0		
			L	Brentford	02.88	1987	4	3	0		
STEWART, Paul A.	Manchester	07.10.64	App	Blackpool	10.81	1981-86	188	13	56	(F)	E Yth Int/E U21-1
			Tr	Manchester C.	03.87	1986-87	51	0	27		
STEWART, Ray S.M.	Perth	07.09.59	Dundee U.	West Ham U.	09.79	1979-87	334	0	60	(RB)	S Sch Int/ S U21-12/S-7
STEWART, W.I. (Billy)	Liverpool	01.01.65	App	Liverpool	01.83					(G)	
			Tr	Wigan Ath.	07.84	1984-85	14	0	0		
			Tr	Chester C.	08.86	1986-87	56	0	0		
STILES, John C.	Manchester	06.05.64	Vancouver W. (Can.)	Leeds U.	05.84	1984-87	45	10	2	(M)	Son of Nobby
STIMSON, Mark	Plaistow	27.12.67	YTS	Tottenham H.	07.85	1986	1	0	0	(FB)	
			L	Leyton Orient	03.88	1987	10	0	0		
STOCKWELL, Mike T.	Chelmsford	14.02.65	App	Ipswich T.	12.82	1985-87	61	11	2	(FB)	
STOKES, Wayne D.	Wolverhampton	16.02.65	Coventry C.(App)	Gillingham	07.82	1982-83	2	1	0	(D)	
				Stockport Co.	10.86	1986	17	1	1		
			Tr	Hartlepool U.	07.87	1987	24	0	0		
STOKLE, David	Hartlepool	01.12.69	YTS	Hartlepool U.	07.88	1986-87	8	0	0	(CD)	
STONEHOUSE, Kevin	Bishop Auckland	20.09.59	Shildon	Blackburn Rov.	07.79	1979-82	77	8	27	(M)	
			Tr	Huddersfield T.	03.83	1982-83	20	2	4		
			Tr	Blackpool	03.84	1983-85	53	2	19		
			Tr	Darlington	07.87	1987	38	5	13		
STORER, Stuart J.	Rugby	16.01.67	YTS	Mansfield T. (YTS)	08.83	1983	0	1	0	(RW)	
			VS Rugby	Birmingham C.	01.85	1985-86	5	3	0		
			Tr	Everton	03.87							
			L	Wigan Ath.	08.87	1987	9	3	0		
			Tr	Bolton W.	12.87	1987	12	3	1		
STOUTT, Stephen P.	Halifax	05.04.64		Huddersfield T. (N/C)	01.84	1983-84	6	0	0	(D)	
			Tr	Wolverhampton W.	04.85	1985-87	91	3	5		
STOWELL, Mike	Preston	19.04.65	Leyland Motors	Everton	12.85					(G)	
			L	Chester C.	09.87	1987	14	0	0		
			L	York C.	12.87	1987	6	0	0		
			L	Manchester C.	01.88	1987	14	0	0		
STRACHAN, Gordon D.	Edinburgh	09.02.57	Aberdeen	Manchester U.	08.84	1984-87	134	5	32	(RM)	S-41/S U21-1
STREETE, Floyd A.	Jamaica	05.05.59	Rivet Sp. (Aylesbury)	Cambridge U.	07.76	1976-82	111	14	19	(CD)	
			Utrecht (Neth.)	Derby Co.	10.84	1984-85	35	0	0		
			Tr	Wolverhampton W.	10.85	1985-87	102	2	1		
STRINGFELLOW, Ian R.	Nottingham	08.05.69	App	Mansfield T.	08.86	1985-87	34	21	12	(F)	Nephew of Mike
STRODDER, Gary J.	Cleckheaton	01.04.65	App	Lincoln C.	04.83	1982-86	122	10	6	(CD)	Son of Colin
			Tr	West Ham U.	03.87	1986-87	39	3	1		
STUART, Mark R.	Hammersmith	15.12.66	Jnrs	Charlton Ath.	07.84	1984-87	85	18	28	(W)	
STUBBS, W. (Billy)	Hartlepool	01.08.66	Seaham Red Star	Nottingham F.	04.87					(F)	
			L	Doncaster Rov.	09.87	1987	8	1	1		
			L	Grimsby T.	03.88	1987	2	5	2		
SUCKLING, Perry J.	Leyton	12.10.65	App	Coventry C.	10.83	1982-83	27	0	0	(G)	E Yth Int/E U21-10
			Tr	Manchester C.	06.86	1986-87	39	0	0		
			Tr	Crystal Palace	01.88	1987	17	0	0		
SULLEY, Chris S.	Camberwell	03.12.59	App	Chelsea	12.77					(LB)	
			Tr	Bournemouth	03.81	1980-85	205	1	3		
			Dundee U.	Blackburn Rov.	03.87	1986-87	47	0	0		

Brian Talbot (Stoke City) The former Ipswich, Arsenal and Watford midfielder.
Match Magazine

Gordon Strachan (Manchester United) Scottish midfield ball winner.
Match Magazine

Paul Stewart (Manchester City) One of the discoveries of last season.
Match Magazine

Mark Stuart (Charlton Athletic) Pictured holding back Oxford United's Robbie Mustoe.
Action Images Ltd

Players Names	Birthplace	Date	Source	League Club	Date Sign'd	Seasons Played	Career Record Apps	Sub	Gls	Pos.	Misc
SUMMERFIELD, Kevin	Walsall	07.01.59	App	West Bromwich A.	01.77	1978-81	5	4	4	(W)	E Yth Int
			Tr	Birmingham C.	05.82	1982	2	3	1		
			Tr	Walsall	12.82	1982-83	42	12	17		
			Tr	Cardiff C.	07.84	1984	10	0	1		
			Tr	Plymouth Arg.	12.84	1984-87	92	16	23		
SUSSEX, Andy R.	Enfield	23.11.64	App	Leyton Orient	11.82	1981-87	126	18	17	(W)	
SUTTON, David W.	Tarleton (Lancs.)	21.01.57	App	Plymouth Arg.	07.74	1973-77	60	1	0	(CD)	
			L	Reading	11.77	1977	9	0	0		
			Tr	Huddersfield T.	03.78	1977-83	242	0	11		
			Tr	Bolton W.	06.85	1985-87	98	0	4		
SUTTON, Steve J.	Hartington	16.04.61	App	Nottingham F.	04.79	1980-87	133	0	0	(G)	
			L	Mansfield T.	03.81	1980	8	0	0		
			L	Derby Co.	10.85	1984	14	0	0		
SWAIN, Kenny M.	Birkenhead	28.01.52	Wycombe W.	Chelsea	08.73	1973-78	114	5	26	(FB)	
			Tr	Aston Villa	12.78	1978-82	148	0	2		
			Tr	Nottingham F.	10.82	1982-84	112	0	2		
			Tr	Portsmouth	07.85	1985-87	113	0	0		
			L	West Bromwich A.	02.88	1987	7	0	1		
SWAN, Peter H.	Leeds	28.09.66	YTS	Leeds U.	08.84	1985-87	42	6	11	(CD/F)	
SWANN, Gary	York	11.04.62	App	Hull C.	04.80	1980-86	176	10	9	(M/FB)	
			Tr	Preston N.E.	11.86	1986-87	74	2	17		
SWINDLEHURST, Dave	Edgware	06.01.56	App	Crystal Palace	01.73	1973-79	221	16	73	(F)	E Yth Int/E U21-1
			Tr	Derby Co.	02.80	1979-82	110	0	29		
			Tr	West Ham U.	03.83	1982-84	52	9	16		
			Tr	Sunderland	08.85	1985-86	59	0	11		
			Cyprus	Wimbledon (N/C)	03.88	1987	2	0	0		
SWORD, Tommy W.	Newcastle	12.11.57	Bishop Auckland	Stockport Co.	11.79	1979-85	236	2	51	(CD)	
			Tr	Hartlepool U.	07.86	1986	18	0	0		
			L	Halifax T.	02.87	1986	8	0	0		
			Tr	Stockport Co.	03.87	1986-87	6	1	1		
TAIT, Mick P.	Wallsend	30.09.56	App	Oxford U.	09.74	1974-76	61	3	23	(M)	
			Tr	Carlisle U.	10.77	1976-79	101	5	20		
			Tr	Hull C.	09.79	1979	29	4	3		
			Tr	Portsmouth	06.80	1980-86	228	12	31		
			Tr	Reading	08.87	1987	35	0	2		
TAIT, Paul R.	Sutton Coldfield	31.07.71	YTS	Birmingham C. (YTS)	08.87	1987	0	1	0	(F)	
TALBOT, Brian E.	Ipswich	21.07.53	App	Ipswich T.	07.70	1973-78	177	0	25	(M)	E U21-1/E-6/E 'B'
			Tr	Arsenal	01.79	1978-84	245	9	40		
			Tr	Watford	06.85	1985-86	46	2	8		
			Tr	Stoke C.	10.86	1986-87	51	3	5		
			Tr	West Bromwich A.	01.88	1987	15	0	2		
TANKARD, Allen J.	Fleet	21.05.69	App	Southampton	05.87	1985-86	5	0	0	(LB)	E Yth Int
TANNER, Michael W.	Bristol	28.10.64		Bristol City	07.85	1985-87	16	3	1	(M)	
TANNER, Nick	Kingswood	24.05.65	Mangotsfield	Bristol Rov.	06.85	1985-87	104	3	3	(LB)	
TAYLOR, Alan D.	Hinckley	14.11.53	Morecambe	Rochdale	05.73	1973-74	55	0	8	(F)	
			Tr	West Ham U.	11.74	1974-78	88	10	25		
			Tr	Norwich C.	08.79	1979	20	4	5		
			Vancouver W. (Can.)	Cambridge U.	10.80	1980-81	17	1	4		
			Vancouver W. (Can.)	Hull C. (N/C)	01.84	1983	13	1	3		
			Tr	Burnley	08.84	1984-85	60	4	23		
			Tr	Bury	06.86	1986-87	55	7	10		
TAYLOR, Andy	Chesterfield	30.12.67	YTS	Chesterfield	07.86	1986-87	7	5	1	(F)	
TAYLOR, Kevin	Wakefield	22.01.61	App	Sheffield Wed.	10.78	1978-83	118	7	21	(M)	
			Tr	Derby Co.	07.84	1984	22	0	2		
			Tr	Crystal Palace	03.85	1984-87	85	2	14		
			Tr	Scunthorpe U.	10.87	1987	35	0	5		
TAYLOR, Les	North Shields	04.12.56	App	Oxford U.	12.74	1974-80	219	0	15	(M)	
			Tr	Watford	11.80	1980-85	167	5	13		
			Tr	Reading	10.86	1986-87	57	4	3		
TAYLOR, P. Mark R.	Hartlepool	20.11.64		Hartlepool U.	01.84	1983-85	42	5	4	(LW)	
			L	Crewe Alex.	12.85	1985	3	0	0		
			Tr	Blackpool	08.86	1986-87	81	0	35		
TAYLOR, R. Mark	Birmingham	22.02.66	YTS	Walsall	07.84	1984-87	70	9	3	(FB)	
TAYLOR, Martin J.	Tamworth	09.12.66	Mile Oak Rovers	Derby Co.	07.86					(G)	
			L	Carlisle U.	09.87	1987	10	0	0		
			L	Scunthorpe U.	12.87	1987	8	0	0		
TAYLOR, R. (Bob)	Easington	03.02.67	Horden CW	Leeds U.	01.86	1985-87	31	5	8	(F)	
TAYLOR, Robert S.	Plymouth	03.12.67	YTS	Portsmouth	08.86					(F)	
			Tr	Newport Co.	03.87	1986-87	38	6	7		
TAYLOR, Shaun	Plymouth	26.03.63	Bideford	Exeter C.	12.86	1986-87	64	0	1	(CD)	
TAYLOR, Steve J.	Royton	18.10.55	App	Bolton W.	10.73	1974-77	34	6	16	(F)	
			L	Port Vale	10.75	1975	4	0	2		
			Tr	Oldham Ath.	10.77	1977-78	45	2	25		
			Tr	Luton T.	01.79	1978	15	5	1		
			Tr	Mansfield T.	07.79	1979	30	7	7		
			Tr	Burnley	07.80	1980-82	80	6	37		
			Tr	Wigan Ath.	08.83	1983	29	1	7		
			Tr	Stockport Co.	03.84	1983-84	26	0	8		
			Tr	Rochdale	11.84	1984-86	84	0	42		
			Tr	Preston N.E.	10.86	1986	5	0	2		
			Tr	Burnley	08.87	1987	38	4	6		
TEMPEST, Dale M.	Leeds	30.12.63	App	Fulham	12.81	1980-83	25	9	6	(F)	
			Tr	Huddersfield T.	08.84	1984-85	63	2	27		
			L	Gillingham	03.86	1985	9	0	4		
			Lokeren (Bel.)	Colchester U.	08.87	1987	44	0	11		
TERRY, Steve G.	Clapton	14.06.62	App	Watford	01.80	1979-87	160	0	14	(CD)	
TESTER, Paul L.	Stroud	10.03.59	Cheltenham T.	Shrewsbury T.	07.83	1983-87	86	12	12	(LW)	
			L	Hereford U.	11.84	1984	4	0	0		

Players Names	Birthplace	Date	Source	League Club	Date Sign'd	Seasons Played	Apps	Sub	Gls	Pos.	Misc
THACKERAY, Andy J.	Huddersfield	13.02.68	Jnrs	Manchester C.	02.86					(M)	
			Tr	Huddersfield T.	07.86	1986	2	0	0		
			Tr	Newport Co.	03.87	1986-87	53	1	4		
THOMAS, Andy M.	Oxford	16.12.62	App	Oxford U.	12.80	1980-85	89	27	32	(M)	
			L	Fulham	12.82	1982	3	1	2		
			L	Derby Co.	03.83	1982	0	1	0		
			Tr	Newcastle U.	09.86	1986-87	24	7	6		
THOMAS, Geoff R.	Manchester	05.08.64	Littleborough P.	Rochdale (N/C)	08.82	1982-83	10	1	1	(M)	
			Tr	Crewe Alex.	03.84	1983-86	120	5	21		
			Tr	Crystal Palace	06.87	1987	41	0	6		
THOMAS, Glen A.	Hackney	06.10.67	App	Fulham	10.85	1986-87	28	0	0	(FB)	
THOMAS, D. Gwyn	Swansea	26.09.57	App	Leeds U.	07.75	1974-83	79	10	3	(M)	W Sch Int/W U21-2
			Tr	Barnsley	03.84	1983-87	172	2	15		
THOMAS, John W.	Wednesbury	05.08.58		Everton	07.77					(F)	
			L	Tranmere Rov.	03.79	1978	10	1	2		
			L	Halifax T.	10.79	1979	5	0	0		
			Tr	Bolton W.	06.80	1980-81	18	4	6		
			Tr	Chester C.	08.82	1982	44	0	20		
			Tr	Lincoln C.	08.83	1983-84	56	11	18		
			Tr	Preston N.E.	06.85	1985-86	69	9	28		
			Tr	Bolton W.	07.87	1987	43	1	23		
THOMAS, Martin R.	Senghenydd	28.11.59	App	Bristol Rov.	09.77	1976-81	162	0	0	(G)	W Yth Int/ W U21-2/W-1
			L	Cardiff C.	07.82	1982	15	0	0		
			L	Southend U.	02.83	1982	6	0	0		
			Tr	Newcastle U.	03.83	1982-87	118	0	0		
			L	Middlesbrough	10.84	1984	4	0	0		
THOMAS, Michael L.	Lambeth	24.08.67	App	Arsenal	12.84	1986-87	48	1	8	(M)	E Yth Int/E U21-3
			L	Portsmouth	12.86	1986	3	0	0		
THOMAS, Mitchell A.	Luton	02.10.64	App	Luton T.	08.82	1982-85	106	1	1	(LB)	E Yth Int/E U21-3
			Tr	Tottenham H.	07.86	1986-87	74	1	4		
THOMAS, Rod C.	Brent	10.10.70	YTS	Watford (YTS)	07.87	1987	1	3	0	(F)	E Sch Int
THOMPSON, Andrew R.	Cannock	09.11.67	App	West Bromwich A.	11.85	1985-86	18	6	1	(M/LB)	
			Tr	Wolverhampton W.	11.86	1986-87	69	2	10		
THOMPSON, Chris D.	Walsall	24.01.60	App	Bolton W.	07.77	1979-82	66	7	18	(M)	E Yth Int
			L	Lincoln C.	03.83	1982	5	1	0		
			Tr	Blackburn Rov.	08.83	1983-85	81	4	24		
			Tr	Wigan Ath.	07.86	1986-87	67	7	12		
THOMPSON, David G.	Morpeth	20.11.68	App	Millwall	11.86	1987	5	0	0	(CD)	
THOMPSON, David S.	Manchester	27.05.62	North Withington	Rochdale	09.81	1981-85	147	8	13	(W)	
			Tr	Notts. Co.	08.86	1986-87	52	3	8		
			Tr	Wigan Ath.	10.87	1987	27	0	3		
THOMPSON, Garry L.	Birmingham	07.10.59	App	Coventry C.	06.77	1977-82	127	7	38	(F)	E U21-6
			Tr	West Bromwich A.	02.83	1982-84	91	0	39		
			Tr	Sheffield Wed.	08.85	1985	35	1	7		
			Tr	Aston Villa	06.86	1986-87	54	1	17		
THOMPSON, Leslie	Cleethorpes	23.09.68	YTS	Hull C.	03.87	1987	5	2	2	(F)	
THOMPSON, Neil	Beverley	02.10.63	Nottingham F. (App)	Hull C.	11.81	1981-82	29	2	0	(LB)	
			Tr	Scarborough	(N/L)	1987	41	0	6		
THOMPSON, Nigel D.	Leeds	01.03.67	App	Leeds U.	12.84	1983-86	6	1	0	(M)	
			L	Rochdale	08.87	1987	3	2	0		
			Tr	Chesterfield	03.88	1987	4	0	0		
THOMPSON, Richard J.	Bristol	11.04.69	Watford (Jnr)	Newport Co.	01.87	1987	10	3	2	(F)	
THOMPSON, Steve J.	Oldham	02.11.64	App	Bolton W.	11.82	1982-87	194	6	29	(M)	
THOMPSON, Steve P.	Sheffield	28.07.55	Boston U.	Lincoln C.	04.80	1980-84	153	1	8	(CD)	
			Tr	Charlton Ath.	08.85	1985-87	95	0	0		
THOMPSTONE, Ian P.	Bury	17.07.71	YTS	Manchester C. (YTS)	06.87	1987	0	1	1	(M)	
THOMSON, R. (Bobby)	Glasgow	21.03.55	Morton	Middlesbrough	09.81	1981	18	2	2	(M)	
			Hibernian	Blackpool	09.85	1985-86	50	2	6		
			Tr	Hartlepool U. (N/C)	08.87	1987	2	1	0		
THORN, Andy	Carshalton	12.11.66	YTS	Wimbledon	11.84	1984-87	106	1	2	(CD)	E U21-4
THORNBER, Steve J.	Dewsbury	11.10.65	Jnrs	Halifax T.	01.83	1983-87	94	10	4	(M)	
THORNE, Steven T.	Hampstead	15.09.68	YTS	Watford	07.86					(M)	
			Tr	Brentford	09.87	1987	1	0	1		
THORPE, Adrian	Chesterfield	25.11.63		Mansfield T. (N/C)	08.82	1982	0	2	1	(F)	
			Heanor T.	Bradford C.	08.85	1985-87	9	8	1		
			L	Tranmere Rov.	11.86	1986	4	1	3		
			Tr	Notts. Co.	11.87	1987	22	1	5		
THORPE, Andy	Stockport	15.09.60	Jnrs	Stockport Co.	08.78	1977-85	312	2	3	(D)	
			Tr	Tranmere Rov.	07.86	1986-87	51	2	0		
			Tr	Stockport Co.	01.88	1987	20	0	0		
TILER, Carl	Sheffield	11.02.70	YTS	Barnsley (YTS)	09.87	1987	0	1	0	(D)	
TILTMAN, Richard G.	Shoreham	14.12.60	Maidstone U.	Brighton & H.A.	11.86	1986-87	10	3	1	(F)	
TINKLER, John	Trimdon	24.08.68		Hartlepool U.	12.86	1986-87	16	6	0	(M)	
TINNION, Brian	Stanley	23.02.68	App	Newcastle U.	02.86	1986-87	18	1	1	(LB)	
TOALE, Ian	Liverpool	28.08.67	App	Liverpool	05.85					(FB)	
			Tr	Grimsby T.	07.87	1987	16	4	0		
TODD, Mark K.	Belfast	04.12.67	YTS	Manchester U.	08.85					(M)	
			Tr	Sheffield U.	06.87	1987	11	1	0		
TOMAN, J. Andy	Northallerton	07.03.62	Bishop Auckland	Lincoln C.	08.85	1985	21	3	4	(W)	
			Bishop Auckland	Hartlepool U.	01.87	1986-87	67	0	22		
TOMLINSON, David I.	Rotherham	13.12.68	App	Sheffield Wed.	12.86	1986	0	1	0	(RW)	
			Tr	Rotherham U.	08.87	1987	6	3	0		
TOMLINSON, Paul	Brierley Hill	22.02.64	Middlewood Rangers	Sheffield U.	06.83	1983-86	37	0	0	(G)	
			L	Birmingham C.	03.87	1986	11	0	0		
			Tr	Bradford C.	06.87	1987	42	0	0		
TOWNSEND, Andy D.	Maidstone	23.07.63	Weymouth	Southampton	01.85	1984-87	77	6	5	(M)	

Players Names	Birthplace	Date	Source	League Club	Date Sign'd	Seasons Played	Career Record Apps	Sub	Gls	Pos.	Misc
TRAVIS, David A.	Doncaster	04.07.64	Hatfield Main	Doncaster Rov. (N/C)	08.84	1984-85	10	2	0	(M)	
			Tr	Scunthorpe U. (N/C)	02.86	1985-86	13	0	1		
			Tr	Chesterfield (N/C)	08.87	1987	6	5	0		
TREVITT, Simon	Dewsbury	20.12.67	YTS	Huddersfield T.	06.86	1986-87	40	8	1	(RB)	
TREWICK, John	Bedlington	03.06.57	App	West Bromwich A.	07.74	1974-80	83	13	11	(M)	E Sch Int/
			Tr	Newcastle U.	12.80	1980-83	76	2	8		E Yth Int
			L	Oxford U.	01.84	1983	3	0	0		
			Tr	Oxford U.	08.84	1984-87	109	2	4		
			Tr	Birmingham C.	09.87	1987	25	1	0		
TRUSSON, Mike S.	Northolt	26.05.59	App	Plymouth Arg.	01.77	1976-79	65	8	15	(M)	
			Tr	Sheffield U.	07.80	1980-83	125	1	31		
			Tr	Rotherham U.	12.83	1983-86	124	0	19		
			Tr	Brighton & H.A.	07.87	1987	13	2	2		
TUCKER, Gordon	Manchester	05.01.68	Shepshed Charter	Huddersfield T.	07.87	1987	19	4	0	(CD)	
TUNKS, Roy W.	Worthing	21.01.51	App	Rotherham U.	03.68	1967-73	138	0	0	(G)	
			L	York C.	01.69	1968	4	0	0		
			Tr	Preston N.E.	11.74	1974-80	277	0	0		
			Tr	Wigan Ath.	11.81	1981-87	245	0	0		
TUPLING, Stephen	Wensleydale	11.07.64	App	Middlesbrough	07.82					(M)	
			Tr	Carlisle U.	07.84	1984	1	0	0		
			Tr	Darlington	10.84	1984-86	105	6	8		
			Tr	Newport Co.	08.87	1987	30	3	2		
TURNBULL, Lee M.	Stockton	27.09.67	YTS	Middlesbrough	09.85	1985-86	8	8	4	(F)	
			Tr	Aston Villa	08.87						
			Tr	Doncaster Rov.	11.87	1987	24	6	1		
TURNER, Chris R.	Sheffield	15.09.58	App	Sheffield Wed.	08.76	1976-78	91	0	0	(G)	E Yth Int
			L	Lincoln C.	10.78	1978	5	0	0		
			Tr	Sunderland	07.79	1979-84	195	0	0		
			Tr	Manchester U.	08.85	1985-87	64	0	0		
TURNER, Paul E.	Cheshunt	13.11.68	App	Arsenal	07.86					(M)	
			Tr	Cambridge U. (N/C)	09.87	1987	7	8	0		
TURNER, Philip	Sheffield	12.02.62	App	Lincoln C.	02.80	1979-85	239	2	19	(M)	
			Tr	Grimsby T.	08.86	1986-87	62	0	9		
			Tr	Leicester C.	02.88	1987	2	3	0		
TURNER, Robert P.	Hartlepool	18.09.66	App	Huddersfield T.	09.84	1984	0	1	0	(F)	
			Tr	Cardiff C.	07.85	1985-86	34	5	8		
			L	Hartlepool U.	10.86	1986	7	0	1		
			Tr	Bristol Rov.	12.86	1986-87	19	7	2		
			Tr	Wimbledon	12.87	1987	0	4	0		
TURNER, Wayne L.	Luton	09.03.61	App	Luton T.	04.78	1978-84	81	3	2	(M)	
			L	Lincoln C.	10.81	1981	16	0	0		
			Tr	Coventry C.	07.85	1985	14	1	1		
			Tr	Brentford	09.86	1986-87	56	0	2		
TUTILL, Stephen A.	York	01.10.69	YTS	York C.	01.88	1987	20	1	0	(CD)	
TWENTYMAN, Geoff	Liverpool	10.03.59	Chorley	Preston N.E.	08.83	1983-85	95	3	4	(CD)	Son of Geoff (Sr)
			Tr	Bristol Rov.	08.86	1986-87	78	3	1		
TYNAN, Paul	Whitehaven	15.07.69	Ipswich T.(App)	Carlisle U.	08.87	1987	2	3	0	(M)	
TYNAN, Tommy E.	Liverpool	17.11.55	App	Liverpool	11.72					(F)	
			L	Swansea C.	10.75	1975	6	0	2		
			Tr	Sheffield Wed.	09.76	1976-78	89	2	31		
			Tr	Lincoln C.	10.78	1978	9	0	1		
			Tr	Newport Co.	02.79	1978-82	168	15	66		
			Tr	Plymouth Arg.	08.83	1983-84	80	0	43		
			Tr	Rotherham U.	07.85	1985-86	32	0	13		
			L	Plymouth Arg.	03.86	1985	9	0	9		
			Tr	Plymouth Arg.	09.86	1986-87	82	1	34		
UZZELL, John E.	Plymouth	31.03.59	App	Plymouth Arg.	03.77	1977-87	262	7	6	(D)	
VALENTINE, Peter	Huddersfield	16.04.63	App	Huddersfield T.	04.80	1981-82	19	0	1	(CD)	
			Tr	Bolton W.	07.83	1983-84	66	2	1		
			Tr	Bury	07.85	1985-87	132	2	7		
VAN DEN HAUWE, Pat	Belgium	16.12.60	App	Birmingham C.	08.78	1978-84	119	4	1	(LB)	W-10
			Tr	Everton	09.84	1984-87	110	0	1		
VARADI, Imre	Paddington	08.07.59	Letchworth	Sheffield U.	04.78	1978	6	4	4	(F)	
			Tr	Everton	03.79	1979-80	22	4	6		
			Tr	Newcastle U.	08.81	1981-82	81	0	39		
			Tr	Sheffield Wed.	08.83	1983-84	72	4	33		
			Tr	West Bromwich A.	07.85	1985	30	2	9		
			Tr	Manchester C.	10.86	1986-87	55	7	26		
VAUGHAN, John	Isleworth	26.06.64	App	West Ham U.	06.82					(G)	
			L	Charlton Ath.	03.85	1984	6	0	0		
			L	Bristol Rov.	09.85	1985	6	0	0		
			L	Wrexham	10.85	1985	4	0	0		
			L	Bristol C.	03.86	1985	2	0	0		
			Tr	Fulham	08.86	1986	44	0	0		
			L	Bristol C.	01.88	1987	3	0	0		
VAUGHAN, Nigel M.	Caerleon	20.05.59	App	Newport Co.	05.77	1976-83	215	9	32	(M)	W U21-1/W-10
			Tr	Cardiff C.	09.83	1983-86	144	5	42		
			L	Reading	02.87	1986	5	0	1		
			Tr	Wolverhampton W.	08.87	1987	33	3	6		
VENISON, Barry	Consett	16.08.64	App	Sunderland	01.82	1981-85	169	4	2	(RB)	E Yth Int/
			Tr	Liverpool	07.86	1986-87	49	2	0		E U21-10
VENUS, Mark	Hartlepool	06.04.67	Sch	Hartlepool U. (N/C)	03.85	1984	4	0	0	(LB)	
			Sch	Leicester C.	09.85	1985-87	58	3	1		
			Tr	Wolverhampton W.	03.88	1987	4	0	0		
VICKERS, Stephen	Bishop Auckland	13.10.67	Spennymoor U.	Tranmere Rov.	09.85	1985-87	84	1	3	(CD)	
VINEY, Keith B.	Portsmouth	26.10.57	App	Portsmouth	10.75	1975-81	160	6	3	(LB)	
			Tr	Exeter C.	08.82	1982-87	267	0	8		
WADDLE, Chris R.	Felling	14.12.60	Tow Law T.	Newcastle U.	07.80	1980-84	169	1	46	(W)	E U21-1/E-34
			Tr	Tottenham H.	06.85	1985-87	99	1	19		
WADE, Bryan A.	Bath	25.06.63	Trowbridge T.	Swindon T.	05.85	1985-87	48	12	18	(F)	

John Trewick (Birmingham City) Midfielder with a wealth of experience.

Mitchell Thomas (Tottenham Hotspur) Defender who followed his former boss, David Pleat, to White Hart Lane. Match Magazine

Gary Thompson (Aston Villa) Pictured here holding off Crystal Palace's Jim Cannon in last seasons match at Selhurst Park. Action Images Ltd

Players Names	Birthplace	Date	Source	League Club	Date Sign'd	Seasons Played	Career Record Apps	Sub	Gls	Pos.	Misc
WAITT, Mick H.	Hexham	25.06.60	Arnold Kingswell Tr	Notts Co. Lincoln C.	12.84 N/L	1984-86	71	11	27	(F)	
WAKENSHAW, Robbie A.	Ponteland	22.12.65	App Tr L Tr Tr	Everton Carlisle U. Doncaster Rov. Rochdale Crewe Alex.	12.83 09.85 03.86 09.86 06.87	1983-84 1985 1985 1986 1987	2 6 8 28 17	1 2 0 1 3	1 2 3 5 1	(W)	E Yth Int
WALFORD, Steve J.	Highgate	05.01.58	App Tr Tr Tr L	Tottenham H. Arsenal Norwich C. West Ham U. Huddersfield T.	04.75 08.77 03.81 08.83 10.87	1975 1977-80 1980-82 1983-86 1987	1 64 93 114 12	1 13 0 1 0	0 3 2 2 0	(D)	E Yth Int
WALKER, Alan	Mossley	17.12.59	Telford U. Tr Tr	Stockport Co. Lincoln C. Millwall Gillingham	08.78 10.83 07.85 03.88	1983-84 1985-87 1987	74 92 7	1 0 0	4 8 0	(CD)	
WALKER, Clive	Oxford	26.05.57	App Tr Tr Tr	Chelsea Sunderland Q.P.R. Fulham	04.75 07.84 12.85 10.87	1976-83 1984-85 1985-86 1987	168 48 16 25	30 2 5 1	60 10 1 8	(LW)	E Sch Int
WALKER, Colin	Rotherham	01.05.58	Gisborne C.(NZ) L Gisborne C. (NZ) Tr Harworth Coliery L L	Barnsley Doncaster Rov. Doncaster Rov(N/C) Cambridge U. (N/C) Sheffield Wed. Darlington Torquay U.	11.80 02.83 11.85 01.86 08.86 12.86 10.87	1980-82 1982 1985 1985 1986 1986 1987	21 12 3 3 2 6 3	3 0 2 0 0 1 0	11 5 0 1 0 0 0	(F)	
WALKER, Derek W.	Perth	24.11.64	Kinnoull Jnrs	Chesterfield	08.86	1986-87	19	4	3	(F)	
WALKER, Des S.	Hackney	21.11.65	App	Nottingham F.	11.83	1983-87	118	4	0	(CD)	E U21-7
WALKER, Phil A.	Kirkby in Ashfield	27.01.57	Mansfield YC Tr L Tr Tr	Chesterfield Rotherham U. Cardiff C. Chesterfield Scarborough	12.77 12.82 09.83 10.84 (N/L)	1977-82 1982-83 1983 1984-85 1987	151 20 2 30 0	15 5 0 8 1	38 3 0 9 0	(F)	
WALKER, Ray	North Shields	28.09.63	App L Tr	Aston Villa Port Vale Port Vale	09.81 09.84 07.86	1982-85 1984 1986-87	15 15 86	8 0 1	0 1 10	(M)	E Yth Int
WALLACE, David L. (Danny)	Greenwich	21.01.64	App	Southampton	01.82	1980-87	206	11	57	(W)	E U21-11/ E Yth Int/E-1
WALLACE, Rodney S.	Greenwich	02.10.69	YTS	Southampton	04.88	1987	3	12	1	(F)	Brother of Danny
WALLER, David H.	Urmston	20.12.63	Tr Tr	Crewe Alex. Shrewsbury T. Chesterfield	01.82 07.86 03.87	1981-85 1986 1987	165 11 39	3 0 1	55 3 19	(F)	
WALLING, Dean A.	Leeds	17.04.69	Leeds U.(App)	Rochdale	07.87	1987	8	4	2	(F)	
WALLINGTON, F. Mark	Sleaford	17.09.52	Jnrs Tr Tr	Walsall Leicester C. Derby Co.	10.71 03.72 07.85	1971 1971-84 1985-86	11 412 67	0 0 0	0 0 0	(G)	E Yth Int/ E U23-2
WALSH, Alan	Hartlepool	09.12.56	Horden C.W. Tr Tr	Middlesbrough Darlington Bristol C.	12.76 10.78 08.84	1977 1978-83 1984-87	0 245 169	3 6 3	0 87 66	(F)	
WALSH, Andrew	Blackburn	15.02.70	Preston N.E. (N/C)	Bury	11.87	1987	0	1	0	(CD)	
WALSH, Colin D.	Hamilton	22.07.62	App Tr	Nottingham F. Charlton Ath.	08.79 09.86	1980-85 1986-87	115 43	24 1	32 9	(M)	S U21-5
WALSH, Gary	Wigan	21.03.68	App	Manchester U.	04.85	1986-87	30	0	0	(G)	E U21-2
WALSH, Ian P.	St. Davids	04.09.58	App Tr Tr Tr Tr	Crystal Palace Swansea C. Barnsley Grimsby T. Cardiff C.	10.75 02.82 07.84 08.86 01.88	1976-81 1981-83 1984-85 1986-87 1987	101 32 45 36 1	16 5 4 5 5	23 11 15 13 0	(F)	W Sch Int/W U21-2 W-18
WALSH, Mario M.	Paddington	19.01.66	App Tr Tr	Portsmouth Torquay U. Colchester U.	01.84 01.85 08.87	1984-86 1987	89 4	11 7	18 2	(F)	
WALSH, Mick C.	Manchester	20.06.56	Jnrs Tr L L Fort Lauderdale (USA) Tr	Bolton W. Everton Norwich C. Burnley Manchester C. Blackpool	07.74 08.81 10.82 12.82 10.83 02.84	1974-80 1981-82 1982 1982 1983 1983-87	169 20 5 3 3 140	8 0 0 0 1 4	4 0 0 0 0 5	(CD)	IR-5
WALSH, Paul A.	Plumstead	01.10.62	App Tr Tr Tr	Charlton Ath. Luton T. Liverpool Tottenham H.	10.79 07.82 05.84 02.88	1979-81 1982-83 1984-87 1987	85 80 63 11	2 0 14 0	24 24 25 1	(F)	E Yth Int/E U21-7/ E-2
WALSH, Steve	Preston	03.11.64	Jnrs Tr	Wigan Ath Leicester C.	09.82 06.86	1092-85 1986-87	123 52	3 1	4 7	(CD)	
WALTERS, Mark	Birmingham	02.06.64	App	Aston Villa	05.82	1981-87	168	13	39	(LW)	E Yth Int/E U21-9/ To Glasgow Rangers 12.87
WALTERS, Steven	Plymouth	09.01.72	Jnrs	Crewe Alex. (Sch)		1987	1	0	0	(M)	
WALTON, Mark A.	Merthy Tydfil	01.06.69	Tr	Luton T. Colchester U.	02.87 11.87	1987	17	0	0	(G)	
WALWYN, Keith I.	Jamaica	17.02.56	Winterton Rgrs. Tr Tr	Chesterfield York C. Blackpool	11.79 07.81 06.87	1980 1981-86 1987	3 245 38	0 0 1	2 118 13	(F)	
WARBURTON, Ray	Rotherham	07.10.67	App	Rotherham U.	10.85	1984-86	3	1	0	(CD)	
WARD, Mark W.	Huyton	10.10.62	App Northwich Vic. Tr	Everton Oldham Ath. West Ham U.	09.80 07.83 08.85	1983-84 1985-87	84 116	0 0	12 5	(RW)	E Semi-Pro Int 1983

Barry Venison (Liverpool) Rising young full-back.

Imre Varadi (Manchester City) Found the net 17 times last season.
Match Magazine

Paul Walsh (Tottenham Hotspur) Signed from Liverpool.
Match Magazine

Mark Ward (West Ham United) Busy little player who was a one-time apprentice at Everton.
Match Magazine

Chris Waddle (Tottenham Hotspur) International star who, with others, will want to forget the European Championship this year.
Match Magazine

231

Players Names	Birthplace	Date	Source	League Club	Date Sign'd	Seasons Played	Apps	Sub	Gls	Pos.	Misc
WARD, Paul T.	Sedgefield	15.09.63	App	Chelsea	08.81					(M/FB)	
			Tr	Middlesbrough	09.82	1982-85	69	7	1		
			Tr	Darlington	09.85	1985-87	124	0	9		
WARD, Peter	Durham	15.10.64	Chester-le-Street	Huddersfield	01.87	1986-87	23	10	2	(F)	
WARE, Paul D.	Congleton	07.11.70	YTS	Stoke C. (YTS)	07.87	1987	1	0	0	(M)	
WARK, John	Glasgow	04.08.57	App	Ipswich T.	08.74	1974-83	295	1	94	(M)	S U21-8/S-29
			Tr	Liverpool	03.84	1983-87	64	6	28		PFA Footballer
			Tr	Ipswich T.	01.88	1987	5	2	0		of Year 1980-81
WARREN, Lee A.	Manchester	28.02.69	YTS	Leeds U.	07.87					(D)	
			Tr	Rochdale	10.87	1987	31	0	1		
WASSALL, Darren P.J.	Birmingham	27.06.68	App	Nottingham F.	06.86	1987	2	1	0	(CD)	
			L	Hereford U.	10.87	1987	5	0	0		
WATSON, Alex F.	Liverpool	06.04.68	App	Liverpool	05.85	1987	2	0	0	(CD)	Brother of David
WATSON, Andrew L.	Huddersfield	03.04.67	App	Huddersfield T.	04.85					(CD)	
			Tr	Exeter C.	07.86	1986-87	41	1	1		
WATSON, David	Liverpool	20.11.61	Jnrs	Liverpool	05.79					(CD)	E U21-7/E-11
			Tr	Norwich C.	11.80	1980-85	212	0	11		Brother of Alex
			Tr	Everton	08.86	1986-87	72	0	7		
WATSON, Tommy R.	Liverpool	29.09.69	YTS	Grimsby T.	06.88	1987	13	6	0	(M)	
WAUGH, Keith	Sunderland	27.10.56	App	Sunderland	07.74					(G)	
			Tr	Peterborough U.	07.76	1976-80	195	0	0		
			Tr	Sheffield U.	08.81	1981-84	99	0	0		
			L	Cambridge U.	11.84	1984	4	0	0		
			L	Bristol C.	12.84	1984	3	0	0		
			Tr	Bristol C.	07.85	1985-87	130	0	0		
WEATHERLY, C. Mark	Ramsgate	18.01.58	App	Gillingham	12.75	1974-87	394	46	47	(CD)	
WEBB, Alan R.	Telford	01.01.63	App	West Bromwich A.	01.80	1981-83	23	1	0	(RB)	
			L	Lincoln C.	03.84	1983	11	0	0		
			Tr	Port Vale	08.84	1984-87	131	1	2		
WEBB, Neil J.	Reading	30.07.63	App	Reading	11.80	1979-81	65	7	22	(M)	Son of Doug
			Tr	Portsmouth	07.82	1982-84	123	0	34		E Yth Int/E U21-3/
			Tr	Nottingham F.	06.85	1985-87	110	0	41		E-7
WEBSTER, Simon P.	Hinckley	20.01.64	App	Tottenham H.	12.81	1982-83	2	1	0	(CD)	
			L	Exeter C.	11.83	1983	26	0	0		
			Tr	Huddersfield T.	02.85	1984-87	118	0	4		
			Tr	Sheffield U.	03.88	1987	5	0	1		
WEGERLE, Roy C.	South Africa	19.03.64	Tampa Bay (USA)	Chelsea	06.86	1986-87	15	8	3	(W)	
			L	Swindon T.	03.88	1987	7	0	1		
WEIR, Michael G.	Edinburgh	16.01.66	Hibernian	Luton T.	09.87	1987	7	1	0	(W)	to Hibernian 1.88
WEIR, Peter R.	Johnstone	18.01.58	Aberdeen	Leicester C.	01.88	1987	18	0	2	(LW)	S-6
WELCH, Keith J.	Bolton	03.10.58	YTS	Rochdale	03.87	1986-87	70	0	0	(G)	
WELLS, Ian M.	Wolverhampton	27.10.64	Harrisons	Hereford U.	06.85	1985-86	47	4	12	(F)	
WELLS, Peter A.	Nottingham	13.08.56	App	Nottingham F.	10.74	1975-76	27	0	0	(G)	
			Tr	Southampton	12.76	1976-82	141	0	0		
			Tr	Millwall	02.83	1982-83	33	0	0		
			Tr	Leyton Orient	07.85	1985-87	130	0	0		
WEST, Colin	Wallsend	13.11.62	App	Sunderland	07.80	1981-84	88	14	21	(F)	
			Tr	Watford	03.85	1984-85	45	0	20		
			Glasgow Rangers	Sheffield Wed.	09.87	1987	23	2	7		
WEST, Colin W.	Middlesbrough	19.09.67	App	Chelsea	09.85	1986-87	8	8	4	(F)	E Yth Int
WEST, Gary	Scunthorpe	25.08.64	App	Sheffield U.	08.82	1982-84	75	0	2	(CD)	E Yth Int
			Tr	Lincoln C.	08.85	1985-86	83	0	4		
			Tr	Gillingham	07.87	1987	42	0	2		
WESTLEY, Shane L.M.	Canterbury	16.06.65	App	Charlton Ath.	06.83	1983	8	0	0	(CD)	
			Tr	Southend U.	03.85	1984-87	114	2	10		
WESTON, Ian P.	Bristol	06.05.68	App	Bristol Rov.	05.86	1986-87	13	3	0	(M)	
WESTWOOD, Gary M.	Barrow	03.04.64	App	Ipswich T.	04.81					(G)	E Yth Int
			L	Reading	09.83	1983	5	0	0		
			Tr	Reading	07.84	1984-87	123	0	0		
WHARTON, Kenny	Newcastle	28.11.60	Grainger Park BC	Newcastle U.	01.79	1978-87	254	18	26	(LB/M)	
WHATMORE, Neil	Ellesmere Port	17.05.55	App	Bolton W.	05.73	1972-80	262	15	102	(F)	
			Tr	Birmingham C.	08.81	1981-82	24	2	6		
			L	Bolton W.	12.82	1982	10	0	3		
			Tr	Oxford U.	02.83	1982-83	33	3	15		
			L	Bolton W.	03.84	1983	7	0	2		
			Tr	Burnley	08.84	1984	8	0	1		
			Tr	Mansfield T.	11.84	1984-86	71	1	20		
			Tr	Bolton W.	08.87						
			Tr	Mansfield T. (N/C)	11.87	1987	0	4	0		
WHEELER, Paul	Caerphilly	03.01.65	App	Bristol Rov.	01.83					(F)	
			Aberaman	Cardiff C.	08.85	1985-87	57	17	9		
WHELAN, Ronnie A.	Dublin	25.09.61	Home Farm	Liverpool	10.79	1980-87	217	10	38	(M)	IR U21-1/IR-25
WHELLANS, Robert	Harrogate	14.02.69	YTS	Bradford C.	06.87					(F)	
			L	Hartlepool U.	12.87	1987	8	3	1		
WHITE, Dale	Sunderland	17.03.68	App	Sunderland	03.86	1985	2	2	0	(F)	E Sch Int
			L	Peterborough U.	12.87	1987	14	0	4		
WHITE, David	Manchester	30.10.67	YTS	Manchester C.	10.85	1986-87	59	9	14	(RW)	E Yth Int/E U21-3
WHITE, Devan W.	Nottingham	02.03.64	Arnold	Lincoln C.	12.84	1984-85	21	8	4	(F)	
			Shepshed Chart.	Bristol Rov.	08.87	1987	39	0	15		
WHITE, Mark I.	Sheffield	26.10.58	Sheffield U. (App)	Reading	03.77	1977-87	265	13	11	(FB/M)	
WHITE, E. Winston	Leicester	26.10.58	App	Leicester C.	10.76	1976-78	10	2	1	(W)	
			Tr	Hereford U.	03.79	1978-82	169	6	21		
			Hong Kong	Chesterfield (N/C)	09.83	1983	0	1	0		
			Tr	Port Vale (N/C)	10.83	1983	0	1	0		
			Tr	Stockport Co. (N/C)	11.83	1983	4	0	1		
			Tr	Bury	12.83	1983-86	125	0	11		
			L	Rochdale	10.86	1986	4	0	0		
			Tr	Colchester U.	02.87	1986-87	54	1	8		

Players Names	Birthplace	Date	Source	League Club	Date Sign'd	Seasons Played	Apps	Sub	Gls	Pos.	Misc
WHITE, Steve J.	Chipping Sodbury	02.01.59	Mangotsfield	Bristol Rov.	07.77	1977-79	46	4	20	(F)	E Sch Int
			Tr	Luton T.	12.79	1979-81	63	9	25		
			Tr	Charlton Ath.	07.82	1982	29	0	12		
			L	Lincoln C.	01.83	1982	2	1	0		
			L	Luton T.	02.83	1982	4	0	0		
			Tr	Bristol Rov.	08.83	1983-85	89	12	24		
			Tr	Swindon T.	07.86	1986-87	46	14	26		
WHITEHEAD, Alan	Bury	20.11.56	Darwen	Bury	12.77	1977-80	98	1	13	(CD)	
			Tr	Brentford	08.81	1981-83	101	1	4		
			Tr	Scunthorpe U.	01.84	1983-86	106	2	8		
			Tr	York C.	10.86	1986-87	40	1	1		
			L	Wigan Ath.	03.87	1986	2	0	0		
WHITEHEAD, Clive R.	Birmingham	24.11.55	Northfield Jnrs	Bristol C.	08.73	1973-81	209	20	10	(RB/W)	E Yth Int
			Tr	West Bromwich A.	11.81	1981-86	157	11	6		
			L	Wolverhampton W.	01.86	1985	2	0	0		
			Tr	Portsmouth	06.87	1987	30	3	2		
WHITEHEAD, Philip M.	Halifax	17.12.69	YTS	Halifax T. YTS)	10.86	1986	12	0	0	(G)	
WHITEHURST, W. (Billy)	Thurnscoe	10.06.59	Mexborough Town	Hull C.	10.80	1980-85	176	17	47	(F)	
			Tr	Newcastle U.	12.85	1985-86	28	0	7		
			Tr	Oxford U.	10.86	1986-87	36	4	4		
			Tr	Reading	02.88	1987	15	0	6		
WHITESIDE, Norman	Belfast	07.05.65	App	Manchester U.	07.82	1981-87	187	13	47	(F)	NI Sch Int/NI-36
WHITLOCK, Mark	Portsmouth	14.03.61	App	Southampton	03.79	1981-85	55	6	1	(CD)	
			L	Grimsby T.	10.82	1982	7	1	0		
			L	Aldershot	03.83	1982	14	0	0		
			Tr	Bournemouth	07.86	1986-87	86	0	1		
WHITTON, Steve P.	East Ham	04.12.60	App	Coventry C.	09.78	1979-82	64	10	21	(F)	
			Tr	West Ham U.	07.83	1983-84	35	4	6		
			L	Birmingham C.	01.86	1985	8	0	3		
			Tr	Birmingham C.	08.86	1986-87	71	1	23		
WICKS, Steve J.	Reading	03.10.56	app	Chelsea	06.74	1974-78	117	1	5	(CD)	E Yth Int/ E U21-1
			Tr	Derby Co.	01.79	1978-79	24	0	0		
			Tr	Q.P.R.	09.79	1979-80	73	0	0		
			Tr	Crystal Palace	06.81	1981	14	0	1		
			Tr	Q.P.R.	03.82	1981-85	116	0	6		
			Tr	Chelsea	07.86	1986-87	32	0	1		
WIFFILL, David P.	Bristol		Bath C.	Manchester C.	04.80					(M)	
			Hong Kong	Bristol Rov. (N/C)	08.87	1987	2	0	0		
WIGLEY, Steve	Ashton-u-Lyne	15.10.61	Curzon Ashton	Nottingham F.	03.81	1982-85	69	13	2	(W)	
			Tr	Sheffield U.	10.85	1985-86	21	7	1		
			Tr	Birmingham C.	03.87	1986-87	54	0	2		
WIGNALL, Steve L.	Liverpool	17.09.54	Liverpool (Jnrs)	Doncaster Rov.	03.72	1972-76	127	3	1	(CD)	
			Tr	Colchester U.	09.77	1977-83	279	2	22		
			Tr	Brentford	08.84	1984-86	67	0	2		
			Tr	Aldershot	09.86	1986-87	77	0	2		
WILCOX, Russell	Hemsworth	25.03.64	App	Doncaster Rov. (App)	05.80	1980	1	0	0	(CD)	E Semi-pro Int 1986
			Frickley Ath.	Northampton T.	08.86	1986-87	80	1	5		
WILDER, Chris J.	Chapeltown	23.09.67	App	Southampton	09.85					(RB)	
			Tr	Sheffield U.	08.86	1986-87	32	4	0		
WILKES, Stephen B.	Preston	30.06.67	App	Wigan Ath.	06.85					(M)	
			Tr	Preston N.E.	08.86	1987	1	2	0		
WILKINS, Dean M.	Hillingdon	12.07.62	App	Q.P.R.	05.80	1980-82	1	5	0	(M)	Brother of Graham/Ray
			Tr	Brighton & H.A.	08.83	1983	2	0	0		
			L	Leyton Orient	03.84	1983	10	0	0		
			PEC Zwolle (Neth)	Brighton & H.A.	07.87	1987	43	1	3		
WILKINS, Ray C.	Hillingdon	14.09.56	App	Chelsea	10.73	1973-78	176	3	30	(M)	E-72/E U21-1 E U23-2/ E F Lge Rep/ To AC Milan (It) 7.84
			Tr	Manchester U.	08.79	1979-83	158	2	7		
WILKINS, Richard J.	Lambeth	28.05.65	Haverhill Rov.	Colchester U.	11.86	1986-87	68	1	11	(M)	
WILKINSON, Paul	Louth	30.10.64	App	Grimsby T.	10.82	1982-84	69	2	27	(F)	E U21-4
			Tr	Everton	03.85	1984-86	19	12	6		
			Tr	Nottingham F.	03.87	1986-87	32	2	5		
WILKINSON, Stephen J.	Lincoln	01.09.68	App	Leicester C.	09.86	1986-87	3	3	1	(F)	
WILLIAMS, Alex	Manchester	13.11.61	App	Manchester C.	11.79	1980-85	114	0	0	(G)	E Yth Int
			Tr	Port Vale	11.86	1986-87	35	0	0		
WILLIAMS, Andy	Birmingham	29.07.62	Solihull Bor.	Coventry C.	07.85	1985-86	3	6	0	(M)	
			Tr	Rotherham U.	10.86	1986-87	72	0	10		
WILLIAMS, Brett	Dudley	19.03.68	App	Nottingham F.	12.85	1985-87	18	0	0	(LB)	
			L	Stockport Co.	03.87	1986	2	0	0		
			L	Northampton T.	01.88	1987	3	1	0		
WILLIAMS, Brian	Salford	05.11.55	App	Bury	04.73	1971-76	148	11	19	(LB/W)	
			Tr	Q.P.R.	07.77	1977	9	10	0		
			Tr	Swindon T.	06.78	1978-80	89	10	8		
			Tr	Bristol Rov.	07.81	1981-84	172	0	20		
			Tr	Bristol C.	07.85	1985-86	77	0	3		
			Tr	Shrewsbury T.	07.87	1987	42	0	0		
WILLIAMS, David M.	Cardiff	11.03.55	Clifton Ath.	Bristol Rov.	08.75	1975-84	342	10	66	(M)	W Yth Int/ W U21-1/W-5
			Tr	Norwich C.	07.85	1985-87	56	4	11		
WILLIAMS, Dean A.	Hempstead (Ex.)	14.11.70	YTS	Cambridge U. (YTS)	07.87	1987	1	0	0	(F)	
WILLIAMS, Gareth J.	Cowes (IOW)	12.03.67	Gosport Bor.	Aston Villa	01.88	1987	1	0	0	(M/FB)	
WILLIAMS, Gary	Wolverhampton	17.06.60	App	Aston Villa	06.78	1978-86	235	5	0	(FB)	
			L	Walsall	03.80	1979	9	0	0		
			Tr	Leeds U.	07.87	1987	31	0	3		
WILLIAMS, Gary	Nantwich	14.05.59	Jnrs	Tranmere Rov. (NC)	09.76	1976	1	0	0	(M/FB)	
			Djurgaardens(Swe.)	Blackpool	08.80	1980	30	1	2		
			Tr	Swindon T.	08.81	1981	37	1	3		
			Tr	Tranmere Rov.	02.83	1982-87	158	8	16		
WILLIAMS, Gary A.	Bristol	08.06.63	App	Bristol C.	08.80	1980-83	98	2	1	(M/FB)	
			Portsmouth (trial)	Swansea C. (N/C)	01.85	1984	6	0	0		
			Bristol Rov. (trial)	Oldham Ath.	08.85	1985-87	42	8	11		

Players Names	Birthplace	Date	Source	League Club	Date Sign'd	Seasons Played	Career Record Apps	Sub	Gls	Pos.	Misc
WILLIAMS, D. Geraint	Treorchy	05.01.62	App	Bristol Rov.	01.80	1980-84	138	3	8	(M)	W Yth Int/
			Tr	Derby Co.	03.85	1984-87	131	1	6		W U21-2/W-3
WILLIAMS, Jeremy S.	Didcot	24.03.60	App	Reading	03.78	1976-87	283	26	17	(RB/W)	
WILLIAMS, W. John	Liverpool	03.10.60	Jnrs	Tranmere Rov.	10.79	1978-84	167	6	13	(CD)	
			Tr	Port Vale	07.85	1985-86	50	0	3		
			Tr	Bournemouth	12.86	1986-87	64	0	5		
WILLIAMS, Keith D.	Burntwood	12.04.57	App	Aston Villa	04.75					(D)	
			Tr	Northampton T.	02.77	1976-80	128	3	6		
			Tr	Bournemouth	08.81	1981-86	99	3	1		
			Bath C.	Colchester U.	12.87	1987	9	1	0		
WILLIAMS, Mike	Deeside	06.02.65	App	Chester C.	02.83	1981-83	30	4	4	(CD)	W Yth Int
			Tr	Wrexham	07.84	1984-87	132	6	3		
WILLIAMS, Neil J.F.	Waltham Abbey	23.10.64	App	Watford	08.82					(W)	
			Tr	Hull C.	07.84	1984-87	75	16	9		
WILLIAMS, Oshor J.	Stockton	21.04.58	Middlesbrough(App)	Manchester U.	08.76					(W)	
			Gateshead	Southampton	03.78	1978-79	4	2	0		
			L	Exeter C.	08.78	1978	2	1	0		
			Tr	Stockport Co.	08.79	1979-84	192	1	26		
			Tr	Port Vale	11.84	1984-85	47	2	6		
			Tr	Preston N.E.	08.86	1986-87	38	1	12		
WILLIAMS, Paul A.	Sheffield	08.09.63	Nuneaton Bor.	Preston N.E.	12.86	1986	1	0	0	(D)	
			Tr	Newport Co.	08.87	1987	26	0	3		
			L	Sheffield U.	03.88	1987	5	1	0		
WILLIAMS, Paul A.	London	16.08.65	Woodford T.	Charlton Ath.	02.87	1987	6	6	0	(F)	
			L	Brentford	10.87	1987	7	0	3		
WILLIAMS, Paul S.	Newton Abbot	20.02.64	Ottery St. Mary	Bristol C.	03.83	1982-83	16	3	1	(F)	
			Saltash U.	Exeter C. (N/C)	08.85	1985-87	8	10	1		
WILLIAMS, Philip D.	Swansea	24.11.66	App	Swansea C.	10.84	1983-87	42	17	5	(W)	
WILLIAMS, Steven B.	Mansfield	18.07.70	YTS	Mansfield T.	06.88	1986-87	3	5	0	(F)	
WILLIAMS, Steve C.	Hammersmith	12.07.58	App	Southampton	07.76	1975-84	277	1	18	(M)	E U21-14/
			Tr	Arsenal	12.84	1984-87	93	2	4		E-6
WILLIAMS, Terry J.	Stoke	23.10.66	App	Stoke C.	10.84	1984-86	6	5	0	(M)	
WILLIAMS, Tommy E.	Winchburgh	18.12.57	App	Leicester C.	12.75	1977-85	236	5	10	(D)	
			Tr	Birmingham C.	08.86	1986-87	62	0	1		
WILLIAMS, Wayne	Telford	17.11.63	App	Shrewsbury T.	11.81	1982-87	202	9	7	(RB)	
WILLIAMS, W.R. (Bill)	Littleborough	07.10.60	Ashe Labs	Rochdale	08.81	1981-84	89	6	2	(CD)	
			Tr	Stockport Co.	07.85	1985-87	97	0	1		
WILLIAMSON, R. (Bobby)	Glasgow	13.08.61	Glasgow Rangers	West Bromwich A.	08.86	1986-87	40	13	11	(F)	
WILLIS, Jim A.	Liverpool	12.07.68	Blackburn Rov.(YTS)	Halifax T.	08.86					(CD)	Brother of Paul
			Tr	Stockport Co.	12.87	1987	10	0	0		
			Tr	Darlington	03.88	1987	9	0	0		
WILLIS, Paul	Liverpool	24.01.70	YTS	Halifax T. (YTS)	10.86	1987	0	1	0	(F)	Brother of Jim
WILMOT, Rhys J.	Newport	21.02.62	App	Arsenal	02.80	1985-86	8	0	0	(G)	W Sch Int/W U21-6
			L	Hereford U.	03.83	1982	9	0	0		
			L	Leyton Orient	05.84	1984	46	0	0		
WILSON, Andrew	Wigan	07.01.65		Wigan Ath. (N/C)	08.87	1987	1	0	0	(M)	
WILSON, Clive A.	Manchester	13.11.61	Jnrs	Manchester C.	12.79	1981-86	107	2	9	(M/LB)	
			L	Chester C.	09.82	1982	21	0	2		
			Tr	Chelsea	05.87	1987	27	4	2		
WILSON, Danny J.	Wigan	01.01.60	Wigan Ath.	Bury	09.77	1977-79	87	3	8	(M)	NI-9
			Tr	Chesterfield	07.80	1980-82	100	0	13		
			Tr	Nottingham F.	01.83	1982	9	1	1		
			L	Scunthorpe U.	10.83	1983	6	0	3		
			Tr	Brighton & H.A.	11.83	1983-86	132	3	33		
			Tr	Luton T.	07.87	1987	38	0	8		
WILSON, Ian W.	Aberdeen	27.03.58	Elgin C.	Leicester C.	04.79	1979-87	277	8	17	(LM)	S-3
			Tr	Everton	09.87	1987	13	3	0		
WILSON, Kevin J.	Banbury	18.04.61	Banbury U.	Derby Co.	12.79	1979-84	106	16	30	(F)	NI-5
			Tr	Ipswich T.	01.85	1984-86	94	4	34		
			Tr	Chelsea	06.87	1987	16	9	5		
WILSON, Paul A.	Bradford	02.08.68	YTS	Huddersfield T.	06.86	1985-86	15	0	0	(LB)	
			Tr	Norwich C.	07.87							
			Tr	Northampton T.	02.88	1987	15	0	1		
WILSON, Phil	Hemsworth	16.10.60	App	Bolton W.	10.78	1979-80	35	4	4	(M)	
			Tr	Huddersfield T.	08.81	1981-86	229	4	16		
			Tr	York C.	08.87	1987	33	3	1		
WILSON, Robert J.	Kensington	05.06.61	App	Fulham	06.79	1979-84	168	7	34	(M)	
			Tr	Millwall	08.85	1985	28	0	12		
			Tr	Luton T.	08.86	1986-87	19	5	1		
			Tr	Fulham	09.87	1987	18	2	3		
WILSON, Terry	Broxburn	08.02.69	App	Nottingham F.	04.86	1987	33	3	5	(M)	S U21-2
WILSON, Ulrich J.	Netherlands	05.05.64	Twente Enschede	Ipswich T.	12.87	1987	5	1	0	(D)	
WIMBLETON, Paul P.	Havant	13.11.64	App	Portsmouth	02.82	1981-83	5	5	0	(M)	E Sch Int
			Tr	Cardiff C.	08.86	1986-87	83	0	17		
WINSTANLEY, Mark A.	St. Helens	22.01.68	YTS	Bolton W.	07.86	1985-87	23	1	1	(CD)	
WINTER, Julian	Huddersfield	06.09.65	App	Huddersfield T.	09.83	1984-87	54	4	3	(M)	
WINTERBURN, Nigel	Nuneaton	11.12.63	App	Birmingham C.	08.81					(LB)	E Yth Int/E U21-1
			Tr	Wimbledon	08.83	1983-86	164	1	8		
			Tr	Arsenal	05.87	1987	16	1	0		
WISE, Dennis F.	Kensington	16.12.66	Southampton(App)	Wimbledon	03.85	1984-87	55	8	14	(W)	E U21-1
WITHE, Chris	Liverpool	25.09.62	App	Newcastle U.	09.80	1980	2	0	0	(LB)	Brother of Peter
			Tr	Bradford C.	06.83	1983-87	141	2	2		
			Tr	Notts. Co.	10.87	1987	35	0	2		
WITHE, Peter	Liverpool	30.08.51		Southport	11.70	1970-71	3	0	0	(F)	E-11
			Tr	Barrow	12.71	1971	1	0	0		
			Arcadia Shep.(SA)	Wolverhampton W.	11.73	1973-74	12	5	3		
			Tr	Birmingham C.	08.75	1975-76	35	0	9		
			Tr	Nottingham F.	09.76	1976-78	74	1	28		

Players Names	Birthplace	Date	Source	League Club	Date Sign'd	Seasons Played	Apps	Sub	Gls	Pos.	Misc
WITHE, Peter (continued)			Tr	Newcastle U.	08.78	1978-79	76	0	25		
			Tr	Aston Villa	05.80	1980-84	182	0	74		
			Tr	Sheffield U.	07.85	1985-87	70	4	18		
			Tr	Birmingham C.	09.87	1987	8	0	2		
WITHERS, David R.	Pontypridd	28.04.67		Newport Co. (N/C)	10.86	1986-87	7	4	1	(F)	
WOOD, Darren	Chesterfield	14.01.68	YTS	Chesterfield	06.87	1986-87	42	3	2	(CD)	
WOOD, Darren T.	Scarborough	09.06.64	App	Middlesbrough	07.81	1981-84	101	0	6	(RB/M)	E Sch Int
			Tr	Chelsea	09.84	1984-87	113	9	2		
WOOD, George	Douglas (I.k.)	26.09.52	East Stirling	Blackpool	01.72	1971-76	117	0	0	(G)	S-4
			Tr	Everton	08.77	1977-79	103	0	0		
			Tr	Arsenal	08.80	1980-82	60	0	0		
			Tr	Crystal Palace	08.83	1983-87	192	0	0		
			Tr	Cardiff C.	01.88	1987	13	0	0		
WOOD, Nicky A.	Oldham	06.01.66	App	Manchester U.	06.83	1985-86	2	1	0	(F)	E Yth Int
WOOD, Paul	Oldham	20.03.70	YTS	Sheffield U.	06.88	1987	0	1	0	(M)	
WOOD, Paul A.	Saltburn	01.11.64	App	Portsmouth	11.82	1983-86	25	22	7	(M)	
			Tr	Brighton & H.A.	08.87	1987	26	5	4		
WOOD, Steve A.	Bracknell	02.02.63	App	Reading	02.81	1979-86	216	3	9	(CD)	
			Tr	Millwall	06.87	1987	23	0	0		
WOODCOCK, A.S. (Tony)	Nottingham	06.12.55	App	Nottingham F.	01.74	1973-79	125	4	36	(F)	E U21-2/E-42
			L	Lincoln C.	02.76	1975	2	2	1		
			L	Doncaster Rov.	09.76	1976	6	0	2		
			FC Köln(WG)	Arsenal	07.82	1982-85	129	2	56		to FC Köln 7.86
WOODS, Chris C.E.	Boston	14.11.59	App	Nottingham F.	12.76						(G)	E Yth Int/E U21-6/
			Tr	Q.P.R.	07.79	1979-80	63	0	0		E-12/to Glasgow
			Tr	Norwich C.	03.81	1980-85	216	0	0		Rangers 6.86
WOODS, Neil S.	Bradford	30.07.66	App	Doncaster Rov.	08.83	1982-86	55	10	16	(F)	
			Glasgow Rangers	Ipswich T.	07.87	1987	12	7	4		
WOODTHORPE, Colin J.	Ellesmere Port	13.01.69	YTS	Chester C.	08.86	1986-87	64	1	2	(LB)	
WORTHINGTON, Frank S.	Halifax	23.11.48	App	Huddersfield T.	11.66	1966-71	166	5	42	(F)	E U23-2/E-8/
			Tr	Leicester C.	08.72	1972-77	209	1	72		E F Lge Rep/
			Tr	Bolton W.	09.77	1977-79	81	3	35		Brother of Dave/Bob
			Tr	Birmingham C.	11.79	1979-81	71	4	30		
			Tr	Leeds U.	03.82	1981-82	32	0	14		
			Tr	Sunderland	12.82	1982	18	1	2		
			Tr	Southampton	06.83	1983	34	0	4		
			Tr	Brighton & H.A.	05.84	1984	27	4	7		
			Tr	Tranmere Rov.	06.85	1985-86	51	8	21		
			Tr	Preston N.E.	02.87	1986-87	10	13	3		
			L	Stockport Co.	11.87	1987	18	1	6		
WORTHINGTON, Gary L.	Cleethorpes	10.11.66	App	Manchester U.	11.84						(F)	E Yth Int/Son of Dave
			Tr	Huddersfield T.	07.86							
			Tr	Darlington	07.87	1987	4	5	3		
WORTHINGTON, Nigel	Ballymena (NI)	04.11.61	Ballymena U.	Notts Co.	07.81	1981-83	62	5	4	(D)	NI Yth Int/NI-21
			Tr	Sheffield Wed.	02.84	1983-87	139	1	2		
WRIGHT, Alan G.	Ashton-u-Lyne	28.09.71	Jnrs	Blackpool (Sch.)		1987	0	1	0	(M)	
WRIGHT, Darren J.	West Bromwich	14.03.68	YTS	Wolverhampton W.	07.85	1985	1	0	0	(FB)	
			Tr	Wrexham	08.86	1986-87	44	5	0		
WRIGHT, Gary	Torquay	21.05.66	Jnrs	Torquay U. (N/C)	08.84	1984	2	0	0	(RB)	
			Chard T.	Torquay U. (N/C)	08.87	1987	1	1	0		
WRIGHT, Ian E.	Woolwich	03.11.63	Greenwich Bor.	Crystal Palace	08.85	1985-87	94	17	38	(F)	
WRIGHT, Mark	Dorchester (Ox.)	01.08.63	Jnrs	Oxford U.	08.80	1981	8	2	0	(CD)	E U21-4/E-19
			Tr	Southampton	03.82	1981-86	170	0	7		
			Tr	Derby Co.	08.87	1987	38	0	3		
WRIGHT, Steve P.	Clacton	16.06.59	Jnrs	Colchester U.	06.77	1977-81	112	5	2	(D)	Son of Peter B.
			HJK Helsinki (Fin.)	Wrexham	09.83	1983-84	76	0	0		
			Tr	Torquay U.	07.85	1985	33	0	0		
			Tr	Crewe Alex.	07.86	1986-87	67	5	3		
WRIGHT, Tommy E.	Dunfermline	10.01.66	App	Leeds U.	01.83	1982-85	73	8	24	(F)	S Yth Int/
			Tr	Oldham Ath.	10.86	1986-87	68	1	15		S U21-1
WRIGHT, W. (Billy)	Liverpool	28.04.58	Jnrs	Everton	01.77	1977-82	164	2	10	(CD)	E U21-6/E-'B'
			Tr	Birmingham C.	07.83	1983-85	111	0	9		
			L	Chester C.	02.86	1985	6	0	1		
			Tr	Carlisle U.	08.86	1986-87	87	0	3		
WRIGHTSON, Jeff G.	Newcastle	18.05.68	App	Newcastle U.	05.86	1986	3	1	0	(D)	
			Tr	Preston N.E.	07.87	1987	23	2	0		
WYLDE, Rodger J.	Sheffield	08.03.54	App	Sheffield Wed.	07.71	1972-79	157	11	54	(F)	
			Tr	Oldham Ath.	02.80	1979-82	109	4	51		
			Sporting Lisbon(Port.)	Sunderland	07.84	1984	8	3	3		
			Tr	Barnsley	12.84	1984-87	50	2	19		
			L	Rotherham U.	03.88	1987	6	0	1		
YALLOP, Frank W.	Watford	04.04.64	App	Ipswich T.	01.82	1983-87	116	6	2	(RB)	E Yth Int
YATES, Dean R.	Leicester	26.10.67	App	Notts. Co.	06.85	1984-87	140	0	15	(CD)	
YATES, Mark J.	Birmingham	24.01.70	YTS	Birmingham C.	07.88	1987	1	2	0	(F)	
YATES, Steven	Bristol	29.01.70	YTS	Bristol Rov. (YTS)	07.86	1986	2	0	0	(CD)	
YOUNG, Eric	Singapore	25.03.60	Slough T.	Brighton & H.A.	11.82	1983-86	126	0	10	(CD)	
			Tr	Wimbledon	07.87	1987	28	1	3		
YOUNG, Kevin	Sunderland	12.08.61	App	Burnley	05.79	1978-83	114	6	11	(LW)	
			L	Torquay U.	11.83	1983	3	0	1		
			L	Port Vale	12.83	1983	28	0	4		
			Tr	Bury	07.84	1984-86	85	3	10		
YOUNG, Richard A.	Nottingham	18.10.68	YTS	Notts. Co.	08.86	1986	18	17	5	(F)	
			Tr	Southend U.	08.87	1987	5	2	0		
ZELEM, Peter R.	Manchester	13.02.62	App	Chester C.	02.80	1980-84	124	0	15	(CD)	
			Tr	Wolverhampton W.	01.85	1984-86	45	0	1		
			Tr	Preston N.E.	03.87	1986	6	0	1		
			Tr	Burnley	08.87	1987	9	1	1		
ZONDERVAN, Romeo	Surinam	04.03.59	Twente Enschede	West Bromwich A.	03.82	1981-83	82	2	5	(M)	Neth Int
			Tr	Ipswich T.	03.84	1983-87	145	0	10		

Mark Wright (Derby County) In action on the right while defending for Southampton against Luton's Mick Harford.　Match Magazine

Eric Young (Wimbledon) The "Dons" central defender climbs above the Watford defence to score.　Action Images Ltd

John Wark (Ipswich Town) Back after four years at Liverpool.　Match Magazine

Ronnie Whelan (Liverpool) Irish international star.　Match Magazine

Steve Williams (Arsenal) Midfield star who joined from Southampton.　Match Magazine

236

Barclays League Fixtures, 1988—89

Copyright © The Football League Limited 1988

Saturday, August 27th, 1988

Division One
Aston Villa v. Millwall
Charlton Ath. v. Liverpool
Derby Co. v. Middlesbrough
Everton v. Newcastle U.
Manchester U. v. Q.P.R.
Norwich C. v. Nottingham F.
Sheffield Wed. v. Luton T.
Southampton v. West Ham U.
Tottenham H. v. Coventry C.
Wimbledon v. Arsenal

Division Two
Brighton & H.A. v. Bradford C.
Chelsea v. Blackburn Rov.
Hull City v. Manchester C.
Leeds U. v. Oxford U.
Leicester C. v. West Bromwich A.
Oldham Ath. v. Barnsley
Shrewsbury T. v. Portsmouth
Stoke C. v. Ipswich T.
Sunderland v. Bournemouth
Swindon T. v. Crystal Palace
Walsall v. Plymouth Arg.
Watford v. Birmingham C.

Division Three
Brentford v. Huddersfield T.
Bristol Rov. v. Wigan Ath.
Bury v. Wolverhampton W.
Cardiff C. v. Fulham
Chester C. v. Blackpool
Chesterfield v. Aldershot
Gillingham v. Swansea C.
Mansfield T. v. Northampton T.
Notts Co. v. Bristol C.
Preston N.E. v. Port Vale
Reading v. Sheffield U.
Southend U. v. Bolton W.

Division Four
Burnley v. Rochdale
Cambridge U. v. Grimsby T.
Carlisle U. v. Peterborough U.
Colchester U. v. York C.
Darlington v. Stockport Co.
Exeter C. v. Wrexham
Leyton Orient v. Crewe Alex.
Lincoln C. v. Hartlepool U.
Rotherham U. v. Doncaster Rov.
Scarborough v. Tranmere Rov.
Scunthorpe U. v. Hereford U.
Torquay U. v. Halifax T.

Monday, August 29th, 1988

Division Two
Barnsley v. Swindon T.
Bradford C. v. Stoke C.
Manchester C. v. Oldham Ath.
Oxford U. v. Hull C.
Portsmouth v. Leicester C.
West Bromwich A. v. Watford

Tuesday, August 30th, 1988

Division Two
Crystal Palace v. Chelsea

Friday, September 2nd, 1988

Division Four
Tranmere Rov. v. Colchester U.

Saturday, September 3rd, 1988

Division One
Arsenal v. Aston Villa
Coventry C. v. Everton
Liverpool v. Manchester U.
Luton T. v. Wimbledon
Middlesbrough v. Norwich C.
Millwall v. Derby Co.
Newcastle U. v. Tottenham H.
Nottingham F. v. Sheffield Wed.
Q.P.R. v. Southampton
West Ham U. v. Charlton Ath.

Division Two
Bournemouth v. Chelsea
Barnsley v. Stoke C.
Birmingham C. v. Leicester C.
Blackburn Rov. v. Oldham Ath.
Bradford C. v. Shrewsbury T.
Crystal Palace v. Watford
Ipswich T. v. Sunderland
Manchester C. v. Walsall
Oxford U. v. Brighton & H.A.
Plymouth Arg. v. Hull C.
Portsmouth v. Leeds U.
West Bromwich A. v. Swindon T.

Division Three
Aldershot v. Gillingham
Blackpool v. Notts. Co.
Bolton W. v. Cardiff C.
Bristol C. v. Chesterfield
Fulham v. Southend U.
Huddersfield T. v. Preston N.E.
Northampton T. v. Brentford
Port Vale v. Chester C.
Sheffield U. v. Bristol Rov.
Swansea C. v. Bury
Wigan Ath. v. Mansfield T.
Wolverhampton W. v. Reading

Division Four
Crewe Alex. v. Scunthorpe U.
Doncaster Rov. v. Exeter C.
Grimsby T. v. Torquay U.
Halifax T. v. Burnley
Hartlepool U. v. Darlington
Hereford U. v. Cambridge U.
Peterborough U. v. Scarborough
Rochdale v. Rotherham U.
Stockport Co. v. Leyton Orient
Wrexham v. Lincoln C.
York C. v. Carlisle U.

Friday, September 9th, 1988

Division Three
Southend U. v. Swansea C.

Division Four
Colchester U. v. Doncaster Rov.

Saturday, September 10th, 1988

Division One
Aston Villa v. Liverpool
Charlton Ath. v. Millwall
Derby Co. v. Newcastle U.
Everton v. Nottingham F.
Manchester U. v. Middlesbrough
Norwich C. v. Q.P.R.
Sheffield Wed. v. Coventry C.
Southampton v. Luton T.
Tottenham H. v. Arsenal
Wimbledon v. West Ham U.

Division Two
Brighton & H.A. v. Bournemouth
Chelsea v. Oxford U.
Hull C. v. Barnsley
Leeds U. v. Manchester C.
Leicester C. v. Ipswich T.
Oldham Ath. v. Birmingham C.
Shrewsbury T. v. West Bromwich A.
Stoke C. v. Blackburn Rov.
Sunderland v. Bradford C.
Walsall v. Crystal Palace
Watford v. Plymouth Arg.

Division Three
Brentford v. Wigan Ath.
Bristol Rov. v. Aldershot
Bury v. Port Vale
Cardiff C. v. Huddersfield T.
Chester C. v. Bristol C.
Chesterfield v. Wolverhampton W.
Gillingham v. Sheffield U.
Mansfield T. v. Fulham
Notts Co. v. Northampton T.
Preston N.E. v. Blackpool
Reading v. Bolton W.

Division Four
Burnley v. York C.
Cambridge U. v. Stockport Co.
Carlisle U. v. Tranmere Rov.
Darlington v. Peterborough U.
Exeter C. v. Halifax T.
Leyton Orient v. Hereford U.
Lincoln C. v. Crewe Alex.
Rotherham U. v. Wrexham
Scarborough v. Rochdale
Scunthorpe U. v. Grimsby T.
Torquay U. v. Hartlepool U.

Sunday, September 11th, 1988

Division Two
Swindon T. v. Portsmouth

Friday, September 16th, 1988

Division Four
Halifax T. v. Carlisle U.
Stockport Co. v. Burnley
Tranmere Rov. v. Cambridge U.
Wrexham v. Colchester U.

Saturday, September 17th, 1988

Division One
Arsenal v. Southampton
Coventry C. v. Charlton Ath.
Liverpool v. Tottenham H.
Luton T. v. Manchester U.
Middlesbrough v. Wimbledon
Millwall v. Everton
Newcastle U. v. Norwich C.
Nottingham F. v. Derby Co.
Q.P.R. v. Sheffield Wed.
West Ham U. v. Aston Villa

Division Two
Bournemouth v. Leeds U.
Barnsley v. Chelsea
Birmingham C. v. Sunderland
Blackburn Rov. v. Swindon T.
Bradford C. v. Oldham Ath.
Crystal Palace v. Shrewsbury T.
Ipswich T. v. Watford
Manchester C. v. Brighton & H.A.
Oxford U. v. Leicester C.
Plymouth Arg. v. Stoke C.
Portsmouth v. Hull C.
West Bromwich A. v. Walsall

Division Three
Aldershot v. Southend U.
Blackpool v. Mansfield T.
Bolton W. v. Bristol Rov.
Bristol C. v. Preston N.E.
Fulham v. Bury
Huddersfield T. v. Gillingham
Northampton T. v. Chesterfield
Port Vale v. Cardiff C.
Sheffield U. v. Chester C.
Swansea C. v. Brentford
Wigan Ath. v. Reading
Wolverhampton W. v. Notts Co.

Division Four
Crewe Alex. v. Darlington
Doncaster Rov. v. Torquay U.
Grimsby T. v. Rotherham U.
Hartlepool U. v. Leyton Orient
Hereford U. v. Scarborough
Peterborough U. v. Lincoln C.
Rochdale v. Exeter C.
York C. v. Scunthorpe U.

Monday, September 19th, 1988

Division Three
Port Vale v. Chesterfield

Division Four
Stockport Co. v. Halifax T.
Tranmere Rov. v. Peterborough U.

Tuesday, September 20th, 1988

Division Two
Chelsea v. Manchester C.
Hull C. v. Blackburn Rov.
Oldham Ath. v. Oxford U.
Shrewsbury T. v. Ipswich T.
Stoke C. v. Portsmouth
Sunderland v. Crystal Palace
Swindon T. v. Bournemouth
Walsall v. Birmingham C.
Watford v. Bradford C.

Division Three
Blackpool v. Bristol C.
Bolton W. v. Fulham
Cardiff C. v. Bury
Huddersfield T. v. Notts Co.
Mansfield T. v. Gillingham
Preston N.E. v. Chester C.
Sheffield U. v. Northampton T.
Wigan Ath. v. Swansea C.
Wolverhampton W. v. Aldershot

Division Four
Cambridge U. v. Lincoln C.
Colchester U. v. Scarborough
Darlington v. Exeter C.
Rochdale v. Doncaster Rov.
Rotherham U. v. Leyton Orient
Scunthorpe U. v. Carlisle U.
Torquay U. v. Burnley
Wrexham v. Grimsby T.
York C. v. Hartlepool U.

Wednesday, September 21st, 1988

Division Two
Brighton & H.A. v. West Bromwich A.
Leeds U. v. Barnsley
Leicester C. v. Plymouth Arg.

Division Three
Bristol Rov. v. Brentford
Reading v. Southend U.

Division Four
Hereford U. v. Crewe Alex.

Friday, September 23rd, 1988

Division Four
Crewe Alex. v. Stockport Co.
Halifax T. v. Tranmere Rov.
Leyton Orient v. Darlington

Saturday, September 24th, 1988

Division One
Aston Villa v. Nottingham F.
Charlton Ath. v. Newcastle U.
Derby Co. v. Q.P.R.
Everton v. Luton T.
Manchester U. v. West Ham U.
Norwich C. v. Millwall
Sheffield Wed. v. Arsenal
Southampton v. Liverpool
Tottenham H. v. Middlesbrough
Wimbledon v. Coventry C.

Division Two
Bournemouth v. Oxford U.
Barnsley v. Manchester C.
Blackburn Rov. v. Birmingham C.
Ipswich T. v. Bradford C.
Leeds U. v. Chelsea
Leicester C. v. Watford
Oldham Ath. v Hull C.
Plymouth Arg. v. West Bromwich A.
Portsmouth v. Crystal Palace
Shrewsbury T. v. Sunderland
Swindon T. v. Brighton & H.A.
Walsall v. Stoke C.

Division Three
Aldershot v. Bolton W.
Brentford v. Sheffield U.
Bristol C. v. Port Vale
Bury v. Mansfield T.
Chester C. v. Huddersfield T.
Chesterfield v. Blackpool
Fulham v. Wigan Ath.
Gillingham v. Reading
Northampton T. v. Bristol Rov.
Notts Co. v. Preston N.E.
Southend U. v. Cardiff C.
Swansea C. v. Wolverhampton W.

Division Four
Burnley v. Colchester U.
Carlisle U. v. Rotherham U.
Doncaster Rov. v. Wrexham
Exeter C. v. Scunthorpe U.
Grimsby T. v. Rochdale
Hartlepool U. v. Cambridge U.
Lincoln C. v. Hereford U.
Peterborough U. v. York C.
Scarborough v. Torquay U.

Friday, September 30th, 1988

Division Three
Wigan Ath. v. Blackpool

Division Four
Cambridge U. v. Carlisle U.
Tranmere Rov. v. Hartlepool U.

Saturday, October 1st, 1988

Division One
Coventry C. v. Middlesbrough
Liverpool v. Newcastle U.
Millwall v. Q.P.R.
Norwich C. v. Charlton Ath.
Nottingham F. v. Luton T.
Sheffield Wed. v. Aston Villa
Southampton v. Derby Co.
Tottenham H. v Manchester U.
West Ham U. v. Arsenal
Wimbledon v. Everton

Division Two
Birmingham C. v. Barnsley
Bradford C. v. Portsmouth
Brighton & H.A. v. Leeds U.
Chelsea v. Leicester C.
Crystal Palace v. Plymouth Arg.
Hull C. v. Walsall
Manchester C. v. Blackburn Rov.
Oxford U. v. Shrewsbury T.
Stoke C. v. Bournemouth
Sunderland v. Oldham Ath.
Watford v. Swindon T.
West Bromwich A. v. Ipswich T.

Division Three
Bolton W. v. Sheffield U.
Brentford v. Gillingham
Bristol C. v. Swansea C.
Cardiff C. v. Bristol Rov.
Chesterfield v. Bury
Huddersfield T. v. Fulham
Mansfield T. v. Notts Co.
Northampton T. v. Aldershot
Preston N.E. v. Southend U.
Reading v. Chester C.
Wolverhampton W. v. Port Vale

Division Four
Colchester U. v. Lincoln C.
Darlington v. Burnley
Hereford U. v. Grimsby T.
Rochdale v. Crewe Alex.
Rotherham U. v. Exeter C.
Scunthorpe U. v. Scarborough
Stockport Co. v. Doncaster Rov.
Torquay U. v. Leyton Orient
Wrexham v. Peterborough U.
York C. v. Halifax T.

Monday, October 3rd, 1988

Division Three
Port Vale v. Huddersfield T.

Tuesday, October 4th, 1988

Division Two
Birmingham C. v. Plymouth Arg.
Chelsea v. Walsall
Crystal Palace v. Ipswich T.
Hull C. v. Leicester C.
Stoke C. v. Shrewsbury T.
Sunderland v. Leeds U.
Watford v. Oldham Ath.

Division Three
Aldershot v. Wigan Ath.
Blackpool v. Northampton T.
Bury v. Reading
Gillingham v. Bristol C.
Notts Co. v. Chesterfield
Southend U. v. Mansfield T.
Swansea C. v. Bolton W.

Division Four
Burnley v. Rotherham U.
Carlisle U. v. Colchester U.
Crewe Alex. v. Cambridge U.
Doncaster Rov. v. Hereford U.
Grimsby T. v. Tranmere Rov.
Halifax T. v. Wrexham
Hartlepool U. v. Rochdale
Leyton Orient v. York C.

Wednesday, October 5th, 1988

Division Two
Bradford C. v. Blackburn Rov.
Brighton & H.A. v. Barnsley
Manchester C. v. Portsmouth
Oxford U. v. Swindon T.
West Bromwich A. v. Bournemouth

Division Three
Bristol Rov. v. Preston N.E.
Chester C. v. Brentford
Fulham v. Wolverhampton W.

Division Four
Exeter C. v. Torquay U.
Lincoln C. v. Scunthorpe U.
Peterborough U. v. Stockport Co.
Scarborough v. Darlington

Friday, October 7th, 1988

Division Four
Tranmere Rov. v. York C.

Saturday, October 8th, 1988

Division One
Arsenal v. Millwall
Aston Villa v. Wimbledon
Charlton Ath. v. Tottenham H.
Derby Co. v. Norwich C.
Everton v. Southampton
Luton T. v. Liverpool
Manchester U. v. Sheffield Wed.
Middlesbrough v. West Ham U.
Newcastle U. v. Coventry C.
Q.P.R. v. Nottingham F.

Division Two
Bournemouth v. Birmingham C.
Barnsley v. West Bromwich A.
Blackburn Rov. v. Crystal Palace
Ipswich T. v. Manchester C.
Leeds U. v. Watford
Leicester C. v. Brighton & H.A.
Oldham Ath. v. Stoke C.
Plymouth v. Bradford C.
Portsmouth v. Oxford U.
Shrewsbury T. v. Hull C.
Walsall v. Sunderland

Division Three
Bolton W. v. Blackpool
Bristol C. v. Fulham
Cardiff C. v. Reading
Gillingham v. Chesterfield
Mansfield T. v. Bristol Rov.
Northampton T. v. Huddersfield T.
Preston N.E. v. Bury
Sheffield U. v. Wolverhampton W.
Wigan Ath. v. Port Vale

Division Four
Burnley v. Exeter C.
Cambridge U. v. Halifax T.
Colchester U. v. Scunthorpe U.
Darlington v. Rotherham U.
Doncaster Rov. v. Hartlepool U.
Grimsby T. v. Peterborough U.
Hereford U. v. Carlisle U.
Rochdale v. Stockport Co.
Scarborough v. Leyton Orient
Torquay U. v. Lincoln C.
Wrexham v. Crewe Alex.

Sunday, October 9th, 1988

Division Two
Swindon T. v. Chelsea

Division Three
Aldershot v. Swansea C.
Brentford v. Southend U.
Notts Co. v. Chester C.

Friday, October 14th, 1988

Division Four
Halifax T. v. Rochdale

Saturday, October 15th, 1988

Division One
Charlton Ath. v. Aston Villa
Coventry C. v. Millwall
Everton v. Derby Co.
Luton T. v. Arsenal
Manchester U. v. Norwich C.
Newcastle U. v. Middlesbrough
Nottingham F. v. Liverpool
Q.P.R v. West Ham U.
Sheffield Wed. v. Wimbledon
Tottenham H. v. Southampton

Division Two
Birmingham C. v. West Bromwich A.
Blackburn Rov. v. Barnsley
Bradford C. v. Crystal Palace
Hull C. v. Sunderland
Ipswich T. v. Oxford U.
Leicester C. v. Stoke C.
Oldham Ath. v. Chelsea
Plymouth Arg. v. Manchester C.
Portsmouth v. Bournemouth
Shrewsbury T. v. Walsall
Watford v. Brighton & H.A.

Division Three
Blackpool v. Sheffield U.
Bristol Rov. v. Notts Co.
Bury v. Brentford
Chester C. v. Cardiff C.
Chesterfield v. Preston N.E.
Fulham v. Aldershot
Huddersfield T. v. Bristol C.
Port Vale v. Bolton W.
Reading v. Mansfield T.
Southend U. v. Gillingham
Swansea C. v. Northampton T.
Wolverhampton W. v. Wigan Ath.

Division Four
Carlisle U. v. Torquay U.
Crewe Alex. v. Doncaster Rov.
Exeter C. v. Grimsby T.
Hartlepool U. v. Wrexham
Leyton Orient v. Colchester U.
Lincoln C. v. Scarborough
Peterborough U. v. Burnley
Rotherham U. v. Tranmere Rov.
Scunthorpe U. v. Cambridge U.
Stockport Co. v. Hereford U.
York C. v. Darlington

Sunday, October 16th, 1988

Division Two
Swindon T. v. Leeds U.

Friday, October 21st, 1988

Division Four
Colchester U. v. Cambridge U.
Doncaster Rov. v. Halifax T.

Saturday, October 22nd, 1988

Arsenal v. Q.P.R.
Aston Villa v. Everton
Derby Co. v. Charlton Ath.
Liverpool v. Coventry C.
Middlesbrough v. Luton T.
Millwall v. Nottingham F.
Norwich C. v. Tottenham H.

Southampton v. Sheffield Wed.
West Ham U. v. Newcastle U.
Wimbledon v. Manchester U.

Division Two
Bournemouth v. Shrewsbury T.
Barnsley v. Ipswich T.
Brighton & H.A. v. Oldham Ath.
Chelsea v. Plymouth Arg.
Crystal Palace v. Hull C.
Leicester C. v. Leicester C.
Manchester C. v. Birmingham C.
Oxford U. v. Blackburn Rov.
Stoke C. v. Watford.
Sunderland v. Swindon T.
Walsall v. Portsmouth
West Bromwich A. v. Bradford C.

Division Three
Aldershot v. Huddersfield T.
Blackpool v. Port Vale
Bolton W. v. Wolverhampton W.
Brentford v. Preston. N.E.
Bristol Rov. v. Chester C.
Gillingham v. Bury
Mansfield T. v. Cardiff C.
Northampton T. v. Bristol C.
Notts Co. v. Reading
Sheffield U. v. Wigan Ath.
Southend U. v. Chesterfield
Swansea C. v. Fulham

Division Four
Burnley v. Leyton Orient
Exeter C. v. Carlisle U.
Grimsby T. v. York C.
Hartlepool U. v. Crewe Alex.
Lincoln C. v. Darlington
Peterborough U. v. Hereford U.
Rochdale v. Scunthorpe U.
Scarborough v. Stockport Co.
Torquay U. v. Rotherham U.
Wrexham v. Tranmere Rov.

Monday, October 24th, 1988

Division Three
Port Vale v. Sheffield U.

Division Four
Stockport Co. v. Hartlepool U.
Tranmere Rov. v. Lincoln C.

Tuesday, October 25th, 1988

Division Two
Birmingham C. v. Stoke C.
Crystal Palace v. Oxford U.
Hull C. v. Chelsea
Ipswich T. v. Portsmouth
Oldham Ath. v. Bournemouth
Plymouth Arg. v. Shrewsbury T.
Sunderland v. Blackburn Rov.
Watford v. Barnsley

Division Three
Bristol C. v. Aldershot
Bury v. Southend U.
Cardiff C. v. Notts Co.
Chesterfield v. Brentford
Fulham v. Northampton T.
Huddersfield T. v. Swansea C.
Preston N.E. v. Gillingham
Wigan Ath. v. Bolton W.
Wolverhampton W. v. Blackpool

Division Four
Cambridge U. v. Scarborough
Carlisle U. v. Burnley
Crewe Alex. v. Grimsby T.
Darlington v. Torquay U.
Halifax T. v. Peterborough U.
Leyton Orient v. Exeter C.
Rotherham U. v. Colchester U.
Scunthorpe U. v. Wrexham
York C. v. Doncaster Rov.

Wednesday, October 26th, 1988

Division Two
Bradford C. v. Leeds U.
Brighton & H.A. v. Walsall
Leicester C. v. Swindon T.
West Bromwich A. v. Manchester C.

Division Three
Chester C. v. Mansfield T.
Reading v. Bristol Rov.

Division Four
Hereford U. v. Rochdale

Friday, October 28th, 1988

Division Three
Southend U. v. Wigan Ath.

Division Four
Colchester U. v. Stockport Co.

Saturday, October 29th, 1988

Division One
Arsenal v. Coventry C.
Aston Villa v. Tottenham H.
Charlton Ath. v. Sheffield Wed.
Derby Co. v. Wimbledon
Everton v. Manchester U.
Luton T. v. Q.P.R.
Middlesbrough v. Millwall
Newcastle U. v. Nottingham F.
Norwich C. v. Southampton
West Ham U. v. Liverpool

Division Two
A.F.C Bournemouth v. Ipswich T.
Barnsley v. Plymouth Arg.
Blackburn Rov. v. West Bromwich A.
Chelsea v. Brighton & H.A.
Leeds U. v. Hull C.
Manchester C. v. Sunderland
Oxford U. v. Bradford C.
Portsmouth v. Oldham Ath.
Shrewsbury T. v. Leicester C.
Stoke C. v. Crystal Palace
Swindon T. v. Birmingham C.
Walsall v. Watford

Division Three
Aldershot v. Chester C.
Blackpool v. Cardiff C.
Bolton W. v. Chesterfield
Brentford v. Port Vale
Bristol Rov. v. Huddersfield T.
Gillingham v. Wolverhampton W.
Mansfield T. v. Bristol C.
Northampton T. v. Reading
Notts Co. v. Fulham
Sheffield U. v. Bury
Swansea C. v. Preston N.E.

Division Four
Burnley v. Cambridge U.
Doncaster Rov. v. Leyton Orient
Exeter C. v. Crewe Alex.
Grimsby T. v. Halifax T.

Hartlepool U. v. Hereford U.
Lincoln C. v. Carlisle U.
Peterborough U. v. Scunthorpe U.
Rochdale v. Darlington
Scarborough v. Rotherham U.
Torquay U. v. Tranmere Rov.
Wrexham v. York C.

Tuesday, November 1st 1988

Division Three
Sheffield U. v. Cardiff C.

Wednesday, November 2nd, 1988

Division Two
Oxford U. v. Sunderland

Friday, November 4th, 1988

Division Four
Cambridge U. v. Exeter C.
Crewe Alex. v. Colchester U.
Halifax T. v. Hartlepool U.
Tranmere Rov. v. Rochdale

Saturday, November 5th, 1988

Division One
Coventry C. v. West Ham U.
Liverpool v. Middlesbrough
Manchester U. v. Aston Villa
Millwall v. Luton T.
Nottingham F. v. Arsenal
Q.P.R. v. Newcastle U.
Sheffield Wed. v. Everton
Southampton v. Charlton Ath.
Tottenham H. v. Derby Co.
Wimbledon v. Norwich C.

Division Two
Birmingham C. v. Portsmouth
Bradford C. v. Bournemouth
Brighton & H.A. v. Shrewsbury T.
Crystal Palace v. Barnsley
Hull C. v. Swindon T.
Ipswich T. v. Leeds U.
Leicester C. v. Manchester C.
Oldham Ath. v. Walsall
Plymouth Arg. v. Blackburn Rov.
Sunderland v. Oxford U.
Watford v. Chelsea
West Bromwich A. v. Oxford U.

Division Three
Bristol C. v. Bolton W.
Bury v. Notts Co.
Cardiff C. v. Gillingham
Chester C. v. Swansea C.
Chesterfield v. Bristol Rov.
Fulham v. Blackpool
Huddersfield T. v. Sheffield U.
Port Vale v. Aldershot
Preston N.E. v. Mansfield T.
Reading v. Brentford
Wigan Ath. v. Northampton T.
Wolverhampton W. v. Southend U.

Division Four
Carlisle U. v. Scarborough
Darlington v. Doncaster Rov.
Hereford U. v. Wrexham
Leyton Orient v. Peterborough U.
Rotherham U. v. Lincoln C.
Scunthorpe U. v. Burnley
Stockport Co. v. Grimsby T.
York C. v. Torquay U.

Monday, November 7th, 1988

Division Four
Tranmere Rov. v. Hereford U.

Tuesday, November 8th, 1988

Division Two
Ipswich T. v. Walsall

Division Three
Aldershot v. Sheffield U.
Brentford v. Notts Co.
Bristol C. v. Wolverhampton W.
Bury v. Chester C.
Chesterfield v. Cardiff C.
Fulham v. Reading
Gillingham v. Blackpool
Huddersfield T. v. Bolton W.
Northampton T. v. Port Vale
Preston N.E. v. Wigan Ath.
Southend U. v. Bristol Rov.
Swansea C. v. Mansfield T.

Division Four
Burnley v. Lincoln C.
Darlington v. Cambridge U.
Grimsby T. v. Doncaster Rov.
Halifax T. v. Colchester U.
Leyton Orient v. Carlisle U.
Rotherham U. v. Scunthorpe U.
Torquay U. v. Rochdale
Wrexham v. Stockport Co.
York C. v. Crewe Alex.

Wednesday, November 9th, 1988

Division Four
Exeter C. v. Scarborough
Peterborough U. v. Hartlepool U.

Friday, November 11th, 1988

Division Three
Shrewsbury T. v. Oldham Ath.

Division Four
Colchester U. v. Torquay U.
Stockport Co. v. York C.

Saturday, November 12, 1988

Division One
Charlton Ath. v. Everton
Coventry C. v. Luton T.
Derby Co. v. Manchester U.
Liverpool v. Millwall
Middlesbrough v. Q.P.R.
Newcastle U. v. Arsenal
Norwich C. v. Sheffield Wed.
Southampton v. Aston Villa
Tottenham H. v. Wimbledon
West Ham U. v. Nottingham F.

Division Two
Bournemouth v. Crystal Palace
Barnsley v. Bradford C.
Blackburn Rov. v. Brighton & H.A.
Chelsea v. Sunderland
Leeds U. v. West Bromwich A.
Manchester C. v. Watford
Oxford U. v. Birmingham C.
Portsmouth v. Plymouth Arg.
Swindon T. v. Ipswich T.
Walsall v. Leicester C.

Division Three
Blackpool v. Aldershot
Bolton W. v. Bury
Bristol Rov. v. Gillingham
Cardiff C. v. Northampton T.
Chester C. v. Chesterfield
Mansfield T. v. Brentford
Notts Co. v. Southend U.
Port Vale v. Swansea C.
Reading v. Preston N.E.
Sheffield U. v. Fulham
Wigan Ath. v. Bristol C.
Wolverhampton W. v. Huddersfield T.

Division Four
Cambridge U. v. Rotherham U.
Carlisle U. v. Darlington
Crewe Alex. v. Tranmere Rov.
Doncaster Rov. v. Peterborough U.
Hartlepool U. v. Halifax T.
Hereford U. v. Halifax T.
Lincoln C. v. Exeter C.
Rochdale v. Wrexham
Scarborough v. Burnley
Scunthorpe U. v. Leyton Orient

Sunday, November 13th, 1988

Division Two
Stoke C. v. Hull C.

Saturday, November 19th, 1988

Division One
Arsenal v. Middlesbrough
Aston Villa v. Derby Co.
Everton v. Norwich C.
Luton T. v. West Ham U.
Manchester U. v. Southampton
Millwall v. Newcastle U.
Nottingham F. v. Coventry C.
Q.P.R. v. Liverpool
Sheffield Wed. v. Tottenham H.
Wimbledon v. Charlton Ath.

Division Two
Bournemouth v. Manchester C.
Bradford C. v. Chelsea
Crystal Palace v. Leicester C.
Hull C. v. Birmingham C.
Ipswich T. v. Brighton & H.A.
Oldham Ath. v. Leeds U.
Oxford U. v. Plymouth Arg.
Portsmouth v. Barnsley
Shrewsbury T. v. Watford
Stoke C. v. Swindon T.
Sunderland v. West Bromwich A.
Walsall v. Blackburn Rov.

Division Three
Bristol C. v. Bolton W.
Bury v. Notts Co.
Cardiff C. v. Gillingham
Chester C. v. Swansea C.
Chesterfield v. Bristol Rov.
Fulham v. Blackpool
Huddersfield T. v. Sheffield U.
Port Vale v. Aldershot
Preston N.E. v. Mansfield T.
Reading v. Brentford
Wigan Ath. v. Northampton T.
Wolverhampton W. v. Southend U.

Division Four
Carlisle U. v. Scarborough
Darlington v. Doncaster Rov.
Hereford U. v. Wrexham
Leyton Orient v. Peterborough U.
Rotherham U. v. Lincoln C.
Scunthorpe U. v. Burnley
Stockport Co. v. Grimsby T.
York C. v. Torquay U.

Tuesday, November 22nd, 1988

Division One
Birmingham C. v. Leeds U.
Blackburn Rov. v. Shrewsbury T.

Friday, November 25th, 1988

Division Four
Colchester U. v. Darlington
Crewe Alex. v. Peterborough U.
Stockport Co. v. Tranmere Rov.

Saturday, November 26th, 1988

Division One
Charlton Ath. v. Nottingham F.
Coventry C. v. Aston Villa
Derby Co. v. Arsenal
Liverpool v. Wimbledon
Middlesbrough v. Sheffield Wed.
Newcastle U. v. Manchester U.
Norwich C. v. Luton T.
Southampton v. Millwall
Tottenham H. v. Q.P.R.
West Ham U. v. Everton

Division Two
Barnsley v. Bournemouth
Birmingham C. v. Ipswich T.
Blackburn Rov. v. Portsmouth
Brighton & H.A. v. Sunderland
Chelsea v. Shrewsbury T.
Leeds U. v. Stoke C.
Leicester C. v. Bradford C.
Manchester C. v. Oxford U.
Plymouth Arg. v. Oldham Ath.
Swindon T. v. Walsall
Watford v. Hull C.
West Bromwich A. v. Crystal Palace

Division Three
Blackpool v. Swansea C.
Bolton W. v. Northampton T.
Bristol Rov. v. Bury
Cardiff C. v. Brentford
Chester C. v. Southend U.
Mansfield T. v. Aldershot
Notts Co. v. Gillingham
Port Vale v. Fulham
Reading v. Chesterfield
Sheffield U. v. Bristol C.
Wigan Ath. v. Huddersfield T.
Wolverhampton W. v. Preston N.E.

Division Four
Cambridge U. v. Leyton Orient
Carlisle U. v. Grimsby T.
Doncaster Rov. v. Burnley
Hartlepool U. v. Exeter C.
Hereford U. v. Rotherham U.
Lincoln C. v. Halifax T.
Rochdale v. York C.
Scarborough v. Wrexham
Scunthorpe U. v. Torquay U.

Tuesday, November 29th, 1988

Division Two
Bournemouth v. Hull C.

Friday, December 2nd, 1988

Division Three
Southend U. v. Port Vale

Division Four
Halifax T. v. Crewe Alex.
Torquay U. v. Cambridge U.
Tranmere Rov. v. Doncaster Rov.

Saturday, December 3rd, 1988

Division One
Arsenal v. Liverpool
Aston Villa v. Norwich C.
Everton v. Tottenham H.
Luton T. v. Newcastle U.
Manchester U. v. Charlton Ath.
Millwall v. West Ham U.
Nottingham F. v. Middlesbrough
Q.P.R. v. Coventry C.
Sheffield Wed. v. Derby Co.
Wimbledon v. Southampton

Division Two
A.F.C Bournemouth v. Blackburn Rov.
Bradford C. v. Birmingham C.
Crystal Palace v. Manchester C.
Hull C. v. Brighton & H.A.
Ipswich T. v. Plymouth Arg.
Oldham Ath. v. Leicester C.
Oxford U. v. Barnsley
Portsmouth v. West Bromwich A.
Shrewsbury T. v. Swindon T.
Stoke C. v. Chelsea
Sunderland v. Watford
Walsall v. Leeds U.

Division Three
Aldershot v. Notts Co.
Brentford v. Bolton W.
Bristol C. v. Reading
Bury v. Wigan Ath.
Chesterfield v. Mansfield T.
Fulham v. Bristol Rov.
Gillingham v. Chester C.
Huddersfield T. v. Blackpool
Preston N.E. v. Cardiff C.
Swansea C. v. Sheffield U.

Division Four
Burnley v. Hartlepool U.
Darlington v. Scunthorpe U.
Exeter C. v. Colchester U.
Grimsby T. v. Scarborough
Leyton Orient v. Lincoln C.
Peterborough U. v. Rochdale
Rotherham U. v. Stockport Co.
Wrexham v. Carlisle U.
York C. v. Hereford U.

Sunday, December 4th, 1988

Division Three
Northampton T. v. Wolverhampton W.

Tuesday, December 6th, 1988

Division Two
Plymouth Arg. v. Brighton & H.A.

Saturday, December 10th, 1988

Division One
Charlton Ath. v. Q.P.R.
Coventry C. v. Manchester U.
Derby Co. v. Luton T.
Liverpool v. Everton
Middlesbrough v. Wimbledon
Newcastle U. v. Wimbledon
Norwich C. v. Arsenal
Southampton v. Nottingham F.
Tottenham H. v. Millwall
West Ham U. v. Sheffield Wed.

Division Two
Barnsley v. Walsall
Birmingham C. v. Crystal Palace
Blackburn Rov. v. Ipswich T.
Brighton & H.A. v. Stoke C.
Chelsea v. Portsmouth
Leeds U. v. Shrewsbury T.
Leicester C. v. Sunderland
Manchester C. v. Bradford C.
Plymouth Arg. v. Bournemouth
Swindon T. v. Oldham Ath.
Watford v. Oxford U.
West Bromwich A. v. Hull C.

Friday, December 16th, 1988

Division Two
Birmingham C. v. Chelsea
Ipswich T. v. Oldham Ath.

Division Four
Crewe Alex. v. Torquay U.
Halifax T. v. Rotherham U.
Rochdale v. Colchester U.
Tranmere Rov. v. Darlington
Wrexham v. Cambridge U.
York C. v. Rotherham U.

Saturday, December 17th, 1988

Division One
Arsenal v. Manchester U.
Coventry C. v. Derby Co.
Liverpool v. Norwich C.
Luton T. v. Aston Villa
Middlesbrough v. Charlton Ath.
Millwall v. Sheffield Wed.
Newcastle U. v. Southampton
Q.P.R. v. Everton
West Ham U. v. Tottenham H.

Division Two
Bournemouth v. Walsall
Barnsley v. Leicester C.
Blackburn Rov. v. Watford
Bradford C. v. Swindon T.
Crystal Palace v. Leeds U.
Manchester C. v. Shrewsbury T.
Portsmouth v. Brighton & H.A.

Division Three
Blackpool v. Bristol Rov.
Bolton W. v. Chester C.
Bristol C. v. Cardiff C.
Fulham v. Preston N.E.
Huddersfield T. v. Bury
Port Vale v. Reading
Sheffield U. v. Southend U.
Swansea C. v. Chesterfield
Wolverhampton W. v. Mansfield T.

Division Four
Doncaster Rov. v. Scunthorpe U.
Grimsby T. v. Leyton Orient
Hartlepool U. v. Carlisle U.
Hereford U. v. Burnley
Peterborough U. v. Exeter C.
Stockport Co. v. Lincoln C.

Sunday, December 18th, 1988

Division One
Nottingham F. v. Wimbledon

Division Two
Plymouth Arg. v. Sunderland
West Bromwich A. v. Stoke C.

Division Three
Aldershot v. Brentford
Northampton T. v. Gillingham
Wigan Ath. v. Notts Co.

Monday, December 26th, 1988

Division One
Aston Villa v. Q.P.R.
Charlton Ath. v. Arsenal
Derby Co. v. Liverpool
Everton v. Middlesbrough
Manchester U. v. Nottingham F.
Norwich C. v. West Ham U.
Sheffield Wed. v. Newcastle U.

Southampton v. Coventry C.
Tottenham H. v. Luton T.
Wimbledon v. Millwall

Division Two
Brighton & H.A. v. Crystal Palace
Chelsea v. Ipswich T.
Hull C. v. Bradford C.
Leeds U. v. Blackburn Rov.
Leicester C. v. Bournemouth
Oldham Ath. v. West Bromwich A.
Shrewsbury T. v. Birmingham C.
Stoke C. v. Manchester C.
Sunderland v. Barnsley
Swindon T. v. Plymouth Arg.
Walsall v. Oxford U.
Watford v. Portsmouth

Division Three
Brentford v. Blackpool
Bristol Rov. v. Wolverhampton W.
Bury v. Bristol C.
Cardiff C. v. Swansea C.
Chester C. v. Wigan Ath.
Chesterfield v. Huddersfield T.
Gillingham v. Fulham
Mansfield T. v. Port Vale
Notts Co. v. Sheffield U.
Preston N.E. v. Bolton W.
Reading v. Aldershot
Southend U. v. Northampton T.

Division Four
Burnley v. Wrexham
Cambridge U. v. Doncaster Rov.
Carlisle U. v. Rochdale
Colchester U. v. Peterborough U.
Darlington v. Halifax T.
Exeter C. v. Hereford U.
Leyton Orient v. Tranmere Rov.
Lincoln C. v. Grimsby T.
Rotherham U. v. Crewe Alex.
Scarborough v. York C.
Scunthorpe U. v. Hartlepool U.
Torquay U. v. Stockport Co.

Wednesday, December 28th, 1988

Division Four
Lincoln C. v. Doncaster Rov.

Friday, December 30th, 1988

Division Two
Oldham Ath. v. Crystal Palace

Division Three
Cardiff C. v. Wigan Ath.
Gillingham v. Port Vale
Reading v. Blackpool

Division Four
Cambridge U. v. Rochdale
Colchester U. v. Hartlepool U.

Saturday, December 31st, 1988

Division One
Aston Villa v. Arsenal
Charlton Ath. v. West Ham U.
Derby Co. v. Millwall
Everton v. Coventry C.
Manchester U. v. Liverpool
Norwich C. v. Middlesbrough
Sheffield Wed. v. Nottingham F.
Southampton v. Q.P.R.
Tottenham H. v. Newcastle U.
Wimbledon v. Luton T.

Division Two
Brighton & H.A. v. Birmingham C.
Chelsea v. West Bromwich A.
Hull C. v. Ipswich T.
Leeds U. v. Plymouth Arg.
Leicester C. v. Blackburn Rov.
Shrewsbury T. v. Barnsley
Stoke C. v. Oxford U.
Sunderland v. Portsmouth
Swindon T. v. Manchester C.
Walsall v. Bradford C.
Watford v. Bournemouth

Division Three
Brentford v. Wolverhampton W.
Bristol Rov. v. Swansea C.
Bury v. Aldershot
Chester C. v. Northampton T.
Chesterfield v. Fulham
Mansfield T. v. Huddersfield T.
Notts Co. v. Bolton W.
Preston N.E. v. Sheffield U.
Southend U. v. Bristol C.

Division Four
Burnley v. Grimsby T.
Carlisle U. v. Stockport Co.
Darlington v. Hereford U.
Exeter C. v. York C.
Leyton Orient v. Wrexham
Rotherham U. v. Halifax T.
Scarborough v. Crewe Alex.
Scunthorpe U. v. Tranmere Rov.
Torquay U. v. Peterborough U.

Monday, January 2nd, 1989

Division One
Arsenal v. Tottenham H.
Coventry C. v. Sheffield Wed.
Liverpool v. Aston Villa
Luton T. v. Southampton
Middlesbrough v. Manchester U.
Millwall v. Charlton Ath.
Newcastle U. v. Derby Co.
Nottingham F. v. Everton
Q.P.R. v. Norwich C.
West Ham U. v. Wimbledon

Division Two
Bournemouth v. Brighton & H.A.
Barnsley v. Hull C.
Birmingham C. v. Oldham Ath.
Blackburn Rov. v. Stoke C.
Bradford C. v. Sunderland
Crystal Palace v. Walsall
Ipswich T. v. Leicester C.
Manchester C. v. Leeds U.
Oxford U. v. Chelsea
Plymouth Arg. v. Watford
Portsmouth v. Swindon T.
West Bromwich A. v. Shrewsbury T.

Division Three
Aldershot v. Cardiff C.
Blackpool v. Bury
Bolton W. v. Mansfield T.
Bristol C. v. Brentford
Fulham v. Brentford
Huddersfield T. v. Southend U.
Northampton T. v. Preston N.E.
Port Vale v. Notts Co.
Sheffield U. v. Chesterfield
Swansea C. v. Reading
Wigan Ath. v. Gillingham
Wolverhampton W. v. Chester C.

Division Four
Crewe Alex. Carlisle U.
Doncaster Rov. v. Scarborough
Grimsby T. v. Colchester U.
Halifax T. v. Scunthorpe U.
Hartlepool U. v. Rotherham U.
Hereford U. v. Torquay U.
Peterborough U. v. Cambridge U.
Rochdale v. Leyton Orient
Stockport Co. v. Exeter C.
Tranmere Rov. v. Burnley
Wrexham v. Darlington
York C. v. Lincoln C.

Friday, January 6th, 1989

Division Four
Tranmere Rov. v. Exeter C.
Wrexham v. Torquay U.

Saturday, January 7th, 1989

Division Three
Aldershot v. Preston N.E.
Blackpool v. Southend U.
Bolton W. v. Gillingham
Bristol C. v. Brentford
Fulham v. Chester C.
Huddersfield T. v. Reading
Northampton T. v. Bury
Port Vale v. Bristol Rov.
Sheffield U. v. Mansfield T.
Swansea C. v. Notts Co.
Wigan Ath. v. Chesterfield
Wolverhampton W. v. Cardiff C.

Division Four
Crewe Alex. v. Burnley
Doncaster Rov. v. Carlisle U.
Grimsby T. v. Darlington
Halifax T. v. Leyton Orient
Hartlepool U. v. Scarborough
Hereford U. v. Colchester U.
Peterborough U. v. Rotherham U.
Rochdale v. Lincoln C.
Stockport Co. v. Scunthorpe U.
York C. v. Cambridge U.

Friday, January 13th, 1989

Division Three
Southend U. v. Fulham

Division Four
Colchester U. v. Tranmere Rov.

Saturday, January 14th, 1989

Division One
Aston Villa v. Newcastle U.
Charlton Ath. v. Luton T.
Derby Co. v. West Ham U.
Everton v. Arsenal
Manchester U. v. Millwall
Norwich C. v. Coventry C.
Sheffield Wed. v. Liverpool
Southampton v. Middlesbrough
Tottenham H. v. Nottingham F.
Wimbledon v. Q.P.R.

Division Two
Brighton & H.A. v. Plymouth Arg.
Chelsea v. Crystal Palace
Hull C. v. Bournemouth
Leeds U. v. Birmingham C.
Leicester C. v. Portsmouth
Oldham Ath. v. Manchester C.
Shrewsbury T. v. Blackburn Rov.
Stoke C. v. Bradford C.
Sunderland v. Oxford U.
Swindon T. v. Barnsley
Walsall v. Ipswich T.
Watford v. West Bromwich A.

Division Three
Brentford v. Northampton T.
Bristol Rov. v. Sheffield U.
Bury v. Swansea C.
Cardiff C. v. Bolton W.
Chester C. v. Port Vale
Chesterfield v. Bristol C.
Gillingham v. Aldershot
Mansfield T. v. Wigan Ath.
Notts Co. v. Blackpool
Preston N.E. v. Huddersfield T.
Reading v. Wolverhampton W.

Division Four
Burnley v. Halifax T.
Cambridge U. v. Hereford U.
Carlisle U. v. York C.
Darlington v. Hartlepool U.
Exeter C. v. Doncaster Rov.
Leyton Orient v. Stockport Co.
Lincoln C. v. Wrexham
Rotherham U. v. Rochdale
Scarborough v. Peterborough U.
Scunthorpe U. v. Crewe Alex.
Torquay U. v. Grimsby T.

Friday, January 20th 1989

Division Four
Halifax T. v. Torquay U.
Stockport Co. v. Darlington

Saturday, January 21st, 1989

Division One
Arsenal v. Sheffield Wed.
Coventry C. v. Wimbledon
Liverpool v. Southampton
Luton T. v. Everton
Middlesbrough v. Tottenham H.
Millwall v. Norwich C.
Newcastle U. v. Charlton Ath.
Nottingham F. v. Aston Villa
Q.P.R. v. Derby Co.
West Ham U. v. Manchester U.

Division Two
Bournemouth v. Sunderland
Barnsley v. Oldham Ath.
Birmingham C. v. Watford
Blackburn Rov. v. Chelsea
Bradford C. v. Brighton & H.A.
Crystal Palace v. Swindon T.
Ipswich T. v. Stoke C.
Manchester C. v. Hull C.
Oxford U. v. Leeds U.
Plymouth Arg. v. Walsall
Portsmouth v. Shrewsbury T.
West Bromwich A. v. Leicester C.

Division Three
Aldershot v. Bristol Rov.
Blackpool v. Preson N.E.
Bolton W. v. Reading
Bristol C. v. Chester C.
Fulham v. Mansfield T.
Huddersfield T. v. Cardiff C.
Northampton T. v. Notts Co.
Port Vale v. Bury
Sheffield U. v. Gillingham
Swansea C. v. Southend U.
Wigan Ath. v. Brentford
Wolverhampton W. v. Chesterfield

Division Four
Crewe Alex. v. Leyton Orient
Doncaster Rov. v. Rotherham U.
Grimsby T. v. Cambridge U.
Hartlepool U. v. Lincoln C.
Hereford U. v. Scunthorpe U.
Peterborough U. v. Carlisle U.
Rochdale v. Burnley
Tranmere Rov. v. Scarborough
Wrexham v. Exeter C.
York C. v. Colchester U.

Friday, January 27th, 1989

Division Four
Colchester U. v. Wrexham

Saturday, January 28th, 1989

Division Three
Brentford v. Swansea C.
Bristol Rov. v. Bolton W.
Bury v. Fulham
Cardiff C. v. Port Vale
Chester C. v. Sheffield U.
Chesterfield v. Northampton T.
Gillingham v. Huddersfield T.
Mansfield T. v. Blackpool
Notts Co. v. Wolverhampton W.
Preston N.E. v. Bristol C.
Reading v. Wigan Ath.
Southend U. v. Aldershot

Division Four
Burnley v. Stockport Co.
Cambridge U. v. Tranmere Rov.
Carlisle U. v. Halifax T.
Darlington v. Crewe Alex.
Exeter C. v. Rochdale
Leyton Orient v. Hartlepool U.
Lincoln C. v. Peterborough U.
Rotherham U. v. Grimsby T.
Scarborough v. Hereford U.
Scunthorpe U. v. York C.
Torquay U. v. Doncaster Rov.

Friday, February 3, 1989

Division Three
Southend U. v. Preston N.E.
Swansea C. v. Bristol Rov.

Saturday, February 4th, 1989

Division One
Arsenal v. West Ham U.
Aston Villa v. Sheffield Wed.
Charlton Ath. v. Norwich C.
Derby Co. v. Southampton
Everton v. Wimbledon
Luton T. v. Nottingham F.
Manchester U. v. Tottenham H.
Middlesbrough v. Coventry C.
Newcastle U. v. Liverpool
Q.P.R. v. Millwall

Division Two
Bournemouth v. West Bromwich A.
Barnsley v. Brighton & H.A.
Blackburn Rov. v. Bradford C.
Ipswich T. v. Crystal Palace
Leeds U. v. Sunderland
Leicester C. v. Hull C.
Oldham Ath. v. Watford
Plymouth Arg. v. Birmingham C.
Portsmouth v. Manchester C.
Shrewsbury T. v. Stoke C.
Walsall v. Chelsea

Division Three
Aldershot v. Northampton T.
Blackpool v. Wigan Ath.
Bristol Rov. v. Cardiff C.
Bury v. Chesterfield
Chester C. v. Reading
Fulham v. Huddersfield T.
Gillingham v. Brentford
Port Vale v. Wolverhampton W.
Sheffield U. v. Bolton W.

Division Four
Burnley v. Torquay U.
Carlisle U. v. Scunthorpe U.
Crewe Alex. v. Hereford U.
Doncaster Rov. v. Rochdale
Exeter C. v. Darlington
Grimsby T. v. Wrexham
Halifax T. v. Stockport Co.
Hartlepool U. v. York C.
Leyton Orient v. Rotherham U.
Lincoln C. v. Cambridge U.
Peterborough U. v. Tranmere Rov.
Scarborough v. Colchester U.

Sunday, February 5th, 1989

Division Two
Swindon T. v. Oxford U.

Division Three
Notts Co. v. Mansfield T.

Friday, February 10, 1989

Division Four
Colchester U. v. Burnley
Stockport Co. v. Crewe Alex.
Tranmere Rov. v. Halifax T.

Saturday, February 11th, 1989

Division One
Coventry C. v. Newcastle U.
Liverpool v. Luton T.
Millwall v. Arsenal
Norwich C. v. Derby Co.
Nottingham F. v. Q.P.R.
Sheffield Wed. v. Manchester U.
Southampton v. Everton
Tottenham H. v. Charlton Ath.
West Ham U. v. Middlesbrough
Wimbledon v. Aston Villa

Division Two
Birmingham C. v. Bournemouth
Bradford C. v. Plymouth Arg.
Brighton & H.A. v. Leicester C.
Chelsea v. Swindon T.
Crystal Palace v. Blackburn Rov.
Hull C. v. Shrewsbury T.
Manchester C. v. Ipswich T.
Oxford U. v. Portsmouth
Stoke C. v. Oldham Ath.
Sunderland v. Walsall
Watford v. Leeds U.
West Bromwich A. v. Barnsley

Division Three
Bolton W. v. Swansea C.
Brentford v. Chester C.
Bristol C. v. Gillingham
Cardiff C. v. Sheffield U.
Chesterfield v. Notts Co.
Huddersfield T. v. Port Vale
Mansfield T. v. Southend U.
Northampton T. v. Blackpool
Preston N.E. v. Bristol Rov.
Reading v. Bury
Wigan Ath. v. Aldershot
Wolverhampton W. v. Fulham

Division Four
Cambridge U. v. Hartlepool U.
Darlington v. Leyton Orient
Hereford U. v. Lincoln C.
Rochdale v. Grimsby T.
Rotherham U. v. Carlisle U.
Scunthorpe U. v. Exeter C.
Torquay U. v. Scarborough
Wrexham v. Doncaster Rov.
York C. v. Peterborough U.

Friday, February 17th, 1989

Division Three
Southend U. v. Brentford

Division Four
Crewe Alex. v. Wrexham
Halifax T. v. Cambridge U.
Stockport Co. v. Rochdale

Saturday, February 18th, 1989

Division One
Charlton Ath. v. Derby Co.
Coventry C. v. Liverpool
Everton v. Aston Villa
Luton T. v. Middlesbrough
Manchester U. v. Wimbledon
Newcastle U. v. West Ham U.
Nottingham F. v. Millwall
Q.P.R. v. Arsenal
Sheffield Wed. v. Southampton
Tottenham H. v. Norwich C.

Division Two
Birmingham C. v. Manchester C.
Blackburn Rov. v. Oxford U.
Bradford C. v. West Bromwich A.
Hull C. v. Crystal Palace
Ipswich T. v. Barnsley
Leicester C. v. Leeds U.
Oldham Ath. v. Brighton & H.A.
Plymouth Arg. v. Chelsea
Portsmouth v. Walsall
Shrewsbury T. v. Bournemouth
Swindon T. v. Sunderland
Watford v. Stoke C.

Division Three
Blackpool v. Bolton W.
Bristol Rov. v. Mansfield T.
Bury v. Preston N.E.
Chester C. v. Notts Co.
Chesterfield v. Gillingham
Fulham v. Bristol C.
Huddersfield T. v. Northampton T.
Port Vale v. Wigan Ath.
Reading v. Cardiff C.
Wolverhampton W. v. Sheffield U.

Division Four
Carlisle U. v. Hereford U.
Exeter C. v. Burnley
Hartlepool U. v. Doncaster Rov.
Leyton Orient v. Scarborough
Lincoln C. v. Torquay U.
Peterborough U. v. Grimsby T.
Rotherham U. v. Darlington
Scunthorpe U. v. Colchester U.
York C. v. Tranmere Rov.

Sunday, February 19th, 1989

Division Three
Swansea C. v. Aldershot

Friday, February 24th, 1989

Division Three
Wigan Ath. v. Wolverhampton W.

Division Four
Colchester U. v. Leyton Orient
Darlington v. York C.
Doncaster Rov. v. Crewe Alex.

Saturday, February 25th, 1989

Division One
Arsenal v. Luton T.
Aston Villa v. Charlton Ath.
Derby Co. v. Everton
Liverpool v. Nottingham F.
Millwall v. Coventry C.
Norwich C. v. Manchester U.
Southampton v. Tottenham H.
West Ham U. v. Q.P.R.
Wimbledon v. Sheffield Wed.

Division Two
Bournemouth v. Portsmouth
Barnsley v. Blackburn Rov.
Brighton & H.A. v. Watford
Chelsea v. Oldham Ath.
Crystal Palace v. Bradford C.
Leeds U. v. Swindon T.
Manchester C. v. Plymouth Arg.
Oxford U. v. Ipswich T.
Stoke C. v. Leicester C.
Sunderland v. Hull C.
Walsall v. Shrewsbury T.
West Bromwich A. v. Birmingham C.

Division Three
Aldershot v. Fulham
Bolton W. v. Port Vale
Brentford v. Bury
Bristol C. v. Huddersfield T.
Cardiff C. v. Chester C.
Gillingham v. Southend U.
Mansfield T. v. Reading
Northampton T. v. Swansea C.
Notts Co. v. Bristol Rov.
Preston N.E. v. Chesterfield
Sheffield U. v. Blackpool

Division Four
Burnley v. Peterborough U.
Cambridge U. v. Scunthorpe U.
Grimsby T. v. Exeter C.
Hereford U. v. Stockport Co.
Rochdale v. Halifax T.
Scarborough v. Lincoln C.
Torquay U. v. Carlisle U.
Tranmere Rov. v. Rotherham U.
Wrexham v. Hartlepool U.

Sunday, February 26th, 1989

Division One
Middlesbrough v. Newcastle U.

Tuesday, February 28th, 1989

Division Two
Bournemouth v. Oldham Ath.
Barnsley v. Watford
Blackburn Rov. v. Sunderland
Chelsea v. Hull C.
Portsmouth v. Ipswich T.
Shrewsbury T. v. Plymouth Arg.
Stoke C. v. Birmingham C.
Swindon T. v. Leicester C.
Walsall v. Brighton & H.A.

Division Three
Aldershot v. Bristol C.
Blackpool v. Wolverhampton W.
Bolton W. v. Wigan Ath.
Brentford v. Chesterfield
Gillingham v. Preston N.E.
Mansfield T. v. Chester C.
Northampton T. v. Fulham
Notts Co. v. Cardiff C.
Sheffield U. v. Port Vale
Southend U. v. Bury
Swansea C. v. Huddersfield T.

Division Four
Burnley v. Carlisle U.
Colchester U. v. Rotherham U.
Doncaster Rov. v. York C.
Grimsby T. v. Crewe Alex.
Hartlepool U. v. Stockport Co.
Rochdale v. Hereford U.
Torquay U. v. Darlington
Wrexham v. Scunthorpe U.

Wednesday, March 1st, 1989

Division Two
Leeds U. v. Bradford C.
Manchester C. v. West Bromwich A.
Oxford U. v. Crystal Palace

Division Three
Bristol Rov. v. Reading

Division Four
Exeter C. v. Leyton Orient
Lincoln C. v. Tranmere Rov.
Peterborough U. v. Halifax T.
Scarborough v. Cambridge U.

Friday, March 3rd, 1989

Division Two
Oldham Ath. v. Shrewsbury T.

Division Four
Halifax T. v. Doncaster Rov.
Tranmere Rov. v. Wrexham

Saturday, March 4th, 1989

Division One
Coventry C. v. Arsenal
Liverpool v. West Ham U.
Manchester U. v. Everton
Millwall v. Middlesbrough
Nottingham F. v. Newcastle U.
Q.P.R. v. Luton T.
Sheffield Wed. v. Charlton Ath.
Southampton v. Norwich C.
Tottenham H. v. Aston Villa.
Wimbledon v. Derby C.

Division Two
Birmingham C. v. Oxford U.
Bradford C. v.Barnsley
Brighton & H.A. v. Blackburn Rov.
Crystal Palace v. Bournemouth
Hull C. v. Stoke C.
Ipswich T. v. Swindon T.
Leicester C. v. Walsall
Plymouth Arg. v. Portsmouth
Sunderland v. Chelsea
Watford v. Manchester C.

Division Three
Bristol C. v. Northampton T.
Bury v. Gillingham
Cardiff C. v. Mansfield T.
Chester C. v. Bristol Rov.
Chesterfield v. Southend U.
Fulham v. Swansea C.
Huddersfield T. v. Aldershot
Port Vale v. Blackpool
Preston N.E. v. Brentford
Reading v. Notts Co.
Wigan Ath. v. Sheffield U.
Wolverhampton W. v. Bolton W.

Division Four
Carlisle U. v. Exeter C.
Crewe Alex. v. Hartlepool U.
Darlington v. Lincoln C.
Hereford U. v. Peterborough U.
Leyton Orient v. Burnley
Rotherham U. v. Torquay U.
Scunthorpe U. v. Rochdale
Stockport Co. v. Scarborough
York C. v. Grimsby T.

Sunday, March 5th, 1989

Division Two
West Bromwich A. v. Leeds U.

Division Four
Cambridge U. v. Colchester U.

Friday, March 10th, 1989

Division Three
Southend U. v. Wolverhampton W.

Division Four
Colchester U. v. Crewe Alex.
Doncaster Rov. v. Darlington
Torquay U. v. York C.

Saturday, March 11th, 1989

Division One
Arsenal v. Nottingham F.
Aston Villa v. Manchester U.
Charlton Ath. v. Southampton
Derby Co. v. Tottenham H.
Everton v. Sheffield Wed.
Luton T. v. Millwall
Middlesbrough v. Liverpool
Newcastle U. v. Q.P.R.
Norwich C. v. Wimbledon
West Ham U. v. Coventry C.

Division Two
Bournemouth v. Bradford C.
Barnsley v. Crystal Palace
Blackburn Rov. v. Plymouth Arg.
Chelsea v. Watford
Leeds U. v. Ipswich T..
Manchester C. v. Leicester C.
Oxford U. v. West Bromwich A.
Portsmouth v. Birmingham C.
Shrewsbury T. v. Brighton & H.A.
Stoke C. v. Sunderland
Swindon T. v. Hull C.
Walsall v. Oldham Ath.

Division Three
Aldershot v. Port Vale
Blackpool v. Fulham
Bolton W. v. Bristol C.
Brentford v. Reading
Bristol Rov. v. Chesterfield
Gillingham v. Cardiff C.
Mansfield T. v. Preston N. E.
Northampton T. v. Wigan Ath.
Notts Co. v. Bury
Sheffield U. v. Huddersfield T.
Swansea C. v. Chester C.

Division Four
Burnley v. Scunthorpe U.
Exeter C. v. Cambridge U.
Grimsby T. v. Stockport Co.
Hartlepool U. v. Halifax T.
Lincoln C. v. Rotherham U.
Peterborough U. v. Leyton Orient
Rochdale v. Tranmere Rov.
Scarborough v. Carlisle U.
Wrexham v. Hereford U.

Monday, March 13th, 1989

Division Three
Port Vale v. Brentford

Division Four
Stockport Co. v. Colchester U.
Tranmere Rov. v. Torquay U.

Tuesday, March 14th, 1989

Division Two
Birmingham C. v. Swindon T.
Crystal Palace v. Stoke C.
Hull C. v. Leeds U.
Ipswich T. v. Bournemouth
Oldham Ath. v. Portsmouth
Plymouth Arg. v. Barnsley
Sunderland v. Manchester C.
Watford v. Walsall

Division Three
Bristol C. v. Mansfield T.
Bury v. Sheffield U.
Cardiff C. v. Blackpool
Chesterfield v. Bolton W.
Fulham v. Notts Co.
Huddersfield T. v. Bristol Rov.
Preston N.E. v. Swansea C.
Wigan Ath. v. Southend U.
Wolverhampton W. v. Gillingham

Division Four
Cambridge U. v. Burnley
Carlisle U. v. Lincoln C.
Crewe Alex. v. Exeter C.
Darlington v. Rochdale
Halifax T. Grimsby T.
Leyton Orient v. Doncaster Rov.
Rotherham U. v. Scarborough
Scunthorpe U. v. Peterborough U.
York C. v. Wrexham

Wednesday, March 15th, 1989

Division Two
Bradford C. v. Oxford U.
Brighton & H.A. v. Chelsea
Leicester C. v. Shrewsbury T.
West Bromwich A. v. Blackburn Rov.

Division Three
Chester C. v. Aldershot
Reading v. Northampton T.

Division Four
Hereford U. v. Hartlepool U.

Friday, March 17th, 1989

Division Four
Halifax T. v. Exeter C.
Stockport Co. v. Cambridge U.
Tranmere Rov. v. Carlisle U.

Saturday, March 18th, 1989

Division One
Arsenal v. Wimbledon
Coventry C. v. Tottenham H.
Liverpool v. Charlton Ath.
Luton T. v. Sheffield Wed.
Middlesbrough v. Derby Co.
Millwall v. Aston Villa
Newcastle U. v. Everton
Nottingham F. v. Norwich C.
Q.P.R. v. Manchester U.
West Ham U. v. Southampton

Division Two
Bournemouth v. Swindon T.
Barnsley v. Leeds U.
Birmingham C. v. Walsall
Blackburn Rov. v. Hull C.
Bradford C. v. Watford
Crystal Palace v. Sunderland
Ipswich T. v. Shrewsbury T.
Manchester C v. Chelsea
Oxford U. v. Oldham Ath.
Plymouth Arg. v. Leicester C.
Portsmouth v. Stoke C.
West Bromwich A. v. Brighton & H.A.

Division Three
Aldershot v. Chesterfield
Blackpool v. Chester C.
Bolton W. v. Southend U.
Bristol C. v. Notts Co.
Fulham v. Cardiff C.
Huddersfield T. v. Brentford
Northampton T. v. Mansfield T.
Port Vale v. Preston N.E.
Sheffield U. v. Reading
Wigan Ath. v. Bristol Rov.
Wolverhampton W. v. Bury

Division Four
Crewe Alex. v. Lincoln C.
Doncaster Rov. v. Colchester U.
Grimsby T. v. Scunthorpe U.
Hartlepool U. v. Torquay U.
Hereford U. v. Leyton Orient
Peterborough U. v. Darlington
Rochdale v. Scarborough
Wrexham v. Rotherham U.
York C. v. Burnley

Sunday, March 19th, 1989

Division Three
Swansea C. v. Gillingham

Friday, March 24th, 1989

Division Two
Oldham Ath. v. Blackburn Rov.
Watford v. Crystal Palace

Division Three
Brentford v. Fulham
Gillingham v. Wigan Ath.

Division Four
Colchester U. v. Grimsby T.

Saturday, March 25th, 1989

Division One
Aston Villa v. West Ham U.
Charlton Ath. v. Coventry C.
Derby Co. v. Nottingham F.
Everton v. Millwall
Manchester U. v. Luton T.
Norwich C. v. Newcastle U.
Sheffield Wed. v. Q.P.R.
Southampton v. Arsenal
Tottenham H. v. Liverpool
Wimbledon v. Middlesbrough

Division Two
Brighton & H.A. v. Oxford U.
Chelsea v. Bournemouth
Hull C. v. Plymouth Arg.
Leeds U. v. Portsmouth
Leicester C. v. Birmingham C.
Shrewsbury T. v. Bradford C.
Stoke C. v. Barnsley
Sunderland v. Ipswich T.
Swindon T. v. West Bromwich A.
Walsall v. Manchester C.

Division Three
Bristol Rov. v. Bristol C.
Bury v. Blackpool
Cardiff C. v. Aldershot
Chester C. v. Wolverhampton W.
Chesterfield v. Sheffield U.
Mansfield T. v. Bolton W.
Notts Co. v. Port Vale
Preston N.E. v. Northampton T.
Reading v. Swansea C.
Southend U. v. Huddersfield T.

Division Four
Burnley v. Tranmere Rov.
Cambridge U. v. Peterborough U.
Carlisle U. v. Crewe Alex.
Darlington v. Wrexham
Exeter C. v. Stockport Co.
Leyton Orient v. Rochdale
Lincoln C. v. York C.
Rotherham U. v. Hartlepool U.
Scarborough v. Doncaster Rov.
Scunthorpe U. v. Halifax T.
Torquay U. v. Hereford U.

Monday, March 27th, 1989

Division One
Arsenal v. Charlton Ath.
Coventry C. v. Southampton
Liverpool v. Derby Co.
Luton T. v. Tottenham H.
Middlesbrough v. Everton
Millwall v. Wimbledon
Newcastle U. v. Sheffield Wed.
Nottingham F. v. Manchester U.
Q.P.R. v. Aston Villa
West Ham U. v. Norwich C.

Division Two
Bournemouth v. Leicester C.
Barnsley v. Sunderland
Birmingham C. v. Shrewsbury T.
Blackburn Rov. v. Leeds U.
Bradford C. v. Hull C.
Crystal Palace v. Brighton & H.A.
Manchester C. v. Stoke C.
Oxford U. v. Walsall
Plymouth Arg. v. Swindon T.
Portsmouth v. Watford
West Bromwich A. v. Oldham Ath.

Division Three
Aldershot v. Reading
Blackpool v. Brentford
Bolton W. v. Preston N.E.
Bristol C. v. Bury
Fulham v. Gillingham
Huddersfield T. v. Chesterfield
Northampton T. v. Southend U.
Port Vale v. Mansfield T.
Sheffield U. v. Notts Co.
Swansea C. v. Cardiff C.
Wigan Ath. v. Chester C.
Wolverhampton W. v. Bristol Rov.

Division Four
Crewe Alex. v. Rotherham U.
Doncaster Rov. v. Cambridge U.
Grimsby T. v. Lincoln C.
Halifax T. v. Darlington
Hartlepool U. v. Scunthorpe U.
Hereford U. v. Exeter C.
Peterborough U. v. Colchester U.
Rochdale v. Carlisle U.
Stockport Co. v. Torquay U.
Tranmere Rov. v. Leyton Orient
Wrexham v. Burnley
York C. v. Scarborough

Tuesday, March 28th, 1989

Division Two
Ipswich T. v. Chelsea

Friday, March 31st, 1989

Division Three
Southend U. v. Sheffield U.

Division Four
Cambridge U. v. Wrexham
Colchester U. v. Rochdale
Torquay U. v. Crewe Alex.

Saturday, April 1st, 1989

Division One
Aston Villa v. Luton T.
Charlton Ath. v. Middlesbrough
Derby Co. v. Coventry C.
Everton v. Q.P.R.
Manchester U. v. Arsenal
Norwich C. v. Liverpool
Sheffield Wed. v. Millwall
Southampton v. Newcastle U.
Tottenham H. v. West Ham U.
Wimbledon v. Nottingham F.

Division Two
Brighton & H.A. v. Manchester C.
Chelsea v. Barnsley
Hull C. v. Portsmouth
Leeds U. v. Bournemouth
Leicester C. v. Oxford U.
Oldham Ath. v. Bradford C.
Shrewsbury T. v. Crystal Palace
Stoke C. v. Plymouth Arg.
Sunderland v. Birmingham C.
Swindon T. v. Blackburn Rov.
Walsall v. West Bromwich A.
Watford v. Ipswich T.

Division Three
Brentford v. Aldershot
Bristol Rov. v. Blackpool
Bury v. Huddersfield T.
Cardiff C. v. Bristol C.
Chester C. v. Bolton W.
Chesterfield v. Swansea C.
Gillingham v. Northampton T.
Mansfield T. v. Wolverhampton W.
Notts Co. v. Wigan Ath.
Preston N.E. v. Fulham
Reading v. Port Vale

Division Four
Burnley v. Hereford U.
Carlisle U. v. Hartlepool U.
Darlington v. Tranmere Rov.
Exeter C. v. Peterborough U.
Leyton Orient v. Grimsby T.
Lincoln C. v. Stockport Co.
Rotherham U. v. York C.
Scarborough v. Halifax T.
Scunthorpe U. v. Doncaster Rov.

Tuesday, April 4th, 1989

Division Two
Chelsea v. Birmingham C.
Hull C. v. Oxford U.
Oldham Ath. v. Ipswich T.
Shrewsbury T. v. Manchester C.
Stoke C. v. West Bromwich A.
Sunderland v. Plymouth Arg.
Swindon T. v. Bradford C.
Walsall v. Bournemouth
Watford v. Blackburn Rov.

Division Three
Brentford v. Bristol C.
Bury v. Northampton T.
Cardiff C. v. Wolverhampton W.
Chesterfield v. Wigan Ath.
Gillingham v. Bolton W.
Mansfield T. v. Sheffield U.
Notts Co. v. Swansea C.
Preston N.E. v. Aldershot
Southend U. v. Blackpool

Division Four
Burnley v. Crewe Alex.
Cambridge U. v. York C.
Carlisle U. v. Doncaster Rov.
Colchester U. v. Hereford U.
Darlington v. Grimsby T.
Leyton Orient v. Halifax T.
Rotherham U. v. Peterborough U.
Scunthorpe U. v. Stockport Co.
Torquay U. v. Wrexham

Wednesday, April 5th, 1989

Division Two
Brighton & H.A. v. Portsmouth
Leeds U. v. Crystal Palace
Leicester C. v. Barnsley

Division Three
Bristol Rov. v. Port Vale
Chester C. v. Fulham
Reading v. Huddersfield T.

Division Four
Exeter C. v. Tranmere Rov.
Lincoln C. v. Rochdale
Scarborough v. Hartlepool U.

Friday, April 7th, 1989

Division Three
Wigan Ath. v. Cardiff C.

Division Four
Halifax T. v. Rotherham U.
Stockport Co. v. Carlisle U.

Saturday, April 8th, 1989

Division One
Arsenal v. Everton
Coventry C. v. Norwich C.
Liverpool v. Sheffield Wed.
Luton T. v. Charlton Ath.
Middlesbrough v. Southampton
Millwall v. Manchester U.
Newcastle U. v. Aston Villa
Nottingham F. v. Tottenham H.
Q.P.R. v. Wimbledon
West Ham U. v. Derby Co.

Division Two
Bournemouth v. Watford
Barnsley v. Shrewsbury T.
Birmingham C. v. Brighton & H.A.
Blackburn Rov. v. Leicester C.
Bradford C. v. Walsall
Crystal Palace v. Oldham Ath.
Ipswich T. v. Hull C.
Manchester C. v. Swindon T.
Oxford U. v. Stoke C.
Portsmouth v. Sunderland
West Bromwich A. v. Chelsea

Division Three
Aldershot v. Bury
Blackpool v. Reading
Bolton W. v. Notts Co.
Bristol C. v. Southend U.
Fulham v. Chesterfield
Huddersfield T. v. Mansfield T.
Northampton T. v. Chester C.
Port Vale v. Gillingham
Sheffield U. v. Preston N.E.
Swansea C. v. Bristol Rov.
Wolverhampton W. v. Brentford

Division Four
Crewe Alex. v. Scarborough
Doncaster Rov. v. Lincoln C.
Grimsby T. v. Burnley
Hartlepool U. v. Colchester U.
Hereford U. v. Darlington
Peterborough U. v. Torquay U.
Rochdale v. Cambridge U.
Tranmere Rov. v. Scunthorpe U.
Wrexham v. Leyton Orient
York C. v. Exeter C.

Sunday, April 9th, 1989

Division Two
Plymouth Arg. v. Leeds U.

Friday, April 14th, 1989

Division Three
Southend U. v. Reading

Division Four
Crewe Alex. v. Rochdale
Halifax T. v. York C.

Saturday, April 15th, 1989

Division One
Arsenal v. Newcastle U.
Aston Villa v. Southampton
Everton v. Charlton Ath.
Luton T. v. Coventry C.
Manchester U. v. Derby Co.
Millwall v. Liverpool
Nottingham F. v. West Ham U.
Q.P.R. v. Middlesbrough
Sheffield Wed. v. Norwich C.
Wimbledon v. Tottenham H.

Division Two
Bournemouth v. Stoke C.
Barnsley v. Birmingham C.
Blackburn Rov. v. Manchester C.
Bradford C. v. Ipswich T.
Crystal Palace v. Portsmouth
Leeds U. v. Brighton & H.A.
Leicester C. v. Chelsea
Oldham Ath. v. Sunderland
Shrewsbury T. v. Oxford U.
Swindon T. v. Watford
Walsall v. Hull C.
West Bromwich A. v. Plymouth Arg.

Division Three
Aldershot v. Wolverhampton W.
Brentford v. Bristol Rov.
Bristol C. v. Blackpool
Bury v. Cardiff C.
Chesterfield v. Port Vale
Fulham v. Bolton W.
Gillingham v. Mansfield T.
Huddersfield T. v. Chester C.
Northampton T. v. Sheffield U.
Preston N.E. v. Notts Co.
Swansea C. v. Wigan Ath.

Division Four
Burnley v. Darlington
Carlisle U. v. Cambridge U.
Doncaster Rov. v. Stockport Co.
Exeter C. v. Rotherham U.
Grimsby T. v. Hereford U.
Hartlepool U. v. Tranmere Rov.
Leyton Orient v. Torquay U.
Lincoln C. v. Colchester U.
Peterborough U. v. Wrexham
Scarborough v. Scunthorpe U.

Tuesday, April 18th, 1989

Division Three
Northampton T. v. Bolton W.

Friday, April 21st, 1989

Division Three
Port Vale v. Bristol C.

Division Four
Colchester U. v. Carlisle U.
Stockport Co. v. Peterborough U.
Wrexham v. Halifax T.

Saturday, April 22nd, 1989

Division One
Charlton Ath. v. Manchester U.
Coventry C. v. Q.P.R.
Derby Co. v. Sheffield Wed.
Liverpool v. Arsenal
Middlesbrough v. Nottingham F.
Newcastle U. v. Luton T.
Norwich C. v. Aston Villa
Southampton v. Wimbledon
Tottenham H. v. Everton
West Ham U. v. Millwall

Division Two
Birmingham C. v. Blackburn Rov.
Brighton & H.A. v. Swindon T.
Chelsea v. Leeds U.
Hull C. v. Oldham Ath.
Ipswich T. v. West Bromwich A.
Manchester C. v. Barnsley
Oxford U. v. Bournemouth
Plymouth Argyle v. Crystal Palace
Portsmouth v. Bradford C.
Stoke C. v. Walsall
Sunderland v. Shrewsbury T.
Watford v. Leicester C.

Division Three
Blackpool v. Chesterfield
Bolton W. v. Aldershot
Bristol Rov. v. Northampton T.
Cardiff C. v. Southend U.
Chester C. v. Preston N.E.
Mansfield T. v. Bury
Notts Co. v. Huddersfield T.
Reading v. Gillingham
Sheffield U. v. Brentford
Wigan Ath. v. Fulham
Wolverhampton W. v. Swansea C.

Division Four
Cambridge U. v. Crewe Alex.
Darlington v. Scarborough
Hereford U. v. Doncaster Rov.
Rochdale v. Hartlepool U.
Rotherham U. v. Burnley
Scunthorpe U. v. Lincoln C.
Torquay U. v. Exeter C.
Tranmere Rov. v. Grimsby T.
York C. v. Leyton Orient

Friday, April 28th, 1989

Division Three
Gillingham v. Bristol Rov.
Southend U. v. Notts Co.

Division Four
Torquay U. v. Scunthorpe U.
Tranmere Rov. v. Stockport Co.

Saturday, April 29th, 1989

Division One
Arsenal v. Norwich C.
Aston Villa v. Middlesbrough
Everton v. Liverpool
Luton T. v. Derby Co.
Manchester U. v. Coventry C.
Millwall v. Tottenham H.
Nottingham F. v. Southampton
Q.P.R. v. Charlton Ath.
Sheffield Wed. v. West Ham U.
Wimbledon v. Newcastle U.

Division Two
Bournemouth v. Barnsley
Bradford C. v. Leicester C.
Crystal Palace v. West Bromwich A.
Hull C. v. Watford
Ipswich T. v. Birmingham C.
Oldham Ath. v. Plymouth Arg.
Oxford U. v. Manchester C.
Portsmouth v. Blackburn Rov.
Shrewsbury T. v. Chelsea
Stoke C. v. Leeds U.
Sunderland v. Brighton & H.A.
Walsall v. Swindon T.

Division Three
Aldershot v. Blackpool
Brentford v. Mansfield T.
Bristol C. v. Wigan Athletic
Bury v. Bolton W.
Chesterfield v. Chester C.
Fulham v. Sheffield U.
Huddersfield T. v. Wolverhampton W.
Northampton T. v. Cardiff C.
Preston N.E. v. Reading
Swansea C. v. Port Vale

Division Four
Burnley v. Doncaster Rov.
Darlington v. Colchester U.
Exeter C. v. Hartlepool U.
Grimsby T. v. Carlisle U.
Halifax T. v. Lincoln C.
Leyton Orient v. Cambridge U.
Peterborough U. v. Crewe Alex.
Rotherham U. v. Hereford U.
Wrexham v. Scarborough
York C. v. Rochdale

Monday, May 1st, 1989

Division Two
Barnsley v. Oxford U.
Birmingham C. v. Bradford C.
Blackburn Rov. v. Bournemouth
Brighton & H.A. v. Hull C.
Chelsea v. Stoke C.
Leeds U. v. Walsall
Leicester C. v. Oldham Ath.
Manchester C. v. Crystal Palace
Plymouth Arg. v. Ipswich T.
Swindon T. v. Shrewsbury T.
Watford v. Sunderland
West Bromwich A. v. Portsmouth

Division Three
Blackpool v. Gillingham
Bolton W. v. Huddersfield T.
Bristol Rov. v. Southend U.
Cardiff C. v. Chesterfield
Chester C. v. Bury
Notts Co. v. Brentford
Port Vale v. Northampton T.
Reading v. Fulham
Sheffield U. v. Aldershot
Wigan Ath. v. Preston N.E.
Wolverhampton W. v. Bristol C.

Division Four
Carlisle U. v. Leyton Orient
Colchester U. v. Halifax T.
Crewe Alex. v. York C.
Doncaster Rov. v. Grimsby T.
Hartlepool U. v. Peterborough U.
Hereford U. v. Tranmere Rov.
Lincoln C. v. Barnsley
Rochdale v. Torquay U.
Scarborough v. Exeter C.
Scunthorpe U. v. Rotherham U.
Stockport Co. v. Wrexham

Tuesday, May 2nd 1989

Division Three
Mansfield T. v. Swansea C.

Division Four
Cambridge U. v. Darlington

Friday, May 5th, 1989

Division Four
Colchester U. v. Exeter C.
Crewe Alex. v. Halifax T.

Saturday, May 6th, 1989

Division One
Charlton Ath. v. Wimbledon
Coventry C. v. Nottingham F.
Derby Co. v. Aston Villa
Liverpool v. Q.P.R.
Middlesbrough v. Arsenal
Newcastle U. v. Millwall
Norwich C. v. Everton
Southampton v. Manchester U.
Tottenham H. v. Sheffield Wed.
West Ham U. v. Luton T.

Division Two
Barnsley v Portsmouth
Birmingham C. v. Hull C.
Blackburn Rov. v. Walsall
Brighton & H.A. v. Ipswich T.
Chelsea v. Bradford C.
Leeds U. v. Oldham Ath.
Leicester C. v. Crystal Palace
Manchester C. v. Bournemouth
Plymouth Arg. v. Oxford U.
Swindon T. v. Stoke C.
Watford v. Shrewsbury T.
West Bromwich A. v. Sunderland

Division Three
Blackpool v. Huddersfield T.
Bolton W. v. Brentford
Bristol Rov. v. Fulham
Cardiff C. v. Preston N.E.
Chester C. v. Gillingham
Mansfield T. v. Chesterfield
Notts Co. v. Aldershot
Port Vale v. Southend U.
Reading v. Bristol C.
Sheffield U. v. Swansea C.
Wigan Ath. v. Bury
Wolverhampton W. v. Northampton T.

Division Four
Cambridge U. v. Torquay U.
Carlisle U. v. Wrexham
Doncaster Rov. v. Tranmere Rov.
Hartlepool U. v. Burnley
Hereford U. v. York C.
Lincoln C. v. Leyton Orient
Rochdale v. Peterborough U.
Scarborough v. Grimsby T.
Scunthorpe U. v. Darlington
Stockport Co. v. Rotherham U.

Saturday, May 13th, 1989

Division One
Arsenal v. Derby Co.
Aston Villa v. Coventry C.
Everton v. West Ham U.
Luton T. v. Norwich C.
Manchester U. v. Newcastle U.
Millwall v. Southampton
Nottingham F. v. Charlton Ath.
Q.P.R. v. Tottenham H.
Sheffield Wed. v. Middlesbrough
Wimbledon v. Liverpool

Division Two
Bournemouth v. Plymouth Arg.
Bradford C. v. Manchester C.
Crystal Palace v. Birmingham C.
Hull C. v. West Bromwich A.
Ipswich T. v. Blackburn Rov.
Oldham Ath. v. Swindon T.
Oxford U. v. Watford
Portsmouth v. Chelsea
Shrewsbury T. v. Leeds U.
Stoke C. v. Brighton & H.A.
Sunderland v. Leicester C.
Walsall v. Barnsley

Division Three
Aldershot v. Mansfield T.
Brentford v. Cardiff C.
Bristol C. v. Sheffield U.
Bury v. Bristol Rov.
Chesterfield v. Reading
Fulham v. Port Vale
Gillingham v. Notts Co.
Huddersfield T. v. Wigan Ath.
Preston N.E. v. Wolverhampton W.
Southend U. v. Chester C.
Swansea C. v. Blackpool

Division Four
Burnley v. Scarborough
Darlington v. Carlisle U.
Exeter C. v. Lincoln C.
Grimsby T. v. Hartlepool U.
Halifax T. v. Hereford U.
Leyton Orient v. Scunthorpe U.
Peterborough U. v. Doncaster Rov.
Rotherham U. v. Cambridge U.
Torquay U. v. Colchester U.
Tranmere Rov. v. Crewe Alex.
Wrexham v. Rochdale
York C. v. Stockport Co.